INTERNATIONAL HANDBOOK OF

PENOLOGY
and
CRIMINAL JUSTICE

INTERNATIONAL HANDBOOK OF

PENOLOGY
and
CRIMINAL JUSTICE

Edited by
Shlomo Giora Shoham
Ori Beck
Martin Kett

2007

CRC Press
Taylor & Francis Group
Boca Raton London New York

CRC Press is an imprint of the
Taylor & Francis Group, an informa business

CRC Press
Taylor & Francis Group
6000 Broken Sound Parkway NW, Suite 300
Boca Raton, FL 33487-2742

© 2008 by Taylor & Francis Group, LLC
CRC Press is an imprint of Taylor & Francis Group, an Informa business

Library of Congress Cataloging-in-Publication Data

International handbook of penology and criminal justice / Shlomo Shoham, Ori
    Beck, Martin Kett, editors.
        p. cm.
    Includes bibliographical references and index.
    ISBN-13: 978-1-4200-5387-6 (alk. paper)
    1. Criminal justice, Administration of. 2. Prisons. 3. Punishment. 4. Crime
prevention. I. Shoham, S. Giora, 1929- II. Beck, Ori. III. Kett, Martin.

HV7405.I59 2008
364--dc22   2007017192

Visit the Taylor & Francis Web site at
http://www.taylorandfrancis.com

and the CRC Press Web site at
http://www.crcpress.com

Table of Contents

Contributors

Charles F. Abel is associate professor of political science and public administration at Stephen F. Austin State University. He is the author of several books and a number of articles in the fields of public law, international political economy, and public administration theory. In addition, he has enjoyed a career as both a city and a county attorney. In his capacity as the university's director of the Center for Applied Social Research, he has established a research stream addressing issues in higher education.

Estella Baker is senior lecturer in law at the University of Sheffield. Her principal research interests lie in the fields of penology and sentencing, European criminal law and justice, and the relationship between criminal justice and governance.

William D. Bales is associate professor at the College of Criminology and Criminal Justice at Florida State University (FSU). Before joining the FSU faculty, he was the director of research for the Florida Department of Corrections. His research and publications are in the areas of sentencing and the effectiveness of different correctional strategies and community re-entry among incarcerated adult and juvenile populations.

Clemens Bartollas is professor of sociology at the University of Northern Iowa, where he has taught for the past twenty-six years. Before pursuing an academic career, he received a theological degree from Princeton Theological Seminary and served Presbyterian churches for nine years during the 1960s. He received his Ph.D. in sociology from Ohio State University in 1973. He has written a number of articles and books, including books on juvenile delinquency, juvenile justice, adult corrections, prison management, criminology, and law enforcement. He has worked with inner-city gangs in Chicago, especially the Gangster Disciples and the Vice Lords, and has done considerable expert witness work in murder and death penalty cases.

Victoria Simpson Beck is assistant professor of criminal justice at Indiana University East. Her published works have appeared in the *International*

Journal of Criminal Justice, the *International Journal of Psychiatry and Law, Police Practice and Research: An International Journal*, and *Violence and Victims*. Her research interests include sex-offender notification policies, juvenile diversion court programs, and corrections. Dr. Beck is the local coordinator for the Prisoners Visitation and Support program in the Federal Medical Corrections Facility in Lexington, Kentucky.

Thomas G. Blomberg is dean and Sheldon L. Messinger Professor of Criminology at the College of Criminology and Criminal Justice at Florida State University. He has published extensively in the areas of penology, social control, victim services, and education and delinquency. His recent books include *Punishment and Social Control: Enlarged Second Edition* (2003), *Data Driven Juvenile Justice Education* (2001), and *American Penology* (2000).

John E. Eck is professor of criminal justice at the University of Cincinnati, where he teaches graduate courses on research methods, police effectiveness, crime prevention, and criminal justice policy. Dr. Eck is internationally known for his studies on problem-oriented policing, the prevention of crime at places, the analysis and mapping of crime hot spots, drug dealing and trafficking control, and criminal investigations. He was a member of the National Academy of Sciences Committee on Police Policy and Research, and a former director of research for the Police Executive Research Forum, where he helped pioneer the development and testing of problem-oriented policing. Dr. Eck is an individual affiliate of the Center for Problem-Oriented Policing and a judge for the British Home Office Tilley Awards for Problem-Solving Excellence. His research interests include explaining and preventing the concentration of crime at locations, the formation of crime patterns, and the development of research processes useful for practitioners involved in crime prevention. Dr. Eck earned his Ph.D. in criminology from the University of Maryland and his bachelor's and master's degrees from the University of Michigan.

David P. Farrington is professor of psychological criminology at the Institute of Criminology, Cambridge University. He is director of the Cambridge Study in Delinquent Development and coinvestigator for the Pittsburgh Youth Study. He is also cochair of the Campbell Collaboration Crime and Justice Steering Group, and is a former president of the American Society of Criminology, the British Society of Criminology, and the European Association of Psychology and Law. He has received the Sellin-Glueck and Sutherland awards of the American Society of Criminology, the Beccaria Gold Medal of the Criminology Society of German-Speaking Countries, the Joan McCord Award of the Academy of Experimental Criminology (AEC), and the prize for distinguished scholarship of the American Sociological Association Criminology Section. He has published twenty-seven books and more than 400 papers on criminological and psychological topics.

Marcus Felson is professor at the Rutgers University School of Criminal Justice. He has served as professor at the University of Southern California and the University of Illinois. He received his Ph.D. from the University of Michigan and his B.A. from the University of Chicago. Professor Felson has been a guest lecturer in numerous countries, including Abu Dhabi, Argentina, Australia, Belgium, Canada, Chile, Denmark, England, Finland, France, Hungary, Italy, Mexico, The Netherlands, New Zealand, Norway, Poland, Scotland, South Africa, Spain, Sweden, Switzerland, and Taiwan. His first book, *Crime and Everyday Life*, is already in its third edition, and he is working on the fourth edition. He is coauthor of *Opportunity Makes the Thief* (with Ronald V. Clarke). His edited books include *Routine Activity and Rational Choice: Advances in Criminological Theory* (edited with Ronald V. Clarke), *Business and Crime* (edited with Ronald V. Clarke), and *Crime Prevention through Real Estate Management and Development* (edited with Rick Peiser). Professor Felson is author of eighty-five professional papers, including "Redesigning hell: Preventing crime and disorder at the Port Authority Bus Terminal." Professor Felson's latest book, *Crime and Nature*, considers how crime can be studied within a larger environmental context.

Roger Hood is professor emeritus of criminology at the University of Oxford and an emeritus fellow of All Souls College. From 1973 to 2003, he was director of the Centre for Criminological Research and a fellow of All Souls. In 2003–2004, he was distinguished visiting professor at the University of Hong Kong, and in 2005 and 2006 he taught at the University of Virginia Law School. In 1986, he was the recipient of the Sellin-Glueck Award of the American Society of Criminology for distinguished international contributions to criminology. He has been appointed CBE, made an Honorary QC, elected a fellow of the British Academy, and awarded the Doctor of Civil Law by Oxford University. As consultant to the United Nations on capital punishment, he has, since 1995, been responsible for preparing and drafting for the secretary-general his five-yearly reports on the status of the death penalty worldwide. He is a member of the British Foreign Secretary's Death Penalty Advisory Panel. Among his books and reports are *A History of English Criminal Law: The Emergence of Penal Policy* (with Sir Leon Radzinowicz, 1986), *Race and Sentencing* (1992), and *The Death Penalty: A Worldwide Perspective* (3rd ed., 2002).

Roy D. King was professor of criminology and criminal justice at the University of Wales, Bangor, where he founded the Centre for Comparative

Criminology and Criminal Justice. He is now professor emeritus and, in 2004, became senior research fellow at the Institute of Criminology at Cambridge, where he also directs the MSt Program on Applied Criminology, Penology, and Management. He is the author of several books and numerous articles, mostly on prisons and imprisonment, and has written widely on prisons in England and Wales, Russia, and the United States, particularly on high-security custody and so-called supermax facilities. His most recent work has been on the prison system of São Paulo, Brazil. He has, at various times, been an expert advisor to Amnesty International, the Council of Europe, and the European Union and to the prison systems of the Russian Federation, Romania, São Paulo, as well as the Federal Bureau of Prisons and Her Majesty's Prison Service. He is currently editing the second edition of *Doing Research on Crime and Justice*.

Steven P. Lab received his Ph.D. in criminology from Florida State University. He is currently professor and chair of criminal justice at Bowling Green State University in Ohio. He is the author of several books, including *Crime Prevention: Approaches, Practices and Interventions* (5th ed.), *Juvenile Justice: An Introduction* (5th ed., with J. T. Whitehead), and *Victimology* (4th ed., with W. G. Doerner), as well as numerous articles and book chapters. His research interests are primarily in the area of crime prevention and the take-up of prevention measures by the public. Dr. Lab is a past president of the Academy of Criminal Justice Sciences.

Chrysanthi Leon is currently a Ph.D. candidate in the jurisprudence and social policy program at the University of California, Berkeley, with an intended completion date of May 2007; she received her J.D. from Boalt Hall School of Law in May 2006 and a B.A. in American studies from Yale University in 1999. An interdisciplinary scholar, Leon works primarily in criminology and the sociology of law. Her current research centers on sex crime and punishment; her other interests include theoretical criminology, alternatives to imprisonment, specialized courts, and judicial policymaking. Works in progress presented at recent meetings of the American Society of Criminology and the Law and Society Association include "Problem-solving courts: Stretching the model of adjudication?" and "'Sex offender to good citizen': Sexual psychopaths as sites of governance." Upcoming presentations will include "Are lawyers different? — The implications of mandated child abuse reporting for the duty of confidentiality" and "Sex offenders and the compulsion to confess." Prior to graduate school, Leon worked for the Friends Committee on National Legislation, a nonprofit lobby group in the public interest. Her work there focused on federal criminal legislation, including the Innocence Protection Act.

David Lester has Ph.D. degrees in psychology (Brandeis University) and social and political science (Cambridge University). He is professor of psychology at the Richard Stockton College of New Jersey. He has served as president of the International Association for Suicide Prevention and written extensively on suicide and other topics in thanatology.

William F. McDonald is professor in the Department of Sociology and Anthropology, and codirector of the Institute of Criminal Law & Procedure at Georgetown University. He earned a doctorate in criminology from the University of California, Berkeley, in 1970. His scholarship on crime and the administration of criminal justice covers virtually all dimensions of those topics including victims, illegal immigrants, police, prosecutors, defense counsel, courts, pretrial processes, sentencing, globalization, and international cooperation. Major publications include *Crime and Law Enforcement in the Global Village* (Anderson 1997), *Plea Bargaining: Critical Issues and Common Practices* (U.S. Government Printing Office 1985), *The Defense Counsel* (Sage 1983), *Plea Bargaining* (with J. A. Cramer; D.C. Heath 1980), *The Prosecutor* (Sage 1979), and *Criminal Justice and the Victim* (Sage 1976). His current research has two focal concerns: the nexus between crime and immigration and the developing institutions of international law enforcement cooperation. Recent publications include "Police and immigrants: Community & security in Post-9/11 America," in *Justice and Safety in America's Immigrant Communities: A Conference Report*, M. King, ed. (Policy Research Institute for the Region 2006); "American and European paths to international law enforcement cooperation: McDonaldization, implosion and terrorism," in *International Journal of Comparative Criminology* (2004 vol. 4); "Traffic counts, symbols & agendas: A critique of the campaign against trafficking of human beings," in *International Review of Victimology* (2004 vol. 11).

Ken Pease is a forensic psychologist by training. He has served as professor of criminology at the University of Manchester and head of the Home Office's Police Research Group. Now retired, his affiliations are with the Jill Dando Institute, the University College London, and the University of Loughborough. He continues to sit on the Home Office's Crime and Technology Reference Group, which advises about science and engineering developments relevant to crime and its control.

William T. Pizzi graduated from Harvard Law School in 1971. He began his legal career as a federal prosecutor in the District of New Jersey. After serving with distinction in that capacity, he joined the faculty at the University of Colorado School of Law in 1975. He is now professor of law at that institution, where he teaches courses in criminal law and criminal procedure. He has written numerous articles in law journals both in the United States and abroad. Many of his articles on subjects such as jury trials, the treatment of crime victims, and plea bargaining take a comparative approach to their subject and have appeared in leading comparative journals such as those at Yale, Stanford, and Michigan. His book, *Trials without Truth*, was published by NYU Press in 2000 and it was translated into Spanish (*Juicios y Mentiras*) in 2004. He has received many awards including his faculty's award for excellence in teaching as well as its award for public service. He has lectured widely, including being a visiting lecturer at law faculties in Norway, Italy, Switzerland, and China.

Henry Pontell is professor of criminology, law and society, and sociology at the University of California, Irvine. His writings in criminology, criminal justice, and law and society span the areas of white-collar and corporate crime, punishment and corrections, deviance and social control, crime seriousness, and most recently, cyber crime and identity fraud. His recent books include *Profit without Honor* (4th ed., Prentice-Hall 2007) and *International Handbook of White-Collar and Corporate Crime* (Springer 2007). A past president of the Western Society of Criminology and vice-president of the American Society of Criminology, he has received the Albert J. Reiss, Jr. Distinguished Scholarship Award from the American Sociological Association and the Donald R. Cressey Award for lifetime contributions to fraud deterrence and detection from the Association of Certified Fraud Examiners.

John Pratt was educated in England at the universities of London (L.L.B. Hons.), Keele (M.A.), and Sheffield (Ph.D.). He is now professor of criminology at the Institute of Criminology, Victoria University of Wellington. He has taught and lectured at universities in the United Kingdom, continental Europe, North America, and Australia. He has undertaken extensive research on the history and sociology of punishment in modern society including *Punishment in a Perfect Society* (1992), *Governing the Dangerous* (1997), and *Punishment and Civilization* (2002). He has also coedited three books: *Dangerous Offenders* (2000), *Crime, Truth and Justice* (2003), and *The New Punitiveness* (2005). His current areas of interest include penal populism (his book, *Penal Populism*, was published by Routledge in 2006) and the sociology of low imprisonment societies. He was editor of *The Australian and New Zealand Journal of Criminology* from 1997 to 2005.

Julian V. Roberts is professor of criminal justice and assistant director at the Centre of Criminology, Faculty of Law, University of Oxford. Prior to joining Oxford, he was a full professor in the Department of Criminology at the University of Ottawa. In 2003, he was awarded a University Research Chair.

In April 2005, he joined the Centre of Criminology, where he currently works. He is a fellow of Worcester College. In 2007, he assumed editorship of *The European Journal of Criminology*.

Stephen M. Rosoff is professor of criminology at the University of Houston, Clear Lake. He is the coauthor of the books *Profit without Honor* and *Looting America*, as well as extensive publications on white-collar crime and elite deviance. Recently, he was a delegate to the United Nations International Crime Conference in Bangkok and was a major participant in a symposium on control fraud at the Lyndon B. Johnson School of Public Affairs at the University of Texas. He has also presented papers in Sydney, Budapest, Milan, and numerous American professional meetings.

Joseph Schafer is associate professor in the Center for the Study of Crime, Delinquency, and Corrections at Southern Illinois University Carbondale. He is a graduate of the University of Northern Iowa and Michigan State University. Schafer is actively involved in researching police organizations, police behavior, and police operations. He is the author of *Community Policing: The Challenges of Successful Organizational Change* (LFB Scholarly 2001). He is the 2006–2007 president of the Society of Police Futurists International (PFI) and a member of the PFI/FBI Futures Working Group, and has served as a scholar-in-residence at the FBI Academy in Quantico, Virginia.

Shlomo Giora Shoham is professor of law at Tel Aviv University. He is a world-renowned criminologist who has published about a hundred books and more than a thousand articles in his areas of specialization. He is the recipient of a decoration from the prime minister of France; he has been awarded the highest prize in American criminology, the Sellin-Glueck award; and in 2003, he was awarded the most prestigious Israeli prize for research in criminology. Professor Shoham has lectured all over the world, including at the renowned universities of Oxford, Harvard, and the Sorbonne.

Jonathan Simon is the associate dean for jurisprudence and social policy and professor of law at the University of California, Berkeley, School of Law, Boalt Hall. Simon is the author of numerous articles on the history and sociology of punishment and the coeditor-in-chief of the journal *Punishment & Society*. His most recent book, *Governing through Crime: How the War on Crime Transformed American Democracy and Created a Culture of Fear*, was published by Oxford University Press in 2006.

Christine Tartaro is associate professor of criminal justice at the Richard Stockton College of New Jersey. She has a B.A. in history from The College of New Jersey and an M.A. and Ph.D. in criminal justice from Rutgers University. She has worked as a researcher for the Police Foundation, the New Jersey Juvenile Justice Commission, and the New Jersey Department of Corrections. She has published articles on jail suicide, direct supervision jails, jail crowding, and correctional suicide litigation. Her research interests include prisons and jails, suicide in correctional facilities, violence in prisons and jails, and crime prevention.

Lawrence F. Travis III is professor of criminal justice and director of the Center for Criminal Justice Research in the Division of Criminal Justice at the University of Cincinnati. He formerly worked as the research director of the Oregon State Board of Parole and as a research analyst with the National Parole Institutes. He is the author of *Introduction to Criminal Justice* (Cincinnati: Anderson), coauthor with Robert Langworthy of *Policing in America* (Englewood Cliffs: Prentice-Hall), and editor of *Policing: An International Journal of Police Strategies and Management*. He has published on a variety of criminal justice topics.

Shanna van Slyke is a doctoral student at Florida State University's College of Criminology and Criminal Justice. She has worked as a graduate research assistant at Florida State University's Center for Criminology and Public Policy Research on funded research projects including the Juvenile Justice Educational Enhancement Program, the Consumer Fraud Institute, and the No Child Left Behind National Earmark Program. Currently, she is involved in research regarding consumer fraud victimization, best practices in juvenile justice education, sentencing white-collar offenders, and natural disasters and community crime rates. Forthcoming publications address the areas of sociolegal developments in consumer fraud, public perceptions of crime seriousness, and prison-based drug treatment.

Courtney A. Waid is a Ph.D. candidate in the College of Criminology and Criminal Justice at Florida State University, where she has taught courses in corrections, juvenile justice, and advanced criminological theory. Her primary research interests include the effectiveness of inmate treatment programs and what works in juvenile detention reform. Previously, she served as a research associate for the Florida Department of Juvenile Justice. Her current area of research concerns the effectiveness of inmate treatment programs, particularly for female offenders.

Gordon P. Waldo received a B.A. in psychology from the University of North Carolina at Chapel Hill and an M.A. and Ph.D. in sociology from Ohio State University. Currently, he is professor and graduate director in the College of

Criminology and Criminal Justice at Florida State University. He has served as chair of the U.S. Sentencing Commission's Drugs and Violence Task Force, research consultant to the National Research Council Panel on Rehabilitation and Deterrence, director of the Southeastern Correctional and Criminological Research Center, senior research advisor to the U.S. Sentencing Commission, associate editor of *Social Forces* and *Criminology*, and academic advisor to Mahidol University (Bangkok, Thailand) in the development of the first doctoral program in criminology in Southeast Asia. He has a long-standing research interest in different rationales for the punishment of offenders.

Lode Walgrave is emeritus professor in criminology at the Catholic University of Leuven (Belgium), where he teaches youth criminology and criminal psychology. He is the director of the Research Group on Youth Criminology, doing research on youth crime, prevention, and juvenile justice. Lode Walgrave was a founding member and chair of the International Network for Research on Restorative Justice and of the International Association for Criminology of Youth. For many years, he has turned his main field of interest to restorative justice. He is especially interested in exploring the social-ethical underpinnings of restorative justice and in searching for an adequate relation between restorative justice and the legal context. He is currently conducting an experiment in family group conferencing (New Zealand style) with serious juvenile offending in Belgium. Though some of his publications are in Dutch, the language of his working environment, Walgrave also published many texts in English on restorative justice issues. He edited several books, including (with Gordon Bazemore) *Restorative Juvenile Justice* (Criminal Justice Press 1999), *Restorative Justice and the Law* (Willan Publishing 2002), and *Repositioning Restorative Justice* (Willan Publishing 2003). He also contributed to most of the recent international readers on restorative justice.

David Weisburd is Walter E. Meyer Professor of Law and Criminal Justice at Hebrew University in Jerusalem and professor of criminology and criminal justice at the University of Maryland, College Park. He is also a senior fellow at the Police Foundation and chair of its Research Advisory Committee. Professor Weisburd has been the principal investigator for a series of major funded studies of policing including the Minneapolis Hot Spots Experiment and the Jersey City Drug Market Analysis Experiment. He is a fellow of the American Society of Criminology, a fellow of the Academy of Experimental Criminology and currently president of the AEC, the cochair of the steering committee of the Campbell Crime and Justice Group, and a member of the Campbell Collaboration International Steering Group. Professor Weisburd was a member of the U.S. National Research Council working group on Evaluating Anti-Crime Programs and its panel on Police Practices and Policies. Professor Weisburd is author or editor of fourteen books and more than sixty scientific articles that cover a wide range of criminal justice research topics, including crime at place, violent crime, white-collar crime, policing, illicit markets, criminal justice statistics, and social deviance.

Brandon C. Welsh is associate professor in the Department of Criminal Justice and Criminology, University of Massachusetts Lowell. He is an author or editor of seven books, including *Saving Children from a Life of Crime: Early Risk Factors and Effective Interventions* (Oxford University Press, 2007), written with David Farrington. He received a Ph.D. in criminology from Cambridge University.

Per-Olof H. Wikström (Ph.D., docent) is professor of ecological and developmental criminology, Institute of Criminology, University of Cambridge. He is the director of the Economic and Social Research Council Cambridge Network for the Study of the Social Contexts of Pathways in Crime (see www.scopic.ac.uk) and the principal investigator of the Peterborough Adolescent Development Study and the Peterborough Community Survey. Professor Wikström was the 1994 recipient of the American Society of Criminology's Sellin-Glueck Award, for outstanding contributions to criminology, and in 2002 he was made a fellow at the Center for Advanced Study in the Behavioral Sciences, Stanford University. Recent publications include *Adolescent Crime: Individual Differences and Life-Styles* (2006, with David Butterworth), *Individuals, Settings, and Acts of Crime: Situational Mechanisms and the Explanation of Crime* (2006), *Doing without Knowing: Common Pitfalls in Crime Prevention* (2006), *The Social Origins of Pathways in Crime* (2005), *Crime as an Alternative* (2004), *Social Mechanisms of Community Influences on Crime and Pathways in Criminality* (2003, with Robert J. Sampson), and *Do Disadvantaged Neighborhoods Cause Well-Adjusted Children to Become Adolescent Delinquents?* (2000, with Rolf Loeber).

Introduction

SHLOMO GIORA SHOHAM

The need for a comparative handbook of penology and criminal justice is clear. To the best of our knowledge, no compilation of essays by the most prominent currently active theoreticians and practitioners exists. The comprehensive nature of this volume relates not only to the many jurisdictions represented in it, but also to the various scholars and researchers from so many different nations and societies who took part in it. Each contributor presents an article reflecting the best-informed thinking in the contributor's area of specialization.

The opening chapter by Thomas G. Blomberg, William D. Bales, and Courtney A. Waid goes into the history of Florida's penal practices, outlining the shift from the old to the new penology. The authors consider claims that the old penology was based on offender transformation, whereas the new penology focuses on offender risk-management. They inquire about Garland's contention that the new penology has evolved into a culture of control, trying to contain recent social disruption, dislocation, and disorder. The authors ask whether the previous focus on offender treatment is completely dead and whether offender risk-management is the future foundation of penology. They conclude, on the basis of an empirical study of the penal practices of Florida, that there is a lingering interest in some offender treatment prospects, coupled with a clear priority upon offender risk-management, imprisonment, community, surveillance, and control. Finally, they conclude that future penology will likely continue to expand its strategies on populations subject to control with both old and new penal practices.

Roy D. King's essay, "Prisons and Jails," reminds us that at the outset of the twenty-first century, more than 9 million people are held in custody, in over two hundred countries around the world. These incarcerations, apart from being a major industrial and social undertaking, affect the lives of the families, friends, and associates of the prisoners. King's essay reviews the universal attributes of prisons. He analyzes the sociology of prisons and the changes in prison staff relationships. He also considers the effects of imprisonment on crime rates. He concludes with the apocalyptic vision that in our rapidly changing world, prisons could yet be seen as relatively benign instruments of control, compared to those we might face in the future; electronic tagging, subcutaneous implants, satellite tracking, and genetic engineering either are available now or will soon be on someone's political agenda.

Christine Tartaro and David Lester highlight the painful and ever-increasing problem of prison and jail suicides. The suicide of the incarcerated generally concerns the public less than the suicide of people in society at large. After all, it is "the suicide of a bunch of animals," who "are not worthy of public concern." This view is now starting to change, partly because the families of prisoners who have committed suicide have successfully managed to sue the authorities. Tartaro and Lester review the frequency of prison and jail suicides; identify risk factors; explain how, where, and when inmates take their lives; and present techniques to prevent custodial suicides. Finally, they urge correctional facilities to adopt these techniques.

Shanna Van Slyke, Gordon P. Waldo, and William Bales have written about monitoring and nontraditional punitive sanctions. The authors first discuss and evaluate fixed fines, day fines, unit fines, and forfeiture. Likewise, they consider registration with criminal justice authorities and nonincarcerative restrictions of liberty, which are becoming increasingly popular for a wide range of offenders. The authors then review a wide variety of punitive and authoritative responses to drunken driving. The next section of the chapter deals with the ever-widening range of civil rights that are lost or restricted upon conviction. The chapter ends with sections on shaming and medical castration. The authors argue finally that for decades, criminologists have been arguing for the more extensive use of evaluation research in the guidance of criminal justice policy. Whether a given sanction is relatively new or has roots in antiquity, all sanctions should be evaluated in terms of whether they meet at least one of the major rationales for punishment. If they do not, then it may be time to consider other alternatives. In the case of most of the sanctions discussed in this chapter, despite hundreds or thousands of years of use, the evaluative research has yet to be done! The message is clear. Even in areas dealing with sanctions that have existed longer than any currently existing criminal justice system, if a practice is to continue, research must be conducted to determine whether or not it meets one of the goals of punishment. If it does not, why should it be continued?

Roger Hood discusses, on a historical and comparative basis, capital punishment and the movement towards its worldwide abolition. He shows how the propagation of the ideals of human rights has led to political and judicial pressures that empower the abolitionist movement. He claims that the position of United States on the death penalty is one of the greatest obstacles to worldwide abolition. He further argues that in addition to the normative considerations involved in the debate about the death penalty, there are also utilitarian considerations. He writes: "It is necessary to approach the question of capital punishment from both normative (moral) and utilitarian points of view, and always in relation to how it is applied in practice. In essence, therefore, the case for retaining the death penalty—and thus resisting the movement to make its abolition an international norm—cannot rest solely on moral, cultural, or religious arguments. It would also have to be shown that it is useful and that it can be applied fairly, and without mistakes or a degree of arbitrariness and cruelty unacceptable to contemporary social and legal values." There is, as this article has tried to make clear, "sufficient evidence to indict capital punishment on all these grounds."

Lawrence F. Travis and Victoria Simpson Beck write about probation, parole, and community corrections on a comparative-international perspective. They begin by discussing the historical development of probation and parole, and then examine the current world trends in their use. The effectiveness of probation and parole is evaluated using the criteria of (1) the effect these sanctions have on public safety, and (2) their contribution to reducing incarceration and related correctional expenditures. The chapter ends with a review of "intermediate sanctions" such as shock incarceration, intensive supervision, electronic monitoring, day reporting, and "broken window" probation. The authors conclude: "What is clear is the centrality of community supervision to contemporary correctional practice. As the pace of development for intermediate sanctions quickens, and the ability to share information about correctional practice and outcome improves, we can expect probation and parole to become ever more common and important components of correctional practice around the world."

Steven P. Lab's essay defines crime prevention as any action designed to reduce the actual level of crime and/or the perceived fear of crime. He then differentiates between three levels of prevention. Primary prevention identifies conditions of the physical and social environment that provide opportunities for or precipitate criminal acts. Secondary prevention engages in early identification of potential offenders and seeks to intervene to prevent crime. Tertiary prevention deals with actual offenders and involves intervention aimed at reducing the probability of subsequent criminality. In dealing with primary prevention, Lab outlines the modern environmental design approaches, neighborhood crime prevention, general deterrence, and social crime prevention. When explaining secondary prevention, Lab explains the need to accurately predict future offending, goes on to survey the methods of situational crime prevention, and studies community-policing strategies. He also gives special attention to the issue of drugs and crime prevention.

Finally, in the section devoted to tertiary prevention, Lab clarifies the issues of specific deterrence, incapacitation, electronic monitoring, and rehabilitation. Lab concludes: "There should be no doubt that crime prevention works. ... The extent of crime prevention's impact, however, varies across time and place, as well as from one approach to another. Indeed, not every program has the same impact in every situation. ... Transplanting that same program to another location may result in the opposite outcome: crime stays the same but fear is reduced. No single approach to crime prevention has proven to be applicable in all situations. Indeed, most interventions appear to work in limited settings with different types of offenders and problems. The greatest challenge, therefore, is to identify the causal mechanisms at work so that effective programs can be replicated in other places and other times."

The situational crime prevention chapter by Marcus Felson outlines the recently popular attempts to intervene in the structured loopholes and design flaws of locations that facilitate crime. Here is an attempt to attack the most accessible link in the etiology of crime.

David P. Farrington and Brandon C. Welsh, writing about the early development of crime prevention, outline programs for preventing delinquency and youth violence shown to be effective in quality evaluation research. The programs aim to prevent the development of criminal potential in individuals, especially by targeting risk factors. The authors specifically review risk-focused prevention programs, family-based prevention programs, school-based prevention programs, and multicomponent interventions. They conclude: "There is good evidence that early family and school interventions—such as general parent education, parent training, child skill training, teacher training, and antibullying programs—can be effective in reducing later delinquency and youth violence. The time is ripe to mount a large-scale evidence-based integrated national strategy for the reduction of crime and associated social problems, including rigorous evaluation requirements, in all countries. This should implement programs to tackle risk factors and strengthen protective factors and could be based on the "Communities that Care" concept. Primary prevention has been effective in improving health and could be equally effective in reducing crime and violence in all countries.

Per-Olof H. Wikström presents an evaluation of the possibility of preventing crime through the threat of punishment. He argues that the complex of "the law, its policing, and threats and administration of punishment" can be regarded as a form of attempted social engineering, which employs deterrence and deterrence-experiences as means to attain compliance. The chapter reviews deterrence theory and its place in the wider context of the etiology of crime. He studies current research and directly tackles the question: "Does deterrence work?" Wikström answers: "Although acknowledging the shortcomings of the empirical evidence, review papers assessing deterrence research nevertheless in most cases come to the conclusion that the legal threat of punishment, by and large, does help prevent crime."

John Pratt writes about retaliation and retribution. He points out that the state, through its criminal justice system, responds to the harm crime causes by retaliating against the harm-doer on behalf of the victim. Thus, the state has institutionalized the otherwise unpredictable retaliation of victims and their kin. John Pratt examines the historical development of retribution in modern society, explains its manifestation in penal sanctions, outlines the main arguments for and against retribution, and studies the circumstances in which one may still find retaliatory practices common outside the criminal justice system. Pratt concludes: "In many countries, there have been a range of measures introduced that provide for more community involvement in penal affairs—plebiscites, for example, in the United States, and community notification procedures regarding the release of sex offenders from prison. Even so, such measures may still not be enough to contain the public mood, disillusioned as it is by the state's self-divestment of authority and acknowledgment that its own bureaucracies were never particularly effective anyway. Under such circumstances, it may well be that some citizens look towards their own forms of retaliation for perceived harms rather than putting their trust in the criminal justice system of the state to address them. Thus, whereas retributionists struggle to contain inflammatory penal trends in the formal criminal justice system at the present time, retaliation against perceived harms and wrongs breaks out beyond it."

Charles F. Abel discusses reparation, compensation, and restitution. He presents a detailed argument to support his claim that reparation constitutes the only adequately explainable, and hence the best, form of punishment. Reparation, paid either as restitution or compensation, is, according to Abel, the most realistic, empirically informed, and unemotional sanction, aimed to satisfy the victim without unduly humiliating the offender. Abel states in conclusion: "Not only must the state take up the role of punisher, but the most efficacious form of punishment is to give people money and let them spend it in ways that they feel affords them the best satisfaction for whatever wrongs they feel they have suffered and whatever values that have been affronted. Therefore, the only forms of punishment that can be explained satisfactorily are those that require reparation through a state-enforced transfer of money."

Joseph A. Schafer and Clemens Bartollas deal with the basic questions concerning the roles assigned to the police in contemporary society. What does society intend for the police to do? What are the means the police are deemed to employ? What aspects of modern policing generate controversy and conflict? Who will control the controllers? Schafer and Bartollas also review the history and development of the police, the structure of police organizations, police culture, and police operations. Schafer and Bartollas' concluding thoughts are: "The police are one of the most visible branches of the government and remain a focus of public awe, respect, vitriol, and scorn. It is common for citizens to have mixed feelings about the police, but few are neutral in their views. The world of the police is, then, a mixed lot. They receive our trust, support, and respect, but also our fear, apprehension, and anger. They routinely confront danger, uncertainty, fear, excitement, revulsion, humor, and boredom. We recognize they are a needed social institution, that they must have discretion, that they must use force, and that they must assert their authority. At the same time, such dimensions of policing create conflict, ill-will, and animosity. Although many problematic aspects of policing have improved in the past century and a half, concern still abounds regarding misconduct, abuse of authority, excessive force, and corruption. This is tempered by the positive feelings people have toward the police, particularly in the aftermath of critical incidents in which police are viewed as heroes and saviors, such as the September 11, 2001 terror attacks."

David Weisburd and John E. Eck ask: "What can police do to reduce crime, disorder, and fear?" They present a typology of current police practices and use it to organize and assess the evidence about police performance on the above criteria. After having reviewed existing practices, Weisburd and Eck conclude with a more general synthesis of the evidence and discuss implications for policing and research on it. They finally state: "Police practice has been centered on standard strategies that rely primarily on the coercive power of the police. There is little evidence to suggest that this standard model of policing will lead to communities that feel and are safer. Although police agencies may support such approaches for other reasons, there is not consistent scientific evidence that such tactics lead to crime or disorder control, or reductions in fear. ... Our review suggests that community policing (when it is not combined with problem-oriented approaches) will make citizens feel safer, but will not necessarily impact upon crime and disorder. In contrast, what is known about the effects of problem-oriented policing suggests promise for reducing crime, disorder, and fear."

William F. McDonald provides a chapter on international policing. He presents the history of transnational law enforcement, explains the considerations involved in the decision to extradite offenders or prosecute them vicariously, shows how ineffective mechanisms of international policing are exploited by criminals, and addresses the issue of desperate victims (or countries) who attempt to bypass the extradition barrier by conducting searches for fugitives, either by themselves, with the aid of police officials, or via bounty-hunters. Finally, McDonald deals with the impact terrorism has had on transnational law enforcement. He states: "In sum, looking at the status of law enforcement and the administration of criminal justice from the perspective of globalization, one sees a patchwork of agreements and tensions among contending geopolitical and legal entities. Although the institutions of transnational cooperation in law enforcement and criminal justice assistance have developed substantially in the recent past, impunity for criminals is a serious reality. For the prosecution of transnational fugitives, many victims today are like victims before the development of the modern police. If they want justice, they have to make their own arrangements. Governmental institutions cannot be relied upon to render justice. Even the states themselves are forced to rely upon heavy-handed, questionable, and politically costly methods to get evidence and to bring offenders to justice."

William T. Pizzi reviews the roles and functions of the prosecution and the defense in Western trial systems. He compares two types of systems: the adversarial system in the common law countries, and the inquisitorial system in the civil law countries. Pizzi presents the structure of both systems, explains the responsibilities of the prosecutor and defense attorneys, and looks at the ethical issues confronting defense lawyers and prosecutors, including the pressure to resolve cases without full trials. Pizzi also tackles the role of the victims in criminal trials.

Julian V. Roberts and Estella Baker write on sentencing. Although sentencing is the raison d'être of the criminal process, judges in many countries enjoy a great degree of discretion in sentencing for most offenses. The authors highlight the nature of such discretion, first indirectly, by reviewing the conflicting nature of the various purposes of sentencing, and then directly, by explaining the parameters of sentencing discretion. The authors then give an overview of a range of methods that states have adopted in an attempt to structure the exercise of this discretion and evaluate their efficacy with respect to a variety of issues, such as previous convictions, sentencing disparity, plea bargaining, and victim input. The final section is devoted to restorative justice. Roberts and Baker conclude: "All together, it is hardly surprising that sentencing policies and practices have been evolving rapidly over the past twenty years, nor that they continue to evolve. There is evidence, for instance, that many American states are beginning to question the utility as well as the justice of the harsher mandatory sentencing laws, particularly those that apply to drug offenders. These laws have resulted in rising prison populations and have disproportionately affected African-American communities. Meanwhile, in other jurisdictions, there is evidence that sentencing is becoming more structured. The fact that sentencing reform remains on the agenda in these as well as many other jurisdictions attests to the difficulty of the issues involved, their continuing political importance, and the lack of satisfaction with attempts that have been made to date to solve the problems that have been outlined in this chapter."

Ken Pease, who writes about victims and victimization, argues that victim programs should foster an internal locus of control among victims, while remaining aware of the issue of victim blame. The author pays great attention to the prevention of repeated crimes against prior victims and suggests how criminal justice resources should be harnessed to that end. He also maintains that progress toward practical victim help and support in the criminal justice system, which is largely indifferent to them, must continue. Pease concludes: "The argument of this chapter has been that stimulating into existence a realistic degree of internal locus of control among victims should be at the core of victim programs. This should be focused upon the prevention of repeated crimes against the prior victim or those linked to that victim by location or vulnerability. This emphasis requires a diminution of stress on the avoidance of victim blame. Victims sometimes recognize their contribution to crime events, and it serves an internal locus of control that this should be so in certain circumstances (and emphatically not in others). The progress towards practical victim support in a criminal justice environment that is largely hostile to them must continue. The involvement of victims in schemes of restorative justice will require more, and more persuasive, evidence of benefit to be safely advocated."

Lode Walgrave follows with a chapter on restorative justice. He opens with the history of restorative justice, presenting both its ancient and modern roots. He then attempts to define restorative justice and find its most common features. Afterward, he reviews and evaluates the different restorative practices or models that are commonly employed in the field. The next three sections are devoted to the study of restorative justice as a form of punishment, to its socioethical foundations, and to the way it should be incorporated into a system of criminal justice. In his concluding remarks, Walgrave sketches the limits to restorative justice and offers a look into the future of the field. He claims: "Developments in criminal justice are a matter of criminal policy, which are only partially dependent on practical and scientific qualities and options, but more still on the cultural and political climate. In almost all Western countries, problems of criminality are currently exploited commercially by dramatizing media and boosted through populist rhetoric by some politicians, which together may lead to a rather simplistic attitude among a great part of the public. Many observers typify the predominating social climate as being intolerant of deviancy and repressive against offending. If that is true, the chances for restorative responses to be generally accepted and promoted would be reduced. ... I have alluded to several scientific explorations of public attitudes that show results that are not at all unfavorable to restorative responses. Therefore, there is no reason to be too pessimistic about the future of restorative justice."

Mark S. Umbreit, Robert B. Coates, and Betty Vos give us an in-depth look at one of the most widely practiced forms of restorative justice, i.e., victim offender mediation (VOM). After explaining what VOM is and how it is practiced, the authors evaluate its effectiveness. They review participation rates, participant satisfaction, diversion rates, recidivism rates, costs, and more. The chapter ends with a look at the implementation of VOM in cases of severe violence. The authors conclude: "Victim offender mediation is a restorative justice process with considerable promise for repairing the harm caused by crime while holding offenders accountable and allowing those affected by the crime to have a voice in its solution. When it is practiced in accordance with its guidelines and values, the research demonstrates that VOM improves victims' involvement and healing, increases the extent to which offenders take responsibility for their behavior and learn from their experience, offers community members a role in shaping a just response to law violation, and contributes to a more positive public attitude toward juvenile and criminal courts."

Finally, we present two case studies designed to give readers a "hands-on" feel for how criminal justice systems deal with specific types of offences. The first case study is by Henry N. Pontell, Stephen M. Rosoff, and Andrew Peterson's chapter about white-collar and corporate crime. The authors open their chapter by citing the widely held view that although the crimes of the wealthy dwarf the painful effects of common crime, high-status white-collar offenders receive much more lenient treatment than blue-collar criminals. They investigate the evidence for this view and show that things are not as clear-cut as is often held. They point out that structural sources of leniency exist on many levels for white-collar and corporate crime and explain why it is difficult to rectify this situation.

The second case study and the last chapter of this book is by Jonathan Simon and Chrysanthi Leon, who write about American sex offender policies since the 1990s. Simon and Leon argue that the cry to get tough on sex offenders has recently become powerful and popular in the United States. They describe its manifestations in the criminal justice system and try to explain the trend.

Punishment and Culture

THOMAS G. BLOMBERG,
WILLIAM D. BALES, AND
COURTNEY A. WAID

Contents

1.1 Introduction

During the 1980s, the United States began to focus less upon offender rehabilitation strategies and increasingly upon the use of various get-tough
imprisonment and other intermediate punishment measures, including
home confinement, electronic surveillance, and daily reporting centers. The
increased reliance upon imprisonment and intermediate punishments
resulted in major increases in the number and proportion of the base population subject to some form of penal control, despite general decreases in
crime rates. In attempts to explain this escalation in penal control, a series
of theoretical frameworks have been proposed. Among these are net-widening, carceral society, minimum security society, maximum security society,
new penology, and most recently the culture of control. Emerging from these
various theoretical interpretations has been a general debate over whether

1

these increasing penal control trends do, indeed, reflect the emergence of a postmodern or new penology or merely the continuation of trends associated with the modern or old penology.

In terms of a postmodern interpretation of contemporary penology, Feeley and Simon (1992) claimed that several distinct features have evolved to distinguish postmodern penology, or what they term the "new penology," from modern penology or "old penology." The authors contended that the old penology was focused upon offender rehabilitation, transformation, or people-changing, whereas the new penology is focused upon offender risk management. Feeley and Simon elaborated that the differences in penal techniques involve a general shift from old penology's reliance upon social technologies to change offender behaviors to new penology's focus upon administrative technologies for offender-management: profiling, auditing, risk screening, and around-the-clock surveillance. Lemert (1993) took exception to Feeley and Simon's claims that penology is in the midst of developing new strategies aimed at increasing control over particular groups of offenders through his examination of contemporary probation practices. Lemert argued that current probation practices are largely unchanged from those practiced throughout the twentieth century. He elaborated that the deterioration in probation supervision that has occurred is because of patterned reductions in probation staff and major increases in caseloads. The end result has been what Lemert called "bankloading," an old practice with a new name that involves probation officers focusing their time and energy upon their most serious cases while largely ignoring the remainder of their caseloads. Lemert concluded that Feeley and Simon's contention "that probation realizes the claims made for it as a part of a new penology or indeed whether its changes have been undertaken as logical consequence of such penology must be doubted" (1993, 460).

Garland (2001) placed the old versus new penology debate into a broader context. He suggested that it is not so much a question of a new or an old penology but rather what has actually taken place in penology. It is in this regard that Garland claimed there has developed an increasingly strident and vindictive "culture of control." Garland elaborated that emerging from late modernity have been a series of social disruptions, dislocations, and disorder that, in turn, have led to an overriding public concern for stability and order. Garland concluded that the quest for stability and order has resulted in a series of penal policies and practices that together have resulted in a "culture of control." The end result is more offenders subject to both new and old penal practices and technologies.

These previous theoretical interpretations of penal trends have been based largely upon fragmented, uneven, and discontinuous empirical documentation. Notably absent from the literature have been more broadly

conceived empirical studies that address systemwide practices, consequences, and trends over time. As a result, whether penology has, in fact,
moved from previous "old" practices into clearly "new" practices remains
questionable. For example, is the previous focus upon offender treatment
indeed dead? Is offender risk management the current and future foundation
of contemporary penology? Or, alternatively, is there a more complicated
blend of penal practices emerging that reflect the ever-continuing ambiguity
and quest for crime control? In an effort to address these questions, this
chapter provides a case study of Florida's penal practices, reforms, and
consequences from 1970 to 2007. Included in the chapter's coverage are
efforts to reform Florida's sentencing practices, use of imprisonment, use
of community supervision, and the emergent penal control and crime inci-
dent-related trends. A salient finding that emerges from this case study is
the documentation of a transition in Florida's penal practices from an indeterminate offender rehabilitation focus that has been blurred over the past
thirty-five years with an increasing emphasis upon offender risk management, imprisonment, and community surveillance. The end result is a lingering interest in certain offender treatment prospects coupled with a clear
priority upon offender risk management, imprisonment, community surveillance, and control.

1.2   Indeterminate to Determinate Sentencing:
1970 to Present

During the past thirty-five years, Florida's penal practices have undergone
numerous changes. In 1970, indeterminate sentencing with parole was the
major prison release mechanism employed by Florida, reflecting the state's
focus upon offender treatment and rehabilitation. During that year, 2,058
(59 percent) inmates were paroled, whereas 1,440 completed their sentences
without supervision. Parole remained the most common prison release
mechanism in 1980 when 4,166 (62 percent) inmates were paroled, and 2,564
completed their sentences. However, in 1983, indeterminate sentencing with
parole as the dominant prison release mechanism came to an abrupt end.
Beginning in the mid-1970s, concern over disparity in sentencing across
racial groups and geographic areas of the state as well as problems with prison
overcrowding contributed to Florida's determinate sentencing movement
(Griswold 1985). After several years of debate and research on various alternatives to indeterminate sentencing, Florida developed a set of sentencing
guidelines that were pilot tested in 1981 (Sundberg, Plante, and Braziel 1983).
When these sentencing guidelines became law in 1983, Florida's long tradition of parole was largely eliminated. To illustrate, in 1990, only 247 (0.7

percent) of the 35,416 inmates released from the state's prisons were granted release by the Florida Parole Board.

Although the 1983 guidelines were promoted as "Truth-in-Sentencing" by policymakers, the lack of adequate prison beds to fully implement determinate sentencing and concerns over future prison overcrowding resulted in the implementation of generous gain-time policies simultaneous to the passage of the new guidelines. Specifically, the new laws allowed inmates to earn up to twenty days per month served in the form of incentive gain-time for good behavior and participation in programs. Additionally, all inmates were awarded unearned gain-time equivalent to one-third of their court-imposed sentence upon entering prison.

The next major shift in Florida's penal policies, namely early prison release, received its impetus from determinate sentencing but did not occur until 1987. At this time, and despite the generous gain-time policies, Florida's prison system was approaching its court-ordered population capacity limits. This was occurring because of a failure by the state to fund prison construction levels commensurate with the numbers of prison admissions resulting from the new determinate sentencing policies. In February 1987, the state responded by implementing an early prison release law that mandated the Florida governor to grant inmates early release credits at a level determined by the Department of Corrections (DOC) to maintain the prison population below its lawful limits. Until 1991, inmates were eligible for the early release program based upon the nature of their current and prior criminal offenses. However, changes to the early release program were implemented as a result of a high-profile case in 1990 in which an inmate with a violent past murdered two Miami police officers within a few days of his early prison release. Specifically, legislation was passed that authorized the Parole Commission to review the histories of all inmates and make the determination of early prison release eligibility. In its various forms, early prison release was in place until December 1994.

In 1994, another major change in sentencing and penal policy resulted from the termination of early prison release and the implementation of new sentencing guidelines. Simultaneous to the new guidelines, unearned gain-time resulting in an automatic one-third sentence reduction was eliminated. Additionally, the statewide administration of the guidelines originally passed in 1983 was transferred from the Florida Supreme Court to the DOC. This included the preparation of guidelines documents, training of judicial personnel, collection of sentencing data, and analysis and reporting on the new sentencing system and the effectiveness of its implementation.

Although the changes in 1994 brought Florida closer to the concept of determinate Truth-in-Sentencing that was envisioned in the 1983 guidelines, this sentencing strategy did indeed become a reality in late 1995. Through grassroots initiatives spurred by public outrage that emerged in response to early prison releases, policymakers enacted legislation that required all offenders sentenced to prison to serve a minimum of 85 percent of their sentence. This law provides the foundation of Florida's determinate sentencing policy today with no discussion of reverting to earlier punishment strategies, despite the fact that Florida's prison population and costs continue to escalate at a rapid pace. See Table 1.1 for a summary listing of Florida's sentencing and related punishment policy changes from 1983 to the present.

Table 1.1 Summary of the History of Florida's Sentencing and Related Punishment Policies

Punishment Policy	Description	Criteria for Placement
1970 Parole	Any offender sentenced to prison with an offense date prior to October 1, 1983, was eligible for release through the Parole Board.	Offense dates prior to October 1, 1983.
1983 Sentencing Guidelines without Early Release	Sentencing guidelines were implemented in 1983 and affected all offenders with offense dates after October 1, 1983, except for those convicted of capital crimes. Eligibility for significant gain-time awards was also enacted including basic gain-time (one-third off the court sentence) and up to twenty days per month served of incentive gain-time.	Offense dates between October 1, 1983, and December 31, 1993, excluding capital cases, that did not receive any early release days under administrative gain-time, provisional credits, or control release.
1983 Sentencing Guidelines with Early Release	Same as above description with the addition of early release credits awarded to selected inmates from February 1987 to December 1994.	Offense dates between October 1, 1983, and December 31, 1993, excluding capital cases, that received any early release days under administrative gain-time, provisional credits, or control release.
1994 Sentencing Guidelines	New sentencing guidelines structure was enacted for offenders with offense dates on or after January 1, 1994. Basic gain-time, which reduced the sentence by one-third, was eliminated.	Offense dates between January 1, 1994, and September 30, 1995.
Minimum 85% of Sentence Served	All offenders with offense dates on or after October 1, 1995, are required to serve a minimum of 85% of the court-imposed sentence.	Offense dates on or after October 1, 1995.

1.3 Prison Practices: 1970 to Present

During the 1960s and 1970s, rehabilitation was recognized as the foundation of the correctional process in Florida's prisons. During this time, rehabilitation was widely accepted as the foremost need of inmates residing in the state's prisons. Furthermore, parole was widely embraced, as it was seen as the sole mechanism for continued offender change and adjustment during community reintegration.

Although it was believed that individualized treatment could continue with the parole process, prison was considered fundamental to the correctional process through its provision of educational, vocational, and substance abuse programs for Florida's inmates. During this period, there was a fundamental reliance on prison, even with the general acknowledgment that parole was a less fiscally taxing method to reforming offenders capable of meeting parole conditions and fulfilling conditions of treatment in the community. Furthermore, the continued reliance on prison persisted despite the rapid influx of inmates into Florida's prisons and the resulting overcrowded conditions that were undermining the effectiveness of prison rehabilitation programs.

As the 1970s progressed, Florida's classification practices not only proliferated but were refined in relation to institutional management needs. The classification teams at each institution were decentralized, with classification officers working directly with inmates in an effort to develop effective individualized offender treatment plans based on the specific needs of each inmate. However, this development was highlighted in the context of public protection and safety, not the offender's amenability to treatment and/or the effectiveness of treatment programming. As a result, the initial shift from the individualized treatment of offenders to risk management was beginning to take place.

During the 1980s, treatment continued, but with a new emphasis upon what was termed "structured treatment." Structured treatment was focused upon the maintenance of institutional order and safety, rather than explicitly preparing inmates for law-abiding behavior upon release. Maintaining order and promoting a safe environment for inmates was viewed as paramount, given the growth in the number of inmates housed in Florida's prisons throughout the 1980s. Table 1.2 shows that in 1975, the imprisonment rate, as measured by the number of offenders in prison per 100,000 persons living in Florida, was 171.3. This rate increased to a level of 205.9 by 1980 and steadily increased throughout the 1980s, as Florida's prisons held 251 and 325 inmates per 100,000 citizens in 1985 and 1990.

Florida's inmate population growth in the 1990s led to the construction of new prison facilities and an increased reliance on privatization throughout

Table 1.2 Number and Rates of Correctional Populations in Florida: 1975 to 2004

Year	Prison Population	Prison Population Rate Per Resident Population	Supervision Population	Supervision Population Rate Per Resident Population	Total Correctional Population	Total Correctional Population Rate Per Resident Population	Percent of Total in Prison	Percent of Total on Supervision	UCR Part 1 Index Crime Rate	Florida Resident Population
1975	14,130	171.3	44,391	635	58,521	773	24.1%	75.9%	7,246	8,248,851
1980	19,722	205.9	47,621	497	67,343	703	29.3%	70.7%	8,388	9,579,497
1985	28,310	251.0	73,866	655	102,176	906	27.7%	72.3%	7,634	11,278,547
1990	42,733	325.0	95,622	727	138,355	1,052	30.9%	69.1%	8,539	13,150,027
1995	61,992	438.1	136,056	962	198,048	1,400	31.3%	68.7%	7,623	14,149,317
2000	71,233	445.7	149,470	935	220,703	1,381	32.3%	67.7%	5,604	15,982,378
2004	81,974	469.3	151,150	865	233,124	1,335	33.6%	66.4%	4,907	17,468,408
Percent change: 1975 to 2004	480.1%	174.0%	240.5%	36.2%	298.4%	72.7%	39.0%	-12.4%	-32.3%	111.8%

the state's correctional system. By 1995, the imprisonment rate was 438.1, and by 2000, 445.7 inmates per 100,000 residents were incarcerated in Florida's prisons. As of June 30, 2004, Florida's imprisonment rate stood at 469.3. The marked increase in the numbers of offenders incarcerated in Florida's prisons in the early 1990s was followed by the construction of a number of new facilities in the mid-1990s. Specifically, in 1990, Florida operated forty-five major prison facilities; however, by 2000, fifty-seven major prison facilities were in operation. Of these fifty-seven prisons, the entire operations of five facilities were and continue today to be managed by private providers. Three of these facilities opened in 1995, and two additional private prisons began housing Florida inmates in 1997.

1.4   From Probation Supervision to Community Supervision: 1970 to Present

Not only have there been major changes in Florida's sentencing practices and resulting increases in the state's prison populations, but community supervision as an alternative to incarceration also underwent major changes. Throughout the 1970s, Florida's community supervision system was fairly straightforward. Felony probation was the only form of community supervision for less serious felony offenders as an alternative to prison. This felony probation practice changed in 1983, with the implementation of new sentencing guidelines and a new determinate sentencing policy. In addition, community control supervision, commonly referred to as "house arrest," was also implemented in 1983 and added to Florida's sentencing guidelines as an alternative to prison. House arrest officers operated with statutorily mandated caseloads of no more than twenty offenders per officer. Electronic monitoring of house arrest offenders was added as a surveillance option in 1987 for the higher risk offenders. Moreover, as electronic surveillance technology advanced, global positioning satellites (GPS) were added in 1998 to allow for twenty-four-hour real-time accountability of the highest risk offenders on house arrest.

The house arrest programs that developed in Florida during the 1980s that were enhanced by electronic monitoring that required offenders to wear an electronic security device, which enabled the tracking of the offender at home. Currently, Florida utilizes more electronic monitoring devices than any other state, except North Carolina (Camp and Camp 2002). Evidence of continued future expansion of electronic monitoring in Florida is indicated by the passage of the Jessica Lunsford Act in 2005, named after a 9-year-old girl who was abducted and killed in February of that same year. Under this legislation, anyone convicted of molesting a child under the age of 12 will face a life sentence with a minimum-mandatory 25-year prison sentence.

When the offender is released back into the community, he or she will be subjected to electronic monitoring for life. Furthermore, any sex offender 18 or older who committed a sexual offense against a victim 15 or younger and those defined as sexual predators who violate their terms of supervision and are returned to supervision are now mandated to be placed on electronic monitoring for the remainder of their term of supervision. The act appropriated $3.9 million in reoccurring funds to increase the number of electronic monitoring devices by 1,200.

As previously mentioned, two types of electronic surveillance are currently utilized: (1) radio frequency (RF) monitoring, and (2) GPS monitoring. When employing RF monitoring devices, DOC uses "active" tamper-alert ankle devices. These devices allow for the computerized surveillance of offenders during the hours they spend within their home. This surveillance is achieved through continuous signaling from the transmitter worn by the offender on his or her ankle and a receiver attached to the offender's home telephone. At a centralized location, a computer receives information concerning all the offenders' movements wearing RF devices. This information is verified via comparison of the offender's movement and his or her work schedule (Baker 2005).

One fundamental limitation of the RF technology is the fact that offenders cannot be monitored while away from their home telephone or residence. Thus, the use of RF devices does not enable DOC to monitor the offenders' whereabouts during approved absences from the home, or while he or she is at work. In order to track the location of the more serious offenders in "near real time" and to provide mapping of the offender's movement for retrieval upon demand from a centralized computer, DOC began employing GPS monitoring in 1998. The rationale behind the adoption of GPS technology was the ability to conduct twenty-four-hour surveillance, as opposed to the in-home-only surveillance that RF technology provides. Currently, DOC employs both "passive" and "active" GPS systems to monitor offender locations. Both systems record offender location at any given time; thus, technologically speaking, the systems do not differ widely. However, active GPS systems notify the probation officer of violations immediately, whereas a passive GPS system provides the probation officer with a printed summary of violations once a day (Florida Corrections Commission 2003).

The use of a GPS system has been promoted as a means to provide increased community protection and security to victims. In some instances, exclusionary boundaries surrounding the place of work or property of a victim are set. In these situations, GPS monitoring alerts system officials when these set boundaries are violated, and in turn, officials can notify the victim of the offense and take appropriate responsive actions. Aside from mapping for information archive retrieval, GPS systems can facilitate two-way communication with the offender and/or victim(s), tamper-of-device notification, and remote laptop tracking (facilitated by a wireless remote). The expectation is that offenders are deterred from violating the conditions of their house arrest, as they are aware that all movements are tracked in "near real time" twenty-four hours a day.

It is important to note that in the early 1983 implementation of the house arrest program, the DOC was concerned about avoiding the pitfall of net-widening. Net-widening refers to the capacity of penal reforms to become implemented as supplements to previous penal practices instead of alternatives, thereby resulting in a larger proportion of population subject to some form of penal control. To avoid net-widening with house arrest and simultaneously provide public safety, DOC drafted very restricted language on offender program eligibility, namely only those offenders found guilty of nonforcible felony offenses. However, statewide opposition from judges to this restrictive eligibility requirement resulted in a modification of the law in which program eligibility was expanded to those offenders found guilty of forcible felony offenses and unspecified "other" offenders deemed suitable for house arrest by sentencing judges. This broad eligibility definition did result in the placement of a number of offenders on house arrest who, in the absence of the program, would have been subject not to prison but rather probation, thereby resulting in net-widening (Blomberg, Bales, and Reed 1993). However, electronic monitoring house arrest has been focused largely upon violent, sexual, and other serious criminal offenders who in the absence of these community surveillance options would have gone to prison (Padgett, Bales, and Blomberg 2006).

Today, Florida employs multiple forms of community supervision with varying degrees of surveillance, caseload sizes, and offender reporting requirements. These include felony probation, administrative probation, drug offender probation, sex offender probation, house arrest, house arrest with electronic monitoring (RF or GPS methods), sex offender house arrest, pretrial intervention, and drug offender pretrial intervention.

1.5   Florida Penal Control Trends: 1970 to 2003

Table 1.3 displays the changes in Florida's use of imprisonment in relation to community alternatives to incarceration from 1975 to 2003. The data illustrate an increasing emphasis on the use of incarceration over community supervision. The prison population has increased by 447.2 percent, while community supervision has increased by 244.6 percent over this time period. Additionally, the percentage of the total offender population subject to incarceration increased by 39.0 percent, while the proportion subject to community supervision actually declined by 12.4 percent. This is particularly revealing given

Table 1.3 Changes in Prison and Community Supervision in Florida: 1975 to 2003

Year	Prison Population	Community Supervision Population	Total Correctional Population	Percent of Total in Prison	Percent of Total on Supervision
1975	14,130	44,391	58,521	24.1%	75.9%
1980	19,722	47,621	67,343	29.3%	70.7%
1985	28,310	73,866	102,176	27.7%	72.3%
1990	42,733	95,622	138,355	30.9%	69.1%
1995	61,992	136,056	198,048	31.3%	68.7%
2000	71,233	149,470	220,703	32.3%	67.7%
2003	77,316	152,985	230,301	33.6%	66.4%
Percent Change: 1975 to 2003	447.2%	244.6%	293.5%	39.0%	−12.4%

Table 1.4 Measures of Rehabilitation Programs in Florida's Prisons: 1970 to 2003

Year	Prison Population	GEDs Earned	GEDs per Inmate Population	Enrollments in Academic and Vocational Programs	Program Enrollments per Inmate Population
1970	8,811	920	10.4%	3,700	42.0%
2003	77,316	1,112	1.4%	25,481	33.0%

that over this period of time, the level of control and surveillance of those offenders subject to community supervision has expanded considerably over the same time period, reflecting Florida's shift from indeterminate sentencing and treatment to determinant sentencing and punishment.

Table 1.4 shows that the percentage of the inmate population earning high school equivalency diplomas (GEDs) has declined from 10.4 percent in 1970 to just 1.4 percent in 2003. Further, the percentage of inmates enrolled in prison academic and vocational programs has declined from 42.0 percent to 33.0 percent over the same period of time. An interesting quote from the DOC's FY1970–1972 *Biennial Report* states that "last year, over 700 inmates were enrolled in a total of 214 college courses, and 19 inmates graduated with an associate of arts degree" (Florida Department of Corrections, 1972, 15). Today, DOC is prohibited from enrolling inmates in any form of college courses.

1.6 Correctional Control and Crime in Florida

In Table 1.2, the number and rates for Florida's correctional population and crime rates from 1975 to 2004 are provided. The table shows that during this twenty-nine-year period, Florida's total correctional population increased by 298 percent, the correctional population rate per 100,000 resident population increased by 73 percent, and the prison population expanded by 480 percent. However, the crime rate actually decreased by 32 percent during this same twenty-nine-year period. Consequently, what these aggregate data and trends suggest is that Florida's correctional population numbers and trends are being driven by factors that extend well beyond Florida's incidents of crime and their associated trends. What appears to have emerged over these years is a culture that is not only receptive to but expects a priority upon multiple methods of crime control.

1.7   Conclusions

The preceding description of Florida's penal policy changes over the past thirty-five years documents a general shift from offender rehabilitation to offender risk management. Florida's long-practiced tradition of indeterminate sentencing to prison with release by parole to the community was subject to considerable debate in the mid-1970s. The debate centered upon multiple concerns including disparity in sentencing and problems with prison overcrowding. Beginning in 1983, a set of pretested sentencing guidelines became law, and in the same year, Florida enacted community control, also known as house arrest. House arrest was intended as a get-tough alternative to prison for nonforcible felony cases, with prisons serving only the more serious and violent offenders who posed the greatest risk to the community. The 1983 sentencing guidelines were promoted as a Truth-in-Sentencing policy. However, problems with prison bed limitations and concerns over future prison overcrowding resulted in the state implementing several prison gain-time policies. In 1987, in reaction to a growing prison population that was near the state's federal court-ordered capacity, Florida implemented an early prison release law designed to keep the state's prison population below its lawful limit.

In 1994, following a high-profile case involving the killing of two police officers by an offender released early from prison, Florida ended early prison release and implemented still-another set of sentencing guidelines. The following year, there was a growing public outcry over early prison release, and Florida responded with a law that required prison inmates to serve at least 85 percent of their sentence. This practice remains in operation today, with Florida's prison population and number of prisons continuing to expand. Further, 10,000 offenders are now under some form of house arrest, with many of these offenders being subject to electronic surveillance. Overall, these trends document that Florida has indeed transitioned its penal policies and practices from offender treatment and rehabilitation toward a more punitive prison and community risk management and surveillance system. However, while this transition has occurred in Florida, there is other activity now taking place that suggests a tempered yet lingering interest in offender treatment and rehabilitation.

To elaborate, at present, the DOC, in collaboration with Florida State University's College of Criminology and Criminal Justice (FSU), is conducting an experimental evaluation of the effectiveness of prison drug treatment. The DOC initiated this study with the proclamation that only a true experimental design involving the random assignment of inmates to control and experimental groups would adequately address the question of whether prison drug treatment is effective, and if such treatment is more or less effective for particular types of inmates. Only one prior prison-based drug treatment study employing a true experimental design with random assignment has been conducted in the United States. However, the study was limited to only one particular drug treatment program in one male prison in California (Wexler et al. 1999a, 1999b). The DOC/FSU study is statewide in the third-largest state prison system in the country, with over 88,000 inmates, and involves all inmates entering prison after January 2006. Additionally, the study will include twenty-five different prisons with as many as three different drug treatment modalities for both men and women.

All inmates are provided a consent form during the reception process, in which they will indicate if they are willing to participate in the study. Those agreeing to participate will be randomly assigned to a treatment or control group. Inmates assessed to be in need of substance abuse programming who are in the treatment group and are located in a facility with treatment slots available receive the type of substance abuse treatment consistent with their level of need, while similar inmates in the control group do not enter treatment. Detailed data will be extracted from the DOC's Offender-Based Information System on inmates released who were assigned to the control and treatment groups. These data will include detailed information on program participation, assessment scores measuring programming needs, and institutional conduct indicators. Also, variables shown to be effective predictors of recidivism will be captured on each inmate including age at release, prior recidivism events, gender, race, educational level, current and prior offenses, custody level, length of time served in prison, psychological condition, and special education needs, as well as re-entry services provided to inmates after prison release.

The study should provide timely and important research findings. Whether prison-based drug treatment is effective in reducing recidivism and facilitating successful community re-entry is the central question that will be answered. Additionally, whether different types of inmates based on gender, age, criminal backgrounds, and so on are more amenable to the effect of drug treatment while incarcerated will be addressed. Finally, the relative effectiveness of different treatment modalities and the length of treatment will be assessed. Given the strength and scope of the research design as well as the level of support for this research from the DOC and other high-ranking government officials in Florida, the findings could result in major changes in the funding and administration of prison-based drug abuse programs in Florida, and perhaps elsewhere.

Florida's past and current incarceration and crime trends closely mirror national trends. For example, as reported by the U.S. Bureau of Justice Statistics (2005), the total inmate population has been increasing for the past several years, reaching 2.1 million in June 2004, or 1 in every 138 U.S. residents incarcerated. While the U.S. crime rate, like Florida's, has declined over the past ten years, the number of admissions to prisons and jails is far greater than the number of inmates released. For example, in relation to the federal prison system, the number of admissions in 2004 exceeded releases by more than 8,000. In sum, the different penal-related laws that have been enacted over the past several decades have culminated in a national reliance upon imprisonment that has resulted in the United States having the highest incarceration rate in the world without considering the growing numbers of offenders subject to community supervision and surveillance.

Florida's current efforts to assess the efficacy of prison drug treatment programs, although suggestive of perhaps a tempering in punishment policies, may instead be more of an aberration. Specifically, given Florida's response to the tragic Jessica Lunsford case, it is evident that even more vindictive punishment policies for sex offenders will be forthcoming not only in Florida, but throughout the United States. At a minimum, what these trends suggest is America's continuing confusion and frustration over crime as well as our continuing debate and uncertainty over how to best protect ourselves from crime. It seems likely that in our ever-continuing quest to provide better public safety, there will be increased reliance upon incarceration coupled with certain forms of strategic treatment as well as ever-more technologically advanced community surveillance. It appears that future penology promises more of the same, namely, a culture that embraces prison and community surveillance as well as selected attempts at treatment, as the ultimate solution to crime continues to be evasive. In sum, given the continuing confusion over the causes and cures for crime, future penology is likely to continue to expand its strategies and population subject to control with both old and new penal practices.

References

Baker, M. 2005. "Electronic monitoring." In *Encyclopedia of Prisons and Correctional Facilities*, edited by M. Bosworth. Thousand Oaks, CA: Sage Publications.

Blomberg, T. G., W. D. Bales, and K. Reed. 1993. Intermediate punishment: Extending or redistributing social control. *Crime, Law, and Social Change* 19: 197.

Bureau of Justice Statistics. 2005. *Prisoners in 2004.* Washington, DC: U.S. Department of Justice.

Camp, C. G., and G. M. Camp. 2002. *The 2001 Corrections Yearbook.* Middletown, CT: The Corrections Institute.

Feeley, M.M., and J. Simon. 1992. The new penology: Notes on the emerging strategy of corrections and its implications. *Criminology* 30: 449.

The Florida Corrections Commission. 2003. *A Review of the Community Control Program and Electronic Monitoring Within the Florida Department of Corrections.* Tallahassee.

The Florida Department of Corrections. 1972. *8th Biennial Report: July 1, 1970 to June 30, 1972.* Tallahassee.

Garland, D. 2001. *The Culture of Crime and Social Order in Contemporary Society.* New York: Oxford University Press.

Griswold, D. B. 1985. Florida's sentencing guidelines: Progression or regression. *Federal Probation* 49: 25.

Lemert, E. M. 1993. Vision of social control: Probation considered. *Crime and Delinquency.* 39: 447.

Padgett, K. G., W. D. Bales, and T. G. Blomberg. 2006. Under surveillance: An empirical test of the effectiveness and consequences of electronic monitoring. *Criminology and Public Policy* 5: 61.

Sundberg, A. C., K. Plante, and D. Braziel. 1983. Florida's initial experience with sentencing guidelines. *Florida State Law Review* 11: 125.

Wexler, H., et al. 1999a. The Amity Prison TC evaluation. *Criminal Justice and Behavior* 26: 147.

Wexler, H. et al. 1999b. Three-year reincarceration outcomes for Amity in-prison therapeutic community and aftercare in California. *The Prison Journal* 79: 321.

Prisons and Jails

ROY D. KING

2

Contents

2.1 Introduction

Five years into the twenty-first century, more than 9 million people are held in custody in more than two hundred countries around the world. Several times that number are directly affected by prisons, either because family members are incarcerated or because they work in prisons; or are involved in their planning, construction, or maintenance; or otherwise service the needs of prisoners and staff. The use of imprisonment is, by any standards, not merely a substantial instrument of social and penal policy; it is also a major industrial and organizational undertaking, and most current signs indicate that it is becoming even more so.

There is undoubtedly a sense in which a prison is a prison is a prison: The fundamental similarities of locking people up against their will for determinate or indeterminate periods of time, for the most part away from their families and the rest of society, are likely to outweigh the myriad ways in which they may differ. But at the same time, there are important differences between jurisdictions in the way imprisonment is employed, and both between and within jurisdictions in the way that prisons are managed; such differences are likely to impact upon prisoners and staff in sometimes profoundly different ways. Such differences will also send out different symbolic messages to the rest of society about the purposes and meaning of imprisonment or, put another way, may reflect on the character of societies and how they view their disgraced or potentially disgraced citizens. In this chapter, I shall try to draw attention both to what might be regarded as the universal or essential attributes of "the prison" and to the ways in which prisons can and do vary. However, it is important to bear in mind that it is obviously going to be necessary for me to be selective, and what is selected will reflect the interests and the knowledge of the author. The themes I will discuss reflect my judgments as to what is important; many of the examples I include will reflect my own direct knowledge, drawn either from my research in specific prisons or jurisdictions, or my examination of them on behalf of various international organizations. As far as possible, I shall try to put these into a wider context, but the reader should be aware that the result will be heavily biased towards what happens in the Anglo-American systems.

The title of this chapter refers both to prisons and jails, and it is appropriate to begin with an elucidation of the differences between those institutions and a brief history of how they have evolved. From there I proceed to a consideration of *the relative use of imprisonment* in section 2.3, and *the changing nature of prison populations* produced by that usage in section 2.4. In section 2.5, I consider the *sociology of prisons* and the way in which staff and prisoner cultures have changed. Section 2.6 discusses issues surrounding *security, order and control, and the supermax phenomenon,* and in the final substantive section, I turn to what is known about the *effects of imprisonment.* In my *Conclusions,* I refer briefly to several other topics that would have been included had space permitted. I conclude by trying to take stock in a consideration of whither the future.

2.2   An Historical Survey of Prisons and Jails

The terms *prison* and *jail* (or *gaol* in the original English spelling) are sometimes used interchangeably, and indeed attempts at making clear definitional distinctions between them tend to founder upon exceptional cases. This is not surprising, given a rather convoluted history and the fact that there has never been any real attempt to disaggregate the concept of imprisonment by inventing special terms to describe different forms. Moreover, the word *prisoner* precisely defines a person legally held captive against his or her will, wherever he or she may be housed. Incidentally, the term *prisoner* is always to be preferred to the term *inmate,* which smacks of management euphemism and which could, in any case, be applied generically to persons held in a wide variety of other residential institutions. I use the term *inmate* only when it is already so enshrined in the literature, for example, in the discussion of inmate culture, where to use other terminology might seem perverse. It is probably best to regard the jail as a subspecies of the more generic prison.

The main distinctions between the nature and functions of jails and prisons can be seen by outlining the current situation in the United States. Today, there are more than 3,000 jails that serve county or other local jurisdictions. They vary enormously in size, reflecting the communities they serve, with more than half having fewer than fifty prisoners on average, and at the other extreme, about seventy-five housing more than a thousand each. They serve multiple functions, but deal with persons held while awaiting trial or sentence, and virtually all prisoners sentenced to terms of one year or less. The term *prison* is reserved for institutions organized on a statewide basis, usually under the authority of a department of corrections or, at the federal level, under the Bureau of Prisons; they deal with prisoners serving determinate sentences of longer than one year and indeterminate sentences. Also, in states that retain the death penalty, they house prisoners on death row. Prisons are usually classified by reference to security or custody levels, to take account of the perceived risks to the public or the good order of the prison, and range from open prisons to maximum security institutions; in recent years, the federal and many state systems have added a new tier of super-maximum (supermax) security prisons. The Bureau of Prisons and some states—namely Connecticut, Delaware, Hawaii, Rhode Island, and Vermont—operate both prisons and jails under a single combined authority, whereas Alaska and West Virginia have a mixture of state and local jails.

It may be helpful to illustrate the functions of these institutions and how they came about by reviewing some of their history in England and Wales. In what follows I use the traditional *gaol* in the context of Britain, and the more international *jail* in the context of the United States and other countries. Early English gaols were institutions that essentially served locally based court jurisdictions. They have probably always been multifunctional, serving to detain the accused pending trial, persons convicted pending sentencing, and sentenced persons pending the execution of the sentence, which in England and Wales was usually something other than imprisonment. Indeed, in the eighteenth century, English courts still had a "bloody code," with an extensive list of crimes entailing capital punishment, or transportation, first to the American colonies and then to Australia. In those days, the gaols were, in the memorable words of Sir Lionel Fox, but the "ante-room to the New World or the next" (Fox 1952). For the purposes of pretrial and presentence detention, physical proximity to the courts was essential. That their function was primarily a temporary holding one was demonstrated by the fact that periodically the King's justices would pass through on circuit to "deliver the gaols"; that is, to try the accused and, depending upon the outcome, either set the accused free, or sentence them to flogging, banishment, or death. Such local gaols were often small, sometimes quite large, but tended to be central and forbidding features of their communities. However, in time many of them were overtaken by economic, social, and demographic change and fell into disuse as isolated relics away from new centers of population.

Such gaols, or some similar places of detention, were probably as old as the concept of justice itself; justice could not be dispensed unless the accused were available to be held to account. At this point, we must briefly digress, because it is important to note that remanding an accused person in custody was not the only way of ensuring attendance at trial. Indeed, in the settled agrarian communities of Anglo-Saxon England, groups of families were held collectively responsible for upholding the law, which included rendering up one of their number accused of wrongdoing on pain of financial penalty. From such beginnings, it gradually became possible for royal courts and local justices to remand accused persons on bail either on their own recognizance (promises to attend, with or without forfeiture of monies if they did not), or the sureties of others on their behalf. The amount of bail reflected the assessment of the risk of failure to attend. In England and Wales, it has not been the practice to pay monies in advance, against the risk of nonattendance, but rather to collect it, or try to, after the event. Today, only a tiny proportion of bail decisions involve monetary sureties, and absconding while on bail has instead become a criminal offense. In the United States, a commercial system developed whereby bail bonds persons would assume the risk by paying the money into court in advance in return for a fee of 10 percent paid by the accused. In recent years, a number of court-administered bail schemes in the United States have somewhat reduced the role of the bail bondsmen. If the terms of bail could not be met, or if the courts determined that the risks of further offending or nonattendance were too great, they could fall back on remands in custody. The relative balance between bail and custody and the making of bail-custody decisions may have a profound effect on the size and nature of modern prison and jail populations and has been the subject of considerable research.

Until the Assize of Clarendon in 1166, Henry II decreed that every county have at least one gaol under the control of his appointed sheriff, thereby introducing a system of criminal justice that has survived in most of its essentials to the present. Until then, there had been a confusing profusion of municipal gaols, local lock-ups, and gaols franchised to lords of the manor, and even gaols operated by the church to service its ecclesiastical courts. Though many of these continued to survive alongside county gaols, they were gradually subjected to increasing control, restriction, and regulation by both the monarch and Parliament. Eventually, too, the responsibility for the gaols passed from the King's sheriff to the local magistracy.

But from very early days, local gaols also served to house petty offenders, drunks, prostitutes, rogues, and vagabonds who served short sentences of imprisonment for breaching the peace or threatening to do so. After the Debtor's Act of 1350, gaols also held persons in an attempt to coerce payment of debts to private creditors—a procedure that was not finally abolished until the 1960s, although in later years the practice survived under the legal fiction that one was in custody for contempt of court orders to pay, and not for the debt itself. In 1777, John Howard, the philanthropic High Sheriff of Bedfordshire (after whom the Howard League for Penal Reform and John Howard Societies in many parts of the world are named), produced his famous report, *The State of the Prisons*, in which he claimed that debtors constituted some 60 percent of the prisoners in the institutions he visited. It was common to speak of some prisons, such as the Fleet in London, as debtors' prisons (and was not unusual for the families to be confined with the debtor). The last gaol used exclusively for debtors—the Queen's—was closed in 1862. Even today, it is still possible to be imprisoned for public debts, such as the nonpayment of taxes and duties of various kinds.

It is a commonplace of modern penology that imprisonment disproportionately embraces the poor and disadvantaged. That is unquestionably true, though for the most part these are poor and disadvantaged persons who have also committed crimes. However, historically the gaols were directly associated not only with debt but also with poverty or, in the terminology of the time, pauperism. The Statute of Labourers in 1349 was designed in part to deal with the shortage of labor, which resulted from the devastation of the population by the Black Death a year earlier, by trying to control the movement of laborers in search of higher wages. As feudal arrangements broke down, persons wandering abroad were seen as a threat to the peace and could find themselves branded as vagabonds, whipped at the pillory, and locked up in gaol. As the face of rural England was changed by the enclosure of common lands, beginning in the sixteenth century and accelerating into the eighteenth century, more agricultural workers were denied their subsistence way of life and became paupers dependent upon the local parish for alms. By the time of Elizabeth I, the problem of paupers had become so entrenched that the first Poor Law was enacted in 1572 with others to follow, culminating in the Poor Law Amendment Act of 1834, putting an end to "outdoor relief." These statutes distinguished between various classes of pauper and provided what were seen as appropriate remedies for their condition: upkeep and relief for the deserving poor and work for those who were unemployed in the poorhouse or workhouse, and punishment for those who could, but would not, work in houses of correction or bridewells, as they came to be called after the royal palace of Bridewell, which was converted for that use. In what has appropriately been called the "great confinement," similar processes were to be found across Europe, and it was not just the poor and the criminal classes who were affected. Those deemed mad were also swept up into asylums.

To some extent, gaols, houses of correction, and workhouses competed for custom in the sense that it was often a matter of chance by which route one found one's way into an institutional setting. Houses of correction over-lapped most directly with the county gaols, often being built next door, and over time became indistinguishable from them. Yet they continued, in name at least, long into the nineteenth century, until they were formally amalgam-ated under the Prison Act of 1865. From that time on, former gaols and houses of correction became known as local prisons. Workhouses survived even longer and remained an ominous specter for many of the working class well into the twentieth century. By then, the principles of "less eligibility" and the rigorous regimes advocated by Bentham and Chadwick—which had, in turn, posed problems for gaols and houses of correction, which surely ought to have even stricter regimes for their even less eligible prisoners—had become more benign, and they served more as asylums for the elderly and infirm.

However, although gaols and houses of correction undoubtedly served a punitive role in relation to the recalcitrant poor and petty offenders, the growth of imprisonment and the establishment of prisons as places for the punishment of convicted felons in England and Wales were inextricably bound up with the uncertainties associated with the sentence of transporta-tion, which had been the preferred method of dealing with felons since its introduction in 1717, and the need to deal with a rising tide of crime. In 1776, with transportation to America no longer an option, a reluctant central government was obliged to provide an alternative. Initially, a solution was found by keeping convicts in the hulks: decommissioned warships moored on the Thames, which had served as temporary lodging for convicts awaiting transportation. During the day, the convicts were put to hard labor in the dockyards and on public works, returning to the hulks, which were managed by a private contractor, at night. But there was a growing interest in the development of national penitentiaries—so called because their design was intended to ensure that those incarcerated therein would be forced to reflect upon, and become penitent about, their crimes.

John Howard and other reformers had shown that the gaols were pesti-lential places where typhus, then known as gaol fever, was rife. Moreover, though nominally under the supervision of sheriffs, and later magistrates, they were in fact run by private gaolers who charged fees for their services, which could extend from bed and board through the provision of gin and ale to the company of prostitutes. More or less anything was available at a price, and the public was more than happy to pay for the opportunity to gawp at the suffering of others. Moreover, there was often little if anything by way of separation of first offenders from recidivists, the convicted from the unconvicted, adults from minors or even males from females. And just as the gaoler and turnkey charged fees, so too might stronger prisoners exploit the weak through claiming their right to "garnish" and "chummage" for the privilege of entering this strange society and having a bed. Such practices fleeced the families of the better-off prisoners and stripped the poor of everything they had, such that sometimes, unable to pay the discharge fee, they festered in prison even after their time had expired. The gaols were, in short, corrupt and unhealthy schools for crime.

Howard was concerned to find ways not just to improve the health and welfare of prisoners but to prevent their further corruption and to lead them on a path towards moral rectitude—a cause that was to engage reformers on both sides of the Atlantic for generations to come. He was impressed by the designs of the architect William Blackburn, which were intended to foster a well-ordered institution by separating offenders, thus facilitating their supervision. Howard had encountered the embodiment of such principles in some of the institutions he had visited in continental Europe, especially in Holland, and he began to argue for the establishment of national penitentiaries in England. A Penitentiary Act was duly passed in 1779, but no government money was forthcoming for the two penitentiaries that were planned, and there was disagreement about where they should be sited. In the absence of developments by the central government, there was a flurry of activity at local level by such influential figures as the Duke of Richmond, in Sussex, and Sir George Onesiphorus Paul in Gloucestershire, to build reformed county gaols and houses of correction.

In 1791, Jeremy Bentham published his brother's plan for a penitentiary, which he called the Panopticon, "a mill to grind rogues honest." By virtue of its circular design, with tiers of open cells facing inwards around the circumference, an officer standing at the center of the Panopticon would have, theoretically at least, the capacity to exercise surveillance over the entire population. For the next twenty years, he repeatedly lobbied for its adoption, modifying both the design and the arrangements for its management; it never found sufficient favor for adoption, in part because of concerns that Bentham himself, as the private contractor, would be the beneficiary of prisoners' labor. Though no such Panopticon was built in the United Kingdom, a few were built elsewhere, the most notable example being at Stateville, Illinois. But, even as Bentham was developing his design, transportation to Australia had become a possibility and enthusiasm for a penitentiary dissipated. The first transports set sail in 1787, but the onset of the Napoleonic Wars, during which ships were needed for other purposes and convicts were conscripted for military service, meant that the process did not really take off until after

1815. Bentham (1802a), still hopeful that his penitentiary scheme would be adopted, criticized the Australian colonies for releasing convicts too soon when they had earned their "ticket of leave": the forerunner of parole. But Bentham was not alone in thinking that transportation to Australia, where there were reports of former convicts becoming prosperous as they took advantage of the opportunities in the new colony, was insufficiently deterrent. Others, however, were later to find it too harsh and a blot on civilization.

Eventually, the first national penitentiary was built at Millbank in 1816: a monstrous and largely unworkable structure housing 1,000 prisoners in a series of pentagonal blocks surrounding a central hexagon. It was a constant source of embarrassment and criticized, in 1835, by the Reverend Whitworth Russell and William Crawford, two of the first prison inspectors appointed to advise the government, for giving insufficient attention to the uplifting possibilities of, *inter alia*, religious instruction. (Incidentally, Russell committed suicide there, in 1847.) Millbank was not demolished until 1893, when it was replaced by Wormwood Scrubs. In 1834, Crawford, a prominent member of the Quaker-inspired Society for the Improvement of Prison Discipline, had presented his monumental report on the penitentiaries of the United States to the Home Secretary. Crawford's was one of the first official examples of cross-fertilization of ideas on crime and punishment between England and the United States. Many more were to follow. But unofficial traffic had preceded it. Crawford was singularly impressed by the design of John Havilland for the Eastern State Penitentiary in Pennsylvania, which leaned on the work of William Blackburn and took some of his principles to their logical conclusion. Seven wings, with tiers of cells on several levels, radiated outwards in a star-shaped design from the prison centre, in which prisoners could be held in completely separate single cells where they might both sleep and work, obviating the possibility of malign influences of prisoners on each other. Solitude combined with religious instruction would bring about penitence and reform. This was preferred to an alternative system that had been developed at Auburn Prison, New York, where prisoners were housed in separate cells at night, but by day were required to work together in workshops organized on factory lines. Under the Auburn system, the association of prisoners with one another during the working day was deemed a necessary evil, but accompanied by a rigidly, not to say brutally, enforced rule of silence to prevent criminal contamination. In what is conventionally described as the battle of the systems—separate versus silent—each had its advocates. In fact, there was less difference between them than is sometimes suggested, but it was the separate system, sometimes taken to relentless extremes, that proved to be the more influential in England, at least at first, whereas in the United States it was the silent system that prevailed, except in Pennsylvania, the Quaker State.

Not everyone who visited the Eastern State Penitentiary viewed it as enthusiastically as did William Crawford. Dickens, for example, was moved to campaign as forcefully against the cruelty of the rational penitentiary as he did about the debtors' prisons (Collins 1962). De Beaumont and de Tocqueville ([1833] 1964) were somewhat bemused by the monomania surrounding penitentiary systems in the United States, and while they thought the Pennsylvania system superior in its purity, it was the cheaper Auburn system that they thought more appropriate as a model for France. But in 1842, the new model prison at Pentonville, London, designed by Colonel Jebb, which closely followed that of Havilland, was opened. It was none too soon. The numbers of persons coming before the courts had risen rapidly over the last two decades, in part because of the introduction of policing under Robert Peel's administration, and the 1837 recommendation of the Molesworth Committee to end transportation. Although transportation lingered on for another twenty years, shorter periods were replaced by sentences of penal servitude. The original Pentonville, a model of architectural determinism, is generally regarded as the perfect architectural realization of the aspirations of those who believed that in a particular prison discipline lay the key to the reform of prisoners. Other prisons, variations on the Pentonville design, quickly followed, some to serve as convict prisons under the control of central government and others to replace moribund county gaols and houses of correction as local prisons. By 1877, the local prisons and the central convict prisons were brought together into a single system to be administered under a Prison Commission, and there followed a period of rationalization in which small, redundant, and inappropriately located prisons were closed down.

It may seem odd to stop this brief historical account in the last quarter of the nineteenth century. Clearly much has happened since. Harding et al. 1985 provides a useful and concise history of the system in England and Wales, whereas McConville 1981, 1994 deal with late eighteenth- and nineteenth-century developments in more detail, and there are many excellent essays on the subject in Morris and Rothman 1995. But in an important sense, the foregoing sets out most of the foundations concerning the establishment of prisons and gaols and their respective functions. Perhaps, too, enough has been said for people to recognize the antecedents of prisons and jails in the United States— as in so many other things, developments in the United States stayed more faithful to the eighteenth-century inheritance than was the case in England—and even for readers to see points of similarity and difference within systems in other countries (for an overview of prison systems in several countries, see Smit and Dünkel 2001).

Responsibility for the integrated prison and gaol system in England and Wales continued to rest with the Prison Commission until 1963, when it was replaced by the Prison Department of the Home Office. Then in 1993, the operation of the prisons was distanced from the Home Office through the creation of the Prison Service Agency, which since 2004 has become subordinate to the National Offender Management Service. However, since the 1870s in England and Wales, local prisons have continued to this day to perform the functions of the old gaols, by holding persons in custody before trial or while awaiting sentence. They also continue to hold sentenced prisoners either for the whole of their sentence, or while they are waiting to be transferred to training prisons, and such prisoners are normally kept separate from the unconvicted, usually in separate wings. Separation, however, is often difficult to sustain because of the constantly fluctuating prison population. In the 1960s, it was planned to develop a system of remand centers to ensure the separation of unconvicted from sentenced prisoners, but only a few were actually built and those that remain are only for young offenders. They coexist alongside the local prisons. Out of the old penitentiaries and convict prisons has developed a system of prisons for sentenced prisoners that have successively been described as central, regional, and training prisons, and which are now classified mainly according to the degree of security they provide, but with several serving specialist functions, for example, as resettlement prisons for those nearing the end of their sentences, or as prisons with special units for exceptional escape risk or difficult to manage prisoners.

Most of the local and training prisons are for adult males, but there are others for women and for young offenders. There have been major changes in the way in which the purposes of imprisonment have been seen since the twin concerns with deterrence, in the form of hard (and often useless) labor, hard fare, and a hard bed on the one hand and moral reform through religious instruction and contemplation on the other, which dominated the nineteenth century. In the twentieth century, these concerns gave way to considerations first about the treatment, training, and rehabilitation of offenders and then with the collapse of the rehabilitative ideal in the face of evidence that "nothing works" in preventing recidivism, to considerations of security, control, and incapacitation. More recently, with a reappraisal of previous evidence and a shift from "nothing works" to "what works," cognitive skills and offending behavior programs have been offered to some offenders, selected through the use of more refined assessments of risks and suitability.

Yet to see these as mutually exclusive phases would be a gross oversimplification. The history of imprisonment has been marked by the tendency of most of those involved in prison operation to have competing and contradictory expectations of what it can and should achieve. Indeed, in the period when reformers were campaigning for the establishment of penitentiaries and advocating one or another competing prison disciplines, their views were often expressed with passion and backed up by extraordinary attention to detail as to possible effects and how they might be measured. Whether they were extolling the virtues of silence and meditation, or the relative merits of those instruments of hard labor such as the tread wheel (on the rotation of which each prisoner might "ascend" 7,200 feet a day) or the crank (whose revolutions could be so minutely calibrated on John Mance's ergonometer), all were convinced that their method would be in the best interests of prisoner and society. As the Reverend Finley in the United States put it: "Could we all be put on prison fare for the space of two or three generations, the world would ultimately be the better for it .... As it is, taking this world and the next together ... the prisoner has the advantage" (cited in Rothman 1971, 84–85). Small wonder, perhaps, as McConville (1995) notes, that the philosopher C. S. Lewis considered it preferable to live under robber barons than moral busybodies; the latter might torment us for our own, with a completely clear conscience.

This bare-bones outline of prison history was traditionally interpreted as though it represented a march of progress from unsanitary, unhealthy, chaotic, and corrupt gaols to clean, healthy, well-ordered, and accountable prisons. Such progress, it was argued, was consistent with the principles espoused in the famous essay on crime and punishment by Cesare Beccaria ([1764] 1963), much applauded by Voltaire as representing a triumph of humane Enlightenment thinking over the arbitrary brutalities of the "bloody code." There are obviously elements of truth in all that, but rarely does history unfold simply as the practical implementation of ideas; anyone surveying the state of contemporary prisons around the world can see whole national systems that remain unsanitary, unhealthy, chaotic, and corrupt. Furthermore, there is clear evidence of arbitrary brutalities even in the most advanced Western democratic systems, e.g., "three strikes" laws and the death penalty, not least in relation to mentally retarded minors.

It is clear from this outline that the development of prisons and their use has been intimately bound up with changes in the social structure of society and the economic relations between social classes or just the advantaged and disadvantaged. Witness the impact of the Black Death; of the enclosure movement; of relations between creditors and debtors; and of confused attempts to deal with the poor, the unemployed, and those who could, but would not, work. It would be extraordinary if the use of imprisonment today did not reflect demographic, economic, and social relations in the wider community, and of course it does. Thus in every society where data exist or research has been carried out, prison populations are mostly from lower social strata, and ethnic minorities are found to a degree radically disproportionate to their weight in the general population. Furthermore, whereas once prisoners were mostly debtors, now they are mainly those involved in the consumption of drugs, the supply of which is low.

Not surprisingly, several writers have sought to theorize this history in terms of the political economy of crime in ways compatible with, if not directly derived from, Marx's class theories. A recent example is by Melossi and Pavarini (1977), but the earliest and most famous of these is by Rusche and Kirchheimer (1939) in their book *Punishment and Social Structure*. Rusche and Kirchheimer sought to move behind the rhetoric of penal reformers to link various forms of punishment—fines, transportation, and imprisonment—to the underlying economic conditions of capitalism and the operation of labor markets. However, the historical basis for their explanation has been criticized and their analysis fails to account for either the differences to be found between different capitalist societies, on the one hand, or the similarities between these and developments in the Soviet Union, on the other.

Revisionist accounts of the history of prisons have been provided by David Rothman (1971, 1980) and Michael Ignatieff (1978). Both locate developments in the ideology of punishment within the history of ideas, and both give prominence to evangelical zeal and the penetration of the structures of punishment by religion and religious figures. Both, however, also seek to relate the evolution of prisons, workhouses, and asylums to wider social influences: Rothman traces American innovations to the hopes and fears of citizens in the new republic, while Ignatieff more explicitly links developments in England to ruling class hegemony.

Most controversial has been the analysis by Michel Foucault (1977), who used selected aspects of this historical canvas to elaborate a philosophical position about the structures and technologies of power in modern society. Foucault argued that the emergence of the prison arose not so much from a desire to punish *less* as a determination to punish *better*—random and brutal punishment of the body was replaced by the systematic control of the mind. In Foucault's analysis, taking Bentham's Panopticon as a starting point, the prison, the workhouse, and the factory were all mechanisms for disciplining and regulating the poor by subjecting them to minute surveillance in what was becoming an ever-more-carceral society. It is pointless to criticize Foucault's theoretical position because of its poor grounding in history and sociology; that is to misconceive his metaphorical analysis, though it has been criticized on both counts. One might note that since Foucault died in 1984, there has been a massive expansion of closed-circuit television (CCTV) surveillance, the introduction of electronic tagging, and proposals for implanting criminals with electronic devices so that they can be monitored by satellite. As an alternative to Foucaultian ideas, Spierenburg (1984) argues that the change from the spectacular theatre of the public scaffold and the pillory to the development of measured punishment that takes place behind high walls, out of public view, reflects a change in public sensibilities. In that regard, it can be seen as part of a process that began earlier and spread much wider in the context of the work of Norbert Elias (1939), on the history of manners and what he called the civilizing process.

Whatever else they have done, these different interpretations of prison history have provoked a stimulating debate about the place of prison in contemporary society.

2.3   The Relative Use of Imprisonment

When the first *World Prison Population List* was published (Walmsley 1999), it was reported that about 8 million persons were held in penal institutions throughout the world, either as detainees awaiting trial, or as convicted offenders. By the time the fifth edition was published (Walmsley 2003), the numbers exceeded 9 million. There are many imperfections in the data assembled by Walmsley. Information is lacking on a number of countries; the data from some countries may be of questionable veracity and are sometimes supplied by unofficial sources; it is not always clear whether remand prisoners and persons confined in juvenile institutions, psychiatric hospitals, and treatment centers for alcohol or drug abusers are included; and the data do not relate to comparable dates. Surprising though it may seem, prison authorities do not always know how many prisoners they have at a given time on the basis of routinely recorded data, but rely on periodic surveys even to establish how many prisoners they have beyond their release dates. Despite such problems, the attempt to provide a global picture offers a rough-and-ready starting point to consider the relative use of imprisonment, although it will be clear that some degree of caution is needed to interpret the basic statistics.

About half of all the prisoners included in the *World Prison Population List* are incarcerated in just three countries: the United States, China, and Russia. It is intriguing that three countries at the opposite poles of the Cold War, with such dramatically different histories, economies, cultures, and patterns of crime, should nevertheless hold, as it were, gold, silver, and bronze medal positions in the world prisoner league. Although the relative positions of these three countries in terms of total prison populations remained unchanged over the five years covered by Walmsley's data, the distances between them did change and even the direction of travel. Over a five-year period, the prison population in the United States grew by over 15 percent, from 1.7 to 2.03 million, though this was a slower rate of increase than in the preceding two decades. The prison population in China also grew, at about half the U.S. rate, from 1.4 to 1.51 million, although these figures relate only to sentenced prisoners and exclude unknown numbers held in pretrial and "administrative" detention. But in Russia, the prison population declined by about 14 percent, from 1 million to 860,000, and has since declined further.

Total numbers of prisoners, without additional information, does not say very much about the relative use of imprisonment in different countries. It has become conventional to use rates of imprisonment per 100,000 population for comparative purposes, which at least standardizes for total population; on that basis, the picture of the top three countries begins to look rather different. Over the period of the five world population lists, the United States has increased its incarceration rate from 645 to 701 per 100,000 population, overtaking Russia, which declined from 685 to 606. China, by contrast (with a population of nearly thrice that of Russia and the United States combined), had incarceration rates that increased from a more modest 115 to 117. However, the inclusion of unknown numbers of prisoners held before trial or in "administrative detention" would change that ratio, possibly dramatically.

The range in incarceration rates is enormous, and some of the changes reported for the same country in successive editions of the prison population list are so large as to be hard to explain. However, grouping by regions tends to iron out the greatest disparities. On that basis, in western and central African states, the median rate is less than 50 per 100,000, whereas in southern African states, it is over 325 per 100,000. In South American countries, the median rate is around 125 per 100,000, but for the Caribbean it is almost 300 per 100,000. On the Indian subcontinent, the rate is just over 50, but in the central Asian states formerly part of the Soviet Union, the rate is almost 400 per 100,000. In southern Europe, the median is about 75 per 100,000, but for central and eastern Europe, formerly part of the Soviet bloc, the rate is approximately 200 per 100,000. The Scandinavian countries range from 60 to 75 per 100,000, with the larger countries of western Europe having rates between 75 and 100, whereas England and Wales have a rate of over 140 per 100,000.

Penal reform organizations sometimes use these incarceration rates as ammunition to suggest that some countries are too punitive, or at least use imprisonment to a disproportionate degree compared to others. They could equally be used, of course, to argue the opposite when compared to another set of countries. But both arguments would be inappropriate, because we know that, in advanced Western societies at least, most crime is committed by young males, and a fairer measure would certainly use rates that took account of the age structure of the population, not just its size. Even that would not provide a measure of punitiveness, because one must know the amount and nature of crime, to which imprisonment constitutes part of the response, before gauging a society's punitiveness (see the discussion of these issues in Pease 1994). I shall illustrate this by reference to a comparison of the use of imprisonment in Russia, the United States, and England and Wales over the ten years from 1992 to 2001 when crime rates, which have been presented elsewhere (King and Piacentini 2005), are taken into account. The figures are presented in Table 2.1.

Table 2.1   Approximate Recorded Crime and Imprisonment Rates per 100,000 Population

		Russia	England and Wales	United States
1992	Crime rate	1,850	10,950	5,250
	Prison rate	480	90	470
2001	Crime rate	2,050	10,600	4,150
	Prison rate	670	130	690

(Note: Crime rates rounded to nearest 50, prison rates to nearest 10.)

The much-criticized imprisonment rate in England and Wales, high by European standards though low in comparison to Russia and the United States, begins to look more modest when set against the high rates of crime: more than twice the rate per 100,000 than the United States and five times the rate in Russia. The imprisonment rate for the United States, on the other hand, looks even more oppressive given the comparatively law-abiding nature of that society as reflected in its relatively low, and falling, level of recorded crime. Although the imprisonment rate in Russia continues to mirror that in the United States, it has held that rate (and since then reduced it further) despite the fact that crime rates there have been going up. It is important to enter caveats about such comparisons. It seems likely that the differences in rates of recorded crime are considerably exaggerated by differences in the degree of sophistication in recording criminal statistics and in the range of offenses that they cover, and the higher rate of crime in England and Wales has a preponderance of lesser offenses, whereas those for the United States and Russia include many more offenses of homicide and rape.

Although there are some countries in the world that are currently in the process of reducing their prison populations, sometimes dramatically (as in Russia in the last five or six years), and others such as Denmark have managed to maintain a steady state, the dominant trend, in more than two thirds of the countries in the world population list, has been upwards. Different countries began the ascent from different starting points, at different times, and proceeded at very different speeds, but there is space here only to consider the trends and the reasons for them in the United States and in England and Wales.

The United States has occupied a unique position, which, over the last three decades, has separated it to such an extent from the rest of the world that it has been characterized as pursuing a policy of "mass imprisonment," which far exceeds the "great confinement" in Europe three centuries earlier. For most of the twentieth century, the incarceration rate in the United States oscillated between 100 and 120 per 100,000: close to the present levels in western Europe. At the beginning of the 1970s, in the wake of the Attica riot in upstate New York, reformers began to talk about a moratorium on prison building, and the incarceration rate was at a historic low of 93 per 100,000. David Rothman (1971, 295) concluded his study of the asylum by suggesting that America was "escaping from institutional responses" and looked forward to a time "when incarceration will be used still more rarely than it is today." But then, in every year since 1972 the rate has increased, at first relatively modestly, then accelerating at a remarkable rate (Zimring and Hawkins 1991). It continues to rise, although the rate of increase has slowed somewhat in the last few years.

Nowhere was the growth in prison numbers more spectacular than in California. As Zimring and Hawkins (1994) report, the prison population in California doubled between 1980 and 1985 and then doubled again between 1985 and 1990. At the beginning of the decade, California's prison population was just half that in England and Wales; by the end, it was twice the size. California's prison population increased more rapidly than that for the United States as a whole, but Zimring and Hawkins calculated that about half of the Californian increase could be accounted for by the national trend, and some further increase would have been expected simply as a result of an increase in population. However, overall the increase could not be accounted for by increases in (nondrug) crime or by overt government policies or legislative initiatives. Instead, they conclude that it was brought about by a revolution in sentencing practice whereby individual sentencers, responding to the public mood and political climate, began to use imprisonment more often in threshold cases—the numerous unremarkable cases of theft, burglary, assault, and drug-related offenses that form the bread and butter of the courts. This effect was then multiplied from the mid-1980s by an explosive increase in drug arrests arising from the "war on drugs"—despite the evidence that drug use had leveled out and was beginning to decline. In a later paper, Zimring (2001) describes the period since 1992 as one in which a new politics of punishment took hold and in which measures such as Megan's Law, Three Strikes and You're Out, and Truth-in-Sentencing added significantly to the length of time served: The mood was not just "lock 'em up" but also "throw away the key," even though crime rates were falling. There are similar, as well as other, interpretations of this phenomenon in the thought-provoking collection edited by David Garland (2001) on mass imprisonment.

There is an ancient cliché that when the United States sneezes, the rest of the world catches cold. Given the strength of the relationships between Margaret Thatcher and Ronald Reagan and between Tony Blair and George W. Bush, it would not be surprising if the United Kingdom were peculiarly prone to infection. Indeed, in England and Wales, the growth followed a somewhat similar pattern, albeit on a more modest scale, and later in the day. After the riots at Strangeways Prison in Manchester and the publication

Table 2.2 Crimes and Prison Population 1991-2001

	British Crime Survey	Police recorded crime	Prison population
1991	15,125,000	5,075,000	44,809
2001	13,037,000	5,527,000	66,301
Percent change	−14	+9	+45

of Lord Justice Woolf's remarkable report (Home Office, 1991b) following his inquiry into the riot and the problems of the prison system, the prison population had been reduced to its lowest level for decades. Not long afterwards, as law and order became an election issue, the penal rhetoric changed. Table 2.2 shows the figures for recorded crimes and the prison population, together with the estimated total crime rate from the British Crime Survey (generally taken to be a better indicator of trends because of the influence of changes in recording practice and other matters that impact on the official figures of crimes known to the police) from 1991 to 2001.

It can be seen from Table 2.2 that the growth in the prison population far outstripped the growth in the official crime rate, which, to judge from the underlying downward trend revealed by the British Crime Survey, probably reflected either more reporting of crimes by the public or better recording by the police, or both, rather than a real increase in crime itself.

How might this growth in the prison population be explained? Hough, Jacobson, and Millie (2003) point out that it could not be explained by an increase in remanding prisoners before trial because the proportion of untried prisoners went down from 16.5 percent at the beginning of the period to 10.2 percent at the end. Nor could it be explained by an increase in the total number of convictions in the criminal courts because these too declined over the period by 1 percent, although it may be significant that there was a massive 92 percent increase in convictions for drug offenses. Rather, what happened was that, in response to urging from politicians who capitalized on the fears of citizens, the courts began to impose longer sentences especially for sexual offenses and for burglary, and to impose sentences of immediate imprisonment or community penalties for offenders who would previously have been discharged, fined, or given suspended sentences, as is shown in Table 2.3.

The result of these changes in sentencing has been to put the prison and probation services under enormous pressure—the former through overcrowding

Table 2.3 Percentage Court Disposals in England and Wales: 1991–2001

	1991	2001
Discharge	17.5	15.5
Fines	37.4	25.9
Community orders	16.7	26.4
Suspended custody	9.7	1.0
Immediate custody	16.5	27.9
Other	2.3	3.2

and difficulties in providing opportunities for work, education, and programs to address offending behavior, and the latter by clogging up case loads with minor offenders who divert resources away from more serious offenders who warrant closer community supervision.

2.4   The Changing Nature of Prison Populations

David Garland's characterization of mass imprisonment involves two essential elements. The first obviously relates to sheer numbers. It implies a rate of imprisonment and a size of prison population markedly above historical and comparative norms. The United States certainly meets those criteria. The second, however, relates to the systematic incarceration of whole groups of the population rather than the imprisonment of individual offenders. The group that Garland and most other writers on the subject have in mind is young, black, urban males, and there is abundant evidence that this group bears the brunt of criminal justice policies in the United States. Garland points out that for this group, imprisonment has become part of the socialization process. Everyone in these neighborhoods has direct knowledge of prison through the experience of family members, friends, or neighbors. To an increasing degree, Hispanics are following in their footsteps. Although Garland wishes to distinguish this from the old Soviet Gulag and suggests that mass imprisonment in the United States is an altogether new phenomenon, it is worth mentioning that when I was actively researching imprisonment in Russia in the early 1990s (King 1994; King and Piacentini 2005), at a time when the incarceration rate for the Russian Federation was higher than that for the United States and had been so for generations, I was struck by the fact that almost every family I met had experience of prison—either because they had themselves been incarcerated or friends or family members had been incarcerated. This contrasts markedly with the United States or the United Kingdom, where it is still the case that the vast majority of the population have no experience whatever of custody. The difference between these situations seems to be that in Russia, the prison permeated the whole of society and impacted upon ethnic majorities and elites as well as minorities, whereas in the United States it has acted upon an underclass, which it helped to create and now perpetuates.

Perhaps we should begin with a glance at what the prison population looked like in the United States in 1970 at the end of the period of stability, and before the takeoff into astronomic growth. There were then nearly 200,000 prisoners serving a year or more, 21,094 in federal prisons and 177,737 in state prisons, plus a further 129,189 in local jails. In the federal system, 4.3 percent were women, compared to 3.3 percent in state prisons and 5.8 percent in the jails. The majority of prisoners were white: 69.6 percent in federal institutions and 56.2 percent in both state prisons and local jails. Black prisoners were already substantially over-represented and accounted for 28.8 percent of federal and 42 percent of state prisoners, and 40.9 percent of those in jails. Persons of Spanish origin accounted for 8.3 percent of federal prisoners, 6.7 percent of state prisoners, and 6.4 percent of jail inmates. Crime was then and still is a young man's game, and this was largely reflected in the age structure of the population in confinement, with about 55 percent being under the age of thirty and only about 4 percent over the age of fifty-five years. Details on the offenses for which people were sentenced are not complete nor supplied in convenient form to summarize for state prisons, and they are not always relevant for the jails, where a substantial proportion were not convicted. But as far as federal prisoners were concerned, the largest group of prisoners, 33.5 percent, were in custody for offenses of dishonesty, excluding white-collar crimes of embezzlement and tax evasion, with a further 21.9 percent convicted of transporting stolen vehicles. Violence accounted for 18 percent and drug offenses for 16.3 percent.

Before I describe the changes in the prison population in the United States, however, I need to draw a distinction between prison populations and prison receptions, because the distinction is vital to unpicking some of the political rhetoric. The distinction is often likened to that between stock and flow in industrial or commercial enterprises. Prisoners are counted as they are received into prison from the courts, and the numbers of receptions in a given year will always be greater than the number of people because some will be received several times—either because they are remanded in custody each time their trial is adjourned for one reason or another or because they may receive a very short sentence of imprisonment, be released, reoffend, and return to prison within the year. This is part of the flow. The other part is persons who have been in custody for longer periods, but are then released either on parole or other early release scheme or at the end of their sentence, some of whom will also return as either parole violators or for new offenses. The prison population refers to the numbers of persons in custody at any one time and is obviously a function of the numbers of persons received and the length of time they stay—with those serving longer sentences accumulating in the prison statistics year by year. Population data may be published either as an average daily population (as in the United Kingdom) or as year-end data or else on the basis of periodic censuses or as estimates based on sampling techniques.

Data on the more than 3,000 U.S. jails are still relatively hard to come by and exist in the form of periodic censuses or estimates based on surveys conducted between censuses, and they rarely include information on discharges. Frase (1998) reports that there were about 13,245,000 jail admissions in 1993, of which 9,796,000 were "new" bookings. On the basis that the average jail population that year was 466,155, it was possible to calculate that the mean length of stay was about thirteen days, albeit with a highly skewed distribution in which large numbers spent very short periods, but a few prisoners had much longer stays forming a long tail (population divided by receptions equals time in years). By mid-year 2003, the jail population had risen to 691,301, having grown at the rate of about 4 percent a year on average over the period (Bureau of Justice 2004). The great majority, 88.1 percent, of the local jail population in 2003 were males, though that proportion has been steadily falling year on year as the numbers of women admitted to the jails have increased. Although whites form the biggest proportion of the jail population at 43.6%, nearly six in every ten are from ethnic minorities: 39.2 percent black, 15.4 percent Hispanic, and 1.8 percent of other ethnic origin. Over the last decade, these proportions have been relatively static. There have, however, been significant changes in the legal status of those detained, with 39.4 percent being convicted, down from about 45 percent a decade earlier, and 60.6 percent being held before trial, up from about 55 percent over the period. It is generally recognized that the growth in jail populations and the skewing towards more blacks and more females really took off in the 1980s under the influence of the war on drugs. But as arrest rates and convictions began to level off in the 1990s, the jail population continued to rise, suggesting that the courts became more punitive in their sentencing.

The data on state and federal prisons while deficient in many respects, are probably more reliable. The latest figures available at the time of writing (Bureau of Justice 2003) relate to 2002, during which year there were 663,521 admissions to state and federal prisons compared to 518,562 a decade earlier: an increase of about 22 percent. Given that the state prison population increased by about 54 percent over the same period and the federal prison population doubled, it is clear that a major factor driving the population increase is longer sentences. In 2002, there were 48,144 admissions to federal prisons and only 42,339 releases, while state prisons admitted 615,377 prisoners and released 569,599. With these kinds of flows, it is not hard to see how the prison population continues to grow even if at a slower rate than during the previous two decades.

The vast majority of state and federal prisoners are males (fifteen times as many men as women) but although both sexes are increasing in the prison population, the numbers of women, just as in the jails, are rising more quickly than the numbers of men: increases of 4.9 percent and 2.4 percent, respectively, in 2002. A decade earlier, men outnumbered women in the prison population by about twenty to one (and in 1970, by thirty to one). One third of these women prisoners are held in just three jurisdictions: Texas, California, and the federal prison system. Whereas in 1970, white prisoners accounted for 57.6 percent of all state and federal prisoners serving a year or more, this had fallen to about 34 percent in 1993 and remained about the same at year-end 2002. Black prisoners, who comprised about 41 percent in 1970, had risen to just over 50 percent in 1992 and remained an absolute majority for some years before falling back to about 45 percent by the end of 2002. The main reason for this latest change in the composition of the prison population has been the rapid growth of Hispanics, who accounted for an estimated 7 percent in 1970, 14 percent in 1993, and 18 percent at year-end 2002. Although the numbers were much lower for females, the racial distribution was broadly similar. In 1970 (when they were not separately identified but were reported as either white or black), the prison population was predominantly young, with 55 percent of the population *under* the age of thirty, but today it is much older. In 2002, almost 60 percent of male prisoners and more than 65 percent of females were *over* the age of thirty, and a group about the size of the total prison population of England and Wales were approaching or above retirement age: a product not just of the graying of America, but of increases in the length of sentences and the fact that those sentenced to longer terms stack up in the prison population year on year.

The broad trends, then, are clear enough. There has been a major change in the composition of the population in state and federal prisons and jails in the United States, so that what was once the preserve of white Americans is now dominated by a preponderance of Afro-Americans with a rapidly growing proportion of Hispanics (and smaller, but still over-represented, groups of Native Americans and Asians). Furthermore, although the prisons and jails are still predominantly male institutions, the number of women in prison has been growing more rapidly so that women now make up about 7 percent of the total.

Considerable attention has been given to the over-representation of Afro-Americans in the prison and jail population, where they appear four times as frequently as their numbers in the general population would warrant. However, Tonry (1994) has argued that this understates the level of racial disproportion because it takes no account of the under-representation of whites. Tonry suggests that rather than use total incarceration rates, it is necessary to use racially disaggregated incarceration rates in order to see the true extent of racial disproportion. On that basis, in 1993, the incarceration rate was 2,124 per 100,000 resident African-Americans, seven times the rate of 320 per 100,000 resident white Americans. There is much debate as to why this should be the case; for example, whether it reflects relative involvement in different types of crime, or whether it is a product of bias and discrimination from arrest to sentencing throughout the criminal justice system. Tonry (1995) has argued persuasively that the outcomes of drug laws and other legislative enactments could and should have been foreseen as likely to bear disproportionately on ethnic minorities who have become the victims of "malign neglect." But he has also argued, no less persuasively, that, when incarceration rates are disaggregated by ethnic groups, racial disproportion is no less in other countries in the English-speaking world. It is simply less visible only because the size of ethnic minorities in the general population is smaller than in the United States. If the size of the minority groups were larger in the wider community, and the (disaggregated) incarceration rates remained the same, then the relative ethnic composition of the prison population would more resemble that in the United States (Tonry 1994).

Several writers (Donziger 1995; Currie 1998; and others) have drawn attention to what these incarceration rates mean for the life chances of young black Americans. Current Bureau of Justice statistics suggest that about one in every ten black males aged between twenty-five and twenty-nine in the United States was in prison in 2002 and that figure rises to more than one in eight if the jail population is included. If the age group is widened to between twenty and twenty-nine, Mauer and Huling (1995) show that one in three black males were either in custody or subject to penal supervision of one kind or another. They estimate that 30 percent of black children born at that time would spend some of their lives in prison, compared to 14 percent of Hispanics and only 4 percent of whites. It is on the basis of these statistics that it has been possible to speak of mass imprisonment impacting systematically upon a whole generation of black citizens. One might add that in the land of the free, concerned to export democracy around the world, not only are such large numbers of its citizens incarcerated but many are subsequently deprived of the right to vote.

It is important to note that the federal prison system has been growing in recent years even more rapidly than state systems and, at year-end 2002, was the largest prison system in the United States, fractionally larger than California and Texas, its nearest rivals. It accounted for 20 percent of the increase in the prison population in 2002–2003, in part because it took over responsibility for felons previously under the jurisdiction of the District of Columbia. Before that, drug offenders brought into custody as a consequence of the war on drugs, a war declared several years after drug use had started to decline, provided the single most important cause of the increase in prison population, and that was most marked in the federal prison system. Whereas in 1970, drug offenders counted for just 16 percent of the 20,000 or so beds in federal prisons, more than half of the 157,000 federal prison places in 2001 were given over to drug offenders, with a quarter to public order offenders (nearly half of those being illegal immigrants) and only a little over 10 percent to violent offenders. For state systems, about half the beds are occupied by violent offenders, whereas about one in five places is taken up by property offenders and a similar number by drug offenders (although many of the property offenses and violent offenses may also have been drug related).

The Bureau of Justice (2004) statistics suggest that the largest growth in the prison population between 1995 and 2001 was accounted for by violent offenders—63 percent of the growth in the prison population—whereas drug offenders accounted for only 15 percent of the growth. That is true, but it can be misleading especially in the hands of mendacious politicians who may seek to create the impression that prisons are increasingly used to deal with the most violent offenders as a last resort. This is where it is important to remember the distinction between prison population and prison receptions. As Tonry (1995) has argued, persons convicted of violent offenses rightly and understandably receive longer sentences and so stack up in the prison population so that the proportion of violent offenders in the population will always be greater than those admitted during the course of the year. Indeed, they can continue to increase as a proportion of the prison population even as they decrease as a proportion of those admitted. A much larger proportion of offenders admitted for nonviolent offenses may, because of their shorter sentences, have a much lesser impact on the prison population.

It would be a surprising indictment of past criminal justice policies, of course, if the vast increases in the prison population brought in large numbers of the most serious offenders who had previously walked free. It stands to reason that such large increases would almost certainly involve sweeping up more people into the criminal justice system and sentencing persons who previously would have received noncustodial penalties to longer and longer periods of imprisonment. As a consequence of such net-widening, there has also been an increase of defaulters on noncustodial penalties who then receive custodial sentences, and parole violators who are returned to prison. Indeed at times, in some jurisdictions, parole violators have vied with persons newly sentenced by the courts for the greater share of admissions to custody.

In England and Wales, certainly, the growth of imprisonment has produced changes, which in some respects and to some degree resemble those that have occurred in the United States. Most markedly, the proportion of nonwhite offenders in the male prison population rose from about 15 percent in 1991 to about 20 percent in 2001, the proportion serving four years or more (the cutoff point for determining long sentences, which also triggers discretionary release by the Parole Board) from 37 percent to 48 percent over the same period, and the proportion over the age of thirty years from 40 percent to 47 percent. For women, who accounted for about 4 percent of the population in 1991 and about 6 percent in 2001, the changes have been less marked, and in one instance in the opposite direction. Between 1991 and 2001, the proportion of women serving four years or more rose from 35 percent to 40 percent, but there was only a very small change in the age structure, and nonwhites actually declined from 30 percent to 26 percent of the population.

The most dramatic change in the offenses for which the prisoners had been sentenced was in relation to drugs. That increase of 92 percent in convictions for drugs offenses that I mentioned above, even without the benefit of a declared war on drugs, had produced a near doubling of the proportion of drug offenders in the prison population from 9 percent in 1991 to 16 percent in 2001. There were consequential slight declines in the proportions of robbers, burglars, thieves, and fraudsters and somewhat larger declines in the proportion of persons convicted of sexual and violent offenses in the prison population.

2.5   The Sociology of Prisons

At the outset, I remarked that there is a sense in which a prison is a prison is a prison but that there are also myriad ways in which they differ and which have consequences for prisoners. In this section, I try to say something about the commonalities and the scope for variation, as we understand from the accumulation of sociological case studies and comparative studies, of what actually goes on in prison. However, I take as my starting point a rather strange experiment reported by the psychologists Haney, Banks, and Zimbardo (1973) on "interpersonal dynamics in a simulated prison" containing three small "cells," which they established in a basement corridor of the psychology department at Stanford University. Out of seventy-five student volunteers who were given a battery of medical, psychological, and social tests, twenty-four students who were strangers to one another were selected for inclusion because they were the most stable, mature, and least involved in antisocial behavior. In the actual experiment, ten of these were allocated to the role of prisoners and were required to wear stocking caps on their heads and loose-fitting smock dresses without underclothes to represent the depersonalization of shaven heads and prison uniforms. They were told that although some of their civil rights would be suspended and they would be confined to their cells twenty-four hours a day, they would not suffer physical abuse and would be guaranteed food, medical care, and three supervised visits to the toilet each day (this was a makeshift prison). Eleven students were allocated to the role of guards, who worked three-person, eight-hour shifts but, when off-duty, were free to go home. Guards were simply told that they must not use physical punishments or be physically aggressive towards prisoners. All participants were paid fifteen dollars a day.

The experiment had to be terminated after six days instead of the intended fourteen, because four "prisoners" suffered extreme emotional depression, crying, rage, and acute anxiety (and another from a psychosomatic condition). Some of the "guards," on the other hand, were disappointed that the experiment had to be ended, because, according to the experiment-ers, "they now enjoyed the extreme control and power which they exercised and were reluctant to give it up." This experiment is widely known and is often quoted with reference to the formation of authoritarian personali-ties—the authors suggesting that their "guards" developed pathological reac-tions because of the power of the social forces operating in the situation to which they were exposed. In this, it stands in a direct line with the experi-ments of Stanley Milgram (1965) a decade earlier, in which he encouraged subjects to administer what they thought were painful electric shocks despite their belief that the recipients were crying in agony. But it is also quoted as though it reflected the inevitable social forces and consequences that flow from the very existence of *the* prison as an institution and has been under-stood in that way by generations of students since.

Craig Haney has gone on to become one of the most distinguished and respected commentators on the psychological consequences of confinement, based on interviews with and clinical assessment of real prisoners, but the Stanford experiment has been strongly criticized on ethical grounds, and in my view rightly so. After all, this was around the time when Jessica Mitford (1973) and others exposed the extent to which real prisoners were being used unethically in medical experiments of one kind or another, and long after the United Nations Standard Minimum Rules for the treatment of prisoners had been promulgated, so one is entitled to ask why the experimenters thought it appropriate to expose students in the way that they did. But it is also vulnerable on scientific grounds. My scientific concern is that the exper-imental conditions they created in no sense represent *the* prison at all. At about the same time as these experiments were being conducted on unsus-pecting California students, my colleague Kelsey Kauffman (who later went on to write one of the earliest and still one of the more important accounts of prison officers) and I took our Yale students for a voluntary seventy-two-hour incarceration at Haddam Academy, then (and perhaps still, for all I know) a former county jail used for staff training purposes by the Connect-icut Department of Corrections (DOC). We were all prisoners, except Kauff-man, who arranged the whole program with DOC. Because both Kauffman and I were experienced prison researchers, we briefed the students first and debriefed them afterwards in some very lively seminars. The guards during our lockup were all professional prison staff from the academy.

Of course, this experience was not totally realistic, neither for the students nor for me. For one thing, there are rather few coeducational prisons. For another, we all knew that this was just pretend and we approached it with good humor, albeit touched by not a little anxiety. Thus my futile attempt to masquerade as a slightly older student was doomed to failure because the guards, having been tipped off by Kauffman, knew I was the tutor and contrived to "find" contraband in my cell and put me on a charge. For still another, I knew (didn't I?) that my wife would be there to collect me after my seventy-two hours of confinement, though the thought that she might run off with someone far more attractive was harder to hold at bay when I was found guilty of possessing the wherewithal for brewing prison "pruno" and thrown in "the hole": a metal cell within a cell used for segregation and punishment. After all, I most emphatically did not have the key to the door. But I suspect that we all learned a great deal more about prisons from this experience than did either the participants or the experimenters at Stanford. We all went through the humiliating routines of strip-searching and cheek-spreading, and attending to the needs of nature in semipublic conditions. But we also became somewhat accomplished (it's harder than you might think) at making and using rat lines for passing goods and messages between cells, for example, and using a mirror to detect the approach of guards, who for the most part treated us as though we were "normal" prisoners in the Connecticut DOC. We agreed on some basic ground rules of prisoner solidarity and survival, including which guards to trust and which would be most likely to deal sympathetically with our requests or complaints.

What was the difference between these two unreal situations, and which better resembled the prison experience? Several things: At Haddam, as at all prisons in my experience, there were rules governing the behavior of guards; the guards had received some training in the discharge of their duties; there was a hierarchical system of control within which guards were supervised by superior officers; and there was some system for holding them to account after the event. To be sure, there are many prison systems where the rules are rudimentary, ill thought-out, and inappropriate; where the guards have the barest minimum of education and training; where supervision by superiors is ineffective or collusive and corrupt; and where mechanisms of accountability are near derisory. But except in parts of the Third World, those would be recognized as deviant cases. In Stanford there were, for all practical purposes, no rules other than an embargo against violence—had there not been, the experimenters might well have found themselves indicted before the courts. It should have come as no surprise that in the absence of rules, training, hierarchies of control, and systems of accountability, people given near absolute power over others behave badly. What the experimenters had set up was something that more closely resembled a concentration camp or an internment camp for prisoners of war than a prison. If there are lessons here, they relate to Guantanamo Bay and Abu Ghraib, though even there some system of accountability has kicked in.

In any event, here I wish to contest the view of the experimenters that the students assigned to guard and prisoner roles came to behave like *real* prison guards and *real* prisoners. Even at that time, there was sufficient prison literature based on observational research to demonstrate that prisoners, far from being universally passive, actually respond to the experience of imprisonment in richly varied and complex ways. True, there was less data available about prison staff, and the stereotype of prison officers as rather brutish authoritarian figures was widely held by those outside prison and even reported in some of the scientific literature, for example, in the study of Pentonville (Morris, Morris, and Barer 1963) (yes, the same New Model Prison from 1842), where they were described as "military martinets." But a moment's serious thought would surely suggest that just as any other occupation offers scope for different types of recruits and different ways of approaching the job, the same might be true for prison officers. In short, the behavior of the student prisoners and guards was being compared with what the investigators *imagined* were the realities, not the realities themselves. What purported to be a scientific experiment about prisons turned out to be a metaphor about unregulated human behavior in much the same way as Foucault's prison was a metaphor for the carceral society. Both need a firmer grounding in the real world. If we take anything from the Stanford experiment, it is that we need rules, and systems of accountability when they are broken, and that without these, human beings possessed of power may tend to abuse it. But despite its apparent scientific garb, the experiment tells us no more about the most basic human behavior in extremity than, say, Golding's *Lord of the Flies*.

What is common to prisons is that prisoners have to come to terms with living their lives in custody against their will for the duration of their sentences. They have to come to terms with being separated from their normal way of life and from their families, and instead, with living with other prisoners and occupying themselves, if at all, from within a restricted range of employment, training, educational, or recreational activities. This whole experience is constrained by rules and regulations that may often make little sense but cover almost every aspect of life and that are administered by prison staff who, unlike themselves, go home at the end of their shift. Not surprisingly, prisoners may respond to this in various ways, but there seem to be three traditional responses, which have achieved archetypal status. They derive essentially from the work of John Irwin, himself once a convicted felon and now a retired university teacher in California and writer of several books on prisons, the first of which he dedicated to the 200,000 convicts then doing time in American prisons (those were the days!) (Irwin 1970). His observations on prison life, understandably, carry a special resonance and a degree of street credibility not normally available to prison sociologists. The three responses are *doing your own time, gleaning,* and *jailing*.

Doing your own time involves trying to get through your prison sentence as little touched by the experience as possible and thus to return to the community so that you can pick up where you left off (always providing that the world outside hasn't changed beyond recognition meanwhile). It requires prisoners to keep their heads down and their noses clean, not to become overly involved in the prisoner community, nor with the staff other than what might be necessary to get by from day to day. Gleaning involves a resolve to use the prison experience and whatever legitimate opportunities it offers in order to return to the community as a changed character. A gleaner may take as many education courses as are offered, or seek to acquire new work or vocational skills, or perhaps get religion while inside. It is often the fate of gleaners that despite, or maybe because of, the fact that they are doing precisely what the authorities may ostensibly want them to do, they may not be believed. It may be said, for example, that he or she only took those courses "in order to get parole." Jailing involves a response whereby the prisoner participates fully in the subterranean life and culture of the prison and makes the prison world his or her own preferred world. Such prisoners might become involved in rackets controlling the supply of contraband goods and services, find themselves in constant friction with staff, or become in competition with other prisoners for reputation. Once on the outside, such prisoners may find themselves like fish out of water and quickly relapse into crime and the security of the prison world, which they know best.

These conceptual characterizations, developed in California, were found to be equally applicable in the context of English prisons by King and Elliott (1977) and have been confirmed in the experience of practitioners and observers in prison systems around the world. Of course, they are not the only possible responses to prison but they remain robust and powerful in that many, though not all, other responses described in the literature could be recharacterized as major or minor variations on, or combinations of, these three themes. And they demonstrate the oversimplification of the Stanford experiment. In reality, the same prisoner may act strategically and learn from his or her experience, at times veering towards one kind of response only to adopt a different response later as he or she navigates through his or her sentence.

But although all prisons have something in common with each other, they also vary widely both between and within jurisdictions, in part reflecting the cultural characteristics of the society in which they are embedded and the policies that give life to the way in which crime and criminals are viewed at particular points in history. At different times, prisons have been expected to punish those incarcerated with or without hard labor, to separate them from bad influences in the hope of reclaiming their souls, or otherwise to reform, re-educate, rehabilitate, treat, train, or simply incapacitate them, or to deter others from experiencing a similar fate. Often they may be expected to perform several of these tasks at one and the same time, and over the last two hundred or so years, a great deal of effort has been expended to try to find effective techniques that could be deployed in furtherance of each of these endeavors. But quite apart from these formal and intended ways in which prisons may differ, there are many other incidental variables, which enter the equation with unintentional consequences. Most importantly, as we have seen, the nature and composition of the prison population changes, and it would be surprising if the sociology of the prison were not profoundly affected by whether the prison population comprised primarily debtors, as in the time of John Howard, or persons confined because of the dependence of themselves or others on drugs, as is the case today in some jurisdictions. To a possibly lesser, but certainly significant, extent (I know of no calculus to determine this precisely), what goes on in prison will also be affected by the numbers, nature, and training of staff, and the extent to which the walls of the prison may be permeated by visits by families, nongovernmental or intergovernmental organizations, the press, and the public. When reading the prison literatures, therefore, it is important to locate what are often case studies clearly in time and place before deciding whether or not what is reported is generalizable.

The early prison literature, primarily American, was perhaps overly concerned with what came to be called the "inmate world," in which the strange and seemingly alien deviant behaviors of prisoners were displayed for a middle class, if primarily academic, audience for the first time (e.g., Schrag 1944). Much of this related to what has generally been referred to as the "Big House": large state or federal penitentiaries, often a legacy of the nineteenth century, whose primary role was custodial and in which there was little by way of classification or programming beyond provision of a few workshops. Of course, all prisons are primarily custodial (a prison from which prisoners can easily escape is surely a contradiction in terms), but as some prisons began to take on a more modern treatment role in what are frequently referred to as correctional facilities in the United States, and training prisons in England and Wales, so the literature became dominated by the potential for tension between custodial and treatment objectives and between custodial and treatment staff (Cressey 1961; Street, Vinter, and Perrow 1966; Kassebaum, Ward, and Wilner 1971). Clemmer (1940), writing in the era of the Big House, provided one of the earliest accounts of the prison community and introduced the concept of *prisonization*—the extent to which new prisoners took on the "inmate culture." According to Clemmer, prisoners became more prisonized the longer they were in prison. Two decades later, Wheeler (1961) and several others in a number of replications explored this process in the context of correctional institutions with some kind of treatment goals. Wheeler posited a U-curve in relation to prisonization, with new prisoners initially expressing conventional values and taking on inmate values as they came closer to the midpoint of their sentence, only to resume more conventional values again as they approached release. Some of these studies, based on pencil-and-paper tests measuring attitudes and values rather than observation of real behaviors, were methodologically flawed and tended to see prisoner responses in as singular and monolithic a way (albeit substantively a very different way) as the responses depicted in the Stanford experiment.

It was not until Irwin's work that systematic attention was given to the varied ways in which prisoners responded to imprisonment based upon observation. However, it is necessary to point to Gresham Sykes's (1958) account of the society of captives, and his collaboration with Sheldon Messenger, as important milestones in prison sociology. Sykes focused, among other things, on the content of the inmate subculture and the values that sustained it, as well as the vital features of imprisonment to which it constituted a response. For Sykes and Messenger (1960), the inmate subculture was embodied in an inmate social code expressing core values about the way prisoners should behave towards each other and to the guards. These included such maxims as don't interfere with the interests of other prisoners; play things cool and do your own time; don't exploit other prisoners; don't weaken; maintain your own dignity whatever the system does; don't suck up to the guards, who should be treated with suspicion, and other similar injunctions. The function of the code was to maintain solidarity among prisoners and was seen as an understandable response to what Sykes (1958) calls "the pains of imprisonment." The pains of imprisonment arose from a series of deprivations: of liberty itself; of the goods and services normally available in the outside world; of heterosexual relationships, except in those jurisdictions that permit conjugal visits; of the autonomy to make decisions over even the simplest matters; and of safety and security, because one may spend one's time with violent persons not of one's own choosing. In this respect, though the pains of confinement might be more extreme, the prison constituted but one example of what Goffman (1961) calls total institutions, from monasteries to mental hospitals, which may vary in their goals and functions but share structural features in common, including ritualized relations between staff and inmates in which inmates develop an underlife in response to processes that deprive and depersonalize them.

This view of inmate culture as a response to the pains of imprisonment was challenged by Irwin, initially in a seminal paper with Donald Cressey (Irwin and Cressey 1962) and later in his book *The Felon* (Irwin 1970), by drawing attention to the obvious fact that prisoners did have an existence outside prison. Many of them had already been heavily involved in thief culture, which had elements in common with the inmate social code. The suggestion was that, in part at least, inmate culture was imported rather than generated from inside. This observation was soon reinforced by Jim Jacobs's

(1974, 1977) work on street gangs behind bars in Stateville Prison in Illinois (one of the few prisons built along the lines of Bentham's Panopticon) and is now blindingly obvious to anyone who observes the way in which repeat offenders returned to custody in large metropolitan prisons or jails greet people inside whom they knew on the streets. What this opened up was the possibility of a much more rounded sociology of the prison, which takes account of the multiplicity of prior biographies of prisoners—and also, of course, of staff—and the way they interact with different kinds of prison policies about treatment or punishment, security, and control as these are filtered down into different kinds of prison regimes. All prison sociology starts from this point, and an early attempt to explore the interaction between biographies of staff and prisoners and the prison regimes and the consequences for order and control when security goals came to override treatment goals is to be found in King and Elliott (1977).

The influence of the inmate social code was still in evidence during the age of the correctional facility, despite the softening of regimes and the well-intentioned activities of correctional counselors, as instanced by the remarks of prisoners reported in Kassebaum, Ward, and Wilner (1971) to the effect that when all is said and done, you are still doing time even if it is in a "pastel prison." But the inmate social code, as Sykes and Messenger well knew, was an ideal-typical construction, representing how prisoners *should* behave rather than how they *do* behave, and it was frequently honored more in the breach than the observance. Though it could sometimes be enforced with ferocity, it was by no means enforced with greater consistency than the criminal code in wider society. However, by the 1970s, prisons in the United States were already changing. The riot in 1970 at Attica Prison in upstate New York drew attention to the problems when a predominantly rural white guard force had custody of a predominantly black and metropolitan prison population. Newly politicized black prisoners participated in prisoners' rights movements, which had some impact upon the legal process and on prison conditions. But as black prisoners began to exceed the numbers of white prisoners in some prisons in New York, California, and Illinois, so white prisoners became fearful not just for their position in inmate society, but also for their lives. The riot at Santa Fe prison in 1980 and its dreadful aftermath indicated the growing power of groups such as the Mexican Mafia and presaged the regrouping of white prisoners, often in racially supremacist organizations such as the Aryan Brotherhood.

What once had seemed to be an ordered social structure with defined norms intended to promote a generalized solidarity among inmates against the staff had begun to crumble, with prisoners from different racial backgrounds set against each other. By 1980, John Irwin was writing about prisons in turmoil, and it was not long before Jim Jacobs (1983) was documenting the surprising ways in which prison sociologists had largely ignored the issue of race relations in their discussions of prison culture, and he questioned whether there were limits to racial integration in prisons. In Britain, too, though the issues about race were much more subdued, escapes and riots meant that the attention of the authorities and, following them, the research community moved elsewhere. In an age of emerging mass imprisonment, attention moved to questions outside the prison: What was driving the growth in prisons? And so far as what went on in prisons was concerned, attention was turned towards questions about how could the rise in population be managed, how could order be maintained, how could escapes be prevented, and was it possible to prevent conditions in prisons deteriorating to unacceptable levels? Research on the prison community seemed something of a luxury and certainly became a rarity, although it is probable that what had been learned about the sociology of prisons was used by managers to break down inmate culture in their search for more effective control.

As American prisons began to divide on racial lines and different ethnic groups brought their own cultures, often with different modalities by which honor and reputation were bestowed, to the prison community, so the traditional values underpinning inmate culture began to be undermined. But there were other factors at work: professional thieves, burglars, and robbers (traditionally the most powerful carriers of thief and convict cultures) were no longer numerically the most dominant groups in prison. As we have seen, a huge growth in prisoners convicted of drug offenses made these prisoners either the majority or a significant minority in federal and many state prisons. For many of these, the need for drugs while in custody over-rode other considerations of solidarity and created lucrative opportunities for those able to supply those needs. Moreover, even racial solidarity began to break down under the pressures of local street gangs, often engaged in turf wars outside, who sought to protect their "homeboys" inside. Impressionistically, at least, the growth in violent crime in the wider American society was mirrored in its prisons by the seeming replacement of instrumental violence to achieve some objective, by expressive violence that often seemed either random or a disproportionate response to perceived grievances. When John Irwin talked about prisons in turmoil in 1980, he was describing a world that could no longer be understood in terms of the old literatures.

One effect of these changes was that, just as it became more necessary to undertake research, it became more difficult to do so. When I conducted research in maximum security prisons in the United States in 1984, I was told that white American sociologists could no longer research these environments without black or Hispanic colleagues, and even then they would be regarded with mistrust. As far as most prison authorities were concerned, notions of diagnosing the problems of prisoners and applying corrective

treatment programs had been abandoned. The best departments of corrections and the Federal Bureau of Prisons retained some vestige of the rehabilitative ideal, but in a much less active form and without this forming a
stated aim of the institution. Educational and other programs were provided
but the onus was placed upon prisoners to recognize their own needs and to
seek or earn programs once they had decided to turn their lives around.
When I returned to research supermax facilities between 1996 and 1999,
educational, recreational, and vocational programs had been drastically curtailed if not eliminated, as politicians aimed both to demonstrate how tough
they were on crime and criminals and to cut costs. Research access was
rigorously controlled. I was accepted, by the authorities, staff, and prisoners,
possibly because I spoke with a pronounced English accent and made it plain
that I was a complete outsider who represented no one other than
myself—someone who knew a fair amount about what went on in prisons
in several countries and was anxious to learn any lessons there might be for
the United Kingdom from the American experience.

In England and Wales, although there have been changes in the composition of the prison population—the increase in drug offenders and minor
criminals who would previously have received noncustodial sentences—issues about race, expressive violence, or street gangs have not surfaced to anything like the same degree or with the same consequences as in
the United States. Moreover, English prisons have been typically run with
higher staff ratios and much closer relationships between prison officers and
prisoners than in many other prison systems. Although there have been
major confrontations between prisoners and staff, especially in the high-
security prisons and institutions for young offenders, it is by no means clear
that these will have followed from prisoners acting out elements of the
inmate code, the presence of which has probably always been somewhat less
evident than would appear to have been the case in the American Big House.
I shall return to questions about disorder in the next section. Suffice it to
say here that, as concerns about treatment and rehabilitation, which dominated the 1950s and early 1960s, were replaced by concerns about security
and control in the minds of prison administrators during the 1970s and
1980s, so conditions in prisons across the system deteriorated (King and
McDermott 1989).

Following the major disturbance at Strangeways Prison in Manchester,
there was an increased commitment to tempering security and control with
considerations of fairness and justice (Home Office 1991a, 1991b). But as
British politicians began to follow the lead of their American counterparts,
ratcheting up the law-and-order rhetoric, so the task of the central administration became reconfigured to one of managing the rapidly increasing
population and trying to ensure that a so-called "decency agenda" was still

pursued even while it was made clear that prisoners had to earn whatever privileges came their way. In an age of "new managerialism," the performance of prisons was evaluated against key performance indicators and targets, and so-called "failing prisons" were encouraged to improve under the threat of being "market tested" against what private contractors might provide. Prison research was increasingly directed and paid for by government, even if it was carried out under contract by university-based researchers.

Nevertheless, in a unique study, Liebling and Arnold (2004), conscious that performance culture focuses too much on what can be easily measured rather than what matters, attempted to measure what they call the moral performance of prisons. They measured regime dimensions, such as the extent to which the prison fostered a sense of fairness, order, safety, well-being, personal development, family contact, and decency, and relational dimensions, such as respect, humanity, trust, and support within staff-prisoner relationships. They argue that at the highest levels of prison management, there are often strongly held values, and these can and do help to shape prison culture, but they have to overcome more negative values located elsewhere. They conclude that in the prisons they studied, the material conditions scored better than relational matters, despite the fact that by common consent it is staff-prisoner interaction that is at the core of the prison experience. In a welcome return to the observational study of the inner life of a medium-security training prison in England, Crewe (2005) provides a finely nuanced account and analysis of the varied ways in which British prisoners behave and the values they hold. In that prison, at least, the ever-present backdrop of drugs; new mechanisms of penal administration offering prisoners incentives and earned privileges, and clearer pathways through their sentences towards parole; and a general improvement in conditions had undermined old bases for solidarity among prisoners and confrontations with staff. It seems likely that this applies in varying degrees throughout the system, though probably to a markedly lesser extent in the high-security estate.

It is important to note that although there are many similarities between British and American prisons arising from historical and language affinities, one should not expect this conceptual apparatus to be transportable to other prison systems without possibly considerable amendment. There is an emerging literature on prisons and prison culture in other societies, but where prison research, nevertheless, is still very much in its infancy (see King 1994; Oleinik 2003; and Piacentini 2004, for example, on Russia; Moczydlowski 1992 and Kaminski 2004 on Poland). In societies such as Russia, where the tradition in metropolitan prisons has been to house prisoners in large communal cells under the control of a prisoner cell boss, or in their corrective labor colonies, where sometimes several hundred prisoners would be under the control of a single member of staff, known as a detachment head, one would expect a rather different social life to emerge. In Brazil, prisoners are sometimes housed in large pavilions, which staff only enter after negotiation with *faxinas,* or prisoner leaders, who are often placemen for the Premier Command of the Capital (PCC), a prison and criminal network that flourishes throughout Sao Paulo, greatly facilitated by the advent of the mobile phone. The *faxinas* control access to prison staff, medical treatment, and the distribution of all goods that are sent in by families. They charge their fellow prisoners for room and board in ways that would resemble eighteenth-century English garnish and chummage, were they not backed up by sometimes-lethal force. Brazil is one of those societies that offer conjugal visits to prisoners, and these take place in the pavilions themselves (Russia, to some extent, is another, though there, they take place in separate and rather homely surroundings). Whatever the benefit from relieving prisoners of the deprivation of heterosexual relationships, as mentioned by Sykes (1958), the Brazilian practice frequently leads to the exploitation of prisoners and pressures either to share their visitors with others or to use them as a conduit for bringing in drugs. The scope for further work on prison communities is potentially endless, and internationally comparative work would be particularly useful.

Much of the sociology of the prison directs our attention to the struggle for power where staff and inmate worlds meet, and it is to issues about security, order, and control that I turn in the next section.

2.6   Security, Order, Control, and the Supermax Phenomenon

In the nineteenth century in England and Wales, the separate system of prison discipline was taken to extremes such that prisoners wore caps with peaks that were pulled down over their faces to form masks whenever they were out of their cells, so that they could not make eye contact with other prisoners. Under the silent system in the United States, when prisoners were out of cells, they were required to walk in lockstep to one side of a line in the corridors, and the rule of silence at meals and in workshops was brutally enforced. Subjugation was the order of the day, and prisons were regimented, and to that degree orderly, places. But it was an order based on coercion, backed up by the use of force, whereby guards may be armed with guns or batons and where the lash was still a lawful punishment for offenses against prison discipline. Though strict discipline and corporal punishment lingered on well into the twentieth century, it was clear that goals of treatment, education, training, or rehabilitation could not be achieved by coercion alone. In order to achieve compliance with such objectives, it was necessary to appeal to some degree of legitimacy about the nature of the requirements placed upon prisoners. The planned use of force has always been and remains an option to regain control, but once the routine (nonemergency) use of force was abandoned, either as an immediate possibility available to staff, or as a consequence of some kind of quasijudicial process following a breach of discipline, then the balance of power shifted. Prisoners were always going to be in a majority, but short of a successful mass outbreak were always likely to suffer the consequences of any insurrection. Experience shows that the authorities always eventually regain control of rioting prisoners even though the prison may have been destroyed and lives may have been lost. For prisoners, freedom ultimately depends upon the lawful completion of their sentences. In principle, the less trouble they bring on themselves the quicker is likely to be their release. Staff, on the other hand, were always going to be in a minority and therefore potentially vulnerable. Although they could likely count on reinforcements coming in emergencies, and upon the support of their superiors, the politicians, and the public for the actions they may reasonably have felt constrained to take, they also knew that in a riot they might be held to account by prisoners for the way they had behaved as guards. In short, most staff and most prisoners recognize that they all have a vested interest in a well-ordered prison, but most also recognize that it is a delicate balance to maintain and one that is never wholly within their own control. Not surprisingly, some of the most interesting work on prisons has addressed these issues of order and control, often in contexts where order had broken down, resulting in either escapes or riots.

It will be helpful, in the discussion that follows, to keep some clear analytical distinctions in mind in relation to issues concerning security, order, and control because the use of these terms in official discourse can often be confusing. I shall use the term *security* to relate specifically to the issues surrounding the central function of keeping prisoners in custody for the duration of their sentence. In this sense, from the staff's point of view, it has to do with the paraphernalia and procedures designed to prevent escapes, and from the prisoners' point of view, to the possibility of overcoming those procedures. *Order* relates to the fulfilled expectation that daily life will continue in predictable ways and in which staff and prisoners at least minimally respect one another. *Control* relates to techniques and procedures deployed formally or informally to foster and maintain a state of order and to restore it once it has been lost or placed under threat. It cannot be stressed too strongly that prisons are for most of the time remarkably orderly places, even though this has often surprised prison researchers.

Two sorts of confusion arise over the use of these terms. First, it is common for prison staff and for prison manuals to use the notion of security in a more generalized sense to relate to matters that might *either* threaten the possibility of escapes *or* a breakdown in social order, *or* both. Thus, in England and Wales, prison officers are required to provide Security Information Reports on any matters that they may regard as suspicious without regard to whether it relates to escapes or a threat to social order. This is seen as a part of what in England is referred to as *dynamic security*—the active involvement of staff in the life of the prisons whereby, using their close relationship with prisoners, they act as the eyes and ears of the prison governor (warden) on the general state of the prison. This dual usage seems to reflect the capacity of the term security in ordinary parlance to cover a sense of personal safety. Thus, home security relates *both* to putting locks and bolts on one's house to meet the requirements of insurance companies *and* the sense that one is or should be free of the dangers from intruders. In the United States, it has become common to refer to members of gangs as members of Security Threat Groups, and in this usage, it is the threat to good order and the safety of other prisoners and staff that is uppermost. Such groups rarely constitute an immediate risk of escape. It is true that the breakdown of social order in the prison, especially if it has taken the form of a riot, can create a situation where escapes may be likely and may have even been engineered with that end in view. But it is suggested that it is better to restrict the term security to matters relating to escapes and the term control to matters related to maintaining or restoring of order—if only because the two have rather different implications for policymakers.

Having raised the question of policy implications, perhaps I should deal with the policy issue dealing with the question of escapes at this point, before moving on to a discussion of control, because the issues about preventing escapes are essentially practical and straightforward. In the United States, and in other countries where perimeter guards may be armed and authorized to use lethal force, the question of escapes tends to be of lower concern than it is in countries such as England and Wales, where prison officers are unarmed. But in either case, the issues are broadly similar. The management problem is to classify prisoners according to risk of escape and the potential harm that would flow from that, to classify prisons according to the security they provide and then to allocate prisoners to the appropriate prisons accordingly. Because security paraphernalia—high walls, razor ribbon, monitoring by closed circuit television, electronic locking and unlocking, higher staff ratios, and so on—are expensive to procure and maintain, it follows that most systems would choose to use them as parsimoniously as possible, through a policy of *concentration*, that is, by concentrating the highest security risks in as few prisons as possible.

Broadly speaking, the United States has always followed a concentration policy apart from a brief period following the federal closure of Alcatraz,

when those prisoners were dispersed temporarily to other federal penitentiaries, although, as I shall argue below, that policy had more to do with
controlling prisoners who were deemed to be dangerous within the prison
system than it did with prisoners who were purely escape risks. In England
and Wales, following the embarrassing escapes of high-profile prisoners in
the 1960s, Mountbatten (Home Office 1966) recommended such a classification of prisoners, with a view to concentrating the highest risks in a new
fortress prison. However, the government was persuaded to follow an alternative policy of *dispersal*—by dispersing high-escape-risk prisoners among
lower security prisoners who were all housed in a growing number of so-
called dispersal prisons, whose security was heavily upgraded. This switch of
policy was based on the recommendations of the Radzinowicz Committee
(ACPS 1968), which, as I have argued elsewhere (King and Morgan 1980;
King 1987), were predicated partly upon the mistaken belief that escape-risk
prisoners, if housed together in a single prison, would become an impossible-
to-manage control problem that might be diluted by dispersing them in
smaller groups to a number of prisons containing lower security risks. It was
also partly based on a laudable desire to adopt what they saw as a more open,
humane, and liberal approach, by developing a relaxed regime within a secure
perimeter. In fact, the dispersal prisons, for complex reasons, became the
most riot- and disturbance-prone institutions in the system—the very thing
they were intended to avoid. Certainly, the system was not parsimonious. In
its first full year of operation, about 6 percent of prisoners were held in the
high-security estate. Gradually, after several attempts to dilute the problem
still further by expanding the dispersal system—which at its height accounted
for over 8 percent of the prison population—an effective policy of greater
concentration has been followed within a reduced high-security estate. In
2002–2003, just over 4 percent of a much larger prison population was
contained in dispersal prisons. In a typically British approach, the change
has gone unremarked, and the terminology of dispersal has remained.

The second kind of confusion relates to the use of the term *control*. In
an important essay, Bottoms (1999) has suggested that prisoners are uncomfortable with the language of control because, when used by prison administrators, it tends to define them as "control problems" and refers to measures
adopted by staff and applied to prisoners. Bottoms argues that prisoners are
much happier with a concept of order because it suggests predictability, which
makes it easier to do their time. However, if it is true that both prisoners and
staff have vested interests in the maintenance of order, then it follows that
prisoners may have techniques and procedures at their disposal that can
influence the situation. Certainly in my experience of discussing these issues
with prisoners, including one who played a prominent role in the Santa Fe
riot, prisoners can be very conscious of their role in the lead-up to and the

aftermath of riots. In that sense, prisoners play an as-yet-much under-researched and largely unacknowledged role in control, the difference being that whereas staff may have formal and informal procedures at their disposal, prisoners may have only the latter. Some of these informal mechanisms used by both staff and prisoners were explored by McDermott and King (1988).

Bottoms (1999), following Braswell, Montgomery, and Lombardo (1994), distinguishes between two types of prison violence, interpersonal and collective, and then suggests that they differ in terms of their relationship to social order in prisons. Interpersonal violence, Bottoms argues, "relates to violent events that take place *within the everyday frameworks of the prison's social order,*" whereas collective violence "brings with it *a significant break-down in the normal patterns of social order in the institution*" (Bottoms 1999, 206, emphasis in original). Bottoms acknowledges that this distinction is not always easy to maintain, and to be sure, any prison manager will be concerned to minimize both, but the distinction is an important one, not just for the purposes of analysis, but because profound consequences seem to flow from them. If the British experience is anything to go by, when collective violence becomes endemic, it calls into question the legitimacy of the whole prison system and eventually triggers a reappraisal of what the system is about. During the 1970s and 1980s, repeated disturbances and riots occurred in the dispersal prisons, which brought into question the way in which the dispersal system functioned in a series of reviews, most importantly that by the Control Review Committee (Home Office 1984). When riots and disturbances spread to lower security prisons in the later 1980s and eventually to local prisons—such as Strangeways in Manchester in 1990—with their high remand populations, the Woolf Report (Home Office 1991b) sought to relegitimate the prison system by balancing concerns about security and control with concerns about justice, fairness, and the legitimate expectations of prisoners who were conceived as having a compact (Woolf, in the end, fought shy of describing it as a contract) with the prison service. Although interpersonal violence can have implications for the legitimacy of the system, it is mostly dealt with through the courts, or some version of due process or quasi due process within the prisons, or through administrative measures, which endeavor to control the violent or disruptive behaviors of particular prisoners. If those measures are themselves seen to be lacking in legitimacy, then interpersonal violence may merge into collective violence.

Some of the finest prison research in recent years has stemmed from a concern to understand the problem of order in circumstances when the prison system of England and Wales was perceived to be losing, or on the brink of losing, control. In the wake of the Report of the Control Review Committee (Home Office 1984), Bottoms was commissioned to undertake research in two dispersal prisons: Albany, which, ever since its inclusion in the dispersal system and its decline into what the press called a "jail of fear" reported on by King and Elliott (1977), had experienced repeated riots; and Long Lartin, one of only two of the seven dispersal prisons then in use not to have had major incidents—or at least none that received much publicity. As a result of their history, the two prisons, each nominally operating as part of the high-security estate, ostensibly offering a coordinated policy for dealing with high-security prisoners, had evolved very different regimes and styles of working. In Long Lartin, a relaxed approach to supervision that allowed prisoners to visit each other's cells was predicated on a management philosophy that assumed "you may have to lose some control in order to gain control" (Bottoms 1999, 211). This style, which stayed more or less faithful to the original Radzinowicz concept, had won the support of prison officers who proudly represented it as the Long Lartin way. Albany staff, on the other hand, had come to terms with repeated crises that had severely eroded their confidence by introducing more and more restrictions on the regime, including freedom of movement. The Albany approach implemented several features of situational crime control by reducing opportunities for disruption. No incoming governor could afford to ignore these traditions. Something of this had already been intuited by the Control Review Committee, but somewhat contrary to expectations, Sparks, Bottoms, and Hay (1996) reported that the results of their research did not show that one prison was self-evidently "better" than the other from the point of view of order, rather that both prisons had established their own version of order, each of which had pluses and minuses depending on one's point of view. A relaxed order in Long Lartin came at the price of quite high levels of intimidation, which would not have been tolerated in Albany, where the cost of a restricted regime came with the benefits of greater safety. But, on their own terms, both prisons could be said to "work" in an orderly way.

Bottoms (1999) draws upon Wrong (1994) for a simplified characterization of three philosophical solutions to the problem of order in wider society: "Hobbes's solution was coercive, Locke's stressed mutual self-interest, and Rousseau of *The Social Contract* gave primacy to normative consensus" (cited in Bottoms 1999, 251). Translated to the world of prisons, the first, coercion, clearly dominated the historic periods of the separate and silent systems as we saw earlier, and it might be tempting to try to classify other periods as ones in which the instrumental concerns of mutual self-interest, or the normative consensus among both staff and prisoners about what was seen as appropriate and legitimate, might predominate. But in prisons as in wider society, there is no reason to assume that the three solutions are mutually exclusive. At any given time, all three might be available as a basis for compliance with any given social order, and any one of them might offer sufficiently compelling reasons for some prisoners to con-

form. Thus Albany was more coercive than Long Lartin in that it operated
on the basis of more severe situational and structural constraints, but both
prisons also operated, although probably not very efficiently at that time,
on the basis of various incentives and disincentives, which helped prisoners
through their sentences and brought a measure of control to staff, thus
serving the instrumental interests of both parties. However, Bottoms artic-
ulates a tension between the dimensions of coercive situational control and
of normative consensus, whereby increased levels of situational control tend
to create a legitimacy deficit. I shall return to this important question of
legitimacy when considering the different policy directions taken by the
prison systems in England and Wales and the United States in relation to
problems of order and control arising primarily, though not exclusively, out
of incidents of interpersonal violence.

I have argued for many years that incidents of interpersonal violence
and what are regarded by the authorities as disruptive or subversive behavior
are as much a product of the interactional environment in which they take
place as they are of the personal characteristics of identified "troublesome"
prisoner. "'Troublesomeness' and similar concepts are not just naturally
occurring phenomena, carried around by individuals as a set of characteristics, identifiable in advance and just waiting to erupt" (King and McDermott 1990, 453). Often, they emerge in a given context, conditioned by the
behaviors of staff and other prisoners, and by rules and regulations that are
sometimes hard to justify but which nevertheless serve to "wind up" prisoners who might otherwise get on with doing their time. This is not to say
that there are no extremely difficult, disturbed, and violent individuals.
There are. But the problem of "trouble" in prisons cannot be reduced to
that. Despite the fact that official discourse on prison control problems
"sometimes pays lip service to the capacity of the system to generate its own
trouble," it "falls back time and again on a model that locates trouble primarily in the dispositions of individual prisoners" (King and McDermott
1990, 449). It is my contention that if indeed trouble in prisons is a product
of the relationship among prisoners, staff, and the regime within which they
both operate, then the way to deal with "control problems" is by operating,
as far as this is possible, on the context in which they occur and not by
transferring selected prisoners to special facilities. In other words, prisons
must learn to "consume their own smoke": staff need to hone and maintain
skills in managing difficult prisoners. Where this does not work, first resort
should be to moving either prisoners or staff to new situations without
adverse consequences, and only as a last resort to establish special facilities
for those who genuinely cannot be dealt with in any other way. Whereas
concentration in special facilities will be the parsimonious and legitimate
solution to security problems, control problems should so far as is possible

be dealt with parsimoniously and legitimately in the situations where they occur.

Historically, policy with regard to troublesome prisoners in England and Wales revolved around initial resort to brief spells in segregation units followed by a return to general population (or normal location, in the parlance of the English system). For persistent "troublemakers" in the dispersal prisons, a system eventually officially called the Continuous Assessment System, but known to all as the "merry-go-round" or the "magic roundabout," involved being "ghosted" out of normal location, first to the prison segregation unit but then, at two- or three-month intervals, a transfer to the segregation unit in another prison, and then another prison, and so on.

Such a system also operated in the United States for a time, where it was referred to as "smelling diesel" because the prisoner was constantly being transferred by road around the system. However, in the early 1980s, the two systems began to diverge in the way in which they dealt with troublesome, difficult, and dangerous prisoners. In the United States, as I indicated earlier, the policy of concentration had long prevailed. In fact, partly because the possibility of armed guards using lethal force factored out concerns about escapes, the American version of concentration had always been driven by dealing with prisoners who were seen as dangers to the *system* rather than dangers to *society*.

The federal penitentiary at Marion, Illinois, came to replace Alcatraz as the depository for prisoners who were seen as the most difficult and dangerous. Because there continued to be numerous incidents of prisoner-upon-prisoner violence even within Marion, a control unit, known as H Unit, was established as a "prison within a prison." In 1983, two prison officers were murdered at the hands of prisoners within the control unit, to which the response was further situational control, and the whole prison was effectively locked down (see Ward and Breed 1986 for a review of the situation leading to and the consequences of the lockdown). In their search for a more effective alternative to Marion, the federal authorities at first looked wistfully to a model, so-called "new generation" prison that had been developed at Oak Park Heights in Minnesota, which successfully operated a rich program of positive regimes for maximum security prisoners who were housed in an ingeniously designed series of small living units, each containing up to 50 prisoners. But as prison populations continued to escalate, state legislatures became more and more concerned to cut costs, and political attitudes hardened such that those standing for election sought to outbid each other in terms of their rhetoric and their policies on law and order.

In a climate that saw expenditure on programs as a waste of taxpayers' money, and attention to human rights and humane regimes as an indication of being soft on crime, the lockdown regime that had operated as a stopgap at Marion began to look like an attractive long-term proposition to many state departments of correction. By declaring a need to deal with prisoners universally, though largely rhetorically, described as the "worst of the worst," it was possible to get funding for so-called super-maximum security or supermax facilities that, at one and the same time, would keep such prisoners securely locked down and, it was said, thereby free the rest of the prison system from their predatory behaviors. In fairly quick order, nearly forty American states began to build new facilities or remodel existing ones as supermax prisons (King 1999). In 1994, the federal authorities opened their own supermax at Florence, Colorado, which replaced Marion.

In England and Wales, events took a different turn. The Control Review Committee clearly recognized the distinction between security and control as defined in this chapter, expressed the view that the creaking dispersal system would be better remodeled to effect greater concentration in two new-generation prisons along the lines of Oak Park Heights, which they had visited in Minnesota, and, crucially, recognized that prisoners who were troublesome in one prison context might not be so in another. In a novel development, the Committee recommended the establishment of a number of small units for dealing with difficult and dangerous prisoners. But the Committee explicitly eschewed the idea of a Marion-style control unit and talked instead of units that would offer different styles of supervision and intervention. The hope was that such units would replace the much-disliked continuous assessment system, and that as far as possible each prison would learn to "consume its own smoke" and to deal with its own control problems so that the new units would be kept as a scarce resource and used as a last resort.

Then in 1994 and 1995, there were once again some serious escapes from dispersal prisons, and after a further general enquiry into prison security, Learmont (Home Office 1995) recommended that consideration be given to building two new American-style supermax facilities: one to effect greater concentration of escape-risk prisoners, and the other, rather strangely, to house control problem prisoners. This was strange because there were at the time no particular control problems in the system, and placing control problem prisoners in a supermax facility would have followed American practice but completely overturned the previous policy of housing such prisoners in small units. In fact, no supermax facility has been built in England and Wales, although as noted earlier there has been greater concentration of escape risks in fewer dispersal prisons, which have all been upgraded in their security provisions. Instead of a supermax for control problems, the Control Review Committee's rather ad hoc small units, though not unsuccessful (see Bottomley 1995), were reorganized into a more progressive system with a clearer statement of objectives and restyled as Close Supervision Centers.

Let me now return to the important question of legitimacy in the close supervision centers in England and Wales and supermax facilities in the

United States—both of which deal ostensibly with the same type of prisoners, namely those that the respective prison systems define as the most difficult to manage and the most dangerous. Some years ago, I conducted a comparative study of Oak Park Heights in Minnesota and Gartree, then a dispersal prison in England, which showed that although both prisons had essentially similar populations, Oak Park Heights had very much higher levels of safety for staff and prisoners than Gartree and also offered a much superior regime in terms of time out of cell, programs, education, and recreation (King 1991). Bottoms (1999) has suggested that this study provided an optimistic answer to the question he posed, as to whether it was possible for a prison with more and more situational controls to operate without suffering a legitimacy deficit. It is worth considering why that was the case, why most American supermax facilities do suffer a legitimacy deficit, and why the Close Supervision Centers in England do appear to operate with at least a reasonable degree of legitimacy.

In Minnesota, when Oak Park Heights was opened, there was some skepticism as to whether there were sufficient prisoners in the system to warrant such a high level of custody. Indeed, the Department of Corrections took in boarders from other states and from the federal prison system, although these were often prisoners who required protection rather than who constituted a danger to others. There were undoubtedly prisoners there who did not fit the profile and who were there to fill up spaces (although the same could be said for Gartree, where the dispersal policy at that time deliberately involved holding some prisoners in higher security conditions than they needed in order to dilute the control problem). Such prisoners called into question the legitimacy of the prison, on grounds that the system was not actually using the facility for the purposes it was established and that it was unfair that the criteria for allocation had been stretched to include them. However, although the prison did have many situational controls built into the design, it did offer very high levels of out of cell activity, access to work, education, and treatment programs, and gave some real responsibility and choices to prisoners but without sacrificing the safety of anyone. Above all, the management philosophy of its warden enjoined staff to treat prisoners in the way in which they would like their son, father, or brother to be treated if they were ever in custody. These ingredients more than outweighed any legitimacy deficit resulting from the overemphasis on security.

The situation that then prevailed in Oak Park Heights contrasted markedly with that in most modern American supermax facilities. In the late 1990s, 1.8 percent of the prison population serving a year or longer—about 20,000 prisoners—was in supermax facilities across the United States. That was almost certainly an underestimate then, and today the figure is probably much higher. In many jurisdictions, there is willful overuse of such facilities, with nine states holding more than 4 percent (and one state 12 percent) of their prisoners in supermax facilities. Although defined as for the worst of the worst prisoners and lip service is paid to the slogan that "bad behavior gets you in and good behavior gets you out," many states have no very clear definition of "good" or "bad behavior," no refined procedures for assessing risks, and no central oversight of entrance or exit to supermax. Often admission to such a facility depends on the single judgment of wardens at other prisons in the system, using their own criteria of prisoners they wish to "ship out." Some departments of correction have rigid rules whereby any assault on a member of staff, no matter how trivial, results in allocation to supermax, either indefinitely or for some, usually long, fixed period. Because the regime is in most cases extremely deprived, whereby prisoners are kept isolated from each other and come out of their cells dressed in jumpsuits, with handcuffs and leg irons, and accompanied by three members of staff, only to use the shower, use the telephone, visit the doctor, or exercise in a dog-run cage, the overuse of such facilities stretches the notion of legitimacy well beyond breaking point as far as most prisoners are concerned.

It has to be said that not all supermax facilities suffer all of the above characteristics, and some are operated with a much more judicious sense of responsibility. It also has to be said that the effects may not be quite as bad as is sometimes claimed (King 2005). But what is particularly worrying is that there are few effective avenues for complaint or for external review. In at least one judgment, the Federal Court for the Northern District of California ruled that what went on in the supermax at Pelican Bay was at the outer limits of what normal human beings could endure, yet did not breach Eighth Amendment rights against cruel and unusual punishment precisely because some "normal" people could endure it. Only for those who were already mentally ill or at risk of becoming so was the regime deemed unfit (*Madrid versus Gomez*, 1995). In these circumstances, it is left to bodies such as Human Rights Watch and Amnesty International to raise questions about the appropriateness of these facilities and the proportionality of what is dispensed therein.

In England and Wales, those prisoners who would be described in America as the worst of the worst are dealt with very differently in the close Supervision Centers. Today fewer than 50 prisoners are held in these facilities—much less than 0.1 percent of the prison population serving a year or longer. Only one small section, currently holding four prisoners, could be described as in a lockdown situation. It operates in a bleak and depressing atmosphere, and when prisoners come out of cells for showers or exercise or some very limited association with other prisoners, they are not normally restrained, although they are sometimes opened up with as many as six officers present, who may either be in shirtsleeves or in riot gear depending upon a risk assessment. A review by Her Majesty's Chief Inspector of Prisons, in marked contrast to the decision on Pelican Bay, determined that the regime in this unit was unacceptable, making it clear that, on behalf of the British people, such (less extreme) practices were not legitimate (HMCIP 1999). The unit was reformed. The other units have rather more facilities and program opportunities, albeit within a secure and controlled environment. Above all, entry and exit from the units is centrally controlled and carefully screened through a Close Supervision Centers Selection Committee, which also regularly reviews progress. Moreover, there is a small, independent advisory group who visit the units regularly, talk to prisoners and staff, and report their findings to the Deputy Director General of the Prison Service. Most prisoners seem to accept that the system, whatever its faults, provides a legitimate and proportionate response to the problems as defined.

2.7   The Effects of Imprisonment

Many people, perhaps the majority, would take the view that people should go to prison for moral reasons, because on the basis of what they have done, they deserve to be punished. For them, the principal question about the use of imprisonment may be limited to questions of proportionality: how long a term and in what conditions is justified by the offense? But for others, imprisonment may be used to bring about other objectives: to bring about a safer society, for example, by deterring, incapacitating, or rehabilitating offenders. Whatever the reason for using imprisonment, there are also likely to be unintended effects, on prisoners, their families, and society. The effects of imprisonment may be judged from many standpoints, but gathering evidence on some of them can be peculiarly intractable, and much depends upon the precise nature of the question asked. Even if the answer to one question about the effects seems clear-cut, it may flatly contradict the answer to another. Weighing the answers and coming to a conclusion about policy is not a matter of science and inevitably brings us back into a moral and political discourse.

Let us start at the deep end and ask whether or not the use of prison has an effect upon crime rates. In an earlier section of this chapter, I argued that it was insufficient to look at differential incarceration rates as though they constituted an index of punitiveness. Although Nils Christie (1995) and others would perfectly reasonably argue that the extent to which a society is prepared to use imprisonment, presumably for whatever purpose and with whatever results, tells us something important about the nature of that society, I suggested that it was important to relate this both to rates of crime in that society and the levels of seriousness of crime. After all, it is to the criminal act that the sentence of imprisonment constitutes a response. In Table 2.1, I displayed the changing crime rates and imprisonment rates in England and Wales, Russia, and the United States over the period 1992–2001 to show the very different relationship between crime and imprisonment in the three countries. In Table 2.2, I looked more closely at the numbers of crimes reported to the British Crime Survey and to the police compared to the size of the prison population in England and Wales over the same period and suggested that imprisonment had greatly outstripped the relatively modest growth in crime, which could itself be explained by a change in reporting by the public and recording by the police. In Table 2.3, I tried to show how that increase in the prison population was driven by a change in sentencing practice, relying much more on immediate imprisonment than monetary penalties. Those are fairly conventional arguments put forward both by academic criminologists and by civil servants involved in the criminal justice system, most of whom have judged the increased use of imprisonment to have been a costly experiment that has little impact on the crime problem, and one that exacerbates the very fears on the part of the public that the policy is, ostensibly, designed to assuage.

However, it is important to understand that had I chosen rather different time periods over which to make the comparisons, a more complicated picture would have arisen. This is not to pander to a public cynicism that "one can prove anything with statistics," because, of course, one cannot. Such an assertion is but a refuge for the lazy. But in examining any set of criminal justice statistics, it is important to understand exactly what is being said. The fact that politicians, or academics for that matter, choose their statistics carefully does not mean that they have proved anything, but it should invite closer and informed scrutiny. I chose the starting date of 1992 because in England, 1992 represented a low point of the prison population, and in Russia, it represented the beginning of my research there and the emergence of the Russian Federation from the old Soviet Union. It had no special significance in the United States.

One writer who has taken a longer time span is the populist polemicist Charles Murray (1997) who, building on the work of James Q. Wilson (1975) and John DiIulio (1991), has argued in defense of Michael Howard, onetime British Home Secretary, who famously declared, and who continues to argue, that "prison works." Murray argues that from about 1955, criminals started to become safer in their acts of crime commission because the chances of getting imprisonment began to decline. Over a forty-year period, on average, the risk of going to prison if you committed a crime fell by 80 percent in England and Wales, and according to Murray, the recent upturn had done little to reverse that trend. In summary, Murray claims, albeit in a qualified way, that this reduction in the risk of imprisonment had led to the steady increase in recorded crime to such a point where the prison population would have to be quintupled to restore the risk of imprisonment back to 1954 levels. Had the ratio of imprisonment to crimes committed been maintained at 1954 levels, the crime rate would never have taken off in the way that it did. In this, England and Wales had followed the policies of the United States, where the lowering of the risk of imprisonment had been more sudden, leading to a precipitous increase in crime that the massive growth in imprisonment has only now begun to stabilize and reverse.

But in reality, the relationship between risk of imprisonment and crime is not as simple as Murray suggests, despite its apparent appeal to common sense. Although the argument appears to be based on both individual and general deterrence, it has been widely accepted ever since the persuasive essay by Beccaria ([1764] 1963) that it is not the severity of punishment that deters but rather the certainty of detection. Murray himself acknowledges that most of the reduction in risk derives not from greater leniency by judges, but from reduced detection rates by police forces and even more from the lower proportion of crimes cleared up that proceed to prosecutions. Of course, Murray deplores both those trends also. But had the level of detections and prosecutions been maintained or increased, it might have been possible to argue that the courts could have become less dependent upon prisons and more reliant on alternatives to custody. In any case, as many writers have argued, if Murray's arguments were sound, one would have expected countries with high risks of imprisonment to have low crime rates. As I noted earlier, there are many caveats that have to be entered when comparing international crime rates and imprisonment rates, but Young (1997) has offered several international examples, including Denmark and Scotland and the Netherlands, that confound that argument, and Donziger (1996) has done the same by comparing North and South Dakota in relation to crime rates generally and Louisiana and Oklahoma in regard to homicide. Tonry and Petersilia (1999) conclude that although research has demonstrated there are deterrent effects of imprisonment, those effects are modest. Whatever impact prison has on crime rates through deterrence is likely to be considerably outweighed by the impact of other social, economic, and cultural factors.

An alternative justification for high levels of incarceration depends upon its incapacitative effects, namely that while prisoners are in custody, they are unable to commit further crimes. This is a truism as far as the general public is concerned, providing one is prepared to ignore accounts of prisoners maintaining their outside criminal activities from inside prison, and it takes no account of crimes committed against prison staff and other prisoners. The argument depends upon estimates of the crimes that would have been committed had the persons concerned remained in the community and often involves a supposition that a relatively small number of offenders commit a disproportionately large number of the total volume of crimes. If such offenders were identified and incapacitated through long or even indeterminate sentences, then a major impact could be achieved on crime rates. Although it is true that some identified offenders turn out to be extremely persistent and prolific, incapacitation theory also depends upon the assumption that others will not emerge to take their place. But in any case, the incapacitation effects of imprisonment have sometimes been wildly exaggerated. Zedlewski (1987), to cite perhaps the most absurd example, took the average of 187 offenses admitted by prisoners in a study by the Rand Corporation and multiplied them by the average costs of crime, to calculate cost savings to be made by locking up each additional prisoner. My concern here is not so much with the cost-benefit analysis, seriously flawed though that was, but with the supposed incapacitation effect. As Zimring and Hawkins pointed out when applying Zedlewski's assumptions to published FBI data, the 237,000 increase in the prison population between 1977 and 1986 should have "reduce[d] crime to zero on incapacitation effects alone. ... On this account crime disappeared some years ago" (cited in Tonry 1995, 27). Most calculations on incapacitation effects suggest that it would take a very substantial increase in imprisonment to produce a very modest effect on total crime. It is worth pointing out that incapacitation effects almost by definition are bound to have diminishing returns: The larger the prison population is at any one time, the safer it is to assume that either the most serious and prolific offenders are inside or, having escaped apprehensions thus far, they are unlikely to be caught in the near future. Additions to the prison population are likely to come by bringing in more marginal, less serious offenders. It probably follows that the additional costs of providing more custodial cases are likely to be greater than any savings to be gained from the crimes thus prevented.

It is possible that imprisonment might have an impact upon the future criminal behavior of those incarcerated, either through the deterrent effect of the experience, or the rehabilitative effect of treatment or training programs of one kind or another, or simply because they have aged and grown out of crime during their time in custody. In fact, disentangling the impact of these three possible variables—and there are several others that might be considered—is no easy task. The usual measure of success, or dependent variable, is whether or not a prisoner is reconvicted within a two-year period after release, though it has to be acknowledged that this is an imperfect proxy for whether or not the exprisoner is further involved in crime. Some years ago, the "nothing works" debate was triggered by an article by Robert Martinson (1974), in anticipation of a research report by Lipton, Martinson, and Wilks (1975), even though the conclusion of his article was not so much that nothing works, but that nothing works much better than anything else. On the basis of meta-analyses of the literature (see Gendreau and Andrews 1990 for a review), the debate turned to a consideration of "what works?" and in recent years there has been a proliferation of cognitive programs designed to address offending behavior based upon more careful matching of programs to offender needs, careful implementation of programs and monitoring of their delivery, and backed up by aftercare and relapse prevention schemes. Results have been mixed, but there are modest grounds for optimism in respect of at least some offenders (see Gaes et al. 1999), though less than for similar programs delivered in the community (see Loeber and Farrington 1998). But such programs reach only a minority of prisoners, and overall reconviction rates remain extremely high—nearly three fifths of all prisoners in England and Wales, for example, are reconvicted within two years, and for young male offenders, the proportion rises to three quarters.

Whatever the effect of imprisonment on crime rates and reconvictions, the collateral, and probably unintentional, effects of imprisonment on prisoners, their families, and society may be profound. In Russia during my research there, prisoners died because conditions were so overcrowded that prisoners lost consciousness for lack of oxygen and could not receive medical attention. Vivien Stern (1998) has drawn attention to the fact that in parts of eastern Europe and central Asia, TB is so widespread in prisons that sentences of imprisonment often amount to unintended death sentences. In England and Wales in recent years, suicide by young offenders and women unable to cope with the experience of custody, often while still on remand, have raised similar concerns about "collateral damage." Taking adults in custody often involves inflicting punishments upon their children, who are deprived of a parent and the support that could have come through income earned through employment, which now has to be supplied at a reduced level through welfare benefits of one kind or another. Because imprisonment often involves breaking up relationships that were already in need of support, the damage can be long lasting. Whether or not prisoners are reconvicted, it is doubtful whether many would have benefited from the prison experience either in terms of their future employment prospects or as rehabilitated citizens, because 4 million or so Americans are now deprived of the vote by virtue of their felony convictions (Fellner and Mauer 1998). And what kind of comment does it make on the nature of our societies when the citizens of some deprived communities, themselves victims of structural economic decline, compete to have prisons built in their backyard as the only means of employment?

I have elsewhere (King 2005) considered the effects of supermax custody from the point of view of prisoners and staff, and the claimed effects on the rest of the prison system and on wider society. With regard to the effects upon prisoners, I reported some counterintuitive results on the basis of my own research. Over half the prisoners I interviewed reported at least some beneficial consequences; for example, it had given them time to think, had taught them the need for patience and control, and had enabled them to turn themselves around. But the overwhelming majority also reported negative psychological effects, similar to what is reported in the literature on sensory deprivation (Haney and Lynch 1997), and most thought they could have got the benefits from a far less draconian regime. At the other extreme, a fifth of the prisoners claimed that they would emerge from the experience bitter and vengeful and would in the future rather be hung for a sheep than a lamb. Most questioned the legitimacy of the system. As for staff, I concluded that the system whereby they remained separated from prisoners by physical and electronic barriers, and only dealt with prisoners who were handcuffed and leg-ironed when they were in the company of two other officers, had led to a substantial deskilling. Few exhibited the qualities, for example, depicted by Liebling and Price (2001). I could find no evidence from my own research and little from the literature that the introduction of supermax had produced a reduction in violence more widely throughout the system. As far as the effects on the rest of society are concerned, I could not help reflecting on the crisis of legitimacy. I was disturbed to learn that departments of correction sometimes organized visits to supermax facilities by schoolchildren so that they might be dissuaded from themselves one day becoming the worst of the worst. But maybe those schoolchildren might take home a different message. As Nelson Mandela (1994) has said, echoing the sentiments of Dostoevsky and Churchill before him: "No one truly knows a nation until one has been inside the jails. A nation should not be judged by how it treats its highest citizens, but its lowest ones."

2.8   Conclusions: Whither the Future?

Having reached the end of this chapter, I am all too aware of the things I have left out and which were more than worthy of inclusion. I could, and probably should, have discussed issues arising from prison overcrowding and the conditions for staff as well as prisoners, as well as health services and problems of suicide and self-harm, of drug abuse, TB, and HIV (see Stern 1993, 1998; Liebling 1999; and McDonald 1999 for illuminating discussions on these topics). A more complete account would certainly have included a systematic discussion of women's imprisonment. Time was when this was a much neglected topic. Today, this is no longer the case, though much of the literature is designed to argue that women have different and special needs in prison. For a state-of-the-art review of the current state of knowledge about women in prison, see Kruttschnitt and Gartner (2003), but we still await a comparative study of imprisonment for both men and women within the same jurisdiction conducted using the same techniques. When such studies have been carried out, we will be in a much better position to know about the relative needs of men and women in prison.

Another area I have neglected is staff—and not just the front-line prison officers or guards but also the various managers and specialists who work in prisons. It is hard to underestimate the importance of good quality staff, and most prison systems pay lip service to their important contribution to the work of the prison. But good studies of the staff world are extremely rare. I referred above to the early and still important American study by Kelsey Kaufmann (1988) of prison officers and their world. Jacobs (1983) is one of the few other American scholars to have devoted systematic attention to prison guards. The best account of prison officers and what characteristics are necessary for the successful accomplishment of their work in the English context is by Liebling and Price (2001).

Nor have I said anything about the modern tendency towards either privatization of prisons or contracting out aspects of correctional services; still less have I discussed the relationship between public- and private-sector provision and the vested interests there may be in the security hardware and other paraphernalia of imprisonment, which may feed into an age of mass imprisonment. Privatization of correctional services has taken a rather different direction in England and Wales from that in the United States or in Australia, and the reader is referred to the account by Harding (1998) for a review of the issues and to Bottomley et al. (1997) for an evaluation of one private-sector English prison.

Finally, I recognize that I should have spoken much more about processes of internal audit, independent inspection, and accountability both to the courts and to various international, governmental, and nongovernmental bodies (see Rodley 1999). For a time, court oversight of American prisons looked to be an effective way of holding prison authorities to account for the conditions in their prisons, but as the interest of courts has waned and their powers curtailed, so American mechanisms for holding departments of correction to account have seemed tokenistic and in the end toothless. In Britain, internal audit, external inspection, and the process of judicial review in the context of the European Convention on Human Rights as embodied in domestic law seem somewhat more effective. See Maguire, Vagg, and Morgan (1985) for an early collection on these issues and the numerous reports by Human Rights Watch and Amnesty International and, in the European context, the work of the European Committee for the Prevention of Torture and Inhuman and Degrading Treatment or Punishment (see Morgan and Evans 1999).

No doubt there are many other omissions, but it is time to ask, What of the future? David Rothman (1971) was not alone when he predicted a continuing decline in the use of imprisonment in America. Before him, Norval Morris (1965) looked forward to the extinction of imprisonment by the end of the twentieth century. And before him, Hermann Mannheim (1942) believed that the days of mass imprisonment were already largely over. They were all wrong. In the circumstances, one might be forgiven for drawing back from making predictions, but it seems fairly safe to say that given existing levels of imprisonment, prisons are not going to go away in the foreseeable future. If the lessons of history seem to show anything, they show that prisons are a remarkably resilient institutional form, and that whatever their faults, and there are many, it is much easier for politicians, the press, and the public to fall back on their use at times when fears of crime, drugs, pauperism, or whatever abound than it is for confidence to be built up in their alternatives. Prisons, it seems, are a necessary evil. Necessary because there are undoubtedly persons who demonstrate by their behaviors a persistent and dangerous threat to law-abiding citizens that, so far at least, have been impossible to contain by other means. Evil because prisons have always contained far more than the comparative few who constitute real and present dangers, and there can be little that is morally uplifting about the state and its servants drastically removing the freedoms of some (usually disadvantaged) citizens marginally to protect the freedoms of more privileged others.

The question, then, is not so much whether prisons will or should exist, but rather about the extent and the conditions of their use. It is difficult to see how countries such as the United States can now row back from the extremely high rates of incarceration currently in use, though it is not impossible that a more rational appreciation of the costs and benefits may yet prevail, and there are minimal signs that this may be happening. It is certainly vital that other countries learn from that experience before they venture too far down the road of mass incarceration. It is also important that fundamental questions of legitimacy be addressed: The recent disclosures of torture at Abu Ghraib and publicity about the conditions in Guantanamo Bay are indicative of what has already been condoned by the courts in domestic American policies about supermax confinement, which have in turn been made possible by the ratcheting up of law-and-order rhetoric by mendacious politicians. This is a bubble that could yet burst, provided enough attention is given to the already considerable body of international jurisprudence concerning human rights and conditions of detention. But it may not. And if not, in the rapidly changing world in which we live, prisons could yet be seen as relatively benign instruments of control compared to those we might face in the future. Electronic tagging, subcutaneous implants, satellite tracking, and genetic engineering are either available now or will soon be on someone's political agenda.

References

ACPS. 1968. The regime for long-term prisoners in conditions of maximum security. In *Report of the Advisory Council on the Penal System (Radzinowicz Report)*. London: HMSO.

Beaumont, G. de, and A. de Tocqueville. 1833, 1964. *On the Penitentiary System in the United States*. Carbondale.

Beccaria, C. 1764, trans. 1963. *On Crimes and Punishments*. Indianapolis: Bobbs-Merril.

Bentham, J. 1802a. Panopticon: Or, the inspection house. In *Works*, Vol. 4, ed. J. Bowring, 37-172. London: Simpkin, Marshall and Co.

Bentham, J. 1802b. Panopticon versus New South Wales, in *Works*, Vol. 4, ed. J. Bowring, 173-248. London: Simpkin, Marshall and Co.

Bottomley, A. K. 1995. *CRC Special Units: A General Assessment*. London: Home Office Research and Planning Unit.

Bottomley, A. K., James, A., 1997. *Monitoring and Evaluation of Wolds Remand Prison, and Comparisons with Public-Sector Prisons in Particular HMP Woodhill*, Hull and Cambridge: Report for the Home Office Research Statistics Directorate.

Bottoms, A. E. 1999. Interpersonal violence and social order in prisons. In *Prisons, Crime and Justice: A Review of Research*, Vol. 26, ed. M. Tonry and J. Petersilia, 205-81. Chicago: University of Chicago Press.

Braswell, M. C., R. H. Montgomery, and L. X. Lombardo, eds. 1994. *Prison Violence in America*. Cincinnati: Anderson.

Bureau of Justice. 2003. *Prisoners in 2002*. Washington, DC: U.S. Department of Justice.

Bureau of Justice. 2004. *Prison and Jail Inmates at Midyear 2003*. Washington, DC: U.S. Department of Justice.

Christie, N. 1995. *Crime Control as Industry: Towards Gulags, Western Style*, London: Routledge.

Clemmer, D. 1940. *The Prison Community*. New York: Holt, Rinehart and Winston.

Collins, P. 1962. *Dickens and Crime*. London: Macmillan.

Crawford, W. 1834. *Report of William Crawford, Esq., on the Penitentiaries of the United States*. Vol. XVI, Parliamentary papers, 593.

Cressey, D. R., ed. 1961, *The Prison: Studies in Institutional Organisation and Change*. New York: Holt Rinehart and Winston.

Crewe, B. 2005. A new inmate code? The origins, functions and effects of contemporary inmate values. In *The Effects of Imprisonment*, ed. A. Liebling and S. Maruna. Cullompton: Willan.

Currie, E. 1998. *Crime and Punishment in America*. Metropolitan Books. New York: Henry Holt and Company.

DiIulio, J. 1991. *No Escape: The Future of American Corrections*. New York: Basic Books.

Donziger, S., ed. 1995. *The Real War on Crime.* The Report of the National Criminal Justice Commission. New York: Harper Perennial.

Elias, N. 1939, tr. 1978. *The Civilising Process: i. The History of Manners* and *ii. State Formation and Civilisation.* Oxford: Oxford University Press.

Fellner, J., and Mauer, M. 1998. Nearly 4 million Americans denied vote because of felony convictions. *Overcrowded Times* 9: 5, 1, 6-13.

Foucault, M. 1977. *Discipline and Punish: The Birth of the Prison.* New York: Pantheon Books.

Fox, L. W. 1952. *The English Prison and Borstal Systems.* London: Routledge and Kegan Paul.

Frase, R. S. 1998. Jails. In *The Handbook of Crime and Punishment,* ed. M. Tonry. New York: Oxford University Press.

Gaes, G., et al. 1999. Adult correctional treatment. In *Prisons: Crime and Justice, A Review of Research,* Vol. 26, ed. M. Tonry and J. Petersilia. Chicago: University of Chicago Press.

Garland, D., ed. 2001. *Mass Imprisonment: Social Causes and Consequences.* London: Sage Publications.

Gendreau, P. and D. Andrews. 1990. Tertiary prevention: What the meta-analysis of the offender treatment literature tells us about what works. *Canadian Journal of Criminology* 32: 173.

Goffman, E. 1961. *Asylums: Essays on the Social Situation of Mental Patients and other Inmates,* New York: Anchor Books.

Haney, C., Banks, C., and Zimbardo, P. 1973. Interpersonal dynamics in a simulated prison. *International Journal of Criminology and Penology* 1: 69.

Haney, C., and M. Lynch. 1997. Regulating prisons of the future: a psychological analysis of supermax and solitary confinement. *New York University Review of Law and Social Change* 23: 477.

Harding, C., et al. 1985. *Imprisonment in England and Wales: A Concise History.* London: Croom Helm.

Harding, R. 1998. Private prisons. In *The Handbook of Crime and Punishment,* ed. M. Tonry. New York and Oxford: Oxford University Press.

HMCIP. 1999. Inspection of close supervision centers, August-September 1999: A thematic inspection. London: Her Majesty's Chief Inspector of Prisons.

Home Office. 1984. Managing the long-term prison system: The report of the control review committee. London: HMSO.

Home Office. 1991a. Custody, care and justice: The way ahead for the prisons service in England and Wales, Cmnd. 1647. London: HMSO.

Home Office. 1991b. Prison disturbances April 1990, Report of an inquiry by the Rt. Hon. Lord Justice Woolf (Parts I and II) and His Honour Judge Stephen Tumim (Part II), Cmnd. 1456. London: HMSO.

Home Office. 1995. Review of Prison Service Security in England and Wales and the Escape from Parkhurst Prison on Tuesday 3rd January 1995. (The Learmont Report), Cmnd. 3020. London: HMSO.

Home Office. 1999. Report of the inquiry into prison escapes and security (Mounbatten Report), Cmnd. 3175. London: HMSO.

Hough, M., Jacobson, J., and Millie, A. 2003. *The Decision to Imprison: Sentencing and the Prison Population.* London: Prison Reform Trust.

Howard, J. 1777. *The State of the Prisons in England and Wales.* Warrington.

Ignatieff, M. 1978. *A Just Measure of Pain: The Penitentiary in the Industrial Revolution, 1750–1850.* New York: Columbia University Press.

Irwin, J. 1970. *The Felon.* Englewood Cliffs, NJ: Prentice-Hall.

Irwin, J. 1980. *Prisons in Turmoil.* Boston: Little Brown.

Irwin, J. 1985. *The Jail: Managing the Underclass in American Society.* Berkeley: University of California Press.

Irwin, J., and D. R. Cressey. 1962. Thieves, convicts and the inmate culture. *Social Problems* 10: 142.

Jacobs, J. 1974. Street gangs behind bars. *Social Problems* 21:3, 395.

Jacobs, J. 1977. *Stateville: The Penitentiary in Mass Society.* Chicago: University of Chicago Press.

Jacobs, J. B. 1983. *New Perspectives on Prisons and Imprisonment.* Ithaca and London: Cornell University Press.

Kaminski, M. 2004. *Games Prisoners Play: The Tragicomic Worlds of Polish Prisons.* Princeton and Oxford: Princeton University Press.

Kassebaum, G., D. Ward, and D. Wilner. 1971. *Prison Treatment and Parole Survival: An Empirical Assessment.* New York: Wiley.

Kauffman, K. 1988. *Prison Officers and Their World.* Cambridge: Harvard University Press.

King, R. D. 1987. New generation prisons: The prison building programme and the future of the dispersal policy. In *Problems of Long-term Imprisonment,* ed. A. E. Bottoms and R. Light. Aldershot: Gower.

King, R. D. 1991. Maximum-security custody in Britain and the USA: A study of Gartree and Oak Park Heights. *British Journal of Criminology* 31:2, 126.

King, R. D. 1994. Russian prisons after Perestroika: End of the Gulag? *British Journal of Criminology* 34, Special Issue, 62.

King, R. D. 1999. The rise and rise of supermax: An American solution in search of a problem? *Punishment and Society* 1:2, 163.

King, R. D. 2005. The effects of supermax custody. In *The Effects of Imprisonment,* ed. A. Liebling and S. Maruna. Cullompton: Willan.

King, R. D., and K. W. Elliot. 1977. *Albany: Birth of a Prison—End of an Era.* London: Routledge and Kegan Paul.

King, R. D., and K. McDermott. 1989. British prisons 1970-1987: The ever-deepening crisis. *British Journal of Criminology* 29:2, 107.

King, R. D., and K. McDermott. 1990. "My geranium is subversive": Notes on the management of trouble in prisons. *British Journal of Sociology* 41, 445.

King, R. D., and R. Morgan. 1980. *The Future of the Prison System.* Farnborough: Gower.

King, R. D., and L. Piacentini. 2005. The correctional system during transition. In *Ruling Russia: Crime, Law and Justice in a Changing Society,* ed. W. Pridemore. Boulder, CO: Rowman and Littlefield.

Kruttschnitt, C., and R. Gartner. 2003. Women's imprisonment. In *Crime and Justice: A Review of Research,* Vol. 30, ed. M. Tonry. Chicago and London: University of Chicago Press.

Liebling, A. 1999. Prisoner suicide and prisoner coping. In *Prisons: Crime and Justice, A Review of Research,* Vol. 26, ed. M. Tonry and J. Petersilia. Chicago: University of Chicago Press.

Liebling, A., and H. Arnold. 2004. *Prisons and Their Moral Performance: A Study of Values, Quality and Prison Life.* Oxford: Oxford University Press.

Liebling, A., and D. Price. 2001. The prison officer. *Prison Service Journal.* Leyhill NB.

Lipton, D., R. Martinson, and J. Wilks. 1975. *The Effectiveness of Correctional Treatment: A Survey of Correctional Treatment Evaluations.* New York: Praeger.

Loeber, R., and D. Farrington. 1998. *Serious and Violent Youthful Offenders: Risk Factors and Successful Interventions.* Newbury Park, CA: Sage.

McConville, S. 1981. *History of English Prison Administration.* London: Routledge and Kegan Paul.

McConville, S. 1994. *English Local Prisons 1860-1900: "Next Only to Death."* London: Routledge.

McConville, S. 1995. Local justice. In *The Oxford History of the Prison,* ed. N. Morris and D. Rothman. New York and Oxford: Oxford University Press.

McDermott, K., and R. D. King. 1988. Mind games: Where the action is in prisons. *British Journal of Criminology* 28:3, 357.

McDonald, D. 1999. Medical care in prisons. In *Prisons: Crime and Justice, A Review of Research,* Vol. 26, ed. M. Tonry and J. Petersilia. Chicago: University of Chicago Press.

Madrid v. Gomez. 1995. Case C90-3094-THE, Class action: findings of fact, conclusions of law and order. U.S. District Court for the Northern District of California, January.

Maguire, M., J. Vagg, and R. Morgan, eds. 1985. *Accountability and Prisons: Opening up a Closed World.* London and New York: Tavistock.

Mandela, N. 1994. *Long Walk to Freedom.* London: Little Brown.

Mannheim, H. 1942. American criminology and penology in war time. *Sociological Review* 34: 222.

Martinson, R. 1974. What works? Questions and answers about prison reform. *Public Interest* 35:2, 22.

Mauer, M., and T. Huling. 1995. *Young Black Americans and the Criminal Justice System.* Washington, DC: The Sentencing Project.

Melossi, D., and M. Pavarini. 1997. *The Prison and the Factory: Origins of the Penitentiary System.* Totowa, NJ: Barnes and Noble.

Milgram, S. 1965. Some conditions of obedience and disobedience to authority. *Human Relations* 18:1, 57.

Mitford, J. 1973. *Kind and Usual Punishment.* New York: Alfred Knopf.

Moczydlowski, P. 1992. *The Hidden Life of Polish Prisons.* Bloomington and Indianapolis: Indiana University Press.

Morgan, R., and M. D. Evans, eds. 1999. *Protecting Prisoners: The Standards of the European Committee for the Prevention of Torture in Context.* Oxford: Oxford University Press.

Morris, N. 1965. Prison in evolution. In *Criminology in Transition—Essays in Honour of Hermann Mannheim,* ed. T. Grygier, H. Jones, and J. Spencer. London: Tavistock Publications.

Morris, N., and D. J. Rothman, eds. 1995. *The Oxford History of the Prison: The Practice of Punishment in Western Society.* New York and Oxford: Oxford University Press.

Morris, T., P. Morris, and B. Barer. 1963. *Pentonville: A Sociological Study of an English Prison.* London: Routledge and Kegan Paul.

Murray, C. 1997. *Does Prison Work?* London: Institute of Economic Affairs and the Sunday Times.

Oleinik, A. 2003. *Organised Crime, Prisons and Soviet Societies.* London: Ashgate.

Pease, K. 1994. Cross national imprisonment rates: Limitations of method and possible conclusions. In *Prisons in Context,* ed. R. D. King and M. Maguire. Oxford: Clarendon Press.

Piacentini, L. 2004. *Surviving Russian Prisons: Punishment, Economy and Politics in Transition.* Cullompton: Willan.

Rodley, N. S. 1999. *The Treatment of Prisoners Under International Law,* 2nd edition. New York: Oxford University Press.

Rothman, D. 1971. *The Discovery of the Asylum: Social Order and Disorder in the New Republic.* Boston: Little, Brown and Co.

Rothman, D. 1980. *Conscience and Convenience: The Asylum and its Alternatives in Progressive America.* Boston: Little Brown.

Rusche, G., and O. Kirchheimer. 1939. *Punishment and Social Structure.* New York: Columbia University Press.

Schrag, C. 1944. *Social Types in a Prison Community.* Unpublished MA thesis, University of Washington. Seattle, WA.

Smit, D., D. Van Zyl, and F. Dünkel. 2001. *Imprisonment Today and Tomorrow: International Perspective on Prisoners' Rights and Prison Conditions*, 2nd edition. The Hague: Kluwer Law International.

Sparks, R., A. Bottoms, and W. Hay. 1996. *Prisons and the Problem of Order*. Oxford: Clarendon Press.

Spierenburg, P. 1984. *The Spectacle of Suffering*. Cambridge and London: Cambridge University Press.

Stern, V. 1993. *Bricks of Shame: Britain's Prisons*. Harmondsworth: Penguin Books.

Stern, V., ed. 1998. *Sentenced to Die? The Problem of TB in Prisons in Eastern Europe and Central Asia*. London: International Centre for Prison Studies.

Street, D., R. Vinter, and C. Perrow. 1966. *Organisation for Treatment*. New York: Free Press.

Sykes, G. M. 1958. *The Society of Captives: A Case Study in a Maximum-Security Prison*. Princeton: Princeton University Press.

Sykes, G. M., and S. Messenger. 1960. Inmate social system. In *Theoretical Studies in the Social Organisation of the Prison*. New York: Social Science Research Council.

Tonry, M. 1994. Racial disproportion in U.S. prisons. In *Prisons in Context*, ed. R. D. King and M. Maguire. Oxford: Clarendon Press.

Tonry, M. 1995. *Malign Neglect: Race, Crime and Punishment in America*. New York: Oxford University Press.

Tonry, M., and J. Petersilia. 1999. American prisons at the beginning of the twenty-first century. In *Prisons: Crime and Justice, A Review of Research*, Vol. 26, ed. M. Tonry and J. Petersilia. Chicago: University of Chicago Press.

Walmsley, R. 1999. World prison population list, Research Findings No. 88. Home Office Research, Development and Statistics Directorate.

Walmsley, R. 2003. World prison population list, Findings 234. Home Office Research, Development and Statistics Directorate.

Ward, D. A., and A. F. Breed. 1986. The United States Penitentiary, Marion, Illinois, in Marion Penitentiary 1985: Oversight hearing before the subcommittee on courts, civil liberties and the administration of justice of the committee on the judiciary, House of Representatives (Ser. no. 26). Washington, DC: U.S. Government Printing Office.

Wheeler, S. 1961. Socialisation in correctional communities. *American Sociology Review* 26: 697.

Wilson, J. Q. 1975. *Thinking About Crime*, New York: Basic Books.

Wrong, D. 1994. *The Problem of Order: What Unites and Divides Society*. Cambridge: Harvard University Press.

Young, J. 1997. Charles Murray and the American prison experiment: The dilemmas of a libertarian. In *Does Prison Work?* ed. C. Murray et al. London: Institute of Economic Affairs and The Sunday Times.

Zedlewski, E. 1987. Making confinement decisions. *Research in Brief Series.* Washington, DC: National Institute of Justice.

Zimring, F. 2001. Imprisonment rates and the new politics of criminal punishment. In *Mass Imprisonment: Social Causes and Consequences,* ed. D. Garland. London: Sage.

Zimring, F., and G. Hawkins. 1991. *The Scale of Imprisonment.* Chicago and London: University of Chicago Press.

Zimring, F., and G. Hawkins. 1994. The growth of imprisonment in California. In *Prisons in Context,* ed. R. King and M. Maguire. Oxford: Clarendon Press.

Suicide in Prisons and Jails

3

CHRISTINE TARTARO AND
DAVID LESTER

Contents

Those studying the social problems of society often ignore those members of the society who are in institutions. For example, when citizens advocate the reduction of violence in society by imprisoning criminals for long terms, they ignore the fact that prisons are often very violent places (Toch 1977).

Violence in prisons is not seen by the general public or by policymakers as relevant to society.

The same used to be true for suicide. Whereas suicide prevention was considered to be a worthy goal for society, suicide by those in prison was typically excluded from public concern. Press reports of famous cases of custodial suicide, such as Hermann Goering's suicide in 1946 after being found guilty of war crimes in the Nuremburg trials or Ulrike Meinhof's suicide in 1976 during her trial for terrorist crimes committed as part of Germany's Baader-Meinhof gang, did little to change this attitude. Indeed, these suicides might have been viewed by some as appropriate outcomes for such criminals.

This attitude has changed in some countries, partly because of the lawsuits brought and won by relatives of defendants and convicts who have committed suicide while in custody and partly because the suicide rate in indigenous peoples in custody, such as Native Americans in the United States and Aborigines in Australia (Lester 1997), has been very high. As information about suicide while in custody accumulates, authorities who fail to take adequate precautions against suicide in their institutions can be held liable.

The inmates of prisons, jails, and police lockups are those individuals in society whose lives are in disarray. Many defendants and convicts have psychiatric disorders. Furthermore, in recent years, psychiatric institutions have tried to "deinstitutionalize" as many of their patients as they can release back into society, and this has resulted in large numbers of psychiatrically disturbed homeless people who commit misdemeanors and crimes, ending up in custody. Jails and prisons have rapidly replaced psychiatric facilities as "shelters" for the psychiatrically disturbed (Butterfield 1998).

The U.S. Bureau of Justice Statistics (U.S. BJS 1999) reported that 7 percent of federal correctional inmates in the United States, 16 percent of state prison inmates, and 16 percent of jail detainees reported a psychiatric condition or had stayed in psychiatric hospitals. Suicide rates are much higher among those with diagnosable psychiatric disorders, and so these inmates are at high risk of suicide while in custody (Maris, Berman, and Silverman, 2000).

In 1998, 70 percent of the inmates in American jails (about 417,000 individuals) had committed drug offenses or used drugs regularly, and over half of all jail and prison inmates (about 56 percent) reported using drugs in the month prior to their offense (U.S. BJS 2000). Suicidal behavior is much more common in drug users than in those who do not use (or abuse) drugs (Lester 2000), and so the higher proportion of drug users in custody would be expected to lead to a high rate of fatal and nonfatal suicidal behavior.

The risk of suicide in custody is made even greater by the impact of imprisonment itself. Entering custody often causes feelings of despair and frustration (Hayes and Rowan 1988), and many inmates are under the influence of alcohol and drugs at the time of arrest and so must undergo withdrawal. Offenders lose contact with family and friends, face the loss of their jobs and a possible long-term incarceration, and may feel that they have lost control over their lives. Imprisonment may also mean the daily threat of assault and rape by other inmates, brutality at the hands of the guards, and emotional and intellectual deterioration resulting from incarceration in a stimulus-impoverished environment. Sykes (1972) labeled such factors "the pains of imprisonment," and they are more commonly called prisonization effects (Walters 2003). The stress of imprisonment is so great that the inmates have to be placed on psychiatric medications, or use illicit drugs, in order withstand the stress (Plourde and Brochu 2002).

3.1   The Incidence of Suicide

Official statistics on suicide have long been criticized as inaccurate (Douglas 1967), and this may be especially true for suicides in custody. For example, Smith (1984) documented a "suicide" in a British prison that was a cover-up of a murder by the officers. Hayes (1989) judged that forty-six deaths in penal institutions in Ohio in 1981–1982 were probably suicides, whereas only twenty-two of these deaths were officially recorded as suicides. Suicides may be covered up and misclassified so as to place the correctional facility and staff in a better light (Welch and Gunther 1997) and to reduce the threat of litigation. Some suicides are recorded as taking place in the hospital to which the inmate is transferred (Hayes 1989), and the absence of a centralized registry for deaths in custody also contributes to the inaccuracy of mortality statistics for inmates (Davis and Muscat 1993).

Tartaro (2004) has noted that, in terms of sheer numbers, more inmates commit suicide in American jails than in American prisons. For example, 113 state and federal prisoners committed suicide in 1985 and 97 in 1986 (U.S. BJS 1988, 1989). In contrast, 453 jail inmates committed suicide in 1985 and 401 in 1986 (Hayes 1989). Most of the estimates of the percentage of deaths in American county jails and state prisons that are a result of suicide range from 18 percent to 26 percent, although occasionally higher percentages are reported. The percentage of deaths in prison due to suicide in Australia, Finland, and Scotland has ranged from 32 percent to 37 percent (Lester and Danto 1993). In the United States, the percentage of deaths in the general public due to suicide is 2.1 percent for males and 14.4 percent for males aged twenty to twenty-nine. Thus, the percentage of death due to suicide in male inmates appears to be higher than for nonincarcerated men.

However, Lester (1987) calculated a suicide rate for all inmates in the United States during 1980–1983 of 24.2 per 100,000 per year for male inmates and 4.7 for female inmates, rates that are similar to those for the general population. Data collected by the U.S. Bureau of Justice Statistics (U.S. BJS 1981–1999) reveal that the average suicide rate in American state prisons was 18.9 for the period 1978–1996. During this period, the peak was 26.7 in 1979 and the lowest was 16.2 in 1995.[1]

Suicide rates have been reported for prisoners in other nations of about 40 in England (Topp 1979), 69 in Belgium (Cosyns and Wilmotte 1974), 81 in Austria (Hoff 1973), and 96 in Canada (Burtch and Ericson 1979), all of which are higher than the suicide rate for the general population in those nations. More recently, Greece has a reported average suicide rate of 112 per 100,000 inmates classified as convicted, on remand, or hospitalized from 1977 to 1996 (Spinellis and Themeli 1997). The average suicide rate for sentenced offenders in Austria between 1975 and 1997 was 81.3 per 100,000 inmates, and the average rate for prisoners on remand was 236 (Fruehwald et al. 2000).

The rates of suicide in jails and police lockups should be considered with caution. O'Toole (1997) discussed measurement issues that are frequently encountered by researchers attempting to discuss the rate of suicide in jails. O'Toole noted that although the average daily population of U.S. jails was approximately 500,000 in 1995, admissions to jails for that year were between 10 and 13 million. Due to the differences in admissions in prisons and jails, O'Toole demonstrated that, although it takes two years for a prison population to turn over, a jail's population turns over twenty to twenty-five times a year. In other words, even if a prison and a jail have the same average daily population and the same number of suicides, O'Toole cautioned against declaring that the suicide rates in the two institutions are equal.

Researchers have identified particular institutional settings that result in high suicide rates. For example, the suicide rate on death row in the United States was 146.5 for the period 1977–1982 (Lester 1986), a remarkably high rate given the tight security for inmates under sentence of death. Lester and Tartaro (2002) studied suicide on the death rows in the United States from 1976 to 1999. The average suicide rate on death row was 113, ranging from zero in 1979 to 312 in 1980. The suicide rate on death row declined over the period studied, and because the population on death row grew during the period, the suicide rate on death row was negatively associated with the death row population.

A high suicide rate of 232 per 100,000 residents has been reported at a state institution for the criminally insane (Haycock 1993). Flaherty (1983) found that juveniles had a suicide rate of 1,578 when placed in adult lockups (in police stations), 641 when placed in adult jails, but only 34 when placed in juvenile detention centers. Clearly juveniles should not be placed in custody in adult facilities.

---

[1] All rates in this chapter are per 100,000 per year.

3.2   Who Commits Suicide?

Many investigators have described small samples of inmates who have committed suicide. For example, Danto (1989) described the typical suicide in an American police lockup as occurring soon after booking (within the first three hours), using hanging in a poorly supervised isolation cell. The victim is usually a white male, under the age of twenty-two, arrested for a relatively minor offense, often intoxicated, belligerent, and confrontational, with no criminal record. Hayes (1983) found a virtually identical profile in a survey of suicides in all the jails in the United States.

The profile for sentenced prisoners is less well described and varies somewhat from prison to prison. In a study of the Maryland state prison system, the typical suicide victim was black, aged twenty-five to thirty-four, sentenced for crimes against people, sentenced to more than eight years, in a maximum security institution, after serving about four years (Salive, Smith, and Brewer 1989). All of these prisoners had been tried, convicted, and sentenced. On the other hand, in England, Topp (1979) found the typical prison suicide victim to be waiting to be sentenced rather than awaiting trial, unmarried, twenty-five to thirty-four years of age, convicted for theft, and in the first month of incarceration. The fact that the above-mentioned profiles for suicidal inmates are different prompts concerns about the reliance on profiles to determine who is at risk for suicide.

Males have higher suicide rates in custody than do females, but this mirrors the difference found in the larger society. Juveniles appear to have a higher risk of suicide (Atlas 1987), as do inmates with a history of drug and alcohol abuse or who are incarcerated while under the influence of these substances (Davis and Muscat 1993; Farmer, Felthous, and Holzer 1996; Liebling 1992, 1993; Loucks 1997).

In some nations, such as Australia, and the Southwestern states of the United States, there has been a great deal of attention focused on suicide among indigenous peoples, typically charged with minor offenses (Lester 1997). Investigators have noted the influence of alcohol intoxication and the stress of being removed from home to a distant jail (Spencer 1989).

Descriptions of the modal or average prisoner suicide do not tell us much, because the profile often resembles the modal prisoner, suicidal or not. What is required are comparisons of those inmates who commit suicide with those who do not. Such research enables the custodial staff to be alert to those inmates who are at greater risk for suicide. In the United States, those inmates who commit suicide resemble those who do not do so in simple demographic characteristics, but they have been charged with more serious crimes and more often with crimes against people (Lester and Danto 1993), and the same appears to be true for Canadian prison suicides (Burtch and Ericson 1979).

Dissemination of the profile of the typical suicidal inmate to correctional staff and administrators sometimes leads them to assume, for example, that only single white males in their early twenties, in the first few hours of incarceration in a jail after committing a minor offense, are at risk for suicide. Thus, they ignore other inmates at risk for suicide (Hayes 1989). Profiles are merely guidelines; exceptions often occur. Liebling (1992) has suggested that correctional staff rely less on profiles and focus more on looking for circumstances that bring about the onset of a suicidal crisis. For example, Blaauw, Winkel, and Kerkhof (2001) found a significant relationship between being a victim of bullying while incarcerated and suicide risk. Stressful situations, such as problems with other inmates, problems with staff, receipt of bad news from home, or receipt of bad news from a lawyer or judge, can be more telling predictors of a suicide attempt than demographic characteristics.

3.3   How Inmates Commit Suicide

The methods for suicide by those in custody depend upon the type of facility in which they are incarcerated. Offenders in police lockups and jails have relatively fewer available tools with which to commit suicide as compared to those in prison. Those in prison have items for personal hygiene and luxury items. They are also serving long sentences and can accumulate many possessions. Inmates in jails are typically there for briefer periods of time and are restricted in the possessions they may have.

In police lockups and jails, suicide frequently occurs shortly after initial incarceration (Frottier et al. 2002; Hayes 1989; Ingram, Johnson, and Hayes 1997), and razors, guns, and medications are not available. Thus, hanging (a generic term for hanging, suffocation, self-suspension, and strangulation) is the only method for suicide available. Over 90 percent of inmates in jails who commit suicide use hanging (Eyland, Corben, and Barton 1997; Hayes 1989; Ingram, Johnson, and Hayes 1997; Marcus and Alcabes 1993; Spinellis and Themeli 1997). Suicides in police lockups tend to involve the victim's clothing, whereas those in jails tend to use their bedding.[2]

Suicidal inmates in prison tend more often to use cutting, but hanging is more often used for fatal suicidal acts (Eyland, Corben, and Barton 1997; Liebling 1992). Hanging is a more lethal method of suicide than cutting, and death from hanging occurs within five to ten minutes after cutoff of oxygen or blockage of blood to the brain (Stone 1999). Perhaps surprising to those with little knowledge of suicide by hanging, it is not necessary to suspend the body from a high place, such as a hook in the ceiling. It is possible to hang oneself using a doorknob placed in the middle of a door. The weight

[2] Bedding is less often provided in police lockups (Hayes 1989).

of the body can create enough pressure from the noose on the neck so as to cut off airflow to the lungs.

3.4   When Suicides Occur

The National Commission on Correctional Health Care (NCCHC) has published standards that identified the following high-risk times for suicide (Hayes 1996): immediately after admission to the facility, immediately after adjudication, following an inmate's return to the facility from court, after receiving bad news regarding his or her family, and after suffering humiliation or rejection. Receiving news of new charges or additional sentences can also precipitate suicidal behavior (White and Schimmel 1995), as can holidays (Hayes 2001).

In jails, it has been reported that 27 percent of suicides occur within three hours after admission, and over 50 percent within the first twenty-four hours (Hayes 1989). Marcus and Alcabes (1993) found that 50 percent of suicides in their urban jail study occurred within three days of a court appearance, when the inmate may have to face the victim, the victim's family, or his or her own family, and face adjudication. Frottier and colleagues (2002) found that suicides in inmates on remand are high during their first twenty days of incarceration, then the rates decline, only to rise again after the inmates have spent over sixty days in jail. The authors speculate that, following the initial shock of incarceration, inmates adjust, but the stress of incarcerated life becomes tiring and unbearable for some inmates after a long period spent in jail.

In prisons, the time frame is quite different. White and Schimmel (1995) found that the average time between admission after sentencing and suicide was about five years. The most common stressors precipitating the suicides were marital or relationship problems, such as the spouse divorcing the inmate, and also concerns about personal safety in the prison. In a study of the Canadian prison system, Schlosar and Carlson (1997) found that inmates sentenced to at least two years of incarceration were more likely to commit suicide during first six months and the last six months of their sentences.

3.5   Where Suicides Occur

A common method for dealing with problem inmates is to isolate them and place them in solitary confinement. Solitary confinement prevents the inmate from being assaulted or from assaulting others, from trafficking in contraband, and from trying to escape. However, isolating inmates also means that there is no cellmate to notice and halt any suicide attempts, and it may increase the inmate's sense of despair (Inch, Rowlands, and Soliman 1995). Over two-thirds of incarcerated suicide victims kill themselves while they are housed by themselves (Eyland, Corben, and Barton 1997; Hayes 1989).

In contrast to this, one of the major issues in corrections is the fact that many custodial institutions are overcrowded. In the United States, for example, the increasing number of prisoners has resulted in high levels of overcrowding in recent years, and the courts have occasionally intervened to force the institutions to release the least dangerous offenders until additional facilities can be constructed. Liebling (1992) has noted that, although overcrowding is a problem that correctional systems must address, overcrowding may reduce the suicide rate of the inmates. However, an increase in inmates in a correctional facility is not always accompanied by a corresponding increase in staffing, so that inmates may not be adequately monitored, thereby increasing the risk of suicidal behavior being undetected (Wooldredge and Winfree 1992).

3.6   Attempted Suicide and Suicide Ideation

In the society at large, it is estimated that there are about eight nonfatal suicide attempts for every completed (fatal) suicide (Maris, Berman, and Silverman 2000). The incidence of attempted suicidal behavior (often called parasuicide or deliberate self-harm, but quite distinct from self-mutilation) appears to be very high among those in custody. Sloane (1973) calculated rates of attempted suicide of 3,200 per 100,000 per year in the jails of Washington, DC, and 1,380 in the prisons. In the jails, Sloane found that those who attempted suicide were younger than the nonsuicidal inmates, had committed more serious offenses, and were more likely to have disciplinary problems, but were less often drug addicts.

Self-mutilation (involving relatively minor damage to the body without the aim of risking death) is also very common in inmates. In a prison in London, Cookson (1977) found about 1.5 acts of self-mutilation a week in a population of 320 women. The self-mutilators had longer sentences and more often had committed violent crimes. They typically used glass to cut themselves while alone in their cells, and the acts were triggered by bad news from the outside and by quarrels with other inmates. It has also been hypothesized that inmates self-mutilate out of boredom and to provide some kind of stimulation, even painful stimulation.

Researchers have cautioned jail practitioners to be careful when dealing with parasuicidal inmates. Although officers might consider such actions as manipulative and a nuisance, research has indicated that these incidents can be quite serious. Power and Spencer (1987) found that few of these parasuicidal actions were close to being lethal, but the lack of available options for self-harm in the correctional system might prompt disturbed inmates to carry out a more dangerous, less controllable type of self-harm that can lead to an accidental death. As was noted earlier, hanging is a very deadly form of self-harm, and it is possible for someone who is attempting to get attention to lose control and die. Furthermore, Dear, Thompson, and Hills (2001) found that at least two-thirds of the parasuicidal inmates in their study had at least moderate suicidal intent at the time of their self-harm. Ivanoff, Jang, and Smyth (1996) also found a positive correlation between parasuicide and suicidal ideation.

3.7   Theories of Inmate Suicide

There is evidence that the same factors that predict or are associated with suicide in the general population are also relevant to suicide in custody. For example, Koller and Castanos (1969) found that Australian prisoners who had a history of attempted suicide were more likely to have lost both parents in childhood or adolescence, an association found for suicidal individuals in general. Stressors for those outside of prison can also trigger suicidal behavior in prison, such as rejection by a lover (Power and Spencer 1987). Suicidal ideation in prisoners is predicted by scores on tests of hopelessness, depression, and stress (Bonner and Rich 1990).

Theories of inmate suicide that focus on the custodial environment have suggested the role of the disgrace of arrest, imitation of the suicidal behavior of other inmates, and the stress of imprisonment, interacting perhaps with a particular personality that predisposes the inmate to suicide (Lester and Danto 1993). However, there has been little theorizing about the causation of suicide in inmates, and more work needs to be done in this area.

3.8   Preventing Custodial Suicide

There are many approaches that correctional systems can take in order to prevent suicide among inmates. We will review these approaches, discuss their appropriateness for different types of custodial facilities, and evaluate their effectiveness.

3.8.1   Screening the Suicidal Inmate

In the past, new admissions to correctional facilities were rarely screened for suicidality or for psychiatric problems. Hayes (1989) found that 89 percent of suicides in jails and 97 percent of those in police lockups had not been evaluated for their suicidal potential before being placed in a cell. In recent years, as the problem of custodial suicide has become a focus of attention, more facilities have established written policies for evaluating new inmates, although the adequacy of these polices and the extent of their implementation have not been studied.

For people in the community calling crisis intervention centers for help, it is mandatory that crisis counselors ask about suicidal ideation and plans, past and present. For new inmates to a facility, especially to police lockups and jails, therefore, an interview should inquire about the inmate's emotional state and include questions about depression and suicidality (Ingram, Johnson, and Hayes 1997; Manning 1989; Marcus and Alcabes 1993; Rowan 1989). Questioning about drug and alcohol use, psychiatric symptoms, both past and present; and any history of psychiatric treatment or drug rehabilitation should also be mandatory. Checking for scars on wrists and the neck (evidence of past suicide attempts) is also a good idea (Ingram, Johnson, and Hayes 1997). Hayes (2001) has listed some of the standard cues known to suicidologists that suggest an increased risk of suicide: changes in appetite, lethargy, expression of strong guilt over the offenses, severe agitation or aggressiveness, changes in mood or behavior, giving away possessions, having unrealistic expectations about the future, and increased difficulty in relating to others. Suicide screeners and other jail staff members should consider these cues to be warning signs of a potential suicide attempt.

It is critical that such an evaluation is conducted before the inmate is placed in a cell—on intake, booking, or admission. Cases of suicides have been reported where the inmate was placed in a cell and the evaluation scheduled to be conducted later. Evaluation of every inmate should also take place on a regular schedule and at times of acute stress (such as a return from a court appearance or bad news from home).

Furthermore, when an inmate is transferred from one place to another, the prior institutional staff should be asked about the inmate's emotional state, behavior, and suicidality in the former institution. Although the person most likely to interview inmates is a staff member, some institutions have experimented with using trained inmates to screen new admissions (Charle 1981).

Hayes (1994) emphasized three important levels of communication that might help in preventing suicide: (1) between the arresting/transporting officer and the jail staff; (2) between and among jail staff members; and (3) between the jail staff members and the suicidal inmate. Good evaluation requires good communication between the staff members conducting the evaluation and the inmate. Thus, the officers in charge of maintaining discipline may not always be the best people to conduct evaluations. Nevertheless, they are the staff members who have the most contact with inmates. The custodial staff can be trained to recognize the clues of impending suicidal behavior, such as the kinds of suicidal communications that potential suicides make. For example, potential suicides may not simply communicate an intention to kill themselves, but merely express hopelessness about the future or give away possessions. Thus, all of the staff members involved with the inmates must be trained in suicide prevention and become convinced of the necessity of passing on information about suicidal cues to other staff members.

As experience with the instruments used to assess suicidality is accumulated, institutions can begin to computerize the data and explore the usefulness of particular measures for their institution with its unique population of inmates. The best screening instruments used for inmates are those used for screening people in other settings for suicidality. Self-report inventories for depression, hopelessness, and suicidal ideation are useful. Recently, Jobes and Drozd (2004) devised a Collaborative Assessment and Management of Suicidality (CAMS) approach, which employs a collaborative assessment in which the clinician and patient work together, and this may prove useful in a custodial setting.

Even if reliable and valid screening instruments are used to evaluate suicide potential, and even if a statistically sound profile of the suicidal inmate is developed for the correctional facility, there will always be false negatives, that is, suicidal inmates who are not identified. More problematic for the staff is that there will also be a large number of false positives, that is, inmates who are judged to be suicidal but who are not. Let us assume that our screening device is 95 percent accurate (which is far better than any existing screening instrument, for which the accuracy is more like 75 percent). Say we have five hundred inmates and that one or two of these may commit suicide in a one-year period. That means that there will be twenty-five false positives, inmates judged to be potential suicides who are not. The facility will have to expend greater resources on these inmates, even though they are not potential suicides. (A 75 percent accuracy will result in 125 nonsuicidal inmates, a quarter of the facility, being placed on suicide watch!) This problem can easily lull custodial administrators into being lax with regard to screening and heeding the information obtained from the screening.

Hayes (1999) has noted that some correctional facilities "punish" inmates who admit to having suicidal ideation. The inmates may lose telephone access, visits, and recreation time. Such correctional facilities may place suicidal inmates in isolation, even though it is foolish to do so; this only increases the inmates' sense of despair and their risk of suicide.

3.8.2 Housing

Housing is a resource that can be used when an inmate is judged to be at risk of suicide or when an inmate denies suicidal ideation but is judged to be concealing such information from the staff. Because most custodial suicides occur while inmates are in isolation, giving suicidal inmates a cellmate is an obvious tactic to prevent suicide. Thus, new admissions to police lockups and jails, for whom the risk of suicide is greatest in the first 24 hours, should be placed in communal cells. This allows new inmates to detoxify if they are under the influence of alcohol or drugs and to adjust to the institution with the help of other inmates. This arrangement is even better if, in long-term institutions, the cellmate has been sensitized to suicidal cues and trained in crisis intervention.

If an inmate who is at risk for custodial suicide must be placed in isolation (for example, for the safety of the other inmates), then adequate monitoring of the inmate must be set up. All cells used to house them should be suicide-resistant. Hayes (1999) makes the distinction between close observation, in which inmates are observed by a staff member at staggered intervals not to exceed fifteen minutes, and constant observation, which means that a staff member is physically present to observe an inmate. The former is recommended for inmates who are not actively suicidal but who have given hints of suicidal ideation or who have a history of self-destructive behavior. The latter should be used for inmates who are actively suicidal, meaning that they have recently threatened suicide or have recently engaged in self-harm. It is important to note that an inmate can commit suicide by hanging/strangulation in a matter of minutes, and so officers must be vigilant.

If an inmate at risk for suicide must be placed in isolation, then a suicideproof cell must be used (Lester and Danto 1993). Such rooms are devoid of materials with which to hang oneself, hooks and protuberances from which to hang oneself, and sharp objects with which to cut oneself. However, such rooms, and the paper clothes required for the inmate, are quite dehumanizing and can increase the inmate's agitation and/or despair. These rooms should only be used for short periods of time.

Older facilities can be modified for suicideproofing by putting scratch-resistant polycarbonate glazing on the inside of metal-bar doors; placing tamperproof covers over vents and all protrusions; removing electrical outlets; and removing exposed pipes, hooks, hinges, and catches (Atlas 1989; Lester and Danto 1993).

It is critical that medical equipment for resuscitation is easily accessible, and this equipment must be checked regularly to ensure that it is in working order. Correctional staff must also be trained to use this equipment, especially the corrections officers who are likely to be the first on the scene.

3.8.3 Monitoring

Many institutions set up monitoring programs for suicidal inmates. Sometimes the inmate may be checked at irregular time intervals, never exceeding fifteen minutes, although fifteen minutes can be sufficient time to hang oneself. Alternatively, the monitoring can be continuous by staff or fellow inmates, either in person or by television monitor. However, observers in institutions have occasionally seen the staff member responsible for continuous monitoring of inmates turn away from the screens, especially when talking to fellow staff members. A cellmate provides continuous monitoring, as long as the cellmate is awake.

Monitoring is especially difficult when institutions are understaffed. If the institution can establish a profile for the timing of suicidal behavior in the institution, which is often between midnight and six in the morning (Hardie 1998), then more staff could be assigned to suicide-prevention work at these times. Trained inmates might be especially helpful to supplement suicide prevention efforts made by the staff.

3.8.4 Suicide-Prevention Programs Run by Inmates

Almost all suicide prevention and crisis intervention programs in communities are staffed by volunteers who are trained paraprofessionals, that is, people whose expertise is not in the mental-health field. Such volunteers are carefully selected and then trained in crisis intervention. The crisis intervention is typically carried out using telephone counseling, although a few centers permit walk-in clients. In the United States, such centers are accredited by the American Association of Suicidology (www.suicidology.org) and worldwide by the Befrienders (www.befrienders.org). The Befrienders suicide-prevention centers are usually called "The Samaritans."

Several Samaritan centers have worked in custodial settings to select and train inmates to work as crisis counselors. For example, in 1995, the Correctional Services of Canada turned to the Samaritans of Southern Alberta to develop a suicide-prevention group in the Drumheller Institution, a federal medium security penitentiary. The administrators from the Samaritan center in Lethbridge selected, trained, and supervised the inmates. The penitentiary suicide-prevention group set up an administrative structure (coordinator, clerk, and secretary) to keep in continual contact with the staff of the local Samaritan center. Surprisingly, the correctional facility agreed to permit the content of the counseling between the inmates and the inmate crisis counselors to remain private. All incoming inmates are informed of the service and the procedures, and the inmate Samaritans are on call twenty-four hours a day to provide emotional support. Schlosar and Carlson (1997) noticed that the atmosphere in this prison changed as inmates saw some of their peers showing compassion and kindness, and more inmates felt comfortable seeking help. At the time of writing, Schlosar and Carlson had eighteen active counselors in the institution, on call twenty-four hours a day, serving 560 male inmates.

Prison inmates may also be recruited to serve as "buddies," with less extensive training and supervision than those in the Samaritan programs. These buddies can be placed in cells with depressed and suicidal inmates, both as a form of surveillance and also to make the inmate feel less isolated. Buddies can be instructed not to intervene or give advice but to report any suicidal cues to a correctional staff member. However, these buddies can be trained in simple crisis counseling skills, such as empathic listening (also known as active listening).

White and Schimmel (1995) reported that 65 percent of federal institutions in the United States use inmate companions. During 1992, 75,363 hours were spent monitoring suicidal inmates throughout the federal prison system. Of this time, staff handled only 28 percent, whereas inmate companions handled 72 percent. The companions are provided with basic training in understanding suicidal behavior, empathic listening, and other communication techniques.

3.8.5 Staff Resistance

As do many members of the general public, correctional staff often sees suicidal behavior as manipulative. As a result, they do not respond to suicidal ideation or attempts in inmates in an appropriate manner. For example, they may be hostile and punitive toward the suicidal inmate, as are some medical staff in emergency rooms that have to treat attempted suicides. It is true that suicide attempts can be manipulative and also that many suicide attempters did not intend to die as a result of their attempt. However, about 15 percent of people with depressive disorders eventually die from suicide, and the same is true for suicide attempters: About 15 percent will eventually die from suicide, compared to about 1 percent of the general population. Thus, suicide attempters are at high risk for subsequent suicide, even if the initial attempt involves minimal self-harm (Dear, Thompson, and Hills 2001). Such myths about suicide should be addressed in the training and continuing education of correctional staff.

3.9 Standards and Training

Several organizations, including the American Medical Association, the National Commission on Accreditation for Law Enforcement, the American Correctional Association (ACA), and the National Commission on Correctional Health Care have proposed standards relating to the emergency response to suicide attempts in correctional institutions (Kappeler 1993). These standards call for written policies detailing responses to suicidal inmates, and they emphasize the need for continued training of staff (Hayes 2001).

NCCHC has the most comprehensive set of standards pertaining to inmate suicide (Hayes 1999). The standards address staff training, intake screening/assessment, housing, levels of supervision, intervention, and administrative review. Although correctional standards are not legally binding, the courts have ruled that the standards serve as guidelines in assessing what is reasonable conduct on the part of corrections agencies (Hayes 1995a, 1995b).

Hayes (1996) surveyed state departments of correction in the United States and found that 79 percent had a suicide-prevention policy, 15 percent had no policy but addressed some of these issues in other agency directives, and 6 percent had no written policies at all. Only 6 percent had written policies that completely met the NCCHC standards.

The U.S. Federal Bureau of Prisons unveiled their suicide-prevention policy in 1982. The policy has five components: (1) initial screening of all inmates; (2) treatment and housing guidelines for suicidal inmates; (3) standardized record keeping, follow-up procedures, and data collection; (4) staff training; and (5) periodic review and audits (White and Schimmel 1995).

All institutions should have established policies and procedures for dealing with suicidal inmates. The policies and procedures should cover inmate screening, staff training, and reactions to suicidal inmates. It is desirable to have an in-house or consulting medical unit with some autonomy from the other units of the institution, and the effectiveness of this medical unit should be monitored continually.

It is also useful to have a psychiatric and counseling unit that can help in evaluating inmates identified as potentially suicidal and that can devise short-term and long-term treatment plans for them. There is some advantage to having this unit independent of the institution, so that the inmates will be more likely to perceive its staff as oriented toward helping the inmates rather than implementing institutional policies. However, this independence is often not feasible.[3]

Having a suicide-prevention policy does not mean that it will be implemented. Liebling (1992) found that less than half of the uniformed staff in one British prison with a suicide-prevention program could explain the policy when asked. Because the uniformed staff are on the "front lines" in preventing suicide, they should receive adequate initial training and refresher courses each year on suicide prevention (Hayes 1999).

---

[3] Note that the Alberta suicide-prevention program, described above, using inmates as crisis counselors, promises confidentiality to the inmates talking to the counselors.

3.10   Civil Liability

American courts have been active in cases involving custodial suicide, with most action in the form of wrongful death or negligence suits based on state tort law (Kappeler 1993). To establish negligence, courts typically try to determine whether the staff's actions or failure to act created an unreasonable risk to the detainee. Four elements are usually considered here: legal duty, breach of duty, proximate cause of injury, and actual injury (Kappeler, Vaughn, and Del Carmen 1991).

3.10.1   Legal Duty

State courts have recognized the staff's responsibility to provide adequate care for inmates. Staff must keep inmates from harm, treat them humanely, and provide medical assistance when necessary (Kappeler, Vaughn, and Del Carmen 1991; Kappeler 1993). Special duty of care is required when a staff member has reason to believe that an inmate poses a risk to him- or herself, particularly those inmates who have a disturbed state of mind and have a diminished ability to protect themselves, and those who are under the influence of drugs or alcohol. Among the factors that lead to such a belief are previous suicide attempts while in custody, statements by an inmate that indicate an intent to harm him- or herself, a history of psychiatric illness, an evaluation by staff that the inmate has suicidal tendencies, and the inmate's level of substance abuse (Kappeler 1993).

3.10.2   Breach of Duty

Courts may determine that staff are in breach of duty when they fail to follow institutional rules and regulations, properly supervise suicidal inmates, provide safe facilities, or fail to call for medical assistance (Kappeler, Vaughn, and Del Carmen 1991). When institutions have written policies, these may serve as the standard that the court can use. In cases when there are no written policies, the courts can use the standards developed by ACA and NCCHC to determine what a standard of care should involve. Thus, institutions need to be aware of the ACA and NCCHC standards, because the courts may hold them to those standards.

3.10.3   Proximate Cause of Injury

This requirement involves the relationship between the inmate's injury and the actions or inaction of the staff. For negligence to be determined, the staff's action or inaction must be proven to be the proximate cause of the inmate's death. For example, if an inmate is determined to be suicidal, but the staff fails to remove the inmate's belt before placing him or her in isolation or in a holding cell, or if the staff neglects to call for medical assistance or attempt first aid, then the staff may be judged to be the proximate cause of the inmate's suicidal death, as was the case in a suicide in New Jersey (Kappeler 1993).

3.11 Conclusions

Although several commentators on suicide prevention in jails and prisons are skeptical about some strategies (e.g., Kennedy and Hormant, 1998), and although research on the problem is typically at a very rudimentary level, it would be foolish to eschew some strategies as ineffective before they have been adequately tested. Researchers need to become more involved with custodial institutions in order to improve the adequacy of the strategies and to evaluate their effectiveness.

Policymakers also need to address several important issues. As more and more psychiatrically disturbed individuals are admitted to jails and prisons in some countries, as a result of the trends toward deinstitutionalizing psychiatric patients and the greater availability of psychiatric medications that permit psychiatric patients to be released into the community, more and more prisoners are going to be psychiatrically disturbed and, therefore, suicidal. The presence of drug- and alcohol-addicted prisoners also increases the likelihood of suicidal inmates. Keeping inmates in prison is expensive, and policymakers should consider alternatives to incarceration for some offenders (such as sentencing offenders to drug treatment instead of jail and providing psychiatric care in halfway houses for some nondangerous offenders).

Finally, failing to establish adequate suicide-prevention policies will cost correctional facilities when they lose lawsuits brought by the inmates' families. Correctional facilities that have not adopted ACA or NCCHC standards should do so, and they should train, retrain, and monitor correctional staff to ensure that these policies are implemented. Correctional facilities will be more successful in these suicide-prevention efforts if they hire qualified research and evaluation professionals to monitor and evaluate their programs.

References

Atlas, R. 1983. *Guidelines for Reducing the Liability for Inmate Suicide.* Miami: Atlas and Associates.

Atlas, R. 1987. *Guidelines for Reducing the Liability for Inmate Suicide.* Miami, FL: Atlas Associates.

Atlas, R. 1989. Reducing the opportunities for inmate suicide. *Psychiatric Quarterly* 60, 161.

Blaauw, E., F. W. Winkel, and J. F. M. Kerkhof. 2001. Bullying and suicidal behavior in jails. *Criminal Justice and Behavior* 28, 279.

Bonner, R. L., and A. R. Rich. 1990. Psychosocial vulnerability, life stress, and suicide ideation in a jail population. *Suicide and Life-Threatening Behavior* 20, 213.

Burtch, B. E., and R. V. Ericson. 1979. *The Silent System.* Toronto: University of Toronto.

Butterfield, F. March 5, 1998. By default, jails become mental institutions. *New York Times.* www.nytimes.com/yr/mo/day/030598prisons-mentalhealth.html.

Charle, S. 1981. How to stop jail suicides. *Police Magazine* 4:6, 49.

Cookson, H. M. 1977. A survey of self-injury in a closed prison for women. *British Journal of Criminology* 17, 332.

Cosyns, P., and J. Wilmotte. 1974. Suicidal behaviors in Belgian penitentiaries. In *Proceedings of the 7th International Conference on Suicide Prevention*, ed. N. Speyer, R. Diekstra, and K. van de Loo, 300. Amsterdam: Swets and Zeitlinger.

Danto, B. L. 1989.The role of the forensic psychiatrists in jail and prison suicides. In *Correctional Psychiatry*, ed. R. Rosner and R. B. Harmon, 61. New York: Plenum.

Davis, M. S., and J. E. Muscat. 1993. An epidemiological study of alcohol and suicide risk in Ohio jails and lockups, 1975-1984. *Journal of Criminal Justice* 21, 277.

Dear, G. E., D. M. Thomson, and A. M. Hills. 2001. Self-harm in prison. *Criminal Justice and Behavior* 27, 160.

Douglas, J. D. 1967. *The Social Meanings of Suicide.* Princeton: Princeton University Press.

Eyland, S., S. Corben, and J. Barton, J. 1997. Suicide prevention in New South Wales correctional centers. *Crisis* 18, 158.

Farmer, K. A., Felthous, A. R., and Holzer, C. E. Medically serious suicide attempts in a jail with suicide prevention program. 1996. *Journal of Forensic Sciences* 41, 240.

Flaherty, M. G. 1983. The national incidence of juvenile suicide in adult jails and juvenile detention centers. *Suicide and Life-Threatening Behavior* 13, 85.

Frottier, P., et al. 2002. Jailhouse blues revisited. *Social Psychiatry and Psychiatric Epidemiology* 37, 68.

Fruehwald, S., et al. 2000. Prison suicides in Austria, 1975-1977. *Suicide and Life-Threatening Behavior* 30, 360.

Hardie, T. J. 1998. Self-harm shows diurnal variation. *Criminal Behavior and Mental Health* 8, 17.

Haycock, J. 1993. Double jeopardy. *Suicide and Life-Threatening Behavior* 23, 130.

Hayes, L. M. 1983. And darkness closes in. *Criminal Justice and Behavior* 10, 461.

Hayes, L. M., 1989. National study of jail suicides. *Psychiatric Quarterly* 60, 7.

Hayes, L. M. 1994. Developing a written program for jail suicide prevention. *Corrections Today* 56:2, 182.

Hayes, L. M. 1995a. National and state standards for prison suicide prevention. In *Prison Suicide: An Overview and Guide to Prevention*, ed. L. M. Hayes, 1. Washington, DC: U.S. Department of Justice.

Hayes, L. M. 1995b. Prison suicide: An overview and a guide to prevention. *Prison Journal* 75, 431.

Hayes, L. M. 1996. National and state standards for prison suicide prevention. *Journal of Correctional Health Care* 3:1, 5.

Hayes, L. M. 1999. Suicide in adult correctional facilities. *Journal of Law, Medicine and Ethics* 27, 260.

Hayes, L. M. 2001. Special Issue: Preventing suicides through prompt intervention. *Jail Suicide/Mental Health Update* 10:3.

Hayes, L. M., and J. R. Rowan. 1988. *National Study of Jail Suicides.* Alexandria, VA: National Center on Institutions and Alternatives.

Hoff, H. 1973. Prevention of suicide among prisoners. In *Jailhouse Blues*, ed. B. Danto, 203. Orchard Lake, MI: Epic.

Inch, H., P. Rowlands, and A. Soliman. 1995. Deliberate self-harm in a young offenders' institution. *Journal of Forensic Psychiatry* 6.1, 161.

Ingram, A., G. Johnson, and I. Hayes. 1997. *Self-Harm and Suicide by Detained Persons.* London: Home Office Police Research Group.

Ivanoff, A., S. J. Jang, and N. J. Smyth. 1996. Clinical risk factors associated with parasuicide in prison. *International Journal of Offender Therapy and Comparative Criminology* 40, 135.

Jobes, D. A., and J. F. Drozd. 2004. The CAMS approach to working with suicidal patients. *Journal of Contemporary Psychotherapy* 34, 73.

Kappeler, V. E. 1993. *Critical Issues in Police Civil Liability.* Prospect Heights, IL: Waveland.

Kappeler, V. E., M. S. Vaughn, and R. V. Del Carmen. 1991. Death in detention. *Journal of Criminal Justice* 19, 381.

Kennedy, D. B., and R. Hormant. 1998. Predicting custodial suicides. *Justice Quarterly* 5, 441.

Koller, K. M., and J. N. Castanos. 1969. Parental deprivation and attempted suicide in prison population. *Medical Journal of Australia* 1, 858.

Lester, D. 1986. Suicide and homicide on death row. *American Journal of Psychiatry* 143, 559.

Lester, D. 1987. Suicide and homicide in USA prisons. *Psychological Reports* 61, 126.

Lester, D. 1997. *Suicide in American Indians.* Commack, NY: Nova Science.

Lester, D. 2000. Alcoholism, substance abuse, and suicide. In *Comprehensive Textbook of Suicidology*, ed. R. W. Maris, A. L. Berman, and M. M. Silverman, 357. New York: Guilford.

Lester, D., and B. Danto. 1993. *Suicide Behind Bars.* Philadelphia: Charles Press.

Lester, D., and C. Tartaro. 2002. Suicide on death row. *Journal of Forensic Sciences* 47, 1108.

Liebling, A. 1992. *Suicides in Prison.* New York: Routledge.

Liebling, A. 1993. Suicides in young prisoners: A summary. *Death Studies* 17, 381.

Loucks, N. 1997. *Research into drugs and alcohol, violence and bullying, suicides and self-injury and backgrounds of abuse.* Edinburgh, Scotland: Scotish Prison Service.

Manning, R. 1989. A suicide prevention program that really works. *American Jails* 3: 1, 18.

Marcus, P. and P. Alcabes. 1993. Characteristics of suicides by inmates in an urban jail. *Hospital and Community Psychiatry* 44, 256.

Maris, R.W., A. L. Berman, and M. M. Silverman. 2000. *Comprehensive Textbook of Suicidology.* New York: Guilford.

O'Toole, M. 1997. Jails and prisons. *American Jails* 11: 2, 32.

Plourde, C., and S. Brochu. 2002. Medication and drug use during incarceration. *International Medical Journal* 9:3, 163.

Power, K. G., and A. P. Spencer. 1987. Parasuicidal behavior of detained Scottish young offenders. *International Journal of Offender Therapy* 31, 227.

Rowan, J. R. 1989. Suicide detection and prevention. *Corrections Today* 51: 5, 218.

Salive, M. E., G. S. Smith, and T. F. Brewer. 1989. Suicide mortality in the Maryland state prison system, 1979 through 1987. *Journal of the American Medical Association* 262, 365.

Schlosar, H., and L. W. Carlson. 1997. Befriending in prisons. *Crisis* 18, 148.

Sloane, B. C. 1973. Suicide attempters in the District of Columbia prison system. *Omega* 4, 37.

Smith, R. 1984. Deaths in prison. *British Medical Journal* 288, 208.

Spencer, J. 1989. Aboriginal deaths in custody. *Australian and New Zealand Journal of Psychiatry* 23, 163.

Spinellis, C. D., and O. Themeli. 1997. Suicide in Greek prisons: 1977 to 1996. *Crisis* 18, 152.

Stone, G. 1999. *Suicide and Attempted Suicide.* New York: Carroll and Graf.

Sykes, G. 1972. *Society of Captives.* Princeton: Princeton University Press.

Tartaro, C. 2004. Suicide in prisons and jails. In *Key Correctional Issues*, ed. R. Muraskin, 72. Upper Saddle River, NJ: Prentice-Hall.

Toch, H. 1977. *Living in Prison.* New York: Free Press.

Topp, D. 1979. Suicide in prison. *British Journal of Psychiatry* 134, 24.

U.S. Bureau of Justice Statistics (BJS). Correctional populations in the United States, 1981-1999. Washington, DC: U.S. Department of Justice.

U.S. BJS. 1988. Correctional populations in the United States, 1985. Washington, DC: U.S. Department of Justice.

U.S. BJS. 1989. Correctional populations in the United States, 1986. Washington, DC: U.S. Department of Justice.

U.S. BJS. 1999. Mental health and treatment of inmates and probationers. Washington, DC: U.S. Department of Justice.

U.S. BJS. 2000. Drug use, testing, and treatment in jails. Washington, DC: U.S. Department of Justice.

Walters, G. D. 2003. Changes in criminal thinking and identity in novice and experienced inmates: Prisonization revisited. *Criminal Justice and Behavior* 30, 399.

Welch, M., and D. Gunther. 1997. Jail suicide and prevention. *Crisis Intervention* 3, 229.

White, T. W., and D. J. Schimmel. 1995. Suicide prevention in federal prisons. In *Prison Suicide*, ed. L. M. Hayes, 48. Washington, DC: U.S. Department of Justice.

Wooldredge, J. D., and L. T. Winfree. 1992. An aggregate-level study of inmate suicides and deaths due to natural causes in U.S. jails. *Journal of Research in Crime and Delinquency* 29, 466.

Hit 'Em Where It Hurts: Monetary and Nontraditional Punitive Sanctions

4

SHANNA VAN SLYKE,
GORDON P. WALDO, AND
WILLIAM BALES

Contents

4.1   Introduction

Although the title of this chapter may seem somewhat vague and ominous, the focus is on the forms of punishment that receive minimal attention in typical discussions of punitive sanctions but are oftentimes widely applied and especially consequential to offenders. Monetary punishments, in particular fines and forfeitures, are used regularly and represent some of the oldest yet newest forms of punishment administered by the criminal justice system. Other topics discussed in this chapter include some nontraditional punitive sanctions, namely: "Registration and Nonprison Restrictions on Liberty," "Driver- and Vehicle-Based Sanctions," "Disenfranchisement and Other Civil Rights Restrictions," "Shaming: Modern Day Branding or Community Reintegration?" "Medical Castration," and "Civil Commitment" of sex offenders.

After the introduction, the chapter is structured in the same basic manner within the discussion of each of these topics. First, a general *description* is provided to introduce the framework and parameters for the discussion as well as defining and describing the specific form of punishment strategy. Second, a brief *history* of the punishment policy is provided to demonstrate where and how it came into existence and some of the more significant changes that may have occurred in its interpretation and popularity during different historical periods. Third, the *prevalence*, or frequency of occurrence, is discussed to give an indication of the importance of the strategy based on its past and current use in the criminal justice system. Fourth, to the extent possible, the *evaluation research* that has been conducted in relation to the effectiveness of each form of punishment as a crime control measure is examined, although in some cases this literature is very sparse or almost nonexistent. Finally, a brief *section summary* is provided to summarize the most important points covered for each type of punishment.

The title of this chapter sounds very inclusive, but because of coverage elsewhere in the book, a number of otherwise relevant topics are intentionally excluded in order to eliminate confusing overlaps and redundancy. These excluded topics include all facets of prison; parole, probation, and conditional release; prerelease, work release, and study release; other halfway-in and halfway-out programs; intensified supervised probation; home confinement and electronic monitoring; day reporting centers and community treatment centers; guidance centers and family therapy programs; restitution and compensation programs; and community service.[1]

Many topics have to be excluded simply because of the selective process of working through a large assortment of materials and the determination of those deemed most important for the immediate purpose. Also, although there is some inclusion and discussion of punitive practices in other countries, penal sanctions in the United States receive a greater emphasis. This is not necessarily because of any greater importance of the practices in the United States, but primarily because of the personal experiences and expertise of the authors and the availability of materials.

4.2   Chapter Overview

4.2.1   Fines

Fines represent an important part of the criminal justice system because they: (1) are one of the oldest forms of punishment, (2) are one of the most flexible forms of punishment, (3) provide the court with a wider range of options for measuring punishment as a continuous rather than a discrete variable, (4) are the most frequently used type of punishment, and (5) are being used in more innovative ways today than at any time in their long history. Some would argue, particularly in the United States, that although fines are used for traffic offenses and some minor misdemeanors, they are not used nearly as extensively as they could be as a form of intermediate sanction. It has also been suggested that fines are discriminatory when they are administered in a "fixed" manner, in that the ability of offenders to pay the fine is not considered.

---

[1] Although some of these measures, electronic monitoring and restitution, for example, may be briefly discussed as they relate to the sanctions covered in this chapter, none of these receive comprehensive coverage.

A discussion of the traditional use of "fixed" fines is included, as well as newer forms of fines such as the structured fine ("day fine" or "unit fine"), which has been used extensively in other countries but, to the dismay of some, has not been used nearly as much in the United States. Additionally, a major new form of fine, which often appears in Internet searches for "intermediate sanctions," is aimed at certain types of corporate offenders in the United States. It is referred to as the Sarbanes-Oxley Act, and a brief discussion of this use of fines is included.

4.2.2 Forfeiture: Failing to Learn from History

Like fines, forfeiture precedes the existence of the criminal justice system and is one of the oldest forms of punishment. In fact, the line between fines and forfeitures in early usage was not always clear. But in contrast to the use of fines, forfeiture virtually disappeared in the U.S. criminal justice system, apparently because of experiences that colonists had with the forfeiture system in England. Considerably later, forfeiture nearly vanished from the criminal justice systems in other countries. But as with many fads and fashions from the past, forfeiture has re-emerged in the United States in recent years as a response to the "war on drugs," and this new use of forfeiture is discussed as well as some of its historical precedents.

4.2.3 Registration and Nonprison Restrictions on Liberty

Registration with criminal justice authorities and nonincarcerative restrictions placed on the liberty of convicted offenders are modern-day phenomenon that are being used more today than ever before. These practices are used with a wide range of offenders, but the most common are sex offenders, career criminals, drug offenders, and traffic offenders. At the present time, career-criminal registration is only used in one state in the United States (Florida) and no other countries; nonetheless, it has a "get tough on crime" appeal that will likely lead to its rapid spread across other states in the United States.

Among sex offenders in particular, legislation providing restrictions on liberty such as community notification of the existence of a sex offender living in the area has become a common practice, spreading in a very short time across the entire United States. Some states also have started DNA registries for sex offenders and other violent criminals as well as other forms of restrictions on liberty.

4.2.4 Driver- and Vehicle-Based Sanctions

As part of the revolt led by the citizen group Mothers Against Drunk Driving (MADD), a wide variety of punitive and ameliorative responses to drunk driving have emerged in recent years. In addition to incarceration and probation, driver license suspension and revocation are perhaps the most common, but a wide range of other responses have surfaced, many that overlap with shaming and forfeiture as punishment. In addition, however, vehicle immobilization devices are increasing in popularity. Among other things, these devices make it difficult or impossible to start a vehicle when the driver is intoxicated.

4.2.5 Disenfranchisement and Other Civil Rights Restrictions

Sometimes referred to as "collateral consequences," there are frequently many things that happen to offenders upon conviction that sometimes go unnoticed by the average person. These include a wide range of civil rights that are lost or modified upon conviction, and in many jurisdictions, these rights are not automatically restored after an offender has "paid his or her debt to society." Sometimes referred to as "civil death," these civil rights restrictions include the right to vote and to run for public office, eligibility for welfare and food stamps, some types of employment, and the right to enter into contracts. Some writers have suggested that disenfranchisement is a kind of "collective sanction" because it is not only a sanction against the individual offender, but also against his or her entire family, community, or sociopolitical group.

4.2.6 Shaming: Modern-Day Branding or Community Reintegration?

In some ways, shaming can be thought of as a form of modern-day branding, flogging, or dunking and, to that extent, can be considered very old, although the contemporary methods and rationales are all relatively new. The pillories of old can also be thought of as an early form of shaming and actually share many similarities with the modern-day use of signs worn around the neck or on the back of an offender professing the nature of his or her criminality, signs placed in the yard of an offender, license plates or bumper stickers placed on a vehicle pronouncing the driver as an offender, written with apologies for their crimes, and the posting of photos on billboards of "johns" convicted of soliciting a prostitute. Re-integrative shaming can be traced as well to some of the customs and early laws of American Indian tribes, but it is not clear that it is being used today in the manner that it was used and intended by the earliest Americans.

4.2.7 Medical Castration

The use of medical castration has existed for nonpunitive purposes for a long time and has been used as a penal sanction at least since the Middle Ages.

In response to a period of highly publicized sex-related crimes in the United States, it has recently received considerable renewed attention. Physical castration has long been used, primarily in European countries for selective use on rapists, pedophiles, and even homosexuals. Although physical castration has been used, the concept of castration became much more acceptable in the United States when chemical castration became a viable alternative in the 1980s. Some states have moved in this direction for certain types of sex offenders; however, there are numerous issues relevant to the use of physical and chemical castration that are still being debated.

4.2.8   Civil Commitment

The process of civil commitment for certain types of societal problems, primarily the mentally ill or mentally handicapped, has been around for a long time. More recently, the civil commitment of sex offenders has emerged in response to several well-publicized heinous cases of sex offenders committing sexual-related murders, usually of young children. The difference between this form of civil commitment and those used for other forms of mental illness in the past is that the current form is imposed at the end of the sex offender's prison sentence in order to maintain custody over him or her, after the prison sentence has expired, for the purpose of treatment.

Overall, the punitive sanctions discussed in this chapter reflect some of the oldest and newest forms of punishment used in contemporary societies. They also reflect some of the most—and least—frequently used sanctions. Moreover, there are numerous points of contention and many disagreements about whether or not each of these punitive sanctions, or at least some forms of them, should be used, and/or how to use them.

4.3   Fines: The Old and the New

4.3.1   Description

The use of the fine is both very old and yet quite new in some of its current implementations. A fine is a type of financial punishment in which the offender is required to pay a sum of money to a governmental entity (federal, state, county, city, etc.) in lieu of or in combination with some other form of punishment. Theoretically, the fine is intended to compensate the governmental entity for the harm committed against it by the offender. According to Morris and Tonry (1990: 123), the fine should be the cornerstone of any system of punishment. Fines differ from restitution in that restitution is intended to directly compensate the victim of crime for the harm committed against him or her by the offender in order to make the victim "whole" again, whereas the fine is intended to compensate the governmental entity for the harm caused to the government by the offense.[2]

4.3.2   Fixed Fines

As used in the United States and many other jurisdictions, a fixed fine (or "tariff fine") is a fine that is based solely on the severity of the offense, with a range of punishment that is usually set in statutes, rules, or sentencing guidelines for each specific offense. This type of fine has been criticized for a long time because of the inherent discriminatory nature of the fining process. Under this system, a fine of a fixed amount is imposed on all defendants regardless of their ability to pay. It is obvious that a fixed sum of money, a $500 fine for example, is a much greater punishment for an unemployed homeless person with three children to care for than it is for a CEO of a major corporation with an annual income in excess of $5,000,000. The U.S. Department of Justice's Bureau of Justice Assistance captures the problem succinctly in the following statement:

> When tariffs are set at low levels, the fines have little punitive or deterrent effect on more affluent offenders. When they are set at higher levels, collecting the fine amount from poor defendants is difficult or impossible, and, in many cases, these defendants are eventually given jail sentences (Bureau of Justice Assistance 1996: 1).

Moreover, in traditional European and American criminal justice systems, failure to pay a fine could result in imprisonment. This obviously has social class implications, and discrimination against the poor is a likely consequence. It is readily apparent that almost by definition, it will be the poor who are going to have the greatest difficulty in paying a fine and avoiding incarceration. In earlier times, this was a major problem, resulting in the oft-heard phrase, later to be used as a book title, "the rich get richer and the poor get prison." Speaking of the 1950s in the United States, Barnes and Teeters (1959: 400-401) stated that "nearly half of all the people in jail at any one time are there for inability to pay their fines." In 1971, the U.S. Supreme Court ruled that the incarceration of indigents solely for their nonwillful payment of a fine was unconstitutional. This does not apply to the willful nonpayment of fines, and courts may order some form of community service if it determines that a defendant is unable to pay a fine (*Tate v. Short* 1971). At approximately the same time, California extended the logic of the Supreme

---

[2] Fines are also used in relation to torts, and in civil law a synonym for "fine" that comes from early English law is "mulct" (Wikipedia 2005).

Court and prohibited the incarceration of indigents under any circumstances, and Delaware went even further and prohibited the incarceration of anyone, regardless of their means, for the nonpayment of a fine (Knopp et al. 1976).

One of the classic textbooks in the field succinctly makes the case for some of the current issues related to the use of the fine as a punishment in the criminal justice system:

> The justifications given for this method of implementing the punitive reaction have varied, but at present they consist of the following: First, the fine is the most easily and thoroughly remissible of any of the penalties; capital punishment, whipping, or imprisonment once administered cannot be remitted effectively, but a fine that has been paid can be repaid. Second, the fine is a most economical penalty; it costs the state practically nothing when used without imprisonment for default. Third, the fine is easily divisible and can be adjusted to the enormity of the offense, the character and wealth of the offender, the state of public opinion, and other conditions more easily than any other penalty. Fourth, it does not carry with it the public stigma and disgrace that imprisonment does, and therefore does not hamper reformation of the offender. Fifth, it affects one of the most general interests of mankind and causes a kind of suffering that is universal; therefore it is efficacious in dealing with the great majority of mankind. Finally, it provides an income for the state, county, or city (Sutherland and Cressey 1978: 324).

Because the fixed fine, which is still the most prevalent form of fine in the United States, has come into question due to its discriminatory nature, several modifications have been proposed and used extensively in other countries, and some have seen limited use in the United States. Terms such as *day fines, structured fines, unit fines,* and *installment fines* are common terms used in various countries. These terms have been used sparingly in the United States, but a number of experiments have been conducted recently in the United States, and these terms have now become part of the criminal justice vocabulary.[3]

[3] According to Hillsman (1998: 4), they are "called 'day fines' in many countries, although they were called 'unit fines' in England while they were being experimented with ... and have been called 'structured fines' in the U.S. because of the tradition in the U.S. of calling any form of sentencing guidelines 'structured sentencing.'" They apparently also were called "means-related fines" in a recent attempt in England to have them reintroduced (see BBC News 2005), and in New Zealand, they are viewed as an extension of the "infringement notice system" (see New Zealand Ministry of Justice 2000).

4.3.3   Structured Fines

The structured fine, frequently called a day fine, is based on two distinctly different concerns. First, as with the fixed fine, the gravity of the offense is determined and a gradient of punishments is assigned based on the seriousness of the crime. Instead of a specific gradient of money being assigned to different levels of harm, however, the punishment gradient is a set of structured-fine units that are attached to the different levels of harm. The more perceived harm, the more structured units of punishment are assigned. The second consideration is to make the punishment, or the amount of pain caused by the fine, equivalent for all offenders regardless of their socioeconomic status. Although this may never be completely possible, and indeed this is the most difficult part of the structured-fine approach, the value of a structured-fine unit is determined by a defendant's net daily income adjusted based on the number of dependents and other special circumstances such as physical and mental disabilities. Once the monetary value of a structured unit is determined, the amount of the fine is obtained by multiplying the number of structured units assigned based on the gravity of the crime by the monetary value of a structured unit and the individual circumstances affecting each offender.

It is apparent where the term *day fine* comes from, because the structured fine is based on the value of an "honest day's work" for each offender dependent on the nature of his or her employment and income. One "day's pay" is frequently the unit used in determining the amount of harm inflicted on society by an offense. Minor offenses may require only two or three days' pay, whereas others may represent several weeks', months', or years' pay. Although the system of structured fines is considerably less discriminatory against the poor, there could still be many situations where a large fine of thirty days or more could pose a serious hardship on poor offenders. "Installment fines" are a way of reducing this hardship by tailoring the payment schedule to fit individual cases. Rather than requiring that a modest thirty-day fine of $25 per day ($25 × 30 days = $750) be paid in order to avoid incarceration, the defendant might be permitted to stay in the community and pay the fine in the same way that many working and middle-class individuals pay for many other things, on the "installment plan."

4.3.4   History

Fines are one of the earliest forms of punishment, and as Lee (1901) reminded us, they were actually in use long before some of the modern-day rationales for punishment were even envisioned. Fines were used in the Anglo-Saxon period in England and were probably in use shortly after the concept of "crime" itself originated. Indeed, the use of fines may well have predated the concept of "punishment" as it has been used in more modern times. For example, in discussing the use of punishment in Anglo-Saxon England, Lee (1901: 10) stated:

> A detected criminal was either fined, mutilated, or killed, but punishment, as we now understand the term, was seldom inflicted; that is to say, the dominant idea was neither to reform the culprit nor to deter others from following in his footsteps ... if a fine were levied, it was more with a view to the satisfaction of the recipients of the money ... than with the intention of causing discomfort or loss to the offender.

Prior to the development of the Magna Carta, "the distinction between civil and criminal law was cloudy (and perhaps nonexistent)" (1989 US, 492 U.S. 257, 8). It would also appear that "amercements" may have been fore-runners of both criminal and civil fines, as well as restitution and forfeiture. In this earlier period, the distinction between crimes and torts was unclear, and this was equally true of the distinction between civil and criminal mon-etary payments. "Amercements were payments to the Crown, and were required of individuals who were 'in the King's mercy,' because of some act offensive to the Crown. Those acts ranged from what we today would con-sider minor criminal offenses ... to 'civil' wrongs against the King. ... Amer-cements were an 'all-purpose' royal penalty" (1989 US, 492 U.S. 257, 7). According to McKechnie (1958: 285-286), an amercement was the "most common criminal sanction in 13th century England."

According to the U.S. Supreme Court:

> Fines and amercements had very similar functions. Fines origi-nated in the 13th century as voluntary sums paid to the Crown to avoid an indefinite prison sentence for a common-law crime or to avoid royal displeasure. ... The fine operated as a substitute for imprisonment. Having no actual power to impose a fine, the court would sentence the wrongdoer to prison. To avoid impris-onment, the wrongdoer would then "make fine" by "voluntarily" contracting with the Crown to pay money, thereby ending the matter. The Crown gradually eliminated the voluntary nature of the fine by imposing indefinite sentences upon wrongdoers who effectively would be forced to pay the fine. Once the fine was no longer voluntary, it became the equivalent of an "amercement."... Although in theory fines were voluntary while amercements were not, the purpose of the two penalties was equivalent, and it is not surprising that in practice it became difficult to distinguish the

two. ... By the 17th century, fines had lost their original character of bargain and had replaced amercements as the preferred penal sanction. The word "fine" took on its modern meaning, while the word "amercement" dropped out of ordinary usage (1989 US, 492 U.S. 257, 21).[4]

In the United States, the use of fines clearly preceded the existence of the Constitution because the Eighth Amendment says, "Excessive bail shall not be required, nor excessive fines imposed, nor cruel and unusual punishments inflicted" (Albers 1999: 467). According to the U.S. Supreme Court, the Eighth Amendment was "based directly on Art. I, 9, of the Virginia Declaration of Rights," which in turn "adopted verbatim the language of the English Bill of Rights," which was written in 1689 (*Solem v. Helm* 1983, 463 U.S. 277, 285, n. 10).[5]

4.3.5   Prevalence

There are several different types of fines in use, and their prevalence or frequency of use varies accordingly.

4.3.6   Fixed Fines

Fixed fines (or tariff fines) are the most common form of punishment and are the primary or sole means of enforcement in the United States for parking violations, traffic violations, environmental crimes, corporate crimes, and more recently the proliferation of Internet spam, just to name a few.[6] They

---

[4] "William Shakespeare, an astute observer of English law and politics, did not distinguish between fines and amercements in the plays he wrote in the late 16th century. In *Romeo and Juliet*, published in 1597, Prince Escalus uses the words 'amerce' and 'fine' interchangeably in warning Montagues and the Capulets not to shed any more blood on the streets of Verona: 'I have no interest in your hate's proceeding, My blood for your rude brawls doth lie a-bleeding; But I'll amerce you with so strong a fine, That you shall repent the loss of mine.' Act III, scene 1, lines 186-189" (1989 US, 492 U.S. 257, 21-22).

[5] "The story of the Excessive Fines Clause begins in the 'early days of English justice, before crime and tort were clearly distinct' (1989 US, 492 U.S. 257, 20). Under the Saxon legal system in pre-Norman England, the victim of a wrong would, rather than seek vengeance through retaliation or 'blood feud,' accept financial compensation for the injury from the wrongdoer. The wrongdoer could also be made to pay an additional sum 'on the ground that every civil deed inflicts a wrong on society in general' (McKechnie 1958: 284-285). At some point after the Norman Conquest in 1066, this method of settling disputes gave way to a system in which all individuals who had engaged in conduct offensive to the Crown placed themselves 'in the King's mercy' so as not to have to satisfy all the monetary claims against them. ... In order to receive clemency, these individuals were required to pay an 'amercement' to the Crown" (1989 US, 492 U.S. 257, 20).

[6] In Tibet, fines are used for couples who violate the "one family, two children" policy. "Ordinary Tibetans are allowed two children, employees of the state only one," and the amount of the fine is 500 Yuan for the first illegal child, which is approximately one year's pay for a farmer (Tibet Online 2005: 3).

have always been used for minor crimes in the United States, but almost never for serious felonies as they are in some other countries. At the present time, fines are being used and considered in innovative ways not previously practiced in the criminal justice system, but most of this has occurred outside of the United States.

When used in more serious felonies, at least in the United States, it is almost always in conjunction with some other form of punishment, usually imprisonment or probation. However, in many European countries, fines are the sole form of punishment for a much broader range of crimes, and for much more serious crimes, and are considered the major alternative to imprisonment (Hillsman 1998: 4).

4.3.7   Day Fines, Structured Fines, and Installment Fines

Other types of fines that are deemed to be less discriminatory have been in use in other countries for many years, beginning in Scandinavia in the 1920s and continuing up to the present in many other European countries (Greene 1993). In the United States, they have recently been proposed and experimented with, but their adoption has been very slow despite being the subject of serious discussion for American criminologists. For example, several criminology texts from the 1950s and 1960s discussed some innovative ways of overcoming the discriminatory nature of the fixed-fine process being used in other countries. Barnes and Teeters (1959: 400-401) referred to the fact that "installment payment of fines has been suggested and in some places has been adopted." In criticizing the approach to fines applied in the United States, Cavan (1962: 647) referred to some of the changes that had occurred in Sweden in the use of fines: "For certain adult offenders, Sweden has devised a unique system of fines. Imprisonment for nonpayment of fines because of poverty has been abolished. A system of day fines is used, whereby each offense calls for the payment of a fine for a given number of days. The amount of the fine, however, is adjusted to the income of the offender. ... Moreover, payments may be made on the installment plan." Barnes and Teeters (1959: 594) also favored a version of structure or day fines when they noted that the "imposition of fines as we understand it today represents one of the most glaring of our discriminations. Invoking a fine, based on the individual's ability to pay, has considerable merit. ... This philosophy of fining could work by establishing units of fines rather than amount."

In trying to establish an early precedent for the use of structured fines, Barnes and Teeters reminded us that the concept has been around for a long time and it had been proposed by many early philosophers. They state:

> Again there is nothing new nor radical in this suggestion. Montesqueu advocated it by stating "A graduation should be estab-

lished between different penalties corresponding to the resources of the offender." Jeremy Bentham held the same idea. Emmanuel du Mouceau, procurator of the Republic of France, stated at Brussels that if a workman is fined the equivalent of four days' labor, it is only fair that a wealthy person, guilty of the same offense, should be obliged to pay four days' income (Barnes and Teeters 1959: 594).

4.3.8 Internal Revenue Service (IRS) Intermediate Sanctions

The most recent innovation in the use of fines in the United States occurs in Section 4958 of the U.S. Internal Revenue Code (the Sarbanes-Oxley Act of 2002). This statute suggested a different interpretation or meaning to the term "intermediate sanctions" as they are to be applied under a specific set of circumstances to tax-exempt organizations. This act permits the IRS to impose excise taxes (or fines) on certain persons who improperly benefit from transactions with an exempt organization. This type of intermediate sanction penalizes the individual who benefits from an improper transaction rather than the organization. Prior to this change in the law the only legal recourse was for the IRS to revoke the organization's exemption status, and it seldom did that unless the problem was very egregious.

According to Mandarino (2003), who has prepared flowcharts to determine whether Section 4958 applies to a transaction, three conditions normally must be met. "First, one party to the transaction must be an 'applicable tax-exempt organization.' Second, the other party to the transaction must be a 'disqualified person.' Third, the transaction or relationship between the two parties must be an 'excess benefit transaction'" (2003: 169).[7]

This use of fines in regard to the IRS code is very new, and its prevalence or impact is not yet known. There are likely to be relatively few cases processed under this statute, and it is unlikely to have a major impact on the average defendant in the criminal justice system, but the financial penalties for those who are processed will likely be substantial. Few cases have made their way through the system thus far, but the first case that worked its way all the way through the appeals process resulted in a dismissal.

4.3.9 Evaluation Research

For fines to have been around as long as they have, it is surprising to find the paucity of research attempting to evaluate their effectiveness as a sentencing alternative. As might be anticipated, for the research that is available,

---

[7] For a detailed discussion of the legal characteristics for all of the concepts involved in the statute, see Runquist 2002.

there is some discrepancy in the results dependent upon the offense and the way the fine is imposed.

4.3.10 Fixed Fines

Gordon and Glaser (1991) examined the use of traditional fines in terms of recidivism, comparing fines with probation, jail time, and combinations of all three. They found no statistically significant differences in recidivism between the different groups, but those who received probation plus a fine did have lower recidivism rates than those who were only given probation, and those who received a combination of jail time, probation, and a fine had lower recidivism rates than those who only received jail time and probation (Gordon and Glaser 1991).

Although there has been more research on the relationship between fines and drunk driving than for most other types of crime, Voas and Fisher (2001: 4) commented that "despite the widespread use of fines in penalizing DWI offenders, little research has been conducted regarding their general or specific deterrent effect in the United States." There are those, such as the California Department of Motor Vehicles (2002), who say that fines do not work for a crime such as driving under the influence (DUI). In a report to the legislature in a section with a heading labeled "What Doesn't Work," they stated, "The following countermeasures, which have long formed the basis of punishment for convicted DUI offenders, have not proven effective in reducing impaired driving—jail or community service [and] fines" (California Department of Motor Vehicles 2002: iv). They also noted that there has been minimal research on the impact of fines as a deterrent, but that which has been conducted fails to find a deterrent effect (California Department of Motor Vehicles 2002: 13).

Tashima and Marelich (1989) studied the use of fines on DUI offenders in California and reported that the results varied depending on the unit of analysis used, but concluded that overall there was minimal support for fines as a deterrent to driving under the influence. Research in Australia by Homel (1980) agreed that fines failed to have an across-the-board impact, but suggested that there was some deterrent effect for young, low-income DUI offenders when heavy fines were imposed. Votey and Shapiro (1983) also found that heavy fines seemed to have some deterrent effect in Scandinavia when related to a defendant's income level. Nichols and Ross (1990) also suggested that, in Australia and Sweden, fines have a deterrent effect if they are based on the seriousness of the offense and the income level of defendants, such that it creates a financial burden on the defendant. However, a paper prepared for the New Mexico legislature suggested that a combination of intermediate sanctions, including fines, might be most effective in reducing DUI: "In many research studies, a combination of license actions, community service, and fines with therapy, education, and monitoring have proven to be the most effective" (University of New Mexico Institute for Social Research 2002).

There is a very intriguing experimental study using a time-series design that was conducted in Israel related to a noncriminal form of rule-breaking. It does not deal with traditional criminal violations, but with the breaking of rules or norms related to tardiness on the part of parents in picking up children from day-care centers. After observing the tardiness of parents in picking up their children for a period of four weeks, a small fine was instituted in six of the ten day-care centers being observed at the beginning of the fifth week. This fine continued until the seventeenth week, when the fine was removed. During the period in which the fine was imposed, an unexpected thing occurred. The rate of tardiness remained the same in the control group, but *increased* by approximately 100 percent in the day-care centers in which the fines were imposed! Also, after the fines were removed, the rate of tardiness did not decline appreciably in the experimental group, essentially remaining at the same level it had jumped to during the fine period. The authors acknowledge that this is probably not a pure test of deterrence theory for a number of reasons, but it certainly challenges some of the common assumptions made in the use of fines as a deterrent (Gneezy and Rustichini 2000).

4.3.11 Structured Fines

Structured fines, or day fines, have not been used extensively in the United States, certainly not in comparison to their use in many Scandinavian and other European countries. Rasmussen and Benson (1994: 134) observed that "despite the apparent appeal of day fines, there is to date no rigorous test in the U.S. to indicate how day fines compare to imprisonment in terms of recidivism and their impact on public safety." There had been an earlier study conducted in Germany that concluded that "ten years after the introduction of the fine on a large scale, our data support the view that the policy has been found politically acceptable, administratively practical, and penologically sound" (Albrecht and Johnson 1980: 12).

There have been several experimental programs in recent years funded by the National Institute of Justice that have examined the effectiveness of this approach, although they may still be subject to the Rasmussen and Benson criticism. The first was a study by Winterfield and Hillsman (1993) on the Staten Island Day-Fine Project, which was implemented between 1987 and 1989. The study concluded that "the day-fine concept could be implemented in a typical American limited-jurisdiction court; day fines could substitute for fixed fines; fine amounts were higher for affluent offenders under the day-fine system; overall revenues increased; [and] high rates of collection could be sustained" (Winterfield and Hillsman 1993: 1). Although recidivism was not the major focus of the study, it is noteworthy that the average number of arrest warrants for nonpayment of fines was lower in the day-fine group (.26) than in the control group (.83), or in comparison with the period immediately prior to the experiment (.55).

In a later study, Worzella (1992) examined the recidivism rates of offenders processed through the Milwaukee Municipal Court Day-Fine Pilot Project and used a comparison group who had received traditional fixed fines. The recidivism rate was essentially the same for both groups in terms of violations of municipal ordinances: Although the day-fine group did have fewer arrest warrants, the difference was not statistically significant. The day-fine group had a higher percentage that paid their fines in full, but this difference also lacked statistical significance (Worzella 1992).

In another study funded by the National Institute of Justice, Turner and Petersilia (1996) examined day fines in multiple sites as sanctions for drug offenders and other felons and misdemeanants. They found that day fines were moderately successful in reducing the rate of technical violations and rearrests, as compared to a group receiving traditional fixed-fine sentences. The day-fine group had a technical violation rate of 9 percent compared to 22 percent for the comparison group, and they had an 11 percent rearrest rate in comparison to a 17 percent rearrest rate for the fixed-fine groups (Turner and Petersilia 1996: 1). According to Hillsman:

> [E]ffectiveness as a deterrent is based on research data that are consistent across studies conducted in different countries, but methodologically weak. ... [F]ines do not appear to be any less effective than sentences of short term incarceration for some ... and ... somewhat more effective than incarceration for others (1998: 2).

4.3.12 Section Summary

In sum, there is limited empirical research on the relationship between fixed fines and recidivism. However, the available research does suggest that fines may have a slight effect in reducing some measures of recidivism in comparison with other forms of punishment. Paradoxically, despite the greater longevity of fixed fines, it would appear that more research has been done on structured fines (day fines) than fixed fines, and it may be true that structured fines have a slightly stronger deterrent effect than do traditional fixed fines. The research is sparse at best, but thus far there is no indication that structured fines are not equal to, or better than, fixed fines in terms of any of the dimensions in which they have been compared. Given the fairness and equity issues noted above, the costs of maintaining the largest prison system in the world, and the success that other countries have had with structured fines, it is clearly time for the United States to seriously contemplate the use of structured fines (day fines) on a large scale as an important but neglected part of the punishment continuum.

4.4   Forfeiture—Failing to Learn from History

4.4.1   Description

Forfeiture, like fines, represents a form of monetary payment to the government whose origins are lost in antiquity, but it differs in that the forfeiture frequently includes property in addition to money. Normally, the term *forfeiture* is thought of as a process that occurs when the government seizes the personal property of a person who has been convicted of a crime as partial punishment or atonement for the commission of the crime. Unfortunately, forfeiture laws are far more complex and have been used in ways that greatly exceed this simple "man-on-the-street" definition. *Webster's Dictionary* defines forfeiture as "the loss of property or money because of a breach of a legal obligation," and this comes closer to its current meaning, but it is still a simplification of the forfeiture process that exists in practice (Merriam-Webster 1997: 457).

The problem occurs because there are several different kinds of forfeiture and, historically, several other interrelated legal concepts that might modify the way the forfeiture process is used. According to the U.S. Department of the Treasury:

> There are two types of forfeiture available to the government: civil forfeiture and criminal forfeiture. A *civil forfeiture* is intended to confiscate property used or acquired in violation of the law; a *criminal forfeiture* is imposed on a wrongdoer as part of his/her punishment following a conviction. The procedures involved in these two types of forfeiture are very different; however, the results are the same, which is the transfer of rights, title, and interest in the property to the United States (2005: 1).

Civil forfeiture is referred to as "*in rem* forfeiture" (against the property) and criminal forfeiture is called "*in personam* forfeiture" (against the individual), but in either case the outcome is the same, the *individual* loses the *property*!

The focus of this chapter, and this book in general, is on the criminal law rather than the civil law system; however, when forfeiture is discussed, it is sometimes difficult to separate them because as the above quote notes, "the results are the same," and it appears that in some cases it is basically an arbitrary decision as to which is used (U.S. Department of Treasury 2005: 1). Moreover, according to the Treasury Department, "*in rem* proceedings are separate legal actions from any criminal action taken against the violator," so in fact it could be either or both civil and criminal actions that are pursued in a given case (2005: 1). Although technically speaking *in rem* forfeiture is not considered punishment, the intertwining of *in rem* and *in personam* forfeiture was further solidified when the U.S. Supreme Court ruled that the use of *in rem* forfeiture was indeed tantamount to punishment and thus subject to the Eighth Amendment limitation on excessive fines (*Austin v. United States* 1993).

4.4.2 History

The history of forfeiture is closely intertwined with the use of fines,[8] and when the earliest uses of forfeiture are examined, the distinctions between fines, civil forfeiture, and criminal forfeiture, and the distinctions between treason, felonies, and misdemeanors, can easily become lost in antiquity.[9] Laughlin pointed to early Mosaic law as the beginning point for forfeiture and quoted from the Bible, "When an ox gores a man or a woman to death, the ox must be stoned, and its flesh shall not be eaten. The owner of the ox, however, shall go unpunished" (Exodus 21:28, quoted by Laughlin 2002: 1). If this was the beginning of forfeiture, however, it would not be considered either civil (*in rem*) or criminal (*in personam*) forfeiture, but rather a different form called *deodand forfeiture*.[10] At the very least, however, forfeiture goes back in English history to the period immediately following the Norman Conquest when William the Conqueror (1066-1087) claimed title to all of the land.[11] He then proceeded to give his supporters (vassals, or lords of the estates) portions of the land that they were to control and protect for the king.

Orderly and peaceful behavior was the expectation for normative behavior, and any discrepancies in behavior were deemed to be violations of the king's peace. Although there is disagreement among historians, it appears that acts of treason and felonies were handled differently. Treason resulted in a penalty of death, and the king received the forfeited property.

---

[8] According to Greek (1992: 124), "The terms fine and forfeiture were often used synonymously in common law."

[9] For an excellent summary of the history of forfeiture in England and the American colonies, see Greek (1992: 124).

[10] Deodand forfeiture refers to a set of circumstances whereby an animate or inanimate object that was the property of one person was instrumental in causing the death of another person. The object would then become the property of the king and normally would be destroyed (Kurisky 1988: 249).

[11] According to Greek (1992: 111), "Blackstone states that forfeiture in England predates the Norman feudal system and has Saxon and ancient Scandinavian roots."

For other felonies, which also carried a death penalty in this early period, the lords of the estates received the forfeiture, which was called an *escheat* (Greek 1992: 109-110).

Another concept that is related to and affects forfeiture is referred to as the *corruption of blood*. According to Greek (1992: 111-112), "Corruption of blood meant that as a result of conviction the criminal's bloodline had been legally severed. ... Not only were his wife and heirs unable to inherit his land or goods, the family was unable to inherit from his parents as well." Another related concept that could impact on forfeiture was the "benefit of clergy." This process represented the only realistic option for avoiding the simultaneous loss of one's life and property following a conviction for a crime. An appeal for benefit of clergy meant that the case would be heard in a church court rather than a Crown court, and for a variety of reasons there was a much greater likelihood of an acquittal in a church court than in the king's court (Greek 1992: 115-116).

As noted previously, forfeiture had disappeared much earlier in the American colonies than in England, but it was structured differently in each of the colonies, and although the use of forfeiture and the other related processes did not disappear at the same time in all of the colonies, for all practical purposes it had disappeared completely in the colonies long before it did in England. Greek stated, "All of the criminal procedures and penalties discussed (forfeiture, corruption of blood, peine forte et dure, deodand) were eventually eliminated in England, but only decades and, in some cases, centuries after they had been rejected by the American colonists" (1992: 118).[12]

As noted above, however, in 1970, after an almost complete absence of 180 years, and after England had finally stopped using forfeiture, the use of civil and criminal forfeiture returned in the United States through the passage of the Comprehensive Drug Abuse Prevention and Control Act (CDAPCA) and the revisions to the Racketeer Influenced and Corrupt Organizations (RICO) Act. The drug war may have been the impetus for the reintroduction of forfeiture laws in the United States, but these laws have expanded far beyond the drug war and in some jurisdictions are being used for a wide range of crimes, among these are drunk driving (Legal Information Institute 1999), gambling, firearms trafficking, stock market fraud, and arson (Legalat-PokerPulse Forums 2004). It is fair to say that as of this writing, asset forfeiture is alive and well in the United States.

4.4.3 Prevalence

A discussion of the prevalence of the use of forfeiture must be divided into at least three periods, and its usage over time also varies greatly across gov-

---

[12] Refer to Greek 1992: 112-115 for a discussion of "peine forte et dure."

ernmental jurisdictions. In the earliest period in Europe, it was a common form of punishment and used as a means of enriching the king's or the estate lord's coffers (Greek 1992). When the early colonists came to America, they were in a state of dormant rebellion about many of the things they didn't like about the English sociolegal system, and the use of forfeiture was one of these points of contention.

The second period in the United States begins with the earliest days of the republic and the framing of the U.S. Constitution and continues until the 1970s. Although in the early days of the Union, "custom duties" were a major source of income, after the Sixteenth Amendment to the Constitution, the early colonists essentially did away with most forms of forfeiture, with some remnants remaining in the system, although used sparingly. In Europe, forfeiture was not removed from the legal system nearly as early as in the United States, but for all practical purposes, it was eventually removed from the system.

The third period began in the United States in the 1970s as part of the war on drugs and has been slowly spreading to some other countries. Although used briefly during Prohibition in the 1920s, the actual re-emergence of forfeiture occurred at the national level with the passing of the Comprehensive Drug Abuse Prevention and Control Act of 1970. This act gave the federal government the authority to use civil *in rem* forfeiture laws to seize property used or acquired in violation of federal drug laws. Many states quickly followed because the governmental entities discovered, just as the king had many years ago, that this was an easy way to fill their coffers and to finance many aspects of law enforcement. This has become a much more lucrative source of income for law enforcement than the "speed traps" used by many communities and has provided an additional incentive to law enforcement agencies to aggressively pursue the enforcement of drug laws. Several amendments to the 1970 law have occurred in recent years, and the Civil Asset Forfeiture Reform Act of 2000 (CAFRA) has attempted to put some controls on the use of civil forfeiture; however, the procedural safeguards of the criminal justice system still do not apply to *in rem* forfeiture practices in the same way they do to *in personam* criminal forfeiture.

At the same time that the CDAPCA was being passed, the Racketeer Influenced and Corrupt Organizations Act was being amended to enhance the use of criminal forfeiture (Laughlin 2002: 3). In this case, the forfeiture is considered a part of the punishment administered by the criminal justice system and therefore requires a conviction based on the normal standard "beyond a reasonable doubt," in contrast to that required under CAFRA of a "preponderance of evidence." According to Laughlin, "One striking similarity between the two forms of forfeiture is the ability of the government to seize control of the property prior to a conviction" (2002: 4).

4.4.4   Evaluation Research

As with many other punitive sanctions, there has been a minimal amount of research conducted on the effectiveness of asset forfeiture laws, particularly in terms of the impact on the war on drugs, which led to the re-emergence of forfeiture laws. At the national level, the primary measure of effectiveness has been the amount of revenue derived from seizures and deposited in the Asset Forfeiture Fund (Executive Office for Asset Forfeiture 1994), but this is a very poor proxy for a true evaluation of the effectiveness of forfeiture in reducing crime.

As forfeiture laws at the state and local levels have expanded to other areas such as drunk driving, however, more research has been generated to assess the specific and general deterrent effects of asset forfeiture, particularly as it is related to vehicle impoundment. A number of these studies have been conducted,[13] and although some have shown positive results, most failed to provide conclusive support for the effectiveness of forfeiture as a deterrent. A study of impoundment and forfeiture laws in California found that "when drivers had their vehicles impounded their subsequent traffic violations and crashes were reduced substantially" (Traffic Tech 2000: 1). The report continued, however: "The vehicle impoundment laws have a specific deterrent effect on the individuals affected by them, but so far do not show a general deterrent effect on everyone else" (Traffic Tech 2000: 3).

Portland's Asset Forfeiture Program is one of the better studies of this type, although for methodological reasons the focus is only on specific deterrence, not general deterrence. The author stated, "Having a vehicle seized reliably predicts a doubled expected time to rearrest for individuals arrested for DWIs," although he acknowledged that "actual forfeiture did not predict any reduction in rearrest over and above that predicted by seizure alone" (Crosby 1996: 28-30).

An interesting ethnographic study of asset forfeiture in the war on drugs was conducted using covert participant observation on the impact of the new forfeiture laws on law enforcement operations. The authors concluded that "asset forfeiture is a dysfunctional policy which, in implementation, has strayed from its original intent and has incurred unintended consequences. Although forfeiture programs generate income, they also cause drug enforcement to serve functions that are inherently contradictory and often at odds with the demands of justice" (Miller and Selva 1994: 313).

More specifically, Miller and Selva suggested that the impact of asset forfeiture laws has changed the behavior of law enforcement in some undesirable ways:

---

[13] For a review of some of these studies, see Crosby (1996).

[A]sset seizure has become the primary objective of drug enforcement ... [and] the process of raising revenues through asset forfeiture often requires police to concentrate on cases that offer little
or no direct social benefit ... [and] the suspects involved in these
cases often are not engaged in serious criminal activity (1994: 331).

4.4.5   Section Summary

Forfeiture is one of the oldest concepts in the criminal justice lexicon of
punishment, although it had largely disappeared until its recent resurrection
in the United States' war on drugs. Although evaluation research on the
effectiveness of forfeiture is sparse, there has been some research in the area
of drunk driving that appears to show a specific deterrent effect, although it
is difficult to separate the use of forfeiture from vehicle seizure in this
research. In the area of drugs, the evidence on forfeiture as a deterrent is
virtually nonexistent, and some of the moral and ethical issues raised by
researchers in this regard are very disturbing.

Laughlin appeared to succinctly summarize the current use of forfeiture
and its probable future use in his statement:

Forfeiture law is well established ... [but] recent changes in the
law ... may be indicative of ... more restrictive ... attitudes. [A]
balance must be struck that will serve to interdict and punish
criminals while preserving our cherished rights of privacy and due
process (2002: 4).

Several authors are even more concerned than Laughlin about the impact
of forfeiture laws. For example, Greek stated:

What are their costs to the Constitutional protections and freedoms we ... take for granted? What will be the effects on international relations that follow from the government's decision to
use military forces for customs enforcement? Are we ... repeating
the very same policies that so angered early American colonists?
(1992: 128).

The concerns raised in the study by Miller and Selva discussed above are
echoed by Blumenson and Nilsen, who are even more critical. Blumenson
and Nilsen blame the drug forfeiture laws for a litany of problems, which
they summarized when stating that:

The law enforcement agenda that targets assets, ... seizures that
are unaccompanied by any criminal prosecution, ... the reverse

stings that target drug buyers rather than drug sellers, the overkill in agencies involved in even minor arrests ... [are] largely the unplanned by-product of this economic incentive structure (1998: 106).

4.5   Registration and Nonprison Restrictions on Liberty

4.5.1   Description

A relatively recent development in criminal justice concerning repeat or serious offenders is the establishment of offender registries and community notification systems.[14] Moreover, following the widely publicized kidnappings and murders of three young Florida and Iowa girls in early 2005 by registered sex offenders, much attention has been drawn to the deficiencies in the then-current system of handling released offenders in the community (Dunkelberger 2005a, 2005b; Ertelt 2005; Goodnough 2005; Herbert 2005; Nolan 2005; Shaffrey 2005). As a consequence, most states now provide additional requirements that accompany registration, such as lifelong electronic monitoring, geographic living and employment restrictions, forced DNA submittals, and penalties for failing to adhere to the conditions of these sanctions.

4.5.2   Registration

Although registration is generally aimed at sex offenders, Florida registration laws also encompass most convicted felons. In particular, most registration laws require that offenders being released into the community be fingerprinted and photographed, as well as being required to provide information

---

[14] Most of the new, harsher sanctions provided for sexual offenders have been sparked by news stories describing the horrific cases of released sex offenders kidnapping, raping, and murdering young children. For example, within two weeks of the discovery of Megan Kanka's body and the public awareness of her accused murderer, New Jersey passed the United States' first Megan's Law (see Farkas and Stichman 2002; Petrunik 2002; Presser and Gunnison 1999). However, after the kidnapping and murder of Florida's Jessica Lunsford, lawmakers concluded that even more restrictions were necessary to prevent another brutal slaying of a child. Jessica's killer, John Couey, was a registered sex offender, but he was not living at his registered address; instead, he was living only yards away from the victim and her family (CNN 2005a). The Jessica Lunsford Act, therefore, was designed to fill the void in registration laws by sending out unannounced notices to the offenders' registered addresses (CNN 2005a; CNN 2005b). In addition, the act punishes violations with a minimum prison sentence of twenty-five years, to be followed by lifetime supervision and electronic monitoring (Dunkleberger 2005a, 2005b). Furthermore, the currently debated national Jessica Lunsford Act provides the penalty of imprisonment for failure to respond to notices (CNN 2005b). Knowingly harboring a sex offender in Florida is also a felony under the Jessica Lunsford Act (CNN 2005b; Dunkleberger 2005a, 2005b).

about their offense, current address, and occupation, all within a specified time frame. In addition, during the investigation of an offense, crime characteristics can be examined and compared to the registry database in order to identify released offenders with similar methods of operation, or to exonerate wrongly accused offenders (Ertelt 2005; Herbert 2005; Johnson 2005). Furthermore, some jurisdictions have passed legislation that mandates that even juvenile sex offenders be placed on the registry (Richmond 2005; Seibel 2005). Registries can be accessed online and typically provide offenders' names, addresses, and photographs (Herbert 2005). Failure to register as a felon in Florida within forty-eight hours is considered a misdemeanor of the second degree and is punishable by up to sixty days in jail. Alternatively, failure to respond to notices, check in with the local county jail, or reregister after changing residence is a felony in Florida and is punishable by either prison or electronic monitoring for up to ten years (Cotterell 2005; Goodnough 2005).

4.5.3 Community Notification

Community notification is designed to keep law enforcement officials and community members aware of the presence of offenders in their community (Herbert 2005; Neff 2005). In particular, notices are sent to members of some communities to inform them of the whereabouts of sex offenders in the United States (Cotterell 2005; Neff 2005; Roos 2005b; Shaffrey 2005). By doing so, preventative actions can be taken, such as the close monitoring of children.

4.5.4 Electronic Monitoring

Permanent or lengthy electronic monitoring is being used in some states for repeat offenders and sexual predators (Dunkelberger 2005a, 2005b; Goodnough 2005; Herbert 2005; Johnson 2005; Lyons 2004; Roos 2005b; WFTV 2005). Paroled sex offenders may be forced to wear electronic bracelets or anklets that allow law enforcement officials to constantly know their precise location, thus enabling the police to know if a known sex offender was in the vicinity when a sex crime occurred (Ertelt 2005; Gearino 2005). Moreover, many of these devices set off an alarm if a sex offender enters a restricted zone where children might congregate, such as a playground (Johnson 2005). Other movement restrictions include schools and parks, and sex offenders are not permitted to work or volunteer at or near these establishments (Herbert 2005; Gearino 2005; Goodnough 2005; Johnson 2005; Neff 2005; Nolan 2005). Additionally, police can be aware of offenders who lie about their daily or nightly activities, such as when and where they work and their place of residence (Herbert 2005; Johnson 2005). Tennessee punishes the removal, tampering, and vandalizing of an electronic monitoring device with a mandatory 180-day jail sentence for the first offense, whereas subsequent offenses are considered felonies and could result in immediate parole or probation revocation (Johnson 2005).

4.5.5 Geographic Isolation

Postprison geographic isolation is another measure currently being used for sex offenders. As a form of halfway house reminiscent of the old transportation system in Europe, the state of Washington sends its released sex offenders to a remote island that is only accessible by boat (Stern 2005). After California residents protested the imminent arrival of released sex offenders into their neighborhoods, lawmakers began considering the use of the Washington island model—despite the $11 million fine levied against Washington for failing to provide adequate rehabilitation services to their isolated inmates (Stern 2005).

4.5.6 DNA Registries

In addition, some states have DNA registries, meaning that eligible offenders are required to submit samples of their DNA in the event that a new crime is committed (Gearino 2005; Goodnough 2005; Roos 2005b). Consequences similar to those for eschewing registration are provided for failure to adhere to DNA registry laws.

4.5.7 History

The roots of registration and other community-based punitive measures aimed at sex offenders lie in the 1970s restorative justice movement that was concerned primarily with rape (Presser and Gunnison 1999). Sex offender registration, in turn, was adapted in order to expand supervisory power over convicted felons in Florida. Although the landmark sex offender registration legislation did not occur until 1996, Washington State passed the Community Protection Act in 1990 that mandated registration, notification, and postprison civil commitment for those offenders deemed to be sexually violent predators (Petrunik 2002). Four years later, the federal government passed the Jacob Wetterling Crimes Against Children and Sexually Violent Offender Act, which gave states the choice of implementing registries or losing 10 percent of their federal law enforcement funds (Petrunik 2002). Community notification became prevalent following the passage of New Jersey's Megan's Law of 1994, which led to the federal Megan's Law of 1996 (Petrunik 2002). Again, states were given the option of setting up community notification systems or losing 10 percent of their federal funding (Petrunik 2002).

4.5.8 Prevalence

All fifty states in the United States require sex offender registration, and forty-seven states require notification (Burdon and Gallagher 2002). In addition, federal law mandates that offenders with child victims are subject to registration and notification for ten years, and sexually violent predators are subject to these requirements for life (Presser and Gunnison 1999). Felon registration in Florida mandates that any offender convicted of a felony through a trial or a plea of *nolo contendere* must register with the sheriff of any county they enter within forty-eight hours (Florida Statutes s. 775.13). The sex offender registration, however, overrides Florida's felon registration such that if a felon is required to register as a sexual predator or a sexual offender, he or she is not required to register as a felon (Florida Statutes s. 775.21, s. 943.0435, s. 944.607).[15]

4.6 Evaluation Research

Unfortunately, although registration, community notification, and the other nonprison restrictions on liberty discussed above have become widespread, virtually no research has been conducted on their effectiveness in reducing crime. However, there are several important points that merit consideration. For example, what is omitted from the above discussion is recognition that a significant proportion of sexual crimes against children are committed by family members (Farkas and Stichman 2002), who are therefore unaffected by these laws. Unfortunately, the problem may be exacerbated by the negative attention to the registered offenders and their families because it is likely that registration and notification laws may actually reduce reporting by family members (Farkas and Stichman 2002). Additionally, these new laws will not be applicable to sex offenders convicted prior to the passage of the laws (Dunkelberger 2005a). Indeed, there are 30,000 sex offenders living in Florida communities who will not be subjected to the recent Jessica Lunsford Act provisions (Dunkelberger 2005a).

These laws are also problematic because sex offender registries are over-inclusive and do not distinguish between those sexual offenders who are still a threat to society and those who no longer pose a threat or never posed a threat (Harvard Law Review 2003). However, based on the perception that there is a particularly high level of recidivism among sex offenders, as well

---

[15] Other exemptions to the Florida felon registry include felons who have had their civil rights restored, felons who received a full pardon for their offense(s), felons who have completed five or more years of incarceration or community supervision, felons who are under the supervision of the federal government, and felons registered as a career offender (Florida Statutes s. 775.261; s. 944.609).

as the seriousness of their potential threat, the Supreme Court ruled that the registries are not overinclusive to the point of denying offenders their right to due process (Harvard Law Review 2003).

Further, the shame and stigma attached to the registries has not been adequately acknowledged or addressed (Harvard Law Review 2003; see section 4.7 below). A body of medical research, however, suggests that such censure may lead to denial, defensiveness, stress, ostracism, and eventual reoffending, especially among pedophiles (Harvard Law Review 2003). Moreover, this negative attention has been cited as a key difficulty in the reintegration of sex offenders back into the community (Burdon and Gallagher 2002; Farkas and Stichman 2002).[16]

4.6.1   Section Summary

In sum, this section discussed such punitive measures as offender registration and community notification, permanent electronic monitoring, living and employment restrictions, and mandatory DNA submittals primarily as they relate to sex offenders. Although these sanctions have been in existence for several years, public attention has recently been heightened as a result of shocking instances involving the brutal assaults and murders of children, which is particularly the case with the issue of sex offenders.

Although the specific crimes that led to these new policies are indeed horrific, the limited empirical and anecdotal evidence suggests that registration and other related restrictions are not effective responses to increasing public demand for safety from sex offenders and career criminals. Rather than targeting those most likely to commit sex offenses (i.e., family members), the newest wave of registration legislation seems to represent yet another misguided legislative response to sensational media accounts of brutality and failures in the present criminal justice system. Although obviously designed with good intentions, these new restrictions may serve to inhibit the exoffender's abilities to return to a normal life in his or her home community following the termination of his or her sentence without targeting the major category of offenders. Registration and community notification may create a stigmatizing effect, whereas living and employment restrictions may seriously hinder the offender's ability to live with his or her family, work in his or her chosen field, or even gain meaningful employment.

---

[16] Additionally, friends and family members of offenders have also experienced harassment (Presser and Gunnison 1999). Still, some research exists that found that harassment of offenders themselves by members of the public is not common (Burdon and Gallagher 2002).

4.7 Driver- and Vehicle-Based Sanctions

4.7.1 Description

In recent years, a variety of innovative alternative sanctions have been created for drunk drivers, especially repeat offenders. In addition to the more traditional punishments of incarceration and probation, some combination of newer sanctions such as distinctive license plates and car stickers, victim-impact panels, traffic schools, vehicle impairment, impoundment, forfeiture, ignition interlock devices, and driver license suspensions and revocations are being used in most jurisdictions in the United States. The majority of states also supplement these new and creative sanctions with preventative law enforcement strategies, such as blanket patrols and sobriety checkpoints, as well as legislative initiatives, such as reducing the legal blood alcohol level. In general, alternative sanctions for drunk drivers fall within one of two basic categories: driver-based or vehicle-based sanctions.

4.7.2 Driver-Based Sanctions

Among driver-based sanctions are hot sheets, administrative license revocation, conditional licensing, community service, victim-impact panels, traffic schools, fines, and home confinement paired with electronic monitoring (Baca et al. 2001: 615; The Century Council 2003; Taxman and Piquero 1998; Voas and DeYoung 2002). *Hot sheets* are drunk driver registries that allow law enforcement personnel to be aware of any convicted repeat drunk drivers who may be driving in their jurisdiction with suspended or revoked licenses (The Century Council 2003). *Administrative license revocation* is the subject of much debate, because this is a penalty that occurs on the spot and is meted out by the police officer. Specifically, the arresting officer can revoke a suspected drunk driver's license as an administrative action prior to a conviction; however, this action is normally followed by a postconviction judicial license revocation (The Century Council 2003; Taylor 2005a; Voas and DeYoung 2002). Alternatively, *conditional licenses* allow the offender to continue driving, but only to preapproved activities, which usually include work and some family-related events (The Century Council 2003; Voas and DeYoung 2002).

Traffic schools vary considerably across states and are not a legal sanction for drunk driving; rather, they are an option a convicted drunk driver may select in order to keep his or her driving record clean, thus avoiding increased insurance payments (GotTrouble.com 1999-2001; MyLawyer.com 2004). Some states require the offender to prove successful completion of a preapproved traffic school in order to avoid harsher penalties, such as imprisonment, whereas other states clear the record of a convicted offender who completes traffic school (MyLawyer.com 2004). *Community service, victim-impact panels, fines,* and *home confinement* with *electronic monitoring* for drunk drivers are no different than for other offenders and are discussed elsewhere.

4.7.3   Vehicle-Based Sanctions

Vehicle-based sanctions consist primarily of special license plates or stickers, breath alcohol ignition interlock devices, vehicle registration cancellation and license plate seizure, vehicle immobilization, vehicle impoundment, and vehicle forfeiture (The Century Council 2003; Cobin and Larkin 1999; Voas and DeYoung 2002). These penalties are designed to prevent a convicted drunk driver from operating a motor vehicle; in particular, these sanctions are helpful safeguards in the event that the offender fails to abide by the terms of his or her driver-based sanctions. *Special license plates* and/or bright-colored stickers may be placed on an offender's vehicle to signal law enforcement officials that a convicted drunk driver is behind the wheel (The Century Council 2003). Breath alcohol ignition interlock devices, similarly, do not absolutely prevent a convicted drunk driver from starting up his or her car; rather, they merely prevent a convicted drunk driver from driving his or her car *while drunk* (The Century Council 2003; Cobin and Larkin 1999; Voas and DeYoung 2002). In particular, these devices require that the offender breathe into them prior to starting the car and will prevent the car from starting if any alcohol is detected. Some states have gone even further, such as requiring that the offender breathe twice: once before starting the car, and again once the car is in motion to prevent another person from breathing for the offender in order to start the car (The Century Council 2003).

The remaining vehicle-based sanctions are basically intended to immobilize the vehicle(s) of arrested or convicted drunk drivers. First, drunk driving could result in *vehicle registration cancellation*, in which the vehicle's registration is invalidated by the state, thus preventing the driver from legally operating their vehicle (The Century Council 2003; Voas and DeYoung 2002). In addition, some states perform *license plate seizures* with drunk drivers, which is a harsher variant of special license plates and stickers.[17] Physical *vehicle immobilization*, on the other hand, can be accomplished by using a device to secure or lock the steering wheel, whereas the drunk driver's vehicle is seized and stored as a result of *vehicle impoundment* (The Century Council 2003; Cobin and Larkin 1999; Voas and DeYoung 2002). *Forfeiture*, which is

---

[17] Some states allow special license plates—such as those previously mentioned—to be substituted for the driver's real license plate, and Minnesota actually requires its police officers to pull over and check out all drivers with these distinctive license plates (The Century Council 2003).

perhaps the most extreme vehicle-based penalty, has already been discussed in an earlier section and will not be examined further at this point.

4.7.4   History

Compared to other sanctions discussed in this chapter, the sanctions in this section have virtually no history. Several factors converged in the 1960s to result in the multitude of alternative sanctions for drunk drivers. The problem of drunk driving first received attention during the 1960s, with rehabilitation being used in the attempt to reduce the incidence of drunk driving fatalities and injuries (Taxman and Piquero 1998). A variety of educational and treatment strategies were adopted based on the recognition that there are several different types of drunk drivers (for example, binge drinkers and social drinkers) (Taxman and Piquero 1998). However, drunk driving accidents did not decrease.

Consequently, starting in the 1980s, more punitive strategies were developed to deter and punish drunk drivers, especially chronic ones (Taxman and Piquero 1998). Organizations created by private citizens whose lives were touched by drunk driving tragedies, such as Mothers Against Drunk Driving and Students Against Drunk Driving (SADD), played a role in what became a national drive to increasingly use severe penalties to combat the problem of drunk driving (Taxman and Piquero 1998; Voas and DeYoung 2002). Administrative license revocations, vehicle impoundment, immobilization and forfeiture, vehicle registration cancellation and license plate seizure, victim-impact panels, and ignition interlock devices were among the multitude of deterrent strategies invoked by states to reduce the incidence of drunk driving (Voas and DeYoung 2002). In fact, recent traffic fatality statistics indicate that drunk driving accidents have indeed decreased over the past two decades (Eisenberg 2003), although the evidence demonstrating the effectiveness of specific strategies has been somewhat mixed.

4.7.5   Prevalence

Within the United States, these alternatives to traditional sanctions for drunk drivers have been used frequently and are available in most states, as well as the District of Columbia, Puerto Rico, and some Native American reservations (The Century Council 2003). For example, forty-one states and the District of Columbia have administrative license revocation laws; thirty-eight states and the District of Columbia have some form of conditional licensing; thirty-four states, the District of Columbia, and the Navajo Nation hold victim-impact panels; nine states allow vehicle immobilization; and fifteen states and the District of Columbia have vehicle impoundment (The Century Council 2003). Importantly, however, these numbers have been steadily increasing.

Europe also provides alternative sanctions for drunk drivers. Aside from those penalties already discussed, one of the newest and most radical sanctions is the "junior license" (Howard 2004). Specifically, after the drunk driver's license is revoked, they may obtain a junior license, which means the offender may only drive a very low-powered car and may not drive on interstates (Howard 2004). Supplemented with a sticker announcing the maximum speed of thirty miles per hour, this penalty has been adopted by Switzerland, Italy, and France (Howard 2004).

4.7.6   Evaluation Research

There has been more research conducted on the effectiveness of strategies designed to reduce the incidence of drunk driving than most other penal sanctions, and in general, the results are somewhat more consistent. In particular, driver-based sanctions appear to be significantly less effective than vehicle-based sanctions, with the exception of home confinement combined with electronic monitoring (The Century Council 2003) and possibly traffic schools (The Century Council 2003). However, there is sufficient evidence indicating that driver-based sanctions are more effective when combined with other types of strategies, such as preventative law enforcement techniques and vehicle-based penalties (The Century Council 2003; Voas and DeYoung 2002).

Hot sheets, administrative license revocations, conditional licensing, and community service all appear to have limited impact unless combined with other sanctions (The Century Council 2003; Voas and DeYoung 2002). Moreover, some negative effects of victim impact panels have been documented for female offenders (Baca et al. 2001), whereas other studies report a positive emotional effect for the victims (The Century Council 2003).

Conversely, the research on most vehicle-based sanctions has tended to generate significant and positive results. Special license plates and distinctive stickers are effective in alerting police of a possible drunk driver, whereas vehicle registration cancellation and license plate seizure have been cited as being low-cost and effective policies, but only if they are properly enforced (The Century Council 2003; Voas and DeYoung 2002). In addition, vehicle immobilization, impoundment, forfeiture, and ignition interlock devices have been demonstrated to significantly reduce recidivism (The Century Council 2003; Cobin and Larkin 1999; Voas and DeYoung 2002). Moreover, some evidence suggests that vehicle immobilization may continue to exert a positive effect on offenders even after the sanction is removed (The Century Council 2003). However, inconsistent application and practical issues associated with these penalties limit their effectiveness. In particular, judges are often reluctant to punish the offender's family by taking away their cars, offenders are frequently unable to afford storage and towing costs, and states have insufficient storage space for seized vehicles (The Century Council 2003). Because these sanctions are usually applied in various combinations, it is less clear which combinations work best, or how effective each individual sanction would be if it was applied as the only sanction.

4.7.7 Section Summary

Although grassroots organizations praise these new punitive and diverse strategies for drunk drivers, many people object that their civil rights are being ignored. For example, one of Washington's newest drunk driver laws allows all breathalyzer tests to be admissible as evidence in court, regardless of their condition (e.g., broken, inaccurate) (Taylor 2005b). In addition, some people argue that the administrative license revocation policy is a violation of due process, as well as double jeopardy. Specifically, the former policy has been attacked on the grounds that the accused is not afforded a trial or jury before his or her license is revoked (Taylor 2005b). The double jeopardy argument holds that the policy allows offenders to be prosecuted and convicted of two different crimes: DUI and driving with a 0.08 percent blood alcohol level, although the offender may only be sentenced for one of these crimes (Taylor 2005b).

New York's 1999 policy of vehicle seizure immediately upon the driver's failure of a breathalyzer test has also met with resistance. For example, a seventy-one-year-old disabled veteran who drinks a couple of beers before he returns to his home explained, "I've been doing this for years. Why all of a sudden do I have to change?" However, it must be borne in mind that, especially compared to other recent penal developments, there is fairly strong evidence that vehicle-based sanctions do effectively reduce the incidence of drunk driving, at least among the population of people subjected to them, and it may also be that they serve a general deterrent function as well.

4.8 Disenfranchisement and Other Civil Rights Restrictions

4.8.1 Description

Often referred to as "collateral consequences" or "civil disabilities," people convicted of a wide range of municipal, state, and federal crimes are likely to incur a variety of civil rights restrictions, including the denial of voting rights, welfare and food stamps, certain types of employment, housing opportunities, student loans, parental custody, and more (Saxonhouse 2004). Amid objections to these policies, the U.S. Supreme Court ruled that such restrictions are not a violation of the Fourteenth Amendment's Equal Protection Clause; thus, states currently have the discretion to impose these punitive sanctions as they deem appropriate (Lippke 2001).

4.8.2   Disenfranchisement

The term *disenfranchisement* refers to the denial of voting rights to convicted felons, although the extent and nature varies significantly by state. Most states ban all criminals convicted of a felony or any other imprisonable offense from voting, and the offense need not have any relation to voting or the electoral process (Fellner 1998). Specifically, states have the right to choose whether they will disenfranchise only those convicted felons who are currently in prison, convicted felons who are on either probation or parole, or even exfelons whose sentences have already expired (Fellner 1998). Additionally, felons may be permanently banned from voting, or they may have their voting rights restored after a specified period of time. However, the process of restoring voting rights is sometimes so complex and intrusive that many exfelons remain disenfranchised; for example, Alabama requires some types of offenders to provide DNA samples in order to regain their voting rights (Fellner 1998).

4.8.3   Other Civil Rights Restrictions

Although some of these restrictions are offense-specific (e.g., drug offenses), others can be imposed on a broader base of offenders. For example, the 1998 Higher Education Act prohibits the provision of financial aid to students with drug convictions (ACLU 2003; Drug Policy Alliance 2003), public housing can be denied to anyone the Department of Housing and Urban Development has "reasonable cause to believe [has] a pattern of drug use" (ACLU 2003), immigrants can be adjudged deportable or inadmissible if they have been convicted of a drug offense (Drug Policy Alliance 2003), the Welfare Reform Act denies cash assistance and food stamps to drug offenders (ACLU 2003), and parental rights can be limited or forfeited upon discovery of drug use (Drug Policy Alliance 2003).

On the other hand, employment restrictions are generally more expansive and may affect a variety of offenders and exoffenders, particularly when employers find applicants to have questionable "moral character" (Saxonhouse 2004). Such restrictions may include prohibitions against employment in health care and education, denial of practitioner licenses, and required criminal background checks (Saxonhouse 2004). In addition, along with drug offenders, some other convicted persons may lose their right to become (or remain) foster or adoptive parents (Drug Policy Alliance 2003).

4.8.4   History

Disenfranchisement and other civil rights restrictions have quite a long history. The denial of civil rights to criminals has its roots in ancient Greek and Roman history, and the practice also resurfaced briefly during the Middle Ages (Mauer

2002). Convicted offenders were stripped of all legal rights—and their heirs were similarly disenfranchised (Mauer 2002). This concept became known as *civil death* or *corruption of blood,* and an example of its effects is the prohibition against passing land from a convict to his or her progeny (Greek 1992; Mauer 2002).

In the United States, disenfranchisement in its current forms can be traced back to the establishment of the nation. At this time, several classes of people were denied the right to vote, including felons, women, blacks, illiterates, and non-property-owners (Mauer 2002). In the decades that followed, particularly following the black right to vote, disenfranchisement assumed a more subtle character. For example, wealthy white voters passed legislation forbidding those who could not afford the poll tax, or who could not pass literacy requirements, from voting (Mauer 2002). These obstacles were followed by another set of voting limitations, this time aimed at those convicted of certain offenses, such as "furtive offenses" (e.g., wife beating) in Alabama, Louisiana, South Carolina, and Virginia, and crimes of "moral turpitude" in Alabama. In fact, Alabama did not eliminate crimes of moral turpitude from the list of disenfranchiseable offenses until 1985 (Mauer 2002). As time has passed, however, disenfranchisement laws have come to affect more and more classes of criminals, even including misdemeanants and those who were never sentenced to prison or probation (Saxonhouse 2004). Given the ever-increasing scope of such legislation combined with the disproportionate number of racial minorities affected by disenfranchisement laws, this type of punitive response has generated significant negative attention, particularly as a result of the 1998 Human Rights Watch/Sentencing Project Report and the outcome of the 2000 presidential election in the United States (Saxonhouse 2004).

4.8.5 Disenfranchisement

In 1998, it was estimated that approximately 3.9 million American adults, or about one in fifty people, were currently affected by disenfranchisement laws (Saxonhouse 2004; Fellner 1998). However, over a quarter of those people were not in prison, on parole, or on probation, which demonstrates the lasting effect of such "collateral consequences" on the social adjustment of exoffenders. All states except Maine, Massachusetts, Utah, and Vermont deny voting rights to imprisoned felons, whereas twenty-nine states do so for convicted felons on probation, thirty-two do so for convicted felons on parole, and fifteen states deny voting rights to exfelons (Fellner 1998). Moreover, fourteen states permanently deny exfelons the right to vote, whereas just about every state disenfranchises them for some specified period of time (ACLU 2003; Saxonhouse 2004). Only Maine and Vermont do not curtail the voting rights of exfelons and allow inmates to vote (ACLU 2003; Political Research Associates 2005).

There is similar diversity with regard to the restoration of voting rights. For example, eight states require a pardon or order from the governor, and two states require parole or pardon board approval (Fellner 1998). Indeed, Mississippi exconvicts have the following options: They "must either secure an executive order from the governor or get a state legislator to introduce the bill on [their] behalf, convince two-thirds of the legislators in each house to vote for it, and have it signed by the governor" (Fellner 1998). Federally disenfranchised exoffenders, on the other hand, must secure a presidential pardon in order to regain their voting rights (Fellner 1998).

4.8.6 Other Civil Rights Restrictions

Approximately 15 percent of the states ban exfelons from public employment, whereas another 10 percent have more lenient restrictions on employment opportunities for convicted felons (Saxonhouse 2004). Sixteen states, or about one-third of the United States, completely abide by the Welfare Reform Act of 1996, although most states have either modified the act or done away with it entirely (ACLU 2003). The Adoptive and Safe Families Act of 1997, on the other hand, has been adopted by every state, and some states have gone so far as to add additional provisions (Drug Policy Alliance 2003).

4.8.7 Evaluation Research

Evaluating these specific "indirect" punitive measures requires a different frame of reference than that required in evaluating the effectiveness of more direct penal sanctions. "Civil death" is not technically a crime control measure, thus it is not designed or intended to have any sort of preventative function (i.e., it is not expected to reduce crime or recidivism). Therefore, one cannot really evaluate the success of disenfranchisement or any other civil rights restrictions in the normal sense of punishment policy effectiveness.

Nevertheless, several arguments against the use of these penalties have been advanced. Prominent among these issues is the fact that approximately 80 percent of polled Americans want exfelons to regain all their rights at some point, and 40 percent wish even those convicts on parole or probation were allowed to vote (Karlan 2004). Moreover, in theory, exfelons are supposed to be able to regain their rights but, in practice, most never do because they don't know how, don't have the financial resources, or don't have other requisite resources (e.g., enough political clout to get pardoned) (Saxonhouse 2004).

Race—and, indirectly, social class—is a key factor in this debate (Karlan 2004; Saxonhouse 2004). Disenfranchisement and the other forms of "civil death" have resulted in the disproportionate representation of minorities among disenfranchised voters (Saxonhouse 2004). Specifically, it is estimated that around one in four black men are permanently disenfranchised in Iowa,

Mississippi, Virginia, and Wyoming, whereas one in three are permanently disenfranchised in Alabama and Florida (Karlan 2004). The effect of permanent disenfranchisement received national attention when it was suggested to be the cause of the Republican—rather than Democrat—victory in the 2000 presidential election (Saxonhouse 2004).

Karlan further argued that disenfranchisement does not just penalize the convicted offender; rather, it also indirectly harms his or her entire community by reducing their political clout (2004). In that sense, disenfranchisement can be viewed as a rather unique "collective sanction" (Karlan 2004). Other opponents to these "collateral consequences" of conviction cite the shame and stigma that often accompanies them (Austin 2004: 173). Not only do these restrictions adversely affect the exoffenders and their communities, but they also cause inconvenience and shame to their families (Austin 2004), which is discussed in the following section.

4.8.8   Section Summary

This section discussed the major forms of "civil death" currently being used in the United States criminal justice system. These include disenfranchisement, or the denial of voting rights; employment restrictions; denial of parental rights; denial of financial aid for secondary education; immigration stipulations; and housing limitations. Just about every state has some combination of these sanctions, although they vary greatly in the nature and extent of these laws (whether these restrictions are permanent or temporary, the type of offense eligible for these restrictions, etc.).

Disenfranchisement and the other civil rights restrictions clearly have a dubious role in the United States criminal justice system. Essentially, they are clearly penalties disproportionately affecting minority (particularly black) and lower socioeconomic members of society. They were not designed to fulfill any type of rehabilitation purposes, and they are not necessarily even indirectly related to the disenfranchised person's offense. Instead, similar to the situation involving the registration of sex and repeat offenders, these measures have a more distinctively punitive orientation than a rehabilitation or crime control function.

4.9   Shaming—Modern-Day Branding or Community Reintegration?

4.9.1   Description

As opposed to some of the other forms of legal punishments discussed in this chapter, shaming has a much longer history. Perhaps the best known incident of shaming—fictional though the account may be—was in Nathaniel Hawthorne's *The Scarlet Letter* (1850), wherein a convicted adulteress is ordered to wear a red "A" on her chest. And while the peak of shaming was around the seventeenth century in the Puritan colonies, a variety of forms still exist in both the United States and abroad today (Harvard Law Review 2004: 2186).

A distinction needs to be made, however, between "reintegrative shaming" and "stigmatizing shaming." The general philosophy behind using reintegrative shaming as a criminal sanction is to create shame and remorse in the offender by bringing together several members of the community so that they may communicate to the offender how his or her offense negatively impacted them (Ahmed and Brathwaite 2004; Hay 2001; Tittle, Bratton, and Gertz 2003; Zhang and Zhang 2004). Stigmatizing shaming, on the other hand, is more similar to branding in that a conspicuous label is attached to the offender for the purpose of public awareness and offender humiliation.

Modern reintegrative shaming practices include holding conferences with juvenile offenders or adult misdemeanants, their victim(s) and family members, and members of the community, and mandating that the offender publicly apologize to his or her victim. The intended purpose is to make offenders more cognizant of the harm created by their act so they will consider the consequences before committing such acts in the future. On the other hand, stigmatizing shaming, such as having drunk drivers carry pictures of their murdered victim(s) in their wallet (Shatzkin 1998) and forcing convicted offenders to wear signs announcing their crime, appears to be gaining popularity. For example, a mail thief was recently ordered by a federal judge to spend eight hours in front of a post office wearing a large sign stating, "I stole mail; this is my punishment" (Colb 2005). In Oakland, efforts to curb prostitution on the demand side led to the new policy of posting pictures of convicted johns on billboards and bus stops (Colb 2004). These types of sanctions have been attacked on the grounds that they may have more negative than positive consequences and therefore serve no crime control function (Colb 2004). However, these are the exceptions rather than the rule. In fact, most of the literature on shaming refers to "reintegrative shaming" and suggests that it is most often used as a diversion tactic for youthful offenders (Campbell and Revering 2002). However, opponents of the sanction argue that shaming is more often than not stigmatizing rather than reintegrative, thereby creating rebellion and increasing criminality (Hund 1999).

4.9.2 History

The roots for shaming may be found in two diametrically opposed backgrounds. *Reintegrative shaming* is largely based on the ideas of indigenous peoples, in particular, the Canadian Natives, Navajos, and Maoris (Campbell and Revering 2002; Hund 1999). Their ideas of conflict resolution and healing circles provide the basis for the current use of reintegrative shaming (Campbell and Revering 2002; James 1993, quoted in Hund 1999). However, *stigmatizing shaming* can be traced back to earlier European shaming, which was often combined with corporal punishments such as flogging, branding, and dunking (Shatzkin 1998). Based on one or both of these shaming traditions—with a few new twists of its own—modern shaming practices began to develop in the United States during the 1980s and 1990s as one of the many alternatives to incarceration (Harvard Law Review 2004).

4.9.3 Prevalence

In 2004, the U.S. Court of Appeals upheld the right of judges to impose shaming punishments. The case that prompted the decision was that of the convicted mail thief mentioned earlier. The defendant, Shawn Gementera, argued that the punishment violated the Sentencing Reform Act and the Eighth Amendment (Colb 2004). However, the court dismissed his claims, instead concluding that shaming is rehabilitative, and not excessively harsh, cruel, or unusual (Colb 2004). Less than a year later, the president of Oakland's City Council announced his new plan to post pictures of convicted johns on billboards and bus stops (Colb 2004). Similarly, in the United Kingdom in recent years, the Divisional Court ruled to do away with provisions set forth in the 1933 Children and Young Persons Act that prevented the media from publishing the names and pictures of convicted juvenile offenders (Spencer 2000). Proponents of the 1933 provisions argued against such "naming and shaming," but the 1997 Parliament revised the provisions such that "naming' is allowed only "if it is satisfied that it is in the public interest to do so" (Spencer 2000). Moreover, reintegrative shaming has been actively used in Australia since 1991 (Campbell and Revering 2002).

4.9.4 Evaluation Research

As with just about every other type of penal sanction, the effectiveness of shaming has been questioned. Essentially, it appears that reintegrative shaming can be effective, especially when large numbers of community members participate; however, stigmatizing shaming has been found by some authors to actually increase crime, especially in the absence of any formal forgiveness of the offender by the victim and community (Hund 1999). Specifically, reintegrative shaming is intended to "encourage offenders to accept responsibility, to internalize laws and community expectations, and then work toward acceptance and support of them" (Lawrence 1991, quoted in Hund 1999), whereas stigmatizing shaming acts to create "outsiders" and put them "in a situation of amplified shame and humiliation ... so they defy society and/or strike out" (Hund 1999).[18]

As previously mentioned, Australia has been using reintegrative shaming for juvenile offenders for over a decade now, and research on their "shaming with compassion" approach found that 95 percent of shamed juveniles do not reoffend (Campbell and Revering 2002). The Anoke, Minnesota, Police Department recently developed a reintegrative shaming program based on the Australian model and boasts of only one recidivist out of seventy juveniles who experienced the shaming penalty (Campbell and Revering 2002). However, recent and well-designed evaluations of specific shaming practices have found minimal support for the effectiveness of either form of shaming and have been unable to determine the exact mechanisms by which shaming is supposed to have a deterrent or rehabilitative effect on offending (Ahmed and Brathwaite 2004; Hay 2001; Tittle, Bratton, and Gertz 2003; Zhang and Zhang 2004).

4.9.5   Section Summary

In sum, the practice of using shaming as a criminal sanction has recently received renewed attention. Essentially, there are two forms: reintegrative and stigmatizing. Reintegrative shaming generally involves the offender, victim(s), members of the community, and a facilitator, and the goal of this method is for the victim(s) and community members to communicate to the offender how his or her criminal or delinquent activities negatively affected them. Ultimately, the parties achieve a reconciliation, which involves the acceptance of the offender's apology and the welcoming of him or her back into the arms of the community. Alternatively, stigmatizing shaming involves no efforts by the criminal justice system to reach an understanding between the offender, victim(s), and community. Rather, specific forms of stigmatizing shaming—much like Hester Prynne's scarlet letter—are simply designed to announce the offender's specific offense to the public, thereby instilling a sense of humiliation in an otherwise recalcitrant offender.

Based on the Australian and Minnesotan experiences, reintegrative shaming appears to be effective in reducing recidivism, especially among youthful offenders and when community participation in the shaming event is significant or prominent, whereas stigmatizing shaming appears to have no ben-

---

[18] Judge John Poe, a Texas judge who has imposed over fifty shaming sanctions in his time on the bench, for example, explained his reasoning behind using shaming sentences with offenders: "The people I see have too good a self-esteem. I want them to feel guilty about what they've done. I don't want them to leave the courthouse having warm fuzzies inside" (Shatzkin 1998). Poe claims his practice of shaming convicted offenders is highly effective, and that he knows of only two shamed offenders who have since committed another crime (Shatzkin 1998).

eficial effects on criminal outcomes whatsoever. However, more recent and empirically sound studies have found considerably less support for the practice of shaming. Moreover, stigmatizing shaming may actually exacerbate the problem by formally labeling the offender as an outsider.

4.10 Medical Castration

4.10.1 Description

The re-emergence of castration as a punitive sanction is another response to the highly publicized crimes committed against young children by released sex offenders, as discussed in the section on "Registration and Nonprison Restrictions on Liberty." Castration is an even more severe means of expressing societal outrage and intolerance over such atrocities, as well as trying to prevent further victimizations of children. Currently, both chemical and surgical castration are possible sanctions in various parts of the United States. *Chemical castration* involves the use of hormones to reduce sexual arousal and urges, whereas *surgical castration* physically removes the males' testes (Russell 1997; Stalans 2004). Although the Supreme Court ruled that involuntary castration was unconstitutional, a number of states require chemical castration as a condition of parole, with offenders having the option of selecting surgical castration instead (Gawande 1997; Petrunik 2002; Russell 1997). Given the wider media, legal, and scholarly coverage on chemical castration relative to surgical castration, this section will primarily address the former, only referring to the latter in order to increase clarity by comparison.

Usually starting approximately a week before the offender's scheduled release from prison, chemical castration is most commonly performed by regular injections of the synthetic hormone medroxyprogesterone acetate (MPA) (Farkas and Stichman 2002; Stalans 2004). The most common form of MPA is Depo-Provera, which, although it acts as a birth control method for women, reduces the blood serum testosterone levels in males (Burdon and Gallagher 2002; Farkas and Stichman 2002; Meisenkothen 1999). As opposed to surgical castration, chemical castration is temporary, and the effects of MPA disappear within seven to ten days of medication cessation (Burdon and Gallagher 2002; Farkas and Stichman 2002; Meisenkothen 1999). Surgical castration, on the other hand, is clearly permanent, although the effects of the procedure can be modified by taking testosterone (Russell 1997).

4.10.2 History

The use of surgical castration (also called orchiectomy) can be traced back thousands of years to ancient societies (Farkas and Stichman 2002; Gawande

1997; Jonckheere 1954; Russell 1997). Castration was used on Greek slaves, Middle Eastern and Asian harem guards, conquered armies, and Italian choir-boys, but in the Middle Ages, it was used as a punitive sanction for rapists and adulterers under the doctrine of "eye for an eye" (Farkas and Stichman 2002; Gawande 1997; Russell 1997). More recently, during the twentieth century, Estonia, Germany, Iceland, the Netherlands, Scandinavia, and Sweden have used physical castration for rapists, pedophiles, and homosexuals (Gawande 1997).

In the United States, forced castration dates back to colonial times when male slaves could face the prospect of surgical castration after having been merely accused of illicit relations with white women (Farkas and Stichman 2002; Serrill 1983). Centuries later, surgical castration was promulgated during the nineteenth-century eugenics movement (Spalding 1998). Advocates of the practice argued for the need to castrate prisoners and others, such as the mentally ill (Farkas and Stichman 2002; Spalding 1998). However, following the discovery of Nazi atrocities during World War II, eugenics and castration declined in popularity and usage (Russell 1997; Serrill 1983). Still, in San Diego in 1975, two child molesters offered to undergo the procedure in exchange for a more lenient sentence; although the judge consented, no doctor willing to perform the procedure could be found (Serrill 1983).

Chemical castration, on the other hand, is a very recent development and first became a realistic sentencing option in 1984, when a Wisconsin judge sentenced a sex offender to MPA treatment as a condition of his probation, although the sentence was rejected during appeals as being a breach of Michigan's probation statute (Spalding 1998). In 1997, California became the first post-World War II U.S. jurisdiction to sanction the use of castration as a punitive response to sexual offenses.

4.10.3 Prevalence

California developed a package of five laws governing the use of chemical castration for sexual offenders (Smith 1998-1999; Stalans 2004). First, the court has discretion in ordering chemical castration for first-time sex offenders with victims under the age of thirteen. Second, chemical castration is mandatory for second-time sex offenders with victims under the age of thirteen. The third section enumerates the offenses to which this legislation applies: sodomy, forcible sodomy or aiding and abetting sodomy or forcible sodomy, committing a lewd or lascivious act on a child by force or violence, oral copulation or aiding and abetting in forcible oral copulation, and penetration of the genital or anal openings with foreign objects. Fourth, the hormone treatment shall begin one week before the offender's scheduled release and shall continue until the offender is deemed by the Department of Corrections to be no longer a danger to the community. Finally, the offender may choose surgical castration and thereby avoid the potential of lifetime hormonal treatments (Smith 1998-1999).

Within six months of the passage of the California law, Florida passed similar legislation, and four other states have since done the same (Petrunik 2002). Florida's statute, however, is not limited to child molesters. Instead, any sexual offender may, upon conviction, be required to receive the hormonal treatment, and any multiple sexual offender may also be forced to undergo chemical castration (Spalding 1998). However, this sentence is only applicable when a court-appointed medical expert deems it medically appropriate, and the trial judge determines the length of the treatment. Failure to comply with treatment constitutes a separate offense, punishable by up to fifteen years in prison (Spalding 1998). Colorado, Georgia, Iowa, Louisiana, Montana, Texas, and Wisconsin have similar legislation (Farkas and Stichman 2002).

The passage of statutes authorizing chemical castration has not necessarily resulted in an onslaught of actual use. In Florida, for example, a major issue regarding chemical castration is how infrequently the sentence is actually imposed. Since 1997, only six convicted sex offenders have been ordered to undergo the treatment, and currently, none of them are actively taking the hormone (Royes 2005). One offender successfully appealed the sentence, another offender is not scheduled for release until 2020 so he may take it then, and the remaining four convicted sex offenders received life sentences so they will never take the drug (Royes 2005). Iowa, where chemical castration is mandatory for repeat sexual offenders of children, has never actually forced a convict to undergo the treatment either (Roos 2005a).

Several European nations also permit the use of chemical castration to control sexual deviance, although there are important limits to the practice. For example, Sweden, Finland, and Germany have minimum age requirements, ranging from twenty to twenty-five (Russell 1997). The use of chemical castration is not necessarily to punish or control convicted sexual offenders per se. Rather, Finland only allows the procedure if it will alleviate the subject's mental anguish over deviant sexual drives, whereas Denmark, Germany, and Norway permit castration if it can be demonstrated that the subject may be compelled to commit sexual crimes due to uncontrollable sexual urges (Russell 1997). Sweden allows chemical castration in the event that the subject poses a threat to society, and the practice is strictly voluntary and requires that the subject be fully informed of all possible side effects (Russell 1997).

4.10.4 Evaluation Research

The evidence supporting the effectiveness of chemical castration is as mixed as the public support for the sanction. Basically, it has been found to be less effective than surgical castration, but more effective than nonpharmacological methods to treat sex offenders (Petrunik 2002), but the evidence is far from overwhelming and there are multiple controversies surrounding the use of castration. First, although MPA treatment research has identified modest reductions in sexual urges and arousal, these studies have generally not been methodologically rigorous or consistent. For example, Stalans noted that MPA evaluations typically lack control groups and use small samples (Stalans 2004).

Another issue is that chemical treatments require weekly doses (Burdon and Gallagher 2002), and many exoffenders refuse the medication or drop out of the treatment (Stalans 2004). Unwilling offenders are unlikely to yield successful treatment outcomes (Smith 1998-1999), and it has been documented that offenders are generally unwilling to undergo this sort of treatment relative to the more common cognitive-behavioral therapy (Stalans 2004). Moreover, the desired effects of the drug disappear within days of treatment cessation (Smith 1998-1999), which clearly represents a security hazard. In addition, none of the chemical castration statutes mandate simultaneous therapy, which research has suggested is critical to the success of the hormonal injections (Burdon and Gallagher 2002; Farkas and Stichman 2002).

Third, resistance on the part of America's medical profession has played no small role in limiting the practice (Farkas and Stichman 2002; Gawande 1997). Although fear of litigation has been cited as the leading reason for doctors' refusals to administer the hormone treatment, such a practice has also been viewed as an affront to physicians' code of ethics (Farkas and Stichman 2002). In fact, some offenders have been forced to attend clinics in Mexico and Canada due to American doctors' adamant refusal to play a part in punitive practices (Gawande 1997; Stonecypher 2000).

Fourth, there are a multitude of possible side effects, and the drug can only be safely prescribed for limited time periods (Stalans 2004). However, it has been suggested that serotonin reuptake inhibitors could fulfill the same preventative functions as MPA, while reducing the number of side effects and lasting for longer periods of time (Stalans 2004).

Fifth, a critical philosophical argument hinges on the fundamental rights of privacy, which includes bodily autonomy and the decision to procreate (Farkas and Stichman 2002; Meisenkothen 1999; Spalding 1998). Although the Supreme Court has decided that the forced administration of medication is allowable as long as it is in the patient's best interest and the patient is a potential threat to himself or society, chemical castration has been viewed as more of a punitive control mechanism than a medical treatment (Farkas and Stichman 2002). Moreover, studies indicate that testosterone has several bodily functions that have no relation to sex drives but that affect appearance and personality (Smith 1998-1999). Thus, MPA could potentially do more than medically cure the offender's deviant sexual proclivities; it could interfere with other bodily processes and functions that are unrelated to the control of sexual urges. Other constitutional considerations that have been raised include involuntary treatment and informed consent, cruel and unusual punishment, due process and equal protection, and double jeopardy (Meisenkothen 1999; Spalding 1998).

Sixth, some argue that many chemical castration statutes are overly inclusive. As previously mentioned, several states allow the procedure as a sanction for a first-time sexual offender. However, research on the effects of MPA treatment suggests that it is only effective with paraphiliacs or those having uncontrollable sexual urges that must be satisfied (Meisenkothen 1999). Alternatively, another related argument is that rape is about power, not sex, thus treatment aimed at reducing a male's sexual urges may have limited positive effects (Serrill 1983).

A final criticism of the treatment is that MPA does not entirely extinguish the male sex drive (Serrill 1983; Smith 1998-1999). MPA-treated sexual offenders may still be capable of sexual intercourse and masturbation (Serrill 1983; Smith 1998-1999). Moreover, even for those sex offenders who do lose their sexual urges, if they have an underlying attraction to children, it is not directly addressed or cured (Serrill 1983; Smith 1998-1999).

On the other hand, proponents of chemical castration for sex offenders argue that it is both safe and effective (Meisenkothen 1999). Supporters of the drug point to studies demonstrating that sex offenders treated with MPA have significantly lower recidivism rates than sex offenders not treated with the drug (Meisenkothen 1999; Smith 1998-1999). In addition, they cite budget statistics suggesting that MPA is more cost-efficient than prison, without sacrificing the safety of children (Smith 1998-1999).

Although there are many arguments over the effectiveness of chemical castration as a form of crime control, more positive reviews of chemical castration have generally been in the form of treated sex offenders' testimonials rather than true evaluation research. For example, a Montana legislator who sponsored the bill explained that her motivation was the request of an incarcerated sex offender: "He pleaded with me to find a way to get him out of prison" and, having knowledge of the treatment, concluded "so why would we not give him the tools to maintain some balance?" (New York Times News Service 1997). Texas Governor (and current President) George W. Bush claimed that his incentive for backing the use of chemical castration came from the request of two incarcerated sexual offenders (Gawande 1997).

In contrast to the positive reviews of voluntary and requested chemical castration, much debate surrounds the use of mandatory treatment. For example, an accused multiple sex offender agreed to chemical castration as part of a plea bargain for a shorter prison sentence, which some could argue represents coerced castration (Associated Press 1999; Stonecypher 2000). The defendant, Hazard Campbell, had to spend two years in a Canadian institution known for treating psychosexual disorders, initiate the procedure, and then return to the United States to serve his twenty-five-year prison sentence (Associated Press 1999; Stonecypher 2000). In California, a convicted sexual pedophile with AIDS appealed his sentence of chemical castration on the grounds he had been denied liberty, privacy, bodily integrity, procreation, and due process of law; however, the El Dorado County Supreme Court upheld the ruling, citing the fourteen-year-old victim's vulnerability and the defendant's criminal forethought and criminal history (McCarthy 2004).

4.10.5   Section Summary

Clearly, castration as a criminal justice system sanction is a controversial issue. Despite its questionable legitimacy, however, its usage has endured throughout several centuries for a variety of purposes. The results of the evaluation research, as well as some anecdotal evidence, seem to suggest that voluntary chemical (or surgical) castration can reduce recidivism among sex offenders to some degree, particularly when combined with some form of therapy (and, for chemical castration, when administered in regular dosages). Similar to other punitive sanctions such as sex offender registration and community notification, however, this type of punitive sanction is not expected to decrease the number of sexual crimes perpetrated by family members, as these offenses are typically not reported and thus would not result in prosecution and conviction. Consequently, the evidence indicates that castration as a punitive measure can be effective, but only when the particular offender elects to undergo the procedure, continues the treatment regularly, and simultaneously submits to psychological treatment. Mandatory castration, on the other hand, has not been demonstrated to be an effective crime control measure, as it can be too easily circumvented, thereby rendering the procedure futile.

4.11   Civil Commitment

4.11.1   Description

Civil commitment has also been used with sex offenders. As discussed in previous sections, horrific cases of sexual crimes against children in the 1990s have received unprecedented media and public attention and an outcry to implement new strategies to prevent sex offenders from victimizing the public, especially children. One of the most controversial policy responses to the

perceived threat of sex offenders repeating their crimes has been the enactment of laws to allow states to invoke the civil commitment of selected sex
offenders after completion of their court-imposed prison or juvenile detention sentence.

Sex offender civil commitment (SOCC) programs are based on the presumption that some sex offenders are mentally ill and, unless treated for their
illness, will continue to be a danger to the community. The SOCC process
is unique in that it focuses on sex offenders who have been sentenced to
prison, and this process is to determine if the offender has a mental abnormality and therefore a high risk of reoffending, thus justifying civil commitment for indeterminate periods of time to a treatment facility upon
completion of the original sentence. The basis of SOCC programs is the
assumption that sex offenders can be psychologically assessed and their level
of risk for committing future sex crimes can be determined. Periodic reviews
of sex offenders in SOCC facilities to determine their treatment progress is
an integral component of ultimately determining when, or if, the offender
can be released back to the community when they no longer pose a threat
to the public (Levenson 2003).

The process by which sex offenders are selected for civil commitment
is similar across all state programs (Lieb and Matson 1998). The procedure
begins with the identification of initially eligible offenders prior to their
release from prison and is followed by multiple assessment and decision
stages. There is an initial screening to determine if offenders meet the criteria
for more in-depth face-to-face evaluations to determine their risk of reoffending. These evaluations employ psychologists and psychiatrists to make
assessments using a variety of established tests to identify the existence and
nature of psychological conditions conducive to sex offending. Based on the
results of this evaluation phase and the recommendations of the mental
health experts, offenders can then be referred to a prosecutor, who determines if there is probable cause for advancing the case to the courts for
consideration of civil commitment. A trial by a judge or jury is then held
to make the final decision whether the person is civilly committed to a
treatment center for an indefinite period of time. Based on periodic reviews
of those committed, the judge makes the decision concerning when the
offender no longer poses a threat of reoffending, and their civil commitment
is terminated.

Consistent with the process used in other state SOCC programs, Florida
has very broad criteria for identifying sex offenders who are eligible for civil
commitment. An offender in a state prison or a juvenile detention facility,
and persons who have been found not guilty by reason of insanity who have
ever been convicted of a sex offense, must be screened by the Sexually Violent
Predator (SVP) program prior to their release from custody (OPPAGA 2000).

An initial screening is conducted several months prior to release by the SVP program administered by the Florida Department of Children and Family Services. This initial phase entails psychological specialists reviewing the sex offender's records including police reports, prior criminal history records, and presentence investigations to assess whether or not the offender should be referred to the next stage. The second stage involves face-to-face clinical testing to determine if the case will be referred to the state attorney to determine whether there is probable cause for civil commitment. If probable cause is determined to exist, a trial by a judge or jury makes the determination of whether the person will receive civil commitment.

4.11.2 History

Although SOCC programs in existence today emerged since 1990, the practice of committing sex offenders to indeterminate terms for treatment purposes is not new. In the 1930s and 1940s, Michigan was the first of twenty-eight states to pass sexual psychopath laws (Wilson 2004). These laws resulted from "an enormous panic about the presumed presence of sex fiends" (Wilson 2004: 379) and allowed for the indeterminate confinement of offenders who were diagnosed as having a sexual dysfunction by psychiatrists. Offenders could be released from a treatment facility when the state determined they were cured of their sexual disorder. Eventually, the psychological field changed its opinions about sex offenders and determined they did not suffer from mental illness and therefore committing them to treatment facilities was no longer a viable policy (Wilson 2004).

In the second wave of legislation, Washington was the first state to pass laws establishing a SOCC program in 1990—only six years after its sexual psychopath law was eliminated. The primary difference between the old sexual psychopath laws and the recent civil commitment law is that the latter allows for the indeterminate commitment and treatment of sex offenders deemed a danger to the community at the end of a criminal sentence of incarceration, whereas the former did not. The first challenge to the new form of sex offender civil commitment that was heard by the U.S. Supreme Court was *Kansas v. Hendricks* in 1997. The court found that the Kansas law "meets the due process requirements of the Constitution and that the act conforms to double jeopardy principles and does not constitute ex post fact law-making" (Wilson 2004: 383).

4.11.3 Prevalence

Sixteen states in the United States have enacted sex offender civil commitment laws since 1990 (Levenson 2004). The states are Arizona, California, Florida, Illinois, Iowa, Kansas, Massachusetts, Minnesota, Missouri, New Jersey,

North Dakota, South Carolina, Texas, Virginia, Washington, and Wisconsin. Additionally, the District of Columbia has enacted a SOCC law (Molett, Arnold, and Meyer 2001), and West Virginia is in the process of considering a SOCC program.

There is no source for national numbers relating to the how many sex offenders have been referred for civil commitment, the number who have been civilly committed, or the cost of these programs. If Florida's experience is indicative of the other state programs responsible for the civil commitment of sex offenders, however, the volume of cases referred and the associated costs are significant. Since the beginning of Florida's Sexually Violent Predator program in 1999 through August 2005, there were 19,472 sex offenders deemed eligible for civil commitment and referred for evaluation. Of this number, only 235 (1.2 percent) have been civilly committed to a treatment facility by the courts (Economic and Demographic Research 2005). The cost of Florida's SVP program in Fiscal Year 1999-2000 alone was $17.8 million, during which nine sex offenders were civilly committed (OPPAGA 2000). A significant expense results from Florida's practice of detaining sex offenders in a facility after the expiration of their prison or juvenile detention sentences while they are being processed through the multistage civil commitment process. Indeed, during the first five years of operation, the state spent $15 million to temporarily detain sex offenders who were ultimately released after the decision was made not to invoke civil commitment (OPPAGA 2000).

4.11.4   Evaluation Research

There has not been an evaluation of the effectiveness of the sex offender civil commitment program at this time. The only research conducted to date was on Florida's Sexually Violent Predator program established under the Jimmy Ryce Act in 1999 (Levenson 2004). The purpose of the study was to determine if offenders chosen for civil commitment are, in fact, more dangerous and pose more of a threat to repeating their sex crimes once released from prison than those not identified for civil commitment. It was hypothesized that offenders selected for civil commitment would be more likely than those not selected to have a mental or personality disorder that impedes their ability to control their sexual behavior and would have higher levels of risk factors that have been shown to predict a greater likelihood of sexual recidivism.

This study examined 450 male sex offenders who were referred to the second stage of the process between July 1, 2000, and June 30, 2001 (Levenson 2004). A total of 2,418 sex offenders were initially referred under the program, with 1,968 (81.4 percent) not considered eligible for the second phase of clinical assessments. Of the study group, 229 (51 percent) were recommended for civil commitment as a result of the clinical assessments and decisions by the team of psychologists and psychiatrists. The study used administrative data from the SVP program, including information from various clinical tests, a host of measures about the offender's prior history, and various characteristics of the offender's victims.

The findings supported the two hypotheses. First, offenders selected for civil commitment during the second stage were significantly more likely than those not selected to have a mental or personality disorder based on various clinical test results. Second, those selected for referral to the state attorney had significantly higher levels of risk factors that indicated a greater likelihood of sexual recidivism. The author supported the need for additional research when stating that "more research from states with SVP commitment statutes is needed, and ultimately, the effectiveness of civil commitment should be measured by its impact on sex offense recidivism" (Levenson 2004: 646). The authors of this chapter heartily concur with Levenson's recommendations because thus far nothing is known about the effectiveness of the sex offender civil commitment program.

4.11.5   Section Summary

SOCC programs, in sum, are designed to ensure that released sex offenders with mental illnesses continue to receive psychological services following their release from prison. A key aspect of SOCC, however, is its indeterminate nature. Specifically, eligible sex offenders may face civil commitment of an indeterminate length; in other words, civilly committed sex offenders must remain in custody until they are determined to no longer represent a risk to the community.

As compared to most of the other sanctions reviewed in this chapter, the emergence of SOCC programs is quite recent, although similar popular perceptions on the very real dangers of sex offenders in the community led the way to the establishment of civil commitment legislation. Unfortunately, SOCC has received very little scholarly attention. The one study that has been conducted yielded promising—albeit indirect—evidence that civil commitment might reduce recidivism among identified sex offenders, but this has not been fully evaluated (Levenson 2004).

4.12   Summary and Conclusions

This chapter has discussed fines, forfeiture, and some nontraditional punitive measures to supplement the materials presented in other chapters of the book. Each section followed the same organizational structure, with a general description of each topic to introduce the concept and provide a definition and description of the specific form of punishment. A brief history of the punishment strategy was provided to indicate where and how it came into existence and some of the more significant changes that have occurred in its use. Prevalence or frequency of occurrence was discussed to provide information about its past and current use in the criminal justice system. The available evaluation research that has been conducted on the effectiveness of each form of punishment was also discussed. A brief summary is presented here, followed by a few concluding observations.

Fines, the payment of money to a governmental entity for harm committed by the offender, represent one of the oldest forms of punishment. Unfortunately, there is limited empirical research on the relationship between the use of fines and recidivism. There is a suggestion in the limited available research that fixed fines may have a slight deterrent effect in reducing some measures of recidivism, but the evidence is not very strong. Despite fixed fines having been in existence for a much longer period of time, more research has been done on structured fines (day fines), and the literature suggests that structured fines may have a stronger deterrent effect than fixed fines. The research is limited, but it would appear that structured fines are equal to or better than fixed fines relative to the generally accepted goals of punishment.

Forfeiture refers to the seizure of an offender's property, presumably following conviction.[19] It is another very old form of punishment, although it had largely disappeared in the Western world until the 1970s, when it was resurrected in the war on drugs by the United States. Evaluation research on forfeiture is very limited and is virtually nonexistent as far as its deterrent effect in the area of illegal drugs is concerned. There has been some research on the relationship between forfeiture laws and drunk driving suggesting that forfeiture, as a form of vehicle seizure, may have some specific deterrent effect, but thus far it is difficult to separate the use of forfeiture from other forms of vehicle seizure.

The discussion of *registration and nonprison restrictions on liberty* covered a series of interrelated issues including offender registration and community notification, permanent electronic monitoring, living and employment restrictions, and mandatory DNA submittals. These sanctions have become much more popular in recent years primarily because of several shocking crimes against children involving known sex offenders.

Despite the increasing popularity, however, there is virtually no research that has examined a true deterrent, incapacitative, or rehabilitative effect for any form of registration or other nonprison restriction on liberty. Although research is limited, an examination of the best available evidence suggests that registration and other related restrictions may not meet any of the normally accepted goals of punishment.

---

[19] As noted in the discussion, forfeiture may occur prior to conviction, and indeed in its current use that may well be a pattern. In fact, even if acquitted, forfeited property is not always returned to the accused person (Wikipedia 2005).

Driver-based and vehicle-based sanctions, particularly license revocation and vehicle immobilization laws, are very new and innovative punitive responses to the problem of drunk driving, particularly when compared to some of the other forms of punishment discussed in this chapter. These sanctions essentially serve as target-hardening approaches because they all make it more inconvenient, difficult, or impossible to drive while drunk.

In recent years, there has probably been more quasiexperimental research conducted on the effectiveness of driver-based and vehicle-based punishment strategies than on all other punishment approaches combined, and it is more sophisticated than much of the other research that has been conducted. Although there are some discrepancies, this research tends to be fairly consistent, especially compared to research on other forms of punishment.

Although the research on driver-based sanctions generally tends to find fairly weak support at best, and no support in many studies, there is some strong and consistent evidence that vehicle-based sanctions do effectively reduce the incidence of drunk driving. Whether this effect is a product of specific deterrence, general deterrence, incapacitation, target hardening, moral appeal, maturational reform, or some process not yet identified is less clear, but there does appear to be a decrease in drunk driving when vehicle-based sanctions are used.

Disenfranchisement and other civil rights restrictions are concerned with rights that are lost as a result of conviction of a crime. Among these are disenfranchisement, or the denial of voting rights; employment restrictions; denial of parental rights; denial of financial aid for secondary education; immigration stipulations; and housing limitations. Some of these, such as disenfranchisement, have a very long history, whereas others like welfare and food stamp restrictions are very recent innovations.

Because none of these sanctions are intended to serve a crime prevention function using the logic or theoretical rationales of deterrence, incapacitation, or rehabilitation, there has never really been any evaluation research conducted on any of these types of punishment. However, many argue that there are debilitating negative consequences related to the use of some of these forms of restrictions.

Shaming as a criminal sanction is an old concept that has recently received renewed attention. Essentially, there are two forms of shaming: reintegrative and stigmatizing. The goal of reintegrative shaming is for the victim and community members to communicate to the offender how his or her actions impacted them in a negative way and to achieve a reconciliation so the offender can be reintegrated into the community. Conversely, stigmatizing shaming involves no attempt to reach an understanding among the offender, victim, and community. These forms of punishment are merely intended to announce the offender's crime to the public and hopefully impact an otherwise recalcitrant offender.

There is a fair amount of research that has been conducted on shaming, and reintegrative shaming has been found to be somewhat effective in reducing recidivism under the Australia and Minnesota models, wherein community participation is present. However, studies relying on more rigorous methodologies have generally found less support for reintegrative shaming. On the other hand, stigmatizing shaming appears to have no positive impact and may actually exacerbate criminality by formally labeling the offender as an outsider.

Although *castration* is a very old practice, its use in the criminal justice system as a means of "incapacitating" sex offenders has become more prominent and acceptable in recent years since the initiation of chemical rather than surgical castration. Although there are many arguments against the use of castration, paradoxically, some of the strongest support for its use comes from anecdotal testimonials provided by treated sex offenders, and not empirical research.

Minimal evaluation research has been conducted on the effectiveness of either form of castration, but the limited research suggests that surgical is more effective than chemical castration, and both are more effective than other nonpharmacological approaches by themselves. Although there are positive reviews of voluntary and requested chemical castration, it is soundly denounced by many professionals in the field and much debate surrounds the use of mandatory castration of either type.

The *civil commitment of sex offenders* is a relatively new concept and, in one sense, is outside of the criminal justice system, but at the same time is stacked on top of everything else the criminal justice system is doing. Civil commitment is designed to ensure that sex offenders with mental illnesses who have completed their prison sentence continue to receive psychological services and to be separated from the community. Specifically, some sex offenders may face civil commitment of an indeterminate length so they remain in custody until they are not considered a risk to community—which, in many cases, is the equivalent of life imprisonment.

Unfortunately, the civil commitment of sex offenders has received very little scholarly attention. The one study that has been conducted was not a direct test of the effectiveness of the process and really does not speak to a deterrent, rehabilitative, or incapacitative effect, although any time offenders are maintained in an incarcerative state, by definition, some incapacitation effect occurs.

In conclusion, although some of the forms of punishment discussed in this chapter are very old (fixed fines, forfeiture, disenfranchisement, shaming, and castration), this is an insufficient reason for assuming they are effective in reducing crime and worthy of retention, or that they are ineffective and should therefore be eliminated. Nor does the fact that a sanction is relatively new (structured fines, registration, nonprison restrictions on liberty, driver-based and vehicle-based sanctions, civil rights restrictions, and civil commitments) indicate that a sanction is effective or ineffective and should be retained or discontinued. Evaluation research is called for, and as this review has indicated, in most cases there is insufficient evidence at this time for making a determination.

At the same time, there are some punitive strategies that research does support, and there are some the criminal justice system might consider discontinuing on other grounds in the absence of empirical evidence to the contrary. For example, structured fines appear to meet punishment goals at least as well as if not better than fixed fines, and countries such as the United States should consider following the lead of some European countries in experimenting more with the use of this approach as an important component of the punishment continuum.

The lack of strong evidence for the effectiveness of forfeiture in deterring drug trafficking is not likely to result in its discontinuation in the near future because of the monetary benefit it provides to law enforcement. As noted above, however, many critics of the drug forfeiture policy blame these policies for a wide range of problems, and a case can be made for their elimination.

It would also appear that the most recent forms of registration legislation represent yet another questionable legislative response to sensational media accounts of brutal crimes and errors of the criminal justice system. These policies restrict the exoffender's abilities to return to a normal life in the community following the termination of sentence. Moreover, registration and community notification may create a stigmatizing effect, whereas living and employment restrictions may seriously hinder the offender's ability to maintain a normal family life or gain meaningful employment. Although grassroots organizations praise some of the new punitive strategies for drunk drivers, many have objected that the offender's civil rights are being violated. Moreover, it is argued that the administrative license revocation policy is a violation of due process, as well as double jeopardy.

Disenfranchisement and the other civil rights restrictions discussed in this section clearly have a dubious role in the United States criminal justice system at best. Essentially, they appear to be penalties disproportionately affecting minority and lower socioeconomic segments of society, blacks in particular. These sanctions were not designed to fulfill any type of deterrent or rehabilitative purpose and are not necessarily related to the disenfranchised person's offense. Instead, similar to the situation involving the registration of sex and repeat offenders, these measures have a more distinctively punitive orientation than a rehabilitative or crime control function.

It is true that several of the sanctions discussed in this chapter likely have an incapacitative impact, but this is almost always the case—simply by definition. Whenever society kills, banishes, or locks offenders away for life, there will almost always be some reduction in crime in the larger society (although perhaps not within the prison system), but at what cost? The incapacitative effect can never be examined or accepted in isolation; it must be weighed against the social, personal, and monetary cost of the punitive sanction applied, as well as in comparison to the other possible and less costly alternatives that are available.

For decades, if not centuries, criminologists have been arguing for the more extensive use of evaluation research in the guidance of criminal justice policy. Whether the sanction is relatively new, or its roots lost in antiquity, all sanctions should be evaluated in terms of whether they meet at least one of the major rationales for punishment. If they do not, then it may be time to consider other alternatives. In the case of most of the sanctions discussed in this chapter, despite hundreds or thousands of years of use, the evaluative research is yet to be done! The message is clear. Even in areas dealing with sanctions that have existed longer than the criminal justice system itself, if the practice is to continue, research must be conducted to determine whether or not the sanction meets one of the goals of punishment. If it does not, why should it be continued?

References

ACLU. 2003. *Collateral Consequences of the War on Drugs*, Drug Policy Litigation Project, New Haven; Drug Policy Alliance, *Barriers to Re-Entry for Convicted Drug Offenders*, April, www.lindesmith.org/library/factsheets/barriers/index.cfm?printpage=1, accessed June 21, 2005.

ACLU. 2005. *Collateral Consequences of the War on Drugs*. Political Research Associates. *Factsheet: The Intended and Unintended Consequences of the Criminal Justice System*, http://www.defendingjustice.org/factsheets, accessed October 31, 2005.

Ahmed, E., and V. Brathwaite. 2004. "What, me ashamed?" Shame management and school bullying. *J. Res. Crime and Delin.* 41, 269.

Albers, M. E. 1999. Legislative deference in Eighth Amendment capital sentencing challenges: The constitutional inadequacy of the current judicial approach. *Case Western Reserve L. Rev.*, 50, 467.

Albrecht, H. J., and E. H. Johnson. 1980. Fines and justice administration: the experience of the Federal Republic of Germany. *Int. J. Comp. and Appl. Criminal Justice* 5, 12.

Associated Press. 1999. Accused rapist to undergo "chemical castration." *Portsmouth Herald*, November 13, www.seacostalonline.com, accessed June 21, 2005.

Austin, R. 2004. "The shame of it all": Stigma and the political disenfranchisement of formerly convicted and incarcerated persons. *Columbia Human Rights L. Rev.* 36, 173.

Austin v. United States, 509 U.S. 602,113 S. Ct. 2801, 125 L. Ed. 2d 488. 1993.

Baca, J., et al. 2001. Victim impact panels: do they impact drunk drivers? A follow-up of female and male, first-time and repeat offenders. *J. Studies on Alcohol,* 62, 615.

Barnes, H. E., and N. K. Teeters. 1959. *New Horizons in Criminology,* 3rd ed., Prentice-Hall, Englewood Cliffs, 1959, 400-401.

BBC News. 2005. Fines plans echo 1991 Tory Policy. http://news.bbc.co.uk/2/hi/uk_news/politics/4173913.2tm, accessed August 24, 2005.

Blumenson, E., and E. Nilsen. 1998. Policing for profit: The Drug War's hidden economic agenda. *U. Chicago L. Rev.* 65, 106.

Burdon, W. M., and C. A. Gallagher. 2002. Coercion and sex offenders: Controlling sex-offending behavior through incapacitation and treatment. *Criminal Justice and Behavior* 29, 87.

Bureau of Justice Assistance. 1996. How to use structured fines (day fines) as an intermediate sanction. Monograph NCJ 156242, 1. Washington, DC: U.S. Department of Justice, Office of Justice Programs.

California Department of Motor Vehicles. 2002. *DUI Countermeasures in California: What Works and What Doesn't, With Recommendations for Legislative Reform.* Report to the Legislature of the State of California, in Accord with Senate Bill 776, Chapter 857, 2001 Legislative Session, September.

Campbell, H. A., and A. C. Revering. 2002. *Holding Kids Accountable: Shaming with Compassion.* International Child and Youth Care Network. www.cyc-net.org/cyc-online/cycol-0402-accountable.html, accessed June 21, 2005.

Cavan, R. S. 1962. *Criminology,* 3rd ed. New York: Thomas Y. Cromwell, 647.

The Century Council. 2003. *Combating Hardcore Drunk Driving.* National Hardcore Drunk Driver Project. www.dwidata.org, accessed June 21, 2005.

CNN. 2005b. Congress gets Lunsford legislation. cnn.allpolitics.printthis.clickability.com, accessed May 5, 2005.

CNN. 2005a. Florida Senate eyes tougher sex offender law. cnn.allpolitics.printthis.clickability.com, accessed May 5, 2005.

Cobin, J. H., and G. L. Larkin. 1999. Effectiveness of ignition interlock devices in reducing drunk driving recidivism. *Am. J. Preventative Med.,* 16, 81.

Colb, S. F. 2004. What a shame: Oakland announces plans to post photos of convicted johns. FindLaw, writ.news.findlaw.com, accessed June 21, 2005.

Colb, S. F. 2005. The U.S. Court of Appeals for the Ninth Circuit upholds a "shaming" penalty. FindLaw, writ.news.findlaw.com, accessed June 21, 2005.

Cotterell, B. 2005. Senator pushes lifelong monitoring of sex offenders. *Tallahassee Democrat,* April 12, www.tallahassee.com, accessed May 5, 2005.

Crosby, I. 1996 *Portland's Asset Forfeiture Program: The Effectiveness of Vehicle Seizure in Reducing Rearrest Among 'Problem" Drunk Drivers.* A Joint Project of The Reed College Public Policy Workshop and the Portland Police Bureau.

Dunkleberger, L. 2005a. Governor signs Lunsford Act, toughening sex offender laws: Law requires longer prison sentences. *Herald Tribune,* www.heraldtribune.com, accessed May 5, 2005.

Dunkleberger, L. 2005b. Report basks sex-offender monitoring: Findings say satellite tracking is best suited for high-risk offenders and predators. *Herald Tribune,* www.heraldtribune.com, accessed May 5, 2005.

Economic and Demographic Research. 2005. *Criminal Justice Estimating Conference.* Joint Legislative Management Committee, February 14, Tallahassee.

Eisenberg, D. 2003. Evaluating the effectiveness of policies related to drunk driving. *J. Policy Anal. and Management* 22, 249.

Ertelt, P. 2005. Bill would require GPS monitoring of sex offenders. *Capitol Bureau,* April 20.

Executive Office for Asset Forfeiture. 1994. *Annual Report of the Department of Justice Asset Forfeiture Program.* Washington, DC: U.S. Department of Justice.

Farkas, M. A., and A. Stichman. 2002. Sex offender laws: Can treatment, punishment, incapacitation, and public safety be reconciled? *Criminal Justice Rev.* 27, 256.

Fellner, J. 1998. *Losing the Vote: The Impact of Felony Disenfranchisement Laws in the United States.* The Sentencing Project and Human Rights Watch, http://www.hrw.org/reports98/vote, accessed October 31, 2005.

Gawande, A. 1997. The unkindest cut: The science and ethics of castration. *Medical Examiner* July 13, slate.msn.com, accessed June 21, 2005.

Gearino, D. 2005. Legislative report: Senate panel approves sex offender reforms. *Globe Gazette,* Des Moines Bureau, April 8.

Gneezy, U., and A. Rustichini. 2000. A fine is a price. *J. Legal Studies.* 29 (January).

Goodnough, A. 2005. After 2 cases in Florida, crackdown on molesters. *The New York Times,* May 1, nytimes.com, accessed May 5, 2005.

Gordon, M. A., and R. Glaser. 1991. The use and effects of financial penalties in municipal courts. *Criminology* 29, 651.

GotTrouble.com. 1999-2001. Traffic tickets. www.gottrouble.com/legal/criminal/traffic_school/traffic_school_1.htm, accessed September 6, 2005.

Greek, C. 1992. Drug control and asset seizures: a review of the history of forfeiture in England and Colonial American. In *Drugs, Crime, and Social Policy,* ed. T. Mieczkowski, 124. Boston: Allyn Bacon.

Greene, J. A. 1993. The day fine system: A tool for improving the use of economic sanctions. New York: Vera Institute of Justice.

Harvard Law Review. 2003. Leading cases: I. constitutional law: 5. sex offender registration. *Harvard L. Rev.* 117, 327.

Harvard Law Review. 2004. Shame, stigma, and crime: Evaluating the efficacy of shaming sanctions in criminal law. *Harvard L. Rev.* 116, 2186.

Hay, C. 2001. An exploratory test of Braithwaite's reintegrative shaming theory. *J. Res. Crime and Delin.* 38, 132.

Herbert, K. 2005. Castor backs Pa. legislation to track sex offenders by GPS. *Philadelphia Inquirer,* April 27.

Hillsman, S. T. 1998. Best practices along the criminal justice process: Criminal fines as an intermediate sanction. Presented at the Beyond Prisons Symposium, Kingston, Ontario.

Homel, R. 1980. *Penalties and the Drink/Driver.*, New South Wales: Department of the Attorney General and New South Wales Bureau of Crime Statistics and Research, Report No. 7.

Howard, C. 2004. Alternative punishments for drunk drivers. www.reflector.com, accessed June 21, 2005.

Hund, A. J. 1999. Participatory reintegrative shaming conferences. *Red Feather J. Postmodern Criminology* 8, critcrim.org/redfeather/journal-pomocrim/vol-8-shaming/hund.html, accessed June 21, 2005.

Johnson, L. L. 2005. Sex offender tracking legislation nears vote. Tennessean.com, cgi.tennessean.com/cgi-bin/print/pr.pl, accessed May 4, 2005.

Jonckheere, F. 1954. L'eunuque dans l'Egypte pharaonique. *Revue d'Historie des Sciences* 7, 139.

Karlan, P. S. 2004. Conviction and doubts: Retribution, representation, and debate over felon disenfranchisement. *Stanford L. Rev.* 56, 1147.

Knopp, F. H., et al. 1976. *Instead of Prisons: A Handbook for Abolitionists.* Syracuse, NY: Prison Research Education Action Project.

Kurisky, G. 1988. Civil forfeiture of assets: A final solution to international drug trafficking? *Houston J. Int. L.* 10, 249.

Loughlin, P. J. 2002. "Does the Civil Asset Forfeiture Reform Act (2000) Bring a Modicum of Sanity to the Federal Civil Forfeiture System?" http://www.ceeol.com/aspx/getdocument.aspx?logid=5&id=b72b1ec4-d28f-47a6-911a-3afc7624f812, accessed June 12, 2007.

Lee, W. L. M. 1901. *History of Police in England.* London: Methuen.

Legal Information Institute. 1999. LII backgrounder on forfeiture. Legal Information Institute, http://straylight.law.cornell.edu/background/forfeiture, accessed August 24, 2005.

LegalatPokerPulse Forums. 2004. The grey zone; Canadian gaming law, http://www.pokerpulse.com/legal/viewtopic.php?p=109&sid=ad728, accessed September 23, 2005.

Levenson, J. S. 2003. Factors predicting recommendations for civil commitment of sexually violent predators under Florida's Jimmy Ryce Act. PhD dissertation, Florida International University.

Levenson, J. S. 2004. Sexual predator civil commitment: A comparison of selected and released offenders. *Intern. J. Offender Therapy and Comp. Criminology* 48, 638.

Lieb, R., and S. Matson. 1998. *Sexual Predator Commitment Laws in the United States: 1998 Update.* Olympia: Washington State Institute for Public Policy, 11.

Lippke, R. L. 2001. The disenfranchisement of felons. *L. and Philosophy* 20, 553.

Lyons, D. 2004. State crime legislation in 2004. *National Conference of State Legislatures.* www.ncsl.org.programs/cj/04crime.htm, accessed May 5, 2005.

Mandarino, J. C. 2003. Notes and comments: intermediate sanctions flow charts. *J. Health L.* 36.

Mauer, M. 2002. *Race, Poverty, and Felon Disenfranchisement.* July/August, Poverty and Race Research Action Council.

McCarthy, R. 2004. Court OKs chemical castration for Tahoe man. *Tahoe Daily Tribune*, December 27, www.tahoedailytribune.com, accessed June 27, 2005.

McKechnie, W. 1958. *Magna Carta: A Commentary on the Great Charter of King John with an Historical Introduction*, 2nd ed., reprint. Glascow: Lenox Hill, 285-286.

Meisenkothen, C. 1999. Chemical castration—breaking the cycle of paraphiliac recidivism. *Social Justice* 26, 139.

Merriam-Webster. 1997. *Merriam-Webster's Collegiate Dictionary.* Springfield, MA: Merriam-Webster, 457.

Miller, J. M., and L. Selva. 1994. Drug enforcements double-edged sword: An assessment of asset forfeiture programs. *Justice Q.* 11, 313.

Molett, M. T., L. Arnold, and W. J. Meyer. 2001. Commitment as an adjunct to sex offender treatment. *Current Opinion in Psychiatry* 14, 549.

Morris, N., and M. Tonry. 1990. *Crime and Justice: A Review of Research*, vol. 12. Chicago: University of Chicago Press, 123.

MyLawyer.com. 2004. Fines, license suspensions, and traffic school. Nolo.com, www.lawguide.com/mylawyer/guideview.asp?layer=3&article=632, accessed September 6, 2005.

Neff, C. 2005. Parent identifies sex offender at school. *The Tribune*, May 4, www.sanluisobispo.com, accessed May 5, 2005.

New York Times News Service. 1997. "Chemical castration" OK'd for Montana inmates. *NewStandard*, April 27, http://www.s-t.com/daily/04-97/04-27-97/a09wn032.htm, accessed September 19, 2006.

New Zealand Ministry of Justice. 2000. Review of monetary penalties in New Zealand: Issues for fines and infringement fines. http:www.justice.govt.nz/pubs/reports/2000/review_money/chapter_5.htm, accessed August 24, 2005.

Nichols, J. L., and H. L. Ross. 1990. The effectiveness of legal sanctions in dealing with drinking drivers. *Alcohol, Drugs, and Driving* 6, 33.

Nolan, J. 2005. Perspective: Tracking convicted sex offenders poses problems for law enforcement. *Perspective* April 8.

OPPAGA. 2000. *The Sexually Violent Predator Program's Assessment Process Continues to Evolve.* Tallahassee, FL: Office of Program Policy Analysis and Government Accountability, Report 99-36.

Petrunik, M. G. 2002. Managing unacceptable risk: Sex offenders, community response, and social policy in the United States and Canada. *Intern. J. Offender Therapy and Comp. Criminology* 46, 483.

Presser, L., and E. Gunnison. 1999. Strange bedfellows: Is sex offender notification a form of community justice? *Crime and Delinquency* 45, 299.

Rasmussen, D., and B. Benson. 1994. *A Review of Program Evaluations.* Report prepared for the Florida Corrections Commission, http://www/fcc.state.fl.us/fcc/reports/intermed/ch2.html, accessed September 15, 2005, 134.

Richmond, T. 2005. Senate approves releasing juvenile sex offenders' identities. *Duluth News Tribune*, April 12, www.duluthsuperior.com, accessed May 5, 2005.

Roos, J. 2005a. Hormone therapy for offenders rarely used. *Des Moines Register*, April 5, desmoinesregister.com, accessed May 5, 2005.

Roos, J. 2005b. Lawmakers weigh "two strikes" provision. *Des Moines Register*, April 8, desmoinesregister.com, accessed May 5, 2005.

Royes, D. 2005. Chemical castration rarely being ordered. *Tallahassee Democrat*, May 31, www.Tallahassee.com, accessed June 27, 2005.

Runquist, L. A. 2002. Intermediate sanctions—FINAL regulations. Runquist and Zybach, http://runquist.com/article_intermedsancts.htm, accessed May 24, 2005.

Russell, S. 1997. Castration of repeat sexual offenders: an international comparative analysis. *Houston J. Intern. L.* 19, 425.

Saxonhouse, E. 2004. Unequal protection: comparing former felons' challenges to disenfranchisement and employment discrimination. *Stanford L. Rev.* 56, 1597.

Seibel, J. 2005. "Amie's Law" on the books: Legislation allows notification of juvenile sex offenders. Journal Sentinel Online, May 2, www.jsonline.com, accessed May 5, 2005.

Serrill, M. S. 1983. Castration or incarceration? Three rapists face what critics call a cruel and useless punishment. *Time*, 122, December 12, 70.

Shaffrey, M. M. 2005. *Congress considers Jessica Lunsford Act to Protect Children.* Journal Washington Bureau. http://findcarrie.conforums.com/index.cgi?board=murder1&num=1111286889&action=display&start=75, accessed June 12, 2007.

Shatzkin, K. 1998. Frustrated magistrates use old fashioned "shame" sentencing minor criminals. Reprinted from the April 26, 1998, issue of the *Los Angeles Times Orange County Edition*, www.worldfreeinternet.net/news/nws106.htm, accessed June 21, 2005.

Smith, K. L. 1998-1999. Making pedophiles take their medicine: California's chemical castration law. *Buffalo Public Interest L. J.* 17, 124.

Solem v. Helm. 1983.463 U.S. 277, 285, n.10.

Spalding, L. H. 1998. Florida's 1997 chemical castration law: A return to the Dark Ages. *Florida State University L. Rev.*, www.law.fsu.edu/journals/lawreview/frames/252/spaltxt.html, accessed June 21, 2005.

Spencer, J. R. 2000. Naming and shaming young offenders. *Cambridge L. J.* 59, 466.

Stalans, L. J. 2004. Adult sex offenders on community supervision: A review of recent assessment strategies and treatment. *Criminal Justice and Behavior* 31, 564.

Stern, E. 2005. Legislature to focus on sex offenders. California Legislative Council, www.modbee.com, accessed May 5, 2005.

Stonecypher, L. 2000. A strange cure for rape. *Kudzu Monthly*, www.kudzumonthly.com, accessed June 21, 2005.

Sutherland, E. H., and D. Cressey. 1978. *Criminology*, 10th ed. Philadelphia: J. B. Lippincott, 324.

Tashima, H. N., and W. D. Marelich. 1989. *A Comparison of the Relative Effectiveness of Alternative Sanctions for First and Repeat DUI Offenders.* Report No. 122. Sacramento, CA: Department of Motor Vehicles.

Tate v. Short. 1971.

Taxman, F. S., and A. Piquero. 1998. On preventative drunk driving recidivism: An examination of rehabilitation and punishment approaches. *J. Criminal Justice* 26, 129.

Taylor, L. 2005a. Bad drunk driving laws, false evidence, and a fading constitution. DUI Blog, www.duiblog.com, accessed June 21.

Taylor, L. 2005b. New DUI law: Inaccurate breath tests are OK. DUI Blog, duiblog.com, accessed June 21.

Tibet Online. 2005. Birth control policies in Tibet. http://www.Tibet.org/Activism/Rights/birthcontrol.html, accessed September 24, 3.

Tittle, C. R., J. Bratton, and M. G. Gertz. 2003. A test of a micro-level application of shaming theory. *Social Problems* 50, 592.

Traffic Tech. 2000. Evaluation of vehicle impoundment on suspended and revoked drivers in California. *Technology Transfer Series*, No. 218. National Highway and Traffic Safety Administration, April, 1.

Turner, S., and J. Petersilia. 1996. *Work Release: Recidivism and Corrections Costs in Washington State: Research in Brief.* Washington, DC: National Institute of Justice, 1.

U.S. Department of Treasury. 2005. *About Forfeiture.* Executive Office for Asset Forfeiture, U.S. Department of the Treasury, http://www.ustreas.gov/offices/enforcement/teoaf/about-forfeiture.shtm, accessed September 23, 1.

University of New Mexico Institute for Social Research. 2002. *Review of the Literature: Best Practices and the State of New Mexico.* Albuquerque: University of New Mexico Institute for Social Research Center for Applied Research and Analysis.

Voas, R. B., and D. J. De Young. 2002. *Accident Analysis and Prevention* 15, 263–270.

Voas, R. B., and D. A. Fisher. 2001. Court procedures for handling intoxicated drivers. *Alcohol Res. and Health* Winter, 4.

Votey, H., and P. Shapiro. 1983. Highway accidents in Sweden: Modeling the process drunken driving behavior and control. *Accident Anal. and Prev.* 15, 523.

WFTV. 2005. Sex offender forced to move out of neighborhood, but can visit. www.wftv.com, accessed May 5, 2005.

Wikipedia. 2005. Fines. http//en.wikipedia.org/wiki/Fines, accessed September 8.

Wilson, F. T. 2004. Out of sight, out of mind: An analysis of *Kansas v. Crane* and the fine line between civil and criminal sanctions. *Prison J.* 84, 379.

Winterfield, L. A., and S. T. Hillsman. 1993. *The Staten Island Day-Fine Project.* Washington, DC: U.S. Department of Justice Office of Justice Programs, National Institute of Justice.

Worzella, D. 1992. The Milwaukee Municipal Court Day-Fine Project, in *Issues and Practices in Criminal Justice*, ed. D. C. McDonald, J. Green, and C. Worzella, 61-76. Washington, DC, National Institute of Justice.

Zhang, L., and S. Zhang. 2004. Reintegrative shaming and predatory delinquency. *J. Res. Crime and Delin.* 41, 433.

The Death Penalty: The Movement toward Worldwide Abolition

5

ROGER HOOD

Contents

5.1 Introduction

I have chosen *the death penalty* rather than *capital punishment* as the title of this contribution simply because the existence in common or statute law of the punishment of death for a criminal offense does not necessarily mean that sentences of death will be imposed, nor if they are imposed that they will be enforced by execution. Even where a sentence of death is mandatory in law, ways are often found to avoid imposing it, for example, by accepting a plea to a lesser noncapital charge. Where it is discretionary, relatively few may be sentenced to death, and even those who are may have their sentences commuted to lengthy terms of imprisonment. Thus, the "sentence to death" may have a far greater impact as a symbol than it has as a punishment that in practice leads ultimately to the extinction of life. Indeed, in colonial America, some persons were sentenced to death but only placed on the scaffold so as to make them experience the disgrace of it and after several hours brought down again (Banner 2002: 76). In contemporary China, an unknown, but probably quite substantial, proportion of those sentenced to death have their sentence suspended for two years on condition of good conduct while in custody. If they do not misbehave, the sentence is commuted to a long period of imprisonment. In Europe, Belgium retained the death penalty on its statute book until 1996, even though no one had been executed since 1918 (for a war crime), and no one for an ordinary crime since 1863 (Toussaint 1999: 20). Then there is the issue of appeals to be taken into account. In the United States, for instance, it has been shown that two-thirds of all death sentences imposed between 1973 and 1995 were overturned on appeal (Liebman et al. 2000: 1844–1850). Thus, the number of persons executed in the United States has only been a small fraction of those originally sentenced to death.

Nevertheless, while the death penalty exists in law, the threat of death as a criminal sanction nearly always carries with it the possibility of execution. As a consequence, prisoners often have to endure during the processes of appeal and clemency proceedings the uncertainty of whether their life will be forfeited. The fact that these proceedings may last for many years while the convicted person awaits his or her fate—the so-called "death row phenomenon"—is a potent aspect of the death penalty,[1] whether or not it is followed by capital punishment. It is for these reasons that this chapter deals with the broader question of the sanction of death, rather than the narrower issue of execution.

5.2 Slow Beginnings

From ancient times until the latter part of the eighteenth century and in all parts of the world, the threat of punishment by death had been widely accepted as the most effective penal weapon of social control. As the historian Stuart Banner has put it:

> The primary purpose of capital punishment was the emphatic display of power, a reminder of what the state could do to those

[1] According to an estimate made by the human rights researcher, Mark Warren, there are between 19,474 and 25,546 persons worldwide under sentence of death, although the number could well be higher. See Amnesty International, *Death Penalty News,* May 2006.

who broke its laws ... The link between cause and effect, between the commission of the crime and the imposition of the death sentence was made as conspicuous as it could be (2002: 13).

In many countries during the seventeenth and eighteenth centuries, death became the appointed punishment for an ever-widening range of offenses, varying enormously in their gravity. For example, in 1810 there were some 220 capital offenses in England. There was no proportionality between the crime committed and the punishment threatened. Every felony, with the exception of petty larceny and maiming, could be punished by death. This was "the bloody code." But whether the offender actually suffered death was practically a lottery. For many, the sentence was commuted to transportation overseas.

Methods of execution had been gruesome and calculated as a public spectacle to inflict terror but also to convey to the audience the consequences of living an immoral life (Banner 2002: 43). In European countries in the seventeenth and eighteenth centuries, criminals were "broken on the wheel" or "with the wheel" (Evans 1996: chap. 5); pressed under weights; boiled to death in oil; torn with red-hot pincers and then torn limb from limb by horses; hanged, drawn, and quartered; or drowned. They were sometimes subject to additional torture in the process. Heads and whole bodies were put on display until they rotted. Such "hanging in chains" or "gibbeting" did not, for example, cease in England until 1832 (Gatrell 1994: 268). In America during colonial times, there were "degrees of death" varying from hanging on the gallows to burning at the stake, dismemberment, or dissection (Banner 2002: 54). In China, convicted offenders were sometimes sawn in half or flayed while alive, or suffered "death by a thousand cuts" (Scott [1950] 1965: chaps. 12–14).

The movement to abolish the death penalty had its roots in the liberal utilitarian and humanistic ideas spawned by the Enlightenment in Europe at the end of the eighteenth century. Cesare Beccaria's famous treatise *On Crimes and Punishments,* published in 1764, advocated the replacement of the bloody code with a graduated system of punishments proportionate to the gravity of the crimes committed: a system that would ensure greater certainty and consistency of punishments meted out in an equitable way. Beccaria argued that the death penalty was both inhumane and ineffective, in that it not only contributed to uncertainty of punishment but also sent out to society the wrong moral message, namely, that it extolled the very practice that the law was trying to prohibit: killing as revenge. It was recognized that death was a disproportionate punishment for crimes less serious than murder, for such a system drew no moral distinction between these crimes and murder and provided no incentive for an offender to choose not to murder but to commit instead a lesser crime, which would not be visited by death. Juries had become reluctant to send people to their deaths for property offenses. Thus, from a utilitarian standpoint, to threaten capital punishment that would only be rarely and haphazardly inflicted was bound to be a less effective deterrent than a more certain and proportionate punishment that was recognized as legitimate by citizens in general and therefore more likely to be enforced. And as for the wide scope of the death penalty, even one of the most vigorous proponents of capital punishment, the English Victorian judge Sir James Stephen, declared: "There is nothing that it is worthwhile to protect at the cost of human life, except human life itself, or the existence of government and society" (Radzinowicz 1968: 339).

Although the question of whether the death penalty should be restricted to fewer crimes and finally abolished altogether was debated widely and with passion in Europe and America (North and South) during the nineteenth century, progress was only achieved gradually and indeed slowly. Leaving aside the short periods of abolition introduced by the liberal rulers of Tuscany and Austria in the 1780s, it was in America that the movement first made a permanent mark. In 1794, the state of Pennsylvania was the first to restrict capital punishment to only the most serious types of murder: felonious murder in the first degree. By the 1860s, the death penalty had been restricted to murder throughout the northern states of the United States, in most parts of Germany, and in England and Wales.[2] In the southern states of the United States, though, it remained a potent punishment for rape and several other offenses against persons and property, such as arson, robbery, and burglary. According to Stuart Banner, between 1870 and 1950, 701 of the 777 people of identified race who were executed for rape were black: "The death penalty was a means of racial control" (2002: 230).

In 1846, Michigan became the first modern state to abolish the death penalty for murder, soon followed by Rhode Island and Wisconsin. As early as 1867, Illinois, followed by most other states, abandoned the mandatory imposition of capital punishment for first-degree murder, so that juries had discretion whether or not to impose it. In South America, Venezuela became the first nation state to abolish the death penalty for all crimes in 1863, and in Europe, Portugal led the way in abolishing it for murder in 1867, followed by the Netherlands, Romania, Italy (it was reinstated by the Fascists in 1927), and Norway. After the First World War, they were joined by Sweden, Denmark, and Switzerland and, after the defeat of their Fascist governments in the Second World War, by Italy in 1947 and the Federal Republic of Germany in 1949.

---

[2] Leaving aside crimes against the state: treason, piracy, and arson in the royal dockyards.

Nevertheless, the plain fact is that by 1957, there were still only ten countries that had abolished capital punishment for all crimes in all circumstances: seven of them being in South America, with (West) Germany being the only large European state that had done so.[3] In addition, a further nine western European countries had abolished capital punishment for murder and other "ordinary" crimes in peacetime: nineteen countries in all, less than a fifth of the U.N. member states.[4] By 1966, the year that the International Covenant on Civil and Political Rights (ICCPR) was approved by the United Nations General Assembly (it did not come into force until March 1976), the number of abolitionist countries still only numbered twenty-six. It was to be another eleven years before the last execution took place in western Europe—in France in 1977.

According to Marc Ancel, the distinguished French jurist, abolition had usually been achieved over time, through a gradual "testing of the waters," so to speak:

> The process of abolition has usually taken a long time and followed a distinctive pattern; first the reduction of the number of crimes legally punishable by death until only murder (and sometimes) treason are left, then systematic use of commutation, leading to *de facto* abolition, and eventual abolition *de jure* (Hood 2002: 24).

It is true that he was not arguing that such a slow step-by-step process was the only way in which abolition could be achieved. Nevertheless, his words were widely interpreted as a normative prescription for how to achieve abolition. Furthermore, he did not take the absolutist position that capital punishment could never be justified. He stated, as if it were not to be doubted, just forty-three years ago, that:

> Even the most convinced abolitionists realise that there may be special circumstances, or particularly troublous times, which justify the introduction of the death penalty for a limited period (Ancel 1962: 3).

---

[3] Venezuela (1863), San Marino (1865), Costa Rica (1877), Ecuador (1906), Uruguay (1907), Colombia (1910), Panama (1922), Iceland (1928), Federal Republic of Germany (1949), Honduras (1956).
[4] Portugal (1867), Netherlands (1870), Norway (1905), Sweden (1921), Denmark (1933) Switzerland (1942), Italy (1947), Finland (1949), Austria (1950). Plus nine states in the United States, two in Australia, and twenty-four in Mexico.

Table 5.1   Status of the Death Penalty at the End of 1988, 1998, 2003, and Mid-June 2007

	Completely abolitionist	Abolitionist for ordinary crimes	Retentionist, but abolitionist *de facto* (ADF)	Actively retentionist
31 December 1988 (180 countries)	35 (19%)	17 (9%)	27 (15%)	101 (56%)
31 December 1998 (193 countries)	70 (36%)	11 (6%)	34 (18%)	78 (40%)
31 December 2003 (194 countries)	79 (41%)	12 (6%)	41 (21%)	62 (32%)
Mid-June 2007 (196 countries)	90 (46%)	9 (5%)	42 (21%)	55 (28%)

5.3   A Leap Forward

Over the next twenty years, the pace of change towards countries adopting abolition was unspectacular but steady: roughly one nation state a year abandoned capital punishment. Then things began to change dramatically. Indeed, there was a transformation. On average, over the twelve years 1988 to 1999, more than three countries a year did so. The pace has slackened a little since then, but has shown no sign, as some have predicted, of coming to a halt (Radzinowicz 1999: 293). As can be seen in Table 5.1, the proportion of countries that were "actively retentionist" (i.e., those that had carried out at least one judicial execution within the past ten years and that had not subsequently declared a permanent moratorium on executions) had fallen from 56 percent in 1988 to 28 percent in June 2007.

Over the same period, the proportion of states that were abolitionist (either for all crimes or for ordinary crimes in peacetime) increased from 28 percent to 51 percent. Also to be observed, especially in relation to Ancel's reservations in 1962, was the enormous increase in the number of countries that had become abolitionist for all crimes in all circumstances, in peacetime as well as wartime, in civilian and military law. In 1988, they numbered thirty-five (67 percent of the fifty-two abolitionist states) but, by June 2007, ninety (91 percent of the ninety-nine abolitionist countries). A list of retentionist and abolitionist countries as of June 2007 can be found in the appendix to this chapter.

Noticeable also is the larger number of retentionist countries that are usually classified as abolitionist *de facto* because no executions had been carried out for at least ten years, or even if executions had been carried out, a moratorium on executions had subsequently been declared and enforced, such as in Russia. However, it must be recognized that not all these countries listed as abolitionist *de facto* are in fact committed to moving towards abolition. Those in the Commonwealth Caribbean, for example, have been thwarted in their desire to proceed with executions only by the sterling work of human rights lawyers in bringing their cases before the Judicial Committee of the Privy Council in London. Other jurisdictions may resume executions after many years. For example, in the United States, Connecticut carried out an execution in 2005, forty-five years after the previous execution, and the U.S. federal government renewed executions after a thirty-eight-year pause when it executed Timothy McVeigh in 2001 after his conviction for the exceptionally egregious Oklahoma City bombing. Nevertheless, thirty, over two-thirds, of the forty-two countries listed in Table 5.1 as *de facto* abolitionist in mid-2006 are regarded by Amnesty International as retaining the death penalty *de jure* yet with no intention of ever carrying out an execution; thus, they are truly abolitionist in spirit and in eventual intention.

Abolition has spread across all of Europe to include all members of the Council of Europe and of the European Union (EU).[5] Belarus is the only European state to retain the death penalty. But as it has applied for membership in the Council of Europe, it can confidently be expected that abolition will come soon. Outside of Europe, it has spread to states in south central Asia. Turkmenistan has completely expunged capital punishment from its laws. Neighboring Kazakhstan, Kyrgyzstan, and Tajikistan have imposed moratoria with a view to abolition, as has Russia since 1996; the president of Uzbekistan has announced that his country will embrace abolition in 2008. Only three small countries in South and Central America retain the death penalty, and all of them can now be regarded as abolitionist *de facto*, not having carried out an execution for at least ten years (Belize, Suriname, and Guyana). When the first edition of my book *The Death Penalty: A Worldwide Perspective* was published in 1988, I could record no abolitionist country in the African region.[6] Now there are fourteen, and a further twenty-one where no judicial executions have been carried out for a decade. There are signs that abolition may come soon to Kenya, Sierra Leone, and possibly Ghana. What is striking about this development is that abolition has usually been achieved swiftly within a few years, often without

---

[5] The Council of Europe was set up in 1949 and now has forty-six member states. It aims "to defend human rights, parliamentary democracy and the rule of law and promote awareness of a European identity based on shared values and standardized social and legal practices." According to the EU Web site: "The European Union (EU) is a family of democratic European countries, committed to working together for peace and prosperity. It is not a State intended to replace existing states, but it is more than any other international organisation. The EU is, in fact, unique. Its Member States have set up common institutions to which they delegate some of their sovereignty so that decisions on specific matters of joint interest can be made democratically at European level. This pooling of sovereignty is also called 'European integration.'"

[6] Which includes Mauritius and the Seychelles.

a country going through all the stages over a considerable period of time, as previously identified by Ancel.

Although in about thirty countries capital punishment can still be imposed according to law for certain dangerous drug offenses, in about the same number of countries for sexual offenses, and in about a dozen countries for nonviolent serious property or economic offenses, the trend has been either to reduce significantly—in some of them to zero—the number of executions for such crimes or to abolish the death penalty completely for them. For example, the new Belarus Criminal Code of 1999 appointed the death penalty for fifteen fewer offenses (in fourteen rather than twenty-nine articles) than had the Code of 1960, and it can now only be imposed "when it is dictated by special aggravating circumstances as well as an exceptional danger posed by the offender." In 2001, the U.N. Human Rights Committee, on receiving a report from the Democratic People's Republic of Korea (North Korea), welcomed the reduction of capital offenses from thirty-three to five "as well as the readiness ... confirmed by the delegation, further to review the issue of capital punishment with a view to its abolition" (United Nations 2000-2001: 99). In China, there has yet to be any reduction in the wide range of offenses—sixty-eight—for which the death penalty may be imposed, but the matter of abolishing the death penalty for all economic crimes is now being openly debated, and a book of essays entitled *The Road to Abolition*, as a signifier of the final goal, was published by the People's Security University Press in 2004 (Bingzhi 2004). In early 2006, consideration of further restricting the scope of capital punishment by abolishing it for economic offenses was also raised in Vietnam. In addition, there has been progress in eliminating mandatory capital statutes, notably in countries of the Commonwealth Eastern Caribbean and in Uganda and Malawi.[7]

Another useful index of change is whether countries that had abolished the death penalty reintroduced it and, whether once having reintroduced it, they carried out executions. This has happened only once. Six years after abolishing capital punishment in 1987, the Philippines Parliament voted to reinstate it, and for ten categories of crime in forty-six defined circumstances. Seven executions were carried out in 1999 and 2000 but no more until the death penalty was abolished again in June 2006, by overwhelming majorities of both the Senate and Congress, with the full support of the president. Gambia and Papua New Guinea both reintroduced the power to impose death sentences in 1991 and 1995, respectively, but no executions have fol-

[7] The U.N. Human Rights Committee in *Carpo v. The Philippines* (No. 1077/2002) held that the mandatory imposition of the death penalty for the broadly defined offense of murder by Article 48 of the Revised Penal Code of the Philippines violated Article 6 of the ICCPR. Views adopted 28 March 2003. For the situation in the Caribbean, see *The Queen v. Peter Hughes* (2002) UKPC 12 para 30; *Patrick Reyes v. The Queen* (2002) UKPC 11, para 43; and *Lambert Watson v. The Queen* (2004) UKPC 34.

lowed. The same is true for the American states of Kansas and New York, which reinstated the death penalty over ten years ago (1994 and 1995, respectively). In both these states, the death penalty statutes were found to violate procedural constitutional requirements in 2003 and 2004, respectively. The legislature of New York has no plans to resuscitate capital punishment.[8]

It is also highly significant that the death penalty was excluded as a punishment by the U.N. Security Council when it established the International Criminal Tribunal in 1993 to deal with atrocities in the former Yugoslavia and, in 1994, the International Criminal Tribunal for Rwanda. Nor is it available as a sanction for genocide, other grave crimes against humanity, and war crimes in the Statute of the International Criminal Court established in 1998.

5.4   The Decline of Executions

As regards the implementation of the death penalty, even among the fifty-six countries that have carried out an execution within the decade ending in 2006, no more than forty-two of them had executed anyone within the five years 2002–2006. For 2006, Amnesty International received reports of executions in only twenty-five countries. And, as far as can be ascertained—and one must read this with a severe "health warning," as many are merely estimates—only twenty-six of these countries executed ten or more people over this period; the other thirteen countries averaged less than two executions each a year. As can be seen from Table 5.2, only eight nations are known to have executed at least a hundred, an average of twenty or more persons a year: China (by far the largest number, the true figure being unknown, as it is a state secret), Democratic Republic of the Congo, Iran, Pakistan, Saudi Arabia (with the highest number per head of population), United States, Vietnam, and Yemen.

Furthermore, there is evidence to suggest that where the abolitionist movement has not persuaded retentionist countries to abandon capital punishment, it may have been responsible in many of them for modifying the frequency with which they have had recourse to executions. Comparing the five years 1994–1998 with 2001–2005, it appears that there were very substantial falls in the number of known executions in several countries, most notably: China, from 12,338 to 7,366; Nigeria, from 248 to 1; Belarus, from 168 to around 12; Singapore, from 242 to 45; Sierra Leone, from 71 to 0; and

[8] See the report of The Committee on Capital Punishment of the Association of the Bar of the City of New York, *Empire State Injustice ... How New York's Death Penalty System Fails to Meet Standards for Accuracy and Fairness,* January 2005. Available at www.death-penaltyinfo.org.

Table 5.2   Judicial Executions Recorded by Amnesty International during the Five Years 2002-2006

Country	Total known executions 2002–2006	Annual average number per million population (2004 estimates)
China	7,736	1.12
Democratic Republic of Congo	215	0.68
Iran	651	1.74
Pakistan	144	0.17
Saudi Arabia	256	1.91
Singapore	45	2.04
United States	308	0.21
Texas	123	1.17
Oklahoma	34	1.94
Vietnam	197	0.46
Yemen	100	1.20

Taiwan, from 121 to 22. And within the past several years, executions have continued to fall. To take some examples: The number of executions in Belarus fell from 29 in 1999 to 0 in 2006. There were 22 executions in Egypt in 2000, but only four were reported in 2006. Forty-one executions were carried out in the province of Taiwan in 1999 and 2000, but none in 2006. The figures for Singapore (the country that had made by far the greatest use of capital punishment in relation to the size of its population—as high as 13.85 per million per annum in the years 1994 to 1998)[9] show a similar sharp downward trend—43 in 1999 to 19 in 2003 and five in 2006. As a result, the annual average number of executions in Singapore has fallen to 2.04 per million in the years 2002–2006.

Executions in public were discontinued in most Western countries in the second half of the nineteenth century (Banner 2002: 136).[10] Yet since 1994, public executions have been carried out in at least seventeen countries, including Iran, Saudi Arabia, and Nigeria. In China, the condemned have been displayed and humiliated in public arenas before large crowds before being taken to the execution grounds to be shot in the head. The U.N. Human Rights Committee has condemned such spectacles as "incompatible with human dignity." Although since 1977 there has been a growing trend to adopt

[9] See United Nations, Economic and Social Council. Capital punishment and implementation of the safeguards guaranteeing protection of the rights of those facing the death penalty. Report of the Secretary-General, UN Docs. E/2005/3, Table 2, 13.

[10] They still persisted in Kentucky in the United States until 1936, when a man was hanged for rape "before a crowd of between 10 and 20 thousand" [Banner 2002: 136], and until 1939 in France, when the last person was guillotined in Paris, as well as in Germany and Italy during the war years.

lethal injection (in thirty-seven of thirty-eight U.S. states, in Taiwan, in Thailand, in some provinces of China, and in the Philippines prior to abolition in 2006), offenders are still decapitated in public in Saudi Arabia; are hanged in public in Iran; and may be stoned to death (for adultery) in Iran, Sudan, and in Northern Nigeria.

5.5   Generating a Worldwide Movement

Why have so many countries joined the movement to remove the death penalty from their armory of penal sanctions over the last twenty years or so? And why have so many of them now become such ardent campaigners for abolition worldwide, even though some of them carried out executions well within living memory? Several countries have only signalled their complete rejection of capital punishment since the mid-1990s, the United Kingdom being one of them, when it abolished the death penalty for treason and piracy and for all offenses under military law as late as 1998, some thirty years after it had abolished it for murder. Executions were still being carried out in east European countries that are now abolitionist until less than (and, in some instances, much less than) twenty years ago: for example, in Croatia until 1987; Hungary and Poland, 1988; Bulgaria, 1989; Estonia, 1991; Azerbaijan, 1993; Georgia, 1994; Lithuania, 1995; and the Ukraine, 1997. Russia, which has yet formally to abolish capital punishment, has had a moratorium on executions in place only since 1996, and not until 1999 were all death sentences commuted to life imprisonment.

The dynamo for the new wave of abolition was the development of international human rights law, arising in the aftermath of the Second World War and the emergence of countries from totalitarian imperialism and colonialism. This created a climate in which citizens of the new democracies readily embraced the notion that citizens should be protected from the power of the state and the tyranny of the opinions of the masses. But although democratization in eastern Europe and elsewhere has clearly been influential, it cannot explain abolition entirely, for three leading democracies, the United States, India, and Japan, retain it. Foremost among the factors that have promoted this new wave of abolition has been the political movement to transform consideration of capital punishment from an issue to be decided solely or mainly as an aspect of national criminal justice policy to the status of a fundamental violation of human rights: not only the right to life, but the right to be free of excessive, repressive, and tortuous punishments (Zimring 2003; Neumayer 2005). This approach rejects the most persistent of the justifications for capital punishment, as described by Richard Evans in his monumental work *Rituals of Retribution:*

> Fundamentally the most powerful and persistent motive for execution has always been retribution, the belief that death can be the only adequate expiation for certain crimes, the feeling that lesser punishments are insufficient, the conviction that those who commit the most serious offenses must pay for them by suffering the ultimate penalty, death (1996: vii).

And it also rejects the utilitarian justification that nothing less severe can act as a sufficient general deterrent to those who contemplate committing capital crimes. This is not only because abolitionists believe that the social science evidence does not support the case for deterrence but also because they would reject the deterrence argument even if it could be shown that there was some evidence in favor of it. They would argue that such deterrence could only be achieved by high rates of execution, mandatorily enforced, and that this would lead to the unjust execution of people who, because of the mitigating circumstances in which their crimes were committed, do not deserve to die. They would also argue that it is precisely when there are strong reactions to serious crimes that the use of the death penalty as an instrument of crime control is most dangerous. Pressure on the police and prosecutors to bring offenders to justice, especially those suspected of committing outrages, is likely to lead to shortcuts, breaches of procedural protections, and simple myopia in investigation once a suspect is identified.

For instance, a Japanese abolitionist lawyer has reported that "almost half of death row inmates were indicted after interrogation without the presence of a lawyer at the police investigation stage'" (Yasuda 2004: 215, 220). And Anatoly Pristavkin, the famous Russian writer, former head of Russia's Pardons Commission, and ardent abolitionist, has stated that prominent jurists in Russia had estimated that wrongful convictions amounted to between 10 and 15 percent of those sentenced to death (1999: 129–137). Similarly, in England, the wrongful convictions of Irishmen following terrorist outrages turned even strong supporters of a return to capital punishment against the idea (Hood 2002: 26). In the United States, investigative journalists uncovered cases of wrongful conviction that had passed through all the lengthy appeal processes without such errors being spotted and in which, with the aid of DNA, convincing evidence of innocence has been forthcoming. The problem appears to be endemic to the systematic use of the death penalty and not simply a reflection of this or that fault in the administration of criminal justice in a particular country. For many abolitionists, even the smallest possibility that an innocent person could be executed would be unacceptable.

More fundamentally, abolitionists who have embraced the doctrine of the right to life would argue that the means could never justify the ends and that the control of serious crime is more appropriately and better achieved through tackling the factors that contribute to it, rather than relying on the inhumane punishment of putting people to death.

5.6 The Developments of Institutions Committed to Abolition

As Leon Radzinowicz pointed out, the crusade against the death penalty has, from its conception, been conceived as a universal goal (1999: 281–282). But it was difficult to achieve without the development of political institutions and international covenants committed to making it a reality. In the long process, lasting from 1948 until 1966, when the International Covenant on Civil and Political Rights was adopted by the U.N. General Assembly (it did not come into force until ten years later), the question of capital punishment in relation to the right to life was keenly debated. What emerged was a compromise allowing for "limited retention," for, as mentioned above, only a minority of states at that time had embraced the abolitionist position. Article 6(1), the draft of which had been agreed to in 1957, stated: "Every human being has the inherent right to life. This right shall be protected by law. No one shall be arbitrarily deprived of his life," and Article 6(2) stated: "In countries that have not abolished the death penalty, sentence of death may be imposed only for the most serious crimes in accordance with the law in force at the time of the commission of the crime ...." In the circumstances pertaining in 1957, it was hardly surprising that it was not possible to define more precisely those offenses for which capital punishment could be retained. Certainly some countries would have preferred a clearer enumeration of the crimes for which it would remain permissible to impose the death penalty instead of relying on the concept of "most serious" (Schabas 2002: 105). This is probably because they recognized that "most serious" could be interpreted differently according to national culture, tradition, and political complexion—the very antithesis of the notion of an attempt to create a *universal* declaration and definition of human rights.

In fact, the term *most serious offenses* in Article 6(2) was nothing more than a "marker" for the policy of moving towards abolition through restriction. Far from indicating that those countries that had not abolished the death penalty could proceed under the protection of Article 6(2), as several countries have subsequently argued, the chairman of the Working Party drafting Article 6 stated: "It is interesting to note that the expression: 'in countries that have not abolished the death penalty' was intended to show *the direction* in which the drafters of the Covenant hoped that the situation would develop," as was the addition of Article 6(6), namely that "Nothing in this article shall be invoked to delay or prevent the abolition of capital punishment by any State party to the present Covenant" (Rodley 2004: 125). The very notion of "progressive restriction" makes it clear that the degree of "seriousness" that would justify the death penalty would need to be evaluated and re-evaluated, always in a narrowing of definition until abolition was eventually achieved (Schabas 2002: 68).[11]

In 1971 and again in 1977, this message, this aspiration, was reinforced by the United Nations General Assembly in resolutions that stated that the main objective of the U.N., in accordance with Article 3 of the Universal Declaration of Human Rights and Article 6 of the International Covenant on Civil and Political Rights (that "every human being has an inherent right to life") is to "progressively restrict the number of offenses for which capital punishment might be imposed, *with a view to its eventual abolition.*"

But this policy would have lacked political force had it not been taken up and insisted upon by two emerging political entities: first the Council of Europe and then the more powerful European Union. And it needed political leadership willing to accept the premises that the execution of citizens, whatever crimes they had committed, was a fundamental denial of their humanity and right to existence, whatever objections might be raised by an appeal to public opinion.

The first move to put this into treaty form, so as to ensure that countries that abolished the death penalty did not reinstate it and to emphasize that the issue was embraced by the right to life, came when the countries of the Council of Europe resolved in 1983 to establish Protocol No. 6 to the European Convention for the Protection of Human Rights and Fundamental Freedoms (ECHR), which abolished the death penalty in peacetime (it came into effect in 1984). Note the date: This was eight years after the U.S. Supreme Court had, in the *Gregg* decision of 1976, affirmed the constitutionality of the new capital punishment statutes that replaced those that it had struck

---

[11] The Human Rights Committee of the UN has, of course, stated that the concept of "the most serious" "must be read restrictively to mean that the death penalty should be a *quite exceptional measure*," and in line with this has, in resolutions and judgments, called for it not to be used for nonviolent financial crimes, nonviolent religious practices or expressions of conscience, sexual relations between consenting adults, drug-related offenses, illicit sex, vague categories of offenses relating to internal and external security, and aggravated robbery where no death ensued. See Schabas 2002, 106-111. The Human Rights Committee with respect to Vietnam noted that, "notwithstanding the reduction of the number of crimes that carry the death penalty from 44 to 29," it could be imposed for "opposition to order and national security violations," both of which "are excessively vague and inconsistent with Article 6(2) of the Covenant." See UN doc. A/57/40 Vol.1, 2002, 82(7), p. 68.

down in the *Furman* decision in 1972 on grounds of arbitrariness, inequity, and racial discrimination in the administration of the death penalty.

Just eighteen years ago, in 1989 (that's how recent it is), the U.N. General Assembly adopted the second optional protocol to the ICCPR, Article 1 of which stated that no one within the jurisdiction of a State party shall be executed. Clause 2 of the article established the important principle that "The death penalty shall not be re-established in States that have abolished it."[12] A year later in 1990, the General Assembly of the Organization of American States adopted the Protocol to the American Convention on Human Rights to Abolish the Death Penalty. Furthermore, any country that has abolished the death penalty and ratified the American Convention on Human Rights is forbidden by the treaty from reintroducing it.

Of particular significance was the adoption, in Vilnius, Lithuania, on 3 May 2002 of Protocol No. 13 to the ECHR. The member states of the Council of Europe resolved "to take the final step to abolish the death penalty in all circumstances, including acts committed in time of war or the imminent threat of war." By May 2007, thirty-nine countries had ratified the protocol and a further six had signed it.[13] All together, by the middle of 2006, seventy-five countries had ratified one of the international treaties or conventions that bars the imposition of capital punishment.

In other parts of the world, regional human rights movements are seeking to follow this example. Thus, in November 1999, the African Commission on Human and People's Rights, meeting in Kigali, Rwanda, "urged states to envisage a moratorium on the death penalty," and the Asian Human Rights Charter adopted in 1998 (under Article 3.7 "Right to Life") declares "all states must abolish the death penalty."

It is of course true that one reason why so many countries have ratified these treaties is because of the political and economic benefits that could be gained if they were to become members of the Council of Europe and the European Union. The pressure was put on them when, in 1994, the Council of Europe (and, four years later in 1998, the European Union) made it a condition of entry that a prospective member state place a moratorium on executions and abolish the death penalty within a short period, interpreted as three years. Important as this has been, it has to be noted that the movement to abolition in eastern Europe had begun before then, beginning with the German Democratic Republic (formerly East Germany) in 1987. In Slovenia in 1989, in the Czech and Slovak Republics in 1990, in Romania after

---

[12] Only a handful of those countries that have ratified the protocol have made a reservation allowing for the death penalty to be imposed in time of war on conviction of a most serious crime of a military nature.

[13] The only European states so far (May 2007) not to have ratified or signed Protocol No. 13 are Azerbaijan and Russia.

the fall of Ceausescu at the end of 1989, and in Hungary in 1990, capital punishment was eliminated when independence was obtained from communist rule. Even in Lithuania, where abolition took somewhat longer to achieve, it was not simply that parliamentarians in 1998 chose "national interests in strategically important international policy" (meaning the possibility of enjoying the benefits of joining the Council of Europe and the EU) over their constituents' preference for capital punishment. As the Lithuanian lawyer Aleksandras Dobryninas has put it: "The attitude to the death penalty in Lithuanian society became a test of the maturity of its democratic outlook and of citizens' willingness to rid themselves of the former totalitarian and inhumane system" (2004: 233–234).

Thus, the message being conveyed by the European confederacy of nations emphasizes its *principled* opposition to the death penalty as a violation of fundamental human rights. Both the Council of Europe and the European Union have declared, "The death penalty has no legitimate place in the penal systems of modern civilized societies, and its application may well be compared with torture and be seen as inhuman and degrading punishment … abolition of the death penalty contributes to the enhancement of human dignity and the progressive development of human rights." The language is uncompromising. The Council of Europe will not accept the argument that capital punishment can be defended on relativistic grounds of religion or culture, or as a matter that sovereign powers ought to be left to decide simply for themselves. They wish abolition to have the status of a universal human rights norm in the same way that slavery, for instance, is defined. This is reflected in the Charter of Fundamental Rights, adopted by the EU in Nice in December 2000, Article 2 of which states that "everyone has the right to life" and "No one shall be condemned to the death penalty or executed," and which also prohibits the extradition of persons charged with a capital offense to retentionist countries unless there is a firm guarantee that the death penalty will not be imposed. This policy of noncooperation has also been embraced by both the South African Constitutional Court and the Canadian Supreme Court, which stated in the case of *United States v. Burns* in 2001:

> While the evidence does not establish an international law norm against the death penalty, or against extradition to face the death penalty, it does show significant movement towards acceptance internationally of a principle of fundamental justice Canada has adopted internally, namely the abolition of capital punishment … It also shows that the rule requiring that assurances be obtained prior to extradition in death penalty cases not only accords with Canada's principled advocacy on the international level, but is also

consistent with the practice of other countries with which Canada generally invites comparison, apart from the retentionist jurisdictions of the United States.

Furthermore, the policy has been endorsed by resolution 2003/11 of the Subcommission on the Promotion and Protection of Human Rights of the U.N. Commission on Human Rights and affirmed by the Commission on Human Rights in its resolution 2004/67 of 21 April 2004. The U.N. Human Rights Committee recently held in *Judge v. Canada* (2003) that countries that had abolished the death penalty had an obligation not to expose a person to the real risks of its application, which would constitute a violation of the person's right to life under Article 6 of the International Covenant on Civil and Political Rights. The significance of this decision lies in the fact that the Committee overturned its previous decision in *Kindler v. Canada* ten years previously in 1993, stating that "since that time there has been a broadening international consensus in favor of abolition of the death penalty, and in states which have retained the death penalty, a broadening consensus not to carry it out" (para. 10.3).

Some European scholars have suggested that, notwithstanding Article 6 of the ICCPR, the time has come to recognize that Article 7, which states categorically that "no one shall be subject to torture or cruel, inhuman or degrading punishment," should be interpreted to ban capital punishment (Nowak 2002: 27, 44). Indeed, in the case of *Öcalan v. Turkey* in March 2003, the European Court of Human Rights endorsed the view that capital punishment amounts to a form of inhuman treatment that can "no longer be seen as having any legitimate place in a democratic society."

The Council of Europe and the EU have both become active in international human rights dialogues to influence so-called third countries to abandon capital punishment. There are regular Human Rights Dialogues and Seminars with China; delegations have gone, for example, to Belarus, Russia, Uzbekistan, and Vietnam. The EU has also been active in lobbying (especially, but not only, state governors in the United States) through diplomatic démarches whenever death sentences are likely to be put into effect. In October 2003, the Parliamentary Assembly of the Council of Europe found the United States and Japan (who have observer status at the Assembly) "in violation of their fundamental obligation to respect human rights due to their continued application of the death penalty." Since then, it has threatened to withdraw their special observer status. There is a further political dimension. The EU resolution on "The Death Penalty in the World" issued in July 2001, calling for a worldwide moratorium on executions, stated that this was "an essential element in relations between the European Union and third countries and one that should be taken into account in concluding agreements with third countries." Both European political entities have, of course, been supported by Amnesty International, and it should be noted that new pressure groups have emerged such as the World Coalition against the Death Penalty, which has so far organized three international congresses — in Strasbourg, Montreal, and Paris.

In particular countries, abolition has usually been achieved not by popular consensus or a demand from the masses, or as the outcome of a sudden cultural shift in social attitudes, but through political and/or judicial leadership, sometimes aided by local pressure groups. For example, in France in 1981, Francois Mitterrand, with the support of his minister of justice-to-be, Robert Badinter, pledged himself ahead of an election to abolish capital punishment despite the fact that opinion polls showed that a majority of the electorate favored retention. He was elected, the death penalty was abolished, and he was re-elected. In eastern European countries, abolition was achieved through the commitment of presidents, as in Georgia, Azerbaijan, and Turkmenistan, or through the determination of Constitutional Courts, as in Hungary and the Ukraine. Such was the course taken in South Africa, when the matter was referred by the new postapartheid government to the newly constituted Constitutional Court in 1995. In *State v. Makwanyane*, the judgment of Justice Arthur Chaskalson, president of the court, rejected "public opinion" as the yardstick for deciding the issue of the death penalty and instead emphasized the need to create in the country a "human rights culture." In a remarkable passage, he stated:

> Public opinion may have some relevance to the enquiry, but in itself is no substitute for the duty invested in the courts to interpret the Constitution and uphold its provisions without fear or favour. ... The very reason for investing the power of judicial review in the courts was to protect the rights of minorities and others who cannot protect their rights adequately through the democratic process. Those who are entitled to claim this protection include the social outcasts and marginalized people in our society. It is only if there is a willingness to protect the worst and weakest amongst us, that all of us can be secure that our own rights will be protected (*State v Makwanyane*, 1995, para. 8).

The tension that has existed on the one hand between popular opinion and its expression through the democratic process and, on the other, the need to protect individuals from the power of the state or the demands of the masses has been well expressed by the distinguished human rights lawyer William Schabas:

While it is desirable that the human rights norms that are en-shrined in international instruments and national constitutions find a favourable echo in public opinion, they surely cannot be dependent on it. Human rights instruments, whether they be international treaties or domestic constitutions, are, first and fore-most, aimed at protection of individuals from the state. Although encompassing a significant collective rights dimension, they begin with the premise that the state itself, even where it expresses the legitimate democratic aspirations of the general public, may at-tempt to oppress the individual for a number of reasons. Conse-quently, unpopular speech and belief need to be sheltered from majorities that would suppress them, ethnic minorities must be guaranteed the right to survive and resist assimilation, and ac-cused criminals require protection from unfair prosecution and biased judges. If public opinion were to be canvassed each time individual rights were in jeopardy, there would be little doubt that human rights would come out the loser. Yet it would contradict the *raison d'être* of human rights law to make its efficacy contin-gent on public opinion, one of the very forces it is aimed at counteracting and neutralising (2002: 328).

5.7   What Hope of Convincing the Remaining Retentionists?

To what extent is resistance to abolition likely to be overcome in the reason-ably near future? It appears to be embedded across Asia and, with the excep-tion of Israel (where it remains for genocide and treason during wartime), throughout the Middle East. Although Cambodia (following the fall of Pol Pot and the institution of a new constitution), Nepal, Bhutan, and the Phil-ippines are the only Asian countries so far to have abolished it, several other countries have restricted the scope and incidence of capital punishment, and the question of abolition is being increasingly voiced. Indeed, executions are reserved in India, where the current chief justice is personally opposed to capital punishment, for the "rarest of rare cases." In South Korea, where there have been no executions since 1998, a bill to abolish the death penalty has been presented before Parliament, and the National Human Rights Commit-tee has recently pronounced in favor of abolition. In Taiwan, too, the minister of justice has publicly declared that he wishes to see an end to executions within a few years. Although the Japanese government has resisted external pressures, the current minister of justice, as well as a predecessor, have declared their personal abhorrence of the death penalty, and the Federation of Bar Associations of Japan has mounted a vigorous campaign for abolition. Within the past five years, the subject has become open to academic debate in China; the Supreme People's Court has decided to review all death penalty cases itself; and with the government preparing to ratify the International Covenant of Civil and Political Rights, some further restrictions on the use of capital punishment can be expected. Even in the Middle East, executions are rare events in several countries, such as the Gulf States, and also in North Africa, including Tunisia and Morocco, neither of which have carried out a judicial execution for at least ten years. As reported in *Death Penalty News* in January 2006, the king of Jordan informed a major Italian newspaper that his country was reviewing its use of capital punishment and that it may become the first state in the region to abolish it.

On the other hand, it cannot be denied that the attempts of the abolitionist nations at United Nations congresses, in the General Assembly, and on the Commission on Human Rights to press forward for a resolution calling for a moratorium of death sentences and executions, so that the effects can be studied, has been met with hostility from many of the retentionist nations, on the grounds that the death penalty is not an issue of universal human rights and that every country should be free to determine its own legal measures and penalties to combat crime. Although there were eighty-one sponsors of the resolution for a moratorium at the U.N. Commission on Human Rights in 2005, sixty-six countries issued a joint statement dissociating themselves on the grounds that there was, in their view, no international consensus that capital punishment should be abolished.[14]

Indeed, several of these countries at different times have characterized such resolutions as a form of cultural imperialism, dictating a particular set of values. Among these countries are those Muslim states that base their criminal justice system on Islamic law. However, a scholar with a deep knowledge of the Muslim faith, the distinguished human rights criminal lawyer M. Cherif Bassiouni, has recently argued that there is nothing in the Koran or the Sunna that requires the death penalty, save perhaps for the crime of brigandage when death occurs: for all other crimes, it is optional, not mandatory. Bassiouni's view is that the interpretation of the Koran has been dominated by traditionalists and fundamentalists, whereas secular reformists and forward-thinking traditionalists would emphasize the need to interpret scripture in the light of scientific knowledge and the Islamic emphasis on mercy in order to create a just and humane society (2004: 169–185). In this regard, it is interesting to note that several secular states with large Muslim majorities have joined the abolitionist movement (Azerbaijan, Bosnia-Herze-

---

[14] See Amnesty International, Death Penalty Developments in 2005. http://web.amnesty.org/pages/deathpenalty-developments2005-eng.

govina, Turkey, Turkmenistan, and Senegal) or are abolitionist *de facto* (Tunisia and Morocco). All the signs give heart to the eventual success of the abolitionist cause.

5.8   The Importance of the United States

Although the United States has not aligned itself with those at the U.N. Human Rights Commission that have stigmatized the abolitionist movement as cultural imperialism, neither has it embraced the aspiration embodied in Article 6 of the ICCPR and U.N. resolutions to abolish the death penalty in due course. The persistence of capital punishment in the United States has become, in my opinion, one of the greatest obstacles to the acceptance of the view that this ultimate penalty inherently and inevitably involves the abuse of human rights. In China, the Caribbean, and no doubt elsewhere, proponents of capital punishment point to the United States to support their view that capital punishment is not inconsistent with democratic values and political freedom. So what prospects are there that the United States might join those nations with which it shares a cultural and political heritage in abandoning capital punishment?

The U.S. government has made its position clear in its response to the seventh U.N. survey in 2005:

> When administered in accordance with all the aforementioned safeguards, the death penalty does not violate international law. Capital punishment is not prohibited by customary international law or by any treaty provisions under which the United States is currently obligated. ... We believe that in democratic societies the criminal justice system—including the punishment prescribed for the most serious and aggravated crimes—should reflect the will of the people freely expressed and appropriately implemented through their elected representatives (U.N. doc. E/2005/3: para. 17).

What makes this attitude so potent in the United States is the embrace of "populist democracy," through which populist sentiment and the views of powerful interest groups are much more keenly felt by elected representatives, including key players in the justice system, such as public prosecutors and judges, who are often elected and subject to re-election by popular vote. Furthermore, leaving aside federal criminal law, the death penalty is a matter for state law, and it has been well documented that there has been little or no appreciation of the import of international treaties and not much, if any, concern for the opinion of foreigners. As Stuart Banner has put it in his history of the death penalty, "The state judges and prosecutors responsible for administering capital punishment were scarcely concerned that citizens of Paraguay and Germany might consider them a bloodthirsty lot"; he was referring to the cases of Angel Breard and Walter La Grand, executed while their cases were still under consideration by the International Court of Justice in relation to the denial of their right to consular assistance under Article 36 of the Vienna Convention on Consular Relations (2002: 303).

David Garland has argued that the reason why the United States, "the last nation in its peer group," has not abandoned capital punishment is not because of "long standing cultural differences" between it and other democratic Western nations that have rejected capital punishment, but rather because of a series of "proximate causes" that have acted on the United States during the time when the divergence between it and European nations over the last twenty to thirty years occurred. He was here referring to "America's distinctive institutions of federalism, popular democracy and constitutional review in the context of a conservative backlash against the *Furman* decision combined with punitive attitudes fuelled by fears of rising crime and violence." He concluded therefore that "America is the last Western nation to complete the abolition process not because of any peculiarly punitive attitudes or any deep-seated cultural commitment but because the political mechanisms for nation-wide abolition do not exist there in the form that they exist in other nations" (Garland 2005: 347). As a result, the death penalty has more of a symbolic meaning than any utilitarian justification.

The negative attitude of the United States government towards international treaties, the refusal to embrace abolition even as an ideal or distant goal (as China has done), and the hesitant approach of the Supreme Court towards claims based on international human rights norms have been significant factors in resisting change. The United States voted against the Second Optional Protocol, and when it ratified the ICCPR in 1992, it entered reservations with regard to Article 6, which prohibits the imposition of capital punishment on a person who is under the age of 18 at the time of the commission of the offense, and to Article 7, concerning cruel or unusual treatment or punishment, which it declared it would only be bound by to the extent that "cruel, inhuman or degrading treatment or punishment" means the "cruel and unusual treatment or punishment prohibited by the Fifth, Eighth, or Fourteenth Amendments to the Constitution of the United States, as interpreted by the U.S. Supreme Court."

However, the U.S. Supreme Court has recently taken notice of the international trends and development in international customary law in interpreting what it calls "evolving standards of decency." First in 2002, in *Atkins v. Virginia*, the court cited the worldwide condemnation of the practice of executing the mentally retarded, as laid down in the U.N. safeguards for those facing the death penalty, among its reasons for deciding that it should now be regarded as "cruel and unusual punishment." And then, in March 2005, the court decided by a majority in *Roper v. Simmons* that the execution of those who had committed offenses as juveniles was unconstitutional and declared that international norms and practice—it had been shown that the United States stood alone among nations in formally approving of the practice—had "provided respected and significant confirmation of the court's determination that the penalty is disproportionate punishment for offenders under 18."

Undoubtedly the weight of international opinion is being felt, as is evident in the judgments of the International Court of Justice against the United States in relation to its failure in the cases of the Paraguayan citizen Angel Breard, the German citizens Karl and Walter La Grand, and in 2005, fifty-one Mexican nationals, to fulfill its obligations under Article 36 of the Vienna Convention on Consular Relations to ensure that consular assistance is provided to foreign nationals arrested for capital and other serious crimes in the United States.[15]

An issue still to be decided by the U.S. Supreme Court is whether the length of time that persons are kept on death row (in most states, prisoners facing the prospect of execution are kept under very restrictive forms of confinement, sometimes for as long as twenty years, before the execution is carried out or an appeal is successful) amounts to cruel and unusual punishment.[16] Here too there is international precedent. In 1993, the Judicial Committee of the Privy Council in London in the case of *Pratt and Morgan v. the Attorney General of Jamaica* held that it would be cruel and degrading punishment to execute a prisoner after a period of five years under sentence of death. Lord Griffiths, delivering the judgment, said:

> There is an instinctive revulsion against the prospect of hanging a man after he has been held under sentence of death for many years. What gives rise to this instinctive revulsion? The answer can only be our humanity: we regard it as an inhuman act to

---

[15] The United States subsequently withdrew in 2005 from the Optional Protocol to the Vienna Convention, which required signatory states to allow the International Court of Justice to adjudicate on treaty obligations.

[16] Justice Breyer, in dissenting from the decision of the court not to hear an appeal from two death row inmates in 1999 (*Knight v. Florida* and *Moore v. Nebraska*), noted, "Both of these cases involve astonishing long delays ... The claim that time has rendered the execution inhuman is a particularly strong one." See the discussion under "Death Row" on the Web site of the Death Penalty Information Center: www. deathpenaltyinfo.org.

keep a man facing the agony of execution over an extended period of time … (4 All E.R. 769 at 783).

And the Canadian Supreme Court in *United States v. Burns*, when considering the death row issue in 2001, declared that "we regard it as an inhuman act to keep a man facing the agony of execution over a long extended period of time … even those who regard its horrors as self-inflicted conceded that it is a relevant consideration."

In reality, the death penalty is rarely enforced in the United States, in relation to the number of persons to whom it could potentially be applied. The substantial fall in the murder rate across the United States during the past decade, in abolitionist and retentionist jurisdictions alike, and the decline in the number of death sentences imposed (from 317 in 1996 to 128 in 2005) and the number of executions (from a high of ninety-eight in 1999 to fifty-nine in 2004 and fifty-three in 2006) suggest that a change is under way. The proportion of the population stating that they favor the death penalty has fallen from around 80 percent a decade ago to around two-thirds, and even less than half when preference can be given to life imprisonment without parole.[17] The concerns expressed in Illinois and other states about the number of innocent persons who have been sentenced to death, backed up by the incontrovertible evidence gathered by Professor Scheck and colleagues in other Innocence Projects through DNA, that truly innocent persons have been sentenced to death (and, many believe, executed), has led to moratoria on executions and commissions set up to enquire how the system may be made "foolproof" (Scheck, Neufeld, and Dwyer 2000).[18] The Illinois Commission concluded unanimously "that no system given human nature and frailties could ever be devised or constructed that would work perfectly and guarantee absolutely that no innocent person is ever sentenced to death" (Hood 2002: 72). In an extraordinary judgment in June 2002, a federal judge, Judge Rakoff, held in the Federal District Court in Manhattan that the death penalty was unconstitutional as it "not only deprives innocent people of a significant opportunity to prove their innocence, and thereby violates procedural due process, but also creates an undue risk of executing innocent people, and thereby violates substantive due process." Although this view was overturned in December 2002 by a Federal Appeals Court for the 2nd Circuit in New York on the grounds that "Binding precedents of the Supreme Court prevent us from finding capital punishment unconstitutional based solely on a statistical or theoretical possibility that a defendant might be innocent,"[19] the argument remains powerful.

[17] See News and Developments: Public Opinion at www.deathpenaltyinfo.org.
[18] See also www.deathpenaltyinfo.org/Innocentlist.html.
[19] See Amnesty International 2003.

The patent flaws in police, prosecutorial, and judicial practice, brought out so vividly in Professor Liebman and his colleagues' analysis of why such a large proportion of death sentences have been overturned, fully justified his stigmatization of capital punishment in the United States as a "broken system" (2000 and 2002).[20] Furthermore, the very high costs involved in capital trials with relatively little success for the state led the New York legislature in April 2005 to decide not to try to re-enact its death penalty statute, which the State Supreme Court had found to have constitutional flaws.

The truth is that capital punishment is becoming more and more marginal. Executions are now confined to a relatively few states. Over the five years 2002 to 2006, just twenty of the thirty-eight states with the death penalty carried out an execution (four of them only one execution, and ten more no more than four executions over the five years). In 2006, executions occurred in fourteen states, only six of them being non-Southern states: California (one), Indiana (one), Montana (one), Nevada (one), Ohio (one), and Oklahoma (4). Thus, in 2006, twenty-four states with the death penalty on their statute books did not execute anybody, and when the twelve wholly abolitionist states and the District of Columbia are added to them, 75 percent (38/51) of U.S. states had no executions in 2006. Another way of looking at this is to note that fifteen of the thirty-eight retentionist states have executed no more than six people since 1976—at the most one every four to five years, and for most of these states with much longer in between. Indeed, 80 percent of all executions have been carried out in just nine states (Texas, Virginia, Oklahoma, Missouri, North Carolina, South Carolina, Georgia, Alabama, and Florida), and over one-third in Texas alone.

Thus, the common picture of the United States, held by foreign observers, of American jurisdictions as a whole strongly supporting capital punishment is misleading. The truth is that in large parts of the country, capital punishment has no more than symbolic retributive status and certainly can have no utility as a measure of crime control. Although some scholars using the methodology of econometrics have claimed to demonstrate the marginally greater deterrent power of executions, their work has been criticized both for its methodology and the inferences drawn from the findings (Hood 2002; Fagen 2005; Donahue & Wolfers 2005).[21] But belief in the deterrent

---

[20] It should be noted that in other countries as well, the number of death sentences affirmed after appeal is usually very low. See, for example, Roger Hood and Florence Seemungal, *A Rare and Arbitrary Fate. Conviction for Murder, the Mandatory Death Penalty and the Reality of Homicide in Trinidad and Tobago* (2006). London: The Death Penalty Project, 31. Available at www.deathpenaltyproject.org.

[21] See also The Death Penalty: No Evidence for Deterrence in *The Economists' Voice*, commenting on articles by Gary Becker and Richard Posner, http://www.bepress.com/ev April 2006. See also Deterrence, News and Developments: www.deathpenaltyinfo.org/deterrence.

power of capital punishment is no longer the main reason why those Americans who support the death penalty do so. Rather, they express strong retributive sentiments. For example, in a recently published debate, a U.S. District judge, who believes in the deterrent effectiveness of capital punishment, nevertheless declared:

> Capital punishment's retributive function vindicates the fundamental moral principles that a criminal should receive his just deserts. Even if capital punishment had no incapacitative and deterrent utility, its use would be justified on this basis alone (Cassell 2003: 183, 197).

Such arguments are open to the ethical challenge posed by those who reject the use of capital punishment as a violation of the human right to be treated with dignity and humanity in all circumstances.

It may be that the use of the death penalty will simply wither away, as it had done in the 1960s to the point where no one was executed in 1968 (Banner 2002: 227). Alternatively, concerted pressure in states where capital punishment only plays a very marginal role, assisted by the arguments referred to above, especially those of mistake and unfairness, may in time lead to more states deciding that abolition is the best policy, and the executing states would become "outliers." Franklin Zimring has opined that "the endgame in the effort to purge the United States of the death penalty has already been launched" (2003: 205). But, as he has stressed, an activist population of people capable of using the evidence to create a change in the climate of opinion will need to be mobilized in order to raise considerably the salience of the issue. And it is worth remembering that the European experience is that, in time, after abolition has occurred, opinions change as people's expectations change. Capital punishment becomes one of the icons of the past, a reminder of more brutal times. The new generation growing up without it has no expectation and less desire for it. Indeed, a YouGov opinion poll of British adults published in the *Daily Telegraph* in January 2006 showed that age was a significant factor affecting support for the reintroduction of capital punishment: 69 percent of the "young" were opposed to it, compared with 41 percent of their "elders." All together, less than half the people polled favored restitution of the death penalty, a substantial decline from earlier years. Since the issue of the return of capital punishment was put to rest following the United Kingdom's ratification of the optional protocols to the ICCPR and ECHR, even the parents of murdered children rarely call for the reinstatement of the death penalty or express dissatisfaction when a convicted killer is sentenced to life imprisonment.

If the strategy of widening the number of abolitionist states were successful, the Supreme Court might even be persuaded to declare that there really has been an evolution in "standards of decency," at home as well as abroad, which deplores the use of capital punishment. Then it would be possible for the federal government to shed what Professor Harold Koh, U.S. Assistant Secretary of State for Democracy, Human Rights and Labor between 1998 and 2001, called its "Achilles' heel" "in almost every multilateral human rights forum" and ratify the Second Optional Protocol to the ICCPR (2002: 1085 at 1105.). But this is just, as it has to be, speculation.

5.9   Conclusions

What this chapter has tried to demonstrate is that the greater emphasis on the "human rights" perspective on the death penalty has added greatly to the moral force propelling the abolitionist movement. Those who still favor capital punishment "in principle" have been faced with yet more convincing evidence of the abuses, discrimination, mistakes, and inhumanity that appear inevitably to accompany it in practice.

Many protagonists of abolition believe that the death penalty is a fundamental violation of the human right to life: in essence, that it is an extreme form of cruel, inhuman, and degrading punishment. But it has to be recognized that not all persons regard this human rights view as valid, especially outside of Europe and the European hegemony. Indeed, many people appear to believe that (at least some) criminals who violate the right to life of others by murdering them deserve to lose their own right to life. And in some countries, this argument is used to justify capital punishment for other grave personal or socially injurious harms. Sometimes capital punishment is said to be sanctioned by religious authority, as in Islamic countries, and sometimes by deeply embedded cultural norms or mindsets, as in many Asian countries.

Yet there remains a large gap between believing that some persons "deserve to die" for the crimes they commit, and believing that a state system for the administration of capital punishment can be devised that meets the high ideals of equal, effective, procedurally correct, and humane justice that civilized societies seek to implement.

It is necessary, therefore, to approach the question of capital punishment from both normative (moral) and utilitarian points of view, and always in relation to how it is applied in practice. In essence, therefore, the case for retaining the death penalty—and thus resisting the movement to make its abolition an international norm—cannot rest solely on moral, cultural, or religious arguments. It would also have to be shown that it is useful and that it can be applied fairly, and without mistakes or a degree of arbitrariness and cruelty unacceptable to contemporary social and legal values. There is, as this chapter has tried to make clear, sufficient evidence to indict capital punishment on all these grounds.

Finally, something must be said about two related issues not covered in this chapter, neither of which can be ignored by anyone concerned with the protection of human rights. The first is the very regrettable fact that abolition of the death penalty and of judicial capital punishment has not always guaranteed that state forces, whether military or police, have respected the rule of law and the right to life in enforcing the law. All too often, governments (even abolitionist governments) have resorted to extrajudicial killing, and in recent times, this has become a policy that is in danger of becoming legitimized as a means of dealing with those defined as "terrorists." At times, the incidence and horrors of extrajudicial executions, sometimes of genocidal proportions, have put the issue of judicial capital punishment in the shade.

The second issue concerns the alternative to capital punishment. It has to be recognized that death should not be replaced by "living death." Indeed, the philosopher John Stuart Mill believed that "the short pang of death" was a less cruel way of punishing a criminal than "immuring him in a living tomb" (Radzinowicz and Hood 1986: 685). Conditions of long-term imprisonment must respect international standards for the humane and progressive treatment of prisoners, even those who have committed the worst of crimes. Furthermore, to offer as an alternative to capital punishment the mandatory use of lifelong imprisonment without the possibility of parole would be, in this author's opinion, to offer one human rights abuse in return for another. Although there may be some prisoners who will probably have to remain in confinement for the rest of their lives, they should be kept to the minimum number necessary for the protection of the public, and the necessity for their detention must still be kept under review. The experience of western European countries is testimony to the fact that a system that promotes the progressive rehabilitation of life-sentenced prisoners, followed by careful selection for release based on a risk assessment, does work very satisfactorily for the majority of prisoners who, in other countries, would face death or a lifetime without hope in prison.

References

Amnesty International. 2003. *Death Penalty Developments in 2002.* ACT 50/002/2003.

Amnesty International. 2006. *Death Penalty News.* January 2006, 7, AI Index, ACT 53/001/2006.

Ancel, M. 1962. *The Death Penalty in European Countries.* Strasbourg: Council of Europe.

Atkins v. Virginia. 2002. 536 U.S. 304.

Banner, S. 2002. *The Death Penalty: An American History.* Cambridge: Harvard University Press.

Bassiouni, M. C. 2004. Death as a penalty in the Shari'a. In *Capital Punishment. Strategies for Abolition,* ed. P. Hodgkinson and W. A. Schabas. Cambridge: Cambridge University Press.

Bingzhi, Z., ed. 2004. *The Road of the Abolition of the Death Penalty in China. Regarding the Abolition of the Non-Violent Crime at the Present Stage.* Renmin University of China, Series of Criminal Jurisprudence (44). Beijing: Press of the Chinese People's Public Security University.

Cassell, P. G. 2003. In defense of the death penalty. In *Debating the Death Penalty,* ed. H. Bedau and P. Cassell. New York: Oxford University Press.

Daily Telegraph. Less than 50pc back death penalty, 3 January 2006, www.telegraph.co.uk/news.

Dobryninas, A. 2004. The experience of Lithuania's journey to abolition. In *Capital Punishment. Strategies for Abolition,* ed. P. Hodgkinson and W. A. Schabas. Cambridge: Cambridge University Press.

Donohue, J. J., and A. Wolfers. 2005. Uses and abuses of empirical evidence in the death penalty debate. *Stan L. Rev* 58.

Evans, R. J. 1996. *Rituals of Retribution: Capital Punishment in Germany 1600-1987.* Oxford: Oxford University Press.

Fagan, J. 2005. *Deterrence and the Death Penalty. A Critical Review of New Evidence, Hearings on the Future of Capital Punishment in the State of New York,* January 21. http://www.deathpenaltyinfo.org/Fagantestimony.pdf.

Garland, D. 2005. Capital punishment and American culture: Some critical reflections. *Punishment and Society* 7(4).

Gatrell, V. 1994. *The Hanging Tree. Execution and the English People 1770-1868.* Oxford: Oxford University Press.

Hodgkinson, P., and W. A. Schabas, eds. 2004. *Capital Punishment. Strategies for Abolition.* Cambridge: Cambridge University Press.

Hood, R. 2002. *The Death Penalty: A Worldwide Perspective,* 3rd ed. Oxford: Oxford University Press.

Kindler v. Canada. 2003. UN doc. CCPR/L/78//D/829/1998.

Knight v. Florida 528 U.S. 990 (1999).

Koh, H. H. 2002. Paying "decent respect" to world opinion on the death penalty. *UC Davis Law Review* 35.

Liebman, J. S. et al. 2002. Capital attrition: Error rates in capital cases, 1973-1995. *Texas Law Rev.* 78.

Liebman, J. S. et al. 2002. *Why is there so much error in capital cases, and what can be done about it?* www.law.columbia.edu/brokensystem/2/index2.html.

Mexico v. USA (Avena). 2004, ICJ, 128.

Moore v. Nebraska. 1999. 528 U.S. 990.

Neumayer, E. 2005. *Death penalty: The political foundations of the global trend towards abolition.* http://ssrn.com/abstract=489628 or DOI: 10.2139/ssrn.489628.

Nowak, M. 2002. Is the death penalty an inhuman punishment? In *The Jurisprudence of Human Rights Law: A Comparative Interpretive Approach,* eds. T. S. Orlin, A. Rosas, and M. Scheinin. Abo Akademi University Institute of Human Rights.

Öcalan v. Turkey. 2003. (46221/99) ECHR 125.

Pratt and Morgan v. Attorney General of Jamaica. 1993.4 ALL E.R. 769 and 783 (PC).

Pristavkin, A. 1999. A vast place of execution—the death penalty in Russia. In *The Death Penalty. Abolition in Europe.* Strasbourg: Council of Europe.

Radzinowicz, L. 1968. *A History of English Criminal Law,* Vol. 4. London: Stevens.

Radzinowicz, L. 1999. *Adventures in Criminology.* London: Routledge.

Radzinowicz, L., and R. Hood. 1986. *A History of English Law, vol. 5 The Emergence of Penal Policy.* London: Stevens.

Rodley, N. 2004. The United Nation's work in the field of the death penalty. In *The Death Penalty—Beyond Abolition.* Strasbourg: Council of Europe.

Roper v. Simmons. 543 U.S. 551. 2005.

Schabas, W. A. 2002. *The Abolition of the Death Penalty in International Law,* 3rd ed. Cambridge: Cambridge University Press, Cambridge.

Schabas, W. A. 2004. Public opinion and the death penalty. In *Capital Punishment. Strategies for Abolition,* ed. P. Hodgkinson and W. A. Schabas. Cambridge: Cambridge University Press.

Scheck, B., P. Neufeld, and J. Dwyer. 2000. *Actual Innocence: Five Days to Execution and other Dispatches from the Wrongfully Convicted.* New York: Doubleday. www.deathpenaltyinfo.org/Innocentlist.html.

Scott, G. R. 1950, reissued 1965. *The History of Capital Punishment.* London: Torchstream Books.

State v. Makwanyane. 1995. (3) SA 391.

The Death Penalty: No Evidence for Deterrence. 2006. *The Economists' Voice,* commenting on articles by Gary Becker and Richard Posner, http://www.bepress.com/ev, accessed April 2006.

Toussaint, P. 1999. The death penalty and the fairy ring. In *The Death Penalty. Abolition in Europe.* Strasbourg: Council of Europe.

UN doc. E/2005/3/Add.1, para. 17.

United Nations. 2000-2001. *Report of the Human Rights Committee* A/56/40 (Vol.1), 86(4), 99.

United States v. Burns. 2001. SCC7 File No 26129.

Yasuda, Y. 2004. The death penalty in Japan. In *The Death Penalty—Beyond Abolition.* Strasbourg: Council of Europe Publishing.

Zimring, F. E. 2003. *The Contradictions of American Capital Punishment.* New York: Oxford University Press.

Appendix: List of Retentionist and Abolitionist Countries

Table A5.1   Countries that Retain the Death Penalty (in June 2007) and have Carried out at least One Judicial Execution within the Past Ten Years (1996–mid-2007) (fifty-five actively retentionist countries)

Afghanistan	India	Saint Kitts and Nevis
Bahamas	Indonesia	Saudi Arabia
Bahrain	Iran	Sierra Leone
Bangladesh	Iraq	Singapore
Belarus	Japan	Somalia
Botswana	Jordan	Sudan
Burundi	Korea, Democratic People's Republic of (North Korea)	Syria
Cameroon	Korea, Republic of (South Korea)	Taiwan (Province of China)
Chad	Kuwait	Thailand
China	Lebanon	Trinidad and Tobago
Comoros	Libya	Uganda
Congo, Democratic Republic of	Malaysia	United Arab Emirates
Cuba	Mongolia	United States of America
Egypt	Nigeria	*Uzbekistan
Equatorial Guinea	Oman	Vietnam
Ethiopia	Pakistan	Yemen
+Guatemala	Palestinian Authority	Zambia
Guinea	Qatar	Zimbabwe
Guyana		

+ In 2005, the president announced he would seek abolition of the death penalty.

* In 2005, the president signed a decree abolishing the death penalty from 1 January 2008.

Table A5.2   Countries that have Abolished the Death Penalty for All Crimes in All Circumstances, in Peacetime and Wartime—June 2007 (ninety countries)

Country or territory	Date of abolition for all crimes	Date of abolition for ordinary crimes	Date of last execution
Albania	2007	2000	1995
Andorra	1990		1943
Angola	1992		n.k.
Armenia	2003		1991
Australia	1985	1984	1967
Austria	1968	1950	1950
Azerbaijan	1998		1993
Belgium	1996		1950
Bhutan	2004		1964
Bolivia	1997	1995	1974
Bosnia and Herzegovina	2001	1997	n.k.
Bulgaria	1998		1989
Cambodia	1989		n.k.
Canada	1998	1976	1962
Cape Verde	1981		1835
Colombia	1910		1909
Costa Rica	1877		n.k.
Côte d'Ivoire	2000		1960
Croatia	1991		1987
Cyprus	2002	1983	1962
Czech Republic	1990		n.k.
Denmark	1978	1933	1950
Djibouti	1995		1977
Dominican Republic	1966		n.k.
Ecuador	1906		n.k.
Estonia	1998		1991
Finland	1972	1949	1944
France	1981		1977
Georgia	1997		1994
Germany (Former German Democratic Republic)	1949 (1987)		1948 (n.k.)
Greece	2004	1993	1972
Guinea-Bissau	1993		1986
Haiti	1987		1972
Holy See (Vatican City State)	1969		n.k.
Honduras	1956		1940
Hungary	1990		1988
Iceland	1928		1830
Ireland	1990		1954
Italy	1994	1947	1947
Kiribati	1979		1979+
Liberia	2005		1993
Liechtenstein	1987		1785
Lithuania	1998		1995

Table A5.2   Countries that have Abolished the Death Penalty for All Crimes in All Circumstances, in Peacetime and Wartime—June 2007 (ninety countries)

Country or territory	Date of abolition for all crimes	Date of abolition for ordinary crimes	Date of last execution
Luxembourg	1979		1949
Malta	2000	1971	1943
Marshall Islands	1986		1986+
Mauritius	1995		1987
Mexico	2005		1937
Micronesia (Federated States of)	1986		1986+
Moldova	1995		1989
Monaco	1962		1847
Montenegro (when Serbia and Montenegro)	2002		1989
Mozambique	1990		1986
Namibia	1990		1988
Nepal	1997	1990	1979
Netherlands	1982	1870	1952
New Zealand	1989	1961	1957
Nicaragua	1979		1930
Norway	1979	1905	1948
Palau	1994		1994+
Panama	1922		1903
Paraguay	1992		1928
Philippines	2006		2000
Poland	1997		1988
Portugal	1976	1867	1849
Romania	1989		1989
Rwanda	2007		1998
Samoa	2004		1962
San Marino	1865	1848	1468
Sao Tome and Principe	1990		1975
Senegal	2004		1967
Serbia (when Serbia and Montenegro)	2002		1989
Seychelles	1993		1976
Slovakia	1990		n.k.
Slovenia	1989		1957
Solomon Islands	1978	1966	1966
South Africa	1997	1995	1991
Spain	1995	1978	1975
Sweden	1972	1921	1910
Switzerland	1992	1942	1944
The former Yugoslav Republic of Macedonia	1991		n.k.
Timor-Leste	1999		1999+

Continued

Turkey	2004	2002	1984
Turkmenistan	1999		1997

Table A5.2   Countries that have Abolished the Death Penalty for All Crimes in All Circumstances, in Peacetime and Wartime—June 2007 (ninety countries)

Country or territory	Date of abolition for all crimes	Date of abolition for ordinary crimes	Date of last execution
Tuvalu	1976		1976+
Ukraine	1999		1997
United Kingdom of Great Britain and Northern Ireland	1998	1965*	1964
Uruguay	1907		n.k.
Vanuatu	1980		1980+
Venezuela	1863		n.k.

Note: n.k. indicates that the information is not available.

+ Date of independence, date of last execution under colonial rule not available.

* Capital punishment for ordinary crimes was abolished in Northern Ireland in 1973.

Table A5.3   Countries that have Abolished the Death Penalty for All Ordinary Crimes—June 2007 (nine countries)

Country	Date of abolition for ordinary crimes	Date of last execution
Argentina	1984	1916
Brazil	1979	1855
Chile	2001	1985
Cook Islands	1965	n.k.
El Salvador	1983	1973
Fiji	1979 (murder) +	1964
Israel	1954	1962
Latvia	1999	1996
Peru	1979	1979

+ Abolished in 2002 for treason, instigating foreign invasion with military force and genocide.

Table A5.4   Countries that Retain the Death Penalty in Law but which may be Regarded as Abolitionist *de facto* on the Grounds that No Executions have been Carried out for at least Ten Years or an Official Moratorium is in Place (forty-two countries)

Country or territory	Date of last execution
Algeria	1993
Antigua and Barbuda	1991
Barbados	1984
Belize	1985
Benin	1987
Brunei Darussalam	1957
Burkina Faso	1988
Central African Republic	1981
Congo (Brazzaville) Republic of	1982
Dominica	1986
Eritrea	1989
Gabon	1989
Gambia	1981
Ghana	1993
Grenada	1978
Jamaica	1988
Kazakhstan (moratorium since Dec. 2003)	2003
Kenya	1987
Kyrgyzstan (moratorium since Dec. 1998)	1998
Lao People's Democratic Republic	1989
Lesotho	1995
Madagascar	1958
Malawi	1992
Maldives	1952
Mali	1980
Mauritania	1989
Morocco	1993
Myanmar	1989
Nauru	1968
Niger	1976
Papua New Guinea	1950
Russian Federation (moratorium since May 1996)	1996
Sri Lanka	1976
St. Lucia	1995
St. Vincent and the Grenadines	1995
Suriname	1982
Swaziland	1983
Tanzania	1994
Tajikistan (moratorium since April 2004)	2004
Togo	1978
Tonga	1982
Tunisia	1991

Note: This does not mean that all of these countries are committed to not resuming executions.

Probation, Parole, and Community Corrections: An International Perspective

6

LAWRENCE F. TRAVIS AND
VICTORIA SIMPSON BECK

Contents

6.1   Introduction

The punishment of crime can take many forms, ranging from financial penalties through the death penalty. It is possible to classify criminal sanctions into at least four major categories of penalties: financial, bodily, custodial, and noncustodial (Reichel 2005). Of all penalties, financial sanctions are probably the most common, in part because they are assigned to the most common but least serious offenses, such as traffic law violations. After financial penalties, the second most common form of criminal sanctions, and the most common for serious offenses, are noncustodial penalties.

Noncustodial penalties are often lumped together into a broad class of practices called community corrections or community supervision. Community corrections is a broad term used to refer to a variety of noninstitutional criminal sanctions, including diversion programs, programs that impose restrictions and punishments on adjudicated offenders while maintaining them in the community, and programs designed to control and assist inmates released early from prison. The general objectives of community corrections are to provide cost-effective methods of controlling adjudicated offenders within the community, in order to ensure community protection and proportionality in punishment, promote rehabilitative and reintegrative measures (McCarthy, McCarthy, and Leone 2001), and restore crime victims.

Community corrections is often the subject of broad criticism due to the perception that it represents a soft approach to criminal sanctioning. Research in the United States has shown that both the public (Newman 1983) and offenders themselves (Gibbs 1985) often consider community corrections dispositions as leniency. Mark Israel and John Dawes (2002) reported similar public perceptions in Australia. Indeed, they noted that "community corrections programmes have been repeatedly characterized as merely 'a slap on the wrist' or, in the Australian idiom, as 'a bag of lollies'" (2002, 6). As a result of this bad public image, community corrections is often unable to compete effectively for scarce criminal justice resources. On the other hand, throughout the world, the ability of community corrections programs to reduce the costs of corrections has been a major impetus for expansion.

Incarceration is a nearly universal sanction for the most serious offenses. One of the most critical problems affecting prisons, internationally, is the escalating number of convicted offenders. Although there appear to be vast differences in international rates of incarceration, with some countries showing increases and others showing decreases, in the majority of countries, rates of incarceration have been increasing substantially since the 1990s (Newman 1999). Figures posted by Roy Walmsley (2001) indicate upwards of 9 million people are being held in penal institutions throughout the world, with a world prison incarceration rate of 140 per 100,000 persons.

Some of the increases in prison populations can be explained by demographic changes or by increases in the number and seriousness of crimes. More likely, however, is the explanation that governments around the world have become more punitive in their response to crime. Millie, Jacobson, and Hough (2003) assessed the increase in prison populations in England and conclude that changes in the law leading to more severe sanctions for some crimes have driven a general increase in the overall prison population in that country. They suggest that legislative efforts to be "tough on crime," even when directed at narrowly defined offenses, translate into generally harsher prison terms across the board.

The increasing size and expense of incarceration supports the development and use of community supervision sanctions. Noncustodial sanctions, especially those involving community supervision or other restrictions on liberty, impose some level of punishment on offenders who would otherwise not be imprisoned (Morris and Tonry 1990). In addition, as with the general movement towards more punitive responses to crime, community supervision broadens the ability of government to exercise some degree of surveillance and control over the population or to widen the net of social control.

Increases in incarceration rates create a variety of problems for penal institutions, including issues of crowding, inadequate control, and soaring costs. Although incarceration appears to be a preferred mode of sanctioning internationally, it is by no means an exclusive punishment. Since the 1800s, noncustodial methods of sanctioning have been touted as a viable alternative to incarceration and its associated social harms and financial costs. Nonetheless, Newman (1999) noted that a greater use of noncustodial sanctions internationally has not resulted in a decrease in the use of prison as a criminal sanction. Ironically, it appears that noncustodial sanctions are used to restrict prison use, instead of reduce prison use. In the United States, for example, recent reforms seeking "Truth in Sentencing" may have the effect of changing the composition of the prison population to include proportionately higher numbers of violent offenders, but not reduce (or possibly even increase) the total prison population (Ditton and Wilson 1999). By the end of 2001, violent offenders accounted for most of the growth in American prison populations, and nearly half of all inmates had been convicted of a violent crime (Harrison and Beck 2003). The balance of this chapter discusses the historical development, application, and status of two core community corrections approaches to criminal sanctioning: probation and parole.

6.2   History of Probation

As cited in Harris (1995a, 4), "Probation is a method of dealing with specially selected offenders and... consists of the conditional suspension of punishment while the offender is placed under personal supervision and is given individual guidance or treatment." The origins of probation can be traced to two distinct traditions: common law, which emphasizes the need to helpfully intervene with offenders, and civil (statute) law, which emphasizes the need to protect the civil rights of offenders.

6.2.1   The Common Law Tradition

In common law countries, such as Britain and the United States, the notion of mitigating the harshness of punishment evolved out of specific practices in England occurring over several centuries. These practices included, for example, the benefit of clergy, which allowed certain accused individuals to appeal to the court for leniency in sentencing by reading from the Bible, and judicial reprieve, which allowed the judge to suspend the sentence of a convicted offender on the condition that the offender display good future behavior. English settlers imported these and similar practices, which became the forerunner of modern probation in the United States.

Modern probation in the United States was further influenced by the efforts of John Augustus, who in 1841 became the first unofficial probation officer. With judicial approval, Augustus would regularly provide bail to, supervise, and assist minor offenders, such as alcoholics. Judicial action against offenders under the care of Augustus was deferred for a period of time. If, at the end of the designated probationary period, the offender had been law-abiding, sober, and industrious, the charges were dropped. The efforts of John Augustus eventually led to the enactment of the first Probation Act in 1878 in the United States, and by the twentieth century, every state had passed probation acts.

Less well known are the actions of Matthew Hill, a court recorder in Birmingham, who began a form of probation for juvenile offenders in that English city in the same year as Augustus started in Boston (Reichel 2005). Hill would release juveniles to the supervision of relatives or volunteers after they had served one day of incarceration. There was an existing practice of releasing youths to their parents or trade masters, but Hill expanded the practice to include any adults who would agree to serve as guardians. Hill selected juvenile offenders who were not wholly corrupt or ruined and assigned them to the care and supervision of guardians. This work with juveniles laid the foundation for the later development of an adult probation process. Thus, in the United States and England, the inception of probation was the result of a humanistic approach to punishment, by mitigating the harshness of the criminal justice system through finding alternatives to custody for minor offenders and youth, and working toward making these offenders better people.

Similar to the United States, the humanistic approach to mitigating the harshness of the criminal justice system was also emphasized in England. The roots of probation in England can be traced to the earlier practice of combining common law surety and recognizance systems to release young offenders into the charge of an employer. Subsequently, in 1876, Ranier suggested to the Church of England Temperance Society that they should extend "the Society's activities to police courts to offer practical help to alcoholic offenders" (Harris 1995a, 32). By 1905, England implemented the Probation of Offenders Act, which involved supervision of defendants in lieu of the imposition of a sentence. Although Canada and India are considered common law countries, in these countries probation acts were established first and supervision followed. In Australia, legislation in 1901 "permitted the conditional release on recognizance of first or marginal offenders"; however, typically, there was no supervision (Harris 1995a, 35).

New Zealand was the first country to emulate the United States by implementing the Probation of First Offenders Act in 1886. By 1920, the New Zealand Probation Act was confirmed as a judicial disposition, allowing for the temporary suspension of sentencing pending good behavior, and providing probation officers with broad supervisory powers, including, for example, approving employment arrangements (Hamai 1995). Although probation had been recognized in a British statute passed in 1879, the statute did not provide for organized, paid supervision of offenders (Timasheff 1941).

6.2.2   The Civil Law Tradition

In much of continental Europe, the civil law tradition influenced the development of probation. In civil law tradition, probation evolved out of the suspension of the execution of a sentence and, originally, did not involve supervision. Rather, the suspension of fine or sentence represented a trial period for first-time offenders, with a fine or sentence imposed only if the defendant engaged in further serious offenses during the suspension.

The civil law tradition reflects the concerns in postrevolutionary France to introduce a principle of strict legality and equality into the penal code, removing judicial discretion (Ville, Zvekic, and Klaus 1997). The principle of strict legality was introduced into the 1791 and 1810 Penal Codes of France, reflecting the belief that the criminal code could not be too precise, and making the judge a mere dispenser of punishment. Following the example set by France, many European criminal codes reflected a similar concern for ensuring sentencing was imposed in respect of a crime and legislating against the abuse of state power. The suspension of sentencing was a major part of Denmark's criminal justice system, since its inception. Belgium empowered courts to impose a suspended sentence in 1888, and Austria and Switzerland in the 1920s. Although Germany did not have an adult probation system prior to World War II, a similar practice, referred to as the power of discontinuance, developed in 1895. The Netherlands, despite a civil law tradition, was strongly influenced by historical and cultural links with Britain; consequently, although suspended sentences were permitted in 1915, supervision was a permissible attachment (Hamai 1995).

6.2.3 International Probation: Similarities

Internationally, probationary supervision periods range anywhere from six months to several years and typically include additional conditions such as refraining from unlawful behavior, working in suitable employment, pursuing education or vocational training, satisfying conditions relating to rehabilitation, reporting to officials as directed, remaining within the jurisdiction, payment of fines and/or restitution, community service, home confinement, and drug testing (Newman 2002). More importantly, by the twentieth century, the existing historical legal differences in probation internationally gave way to a convergence when many of the civil law countries added supervision to suspension (van Kalmthout and Derks 2000). For example, Denmark was "one of the first countries to introduce supervision (by volunteer charitable organizations)" in 1905, France added supervision in 1958, and Austria added supervised probation in 1980 (Harris 1995a, 47; Ville, Zvekic, and Klaus 1997). Harris (1995a, 41) reports that during this same time period, common law countries gave way to the civil law tradition:

> The idea that responsibility for determining the proper response to infraction should be based on professional expertise and values, though seen as inevitable and progressive in the 1950s, inexorably gave way to a return to legalism and due process and therefore to the relocation of responsibility for detailed decision-making into the courts. In no common law country can probation any longer be considered a common law disposal.

Thus, "in common law countries probation moved from informal and marginal beginnings to become a dimension of law and policy, in civil law countries the reverse process occurred" (Ville, Zvekic, and Klaus 1997, 49).

6.2.4 International Probation: Differences

Despite the convergence of civil law and common law in the development of probation, broad differences still exist as the evolution of probation has been further influenced by cultural context (social, political, and ideological climates and economic resources). For example, in India economic issues, weak central control over states, and other cultural factors render probation marginal (Hamai 1995). However, in other countries, such as the United Kingdom, Canada, and the United States, probation is a formalized process administered by governmental agencies reflecting cultural expectations of punishment and social control (Ville, Zvekic, and Klaus 1997).

(a) *Formalized probation systems.* The emphasis on reintegration in Canada has resulted in prisons being used as a last resort, barring serious crimes such as murder; thus, the majority of offenders have served four or five probationary terms prior to receiving a prison sentence (Newman 2002). In the United States, currently, probation is one of the most widely utilized sentencing dispositions, yet it reflects a general retributive approach to criminal sanctioning, with a primary focus on risk management. At the end of 2001, approximately 4 million men and women were on probation in the United States, representing a record high (Glaze 2002). Similar to the United States, there is an increasing focus on crime prevention and risk management activities in the United Kingdom (Nash 1998). Further, although historically probation in England and Wales was imposed as an alternative sentence, it is currently being used as a sentence disposition (Newman 2002). Hong Kong, on the other hand, has managed to preserve the original rehabilitative philosophy behind the creation of probation. Although modeled on the U.K. system, the Hong Kong system of probation is statutorily based, was first applied only to juvenile offenders, and became available to adult offenders in 1956 under the Probation of Offenders Ordinance (Chui 2003).

Probation was first introduced in Venezuela in 1980 and may be assigned as an alternative to prison for first-time offenders, with prison sentences no greater than eight years, and under certain other conditions. Probation in Venezuela is not a sentencing alternative for trial judges, because it is not listed as an option in the penal code. Once convicted, however, sentenced offenders may petition for probation (Newman 2002).

(b) *Informal probation systems.* In Papua New Guinea, probation incorporates community customs with elements of punishment and social control, and utilizes volunteer probation officers to assist and supervise offenders. Probation services in Japan also rely mostly on volunteers. Other countries, such as Bangladesh, also place an emphasis on community involvement, which is perceived to be essential to make probation work. In fact, in Kenya, community probation officers live and work in the community they serve, and services emphasize reintegration within the context of a multiagency approach. The Netherlands address the welfare needs of offenders while working in close collaboration with criminal justice agencies (Ville, Zvekic, and Klaus 1997).

6.3   Suspension of Sentence for a Probationary Period

Similar to probation, some countries, under certain conditions, allow for the suspension of a sentence for a "probationary period." For example, in Mexico, there is no probation system; however, the legal system provides for suspended sentences with probation as long as the penalty is no longer than four years and the offender has met certain conditions. In Mexico, probation suspends penalties and fines. Costa Rica and Brazil provide for the suspension of procedure, in certain cases, based on the testing of conduct of the accused and only when the defendant admits the charges. To be considered for suspension of sentence ('suspensao condicional da pena') in Brazil, the penalty cannot exceed two years; in Costa Rica, the suspension must be requested by the accused, prior to trial. China has a process called Guanzhi, which is imposed only for minor offenses and allows offenders to remain in their community and continue working while under supervision of public security agents (Newman 2002).

6.4   History of Parole

Parole as a form of community corrections has two meanings. First, the word *parole* relates to the early release of incarcerated persons. Second, parole refers to the process of supervision of offenders after release from incarceration. Parole release is probably the most maligned element of the criminal justice system, receiving criticism for both excessive leniency and unwarranted harshness. Parole provides the conditional release of inmates, at the discretion of some parole authority, to serve the remainder of their sentences under community correctional supervision. Historically, parole emerged from the concept of the system of marks, an early 19th-century practice of indeterminate sentencing that allowed for early release of inmates exhibiting good behavior (Roth 2005).

The practice of parole release was conceived by Captain Alexander Maconochie, of Great Britain, who is considered to be the "father of parole." While assigned to England's prison colony at Van Diemen's Land (now Tasmania), Maconochie developed the system of marks, which allowed for convicts to be sentenced to a certain amount of labor rather than specific period of time. Under the mark system, convicts could earn marks for good conduct and work or lose marks for bad behavior.

Similar to the system of marks, good-time laws were created 1817 in the United States. Good-time laws allowed for sentence reductions for good work and behavior. Tennessee was one of the first states to implement a good-time reduction of prison sentences in 1836, and the practice gained wider popularity in the United States throughout the 19th century (Ville, Zvekic, and Klaus 1997).

6.5 International Parole: Commonalities and Differences

Parole release is not widely used throughout the world and is a practice concentrated mostly in developed, Western countries. In order to be released on parole, most existing parole systems require prisoners to show improvement in their behavior/attitude and demonstrate prosocial behavior through work and by engaging in prison programs and/or educational/re-educational programs. Some systems may also require that prior to being released on parole, the inmate has a place to stay and a job. Cross-country variation in parole exists in terms of (a) eligibility for parole, (b) portion of sentence served prior to parole eligibility, (c) the length of parole supervision, and (d) formalization of parole.

6.5.1 Cross-Country Variation in Eligibility for Parole

In some countries, the use of parole is applied discriminatorily based on, for example, length of sentence, income, and/or seriousness of offense. In England and Wales, parole release is based on sentence length and is limited to inmates with sentences exceeding four years. Conditional release on parole in Mexico, however, is not only based on sentence length but on income as well. Parole in Mexico is permitted only when the maximum penalty is no more than three years for high-income inmates and four years for low-income inmates, after one-third of the total sentence has been served. The parole system in Finland differentiates based on number of convictions, with shorter amounts of time served for first offenders, prior to parole consideration. The Ukraine's system of parole differentiates based on the seriousness of the offense, with serious offenders having to serve more time before being eligible for parole. In New Zealand, serious violent offenders may be excluded from parole, and Denmark excludes individuals sentenced to life in prison from parole (Newman 2002).

6.5.2   Cross-Country Variation in Time Served Prior to Parole

There is also cross-country variation in the amount of time prisoners must serve, prior to being considered for release on parole. For example, in countries such as Australia, parole has been affected by Truth in Sentencing legislation, requiring inmates to serve a substantial portion of their sentence before being eligible for parole, and has resulted in significant increases in prison populations. State prison populations in the United States have been influenced by Truth in Sentencing legislation along with mandatory sentencing legislation and the abolition of parole release in fourteen states and the federal jurisdiction in the last quarter of the twentieth century. On the other hand, in some countries, such as Taiwan, parole criteria have been relaxed in order to reduce prison crowding and associated management issues. Although Israel does not have a parole system, the overcrowding of prisons has resulted in laws authorizing administrative release of prisoners (Newman 2002).

In general, variation in the amount of time served for long-term sentences (one year to life, depending on the country) ranges from one-third (Brazil, Federated States of Micronesia, New Zealand, Papua New Guinea, Slovenia, South Korea, and Taiwan) to one-half (China, Czech Republic) to two-thirds (Canada, Norway). Finland allows first-time prisoners to be released on parole after having served one-half of their sentences; whereas all others must serve at least two-thirds of their sentence. Italy allows for the conditional release of prisoners on parole, after serving "part" of their sentence, whereas Denmark allows for the release of inmates on parole after having served between one-half and two-thirds of their sentence. In the Ukraine, parole is permitted only after one-half, two-thirds, or three-quarters of the sentence has been served, depending upon the seriousness of the crime (Newman 2002).

In addition to discretionary release by parole, the second definition of parole relates to postrelease supervision. As Ditton and Wilson (1999) observed about the United States, "While discretionary release from prison by a parole board has been eliminated by some states, post-release supervision still exists and is generally referred to as community or supervised release." Even in nations that do not have a separate "parole system" with release and supervision powers vested in a parole authority, it is not uncommon for prisoners released prior to the expiration of their full term to be required to submit to supervision by the probation department (van Kalmthout and Derks 2000). In those cases, released inmates experience "parole supervision" for all intents and purposes.

6.5.3   Cross-Country Variation in Length of Parole Supervision

In England and Wales, inmates with shorter sentences are released from parole supervision after 50 percent of their sentence term has expired, whereas long-term prisoners are supervised until 75 percent of their sentence term has expired. The length of parole supervision in the Czech Republic is between one and seven years, as defined by the court. In Canada, inmates released on parole are subject to supervision until their time warrant expires (Newman 2002).

6.5.4   Cross-Country Variation in the Formalization of Parole

In Canada, both provincial and national inmates may be released on parole, under the Parole Acts of 1959 and 1977. Technically, however, inmates released early from prison are not on "parole," as there is no parole board (national or provincial) making release decisions. Under the federal Mandatory Release Program, inmates must serve two-thirds of their sentence prior to being released under supervision. In Canada, the parole officer merely serves as a resource, helping the releasee obtain housing and employment and helping with personal problems. Similarly, aftercare (parole) in Japan is administered by the Rehabilitation Bureau of the Ministry, which is supplemented by community volunteers. In India, parole takes the form of emergency leave (15 days yearly) and ordinary leave (30 days yearly) for participation in family events and problems (marriages, funerals, home repairs) (Newman 2002).

6.6   Systems Similar to Parole

Although not all countries have parole systems, several allow for the remission of a sentence and early release from prison. In general, sentence remissions are not a right (with the possible exception of the Republic of Ireland), but rather a concession to motivate cooperation and prosocial behavior within the prison system. Thus, remissions tend to be predicated on good behavior, participation in prison programs, prison work, and educational and re-educational programs. Some countries allow conditional remission and release (i.e., release can be revoked), whereas other countries place no conditions on early release (i.e., release cannot be revoked) (Newman 2002).

The Republic of Colombia, Costa Rica, Northern Ireland, the Slovak Republic, and Venezuela provide systems of early conditional release from prison. In the Netherlands, inmates serving a sentence of one year or longer are released after serving two-thirds of their sentence with no conditions (i.e., release cannot be revoked). Several other countries provide unconditional remission. For example, South Africa, in addition to providing parole, also allows for unconditional early release, for a maximum remission time of one-third of a prison sentence for prisoners sentenced to two or more years. France provides a system of early release through the Penalty Application Commission, under which sentence reductions may not exceed seven days per month for incarceration over one year (Newman 2002).

The Republic of Ireland, in theory, has automatic remission for good behavior, after serving one-fourth of the prison sentence. In Hungary and Israel, there are no automatic remissions; however, in Israel inmates may receive time off for good behavior after serving two-thirds of their sentence. In Kenya, Nigeria, and Hong Kong, inmates may gain time off for good behavior, but lose time for misconduct. Russia allows for early release (or less restrictive punishment) for "excellent" behavior and "honest" labor (Newman 2002).

Finally, in countries without parole or remission, inmates may be allowed to leave the prison for limited periods of time under certain conditions. In Poland, for example, prisoners can be granted permission to leave the prison for an important reason or as a reward for good behavior. In general, leaves from prison in Poland are granted for a maximum of five days. Although Malta allows for reductions in sentence for up to four months per year, based on good behavior, Malta also provides presidential amnesties on special occasions. Russia also allows for furloughs, early release, and less restrictive punishments for "excellent" behavior and "honest" labor. Although Israel does not provide for total or partial remission, time off is granted for prisoners who have served two-thirds of their sentence and have exhibited good behavior. In response to prison crowding, Israel does provide for administrative release under strict criteria (Newman 2002).

6.7 Current Trends in Probation

Although a body of literature on probation from different countries does exist (for a discussion, see Hamai 1995 or van Kalmthout and Derks 2000), the existing cultural differences in probation make comparative studies on a cross-national basis difficult. Consequently, there are very few cross-national probation studies. Nonetheless, the few existing comparative studies suggest the following international trends in probation:

- In most countries, the responsibility for probation falls between national and local governments.
- Most countries allow for additional requirements to probation orders.
- The age of criminal responsibility and, thus, the age at which probation service becomes involved with juveniles varies between nine and fourteen, and is distinct from adult probation.
- Probation is predominantly used for middle-range offenders (e.g., nonviolent property offenses, vehicle theft), although most countries permit probation to be used for serious offenses where mitigating factors exist.
- In most countries, the length of probation is varied and typically ranges from six months to three years.
- Although comparisons of probation custody rates do not present a clear picture, in the majority of countries, there has been a steady increase (see Table 6.1).

A recent examination of trends in rates of probation is provided by the Seventh United Nations Survey on Crime Trends and the Operations of Criminal Justice Systems, representing the responses from 92 countries (approximately one-half) around the world (Walmsley 2002).

6.8   Current Trends in Parole

As was the case with probation, there is little comparative literature on parole, and the existing cultural differences in parole, as noted above, make comparative studies difficult. The existing comparative information provides for the following observations:

- 41 percent of the countries listed as offering adult release/parole service have experienced substantial increases in adult parole populations between 1999 and 2000, while the balance of the countries have experienced a decrease, remained about the same, or failed to provide information.
- The United States experienced the greatest increase in adult release/parole population, followed by the Ukraine.
- 33 percent of the countries listed as offering juvenile release/parole have experienced increases in juvenile release/parole service, while the balance of the countries have experienced a decrease, remained about the same, or failed to provide information (see Table 6.2).
- The greatest increase in use of juvenile release/parole occurred in Japan, followed by the Ukraine; however, use of juvenile probation was not included in this report.

Table 6.1   Adults Placed on Probation on Given Day

Country	Average of number value			Average of per 100,000 capita		
	1998	1999	2000	1998	1999	2000
Azerbaijan	3421	3524	3463	43.23266	44.14381	43.02398
Belarus	17385	16920	15844	172.1287	169.2	158.44
Canada	100982	102147	—	334.3775	334.9082	—
Chile	3584	4028	3462	24.21622	26.85333	22.77632
Cyprus	62	49	11	8.277704	6.498674	1.453104
England & Wales	117600	127200	—	224.308	241.4125	—
Estonia	1282	3944	5187	91.17871	284.4224	378.8897
Finland	1428	1326	1287	27.71201	25.6728	24.85996
Hong Kong, China (SAR)	2668	2684	2827	40.14686	39.93632	41.59188
Hungary	163	186	174	1.613861	1.841584	1.74
Iceland	14	19	16	5.109489	6.846847	5.69395
Ireland	2312	2363	2030	62.28448	62.97974	53.50554
Jamaica	389	651	1136	15.10093	25.13514	43.1447
Japan	14712	15105	15593	11.67619	11.8937	12.27795
Kazakhstan	27778	8079	27315	183.9603	54.22148	183.3221
Korea, Republic of	34755	32713	28278	74.90302	69.75053	59.78436
Kyrgyzstan	410	315	210	8.547009	6.475353	4.272635
Lithuania	13430	13610	10616	362.6789	367.9373	287.3072
Maldives	20	4	3	7.616726	1.485388	1.086957
Mexico	36256	29291	23283	38.08403	30.32195	23.75816
Russian Federation	454811	544665	458857	309.3952	373.0582	314.2856
Slovakia	2080	2095	2134	38.58526	38.83139	39.50542
Spain	62	100	111	0.15736	0.253807	0.281013
Ukraine	46292	25327	36748	92.03181	50.75551	74.23838
United States of America	3384359	3740808	3807993	1230.676	1345.614	1350.352
Venezuela	—	—	1493	—	—	6.169421

- Recent trends in parole are provided by the Seventh United Nations Survey on Crime Trends and Operations of Criminal Justice Systems (Walmsley 2002).

Not surprisingly, the United Nations data generally show a trend towards larger numbers of people under community supervision each year (see Tables 6.3 and 6.4). Although there are some fluctuations in particular countries or in population sizes from year to year, the broad trend is towards increased use of community supervision. As the costs of incarceration increase and more and more of the world's governments and people come to define capital and corporal penalties as inappropriate, community supervision gains prominence as a means of punishing crime.

Whether probation or parole, the defining characteristic of these penalties is that they entail supervised conditional release. Persons placed on

Table 6.2 Juveniles Placed on Probation on Given Day

Country	Average of number value			Average of per 100,000 capita		
	1998	1999	2000	1998	1999	2000
Belarus	4245	4082	3807	42.0297	40.82	38.07
Canada	33325	30722	—	110.3477	100.7279	—
Cyprus	25	28	23	3.337784	3.713528	3.038309
England & Wales	9300	9800	—	17.73865	18.59939	—
Estonia	409	771	801	29.089	55.60083	58.50986
Finland	254	176	198	4.929167	3.407551	3.824609
Hong Kong, China (SAR)	910	878	811	13.69327	13.06412	11.93173
Hungary	12	15	24	0.118812	0.148515	0.24
Iceland	2	—	3	0.729927	—	1.067616
Ireland	770	788	677	20.74353	21.00213	17.84396
Italy	1249	1412	1434	2.168403	2.451389	2.485269
Jamaica	549	369	553	21.31211	14.2471	21.00266
Japan	39054	39433	38823	30.99524	31.04961	30.56929
Korea, Republic of	11755	13630	16672	25.33405	29.06183	35.24736
Kyrgyzstan	68	70	83	1.417553	1.438967	1.688708
Lithuania	—	—	722	—	—	19.53992
Maldives	8	1	—	3.046691	0.371347	—
Mexico	634	798	959	0.665966	0.826087	0.978571
Qatar	78	136	81	14.28571	24.06611	13.84876
Russian Federation	94170	108002	84758	64.06122	73.97397	58.05342
Slovakia	83	79	84	1.5397	1.464286	1.55504
Spain	—	2	3	—	0.005076	0.007595
Sweden	165	123	151	1.864028	1.388669	1.702559
Ukraine	4019	4224	5112	7.99006	8.46493	10.32727
Zambia	123	58	62	1.27254	0.586973	0.613861

probation or parole are expected to abide by a set of conditions or behavioral rules. Most often these include restrictions on criminal behavior, requirements of law-abiding behavior, and participation in rehabilitation or self-improvement programs. Failure to abide by these conditions is punishable by a revocation of liberty and the imposition (reimposition, in the case of parole) of incarceration. Adherence to the conditions of release is monitored through supervision by government agents.

6.9   The Effectiveness of Supervision

A quarter century ago, Andrew von Hirsch and Kathleen Hanrahan (1978) argued that there was little reason to continue the practice of parole supervision. They suggested that the research to date did not support parole supervision as a crime-control strategy and that parole officers were not very effective in providing needed services to parolees. Others have also criticized parole super-

Table 6.3 Adults Placed on Release/Parole on Given Day

Country	Average of number value			Average of per 100,00 capita		
	1998	1999	2000	1998	1999	2000
Azerbaijan	40	49	71	0.505497	0.613804	0.882097
Belarus	7287	6473	8288	72.14851	64.73	82.88
Botswana	2	3	5	0.128064	0.188903	0.31211
Bulgaria	1076	1226	1085	13.03137	14.93665	13.28524
Canada	9938	9995		32.90728	32.77049	—
Chile	2516	2164	1836	17	14.42667	12.07895
Estonia	360	360	354	25.60401	25.96148	25.85829
Finland	1190	1165	1231	23.09334	22.55566	23.77825
Georgia	562	633	1847	10.32709	12.59952	36.76354
Hong Kong, China (SAR)	1903	1638	1561	28.63549	24.37246	22.96601
Hungary	4108	4312	5495	40.67327	42.69307	54.95
Iceland	149	126	112	54.37956	45.40541	39.85765
Ireland	56	72	71	1.508621	1.918977	1.871376
Italy	317	225	200	0.550347	0.390625	0.34662
Jamaica	61	77	73	2.368012	2.972973	2.772503
Japan	6302	6317	6625	5.001587	4.974016	5.216535
Kazakhstan	9762	9255	11814	64.64901	62.11409	79.28859
Korea, Republic of	4790	8559	8035	10.32328	18.24947	16.98732
Kyrgyzstan	1200	1701	2310	25.01563	34.9669	46.99898
Latvia	910	923	723	37.15802	38.29876	30.48061
Lithuania	2873	2986	2647	77.58574	80.72452	71.63735
Macedonia, FYR	175	227	290	8.684864	11.25434	14.27868
Maldives	1	1		0.380836	0.371347	—
Mexico		1706	3118	—	1.766046	3.181633
Moldova, Republic of	446	351	212	10.37451	8.181818	4.950957
Netherlands	85	87	86	0.541401	0.550633	0.540881
Philippines	2630	3980	3099	3.612637	5.363881	4.099206
Qatar	21	11		3.846154	1.946524	—
Slovenia	458	613	700	23.10098	30.87384	35.21127
Spain	7076	6901	6364	17.95939	17.51523	16.11139
Sri Lanka	99	116	112	0.526596	0.610526	0.57732
Thailand	18687	24127	19321	31.24916	40.07807	31.83031
Turkey	1942	1836	1363	3.063091	2.855365	2.087289
Ukraine	12434	14397	20117	24.71968	28.8517	40.6404
United States of America	638203	641693	652199	232.0738	230.8248	231.2762
Zimbabwe	74	69	61	0.606557	0.556452	0.484127

vision (Gottfredson, Mitchell-Herzfeld, and Flanagan 1982). Because those on parole are required to obey a range of behavioral conditions, they can be returned to prison for "technical violations," breaking the rules of supervision that do not involve any new criminality. When technical violations are counted as "failures," parolees have more chances to "fail" than do nonparolees, who must be convicted of new crimes to be incarcerated. As a result of differences

Table 6.4   Juveniles Placed on Release/Parole on Given Day

Country	Average of number value			Average of per 100,000 capita		
	1998	1999	2000	1998	1999	2000
Azerbaijan	2	—	—	0.025275	—	—
Belarus	604	749	811	5.980198	7.49	8.11
Bulgaria	21	7	3	0.25433	0.085283	0.036733
Estonia	34	18	14	2.418156	1.298074	1.022644
Finland	1	—	1	0.019406	—	0.019316
Georgia	32	15	37	0.588019	0.298567	0.736465
Hong Kong, China (SAR)	1456	1315	1203	21.90923	19.56641	17.69898
Hungary	220	205	230	2.178218	2.029703	2.3
Ireland	5	1	4	0.134698	0.026652	0.10543
Japan	5813	6423	6977	4.613492	5.05748	5.493701
Kazakhstan	335	252	302	2.218543	1.691275	2.026846
Korea, Republic of	654	740	855	1.409483	1.577825	1.807611
Kyrgyzstan	60	95	85	1.250782	1.952884	1.7294
Latvia	97	106	71	3.9608	4.39834	2.993255
Lithuania	—	—	7	—	—	0.189445
Macedonia, FYR	2	4	—	0.099256	0.198314	—
Maldives	2	—	1	0.761673	—	0.362319
Mexico	1763	1189	816	1.851891	1.230849	0.832653
Moldova, Republic of	28	48	17	0.651314	1.118881	0.397011
Slovenia	6	3	—	0.302633	0.151095	—
Spain	25	20	25	0.063452	0.050761	0.063291
Sweden	3	2	—	0.033891	0.02258	—
Turkey	22	7	1	0.0347	0.010886	0.001531
Ukraine	1144	1290	1381	2.274354	2.58517	2.789899

in the definition of success and failure, the research on supervision effectiveness shows mixed findings. It is difficult, if not impossible, to decide whether parole supervision is an effective crime prevention method (Flanagan 1985).

Critics have raised similar concerns about the effectiveness of probation supervision. Joan Petersilia and her colleagues (1986) concluded that a 65 percent rate of new criminality among their sample of probationers showed that supervision of felons was not effective at protecting public safety. She summarized the results of this study (1986, 2):

> These results would seem to support the contention that routine probation is not an appropriate or effective sanction for convicted felons. It evidently could not provide the kind of supervision that might have prevented the majority of our sample of felony offenders from returning to crime.

Vito (1986) replicated the study with a sample of Kentucky probationers. McGaha, Fichter, and Hirschburg (1987) replicated the study with probationers in Missouri, and Goldstein, Burrell, and Talty (1985) examined probationers in New Jersey. All of these studies reported that probationers in their samples did not pose as great a threat to public safety as those examined in Petersilia's study in California. When rearrest is used as the criterion, a review of several studies of probation effectiveness reported rearrest rates ranging from 12 to 65 percent (Geerken and Hayes 1993).

To answer the question of whether community supervision is effective, we must first determine what we mean by effectiveness. Clear and Dammer (2002) observed that the typical measure of effectiveness is "recidivism." Alan Harland (1996, 2–3) noted that the definition of what works depends on the perspective of the individual asking the question. Elected officials and citizens define "effectiveness" as reducing rates of recidivism. Policymakers may see it as lowering rates of commitment or lengths of stay for prison and jail inmates. Budget officials might see effectiveness as managing offenders at a lower cost, whereas retributivists would define effectiveness as a system of sanctions matching punishment with the crime and blameworthiness of the offender. In short, probation, parole, and other community supervision practices are effective to the degree that they: (1) can control risk of new crime (public safety), (2) reduce incarceration and correctional costs, and/or (3) match punishments with offenders.

6.10 Public Safety

There has been increased attention paid to the ability or inability of community correctional programs to protect the public. Bennett (1991, 95) observed, "The public is upset, and perhaps rightly so, that people placed on regular probation often do not receive either help or supervision because of large caseloads and inadequate supervision." The critical question is how safe is safe enough? Jones (1991) described how risk levels can range from a definition of no new criminality through acceptance of levels of crime no greater than those among persons incarcerated. Harland and Rosen (1987) suggested that minimizing public risk is the primary goal of most intermediate sanctions. Thus, although no new crime would be preferred, achieving similar levels of new crime among a population that is diverted from prison that is less than (or no more than) the level among incarcerated offenders may be "safe enough."

John Worrall and his associates (2004) studied the link between the size of the probation caseload and the crime rate in California counties. Although they conclude that the size of the probation caseload is positively associated with the rate of property crime, it is not possible to tell if crime rate causes probation or vice versa. Still, there is no evidence that large probation caseloads are associated with reductions in crime. Worrall et al. (2004) observed that large caseloads are also associated with reduced levels of treatment and reintegration services for probationers. It may be the administration of supervision (large numbers of offenders assigned to too few officers) that explains failure. Others contend that smaller caseloads provide close supervision, which translates into higher rates of technical violations and, thus, higher rates of failure. Nicole Piquero (2003) suggested that probationers receiving closest supervision are more likely to fail early than those not subjected to such intensive supervision.

6.11 Reducing Incarceration and Correctional Costs

As Jones (1991) observed in Kansas, an important consideration in the use of probation and parole, and the development of other community supervision sanctions, is a desire to reduce prison crowding and correctional costs. Clear and Byrne (1992) flatly said, "The frank bottom line for the intermediate sanction movement must be whether it is able to reduce overcrowding in corrections." One force supporting the increased use of community supervision is the need to deal with large numbers of offenders. If we had excess prison space, we might simply incarcerate offenders who required tougher punishment than probation. We do not have that excess, and we cannot afford to build enough prisons to house all of these offenders.

Probation, parole, and alternative sanctions in the community can reduce demand for prison space (Gowdy 1993). On the other hand, creating more severe community-based sanctions may result in net-widening. Net-widening is the term used to describe the situation when programs designed to divert offenders from criminal justice interventions or severe sanctions actually result in more people being subjected to some formal intervention. If probation is designed to divert offenders from prison, but also results in offenders (who otherwise would have simply been warned and released) being sentenced to terms of supervision, then the "net" of criminal justice intervention has been widened. Morris and Tonry (1990) argued that one result of alternative sanctions has been to make sentences more severe for those who would not have gone to prison anyway. When alternative sanctions widen the net, they do not attain the goal of reducing correctional costs and prison crowding. Beck and Mumola (1999) reported that one of the reasons for prison population growth was the large number of parole violators returned to prison. As Rhine (1997) pointed out, the new, risk-centered community supervision strives to identify and arrest probationers and parolees who violate conditions of release. When the strategy is successful, the "failure" rates for probation and parole increase, and more community supervision violators are sent to prison, possibly for longer terms.

6.12   Matching Punishments with Offenders

The third goal of supervision in the community is to create a range of penalties that can be appropriately applied to the range of offenses and offenders who come before the courts. The traditional choice between probation and incarceration is seen by many as inadequate to the wide array of crimes and criminals that exists. Morris and Tonry (1990) argued: "A variety of intermediate punishments, along with appropriate treatment conditions, should be part of a comprehensive, integrated system of sentencing and punishment." A growing emphasis on developing a range of punishments has led to the creation of what are called "intermediate penalties."

6.13   The Development of Intermediate Sanctions

Because of the tradition of probation coming before incarceration and parole coming after, probation and parole can be considered "bookends of imprisonment." This traditional distinction between probation and parole has diminished in recent years, especially in the United States. Indeed, the advent of what are known as "intermediate sanctions" has also lessened the distinction between community supervision and incarceration.

In the United States, nearly three-quarters of the population under correctional supervision of any sort are to be found in community supervision programs. Because of the relative ease with which probation and parole supervision can be extended to larger numbers of offenders, it is likely that community supervision will become the dominant sanction for criminal behavior around the world. Both probation and parole allow for at least partial control of criminal offenders, the provision of services, and the imposition of punitive sanctions at low cost. In a shrinking world where information is more easily shared, these attributes of community supervision will attract attention from governments wrestling with increasing crime and reduced correctional resources.

The development of a range of sanctions in the United States over the past three decades has expanded the scope of community corrections. Partly in response to criticisms of probation and parole as being too "lenient" or inadequately punitive, new sanctions have emerged that fall somewhere between traditional community supervision and imprisonment. As Morris and Tonry (1990) have phrased it, "We are both too lenient and too severe; too lenient with many on probation who should be subject to tighter controls in the community, and too severe with many in prison and jail who would present no serious threat to community safety if they were under control in the community." What was needed, they argued, were intermediate sanctions—punishments with a severity that falls somewhere between traditional probation and imprisonment.

6.14   Intermediate Sanctions in the United States

Intermediate sanctions were developed for offenders whose crimes were not serious enough for incarceration, but who merited a punishment harsher than ordinary probation. The stated objectives of intermediate sanctions, like those of community supervision, are to provide public safety, offer a punishment alternative to imprisonment, reduce correctional costs, reduce prison crowding, and rehabilitate the offender. Virtually every discussion of intermediate sanctions in the United States notes a crisis in corrections (e.g., booming prison populations and fiscal constraints) as the impetus for this reform. Cullen and his colleagues (1996) contended, however, that this particular response to the penal crises was the result of the social and political context in the United States. They argued that if the penal crisis had occurred in the 1960s (the era of the Great Society), the response may have been to reduce sentence lengths, and perhaps, there would have been a movement toward deinstitutionalization. Because of the political "get tough on crime" rhetoric of the 1980s, however, intermediate sanctions appealed to liberals and conservatives alike. Liberals could take solace in the fact that a method of punishment was being provided that offered less use of incarceration. The conservative appeal arose out of the promise of control at a reduced cost. Among others, common intermediate sanctions in the United States today include shock incarceration, intensive supervision, electronic monitoring, and day reporting, which are more severe than traditional probation or parole supervision.

Harris and her colleagues (2001) investigated the use of intermediate sanctions in one county to assess the way in which a range of intermediate sanctions were applied. They reported a significant but weak relationship between severity of sanction and seriousness of offense. They interpreted this to mean that having a range of intermediate sanctions supports efforts to match penalties to crimes, but other factors influence the application of penalties in specific cases. They concluded that absent a range of intermediate penalties, it might not be possible to link crimes and punishments in any meaningful fashion.

6.15   Shock Incarceration

Shock probation and shock parole are used in an attempt to deter offenders from continued criminality by ordering a prison sentence that is later "commuted" to a period of supervision. The initial incarceration sentence is expected to "shock" the offender by the severity of the punishment. It also informs offenders what to expect if they continue to break the law (Vito 1985). For example, a judge may order a long prison term but, within a few months, change the penalty to a probation period. In some states, the inmate can petition the court for shock probation, whereas in others, shock probation is solely at the discretion of the judge.

Shock parole also involves an early release from a relatively long prison term. The difference is that the parole authority, not the judge, grants release supervision. A convicted offender who receives a ten-year prison sentence could receive shock probation from the judge after four or five months. In several states, if shock probation is not granted, the parole authority is allowed to grant early or shock parole.

The effectiveness of shock programs is unclear. Many of the programs provide no shock value because offenders expect to be released. Ideally, the incarcerated offender is "shocked" when released. The only surprise in practice may come if there is no early release. The combination of a short prison term followed by community supervision attempts to gain the benefits of both incarceration and supervision. In theory, shock probation and parole warn the offender that without the kindness of the judge or parole authority, the offender would be serving a long prison term. In effect, the released inmate is expected to realize that he or she is living "on borrowed time" and will face a long term of incarceration if supervision is unsuccessful. Camp and Camp (1996) reported that probation agencies in one-half of the state and federal jurisdictions operate shock probation programs.

A variation on the practice of shock probation and parole has been the prison boot camp (Anderson, Dyson, and Burns 1999). These programs are sometimes referred to as "shock incarceration," because the conditions of incarceration are designed to be more severe but limited in duration. Boot camp programs in prisons subject inmates to austere conditions including physical conditioning and strict discipline combined with hard labor. A total of 12,751 inmates were participating in boot camp programs operating in ninety-five correctional facilities across the United States at midyear 2000.

Most boot camp graduates are released to community supervision as probationers or parolees. Mackenzie and Parent (1991) evaluated the effect of boot camps on prison crowding. They observed that when careful selection criteria are developed, camps can reduce the number of inmates admitted to regular prison terms. Further, Mackenzie and Shaw (1990) reported that graduates of boot camps appear to have more socially positive attitudes than other prisoners. They suggested that boot camps may meet offender needs in ways that reduce the likelihood of future crime. In contrast, Faith Lutze (1998) found that although boot camp programs provide stricter controls on inmate behavior in prison, they are no more likely to support personal growth and development among inmates than traditional minimum-security incarceration. That is, boot camp participants do not differ from regular prisoners in terms of their learning ways to avoid future problems with the law. In a later study, Lutze (2001) reported that the increased severity of boot camp was associated with negative attitudes and adaptations to prison, if the program did not also provide support for future improvement for inmates. Being "tough" for the sake of being tough was perhaps seen by the inmates as unnecessary and unfair. As Mackenzie and Parent (1991) noted, legislators may support boot camp programs because the conditions in these programs are more punitive than in the typical prison, and thus shorter terms are seen as equally tough on crime. The available evidence indicates that boot camps do not reduce rates of new crime (recidivism) by program graduates and may actually hinder inmates in making a positive adjustment (Mackenzie 1997).

Split and combination sentences are similar to shock probation. A split sentence is one divided (split) between a period of incarceration and a period of probation supervision. Because of the great flexibility that judges are allowed in determining the conditions of probation, split sentences are relatively widely used. This is true even in jurisdictions where there is no law that specifically authorizes split sentencing. Split or combination sentences allow judges to alter the severity of a probation penalty. A judge may believe an offender should spend some time incarcerated but not wish to send a minor offender to prison for a long period. In 2003, 8 percent of persons placed on probation received a split sentence, while just over half were sentenced directly to probation. Of all those on probation in the United States in 2003, 22 percent had a sentence that combined probation and incarceration.

6.16   Intensive Supervision

Intensive supervision programs (ISPs) seek to provide more control and service to offenders who otherwise would be incarcerated (Travis 1984). In practice, these programs rely upon lower client-to-officer ratios, and thus, they assume a higher level of supervision and service delivery (Cullen, Wright, and Applegate 1996; Latessa 1980). Evaluations of intensive supervision programs show some promise of their effectiveness. However, they do not show that intensive supervision yields better results for the intensive populations than does regular supervision for the regular caseload (Mackenzie 1997). Intensive supervision programs are among the most popular intermediate sanctions in the United States. California was the first state to implement

ISPs in the 1960s, and today, ISPs exist in every state. Throughout their history, there have been three prominent models tied to three specific ideo-logical eras in the United States (Fulton et al. 1997).

The first generation of ISPs were developed in the 1960s under the rehabilitative ideology and focused on rehabilitative interventions with small caseloads. Evaluations indicated that these programs were more costly than regular probation and no more effective in reducing recidivism (Fulton et al. 1997). The State of Georgia reintroduced the use of ISPs (the second generation) in 1982 as a response to prison crowding. Most states followed suit in the 1980s and used ISPs as an alternative to prison. This generation of ISPs reflected the penal harm principles of the time, emphasizing punish-ment, control, and increased surveillance of offenders. Probation officers were less concerned with rehabilitation and more concerned with enforce-ment and revocation. Given the high rate of revocation that accompanied the Georgia model, this generation proved to be no better in reducing recid-ivism than the earlier generation. Nonetheless, the Georgia model is still the predominant model used in the United States today (Fulton et al. 1997).

The third generation of ISPs is the American Probation and Parole Asso-ciation (APPA) Prototypical model, which was implemented in the early 1990s as a result of increasing research evidence indicating a relationship between participation in effective treatment and lower recidivism rates. This model was intended to accomplish short-term crime control and long-term behavioral change. Under the APPA model, the probation officer acts as an advocate and tries to link the offender to treatment services. The probation officer also realizes that a full range of services must be applied to the offender, including surveillance and enforcement. The APPA model has done no better than its predecessors in reducing recidivism, but correctional administrators appreciate that it provides additional resources and gives them more options. Probation officers like the APPA model because they often believe that this treatment-control style is the way ISPs should have been operated all along (Fulton et al. 1997).

Whether or not ISPs reduce prison crowding is unclear. Erwin (1986) argued that, based on certain characteristics, Georgia ISP participants more closely resembled the prison population than the probation population. Petersilia and Turner (1993) suggested that because of the high rates of revocation exhibited by ISP participants in their study, intensive supervision programs may actually exacerbate the prison crowding problem.

Further, ISPs do not appear to achieve the goal of rehabilitating offenders, unless the sanction has been coupled with treatment. Petersilia and Turner (1993) found that at no site did intensive supervision participants experience arrest less often, a longer time to arrest, or arrest for a less serious offense than the control group. Fulton et al. (1997) noted, however, that the initial evaluation of the APPA model of intensive supervision programs indicated that a major source of variation in recidivism was the level of services provided.

Typically, an intensive supervision program requires the probationer to have more contacts with his or her probation officer. By reducing the size of caseloads, we expect officers to be more vigilant in intensive supervision programs (Byrne 1986). The net effect of these differences is to make the penalty more painful. The probationer experiences more intrusions by the officer. The penalty is also more incapacitative. The offender is more closely watched, and thus he or she is prevented from relapsing into crime. Intensive supervision programs in which the level of service delivery actually increased do appear to be modestly effective. What may be most important is how the mental picture caused by the label "intensive supervision" may make it politically possible to retain relatively serious or persistent offenders under community supervision, as opposed to incarcerating them (Clear and Shapiro 1986). This is consistent with the traditional role of community supervision as the "overflow valve" for prison populations.

6.17   Electronic Monitoring

There are two types of electronic surveillance systems in use today (National Institute of Justice 1999; Ford and Schmidt 1985; Huskey 1987; Schmidt 1987): active and passive surveillance. The supervising agency takes positive steps to monitor the offender in active systems. This typically involves fitting the offender with a transmitting device that sends a tone over the telephone. When called, the offender must answer the phone and place the transmitter in a special telephone connection to transmit a message to the calling computer. In the passive system, the transmitter attached to the offender emits a continuous signal and must be kept within range of an amplifier/transmitter or the signal will not reach a monitoring computer. This continuously signaling system usually requires the offender to remain within 150 to 200 feet of the fixed amplifier, normally installed in the offender's home (Huskey 1987).

Baumer, Maxfield, and Mendelsohn (1993) evaluated electronically monitored home detention programs, finding that these programs differed in their effectiveness based upon the agency under which they were operated and the characteristics of the people placed on monitoring. Pretrial detainees were more likely to violate program conditions, but these offenders were more clearly diverted from jail. Some evidence suggested that one effect of electronically monitored home confinement was to encourage offenders to seek employment. Finally, the assessment indicated that offenders on home confinement were not as securely prevented from committing new crimes as are those who are incarcerated in jails or prisons.

There are critics who suggest that monitoring is an insufficient penalty for many offenders, contending that this leniency reduces the deterrent effect of the law. Others argue that monitoring technology allows the release from incarceration of "dangerous" offenders who pose too great a risk to the community. In contrast, some criticize the technology as too oppressive, violating current standards of privacy, and infringing on constitutional rights to protection against unreasonable searches and seizures. Finally, some fear electronic monitoring, in practice, will be used to increase the severity of community supervision for those who would otherwise have been released to traditional probation or parole.

Proponents of surveillance argue that the technology enhances public safety by ensuring supervision of offenders in the community. Further, surveillance itself deters offenders from committing crimes. Similarly, proponents suggest that the ability to monitor offenders results in a lessening of penalty severity; continual supervision allows judges and parole boards to leave these offenders in the community. Although the current focus may be on the electronics of contemporary surveillance, at base, the questions and criticisms are the same ones that have always surrounded community supervision.

Electronic monitoring as a sanction, alone or in combination with other forms of community supervision, appears to be here to stay. Harry Boone (1996) reported results of a survey where over 90 percent of judges and policymakers said they felt electronic monitoring was here to stay, with almost two-thirds noting that they believed the use of electronic monitoring would grow in the future. Most observers believe that electronic monitoring is a cost-effective alternative to incarceration for many offenders (Evans 1996). Camp and Camp (1996, 160) reported that more than 90 percent of probation agencies responding to their survey indicated they used electronic monitoring, with a capacity of monitoring more than 12,000 offenders. At midyear 2003, over 12,500 jail inmates were supervised outside the jail facilities through electronic monitoring (Harrison and Karberg 2004). The typical offender was monitored for a period of about three months. It is not clear how well electronic monitoring can meet the goals of fairness, retribution, and a reduction in future crime (Cohn, Biondi, and Flaim 1996). Thus far, evaluations of electronic monitoring have not shown these programs to have an impact on future crime (Austin and Hardyman 1991; Mackenzie 1997).

6.18   Day Reporting

Day reporting is of relatively recent origin. The first day reporting program in the United States was started in Massachusetts in 1986 (McDevitt 1988). Designed as an early release alternative for prison and jail inmates, participants were required to report to the center each day, prepare an itinerary for their next day's activities, and report by telephone to the center throughout the day (Larivee 1990). By 1992, six centers with an average population of several hundred offenders were in operation. By the middle of 2003, jails reported supervising almost 8,000 offenders in day reporting programs across the United States.

Parent (1990) reported that day reporting programs were operational in six states by the late 1980s. The programs (and the clients they served) varied. McDevitt and Miliano (1992) observed that programs tend to have similar components, including frequent contact, formalized scheduling, and drug testing. Day reporting represents a significant increase in surveillance and contact over even intensive supervision programs. By 1994, over a hundred centers were operating in the United States (Parent et al. 1995).

Day reporting clients typically make at least one in-person and several telephone contacts with center staff daily, but are allowed to remain in the community throughout much of the day. Most programs are limited to between two and four months in duration, followed by a period of probation or parole supervision. Often, day reporting clients work with program staff to develop and obtain substance abuse treatment, psychological treatment, and employment services. The programs have not been adequately evaluated but promise to reduce prison crowding and costs, protect community safety, and provide needed services to offenders.

6.19 Broken Windows Probation

Perhaps the most recent suggested reform in community supervision in the United States is "broken windows probation." This reform seeks to expand the role of probation officers and agencies in a range of community activities and problems, with the goal of changing the environment in which offenders reside and thereby reducing chances of new crimes. Building on the notion of community decline embodied in the "broken windows theory" of policing (Wilson and Kelling 1982), advocates of broken windows probation urge the development of partnerships between probation and other law enforcement and community agencies.

The product of the Reinventing Probation Council (www.manhattan-institute.org), the broken windows probation model focuses on what is called "place-based" supervision. The attention of the supervising agent and agency is directed at the community in which the offender resides and works. Probation efforts are to be directed at connecting offenders with prosocial influences in their communities and with supporting prosocial influences in those communities. No longer will managing individual cases be sufficient. In theory, strong neighborhoods with strong informal social controls and a range of legitimate options and opportunities will keep probationers from returning to crime. The job of the probation agency is to work with other community and governmental organizations to build strong communities.

If implemented as envisioned, offenders would be assigned to supervision caseloads based on their residential or employment address. Supervising officers would devote at least as much attention to working with police, employers, family, and other community resources as they would dealing directly with the individual offender. As Rhine and his colleagues (2001, 33) summarized it:

> There is no doubt that the adoption of the strategies that occupy the center of the "Broken Windows" model will require a loosening of organizational structure and a major redirection in the management practices associated with many probation agencies today. This will necessarily involve a decentralization of tasks, greater reliance on automated information systems, an outcomes-based or results-driven focus, and the cultivation of wide-ranging staff competencies that facilitate building partnerships within and linking offenders to the communities in which they live.

Although the full model of broken windows probation has not been implemented and evaluated anywhere, parts of the model have been implemented in some places. The apparent success of partnerships between community supervision agencies and others in reducing firearms homicides among youth in Boston, the ability of the probation department in Dallas to screen and refer probationers for substance abuse and mental health needs, and similar practices were cited by the Reinventing Probation Council as evidence of the ability of a broken windows approach to improve the effectiveness of probation.

Not surprisingly, there are critics of the broken windows model. Faye Taxman and James Byrne (2001) argued that the movement to broken windows probation will result in fewer treatment services to offenders, more restrictive supervision, more severe penalties, and higher rates of recidivism. They suggest that the current evidence regarding what are the "best practices" in community supervision does not support the model. Rather, they argue for greater attention to individual offender treatment needs. In their view, the broken windows probation model is "a throwback to the 'get tough' surveillance-oriented community sanctions championed during the late '80s and early '90s" (Taxman and Byrne 2001).

6.20   Conclusions

Time will tell if the broken windows model of community supervision will take root and what effects it might have. No matter the outcome of the current discussion about the best future direction for probation and parole, what is clear is the centrality of community supervision to contemporary correctional practice. As the pace of development for intermediate sanctions quickens, and the ability to share information about correctional practices and outcomes improves, we can expect probation and parole to become ever more common and important components of correctional practice around the world.

References

Anderson, J. F., L. Dyson, and J. C. Burns. 1999. *Boot camp: An intermediate sanction.* Lanham, MD: University Press of America.

Austin, J., and P. Hardyman. 1991. *The use of early parole with electronic monitoring to control prison crowding.* Washington, DC: National Institute of Justice.

Baumer, T., M. Maxfield, and R. Mendelsohn. 1993. A comparative analysis of three electronically monitored home detention programs. *Justice Quarterly* 10(1), 121.

Beck, A. J., and C. J. Mumola. 1999. *Prisoners in 1998.* Washington, DC: Bureau of Justice Statistics.

Bennett, L. A. 1991. Security in the community: The public wants accountability. *Corrections Today* 53(4), 92.

Boone, H. 1996. Electronic home confinement: Judicial and legislative perspectives. *APPA Perspectives* 18.

Byrne, J. M. 1986. The control controversy: A preliminary examination of intensive probation supervision programs in the United States. *Federal Probation* 50(2), 4-16.

Camp, G., and C. Camp. 1996. *The Corrections Yearbook 1996.* South Salem, NY: Criminal Justice Institute.

Chui, W. H. 2003. Experience of probation supervision in Hong Kong: Listening to the young adult probationers. *Journal of Criminal Justice* 3, 567.

Clear, T. R., and J. M. Byrne. 1992. The future of intermediate sanctions: Questions to consider. In *Smart sentencing: The emergence of intermediate sanctions,* ed. James M. Byrne, Arthur J. Lurigio, and Joan Petersilia, 319. Beverly Hills, CA: Sage.

Clear, T. R., and H. R. Dammer. 2002. Probation. In *Encyclopedia of Crime and Punishment,* Volume 3, ed. David Levinson, 1259. Thousand Oaks, CA: Sage.

Clear, T. R., and C. Shapiro. 1986. Identifying high risk probationers for supervision in the community: The Oregon model. *Federal Probation* 50(2), 42.

Cohn, A. W., L. G. Biondi, and L. C. Flaim. 1996. The evaluation of electronic monitoring programs. *APPA Perspectives* 28.

Cullen, F. T., J. P. Wright, and B. Applegate. 1996. Control in the community: The limits of reform. In *Choosing correctional options that work*, ed. Alan T. Harland, 69. Thousand Oaks, CA: Sage.

Ditton, P. M., and J. Wilson. 1999. *Truth in Sentencing in State Prisons*. Washington, DC: U.S. Bureau of Justice Statistics.

Erwin, B. S. 1986. Turning up the heat on probationers in Georgia. *Federal Probation* (50)2, 17.

Evans, D. G. 1996. Electronic monitoring: Testimony to Ontario's standing committee on administration of justice. *APPA Perspectives* 8.

Flanagan, T. 1985. Questioning the other parole: The effectiveness of community supervision of offenders. In *Probation, Parole, and Community Corrections: A Reader*, ed. Lawrence F. Travis, III, 167. Prospect Heights, IL: Waveland.

Ford, D., and A. Schmidt. 1985. *Electronically monitored home confinement*. NCJRS Update (November).

Fulton, B., E. J. Latessa, A. J. Stichman, and L. Travis. 1997. Up to speed: The state of ISP: Research and policy implications. *Federal Probation* 61(4), 65.

Geerken, M., and H. Hayes. 1993. Probation and parole: Public risk and the future of incarceration alternatives. *Criminology* 31(4), 549.

Gibbs, J. 1985. Clients' views of community corrections. In *Probation, Parole, and Community Corrections: A Reader*, ed. Lawrence F. Travis, III, 97. Prospect Heights, IL: Waveland.

Glaze, L. 2002. *Probation and Parole in the United States*. Washington, DC: U.S. Bureau of Justice Statistics.

Goldstein, H., W. Burrell, and R. Talty. 1985. Probation: The Rand report and beyond. *APPA Perspectives* 9(2), 11.

Gottfredson, M., S. Mitchell-Herzfeld, and T. Flanagan. 1982. Another look at the effectiveness of parole supervision. *Journal of Research in Crime and Delinquency* 18(2), 277.

Gowdy, V. 1993. *Intermediate Sanctions*. Washington, DC: National Institute of Justice.

Hamai, K., ed. 1995. *Probation Round the World: A Comparative Study*. New York: Routledge.

Harland, A.T., ed. 1996. *Choosing correctional options that work*. Thousand Oaks, CA: Sage.

Harland, A.T., and C. Rosen. 1987. Sentencing theory and intensive supervision probation. *Federal Probation* 51(4), 33.

Harris, P., P. Rebecca, and S. Rapoza. 2001. Between probation and revocation: A study of intermediate sanctions decision-making. *Journal of Criminal Justice* 29(4), 307.

Harris, R. 1995a. Probation round the world: Origins and development. In *Probation Round the World: A Comparative Study*, ed. Koichi Hamai. New York: Routledge.

Harris, R. 1995b. Studying probation: A comparative approach. In *Probation Round the World: A Comparative Study*, ed. Koichi Hamai. New York: Routledge.

Harrison, P. M., and A. J. Beck. 2003. *Prisoners in 2002*. Washington, DC: U.S. Bureau of Justice Statistics.

Harrison, P. M., and J. C. Karberg. 2004. *Prison and Jail Inmates at Midyear 2003*. Washington, DC: Bureau of Justice Statistics.

Huskey, B. L. 1987. Electronic monitoring: An evolving alternative. *APPA Perspectives* 11(3), 19.

Israel, M., and J. Dawes. 2002. 'Something from nothing': Shifting credibility in community correctional programmes in Australia. *Criminal Justice* 2(1), 5.

Jones, P. 1991. The risk of recidivism: Evaluating the public-safety implications of a community corrections program. *Journal of Criminal Justice* 19(1), 49.

Larivee, J. J. 1990. Day reporting centers: Making their way from the U.K. to the U.S. *Corrections Today* 52(6), 84.

Latessa, E. J. 1980. Intensive diversion unit: An evaluation. In *Criminal justice research*, ed. B. Price and P. J. Baunach, 101. Beverly Hills, CA: Sage.

Lutze, F. 1998. Are shock incarceration programs more rehabilitative than traditional prisons? A survey of inmates. *Justice Quarterly* 15(3), 547.

Lutze, F. 2001. The influence of a shock incarceration program on inmate adjustment and attitudinal change. *Justice Quarterly* 29(3), 255.

McCarthy, B. R., B. J. McCarthy, and M. C. Leone. 2001. *Community based corrections*, 4th ed. Belmont, CA: Wadsworth/Thompson Learning.

McDevitt, J. 1988. *Evaluation of the Hampton County Day Reporting Center*. Boston: Crime and Justice Foundation.

McDevitt, J., and R. Miliano. 1992. Day reporting centers: An innovative concept in intermediate sanctions. In *Smart sentencing: The emergence of intermediate sanctions*, ed. James M. Byrne, Arthur J. Lurigio, and Joan Petersilia, 152-165. Beverly Hills, CA: Sage.

McGaha, J., M. Fichter, and P. Hirschburg. 1987. Felony probation: A re-examination of public risk. *American Journal of Criminal Justice* 12(1), 1.

Mackenzie, D. 1997. Criminal justice and crime control. In *Preventing Crime: What Works, What Doesn't, What's Promising?* ed. Lawrence Sherman, Denise Gottfredson, Doris MacKenzie, John Eck, Peter Reuter, and Shawn Bushway. Washington, DC: National Institute of Justice.

Mackenzie, D., and D. Parent. 1991. Shock incarceration and prison crowding in Louisiana. *Journal of Criminal Justice* 19(3), 225.

Mackenzie, D., and J. Shaw. 1990. Inmate adjustment and change during shock incarceration: The impact of correctional boot camp programs. *Justice Quarterly* 7(1), 125.

Millie, A., J. Jacobson, and M. Hough. 2003. Understanding the growth in the prison population in England and Wales. *Criminal Justice* 3(4), 369.

Morris, N., and M. Tonry. 1990. *Between prison and probation: Intermediate punishments in a rational sentencing system.* Oxford University Press.

Nash, M. 1998. Managing risk—achieving protection? The police and probation agendas. *International Journal of Public Sector Management* 11(4), 252.

National Institute of Justice. 1999. Keeping track of electronic monitoring. *National Law Enforcement and Corrections Technology Center Bulletin* October. Washington, DC.

Newman, G. R. 1983. *Just and Painful.* New York: Macmillan.

Newman, G. R., ed. 1999. *The Global Report on Crime and Justice.* United Nations Office for Drug Control and Crime Prevention, Center for International Crime Prevention. New York: Oxford University Press.

Newman, G.R., ed. 2002. *U.S. The World Factbook of Criminal Justice Systems.* Department of Justice, Office of Justice Programs, Bureau of Justice Statistics (1993-2002). http://www.ojp.usdoj.gov/bjs/abstract/wfcj.htm, accessed June 2004.

Parent, D. G. 1990. *Day Reporting Centers for Criminal Offenders: A Descriptive Analysis of Existing Programs.* Washington, DC: U.S. Department of Justice.

Parent, D. G., J. M. Byrne, V. Tsarfaty, L. Valade, and J. Esselman. 1995. *Day Reporting Centers,* Volume 1: *Issues and Practices.* Washington, DC: National Institute of Justice.

Petersilia, J. 1985. *Probation and Felony Offenders.* Washington, DC: U.S. Department of Justice.

Petersilia, J., and S. Turner. 1993. *Evaluating Intensive Supervision Probation/Parole: Results of a Nationwide Experiment.* Washington, DC: National Institute of Justice.

Petersilia, J., S. Turner, and J. Peterson. 1986. *Prison versus Probation in California: Implications for Crime and Offender Recidivism.* Santa Monica, CA: Rand.

Piquero, N. 2003. A recidivism analysis of Maryland's community probation program. *Journal of Criminal Justice* 31(4), 295.

Reichel, P. 2005. *Comparative Criminal Justice Systems,* 4th ed. Upper Saddle River, NJ: Pearson/Prentice-Hall.

Rhine, E. F. 1997. Probation and parole supervision: In need of a new narrative. *Corrections Management Quarterly* 1(2), 71.

Rhine, E. F., G. Hinzman, R. R. Corbett, D. R. Beto, and M. Paparozzi. 2001. A call for transforming community supervision. *APPA Perspectives* Spring: 30.

Rhine, E., G. Hinzman, R. Corbett, D. Beto, and M. Paparozzi (2001). The "broken windows" model of probation: A call for transforming community supervision. *Perspectives* 25(2): 30–33.

Roth, M. P. 2005. *Crime and Punishment: A History of the Criminal Justice System.* Belmont, CA: Wadsworth/Thompson Learning.

Schmidt, A. 1987. Electronic monitoring: Who uses it? How much does it cost? Does it work? *Corrections Today* 49(7), 28.

Taxman, F., and J. Byrne. 2001. Fixing broken windows probation. *Perspectives* 25(2): 22–29.

Timasheff, N. 1941. *One Hundred Years of Probation, 1841-1941: Parts I and II.* New York: Fordham University Press.

The Reinventing Probation Council (1999). "Broken Windows" Probation: The Next Step in Fighting Crime. New York, NY: Manhattan Institute.

Travis, L.F., III. 1984. Intensive supervision in probation and parole. *Corrections Today* 46(4), 34.

van Kalmthout, A. M., and T. M. Derks. 2000. *Probation and Probation Services: A European Perspective.* Nijmegen, The Netherlands: Wolf Legal Publishers.

Ville, R., U. Zvekic, and J. F. Klaus, eds. 1997. *Promoting Probation Internationally.* Rome/London: United Nations Interregional Crime and Justice Research Institute, Commonwealth Secretariat.

Vito, G. F. 1985. Probation as punishment: New directions. In *Probation, Parole and Community Corrections*, ed, Lawrence F. Travis III, 73. Prospect Heights, IL: Waveland.

Vito, G. F. 1986. Felony probation and recidivism: Replication and response. *Federal Probation* 50(4), 17.

von Hirsch, A., and K. Hanrahan. 1978. *Abolish Parole?* Washington, DC: U.S. Department of Justice.

Walmsley, R. 2001. *An overview of world imprisonment: Global prison populations, trends and solutions.* http://www.kcl.ac.uk/depsta/rel/icps/world_ imprisonment.doc, accessed June 16, 2004.

Walmsley, R. 2002. *The Seventh United Nations Survey on Crime Trends and the Operations of the Criminal Justice System (1998-2000).* United Nations Office on Drugs and Crimes. http://www.unodc.org/unodc/cime_cicp_survey_ seventh.html#responses, accessed June 16, 2004.

Wilson, J. Q., and G. L. Kelling. 1982. Broken windows: Police and neighborhood safety. *Atlantic Monthly* 249 (March): 29.

Worrall, J., P. Schram, E. Hays, and M. Newman. 2004. An analysis of the relationship between probation caseloads and property crime rates in California counties. *Journal of Criminal Justice* 32(3), 231.

Crime Prevention

STEVEN P. LAB

7

Contents

7.1   Introduction

Crime prevention is not a new idea. Indeed, for as long as people have been victimized, there have been attempts to protect one's self and one's family. The term *crime prevention*, however, has only recently come to signify a set of ideas for combating crime. Many people suggest that crime prevention today is new and unique, particularly in terms of citizen participation. In reality, many recent activities classified as crime prevention can be seen throughout history. "New" crime prevention ideas and techniques are often little more than reincarnations of past practices or extensions of basic approaches in the (distant) past. It is only in the relatively recent past that the general citizenry has *not* been the primary line of defense against crime and victimization.

The earliest responses to crime were left to the individual and his or her family. Retribution, revenge, and vengeance were the driving forces throughout early history. The Code of Hammurabi (approximately 1900 B.C.) outlined retribution by the victim and his or her family as the accepted response to injurious behavior. *Lex talionis*, the principle of "an eye for an eye," was specifically set forth as a driving principle in the Hammurabic law. Such laws and practices provided legitimacy to individual citizen action.

The existence of formal systems of social control is relatively new. Early "policing," such as in the Roman Empire and in France, was concentrated in the cities, conducted by the military, and dealt with issues of the central state and the nobility (i.e., king) (Holden 1992; Langworthy and Travis 1994). The general public was left to continue self-help methods.

Crime prevention emerged with the development of formal police organizations. Central to the establishment of the Metropolitan Police in 1829 London was the idea of crime prevention. Sir Robert Peel, who was the driving force behind the Metropolitan Police Act, and Charles Roman, the commissioner of the new organization, both saw crime prevention as the basic principle underlying police work (LaGrange 1993). Even earlier attempts at formal policing, such as that in seventeenth century Paris, emphasized crime prevention through methods such as preventive patrol, increased lighting, and street cleaning (Stead 1983).

Although individual action and self-help dominated throughout most of history, it should not be construed as indicative that protective actions were solely a matter of retribution and revenge. There are numerous examples of approaches that were preventive in nature. Easy examples were the use of walls, moats, drawbridges, and other physical design features around cities that protected the community from external invasion. Surveillance, as provided by "watch and ward," allowed the identification of problems before they got out of hand. Yet another early prevention approach was the restriction of weapon ownership as a means of eliminating violent behavior (Holden 1992).

The advent of the twentieth century saw the growth of scientific study of crime and criminal behavior, and the movement away from simple responses to crime (such as repression, vengeance, and retribution) to actions that attack the causes of deviant behavior. The development of the juvenile court and its efforts to combat the problems of poverty, lack of education, and poor parenting among the lower classes was clearly an attempt at prevention. The growth of rehabilitation was another move toward preventing criminal behavior.

Crime prevention is an idea that has been around for as long as there has been crime. Although the form has changed and the term *crime prevention* is relatively new, the concern over safety is age old. It has only been in the relatively recent past that society has moved to a system of police, courts, and corrections that has assumed the primary responsibility for crime. The criminal justice system, however, has been unable to prevent or control crime. Simply increasing the funding for the system has not improved its ability to stop crime. Crime is a societal problem, not just a criminal justice system problem.

Since the late 1960s, there has been a growing movement toward bringing the citizenry back as active participants in crime prevention. Although many see this type of community action as new, in reality it is more a movement back to old traditions of individual responsibility than it is a revolutionary step forward in crime control. Crime prevention must utilize the wide range of ideas and abilities found throughout society. Community planning, architecture, neighborhood action, juvenile advocacy, security planning, education, and technical training, among many other system and nonsystem activities, all have a potential impact on the levels of crime and fear of crime. The realm of crime prevention is vast and open for expansion.

This chapter attempts to provide an overview of the many concepts and approaches making up crime prevention. After offering a definition for *crime prevention* and a model of crime prevention practices, the chapter presents discussions of some of the most recognizable crime prevention initiatives. Included in this discussion are environmental design approaches, community organizing/neighborhood watch, general deterrence, social crime prevention, prediction for secondary prevention, situational crime prevention and community policing, interventions focusing on drug use and abuse, and avenues of addressing recidivistic behavior. The chapter focuses mainly on primary and secondary prevention. The goal is to present a sampling of prevention approaches, outline the selected programs and issues, present the research and evaluations that have been carried out on the programs (if any have been done), and critically examine the prevention effort and the potential of the approach to affect crime and the fear of crime.

7.2 Defining Crime Prevention

The definition of crime prevention varies from study to study and program to program. Crime prevention must attack both the real and perceived levels of crime and victimization. Most definitions of crime prevention incorporate the ideas of lessening the actual levels of crime or prohibiting further increases in crime (see Akers and Sagarin 1972; Empey 1977; National Crime Prevention Institute 1978; Whisenand 1977). Few, however, deal with the problem of fear of crime and perceived crime and victimization. The definition used in this chapter, therefore, is

> Crime prevention entails any action designed to reduce the actual level of crime and/or the perceived fear of crime.

These actions are not restricted to the efforts of the criminal justice system and include activities by individuals and groups, both public and private. Just as there are many causes of crime, there are many potentially valuable approaches to crime prevention.

7.2.1 A Crime Prevention Model

Crime prevention can be divided into three approaches, similar to that found in public health models of disease prevention (see Brantingham and Faust 1976; Caplan 1964; Leavell and Clarke 1965; Shah and Roth 1974). Each of the three areas of prevention—primary, secondary, and tertiary—attacks the problem at different stages of development. From the public health viewpoint, primary prevention refers to actions taken to avoid the initial development of the disease or problem. This would include vaccinations and sanitary cleanups by public health officials. Secondary prevention moves beyond the point of general societal concerns and focuses on those individuals and situations that exhibit early signs of disease. Included at this stage are screening tests such as those for tuberculosis or systematically providing examinations to workers who handle toxic materials. Tertiary prevention rests at the point where the disease or problem has already manifested itself. Activities at this stage entail the elimination of the immediate problem and taking steps designed to inhibit a reoccurrence in the future. The various approaches to crime prevention are directly analogous to this public health model.

Primary prevention "identifies conditions of the physical and social environment that provide opportunities for or precipitate criminal acts" (Brantingham and Faust 1976). The types of prevention approaches subsumed here include environmental design, neighborhood watch, general deterrence, private security, education about crime and crime prevention, and attempts to change the underlying social conditions related to crime and deviance. Secondary prevention "engages in early identification of potential offenders and seeks to intervene" (Brantingham and Faust 1976) prior to commission of illegal activity. Implicit in secondary prevention is the ability to correctly identify and predict problem people and situations. Perhaps the most recognizable form of secondary prevention is the idea of situational crime prevention, which seeks to identify existing problems at the micro level and institute interventions that are developed specifically for the given problem. Also included under secondary prevention is community policing, which relies heavily on citizen involvement in a problem-solving approach to neighborhood concerns.

According to Brantingham and Faust (1976), tertiary prevention "deals with actual offenders and involves intervention... in such a fashion that they will not commit further offenses." The majority of tertiary prevention rests within the workings of the criminal justice system: arrest, prosecution, incarceration, treatment, and rehabilitation.

7.2.2 Alternate Models

Although this chapter uses the primary/secondary/tertiary model to organize the discussion of crime prevention, other models exist. One model is a variation on this tripartite view offered by van Dijk and de Waard (1991). Their model adds a second dimension of victim-oriented, community/neighborhood-oriented, and offender-oriented approaches. For example, primary prevention techniques can be divided into actions that target victims, the community, or potential offenders. The authors attempt to refine the public health-based classification system. Crawford (1998) offered another two-dimensional typology, which again uses the primary/secondary/tertiary view as a starting point and adds a distinction between social and situational approaches within each category. Both of these proposed models, as well as others not discussed here, offer alternative views of crime prevention and ways of conceptualizing crime prevention interventions. They offer more complex views, however, which are not necessary for examining the realm of crime prevention. Consequently, this chapter opts to use the more simplified classification scheme of primary, secondary, and tertiary prevention.

7.3 Primary Prevention

Primary prevention deals with eliminating influences in the physical and social environment that engender deviant behavior. Such programs do not target individuals who are already criminal or prone to criminal behavior, except in a most indirect sense. Instead, primary prevention programs work with general physical and societal factors that provide the opportunity for deviance to occur. The following discussion reflects varying methods aimed at removing or mitigating the criminogenic aspects of communities and the larger society.

7.3.1 The Physical Environment and Crime

The advent of modern crime prevention can be traced to the attention paid to architectural and physical design changes and their impact on crime in the 1970s. Changing the physical design of a home, business, or neighborhood has the potential of affecting crime in a variety of ways. One possibility is that the changes will make it more difficult to carry out a crime and reduce the payoff in relation to the effort. Another potential impact is that the risk of being seen and caught while committing an offense may be enhanced. Finally, the physical design changes may prompt local residents to alter their behavior in ways that make crime more difficult to commit.

Efforts to alter the physical design to impact crime are generally referred to as crime prevention through environmental design (CPTED). The basic ideas of CPTED grew out of Oscar Newman's concept of *defensible space*, which proposed "a model which inhibits crime by creating a physical expression of a social fabric which defends itself" (Newman 1972). The idea is that the physical characteristics of an area can influence the behavior of both residents and potential offenders. For residents, the appearance and design of the area can engender a more caring attitude, draw the residents into contact with one another, lead to further improvements and use of the area, and build a stake in the control and elimination of crime. For potential offenders, an area's appearance can suggest that residents use and care for their surroundings, pay attention to what occurs, and will intervene if an offense is seen.

Four key elements of defensible space are territoriality, natural surveillance, image, and milieu (Newman 1972). Each of these factors influences the criminogenic nature of the area. Territoriality refers to the ability and desire of legitimate users of an area to lay claim to the area through the establishment of real or perceived boundaries, the recognition of strangers and legitimate users of the area, and a general communal atmosphere among the inhabitants. Natural surveillance involves designing an area that allows legitimate users to observe the daily activity of friends, strangers, and potential offenders. Image refers to building a neighborhood or community that does not appear vulnerable to crime and is not isolated from the surrounding community. Finally, milieu suggests that the placement of a community within a larger low-crime, high-surveillance area will inhibit criminal activity. All of the aspects of defensible space seek to present the area as a high-risk venture for those seeking to commit crime.

Although much of the discussion about physical features deals with the correct design to allow surveillance and feelings of goodwill among legitimate users, there is also the question of physical signs of disorder that may actively promote an area as ripe for criminal activity. Signs of disorder, however, are not restricted to physical features. There also are social signs of disorder. Various authors (for example, Hunter 1978; Skogan 1990; Taylor and Gottfredson 1986; Wilson and Kelling 1982) have presented indicators of physical disorder, including broken windows, abandoned buildings, vacant lots, deteriorating buildings, litter, vandalism, and graffiti. Similarly, they offer social indicators such as loitering juveniles, public drunkenness, gangs, drug sales and use, harassment (such as begging and panhandling), prostitution, and a lack of interaction between people on the street. Perkins and Taylor (1996), Taylor et al. (1995), and Spelman (1993) suggested that physical disorder can contribute to the growth of social disorder. Examples of such instances would be nonresidential property or abandoned structures interrupting a housing block (Taylor 1988). The physical feature may inhibit social interaction among residents and allow for social incivilities to arise.

These physical and social indicators are typically referred to as signs of incivility. Incivility in a neighborhood has been proposed as evidence that the residents are not concerned, or at least are less concerned, about what is happening around them than persons in areas not characterized by incivility (Lewis and Salem 1986). Signs of disorder may lead residents to withdraw into their homes and abandon cooperative efforts at improving the neighborhood (Skogan 1990; Taylor 1988). In essence, signs of incivility attract potential offenders to the neighborhood. The idea of incivilities can be viewed as another part of Newman's "image." For the offender, signs of incivility are indicative of lower risk (Taylor and Gottfredson 1986). Efforts to minimize incivility through improvement of the physical and social environment, therefore, should increase perceived risk and decrease crime and fear of crime.

A great deal of physical design initiatives revolve around access control/target hardening and surveillance. Access control seeks to allow only those persons who have legitimate business in an area to enter. This reduces the opportunity for crime by increasing the effort needed to enter and exit a building or area for the purpose of committing crime. Many access control strategies are referred to as target hardening. That is, they are efforts that make potential criminal targets more difficult to victimize. The use and/or installation of locks, bars on windows, unbreakable glass, intruder alarms, fences, safes, and other devices makes crime harder to carry out. Neighborhood designs that could make offending more difficult include limited numbers of entrances, limited numbers of through streets, and the establishment of cul-de-sacs and dead-end streets. These actions would limit the flow of traffic through an area by strangers and enhance the ability to recognize legitimate users. It also eliminates escape routes for offenders who do enter the area.

Other forms of access control/target hardening take an indirect approach to crime control. The placement of identifying marks on personal property makes stolen goods harder to fence and easier to identify and return to victims. The use of warning signs, closed-circuit television (CCTV) cameras, and lighting may act as psychological deterrents that increase perceived risk. Indeed, cameras need not be operable, as in many department stores, to serve a target hardening function.

Surveillance entails any action that increases the chance that offenders will be observed by residents. Placing windows and doors in such a fashion to allow residents to see activity is one means of improving surveillance (Newman 1972). The installation of lights should enhance the ability to see what occurs in the area. Increasing outdoor activity and pedestrian traffic increases the number of "eyes on the street." Underlying these suggestions is the assumption that, if a crime or suspicious individual is seen, the observer will inform the police or take some other action designed to eliminate crime.

7.3.2   Evaluation of Physical Design

Examination of the existing evidence on physical design shows some promising results, along with a number of instances where the impact of the techniques is inconsistent. In general, research on lighting has produced inconsistent results, with the greatest differences in outcome appearing between early studies and those done more recently in the United Kingdom. Various early studies in the United States reported no impact, or even increased crime after lighting changes (Atlanta 1975; Lewis and Sullivan 1979; Mayor's Criminal Justice Coordinating Council 1977; Reppetto 1974; Tien et al. 1977). More recent studies, particularly those of Painter and her colleagues (Painter 1993; Painter and Farrington 1997, 1999a, 1999b), find a positive impact of lighting. Lighting appears to have its greatest impact on burglary, theft, and fear of crime in residential areas.

Surveillance can also be enhanced through the use of closed-circuit television. As a crime prevention tool, CCTV has received little attention in the United States but is in widespread use in the United Kingdom. Oc and Tiesdell (1997) noted that over eighty town or city centers in the United Kingdom had CCTV in operation, and an additional two hundred CCTV programs operated in other public places. The British government funded over 550 CCTV programs in the mid- to late 1990s, with funding for additional programs allocated from 1999 to 2001 (Phillips, 1999). Evaluations of CCTV in town centers, housing areas, car parks, and businesses show inconsistent results. Although some evaluations show reductions in burglary, theft, and robbery, others do not (Beck and Willis 1999; Brown 1995; Ditton and Short 1999; Tilley 1993; Tonglet 1998; Welsh and Farrington 2002). The most consistent positive finding is reduction in fear of crime.

Despite the great proliferation of property identification programs (typically called Operation Identification), there is little empirical research on most programs. The basic idea behind these projects is to increase the difficulty for offenders to dispose of marked items. Few programs, however, are able to entice more than a small fraction of the population to participate (Heller et al. 1975). Evaluations of property marking have failed to reveal any consistent impact on burglary or theft.

Alarms represent one possible deterrent to offending that is effective at reducing burglary in homes and businesses. Silent alarms have increased the numbers of arrests and the clearance rate, as well as reduced household burglary (Buck, Hakim, and Rengert 1993; Cedar Rapids Police Department 1975). Interviews with offenders also reveal that they check on the presence or absence of alarms during the planning stages of their offenses (Reppetto 1974; Bennett and Wright 1984).

Access control also can be improved through the installation of various devices that make entry more difficult, such as locks, doors, and unbreakable glass. Evaluations of the effect of various methods aimed at making entry more difficult generally reveal positive results (Bennett and Wright 1984; Home Office 2003b, 2003d; Seattle 1975). At the same time, offenders often find alternative targets or methods to circumvent the security devices.

Besides individual design features, CPTED also takes a more global view of altering the design of entire neighborhoods. Research on these broader-based approaches also reveals positive results. Alteration of street layouts and traffic patterns, for example, reveals reduced crime and lower fear of crime among subjects living in those areas (Beavon, Brantingham, and Brantingham 1994; Bevis and Nutter 1977; Bowers, Johnson, and Hirschfield 2003; Newman and Wayne 1974). Streets and areas that are easily accessible to pedestrian and auto traffic tend to experience higher levels of actual crime and fear of crime. The construction of cul-de-sacs, dead-end streets, alley gates, and streets that promote a feeling of ownership will have positive effects for crime prevention.

Numerous evaluations of CPTED have been undertaken in relation to public housing developments, residential estates/subdivisions, and neighborhoods (Booth 1981; Fowler, McCalla, and Mangione 1979; Home Office 2003b, 2003d; Newman 1972; Newman and Franck 1980; Normoyle and Foley 1988; Poyner 1994). Results of these analyses offer mixed results. Although some evaluations find reductions in burglary, theft, and robbery, others report no changes in the offense levels. The most consistent finding is that improvements in an area tend to reduce fear of crime and increase residents' satisfaction.

Although it appears that physical design features can impact crime and fear, there is no guarantee that proper design will produce the desired results. Merry (1981) noted that "good defensible space design neither guarantees that a space will appear safe nor that it will become a part of a territory which residents defend effectively." In essence, an area may be defensible but undefended.

7.3.3 Evaluations of Incivility

Although signs of disorder and incivility have been accepted almost without question as a cause of crime and fear in society, the research is not so promising. Recent analyses question the extent to which eliminating signs of disorder, particularly physical signs, will have an impact. Covington and Taylor (1991) and Taylor (1997) pointed out that the relationship between disorder and fear is highly contingent on how disorder is measured. Specifically, they noted that area disorder measured objectively by independent raters is only marginally related to fear and resident behavior. A strong relationship between disorder and fear (and possibly behavior) appears only when *perceived* incivilities are considered, as subjectively reflected in surveys of residents. Consequently, efforts to reduce physical disorder would have only minimal impact on fear (Taylor 1997). The challenge is to identify methods of altering the *perceptions* of disorder. Although the impact of disorder and incivilities on crime, fear, and citizen behavior may be minimal, many reasons remain for working to reduce signs of incivility. Perhaps the best reason is that nobody should have to live in areas with such problems.

7.3.4 Summary

These various discussions should not be interpreted as indicating that there is no positive effect of defensible space features on crime and fear of crime. An array of studies has found various design features and crime prevention techniques that impact on crime and fear. There are, however, a substantial number of studies that produce negative or equivocal results. These contradictory findings may stem from the inability to bring about, or lack of attention paid to, changes in intervening factors, such as social cohesion and feelings of territoriality. The basic premise of Newman's argument is that the physical environment engenders feelings of territoriality and citizen control, which then impact on crime. Any failure of physical design, therefore, may be due to an inability of the individual implementation program to bring about these intervening factors.

7.4 Neighborhood Crime Prevention

The failure of physical environmental design changes to impact crime and fear may be directly attributable to the inability of such activities to motivate residents and legitimate users to act against crime. Neighborhood crime prevention, however, seeks to directly influence citizen participation in crime prevention and the reduction of crime and fear. Neighborhood crime prevention can take a variety of forms that are broader in scope than those discussed in connection with physical design. The possible techniques include neighborhood watch, neighborhood advocacy, citizen patrols, and physical design.

A wide variety of neighborhood crime prevention strategies have been proposed and implemented over the years. The past thirty years have seen a great proliferation of programs in the United States and Great Britain. Although many programs in both countries have been instigated and aided by various government agencies or policies, other programs emerged from the simple realization by citizens that the formal criminal justice system was incapable of solving the crime problem on its own. Regardless of the source of stimulation, neighborhood crime prevention has become a major aspect of crime prevention.

The basic goal of neighborhood crime prevention is increasing community awareness and problem-solving. This can be accomplished through a variety of methods. Foremost among these is the bringing together of neighbors and residents of an area. Often, the resulting groups and activity are referred to as *neighborhood watch*. Mutual problems and goals among participating individuals lead to increased feelings of communal needs and, possibly, joint action. Neighborhood watch, ideally, is proactive in design. That is, it sets out to identify problems before they occur or, at the very least, as they occur. Neighborhood involvement is meant to recognize and circumvent those problems that lead to an area's decline and accompanying increased crime.

In its most effective form, neighborhood watch and similar programs should provide informal (and possibly formal) social control in the community. Bursik and Grasmick (1993) noted that many neighborhoods are socially disorganized and, consequently, are unable to exert any control over residents or visitors. The authors argued that neighborhoods need to draw on resources from a variety of sources in an effort to build social control. Friendships, families, local businesses, churches, schools, and interpersonal networks are examples of local resources upon which neighborhoods can draw and build (Bursik and Grasmick 1993). Neighborhood watch is one incarnation of social control in a neighborhood.

One way that neighborhood watch contributes to social control is through the heavy use of surveillance. Successful surveillance requires the ability to distinguish legitimate from illegitimate users of an area. The surveillance goal of neighborhood watch is greatly enhanced through the institution of various activities. Many neighborhood watch programs include citizen patrols, whistle stop programs, education programs, neighborhood advocacy, neighborhood clean-up, environmental manipulations, and property identification. These actions often are initiated by the community and not by outside organizations.

Although neighborhood or block watches are common, the exact number of such organizations is not known. A 1992 national survey of the United States found that 31 percent of all respondents belong to some form of neighborhood crime prevention organization (O'Keefe et al. 1996). Data for England and Wales suggest that there are over 140,000 neighborhood watch schemes, with more than 6 million participating households (Crawford 1998).

One notable movement in the area of neighborhood anticrime programs involves the proliferation of community antidrug (CAD) programs in the United States since the late 1980s. In response to the surge in drug use, particularly cocaine and crack in inner cities during the early 1990s, residents banded together with each other, the police, and various agencies and organizations to attack drug use, drug sales, and related problems (Davis, Lurigio, and Rosenbaum 1993). Many of the neighborhood efforts use surveillance tactics, report to the police, work with agencies to clean up the area, provide information to residents, institute antidrug programs, and participate in citizen patrols.

Citizen patrols are often a key element of neighborhood watch and represent an active role in surveillance efforts. As the title implies, local residents patrol their neighborhoods and inform the authorities if they see any questionable activity. They are discouraged from physically intervening into any suspicious activity they may find. As with block watches, no clear number of citizen patrols is available.

The police play a major role in many community crime prevention activities and organizations. The police may actually be the initiators and/or leaders of neighborhood watch and other programs. This is largely due to the fact that there is interdependence between citizens and the police. It is also important to remember that neighborhood organizations are not meant to replace the legal authorities. The intent is to supplement police activities with the eyes, ears, and ideas of community residents. Both the residents and the police, therefore, must share the burden of promoting neighborhood organization and involvement. One way for the police to accomplish this goal is to encourage the populace to take part in controlling crime and calling the police.

7.4.1 Evaluation of Neighborhood Crime Prevention

Evaluation of neighborhood crime prevention efforts typically entails two distinct measures of effectiveness. The most logical measure is the impact these activities have on crime and the fear of crime. A second measure of effectiveness is the impact of neighborhood organizing on factors such as social cohesion, a sense of territoriality, and neighborliness. Crime rates and fear of crime change to the extent that these intervening factors are enhanced.

Studies of neighborhood crime prevention often include an evaluation of the effectiveness of the organization effort. The outcome measures range from simple documentation of existing groups and numbers of participants to some statement about the quality of individual involvement. A few studies rely exclusively upon these process evaluation measures and fail to consider the actual impact on crime and fear.

Community cohesion is often measured as improved relations between the police and residents. Evaluations show that neighborhood watch participants have higher evaluations of the police (Brown and Wycoff 1987; Laycock and Tilley 1995; Shernock 1986; Skogan and Wycoff 1986; Williams and Pate 1987; Wolfer 2001), possibly due to the increased interaction between citizens and the police that is not oriented around confrontation. Community watch programs bring citizens and officers together in a symbiotic, mutual problem-solving activity. Attempts to more directly assess changes in community cohesion and communal support, however, show mixed results. Whereas Bennett (1987, 1990) reported social cohesion increased in one area of London and decreased in another, Rosenbaum, Lewis, and Grant (1985) revealed no change in community cohesion for three areas and decreased cohesion in the fourth neighborhood. Similarly, Lewis, Grant, and Rosenbaum (1988) found no change in the frequency of informal discussion between residents in neighborhood watch areas.

The primary interest in neighborhood crime prevention is reduced levels of crime and fear of crime. Community crime prevention techniques are aimed primarily at the property offenses of burglary, larceny, and robbery. Little, if any, impact should be found on crimes of interpersonal violence because many personal crimes occur between individuals who know one another and within the home. Increased surveillance will not alleviate crimes when the offender and victim are residents or legitimate users of the area.

Official crime records reveal a positive impact of neighborhood watch programs on crime. Most studies report a lower level of crime (particularly property offenses) in the target communities than control areas and/or decreases compared to preprogram levels (Home Office 2003a, 2003c; Latessa and Travis 1987; Kodz and Pease 2003; Perry 1984). Not all studies using official records, however, reveal uniformly lower levels of crime in crime prevention communities (Bennett 1990; Henig 1984). Victim survey data has also been used in assessment of neighborhood watch programs. These studies typically report strong support for neighborhood watch and lower levels of crime and fear (Cook and Roehl 1983).

The Kirkholt burglary prevention project and the Safer Cities program in the United Kingdom are two recent examples of effective community and neighborhood interventions. Kirkholt, a clearly defined residential area comprised of over 2,200 dwellings near Manchester, which is owned by the local governmental authority, experienced a burglary rate more than twice that of other high-risk areas in England (Forrester, Chatterton, and Pease 1988). The burglary prevention activities used in the area included the removal of prepayment heating fuel meters in homes, improvements in physical security devices, the use of community teams to conduct security surveys, and the establishment of "cocoon neighborhood watch" (very small groups of homes banded together for surveillance and support). In the Safer Cities program, the British government provided funds for local initiatives aimed at reducing crime and the fear of crime, and the creation of safer cities. Monies were allocated in an attempt to build multiagency partnerships for fighting social, physical, and economic problems in urban areas (Sutton 1996; Tilley 1992). Each individual program included a coordinator, police participation, various agency representatives, and a steering committee. Many of the interventions initiated under the Safer Cities programs included ideas found in other projects such as Kirkholt. Target hardening, property marking, community mobilization, the use of signs and other media, and neighborhood watches were common activities (Tilley and Webb 1994).

Evaluations of the Kirkholt and Safer Cities initiatives reveal generally positive results. Evidence shows that the level of burglary was significantly reduced (Ekblom, Law, and Sutton 1996; Forester et al. 1990; Tilley and Webb 1994), as was repeat victimization against targets. Publicity concerning an area's activities was seen as an important part of making an impact for the larger community (Tilley and Webb 1994). Greater impacts on crime were evident in areas where more action was undertaken.

Besides attempting to eliminate or reduce crime, neighborhood crime prevention programs have the potential to impact the fear of crime. Many evaluations investigate changes in fear, often through victim surveys that ask residents about their feelings of safety in the community and their perceived risk of future victimization. Reported reductions in fear of crime can be very dramatic, with 25 percent, 50 percent, and even 75 percent of respondents claiming less fear subsequent to program initiation (Cook and Roehl 1983; Ekblom, Law, and Sutton 1996; Tilley and Webb 1994). Even efforts to establish neighborhood crime prevention programs in hard-to-organize areas or attempts to implement prevention with limited community support demonstrate the fear-reducing capabilities of such endeavors. For example, a concerted effort to organize ten high-crime, high-fear inner-city neighborhoods in nine cities resulted in significantly reduced fear in six of the ten neighborhoods (Bennett and Lavrakas 1989).

Community antidrug programs represent a recent incarnation of community crime prevention initiatives that utilize many of the same forms of intervention found in neighborhood watch initiatives. As with other community crime prevention initiatives, CAD seeks to draw residents together to fight drug problems. Although there is some evidence that antidrug programs are impacting positively on social cohesion, the research results are mixed. Lurigio and Davis (1992) reported significant increases in social cohesion in three cities, whereas Roehl et al. (1995) and Davis et al. (1991) noted that actual participation by residents is low (often less than 10 percent) and many programs operate with only a small core group of dedicated individuals. The more important issue is whether CAD programs are able to reduce the levels of crime and other problems. In general, evaluations in different neighborhoods and housing developments report overall positive results, with fewer drug problems and greater satisfaction with the area (Davis et al. 1991; Popkin et al. 1999; Rosenbaum et al. 1997).

7.4.2   Citizen Participation and Support

The results of research on neighborhood crime prevention should be qualified in light of information on citizen participation. Many findings are presented as generalizable to all neighborhoods. The findings, however, may not be applicable to all subgroups of the population. Indeed, some studies find changes only for program participants.

It is important to note that participation is not even across all subgroups of the population and that participation is centered more among those who have more (property) at risk, view crime as a problem, and are involved in other social groups (Bennett 1989; Lavrakas and Herz 1982; Skogan and Maxfield 1981). High-crime, heterogeneous, transient areas generate feelings of fear, distrust, suspicion, and anxiety that tend to isolate people from one another and lead to a lack of participation in organized crime prevention activities (Skogan and Maxfield 1981). Participation also varies according to the type of prevention program (Hope and Lab 2001; Lab 1990). This means that the potential impact of neighborhood watch and community crime prevention is untested in many areas and on the populations where the greatest margin for change exists. It is in these areas where engendering participation is most challenging, in part because of a vicious cycle between involvement and fear/crime. That is, fear and perceived risk may lead people to retreat into their homes and avoid other people, which in turn mitigates the possibility of group action to address fear and victimization.

7.4.3 Summary

The evidence tends to support the basic idea of neighborhood crime prevention as a means of combating crime and the fear of crime. Research generally presents neighborhood watch and its component activities as effective methods to reduce crime, victimization, and fear of crime. The magnitude of the changes, however, often appears to vary greatly from study to study. The discrepant results can be attributed to several factors. Foremost among the causes is the fact that the neighborhood initiative was not successfully implemented. That means that the failure is not in the crime prevention program itself, but is from a failure to mobilize the citizens, initiate the intervention, or bring the measures to bear on the problem.

7.5 General Deterrence

Any discussion of primary prevention would not be complete without a look at the deterrent effects of punishment. Recall that primary prevention attempts to eliminate or reduce the level of deviant behavior prior to its occurrence. Most people today feel that official agencies of social control are, or should be, responsible for eliminating crime. Indeed, the actions of criminal justice agencies are aimed at the elimination of crime through deterrence.

One of the leading writers on the subject defines *deterrence* as "influencing by fear" (Andenaes 1975). According to this writer, potential offenders decide to refrain from committing criminal acts due to a fear of apprehension and punishment. The likelihood of deterrence increases as the risk of punishment increases. An actual experience of punishment does not have to occur before an individual can be deterred. Instead, Andenaes (1975) assumed that the threat of punishment would be enough if the proper circumstances exist. The idea of "threat" and interest in diverting initial or future activity prompted Andenaes to refer to deterrence as "general prevention." It is prevention of the potential offense by use of fear.

7.5.1 Type of Deterrence

Deterrence can be broken down into two distinct types: specific and general. *Specific deterrence* refers to efforts that keep the individual offender from violating the law again in the future. The hope is that the experience of punishment will deter the individual who has been punished from future illegal activity. The offender who is incarcerated for burglary is expected to be deterred by the experience from committing any further acts of burglary once he or she is released from the institution. The punishment is not expected to impact on anyone besides the targeted individual. In a strict sense, the deterrent action also should only impact on the same criminal act. One would not expect that other deviant acts, such as rape or assault, to be affected by punishment for burglary. Property crimes like larceny may see a change due to the punishment of burglary but not to the same extent as for burglary. Because of its focus on reported or future reoffending, specific deterrence is a form of tertiary prevention and taken up later in the chapter.

General deterrence, on the other hand, aims to impact on more than the single offender. The apprehension and punishment of a single individual hopefully serves as an example to other offenders and potential law violators. In this instance, the incarceration of a single burglar should deter other individuals from committing burglary. The focus is on stopping the initial offense, which may be committed by a citizen.

Both types of deterrence assume a rational offender. Any deterrent effect rests upon the ability of an offender to make choices of whether or not to violate society's behavioral standards. Accordingly, the inability to make rational decisions would mitigate any effect of deterrence. Rationality also assumes that potential offenders are *hedonistic* (i.e., they seek pleasure and avoid pain). Punishment is assumed to be painful to the individual, and the outcome of criminal activity represents the pleasure component. Deterrence seeks to offset any pleasure received in the crime by introducing an equal or slightly higher level of pain. Such an action should result in an elimination of further law violation. General deterrence, resting heavily on the assumption of a rational individual, suggests that the pain experienced by one person will be seen as potential pain by persons contemplating a similar act.

The deterrent effect of punishment relies on the existence of three factors. These are the severity, certainty, and celerity of the punishment. *Severity* entails making certain that punishments provide enough pain to offset the pleasure received from the criminal act. *Certainty* deals with the chances of being caught and punished for one's behavior. *Celerity* refers to the swiftness of the societal response.

7.5.2   The General Deterrent Effect of Legal Sanctions

A great deal of research has been conducted on the impact of legal sanctions on levels of crime in society. This research has taken the form of both cross-sectional analyses (which compare jurisdictions with different laws) and longitudinal evaluations (which look at crime levels before and after changes in the law). The literature also looks at the impact of people's perceptions on the certainty, severity, and celerity of arrest and punishment.

The deterrence literature fails to find any strong compelling arguments that the law and sanctions have any major impact on the level of offending. The most clear-cut finding seems to indicate that increased certainty of apprehension and punishment results in reduced offending. Severity appears to have little influence on behavior. This result may be due to the lack of knowledge that individuals have about the actual sanctions and the chances of being caught and receiving the punishment. The literature on perceptions of arrest and punishment, however, fails to clarify the impact of deterrence. The research findings reflect the fact that perceptions are based on past experiences much more than future activities are based on present perceptions. Again, certainty seems to hold the most power.

The finding that certainty of apprehension and punishment is the most important factor suggests that any deterrent effect must rest on efforts by the criminal justice system and society to increase the level of risk for offenders. At the same time, changes that increase perceptions of risk, whether through experience, avoidance, or something else, also contribute to deterrence. This risk can come from the crime prevention techniques discussed elsewhere in this chapter. Failure to increase the risk of apprehension and punishment does not mean that the crime rate will rise. Rather, it indicates that the sanctioning power of the criminal justice system alone is not enough to keep motivated individuals from offending.

This discussion offers only a brief glimpse of deterrence and its potential for preventing crime. A great deal more can be said about deterrence and the research on both the general and specific deterrent impact of the law and sanctions. Those discussions are found elsewhere in this book.

7.5.3 Social Crime Prevention

So far throughout the discussion of primary prevention, there has been an implicit assumption that crime is an aberration that can be eliminated through various interventions. Most of the ideas suggest that relatively simple efforts, such as making physical improvements in communities, organizing residents to combat crime, convincing citizens to take precautions and participate in anticrime measures, and engendering deterrence, can have a significant impact on crime and fear. Indeed, research shows that primary prevention techniques can be and are effective. At the same time, however, there are numerous examples of programs that fail to impact crime or fear, or have an impact only in the short term.

One primary prevention topic that we have not yet discussed is that dealing with larger social issues. *Social prevention* ideas rest on the assumption that true changes in crime and fear can be achieved only through attacking and altering larger societal problems and issues. Advocates of social prevention approaches point to problems of structural inequality, poor education, unemployment and/or poor employment options, economic and social powerlessness, and other related concerns. They also criticize most crime prevention programs for failing to address these root causes of crime, opting instead to implement programs that will have only minimal impacts. These advocates would also argue that social prevention is the best example of what "primary" prevention is supposed to be.

Many social prevention arguments typically begin by pointing out that crime is not evenly distributed in society. Hope (1997) provided evidence from the British Crime Survey (BCS) that property crime is highly concentrated among a relatively small proportion of the population. This concentration appears in various related ways. First, victimization is more prevalent among the poor in society. Second, there is a strong spatial dimension to victimization (Hope 1997; Rosenbaum 1991). Third, the concentration is not just in terms of certain people being victimized, but also in terms of being victimized with greater frequency (Hope 1997). Finally, victimization is disproportionately felt by minorities and poorly educated and unemployed or underemployed members of society (Rosenbaum 1991). The problem of crime and fear, therefore, is not equally felt by everyone in society.

Of greater importance than simply noting the concentration of crime are the reasons for that concentration. Poverty, joblessness or underemployment (low-paying or low-status jobs), poor educational opportunities, lack of development, and similar factors all contribute to area crime. Each of these factors led to the abandonment of neighborhoods and, in turn, influence the social make-up of a community. Faced with few, if any, legitimate opportunities, residents of these areas increasingly turn to illegitimate activities, such as crime and substance abuse (Rosenbaum 1991). As these activities increase in an area, chances of reinvestment become even more remote. Schools are abandoned or left in disrepair. Families are increasingly headed by a single parent, often the mother. Parks and playgrounds are taken over by gangs, litter, and graffiti. A vicious downward spiral is entered, with few expectations that it can be reversed.

The absence of jobs and opportunities also impacts on behavior in a more direct fashion. Rosenbaum (1991) noted that employment, or the prospect of employment, serves as a reward for finishing school, staying out of trouble, and working hard. As inner cities lose businesses and industry, these rewards disappear and there is less incentive to maintain good behavior. At the same time, there are growing incentives to participate in bad behavior. The wages for drug dealing, for example, far exceed the compensation offered by the few businesses that still exist in inner cities. Individuals who are confined to these areas, therefore, shift their behavior to the activities that bring a reward (Rosenbaum 1991).

Reversing the trend in problem communities requires a great deal of effort and ability not typically found in those areas. Numerous authors note the lack of power held by residents of these marginal communities (Hope 1997; Phillips 1991; Schwendinger and Schwendinger 1993; Sutton 1994). Even if residents are able to come together, identify problems, and decide to take action, they have few resources upon which to draw and even fewer chances of securing the help and resources from the larger community. The communities and residents face a circular problem. Their lack of power comes from various factors, including poverty, social alienation, joblessness, substance abuse, poor education, and family conflict. This powerlessness, however, makes it difficult to overcome these problems. The powerless community needs jobs, education, reinvestment, and other changes in order to eliminate the problems that cause powerlessness (Phillips 1991).

Some authors place a great deal of the blame for these conditions on government initiatives. The consolidation of the poor, unemployed, under-educated, and disenfranchised into public housing in close proximity with one another and separated from the rest of society promotes the development of different views about education, work, family, conformity, and other factors (Hope 1997; Sampson and Wilson 1995). Schwendinger and Schwendinger (1993) argued that the underemployed have been consciously abandoned by the government. Social policies have contributed to the plight of different groups in society.

Given these facts, a number of questions arise for crime prevention and other methods of social control. First, what impact will traditional responses of the criminal justice system have on crime and fear? Second, to what extent should we expect that typical crime prevention efforts, such as those outlined so far, would be successful? Finally, what should the societal response be to crime?

7.5.4   Limitations of Present Responses

Those who advocate social prevention point to the rhetoric of many crime initiatives as an indication of the short-sightedness of the policies. What typically occurs is that social control agents end up focusing on symptoms rather than the root causes (Schwendinger and Schwendinger 1993; Sutton 1994). Instead of trying to address why people use drugs, most interventions simply try to eliminate the availability of drugs. Instead of identifying the reasons why people turn to property crime rather than work, the criminal justice system seeks to arrest and punish those individuals.

Crime prevention programs often fall prey to the same trap of focusing on symptoms. Most crime prevention programs pursue a variety of approaches that, unfortunately, tend to target or alleviate the symptoms without addressing the causes (Sutton 1994). For example, many programs seek to make offending less attractive to the offender through such methods as increasing the risk of being caught or eliminating the payoff to be gained. The reason for the offending is never truly addressed. Other efforts tend to build fortresses around the nonoffenders and leave the problems "outside." Although this may protect certain individuals and groups, a fortress mentality does little to solve the root problems in the community. Similarly, focusing on disorder typically results in efforts to clean up an area and drive out the problems rather than understanding the causes of the problems and taking steps to eliminate those factors.

Social prevention argues that the majority of past and present crime policy and crime prevention initiatives lack a clear social agenda. Colvin (1991), the Schwendingers (1993), Tonry and Farrington (1995), and many others noted that important broad social issues have been ignored in the past, and emphasis has been placed on more immediate, isolated, and small-scale responses to crime. Gilling (1994) suggested that this orientation is due largely to the fact that problems of crime and disorder have been left in the hands of the police and other criminal justice system agents. Although well meaning, these individuals and groups lack the expertise, training, resources, and orientation needed to uncover and address the underlying causes of social problems.

7.5.5   A Social Prevention Approach to Crime

From a social prevention orientation, society needs to address problems at the *macro level*. What this means is that the root causes of crime need to be ameliorated. Among the problems to be addressed are unemployment, underemployment, poor educational opportunities, the breakdown of the family, structural inequality, discrimination, the diminution of socializing institutions (such as religion), and governmental initiatives that harm individuals and groups. What is needed according to social prevention, however, is a reorientation of societal efforts to making these efforts the cornerstone of social policy.

One early example of a social prevention approach is the Chicago Area Project (CAP). CAP grew out of work by Shaw and McKay (1942) in which they noted that high-crime areas did not have the community atmosphere necessary to exert control over its citizens or to improve the conditions of the area. The primary goal of CAP was the organization of the community into a self-serving, self-help neighborhood. The formal project was intended as a guide and source of assistance for building community concern and cohesion. Neighborhood residents were expected to identify the problems and solutions as well as carry out the plan of action. Improving the appearance of the neighborhood, restricting juvenile access to bars and poolrooms, obtaining city services, sponsoring educational/training programs for immigrants and others in need, bringing community members together in planning changes, involving area youth in nondeviant activities, and assisting both predelinquent youths and individuals who had already run afoul of the legal system were key activities for improving the community. Adjudicated individuals were targeted for employment and other assistance upon their release from prison. There was a clear attempt to build an ongoing, thriving community.

The fact that CAP set out to make general social changes and did not focus only on crime sets the program in the realm of social prevention initiatives. In CAP, delinquency and criminality served to identify those areas most in need of assistance and areas where deviance flourished. They did not, however, constitute the entire focus of the programs. Rather, the symptoms (crime) were secondary to the root problems. Analysis of the project showed reduced levels of deviant activity in target areas, especially for juvenile delinquency (Schlossman, Zellman, and Shavelson 1984; Schlossman and Sedlak 1983).

As is evident from the discussion thus far, there are many issues that require attention in society. Colvin (1991) offered a social prevention plan that covers a wide range of activities and demonstrates that a comprehensive social prevention program will have many elements. These elements range from providing emergency financial assistance to changing the tax system.

Many individuals have immediate short-term needs that include issues such as unemployment, low wages, homelessness, and other acute problems (Colvin 1991). The emphasis is on tying the immediate help to longer term solutions. For example, it would be preferable to subsidize a person's income instead of simply providing a welfare payment. The income subsidy should be a first step in building meaningful, well-paying jobs.

Parent-effectiveness programs are another social prevention idea. Colvin (1991) talked about building social bonds within the family and passing those values on to youths. In many areas, the challenge is to keep the family intact. Rosenbaum (1991) noted that many welfare policies work to destroy the family by making it monetarily lucrative for the father to leave the home, the mother to have more children, and the adults to refrain from accepting employment. This situation makes it difficult to provide children with values favoring hard work, accomplishment, loyalty, responsibility, and other social values.

Education is a key element of social prevention, in terms of both basic reading, writing, and math skills, and vocational training. Schools should be provided with the resources to hire the best teachers, purchase required materials, and offer up-to-date training (Colvin 1991). Educational institutions need to provide youths and adults with the technical skills to prepare them for future jobs (Schwendinger and Schwendinger 1993). Schools can also provide conflict management training, social skills training, and other preparation for basic life experiences. All of these measures require a commitment of time, energy, and resources on behalf of society, which at the present time is not forthcoming.

Improved education and training is only worthwhile if there is a concomitant emphasis on providing meaningful employment. Schwendinger and Schwendinger (1993) called for a *full employment policy*, which addresses both the provision of jobs and meaningful income. One method for supplying jobs would be to mobilize the work force in building the physical and social infrastructure of communities. Expanded housing, improved and accessible health care, increased educational opportunities, and myriad other social needs require additional, trained workers (Rosenbaum 1991; Schwendinger and Schwendinger 1993).

Colvin (1991) also called for implementing a progressive tax system. Such a system would return the United States to a period where the wealthy paid a higher portion of their earnings in taxes than they do today. Colvin (1991), the Schwendingers (1993), and others pointed out that corporations and wealthy individuals have seen their tax burden significantly diminish over time, while taxes on the middle class have increased. The renewed funds should be channeled into human development programs and improving the physical infrastructure (Colvin 1991). This would begin to address the structural inequality in society (Hope 1997) and narrow the gap between the rich and the poor.

Social prevention requires that an entire range of interventions be undertaken at the same time. Altering a person's sense of responsibility, providing meaningful education programs, guaranteeing employment at a reasonable wage, and building the physical and social infrastructure of the community as a support network to families and individuals all rely on one another. The failure of one element detracts from the ability of the other parts to make a difference. A good education coupled with no job prospects, for example, leads to nowhere. Social prevention requires broad social changes in the structures that promote crime.

7.5.6 The Prospects for Social Prevention

If social prevention is needed to solve the crime problem (among others), why are these efforts not fully under way in society? There are a number of possible reasons and concerns with broad-based social prevention measures such as those discussed in this chapter. First, there is a strong political component that needs to be considered. Many social prevention ideas are counter to the status quo, particularly of those in power. Second, social prevention seeks to make major changes in society, which may not present significant payoffs for many years (Gilling 1994; Rosenbaum 1991). Unfortunately, most people expect immediate improvements. Impatience is antithetical to social prevention. Third, some critics reject social prevention because of its utopian appearance (Gilling 1994). Many people believe that crime and disorder are an integral part of modern society, and all we should expect is to contain the problem. Fourth, there remains a great deal of ambiguity over whether making the large social changes will greatly improve the crime problem. This uncertainty comes from the lack of agreement over the underlying causes of crime (Gilling 1994). Related to this concern is the final issue of society believing that offenders need to be punished (Rosenbaum 1991). In essence, there are those who see the cause of crime not in the social structure, but in the choice of the individual.

7.5.7 Summary

This brief discussion of social prevention offers a divergent view of how society should address crime from that found in most other prevention discussions. What should also be evident, however, is that many elements of a social prevention approach appear, in some form, in other crime prevention efforts. Organizing communities is a major goal of anticrime and antidrug efforts. Schools and educational programs are intimately involved in conflict resolution, drug programming, vocational training, and many other efforts that should influence society and individual behavior. At the same time, however, it is clear that most crime prevention actions, and certainly the primary functions of the criminal justice system, are not geared toward making fundamental changes in society that are sought under social prevention.

7.6 Secondary Prevention

The orientation of secondary prevention focuses activity on individuals, places, and situations that have a high potential for deviance. Secondary prevention is concerned with intervening in those situations and with those persons who display a tendency toward criminal behavior. Similar to primary prevention, the emphasis is still on preventing crime prior to its initial occurrence. Perhaps the core concern for secondary prevention, therefore, is the prediction of future criminal activity.

7.6.1 Prediction for Secondary Prevention

Secondary prevention techniques rest heavily on the idea of identification and prediction. Rather than intervene with entire communities or neighborhoods, or establish programs to reach the general public, secondary prevention techniques rely on efforts to identify potential offenders, places, or situations that have a higher likelihood for criminal activity. One primary problem for secondary prevention, therefore, is proper identification and prediction. Predicting who will and who will not become deviant, where and when crime will occur, who will be a victim, what items will be targeted by offenders, and related topics is often a difficult or involved effort. The following discussion looks at predicting offending behavior; analyzing risk factors for deviance; and identifying places, times, and individual victimization.

7.6.2 Predicting Future Offending

Making predictions about future behavior, whether deviant or conventional, can be accomplished in a variety of ways. Three major methods of prediction are clinical prediction, actuarial prediction, and criminal career research. Clinical predictions are based on a rater's evaluation of an individual, usually after interviews and direct examination of the subject and his or her records. Clinical predictions have predominated in criminal justice, particularly in terms of sentencing and treating individuals. Research on the clinical prediction of violence reveals a great tendency for false determinations, both positive and negative (Monahan 1981).

Actuarial prediction refers to making predictions based on known parameters in the data. The key to actuarial prediction is the identification of the appropriate predictive items. Factors typically used include age, race, sex, socioeconomic status, educational status, IQ, criminal history, the immediate offense, family background, and psychological test results. Actuarial prediction has been a more recent choice in criminal justice, given the availability of large amounts of data and problems with clinical techniques. Research on actuarial prediction reveals lower levels of error than that found in clinical studies. At the same time, actuarial predictions can be wrong 25 to 50 percent of the time. The result of both clinical and actuarial prediction is some degree of false predictions.

The third approach attempts to identify individuals based on their criminal careers. A wide array of studies point out that past delinquent/criminal behavior is perhaps the best predictor of future deviant behavior (Blumstein, Farrington, and Moitra 1985; Farrington 1983; Gottfredson and Gottfredson 1986; Stouthamer-Loeber and Loeber 1989). Criminal career research uses known patterns of deviant behavior to establish the probability of offending for similar subjects.

Unfortunately, studies of criminal careers typically fall short of their goal. There is a lack of specialization in offending and an absence of patterns in deviant behavior. Perhaps the one fact that most researchers agree on is that chronic offenders (typically defined as having five or more police contacts) tend to continue committing crime. Indeed, chronic juvenile offenders are more likely to become serious adult offenders.

7.6.3 Risk Factors and Prediction

A more recent trend in identifying who will commit offenses involves the identification of *risk factors* related to deviant behavior. Risk factors, however, are only indicators or flags that can signal the need for increased attention or possible assistance for individuals. They do not definitively identify who will and who will not offend in the future. The identification of potential risk factors is not a new idea. Most criminological theory is based on the idea of identifying the best predictors of criminal activity in order to develop appropriate interventions.

Many researchers attempt to use various risk factors as predictors of later deviance. Research shows that many items (such as family factors, peer influences, community conditions, and psychological problems) correlate with delinquency and criminality. Various studies (Browning and Loeber 1999; Lipsey and Derzon 1998; Kelly et al. 1997) suggest that risk factors are useful tools in identifying potential problem individuals. What is rarely identified is the accuracy of predictions that rely on these risk factors. Explicit attempts to assess accuracy do not always provide promising results (Lipsey and Derzon 1998). Most analyses identify risk factors based on prior correlational analyses and fail to test the adequacy of any predictions based on those findings. Risk factors should be used as indicators of possible future problem behavior. They should not be viewed as good predictors of behavior. Indeed, many individuals, particularly youths, may exhibit many of the risk factors but fail to ever act in socially inappropriate ways.

7.6.4 Predicting Places and Events

Prediction for secondary prevention does not have to be limited to predicting which individuals in which situations will turn to delinquency or criminality.

It is also possible to consider predicting the where and when of offending. This activity is also not a new or unique idea. Indeed, it is common for police agencies to distribute their resources differentially across their jurisdiction and at different times of the day. In recent years, researchers have employed new and developing technologies and data sources for identifying the where and when of offending. "Hot spot" analysis and studies of repeat victimization are examples of predicting the time and place of offending.

It has long been common practice for the police to identify locations and times that are more prone to criminal activity. The most recent example of this activity entails hot spot research. Sherman (1995) defined *hot spots* as "small places in which the occurrence of crime is so frequent that it is highly predictable, at least over a one year period." Analyzing calls for police service in Minneapolis, Sherman, Garten, and Buerger (1989) reported that 50 percent of all calls for service come from only 3 percent of the locations. Notably, all domestic disturbance calls appear at the same 9 percent of the places; all assaults are at 7 percent of the locations; all burglaries occur at 11 percent of the places; and all robbery, sexual misconduct, and auto theft calls appear at 5 percent of the possible locations.

Attempts to identify hot spots are also useful in pointing out what types of crimes and locations coincide. Block and Block (1995) reported that hot spots often surround elevated transit stops and major intersections in Chicago. These are locations where potential victims can be located and potential offenders have options for escape. Rengert (1997) uncovered an important qualifier in hot spots when he found that the locations of auto theft hot spots change according to different times of the day and night. Tourist attractions and educational institutions are hot spots during the day, whereas entertainment venues, bars, and other adult nightspots become greater target areas in the evenings and at night (Rengert 1997). The addition of a temporal characteristic to hot spots shows that the time and place of crime is variable.

A finding that crime concentrates in certain locations or at certain times suggests that the targeting of hot spots may be an effective starting point for crime prevention. The identification of a hot spot should prompt analyses to uncover what factors make a location a good spot for crime (Spelman 1995) and offer insight into preventive responses. One set of tools, which is becoming a central component to police planning, is computer mapping programs. Mapping and hot spot research can supply information not only on crime but also on information about the neighborhood, site, or time at which an activity is taking place.

Another way to predict the occurrence of crime is to identify *repeat victimization*. Repeat victimization can be considered in terms of either people or places being victimized at least a second time within some period subsequent to an initial victimization event. The assumption is that evidence of recurring victimization can be used for targeting preventive actions.

A variety of studies note that repeat victimization is not an uncommon event. In one early examination of burglary, Polvi et al. (1990) claimed that the risk of being a repeat burglary victim is twelve times higher than expected, and this risk is more pronounced immediately after an initial burglary. Ellingworth, Farrell, and Pease (1995), using British Crime Survey data, found that roughly one-quarter to one-third of all property crime is committed against people victimized five or more times within a one-year period of time. Pease (1988) noted that only 2 percent of the BCS respondents account for 41 percent of the property victimizations, whereas 1 percent are the targets for 59 percent of the personal crimes. These levels of repeat victimization are probably underreports because they rely on repeats only within a one-year time frame, which minimizes the potential for repeats before or after the survey boundaries (Farrell et al. 2002).

Explanations for repeat victimization can generally be divided into two categories: risk heterogeneity and state dependence (Farrell, Phillips, and Pease 1995). Risk heterogeneity suggests that the prior victimization or some other factor identifies the victim or location as an appropriate target for further victimization. Event dependency refers to situations where (usually) the same offender commits another offense based on the past experiences with that victim or location. Successful past offending leads to another attempt against the same target. Both arguments find support in Gill and Pease's (1998) study of incarcerated robbers. Their subjects indicated that repeat victimizations are related to information from past offenses (theirs or others) and planning.

Targeting prevention activities at past victims has a great potential for reducing the incidence of subsequent offending against those targets and may possibly reduce the absolute level of victimization (Pease 1988). For example, the Kirkholt burglary prevention program worked with current victims as a means of reducing further burglaries. Evidence suggests that this effort successfully reduced further offending. Targeting past victims and locations also provides good information on how to intervene. The analysis of past offenses can provide information on the mode of entry, time of offending, property targeted, and other factors that can form the basis for preventive actions (Ratcliffe and McCullagh 1999). Clarke, Perkins, and Smith (2001) suggested that studies of repeat victimization can also provide insight to the decision-making process of the offenders. Evidence from an analysis of repeat burglary supports the idea that burglars repeat their offense after a period of time in order to steal the items that have been purchased to replace the goods taken in the first offense (Clarke, Perkins, and Smith 2001).

Despite the increased interest in repeat victimization, there are two issues that require more attention. First, not all criminal acts are followed by another one against the same location or individual. Identifying which acts will result in a repeat victimization prior to the subsequent act is an elusive task. A second issue deals with virtual repeats (Pease 1998). A virtual repeat involves a follow-up victimization of a similar person, place, or item after the initial action. Johnson and Bowers (2002) illustrated this possibility when they found that a local residential burglary elevates the risk of burglary for other proximate homes. The question is how do you address these issues within a prevention initiative?

Hot spot research, repeat victimization, and related topics represent innovative approaches to narrowing the individuals or situations that can be targeted by crime prevention activities. The idea of allocating resources by time and place is common in policing. It should be no more difficult to borrow that idea and apply it to general preventive efforts used by the criminal justice system or any other group or agency. Both hot spot and repeat victimization analyses offer insight into the where and when issues of instituting crime prevention.

7.6.5 Summary

Prediction is an important part of crime prevention—particularly secondary prevention. This is true especially for attempting to intervene with individuals and situations where a high propensity for criminal and deviant behavior exists.

7.7 Situational Crime Prevention

The targeting of crime prevention efforts is nowhere more evident than under the rubric of situational crime prevention. Instead of attempting to make sweeping changes in an entire community or neighborhood, situational prevention is aimed at specific problems, places, persons, or times. The situational approach assumes that a greater degree of problem identification and planning will take place prior to program implementation, and that the impact will be more focused and, perhaps, identifiable. The identification of places and individuals at risk of victimization, especially focusing on repeat victimization, is central to a great deal of situational prevention.

Clarke (1983) offered the following definition of situational prevention:

> Situational crime prevention can be characterized as comprising measures (1) directed at highly specific forms of crime (2) that involve the management, design, or manipulation of the imme-

diate environment in as systematic and permanent a way as possible (3) so as to reduce the opportunities for crime and increase
the risks as perceived by a wide range of offenders.

The key part of the definition is the third caveat: "reduce the opportunities" and "increase the risks as perceived by … offenders." Situational prevention rests on the idea that it is possible to make changes in the environment
that will make offending less attractive to potential offenders. The theoretical
basis of situational prevention is the rational choice, routine activities, and
lifestyles perspectives. Each of these approaches addresses the ability of offenders to respond to crime opportunities. Although it is common for discussions
of these perspectives to focus on potential offenders, the potential victim is
also an important part of the equation. The cornerstone of situational crime
prevention is the belief that offenders are capable of making choices. Rational
choice theory posits that individuals make decisions on whether to commit
an offense based on an array of inputs, including the effort involved, the
potential payoff, the degree of peer support for the action, the risk of apprehension and punishment, and the needs of the individual (Clarke and Cornish
1985; Cornish and Clarke 1986a, 1986b). This does not mean that every
offender makes a totally free-willed choice to commit a crime. Rather, what
it suggests is that individuals do not simply commit an offense every time an
opportunity presents itself. Potential offenders make a calculated decision
about crime, which is mediated by factors such as those noted above. The fact
that offenders make choices is apparent in various studies of burglars (Bennett
1986; Cromwell, Olson, and Avary 1991; Wright and Decker 1994).

The source of the information upon which an offender bases decisions,
whether consciously or subconsciously, comes from the daily routines of the
individual. Routine activities theory, as proposed by Cohen and Felson
(1979), argues that the daily activity of individuals results in the convergence
of motivated offenders with suitable targets in the absence of guardians. This
convergence provides opportunities for crime to occur. The lifestyle perspective grows out of research on victimization and specifically focuses on the
activity of the victim as a contributing factor in criminal acts. For example,
frequenting a bar in which violent fights are common increases the risk an
individual will be involved in such a confrontation. Similarly, working in a
convenience store located in a high-crime neighborhood enhances the possibility of being a robbery victim. In both situations, the individual's lifestyle
impacts on the potential of becoming a victim or a repeat victim. More
broadly, one's lifestyle has the potential to offer opportunities to commit
crime as well as become a victim.

Besides drawing on a number of relatively new theoretical approaches,
situational prevention also distinguishes itself by approaching problems in a

very systematic fashion. Essentially four steps are involved: (1) study the problem, (2) identify possible responses, (3) implement the intervention, and (4) evaluate and adjust the intervention. Situational prevention starts with a specific, identifiable crime problem. That problem is then subjected to study, drawing on as wide an array of information and individuals as possible. Based on the findings of the analysis, an intervention is identified and implemented. At this point, the prevention process continues with an evaluation of the program impact, with the intent of making changes in the response, if necessary. Situational prevention, therefore, is a dynamic process of problem identification, response identification, program implementation, and evaluation and adjustment.

In one of the earliest presentations on situational prevention, Clarke (1983) provided a simple three-pronged approach to interventions: surveillance, target hardening, and environmental management. Since that early discussion, Clarke and colleagues (1992; Clarke and Homel 1997; Cornish and Clarke 2003) have built a typology of situational techniques that has expanded to twenty-five categories of prevention activities. The techniques range from increasing the effort, to increasing the risks to offenders, to reducing the potential rewards, to reducing provocations to offend, to removing the excuses for offending.

Although situational prevention is addressed in more depth later in this book, several observations will be made here based on studies of situational prevention. First, there is an emphasis on property crimes, which is to be expected given the theoretical bases underlying the approach. Second, a wide array of interventions appears in the literature. This diversity suggests that the prevention initiatives truly are "situational" in nature and cannot be simply applied to the same crime that appears in different places at different times. Third, research successfully demonstrates the effectiveness of programs that target effort, risk, and reward. Situational crime prevention offers an approach that seeks to target specific problems with individualized interventions. As such, these techniques epitomize the ideas of secondary prevention. This does not mean that we are looking at entirely new forms of interventions. Indeed, many situational techniques are the same ideas appearing under primary prevention. The success of situational approaches has moved these ideas into the forefront of many crime prevention discussions and will continue to receive a great deal of attention in the future.

7.7.1 Community Policing and Partnerships

The inability of the police to handle the crime problem alone and the recognition that crime and disorder cannot be dealt with solely through the arrest and prosecution of offenders has led to the development of community policing and other partnership initiatives. In many respects, community policing and partnerships mirror ideas found in situational prevention. A key assumption is that there are factors underlying the crime and disorder problems in the community. The typical police response to the problems, that being arrest and prosecution, does little to address the causes of the problems. These new approaches seek to identify problems and potential solutions, as well as implement interventions. As such, community policing and partnerships fall squarely in the realm of secondary prevention. They target high-risk situations.

Community policing finds its roots in a variety of past programs and practices. One of these is the revival of foot patrol. Research shows that foot patrol has had a mixed impact on crime (Bowers and Hirsch 1987; Esbensen 1987; Police Foundation 1981; Trojanowicz 1983), although it appears to reduce the level of citizens' fear and improve attitudes toward the police (Brown and Wycoff 1987; Police Foundation 1981; Trojanowicz 1983). Variations on foot patrol, such as bicycle patrol and store-front offices, serve much the same purpose. The police are also a key ingredient to both the establishment and maintenance of neighborhood watch and citizen crime prevention initiatives. Underlying these activities has been the recognition that the police cannot solve crime on their own or address the increased calls for assistance by the public. The police need to build better relations with citizens and increase the involvement of citizens in crime prevention and crime policy.

Police sweeps or intensive patrol operations that target specific problems in localized areas are also activities that presage community policing. Sherman (1990), for example, pointed out that a massive police crackdown in one area of New York effectively reduced drug crimes, robbery, and homicide, although the impact did not persist long after the effort ended. Similarly, a police crackdown on a drug market in Lynn, Massachusetts, was successful at reducing drug-related crimes in the area (Kleiman and Smith 1990). In these cases, the police simply used their traditional powers of arrest, albeit in a concerted effort, to impact the crime problem. The localized character of the interventions is a key element in community policing initiatives.

7.7.2 Defining Community Policing

Defining community policing has proved to be an elusive goal. Although a single definition has not emerged, several authors offer definitions that tap the essential elements of most discussions. Weisel and Eck (1994) defined community policing as "a diverse set of practices united by the general idea that the police and the public need to become better partners in order to control crime, disorder, and a host of other problems." Similarly, Wilkinson and Rosenbaum (1994) stated that

> "Community Policing" represents a fundamental change in the basic role of the police officer, including changes in his or her *skills, motivations,* and *opportunity* to engage in problem-solving activities and to develop new partnerships with key elements of the community.

The various definitions of community policing generally include several essential features. These are community involvement, problem solving, a community base, and redefined goals for the police.

First, community policing requires cooperation between the police and other members of the community. Second, there must be an emphasis on *problem solving,* rather than simply dealing with the crime that occurs through investigation and arrest. Community policing challenges officers to identify the underlying causes and contributors to the crime and seek out solutions to those problems. This is basically the argument underlying problem-oriented policing. Policing must approach issues and problems differently based on the uniqueness of each situation. Invoking the criminal code is only one avenue for dealing with societal issues. Instead, different problems require alternative solutions or interventions. The police, therefore, need to identify and pursue solutions to the root problem.

The third critical feature of community policing is the decentralization of the police operation. Community policing typically means assigning officers to a specific neighborhood, with the expectation that the officers will get to intimately know the community, its problems, and its citizens. Finally, community policing entails altering the goals of policing. Besides arrests, as in traditional evaluations of the police, community police programs can be judged by reduced crime, the elimination of problem properties, increased feelings of safety, less neighborhood disorder, more community cohesion, and many other outcomes. It is important to note that community policing should emphasize the ends, rather than the means to the ends. That is, instead of focusing on how things get done, the primary concern is the elimination of the root problem. Other key features of community policing offered in the literature are a less rigid organizational structure, a focus on disorder, different training for officers, mobilization, collaboration, de-emphasizing calls for service or arrests, and recognizing the complexity of criminal behavior (Carter 1995; Eck and Rosenbaum 1994; Walker 1999; Watson, Stone, and DeLuca 1998).

Although it is not possible to provide a universally accepted definition of community policing, it is possible to identify what community policing is *not*. Community policing is not police-community relations. It is also not simply moving police officers to foot patrol or store-front offices. Nor is it simply targeting a problem or location using traditional police techniques. Rather, community policing requires more fundamental changes in police operations.

7.7.3 Problem Identification

Perhaps the central task of community policing or any partnership is the identification of problems and their solutions. Eck and Spelman (1989) offered a four-step process for problem solving. These steps are scanning, analysis, response, and assessment (SARA). Scanning entails the identification of the problem, issues, and concerns in the community. This information may arise from the observations officers make as they work in the community, from residents or businesses who bring problems to the officers, from other agencies (such as schools or hospitals) in the community, or from the systematic study of data and information on the area.

In the analysis stage, more than just the police need to be involved. The array of individuals and agencies participating will vary by the problem. For example, if drug dealing is centered in a house, apartment, or public housing building, the police, landlords, housing authority personnel, health department, and/or city attorney need to be involved in the problem analysis. If the drug activity centers on youths, it may be advisable to include the schools, probation office, or youth groups in the process. The diverse participants will bring different information and viewpoints to the process.

This cooperative interaction will result in unique responses to the different problems. Just as in the analysis stage, the participants involved in implementing the response will vary. In some cases, the police may have little day-to-day involvement in the intervention because the identified response requires expertise and abilities that the police do not have. An example of this would be the use of civil litigation against owners of property where drug use is allowed to continue. The final step, assessment, is essential to the success of community policing (Eck and Spelman 1989). The interventions need to be evaluated for their effectiveness. This evaluation provides important feedback to the process and to improving (or altering) the intervention.

7.7.4 Impacts of Partnerships

The move toward community policing and partnership programs is growing throughout the United States, Canada, Great Britain, and many other countries (see Lab and Das 2003). The partnerships and programs appear under a variety of headings and involve police in a wide range of capacities. These partnerships vary greatly, largely due to the emphasis on identifying interventions that address a specific problem. Although relatively little outcome evaluation has been undertaken on community policing and partnership initiatives, the following paragraphs will provide some insight.

Despite the great amount of money and effort put into promoting community policing, many police departments do little to actually include the public and other agencies in problem-solving activities. This does not mean that some police departments are not attempting to build true partnerships through community policing. The Chicago Alternative Police Strategy (CAPS) is a good example of successfully implementing a community-oriented policing approach. The program began in five of the city's twenty-five police beats in 1993 and included assigning officers to permanent neighborhood beats, the involvement of residents in the identification of problems and potential solutions, and reliance on other agencies (both public and private) to address identified issues (Hartnett and Skogan 1999). As expected, the response to problems varied from neighborhood to neighborhood. Improved police enforcement appeared throughout the project and often focused on drug problems. Efforts to clean up problem locations and generally improve the physical conditions of neighborhoods represent a major initiative in the program. Mobilizing residents to provide surveillance, work with one another, call the police, and take other actions also appear throughout the project. These actions successfully reduced the signs of physical decay, impacted on the extent of visible gang and drug activity, reduced area crime rates, and improved residents' attitudes and assessments of the police and the city (Skogan and Hartnett 1997).

Unfortunately, most evaluations tend to be process evaluations that look at the number of community policing officers hired and put on the street or the assignment of officers to "community" or neighborhood offices or beats. Most evaluations fail to assess the degree of problem solving taking place; the number and breadth of community members or agencies being involved in problem identification and problem solving; or the changes in crime, fear, or disorder related to the problem-solving efforts.

Recently, Zhao and his colleagues (2002, 2003) analyzed the impact of community policing on arrests and crime. Based on city-level data, they reported that agencies receiving community policing funds make a significantly greater number of arrests (Zhao, Scheider, and Thurman 2003), and those cities experience significantly lower levels of violent and property crimes (Zhao, Scheider, and Thurman 2002). What these analyses do not reveal is the actual community policing activities and the types of partnering efforts that bring about these changes. It does suggest, however, that community policing creates positive change.

An interesting partnership for dealing with problems, particularly drug issues, involves the use of civil abatement procedures. This approach seeks to involve landlords, citizens, health departments, zoning boards, and city/county attorneys in the application of civil (and sometimes criminal) codes. The advent of these efforts can be traced to work in Portland, Oregon, in 1987 (Davis and Lurigio 1998). In terms of drug crimes, these efforts seek to eliminate the use of locations for drug sales or drug use. Property owners can be fined, buildings can be confiscated or boarded up, tenants can be evicted, or structures can be demolished as a result of abatement procedures. Abatement attempts to reduce crime by altering the opportunities for the actions (Mazerolle and Roehl 1998).

Civil abatement has been evaluated in both Oakland and San Diego, California. In both locations, pressure was brought to bear on the owners of property when drug offenses took place. The results show that civil abatement was successful at building coalitions of citizens and agencies, and at lowering the levels of crime and disorder (Eck and Wartell 1998, 1999; Mazerolle and Roehl 1998). Civil abatement, however, can be a long and cumbersome process, particularly if the property owner opts to fight the procedures through the courts. Although many landlords comply with abatement, landlords often oppose the programs and perceive themselves as victims in the process (Smith and Davis 1998).

Three major U.S. initiatives for partnership building are the Comprehensive Communities Program (CCP), the Strategic Approaches to Community Safety Initiative (SACSI), and Project Safe Neighborhoods (PSN). Each of these projects has similar features. The key to the programs is to use a problem-solving approach that includes a wide array of community individuals, agencies, and/or groups. In all three of these initiatives, the partnerships are made up primarily of official criminal justice personnel, with the public being involved mainly through educational outreach. The evaluations of the projects are mainly process evaluations. When outcome measures are considered, the evaluations generally fail to provide data for comparable control areas (Bureau of Justice Assistance 2001). It is not possible, therefore, to know whether the partnerships are effective at reducing crime.

The passage of the U.K. Crime and Disorder Act in 1998 mandated the establishment of community partnerships to combat crime and related problems. These partnerships are meant to include the local police and a variety of community constituencies, including housing authorities, victims, health professionals, probation offices, and others. A key component of the act is that each partnership is to carry out a crime audit (data collected for planning and evaluation purposes) every three years, based on data from a variety of sources, such as police statistics, victimization surveys, probation data, education, and environmental health. The police are mandated to consult with the partnership and use the data to form prevention strategies and evaluate those strategies (Walklate 1999). Although outcome evaluations have yet to be completed, process evaluations note that some attempts to form partnerships have met with less than full success, the police are often the major contributor to the process, and the exact role of the participants is often poorly outlined (see, for example, Hughes 2002; Phillips 2002; Tierney 2001).

7.7.5 Summary

Participants tend to develop a positive attitude toward community policing and partnership efforts (Rosenbaum 2002; Skogan 1995). Despite the positive experiences, however, the lack of an extensive track record for partnerships and the fact that relatively few outcome evaluations have been completed make it difficult to sell the idea. Training and education of the various participants in community policing and partnerships is essential to both the effectiveness of the efforts and their acceptance (Sadd and Grinc 1996; Skogan 1995; Skolnick and Bailey 1988). Members of the partnership and the public need to be educated about community outreach, coalition building, and problem identification. The absence of such training results in many community policing and partnership initiatives becoming unilateral activities by the police, or poorly coordinated and implemented efforts (Buerger 1994; Moore 1994; Sadd and Grinc 1994, 1996; Skogan 1995, 1996).

The police need to partner with other criminal justice agencies, community groups, and the citizenry if they are to have an impact on the underlying causes for crime. These collaborations have the potential of bringing a wide array of new and innovative ways of looking at problems, as well as proposing solutions to those problems. They also bring to the table different skills, abilities, and resources that can be used to implement the proposed solutions.

7.8   Drugs, Crime, and Crime Prevention

The interplay between drugs and crime is a continuing topic in criminal justice. Violent crime stemming from the drug trade in U.S. cities has regularly appeared on the evening news and in the printed media. The U.S. government has responded to this increased concern by continuing its "war" on drugs. Efforts to reduce the supply of drugs have been the primary means of attack in this war. This emphasis on supply reduction targets the drugs at various points: arrests of the street-level dealer, identifying and prosecuting the drug "kingpin," and drug interdiction at the borders to the country. Less emphasis is placed (at least at the federal level) on the treatment of substance abusers or the prevention of initial use.

The issue of drug use/abuse is best addressed within the framework of secondary prevention. Drug use is one means of predicting or identifying potential problems in society. Targeting those involved in drug use may serve to alleviate the problems (crime and otherwise) that stem from drug use. As with many interventions, those tied to drug issues do not fall exclusively in the realm of secondary prevention. Efforts to work with current users are themselves tertiary in nature. Other methods aimed at preventing initial use may be construed as primary prevention, especially if implemented on a broad scale. The fact that the actual concern in dealing with drugs often lies with related crime and societal problems, however, means that drug issues are most properly dealt with in terms of secondary prevention.

7.8.1   Drug Use and Crime

Data on drug use suggest that illicit drug use is not as widespread as the media portrays. Most drug use appears to be experimental or occasional in nature (Johnston, O'Malley, and Bachman 2003). At the same time, the data on offenders point out that drug use is common among those who are apprehended for crimes (National Institute of Justice 2003). Although not necessarily representative of all offenders, those who are caught make up a large group of individuals. Drug use may be considered a risk factor in other criminal behavior. That is, the use of drugs may be a predictor of other deviant activity.

The connection between drug use and crime has received a great deal of attention, although the actual relationship has been hypothesized to take a variety of forms. White (1990) outlined four possible models for the relationship. First, drug use causes criminal activity. Second, criminal activity causes drug use. Third, there is a reciprocal relationship in which both drug use and criminal activity cause one another. Finally, the relationship between the two is spurious with other factors (possibly the same ones) causing drug use and crime. The bottom line of these models is answering the question: Which comes first?

Studies on the temporal order of drug use and crime reveal a complex relationship. Numerous studies suggest that involvement in criminal behavior precedes drug use. The most significant of these is the longitudinal National Youth Survey (NYS), which shows a general progression in behavior starting with minor delinquency and leading to alcohol use, index offenses, marijuana use, and polydrug use, in that order (Huizinga, Menard, and Elliott 1989). Claims supporting the temporal priority of drug use typically rely on studies of drug addicts or high-rate users of drugs. These analyses commonly note that addicts and serious drug users commit up to four to six times more crime when they are actively using drugs (Ball, Shaffer, and Nurco 1983; Collins, Hubbard, and Rachal 1985). It is also plausible to argue that the actual relationship between crime and drug use is reciprocal. That is, criminal activity leads to drug use and drug use leads to criminal activity. Support for a reciprocal relationship can be found in many studies (Anglin and Hser 1987; Anglin and Speckart 1988; Collins, Hubbard, and Rachal 1985; Nurco et al. 1988; van Kammen and Loeber 1994).

The most accepted argument is the claim that the relationship between drug use and delinquency is spurious. This simply means that, although use and crime exist at the same time and vary in a similar fashion, neither is the ultimate cause of the other. Rather, they are caused by either the same common factors or by different factors (Huba and Bentler 1983; Huizinga, Menard, and Elliott 1989; Kandel, Smicha-Fagan, and Davies 1986).

The fact that drug use is related to criminal activity cannot be disputed. The inability to definitively identify a causal sequencing between drug use and crime does not render the relationship useless to crime prevention. A strong correlation between the two behaviors means that drug use can be used as a predictor of other criminal behavior (Elliott and Huizinga 1984; Kandel, Smicha-Fagan, and Davies 1986; Newcomb and Bentler 1998). The research suggests that each behavior contributes to the other, thereby providing insight for intervention and treatment. It may be possible to attack crime by attacking drug use. Certainly, targeting drug users for intervention means dealing with those who are at higher risk of participating in other criminal activities.

7.8.2   Interventions and Prevention

Interventions aimed at limiting drug use and related crime take a variety of forms. Most of the approaches can be subsumed in three general areas: law enforcement, treatment, and prevention. The law enforcement efforts typically focus on disrupting the availability of illegal substances, particularly by focusing on high-crime areas or at-risk groups (such as gangs). These efforts fall under the heading of secondary prevention. Treatment programs, however, by dealing with current drug users, are more closely aligned with tertiary prevention. To the extent that the treatment may reduce/eliminate related offending, the programs can be considered as secondary prevention. The truly preventive programs are those that seek to prevent the use of drugs in the first place and, subsequently, lower the overall levels of crime.

7.8.3   Law Enforcement

Police crackdowns on drug availability are common responses. New York City's Operation Pressure Point involved saturating a known "drug supermarket" with police officers and resources. The police operation was credited with thousands of arrests; the elimination of the drug supermarket; and significant reductions in robbery, burglary, and homicide (Kleiman 1988). Unfortunately, the program led some dealers and buyers to find new areas for doing business (i.e., displacement), and the program lasted only as long as the police maintained their heightened presence (Johnson et al. 1990; Kleiman and Smith 1990).

Gangs represent a high-risk group for drug use, sales, and criminal behavior. The Los Angeles Community Resources Against Street Hoodlums (CRASH) program is a prime example of police targeting of gang behavior. These efforts, however, have not shown an impact on the drug problem or other gang behavior, including gang homicides (Kleiman and Smith 1990). The size and scope of the drug problem appear to be more than simple police enforcement can handle. Assumptions that law enforcement efforts will significantly reduce the supply of drugs for any long period of time are ill conceived.

7.8.4   Treatment

Drug treatment can take a wide variety of forms and may entail greatly divergent approaches. Most interventions fall into one of four general types: maintenance programs, therapeutic communities, outpatient drug-free programs, and detoxification. Although each of these groupings promote a different major emphasis, many interventions contain features of more than one type, such as counseling and therapy, which appear in virtually all of the programs. Maintenance programs most often appear in the form of methadone maintenance. These are outpatient programs that involve the provision of methadone to heroin/opiate addicts. Over time, those on maintenance will no longer experience the highs and lows of addiction to other drugs and, hopefully, not suffer withdrawal pains. A primary assumption underlying these programs is that the patient is unable to function without some form of drug use and that methadone is an acceptable substitute for other, more damaging drugs. Evaluations of the effectiveness of maintenance programs show generally positive results (Anglin and McGlothlin 1984; Ball et al. 1987; Hser, Anglin, and Chou 1988).

Therapeutic communities emphasize providing a supportive, highly structured atmosphere within which individuals can be helped to alter their personality and develop social relationships conducive to conforming behavior (Anglin and Hser 1990). These residential programs operate as surrogate families for clients. In many cases, therapeutic communities are run by current or past clients. Programs include intensive group therapy sessions, education, vocational training, and/or mandatory employment. The research on therapeutic communities consistently show lowered drug use and criminal activity (Anglin and Hser 1990; Coombs 1981; DeLeon 1984; DeLeon and Rosenthal 1989; Inciardi 1996).

Outpatient drug-free programs often resemble therapeutic communities in most respects except for the residential component. Individual and group counseling is the cornerstone of these programs. Social skills training, vocational programming, social interaction, referral to other sources of assistance, and possibly short-term drug maintenance are also common components

(Anglin and Hser 1990). Alcoholics Anonymous and Narcotics Anonymous are well-known examples of this type of program. The impact of these programs is highly questionable because clients can drop out at any time. Evaluations based only on those individuals who remain in the treatment may look good, but the results reflect only the small number of clients who truly wish to succeed.

Finally, detoxification refers to the use of drugs in an effort to remove an individual from an addiction to another illicit drug. As opposed to maintenance programs, detoxification uses drugs in a short-term program of controlled withdrawal. The basic idea is to wean the client from the addiction with the minimal amount of discomfort and pain. Detoxification may be accompanied with counseling, referral, or other services. Although some evaluations show that detoxification is successful at eliminating drug use in the short term, detoxification has not been adequately evaluated over the long term.

7.8.5 Prevention Programs

Prevention programs that aim to keep individuals from initially using drugs usually target juveniles. It is during adolescence that most persons experiment with and enter into patterns of drug use. Prevention modalities cover a range of issues and approaches, including the dissemination of factual information about drugs and their consequences, the building of self-esteem, taking responsibility for making choices, and learning how to handle peer pressure. Most often, prevention programs incorporate more than one approach.

Education/information/knowledge programs are common and popular prevention strategies. These approaches focus their efforts on providing factual information about drugs, drug use, and the consequences of drug use. The basic assumption is that this knowledge will allow the individual to make an informed choice, and that, armed with these facts, most individuals will opt to avoid drugs.

Evaluations provide mixed results concerning these programs. Although the programs are effective at increasing subjects' knowledge about drugs (Botvin 1990), they have shown little, if any, impact on behavior (Abadinsky 1989; Botvin 1990; Botvin and Dusenbury 1989; Eiser and Eiser 1998; Kinder, Pape, and Walfish 1980; Swadi and Zeitlin 1987; Tobler 1986). It is also possible that the knowledge leads many youths to experiment with drugs in order to "find out for themselves" about drugs.

Perhaps the most widespread prevention approach today is resistance skills training. The most well-known of these programs is the Drug Abuse Resistance Education (DARE) program. Resistance skills training involves a set of ideas dealing with recognizing problematic situations and issues, dealing with peer pressure, recognizing pressure from media presentations,

knowing proper responses to temptations, building self-esteem and assertiveness, and knowing how and when to take a stand. The implicit assumption
in this type of prevention is that drug use is largely a function of situation
and peer involvement. Youths need to learn how to recognize peer pressure
and how to make proper decisions in the face of that pressure. Research on
the impact of resistance skills training is mixed. Studies focusing on tobacco,
alcohol, and marijuana use show that the program is successful at reducing
the number of youths who use those substances (Botvin and Eng 1980, 1982;
Botvin, Eng, and Williams 1980; Botvin et al. 1983; Botvin et al. 1984).
Although these results present positive outcomes, evaluations of DARE fail
to find any significant impact on drug use behavior (Clayton, Cattarello, and
Walden 1991; Ringwalt, Ennett, and Holt 1991; Rosenbaum et al. 1994;
Rosenbaum and Hanson 1998).

The evidence on prevention programs suggests that the impact is often
minimal. Resistance skills training presents mixed results. Programs that
emphasize providing factual information about drugs fail to have much
impact. Other programs that stress self-esteem, self-awareness, and interpersonal growth in the absence of specific strategies for dealing with drugs
(typically referred to as affective education programs) also demonstrate minimal influence on drug use (Botvin 1990; Schaps et al. 1986; Tobler 1986).
Although there appears to be hope for the prevention of drug use, most of
the programs need to be evaluated with longer follow-up periods and better
research designs.

7.8.6 Summary

The relationship between drug use and criminal activity is a complex one.
Although the extent to which drug use causes crime or crime causes drug
use is not clear, there is a strong correlation between the two activities. This
suggests that knowledge of one can be used to attack the other. From the
standpoint of secondary crime prevention, drug use can be used as a predictor
of individuals at a higher risk of committing other criminal acts. To the extent
to which drug use is a cause or contributor to criminal activity, drug prevention and treatment programs may be effective at limiting or eliminating
other crime. Effective interventions do exist, although most need further
analysis over longer periods of time in order to definitively outline their
impact and potential.

7.9 Tertiary Prevention

Tertiary crime prevention deals with the elimination of recidivistic behavior
on the part of offenders. The emphasis is on actions taken to keep the

confirmed offender from further harming society. Although the identification of individuals for insertion into tertiary prevention measures is straightforward (i.e., past deviant behavior), prediction is still an important component of many tertiary prevention approaches. Prediction at this stage of prevention focuses on predicting recidivism and not initial offending.

For the most part, tertiary prevention rests within the confines of the formal justice system. Typical tertiary approaches are specific deterrence, incapacitation, and rehabilitation. Specific deterrence involves the imposition of sanctions upon the individual in the hopes that these actions will keep that specific individual from further engaging in crime once the punishment has ceased. Incapacitation typically looks at the reduction in crime attributable to the confinement of an offender. Physical control over a person's behavior makes the commission of criminal actions in larger society an impossibility. Incapacitation can also be accomplished through the use of electronic monitoring systems (EMSs). Finally, an alternative goal of criminal justice intervention is rehabilitation. Despite claims that rehabilitation has little preventive impact, it continues to be a major focus of system effort. The following discussion is limited to brief discussions of deterrence, incapacitation, and rehabilitation. Other chapters offer more in-depth discussions.

7.9.1 Specific Deterrence

Specific deterrence is aimed at the individual offender and his or her future behavior. It seeks to prevent the offender from further deviant actions through the imposition of punishments that will negate any pleasure or advantage gained by participation in criminal activity. Relatively little research has been devoted to the study of specific deterrence.

Intuitively, specific deterrence should be a logical outcome of system intervention. Although many types of punishment are imposed by the criminal justice system, incarceration is assumed to have the greatest potential for deterring the individual from future criminal acts. This does not mean that fines, probation, community service orders, cease-and-desist orders, and other penalties have no deterrent value. These other forms of punishment, however, leave the individual his or her freedom and generally represent more lenient attitudes toward the behavior in question.

Many evaluations of specific deterrence look to the effect of imprisonment on subsequent offending. The easiest form of evaluation considers the recidivism rate of those individuals who have spent some period of time in an institution. These analyses generally suggest that length of incarceration is unrelated to recidivism (Babst, Koval, and Neithercutt 1972; Berecochea and Jaman 1981; Weisburd, Waring, and Chayet 1995).

Several studies of specific deterrence examine the differential impact of police decisions on subsequent spouse abuse. The Minneapolis Domestic

Assault experiment (Sherman and Berk 1984) investigated the deterrent effect of arrest, separation, and police counseling in misdemeanor spouse abuse situations. A six-month follow-up period revealed that arrests result in lower recidivism levels using both official and self-report measures of subsequent behavior (Sherman and Berk 1984). Various methodological problems led to several replications that revealed different results. The follow-up studies that corrected for the flaws in the original project show that arrests have no greater impact on future activity than does separating or counseling the parties involved in the dispute (Dunford, Huizinga, and Elliott 1990; Hirschel et al. 1991).

The studies of specific deterrence do not present promising results. At best, analyses present contradictory findings of a deterrent effect of punishment and system intervention. Problems within the study designs appear to be the major reasons for the varying findings. Foremost is the inability of researchers to randomly assign punishments or choose representative subjects. A second problem is the failure to consider possible confounding influences of participation in rehabilitative programs while incarcerated. The rarity of evaluations on specific deterrence suggests that there is little interest in examining the effectiveness of this preventive approach.

7.9.2　Incapacitation

Although imprisonment may not deter an individual from committing deviant acts again in the future, it does keep the subject from committing crimes against society while in the institution. Simply put, incarceration provides incapacitation by exerting total, continuous control over the individual, thus precluding behavior that is harmful to society. Incapacitation can take two different forms: collective and selective. Collective incapacitation refers to the imposition of sentences upon everyone exhibiting the same behavior with no concern for the future potential of the individual. Selective incapacitation emphasizes identifying the high-risk offenders and subjecting only that group to extended incarceration.

The evidence on collective incapacitation offers results ranging from small effects on the level of crime to large changes. Clarke (1974) claimed that incarcerating boys prior to age eighteen avoids 5 percent of the index offenses for white youths and 15 percent of the index offenses for nonwhites. Greenberg (1975) estimated that doubling the amount of time adults spend in prison would only decrease crime by 0.6 percent to 4.0 percent. Finally, Peterson and Braiker (1980), using self-report data, found that incarceration reduces the level of burglary by only 6 percent and auto theft by 7 percent.

Although it is apparent that at least some degree of a collective incapacitation effect is possible, the dollar costs of achieving this result may be significant. Cohen (1978) estimated that a 10 percent reduction in the California index crime rate requires a corresponding 157.2 percent increase in the prison population. The smallest change related to a decrease in index crimes appears in Mississippi, where it is still necessary to increase the incarcerated population by 33.7 percent. It is clear that incapacitation exacts a high cost in terms of the number of offenders that need to be incarcerated, as well as the monetary cost of housing these offenders.

Selective incapacitation differs from collective efforts by imposing punishment on a select few individuals. The emphasis is on the identification of offenders who are at high risk for future criminal activity. The idea of selective incapacitation received its greatest boost when Greenwood (1982) claimed that by reducing the time served by low- and medium-risk inmates and increasing the terms for high-risk offenders, it is possible to reduce robbery by 15 percent while lowering the California prison population by 5 percent. He compared this to a collective incapacitation approach, which would require a 25 percent increase in the prison population to achieve the same 15 percent reduction in robberies.

A number of problems permeate the issue of selective incapacitation. The foremost concern is the questionable ability to predict future behavior. The predictions also assume that both the rate of offending for the subjects and the rates of arrest, conviction, and incarceration remain constant over time. These assumptions are very questionable. Variation in these factors makes estimates of incapacitation problematic. Finally, there is a serious question concerning the right of society to punish high-risk individuals for their potential dangerousness (not just their actual) behavior. In summary, although selective incapacitation holds much intuitive appeal, there does not seem to be a solid empirical basis for invoking the process at this time.

7.9.3 Electronic Monitoring Systems

The use of electronic monitoring systems as a means of controlling behavior of the accused or convicted is a growing trend. Interest in EMS can be traced to the experimental development and use of an electronic bracelet by Jack Love, a New Mexico judge. The device was first used in 1983 on a small group of offenders in New Mexico (Niederberger and Wagner 1985). The primary aim of the EM systems was to monitor compliance with curfews and home confinement (Vaughn 1989). Interest in this novel technique quickly prompted the development of similar devices by various companies and the adoption or testing of the technology in jurisdictions across the country.

Proponents of electronic monitoring point to a variety of advantages stemming from its use. EMS can possibly alleviate the overcrowding of correctional institutions, while enhancing the ability to supervise offenders in the community better than the simple use of probation or parole. The system also reduces the costs of monitoring offenders in the community. Additionally, electronic monitors assist reintegration into society by allowing offenders to remain in the community, maintain family and friendship ties, and support the family.

Evaluations of EMS suggest it is a viable method for handling both adults and juveniles at postconviction and pretrial stages of intervention. Studies consistently reveal few new crimes, low violation rates, and the dominance of technical violations (Ball, Huff, and Lilly 1988; Bonta, Wallace-Capretta, and Rooney 2000; Cooprider and Kerby 1990). One major problem with the evaluations is the failure of most studies to randomly assign subjects to EMS and non-EMS status. A second qualifier entails the fact that many studies do not have adequate, or any, control groups with which to compare EMS clients. Although EMS has been successful at keeping violation rates and new offending low, the espoused goal of reducing overcrowding in jails and prisons has not been realized.

7.9.4 Rehabilitation

The final form of tertiary prevention discussed here is rehabilitation. Indeed, throughout most of the twentieth century, the major method of achieving tertiary prevention was the rehabilitation of offenders. Despite the move toward increased punitiveness since the 1970s, rehabilitation has remained a driving interest in the correctional field. Given this, one would assume that there is clear evidence of successful intervention. The state of the evidence, however, is not as clear.

Debate over the effectiveness of rehabilitation generally stems from Martinson's (1974) observation that "with few and isolated exceptions, the rehabilitative efforts that have been reported so far have had no appreciable effect on recidivism." This single statement was based on an examination of literature on rehabilitation appearing between 1945 and 1967. The finding of little or no effect of rehabilitation on recidivism also appeared in a variety of subsequent reports (Gensheimer et al. 1986; Lab and Whitehead 1988; Sechrest, White, and Brown 1979; Wright and Dixon 1977). Based on these reviews, which span a variety of decades and rehabilitative strategies, the conclusion that rehabilitation has little impact seems to be an acceptable notion.

Not all researchers, however, are ready to sound the death knell for rehabilitation. Various researchers claimed that there are many instances where rehabilitation is effective (Garrett 1985; Graziano and Mooney 1984; Mayer et al. 1986; Palmer 1975). The strongest argument for rehabilitation is offered by Andrews et al. (1990), who argued that treatment programs that correctly match subjects with the correct intervention can have a significant impact on recidivism. In a series of papers, Lipsey (1990; 1999; Lipsey and Wilson 1993, 1998) reported on an extensive evaluation of the rehabilitation literature, which finds positive impacts from rehabilitative treatment. Lipsey

(1990) argued that research on the impact of rehabilitation needs to consider the type of treatment, the setting in which it is delivered, the method of evaluation, and other factors when assessing the evidence.

There is still a great deal of debate on the impact of rehabilitation on recidivism, although most reviews claim to find at least some positive support for rehabilitation. Strong claims of success typically rely on outcome measures besides recidivism, such as improved educational attainment and increased self-esteem. Perhaps the key to developing effective interventions is matching the appropriate subjects to the proper treatment (Andrews et al. 1990). Unfortunately, the ability to make such selections remains an elusive problem. The majority of programs do not know which clients are best served by their treatment nor do they know how to identify the proper subjects once they are aware of differential program impact. As a result, tertiary crime prevention can be achieved only in a limited way through rehabilitation.

7.10   Conclusions

Crime prevention encompasses a wide diversity of ideas and approaches. Indeed, no two individuals will necessarily see or define crime prevention in exactly the same way. Throughout this chapter, an attempt has been made to offer a variety of perspectives on crime prevention and on the evidence of the effectiveness of the interventions. There should be no doubt that crime prevention works. Effective interventions are evident throughout the earlier discussions. The extent of crime prevention's impact, however, varies across time and place, as well as from one approach to another. Indeed, not every program has the same impact in every situation. Crime may be reduced in one place although there is no impact on the fear of crime. Transplanting that same program to another location may result in the opposite outcome: Crime stays the same but fear is reduced. No single approach to crime prevention has proven to be applicable in all situations. Indeed, most interventions appear to work in limited settings with different types of offenders and problems. The greatest challenge, therefore, is to identify the causal mechanisms at work so that effective programs can be replicated in other places and other times.

More attention needs to be paid to the evaluation component of prevention programs. First, many programs have not been subjected to any evaluation beyond simple description of the process used in establishing the intervention and the success of that process in terms of the number of meetings held and the level of attendance. Such superficial evaluation tells us nothing about the impact on crime and fear of crime, although the programs are often touted as successful because of the organizing efforts. A second evaluation problem is the lack of appropriate control or comparison groups in the research. Where reductions in criminal behavior do appear, the studies often fail to adequately assess the changes in relation to an area or group that is not the subject of the intervention. Thus, it is difficult, if not impossible, to make an informed judgment on the success or failure of the project.

The problem of evaluation is further complicated by the introduction of many actions at the same time. For example, physical design changes, neighborhood watch, citizen patrols, Operation ID, and media campaigns often overlap. It becomes impossible to evaluate which, if any, intervention has a positive (or negative) impact on crime. Knowing what aspect of the project worked best is an important piece of information.

A fourth evaluation issue is to recognize that not every crime prevention technique can be expected to have an equal or positive impact in all possible situations. Some techniques are better suited for certain problems and places than others. Evaluations need to carefully assess the match between techniques and the location and timing of their implementation. A final concern for evaluation deals with the time frame in which a technique is expected to make a difference. Many interventions are evaluated shortly after implementation. The expectation is that the program should have an immediate impact on crime, fear, and other factors. In reality, however, many changes take time to appear.

The ideas and topics addressed in this book are among the many possible prevention approaches that are used and are emerging to address the persistent problems of crime and fear in society. Such efforts will continue to grow. The effectiveness of these ideas rests on quality evaluation and a willingness to adapt and change. Only through research and modifications can the programs evolve into effective interventions. Evaluation of crime prevention techniques will remain a pivotal issue in dealing with crime and fear of crime throughout the future.

References

Abadinsky, H. 1989. *Drug Abuse: An Introduction.* Chicago: Nelson-Hall.

Akers, R. L., and E. Sagarin. 1972. *Crime Prevention and Social Control.* New York: Praeger.

Andenaes, J. 1975. General prevention revisited: research and policy implications. *Journal of Criminal Law and Criminology* 66, 338-365.

Andrews, D. A., I. Zinger, R. D. Hoge, J. Bonta, P. Gendreau, and F. T. Cullen. 1990. Does correctional treatment work?: A clinically relevant and psychologically informed meta-analysis. *Criminology* 28, 369-404.

Anglin, M. D., and Y. Hser. 1987. Addicted women and crime. *Criminology* 25, 359-397.

Anglin, M. D., and Y. Hser. 1990. Treatment of drug abuse. In *Drugs and Crime*, ed. M. Tonry and J. Q. Wilson. Chicago: University of Chicago Press.

Anglin, M. D., and W. H. McGlothlin. 1984. Outcome of narcotic addict treatment in California. In *Drug Abuse Treatment Evaluation: Strategies, Progress and Prospects*, ed. F. M. Times and J. P. Ludford. Washington, DC: National Institute on Drug Abuse.

Anglin, M. D. and G. Speckart. 1988. Narcotics use and crime: A multisample, multimethod analysis. *Criminology* 26, 197-233.

Atlanta, City of Street Lighting Project: Final Evaluation Report. 1975. Washington, DC: National Criminal Justice Reference Service.

Babst, D. V., M. Koval, and M. G. Neithercutt. 1972. Relationship of time served to parole outcome for different classifications of burglars based on males paroled in fifty jurisdictions in 1968 and 1969. *Journal of Research in Crime and Delinquency* 9, 99-116.

Ball, J. C., E. Corty, R. Bond, and A. Tommasello. 1987. The reduction of intravenous heroin use, non-opiate abuse and crime during methadone maintenance treatment—Further findings. Paper presented at the Annual Meeting of the Committee on Problems on Drug Dependency, Philadelphia.

Ball, J. C., J. W. Shaffer, and D. N. Nurco. 1983. The day-to-day criminality of heroin addicts in Baltimore: A study in the continuity of offense rates. *Drug and Alcohol Dependence* 12, 119-142.

Ball, R. A., C. R. Huff, and J. R. Lilly. 1988. *House Arrest and Correctional Policy: Doing Time at Home.* Newbury Park, CA: Sage.

Beavon, D. J. K., P. L. Brantingham, and P. J. Brantingham. 1994. The influence of street networks on the patterning of property offenses. In *Crime Prevention Studies*, vol. 2., ed. R. V. Clarke. Monsey, NY: Criminal Justice Press.

Beck, A., and A. Willis. 1999. Context-specific measures of CCTV effectiveness in the retail sector. In *Surveillance of Public Space: CCTV, Street Lighting and Crime Prevention*, ed. K. Painter and N. Tilley. Monsey, NY: Criminal Justice Press.

Bennett, S. F., and P. J. Lavrakas. 1989. Community-based crime prevention: An assessment of the Eisenhower Foundation's neighborhood program. *Crime and Delinquency* 35, 345-364.

Bennett, T. 1986. Situational crime prevention from the offender's perspective. In *Situational Crime Prevention: From Theory into Practice*, ed. K. Heal and G. Laycock. London: Her Majesty's Stationery Office.

Bennett, T. 1987. *An Evaluation of Two Neighborhood Watch Schemes in London.* Cambridge: Institute of Criminology.

Bennett, T. 1989. Factors related to participation in neighbourhood watch schemes. *British Journal of Criminology* 29, 207-218.

Bennett, T. 1990. *Evaluating Neighborhood Watch.* Aldershot, U.K.: Gower.

Bennett, T., and R. Wright. 1984. *Burglars on Burglary*. Brookfield, VT: Gower.

Berecochea, J. E., and D. R. Jaman. 1981. *Time Served in Prison and Parole Outcome: An Experimental Study*. Report No. 2. Sacramento: California Department of Corrections.

Bevis, C., and J. B. Nutter. 1977. *Changing Street Layouts to Reduce Residential Burglary*. St. Paul, MN: Governor's Commission on Crime Prevention and Control.

Block, R. L., and C. R. Block. 1995. Space, place and crime: Hot spot areas and hot places of liquor-related crime. In *Crime and Place*, ed. J. E. Eck and D. Weisburd. Monsey, NY: Criminal Justice Press.

Blumstein, A., D. P. Farrington, and S. Moitra. 1985. Delinquency careers: Innocents, desisters, and persisters. In *Crime and Justice*, vol. 6, ed. M. Tonry and N. Morris. Chicago: University of Chicago Press.

Bonta, J., S. Wallace-Capretta, and J. Rooney. 2000. A quasi-experimental evaluation of an intensive rehabilitation supervision program. *Criminal Justice and Behavior* 27, 312-329.

Booth, A. 1981. The built environment as a crime deterrent: A reexamination of defensible space. *Criminology* 18, 557-570.

Botvin, G. J. 1990. Substance abuse prevention: Theory, practice and effectiveness. In *Drugs and Crime*, ed. M. Tonry and J. Q. Morris. Chicago: University of Chicago Press.

Botvin, G. J., E. Baker, N. Renick, A. D. Filazzola, and E. M. Botvin. 1984. A cognitive-behavioral approach to substance abuse prevention. *Addictive Behaviors* 9, 137-147.

Botvin, G. J., and L. Dusenbury. 1989. Substance abuse prevention and the promotion of competence. In *Primary Prevention and Promotion in the Schools*, ed. L. A. Bond and B. E. Compas. Newbury Park, CA: Sage.

Botvin, G. J., and A. Eng. 1980. A comprehensive school-based smoking prevention program. *Journal of School Health* 50, 209-213.

Botvin, G. J., and A. Eng. 1982. The efficacy of a multicomponent approach to the prevention of cigarette smoking. *Preventive Medicine* 11, 199-211.

Botvin, G. J., A. Eng, and C. L. Williams. 1980. Preventing the onset of cigarette smoking through life skills training. *Journal of Preventive Medicine* 9, 135-143.

Bowers, K. J., S. D. Johnson, and A. F. G. Hirschfield. 2003. *Closing off opportunities for crime: An evaluation of alley-gating*. Under submission.

Bowers, W. J., and J. H. Hirsch. 1987. The impact of foot patrol staffing on crime and disorder in Boston: An unmet promise. *American Journal of Police* 6, 17-44.

Brantingham, P. J., and F. L. Faust. 1976. A conceptual model of crime prevention. *Crime and Delinquency* 22, 284-296.

Brown, B. 1995. *CCTV in Town Centres: Three Case Studies*. London: Home Office Police Research Group.

Brown, L. P., and M. A. Wycoff. 1987. Policing Houston: Reducing fear and improving service. *Crime and Delinquency* 33, 71-89.

Browning, K., and R. Loeber. 1999. *Highlights of Findings from the Pittsburgh Youth Study.* OJJDP Fact Sheet, No. 95. Washington, DC: Office of Juvenile Justice and Delinquency Prevention.

Buck, A. J., S. Hakim, and G. F. Rengert. 1993. Burglar alarms and the choice behavior of burglars: A suburban phenomenon. *Journal of Criminal Justice* 21, 497-508.

Buerger, M. E. 1994. The limits of community. In *The Challenge of Community Policing: Testing the Promises*, ed. D. P. Rosenbaum. Thousand Oaks, CA: Sage.

Bureau of Justice Assistance Comprehensive Communities Program. 2001. Program Account. Washington, DC: U.S. Department of Justice.

Bursik, R. J., and H. G. Grasmick. 1993. *Neighborhoods and Crime: The Dimensions of Effective Community Control.* New York: Lexington.

Caplan, G. 1964. *Principles of Preventive Psychiatry.* New York: Basic Books.

Carter, D. L. 1995. Community policing and DARE: A practitioner's perspective. *BJA Bulletin* (June).

Cedar Rapids Police Department. 1975. *Cedar Rapids Police Department Installation, Testing, and Evaluation of a Large-scale Burglar Alarm System for a Municipal Police Department—A 2nd Phase Completion Report.* Cedar Rapids, IA.

Clarke, R. V. 1983. Situational crime prevention: Its theoretical basis and practical scope. In *Crime and Justice*, vol. 4, ed. M. Tonry and N. Morris. Chicago: University of Chicago Press.

Clarke, R. V. 1992. *Situational Crime Prevention: Successful Case Studies.* Albany, NY: Harrow and Heston.

Clarke, R. V., and D. Cornish. 1985. Modeling offenders' decisions: A framework for policy and research. In *Crime and Justice*, vol. 4, ed. M. Tonry and N. Morris. Chicago: University of Chicago Press.

Clarke, R. V., and R. Homel. 1997. A revised classification of situational crime prevention techniques. In *Crime Prevention at a Crossroads*, ed. S. P. Lab. Cincinnati: Anderson.

Clarke, R. V., E. Perkins, and D. J. Smith, Jr. 2001. Explaining repeat residential burglaries: An analysis of property stolen. In *Repeat Victimization*, ed. G. Farrell and K. Pease. Monsey, NY: Criminal Justice Press.

Clarke, S. 1974. Getting 'em out of circulation: Does incarceration of juvenile offenders reduce crime? *Journal of Criminal Law and Criminology* 65, 528-535.

Clayton, R. R., A. Cattarello, and K. P. Walden. 1991. Sensation seeking as a potential mediating variable for school-based prevention interventions: A two-year follow-up of DARE. *Journal of Health Communications* 3, 229-239.

Cohen, J. 1978. The incapacitative effect of imprisonment: A critical review of the literature. In *Deterrence and Incapacitation: Estimating the Effects of Criminal Sanctions on Crime Rates*, ed. A. Blumstein, J. Cohen, and D. Nagin. Washington, DC: National Academy Press.

Cohen, L. E., and M. Felson. 1979. Social change and crime rate trends: A routine activities approach. *American Sociological Review* 44, 588-608.

Collins, J. J., R. L. Hubbard, and J. V. Rachal. 1985. Expensive drug use and illegal income: A test of explanatory hypotheses. *Criminology* 23, 743-764.

Colvin, M. 1991. Crime and social reproduction: A response to the call for 'outrageous' proposals. *Crime and Delinquency* 37, 436-448.

Cook, R. F., and J. A. Roehl. 1983. *Preventing Crime and Arson: A Review of Community-Based Strategies.* Reston, VA: Institute for Social Analysis.

Coombs, R. H. 1981. Back on the streets: Therapeutic communities' impact upon drug abusers. *American Journal of Alcohol Abuse* 8, 185-201.

Cooprider, K. W., and J. Kerby. 1990. A practical application of electronic monitoring at the pretrial stage. *Federal Probation* 54, 28-35.

Cornish, D. B., and R. V. Clarke. 1986a. *The Reasoning Criminal.* New York: Springer-Verlag.

Cornish, D. B., and R. V. Clarke. 1986b. Situational prevention, crime displacement and rational choice theory. In *Situational Crime Prevention: From Theory into Practice*, ed. K. Heal and G. Laycock. London: Her Majesty's Stationery Office.

Cornish, D. B., and R. V. Clarke. 2003. Opportunities, precipitators and criminal decisions: A reply to Wortley's critique of situational crime prevention. In *Theory for Practice in Situational Crime Prevention*, ed. M. J. Smith and D. B. Cornish. Monsey, NY: Criminal Justice Press.

Covington, J., and R. B. Taylor. 1991. Fear of crime in urban residential neighborhoods: Implications of between- and within-neighborhood sources for current models. *Sociological Quarterly* 32, 231-249.

Crawford, A. 1998. *Crime Prevention and Community Safety: Politics, Policies and Practices.* London: Longman.

Cromwell, P. F., J. N. Olson, and D. W. Avary. 1991. *Breaking and Entering: An Ethnographic Analysis of Burglary.* Newbury Park, CA: Sage.

Davis, R. C., and A.J. Lurigio. 1998. Civil abatement as a tool for controlling drug dealing in rental properties. *Security Journal* 11, 45-50.

Davis, R. C., A.J. Lurigio, and D. P. Rosenbaum. 1993. *Drugs and the Community: Involving Community Residents in Combatting the Sale of Illegal Drugs.* Springfield, IL: Charles C. Thomas.

Davis, R. C., B. E. Smith, A. J. Lurigio, and W. G. Skogan. 1991. *Community Response to Crack: Grassroots Anti-Drug Programs.* Washington, DC: National Institute of Justice (NIJ).

DeLeon, G. 1984. Program-based evaluation research in therapeutic communities. In *Drug Abuse Treatment Evaluation: Strategies, Progress and Prospects*, ed. F. M. Tims and J. P. Ludford. Washington, DC: National Institute on Drug Abuse.

DeLeon, G., and M. S. Rosenthal. 1989. Treatment in residential therapeutic communities. In *Treatment of Psychiatric Disorders: A Task Force Report of the American Psychiatric Association*, vol. 2, ed. H. Kleber. Washington, DC: American Psychiatric Association.

Ditton, J. and E. Short. 1999. Yes, it works, no, it doesn't: Comparing the effects of open-street CCTV in two adjacent Scottish town centres. In *Surveillance of Public Space: CCTV, Street Lighting and Crime Prevention*, ed. K. Painter and N. Tilley. Monsey, NY: Criminal Justice Press.

Dunford, F. W., D. Huizinga, and D. S. Elliott. 1990. The role of arrest in domestic assault: A pilot study. *Justice Quarterly* 7, 631-654.

Eck, J. E., and D. P. Rosenbaum. 1994. The new police order: Effectiveness, equity, and efficiency in community policing. In *The Challenge of Community Policing: Testing the Promises*, ed. D. P. Rosenbaum. Thousand Oaks, CA: Sage.

Eck, J. E., and W. Spelman. 1989. A problem-oriented approach to police service delivery. In *Police and Policing: Contemporary Issues*, ed. D. Kenney. New York: Praeger.

Eck, J. E., and J. Wartell. 1998. Improving the management of rental properties with drug problems: A randomized experiment. In *Civil Remedies and Crime Prevention*, ed. L. G. Mazerolle and J. Roehl. Monsey, NY: Criminal Justice Press.

Eck, J. E., and J. Wartell. 1999. *Reducing Crime and Drug Dealing by Improving Place Management: A Randomized Experiment*. NIJ Research Preview. Washington, DC: National Institute of Justice.

Eiser, C., and J. R. Eiser. 1998. *Drug Education in Schools*. New York: Springer-Verlag.

Ekblom, P., H. Law, and M. Sutton. 1996. *Safer Cities and Domestic Burglary*. London: Home Office Research and Statistics Directorate.

Ellingworth, D., G. Farrell, and K. Pease. 1995. A victim is a victim is a victim?: Chronic victimization in four sweeps of the British Crime Survey. *British Journal of Criminology* 35, 360-365.

Elliott, D. S., and D. H. Huizinga. 1984. *The Relationship between Delinquent Behavior and ADM Problems*. Boulder, CO: Behavioral Research Institute.

Empey, L. T. 1977. Crime prevention: The fugitive utopia. In *Crime: Emerging Issues*, ed. J. A. Inciardi and H. A. Siegel. New York: Praeger.

Esbensen, F. 1987. Foot patrols: Of what value? *American Journal of Police* 6, 45-65.

Farrell, G., C. Phillips, and K. Pease. Like taking candy: Why does repeat victimization occur? *British Journal of Criminology* 33, 384-399.

Farrington, D. P. 1983. Offending from 10 to 25 years of age. In *Prospective Studies of Crime and Delinquency*, ed. K. T. van Dusen and S. A. Mednick. Boston: Kluwer-Nijhoff.

Forrester, D. H., M. R. Chatterton, and K. Pease. 1988. *The Kirkholt Burglary Prevention Demonstration Project*. Home Office Crime Prevention Paper no. 13. London: Her Majesty's Stationery Office.

Forrester, D. H., S. Frenz, M. O'Connell, and K. Pease. 1990. *The Kirkholt Burglary Prevention Project: Phase II.* London: Home Office.

Fowler, F., M. E. McCalla, and T. W. Mangione. 1979. *Reducing Residential Crime and Fear: The Hartford Neighborhood Crime Prevention Program.* Washington, DC: National Institute of Law Enforcement and Criminal Justice.

Garrett, C. J. 1985. Effects of residential treatment on adjudicated delinquents: A meta-analysis. *Journal of Research in Crime and Delinquency* 22, 287-308.

Gensheimer, L. K., J. P. Mayer, R. Gottschalk, and W. S. Davidson. 1986. Diverting youth from the juvenile justice system: A meta-analysis of intervention efficacy. In *Youth Violence: Programs and Prospects,* ed. S. J. Apter and A. P. Goldstein. New York: Pergamon.

Gill, M., and K. Pease. 1998. Repeat robbers: Are they different? In *Crime at Work: Increasing the Risk for Offenders,* ed. M. Gill. Leicester, England: Perpetuity Press.

Gilling, D. 1994. Multi-agency crime prevention in Britain: The problem of combining situational and social strategies. In *Crime Prevention Studies,* vol. 3, ed. R. V. Clarke. Monsey, NY: Criminal Justice Press.

Gottfredson, S. D., and D. M. Gottfredson. 1986. Accuracy of prediction models. In *Criminal Careers and 'Career Criminals,'* vol. 2, ed. A. Blumstein, J. Cohen, J. A. Roth, and C. A. Visher. Washington, DC: National Academy Press.

Graziano, A. M., and K. Mooney. 1984. *Children and Behavior Therapy.* New York: Aldine.

Greenberg, D. 1975. The incapacitative effect of imprisonment: Some estimates. *Law and Society Review* 9:541-580.

Greenwood, P. W. 1982. *Selective Incapacitation.* Santa Monica, CA: Rand Corp.

Hartnett, S. M., and W. G. Skogan. 1999. Community policing: Chicago's experience. *National Institute of Justice Journal* 3-11.

Heller, N. B., W. W. Stenzel, A. D. Gill, R. A. Kolde, and S. R. Shimerman. 1975. *Operation Identification Projects: Assessment of Effectiveness.* Washington, DC: Law Enforcement Assistance Administration.

Henig, J. R. 1984. *Citizens Against Crime: An Assessment of the Neighborhood Watch Program in Washington, DC.* Washington, DC: George Washington Univ., Center for Washington Area Studies.

Hirschel, J. D., I. W. Hutchinson, C. W. Dean, J. J. Kelly, and C. E. Pesackis. 1991. *Charlotte Spouse Assault Replication Project: Final Report.* Charlotte: University of North Carolina at Charlotte.

Holden, R. N. 1992. *Law Enforcement: An Introduction.* Englewood Cliffs, NJ: Prentice-Hall.

Home Office. 2003a. *Reducing Burglary Initiative Project Summary.* Rochdale, Supplement 1 to Findings #204, London: Home Office.

Home Office. 2003b. *Reducing Burglary Initiative Project Summary.* Fordbridge, Solihull, Supplement 2 to Findings #204, London: Home Office.

Home Office. 2003c. *Reducing Burglary Initiative Project Summary.* Yew Tree, Sandwell, Supplement 3 to Findings #204, London: Home Office.

Home Office. 2003d. *Reducing Burglary Initiative Project Summary.* Stirchley, Birmingham. Supplement 4 to Findings #204, London: Home Office.

Hope, T. 1997. Inequality and the future of community crime prevention. In *Crime Prevention at a Crossroads*, ed. S. P. Lab. Cincinnati: Anderson.

Hope, T., and S. P. Lab. 2001. Variation in crime prevention participation: Evidence from the British Crime Survey. *Crime Prevention and Community Safety: An International Journal* 3(1), 7-22.

Hser, Y., M. D. Anglin, and C. Chou. 1988. Evaluation of drug abuse treatment: A repeated measure design assessing methadone maintenance. *Evaluation Review* 12, 547-570.

Huba, G.J., and P. M. Bentler. 1983. Causal models of the development of law abidance and its relationship to psycho-social factors and drug use. In *Personality Theory, Moral Development and Criminal Behavior*, ed. W. S. Laufer and J. M. Day. Lexington, MA: D.C. Heath.

Hughes, G. 2002. Crime and disorder reduction partnerships: The future of community safety? In *Crime Prevention and Community Safety: New Directions*, ed. G. Hughes, E. McLaughlin, and J. Muncie. Thousand Oaks, CA: Sage.

Huizinga, D. H., S. Menard, and D. S. Elliott. 1989. Delinquency and drug use: Temporal and developmental patterns. *Justice Quarterly* 6, 419-456.

Hunter, A. 1978. Symbols of incivility: Social disorder and fear of crime in urban neighborhoods. Paper presented at the American Society of Criminology Annual Meeting, Dallas.

Inciardi, J. A. 1996. A corrections-based continuum of effective drug abuse treatment. *NIJ Research Preview.* Washington, DC: U.S. Department of Justice.

Johnson, B. D., T. Williams, K. A. Dei, and H. Sanabria. 1990. Drug abuse in the inner city: Impact on hard-drug users and the community. In *Drugs and Crime*, ed. M. Tonry and J. Q. Morris. Chicago: University of Chicago Press.

Johnson, S. D., and K. J. Bowers. 2002. Domestic burglary repeats and space-time clusters: The dimensions of risk. *European Journal of Criminology* 2002.

Johnston, L. D., P. M. O'Malley, and J. G. Bachman. 2003. *Monitoring the Future National Survey Results on Drug Use, 1975-2002.* Washington, DC: National Institute on Drug Abuse.

Kandel, D. B., O. Smicha-Fagan, and M. Davies. 1986. Risk factors for delinquency and illicit drug use from adolescence to young adulthood. *Journal of Drug Issues* 16, 67-90.

Kelly, B. T., R. Loeber, K. Keenan, and M. DeLamatre. 1997. Developmental pathways in boys' disruptive and delinquent behavior. *Juvenile Justice Bulletin.*

Kinder, B. N., N. E. Pape, and S. Walfish. 1980. Drug and alcohol education programs: A review of outcome studies. *International Journal of the Addictions* 15, 1035-1054.

Kleiman, M. A. R. 1988. Crackdowns: The effects of intensive enforcement on retail heroin dealing. In *Street Level Drug Enforcement: Examining the Issues*, ed. M. Chaiken. Washington, DC: National Institute of Justice.

Kleiman, M. A. R., and K. D. Smith. 1990. State and local drug enforcement: In search of a strategy. In *Drugs and Crime*, ed. M. Tonry and J. Q. Morris. Chicago: University of Chicago Press.

Kodz, J., and K. Pease. 2003. *Reducing Burglary Initiative: Early Findings on Burglary Reduction*. Findings #204. London: Home Office.

Lab, S. P. 1990. Citizen crime prevention: Domains and participation. *Justice Quarterly* 7, 467-492.

Lab, S. P., and D. K. Das. 2003. *International Perspectives on Community Policing and Crime Prevention*. Upper Saddle River, NJ: Prentice-Hall.

Lab, S. P., and J. T. Whitehead. 1988. An analysis of juvenile correctional treatment. *Crime and Delinquency* 34, 60-85.

LaGrange, R. L. 1993. *Policing American Society*. Chicago: Nelson-Hall.

Langworthy, R.H., and L. F. Travis, III. 1994. *Policing in America: A Balance of Forces*. New York: Macmillan.

Latessa, E. J., and L. F. Travis. 1987. Citizen crime prevention: Problems and perspectives in reducing crime. *Journal of Security Administration* 10, 38-50.

Lavrakas, P., and E. J. Herz. 1982. Citizen participation in neighborhood crime prevention. *Criminology* 20, 479-498.

Laycock, G., and N. Tilley. 1995. *Policing and Neighbourhood Watch: Strategic Issues*. London: Home Office Police Research Group.

Leavell, H. R., and E. G. Clarke. 1965. *Preventive Medicine for the Doctor in His Community: An Epidemological Approach*, 3rd ed. New York: McGraw-Hill.

Lewis, D. A., J. A. Grant, and D. P. Rosenbaum. 1998. *The Social Construction of Reform*. Evanston, IL: Northwestern University Press.

Lewis, D.A., and G. Salem. 1986. *Fear of Crime: Incivility and the Production of a Social Problem*. New Brunswick, NJ: Transaction.

Lewis, E. B., and T. T. Sullivan. 1979. Combating crime and citizen attitudes: A study of the corresponding reality. *Journal of Criminal Justice* 7, 71-79.

Lipsey, M. W. 1990. Juvenile delinquency treatment: A meta-analytic inquiry into the variability of effects. Paper presented at the American Society of Criminology Annual Meeting, Denver.

Lipsey, M. W. 1999. Can rehabilitative programs reduce the recidivism of juvenile offenders?: An inquiry into the effectiveness of practical programs. *Virginia Journal of Social Policy and Law* 6, 611-641.

Lipsey, M. W., and J. H. Derzon. 1998. Predictors of violent or serious delinquency in adolescence and early adulthood: A synthesis of longitudinal research. In *Serious and Violent Juvenile Offenders: Risk Factors and Successful Interventions*, ed. R. Loeber and D. P. Farrington. Thousand Oaks, CA: Sage.

Lipsey, M. W., and D. B. Wilson. 1993. The efficacy of psychological, educational, and behavioral treatment. *American Psychologist* 48, 1181-1209.

Lipsey, M. W., and D. B. Wilson. 1998. Effective interventions for serious juvenile offenders: A synthesis of research. In *Serious and Violent Juvenile Offenders: Risk Factors and Successful Interventions*, ed. R. Loeber and D. P. Farrington. Thousand Oaks, CA: Sage.

Lurigio, A. J., and R. C. Davis. 1992. Taking the war on drugs to the streets: The perceptual impact of four neighborhood drug programs. *Crime and Delinquency* 38, 1992, 522-538.

Martinson, R. 1974. What works? Questions and answers about prison reform. *The Public Interest* 35, 22-54.

Mayer, J. P., L. K. Gensheimer, W. S. Davidson, and R. Gottschalk. 1986. Social learning treatment within juvenile justice: A meta-analysis of impact in the natural environment. In *Youth and Violence: Problems and Prospects*, ed. S. J. Apter and A. P. Goldstein. New York: Pergamon.

Mayor's Criminal Justice Coordinating Council. 1977. *The Limits of Street Lighting: The New Orleans Experiment in Crime Reduction*. New Orleans.

Mazerolle, L. G., and J. Roehl. 1998. Civil remedies and crime prevention: An introduction. In *Civil Remedies and Crime Prevention*, ed. L. G. Mazerolle and R. Roehl. Monsey, NY: Criminal Justice Press.

Merry, S. E. 1981. Defensible space undefended: Social factors in crime control through environmental design. *Urban Affairs Quarterly* 16, 397-422.

Monahan, J. 1981. *The Clinical Prediction of Violent Behavior*. Washington, DC: U.S. Department of Health and Human Services.

Moore, M. H. 1994. Research synthesis and policy implications. In *The Challenge of Community Policing: Testing the Promises*, ed. D. P. Rosenbaum. Thousand Oaks, CA: Sage.

National Crime Prevention Institute (NCPI). 1978. *The Practice of Crime Prevention*. Louisville, KY: NCPI Press.

Newcomb, M. D., and P. M. Bentler. 1998. *Consequences of Adolescent Drug Use*. Newbury Park, CA: Sage.

Newman, O. 1972. *Defensible Space*. New York: Macmillan.

Newman, O., and K. A. Franck. 1980. *Factors Influencing Crime and Instability in Urban Housing Developments*. Washington, DC: National Institute of Justice.

Newman, O., and F. Wayne. 1974. *The Private Street System in St. Louis*. New York: Institute for Community Design Analysis.

Niederberger, W. V., and W. F. Wagner. 1985. *Electronic Monitoring of Convicted Offenders: A Field Test Report*. Washington, DC: National Institute of Justice.

Normoyle, J. B., and J. M. Foley. 1988. The defensible space model of fear and elderly public housing residents. *Environment and Behavior* 20, 50-74.

Nurco, D. N., T. W. Kinlock, T. E. Hanlon, and J. C. Ball. 1988. Nonnarcotic drug use over an addiction career: A study of heroin addicts in Baltimore and New York City. *Comprehensive Psychiatry* 29, 450-459.

Oc, T., and S. Tiesdell. 1997. *Safer City Centres: Reviving the Public Realm.* London: Paul Chapman.

O'Keefe, G. J., D. P. Rosenbaum, P. J. Lavrakas, K. Reid, and R. A. Botta. 1996. *Taking A Bite Out of Crime: The Impact of the National Citizens' Crime Prevention Media Campaign.* Thousand Oaks, CA: Sage.

Painter, K. 1993. Street lighting as an environmental crime prevention strategy. In *Proceedings of the International Seminar on Environmental Criminology and Crime Analysis,* ed. D. Zahm and P. Cromwell. Coral Gables, FL: Florida Criminal Justice Executive Institute.

Painter, K., and D. P. Farrington. 1997. The crime reducing effect of improved street lighting: The Dudley project. In *Situational Crime Prevention: Successful Case Studies,* 2nd ed., ed. R. V. Clarke. Gulderland, NY: Harrow and Heston.

Painter, K., and D. P. Farrington. 1999a. Improved street lighting: Crime reducing effects and cost-benefit analysis. *Security Journal* 12, 17-32.

Painter, K., and D. P. Farrington. 1999b. Street lighting and crime: Diffusion of benefits in the Stoke-on-Trent project. In *Surveillance of Public Space: CCTV, Street Lighting and Crime Prevention,* ed. K. Painter and N. Tilley. Monsey, NY: Criminal Justice Press.

Palmer, T. 1975. Martinson revisited. *Journal of Research in Crime and Delinquency* 12, 133-152.

Pease, K. 1988. *Repeat Victimization: Taking Stock.* London: Home Office Police Research Group.

Perkins, D. G., and R. B. Taylor. 1996. Ecological assessments of community disorder: Their relationship to fear of crime and theoretical implications. *American Journal of Community Psychology* 24, 63-107.

Perry, K. 1984. Measuring the effectiveness of neighborhood crime watch in Lakewood, Colorado. *Police Journal* 57, 221-233.

Peterson, M. A., and H. B. Braiker. 1980. *Doing Crime: A Survey of California Prison Inmates.* Santa Monica, CA: Rand Corp.

Phillips, C. 1999. A review of CCTV evaluations: Crime reduction effects and attitudes towards its use. In *Surveillance of Public Space: CCTV, Street Lighting and Crime Prevention,* ed. K. Painter and N. Tilley. Monsey, NY: Criminal Justice Press.

Phillips, C. 2002. From voluntary to statutory status: Reflecting on the experience of three partnerships established under the Crime and Disorder Act 1998. In *Crime Prevention and Community Safety: New Directions,* ed. G. Hughes, E. McLaughlin, and J. Muncie. Thousand Oaks, CA: Sage.

Phillips, M. B. 1991. A hedgehog proposal. *Crime and Delinquency* 37, 555-574.

Police Foundation. 1981. *The Newark Foot Patrol Experiment.* Washington, DC: The Police Foundation.

Polvi, N., T. Looman, C. Humphries, and K. Pease. 1990. Repeat break and enter victimization: Time course and crime prevention opportunity. *Journal of Police Science and Administration* 17, 8-11.

Popkin, S. J., V. E. Gwiasda, D. P. Rosenbaum, J. M. Amendolia, W. A. Johnson, and L. M. Olson. 1999. Combating crime in public housing: A qualitative and quantitative longitudinal analysis of the Chicago Housing Authority's anti-drug initiative. *Justice Quarterly* 16, 519-558.

Poyner, B. 1994. Lessons from Lisson Green: An evaluation of walkway demolition on a British housing estate. In *Crime Prevention Studies,* vol. 4, ed. R. V. Clarke. Monsey, NY: Criminal Justice Press.

Ratcliffe, J., and M. McCullagh. 1999. Burglary, victimization and social deprivation. *Crime Prevention and Community Safety: An International Journal* 1, 37-46.

Rengert, G. F. 1997. Auto theft in central Philadelphia. In *Policing for Prevention: Reducing Crime, Public Intoxication and Injury,* ed. R. Homel. Monsey, NY: Criminal Justice Press.

Reppetto, T. A. 1974. *Residential Crime.* Cambridge, MA: Ballinger.

Ringwalt, C. L., S. T. Ennett, and K. D. Holt. 1991. An outcome evaluation of project DARE. *Health Education Research: Theory and Practice* 6, 327-337.

Roehl, J. A., H. Wong, R. Huitt, and G. E. Capowich. 1995. *A National Assessment of Community-based Anti-drug Initiatives: Final Report.* Pacific Grove, CA: Institute for Social Analysis, 1995.

Rosenbaum, D. P. 1991. The pursuit of "justice" in the United States: A policy lesson in the war on crime and drugs? In *Community Crime Prevention: Shaping the Future,* ed. D. J. Loree and R. W. Walker. Ottawa: Royal Canadian Mounted Police.

Rosenbaum, D. P. 2002. Evaluating multi-agency anti-crime partnerships: Theory, design and measurement issues. In *Evaluation for Crime Prevention,* ed. N. Tilley. Monsey, NY: Criminal Justice Press.

Rosenbaum, D. P., R. L. Flewelling, S. L. Bailey, C. L. Ringwalt, and D. L. Wilkinson. 1994. Cops in the classroom: A longitudinal evaluation of Drug Abuse Resistance Education (DARE). *Journal of Research in Crime and Delinquency* 31, 3-31.

Rosenbaum, D. P., and G. S. Hanson. 1998. Assessing the effects of school-based drug education: A six-year multilevel analysis of project DARE. *Journal of Research in Crime and Delinquency* 35, 381-412.

Rosenbaum, D. P., P. J. Lavrakas, D. L. Wilkinson, and D. Faggiani. 1997. *Community Responses to Drug Abuse National Demonstration Program: An Impact Evaluation.* Washington, DC: National Institute of Justice.

Rosenbaum, D. P., D. A. Lewis, and J. A. Grant. 1985. *The Impact of Community Crime Prevention Programs in Chicago: Can Neighborhood Organizations Make a Difference?* Evanston, IL: Northwestern University.

Sadd, S., and R. Grinc. 1994. Innovative neighborhood oriented policing: An evaluation of community policing programs in eight cities. In *The Challenge of Community Policing: Testing the Promises*, ed. D. P. Rosenbaum. Thousand Oaks, CA: Sage.

Sadd, S., and R. Grinc. 1996. *Implementation challenges in community policing: Innovative neighborhood-oriented policing in eight cities*. NIJ Research in Brief. Washington, DC: U.S. Department of Justice.

Sampson, R. J., and W. W. Wilson. 1995. Toward a theory of race, crime, and urban inequality. In *Crime and Inequality*, ed. J. Hagan and R. D. Peterson. Stanford, CA: Stanford University Press.

Schaps, E., J. M. Moskowitz, J. H. Malvin, and G. A. Schaeffer. 1986. Evaluation of seven school-based prevention programs: A final report of the Napa project. *International Journal of the Addictions* 21, 1081-1112.

Schlossman, S., and M. Sedlak. 1983. *The Chicago Area Project Revisited*. Santa Monica, CA: Rand Corp.

Schlossman, S., G. Zellman, and R. Shavelson. 1984. *Delinquency Prevention in South Chicago: A Fifty-year Assessment of the Chicago Area Project*. Santa Monica, CA: Rand Corp.

Schwendinger, H., and J. Schwendinger. 1993. Giving crime prevention top priority. *Crime and Delinquency* 39, 425-446.

Seattle Law and Justice Planning Office. 1977. *Evaluation Report: Target Hardening*. Washington, DC: Law Enforcement Assistance Administration.

Seattle Public Schools Communities That Care Works! http://www.seattle-schools.org/area/ctc/CTCworks.xml, accessed November 14, 2003.

Sechrest, L., S. O. White, and E. D. Brown. 1979. *The Rehabilitation of Criminal Offenders: Problems and Prospects*. Washington, DC: National Academy Press.

Shah, S. A., and L. H. Roth. 1974. Biological and psychophysiological factors in criminality. In *Handbook of Criminology*, ed. D. Glaser. Chicago: Rand-McNally.

Shaw, C. R., and H. D. McKay. 1942. *Juvenile Delinquency in Urban Areas*. Chicago: University of Chicago Press.

Sherman, L. W. 1990. Police crackdowns: Initial and residual deterrence. In *Crime and Justice*, vol. 12, ed. M. Tonry and N. Morris. Chicago: University of Chicago Press.

Sherman, L. W. 1995. Hot spots of crime and criminal careers of places. In *Crime and Place*, ed. J. E. Eck and D. Weisburd. Monsey, NY: Criminal Justice Press.

Sherman, L. W., and R. A. Berk. 1984. The specific deterrent effect of arrest for domestic assault. *American Sociological Review* 49, 261-272.

Sherman, L. W., P. R. Garten, and M. E. Buerger. 1989. Hot spots of predatory crime: Routine activities and the criminology of place. *Criminology* 27, 27-56.

Shernock, S. K. 1986. A profile of the citizen crime prevention activist. *Journal of Criminal Justice* 14, 211-228.

Skogan, W. G. 1990. *Disorder and Decline: Crime and the Spiral of Decay in American Neighborhoods.* New York: Free Press.

Skogan, W. G. 1995. *Community policing in Chicago: Year two.* NIJ Research Preview, Washington, DC: U.S. Department of Justice.

Skogan, W. G. 1996. The community's role in community policing. *NIJ Journal* 231, 31-34.

Skogan, W. G., and S. M. Hartnett. 1997. *Community Policing: Chicago Style.* New York: Oxford University Press.

Skogan, W. G., and M. G. Maxfield. 1981. *Coping with Crime: Individual and Neighborhood Reactions.* Beverly Hills, CA: Sage.

Skogan, W. G., and M. A. Wycoff. 1986. Storefront police offices: The Houston field test. In *Community Crime Prevention: Does It Work?* ed. D. P. Rosenbaum. Beverly Hills, CA: Sage.

Skolnick, J. H., and D. H. Bailey. 1988. Theme and variation in community policing. In *Crime and Justice,* vol. 10, ed. M. Tonry and N. Morris. Chicago: University of Chicago Press.

Smith, B. E., and R. C. Davis. 1998. What do landlords think about drug abatement laws? In *Civil Remedies and Crime Prevention,* ed. L. G. Mazerolle and R. Roehl. Monsey, NY: Criminal Justice Press.

Spelman, W. 1993. Abandoned buildings: Magnets for crime? *Journal of Criminal Justice* 21, 481-296.

Spelman, W. 1995. Criminal careers of public places. In *Crime and Place,* ed. J. E. Eck and D. Weisburd. Monsey, NY: Criminal Justice Press.

Stead, P. J. 1983. *The Police of France.* New York: Macmillan.

Stouthamer-Loeber, M., and R. Loeber. 1989. The use of prediction data in understanding delinquency. In *Primary Prevention and Promotion in the Schools,* ed. L. A. Bond and B. E. Compas. Newbury Park, CA: Sage.

Sutton, A. 1994. Crime prevention: Promise or threat? *Australian and New Zealand Journal of Criminology* 27, 5-20.

Sutton, M. 1996. *Implementing Crime Prevention Schemes in a Multi-agency Setting: Aspects of Process in the Safer Cities Programme.* London: Home Office Research and Statistics Directorate.

Swadi, H., and H. Zeitlin. 1987. Drug education to school children: Does it really work? *British Journal of Addiction* 82, 741-746.

Taylor, R. B. 1988. *Human Territorial Functioning.* New York: Cambridge University Press.

Taylor, R. B. 1997. Crime, grime and responses to crime: Relative impacts of neighborhood structure, crime, and physical deterioration on residents and business personnel in the Twin Cities. In *Crime Prevention at a Crossroads*, ed. S. P. Lab. Cincinnati: Anderson.

Taylor, R. B., and S. Gottfredson. 1986. Environmental design, crime, and prevention: An examination of community dynamics. In *Communities and Crime*, ed. A. J. Reiss and M. Tonry. Chicago: University of Chicago Press.

Taylor, R. B., B. A. Koons, E. M. Kurtz, J. R. Greene, and D. D. Perkins. 1995. Street blocks with more nonresidential land use have more physical deterioration: Evidence from Baltimore and Philadelphia. *Urban Affairs Review* 31, 120-136.

Tien, J. M., V. F. O'Donnell, A. I. Barnett, and P. B. Mirchondani. 1977. *Street Lighting Projects: National Evaluation Program, Phase I Summary Report*. Washington, DC: National Institute of Law Enforcement and Criminal Justice.

Tierney, J. 2001. Audits of crime and disorder: Some lessons from research. *Crime Prevention and Community Safety: An International Journal* 3(2), 7-18.

Tilley, N. 1992. *Safer Cities and Community Safety Strategies*. Crime Prevention Unit Paper 38. London: Home Office.

Tilley, N. 1993. *Understanding Car Parks, Crime and CCTV: Evaluation Lessons from Safer Cities*. London: Home Office Police Research Group.

Tilley, N., and J. Webb. 1994. *Burglary Reduction: Findings from Safer Cities Schemes*. London: Home Office Police Research Group.

Tobler, N. S. 1986. Meta-analysis of 143 adolescent drug prevention programs: Quantitative outcome results of program participants compared to a control or comparison group. *Journal of Drug Issues* 16, 537-567.

Tonglet, M. 1998. Consumers' perceptions of shoplifting and shoplifting behavior. In *Crime at Work: Increasing the Risk for Offenders*, vol. 2, ed. M. Gill. Leicester, England: Perpetuity Press.

Tonry, M., and D. P. Farrington. 1995. Strategic approaches to crime prevention. In *Building a Safer Society: Strategic Approaches to Crime Prevention*, ed. M. Tonry and D. P. Farrington. Chicago: University of Chicago Press.

Trojanowicz, R. 1983. *An Evaluation of the Neighborhood Foot Patrol Program in Flint, Michigan*. East Lansing: Michigan State University.

van Dijk, J. M., and J. deWaard. 1991. A two-dimensional typology of crime prevention projects. *Criminal Justice Abstracts* 23:483-503.

van Kammen, W. B., and R. Loeber. 1994. Are fluctuations in delinquent activities related to the onset and offset in juvenile illegal drug use and drug dealing? *Journal of Drug Issues* 24, 9-24.

Vaughn, J. B. 1989. A survey of juvenile electronic monitoring and home confinement programs. *Juvenile and Family Court Journal* 40, 1-36.

Walker, S. 1999. *The Police in America: An Introduction*, 3rd ed. Boston: McGraw-Hill.

Walklate, S. 1999. Some questions for and about community safety partnerships and crime. *Crime Prevention and Community Safety: An International Journal* 1(3), 7-16.

Watson, E. M., A. R. Stone, and S. M. DeLuca. 1998. *Strategies for Community Policing.* Upper Saddle River, NJ: Prentice-Hall.

Weisburd, D., E. Waring, and E. Chayet. 1995. Specific deterrence in a sample of offenders convicted of white-collar crime. *Criminology* 33, 587-607.

Weisel, D. L., and J. E. Eck. 1994. Toward a practical approach to organizational change: Community policing initiatives in six cities. In *The Challenge of Community Policing: Testing the Promises,* ed. D. P. Rosenbaum. Thousand Oaks, CA: Sage.

Welsh, B. C., and D. P. Farrington. 2002. *Crime Prevention Effects of Closed Circuit Television: A Systematic Review.* London: Home Office.

Whisenand, P. M. 1977. *Crime Prevention.* Boston: Holbrook Press.

White, H. R. 1990. The drug use-delinquency connection in adolescence. In *Drugs, Crime and the Criminal Justice System,* ed. R. Weisheit. Cincinnati: Anderson.

Wilkinson, D. L., and D. P. Rosenbaum. 1994. The effects of organizational structure on community policing: A comparison of two cities. In *The Challenge of Community Policing: Testing the Promises,* ed. D. P. Rosenbaum. Thousand Oaks, CA: Sage.

Williams, H., and A. M. Pate. 1987. Returning to first principles: Reducing fear of crime in Newark. *Crime and Delinquency* 33, 53-70.

Wilson, J. Q., and G. Kelling. 1982. Broken windows. *Atlantic Monthly* (March), 29-38.

Wolfer, L. 2001. Strengthening communities: Neighborhood watch and the elderly in a Pennsylvania town. *Crime Prevention and Community Safety: An International Journal* 3(3), 31-40.

Wright, R. T., and S. H. Decker. 1994. *Burglars on the Job: Streetlife and Residential Break-ins.* Boston: Northeastern University Press.

Wright, W. E., and M. C. Dixon. 1977. Community prevention and treatment of juvenile delinquency. *Journal of Research in Crime and Delinquency* 14, 35-67.

Zhao, J. S., M. C. Scheider, and Q. Thurman. 2002. Funding community policing to reduce crime: Have COPS grants made a difference? *Criminology and Public Policy* 2, 7-32.

Zhao, J. S., M. C. Scheider, and Q. Thurman. 2003. A national evaluation of the effect of COPS grants on police productivity (arrests) 1995-1999. *Police Quarterly* 6, 387-409.

Situational Crime Prevention[1]

8

MARCUS FELSON

Contents

[1] This chapter was first published in the author's *Crime and Everyday Life*, 3rd ed., London: Sage, 2002, chap. 10. Reprinted by permission.

8.1   Introduction

Great Britain's Home Office is roughly equivalent to the U.S. Department of Justice. Within this agency was the small Research Unit, located during the 1970s at Romney House on Marsham Street, a five-minute walk from Scotland Yard. There, in 1973, a thirty-one-year-old research officer named Ronald Clarke had just completed a study of why youths abscond from borstals (American translation: why juvenile delinquents run away from reform school).

The usual social science variables did not successfully explain why some boys ran away whereas others stayed put. But Clarke learned that most boys ran away on weekends, when staffing and supervision were light. Because these were not prisons and staff members were not guards, their influence was largely informal. Merely by their presence, adults could prevent a certain amount of trouble, including absconding. With these results, Clarke began to think of crime in general as the result of human situations and opportunities.

In 1976, with Pat Mayhew, A. Sturman, and J. M. Hough, Clarke published *Crime as Opportunity*, which offered many inexpensive ways to reduce crime by removing the opportunity to carry it out. Over time, this has become known as situational crime prevention. Clarke later headed the Research and Planning Unit of the Home Office. Under his leadership, several British researchers inside and outside the government created or discovered real-life crime prevention experiments that helped provide a major alternative theory of crime and practical guidelines for its prevention.

Clarke has encouraged or assisted others to study situational prevention examples with systematic data and to write up these studies. As it has evolved, situational crime prevention today includes at least sixteen categories of prevention (Clarke 1997c, 1999) and perhaps more than a hundred case studies. Situational crime prevention seeks inexpensive means to reduce crime in three general ways:

- Design safe settings.
- Organize effective procedures. That includes planning and carrying out the best management principles.
- Develop secure products. That means making cars, radios, and other products more difficult to steal or abuse.

Indeed, the crime prevention repertoire is growing so greatly that it offers alternatives should one measure be politically or ethically problematic (see Felson and Clarke 1997b; von Hirsch, Garland, and Wakefield 2000). Settings, procedures, and products cover a wide range of crime prevention ideas, which no one person could learn in an entire lifetime. With Clarke's multitude of examples, it is no longer possible to dismiss situational prevention as simply installing a better lock. Certainly, this field has produced many subtleties and surprises, dozens of books and monographs, and hundreds of articles. It is harder for intellectuals to dismiss a field after several of them have written books about it (Sullivan 2000; von Hirsch, Garland, and Wakefield 2000). British Home Office researchers have contributed much of the systematic crime prevention measures now available. Their work has been supplemented by studies in the Netherlands, Sweden, and Canada, often in dialogue with the British. Sadly, the American representation has been sparse, yet Clarke moved to the United States to become a professor. It is increasingly evident that situational crime prevention offers society the best chance for a quick and inexpensive way to reduce crime slice by slice. Thus, Clarke not only provides specific examples but also principles for inventing your own crime prevention measures.

8.2 Situational Prevention and Crime Science

Clarke and his associates adopted the following policy:

Do not worry about academic theories. Just go out and gather facts about crime from nature herself (e.g., by observing or by interviewing offenders). (This is not to say you should throw all your education to the wolves. It merely tells you that science has to gather facts and learn from them.)

Focus on very specific slices of crime, such as vandalism against telephones or soccer violence. Even the crime of "vandalism" would be far too broad!

Do not try to improve human character. You are certain to fail.

Try to block crime in a practical, natural, and simple way, at low social and economic cost.

Do small-scale experiments, especially looking for natural environments to study each slice of the crime prevention puzzle.

Use very simple statistics and charts that let you see each comparison quite directly.

Perhaps we could sum up his approach in three words: "Don't get fancy."

Clarke sometimes claims that he really has no interest in theory, that his only goal is to find practical ways to prevent crime. This surprises many conventional criminologists, but being practical poses a very good discipline on us all. Make it work! If it does not work, it probably is not very good science in the first place. If it does work, science will improve, too.

Another reason that I consider situational prevention a contribution to crime prevention is that it helps us understand offenders, targets, guardians, and their convergences. Clarke seeks to accomplish prevention by making each criminal act appear

- Difficult
- Risky
- Unrewarding
- Inexcusable

That breaks down crime into components that can then be explored—exactly what science is all about. The last of the four is closely linked to "neutralization theory," which considers how offenders excuse their own actions. (Removing these rationalizations or excuses helps prevent crimes. Supermarkets often train their employees in the different types of theft in order to remove the idea that "minor pilfering" is not stealing.)

8.3 Preventing Property Crime

A good deal of this chapter presents specific examples of successful situational prevention. I have selected these to tell a story. I include crime prevention methods that were discovered accidentally, those involving criminologists, and others involving people who never heard of situational crime prevention but did it anyway. Whether planned or not, people have acquired a variety of crime prevention experience well worth sharing.

8.3.1   Trouble on Double-Deck Buses

Our illustration of situational prevention begins with the problem of vandalism against Britain's traditional red double-deck buses. The Home Office researchers learned that most of the vandalism was on the upper deck, usually in the back row, where supervision was least likely to occur (Clarke 1978). They also learned that the traditional British bus conductor had a major role in preventing vandalism. A bus conductor would ascend the stairs to the upper deck to collect fares and thus serve as a guardian against the crime of vandalism.

Because some companies had removed the conductor to save money, whereas other companies had not, this was a natural experiment. Those buses with conductors had less vandalism, but they also had more assaults on conductors. This is an instance of how crime prevention can sometimes backfire, solving one crime but leading to another. This example also establishes that situational crime prevention is far from obvious, sometimes producing unexpected results.

8.3.2   Correcting the Criminal Use of Telephones

Ronald Clarke and associates are developing a growing literature on the criminal side of telephones and what to do about it (see Table 8.1).

They have shown that obscene phone calls can be thwarted by caller identification services; drug transactions are impaired by pay phones that only call out; fraudulent international calls from pay phones are impossible when phones exclude common paths for the fraud; and stolen or cloned cell phones can be designed to fail for anybody but the owner. Clarke, Kemper, and Wyckoff (2001) documented more than $1.3 billion in cell phone fraud

Table 8.1   Phone-Related Crime and Situational Solutions

Phone crime problem	Technical solution	Reference
Obscene phone calls	Caller ID	Clarke 1997a
Drug transactions	Only call out	Natarajan, Clarke, and Johnson 1995
Fraudulent long-distance calls from pay phones	Programmed to exclude common frauds	Bichler and Clarke 1996
Stolen or cloned cell phones	Designed to fail when stolen	Clarke, Kemper, and Wyckoff 2001

losses during 1995 to 1996. Five technical changes were designed to cut off fraud quickly:

1. Computer profiling to detect strange call patterns
2. Personal identification numbers (PINs)
3. Precall validation by computer checks
4. Radio wave checks
5. Encrypted checks of each phone

These adjustments resulted in a 97 percent cut in cell phone fraud.

Telephones are important facilitators in drug transactions. Managai Natarajan, Ronald Clarke, and Mathieu Belanger, in ongoing work, are paying close attention to the use of telephones for doing illegal work. Some localities have thwarted outdoor retail drug dealing by having pay phones

- Moved inside of business for extra supervision
- Programmed to call out but not receive calls
- Removed entirely

8.3.3   Car Theft Is Preventable

Additional information about thwarting motor vehicle theft is found in several studies (Brown 1995; Brown and Billing 1996; Southall and Ekblom 1985). Clarke and Harris (1992) listed numerous technical changes that the auto industry can contribute to help reduce auto theft. Several of these are already common in cars today. Many cars have better security locks for steering columns, doors, and the hood. Door buttons today are more difficult to pull up with a clothes hanger. Window glass is often harder to break. Many models make it difficult to leave your key in the ignition. Smart keys, elimination of external keyholes, and electronic immobilization after break-ins are no longer confined to the most expensive models. Manufacturers have improved some of those models listed as most stolen by the Highway Loss Date Institute (see Exhibit 8.1). Tremendous strides in car tape player security have combined with lower fence values, thereby interfering with their theft. The time it takes to steal a car has increased, and the pure amateur has more problems than ever. Brown and Billing (1996) showed that more secure cars led to less theft in Britain, and the American auto industry experience shows that cars with disastrous theft problems can be redesigned for crime prevention and their good names restored. By the time you read this, a new design will have been developed, probably for a model that got into the national media as thieves' favorite.

On the other hand, many new cars have expensive airbags, which are quickly pried out and sold for about $1,000 for installation in cars at repair shops, and computers provide new targets as well. This illustrates what Ekblom referred to as an "arms race" between offenders and forces of crime control. Crime is never permanently prevented, but neither do we get anywhere against crime when we do not try.

Beyond the automobile industry, inexpensive technology already exists to put a personal identification number into every new and valuable electronic item, such as a television set or videocassette recorder. The product would not work outside your home unless you entered the right number. It would lose its value to a thief. It also should be possible to program something within your electrical system so an appliance removed from your home would not work elsewhere without punching in the code. Industry could make a major contribution to society by designing and selling more products that go kaput when stolen (Felson 1997).

8.3.4 A Serendipitous Finding about Motorcycle Theft

American motorcyclists keep complaining about having to put on their helmets and campaigning to stop helmet laws. If they only knew. Wherever helmet safely laws were enacted and enforced, thefts of motorcycles went down greatly.

To understand why, note that many motorcycle thefts are for joyriding and occur on the spur of the moment. The likely offenders usually do not have a big motorcycle helmet with them at the time they see a shiny motorcycle. When Germany enacted and enforced its motorcycle helmet law, thefts went down and stayed down, with no indication of displacement to other vehicle theft (Mayhew, Clarke, and Eliot 1989).

We see that significant crime prevention can occur completely without planning. Even a very simple change in the law can have a great impact. Because wearing a helmet is highly visible behavior, it provides tangible evidence that the law is being followed and that the motorcycle probably is not stolen.

8.3.5 Saving Billions on Retail Theft

Not all prevention occurs with across-the-board laws enacted centrally. Some crime prevention requires more "personal service." For example, a retail store has to take into account its particular doors, layout, pedestrian flow, and hours of operation in planning for prevention. Good management and crime prevention go hand in hand within retail stores. A well-managed and well-organized retail store will not only have less shoplifting and employee theft but will usually enjoy more sales and better morale among employees.

Retail stores use many prevention methods. More frequent interventions and audits help to discourage employee theft. Requiring that all merchandise be bagged and then stapled shut makes it harder for a customer to slip something unpaid for into his or her bag. Designing exit routes carefully encourages people to pay for their merchandise as they walk out. Tags that beep when not deactivated discourage shoplifters. Electronic systems for detecting merchandise are increasingly available at low prices, paying for themselves in loss reduction within a year or two. Robert DiLonardo's (1997) evaluation showed that tags can be tremendously successful in reducing thefts from stores. Barry Masuda (1993, 1997) showed that employee theft also can be reduced.

Retailers can easily lose thousands of dollars in merchandise out the door. In a few seconds, thieves can grab stacks of expensive garments and run to a waiting car. The well-managed store combines comprehensive planning with situational prevention to prevent such losses. For the back door, it is essential to schedule deliveries carefully so people do not take away more than they deliver. For the front door, a clever merchant learned to alternate the direction of hangers on the rack so they lock when grabbed. This small but ingenious idea is clearly superior to letting people steal and then waiting for the criminal justice system to find and punish them.

Our knowledge about retail crime has increased greatly in recent years (Beck and Willis 1995, 1999; Clarke 1996; Gill 1994; Hayes 1997a, 1997b). A broader field of business crime analysis is offered in two collections of essays (Felson and Clarke 1997a; Felson and Peiser 1998). As you read these sources, you will realize that crime prevention should not simply be left to the public sector, although public officials can do an excellent job of preventing crime when they put their minds to it.

8.3.6 Refusing to Accept Subway Graffiti

For many years, subway trains of New York City were covered inside and out with graffiti and surely were among the ugliest anywhere. Moreover, the transit system was in chaos, ridership was dropping, and employee morale was low. Many efforts and policies had failed to correct the problems.

Then David Gunn became president of the New York City Transit Authority and announced the Clean Car Program. The aim of the program was to clean off graffiti immediately. Graffiti painters thus would get no satisfaction from their work traveling all over town. New York City's subway cars never returned to the graffiti levels before the program (Sloan-Howitt and Kelling 1997). One lesson of the program: Find out exactly what potential offenders want from crime and take it away from them.

Another subway system far distant from New York City prevented graffiti in fixed locations using a very different plan. The Swedish government calls the Stockholm Metro the world's longest art gallery. More than half of its stations have artwork, including mosaics, paintings, engravings, and bas-reliefs. They may not win aesthetic fame, but the artists knew how to beat the graffiti painters with textures and colors. Each of these techniques was used: multicolors, surfaces that are either unusually rough or highly polished, and walls that are either sharply uneven or blocked with metal grills.

8.3.7 Art Theft Appreciation

Art theft is surprisingly common in New York City art galleries. Truc-Nhu Ho (1998) studied 229 such thefts from forty-five art dealers. Although the statistics are limited, they show that art thefts fit patterns (see Conklin 1994). Art thieves

- Detest abstract art
- Avoid galleries with security checks
- Hate galleries near active nightlife
- Turn up their noses at large objets d'art
- Appreciate realistic paintings and sculptures
- Prefer galleries on the ground floor on quiet streets
- Resonate with art that has price tags affixed

The discerning art dealer should study art through the eyes of thieves.

8.3.8 Putting Lighting into Focus

It is not simple to say, "Turn on the lights."

In the 1970s, it was very common for cities to fight crime by scattering streetlights without plan. Consider the logic for why this failed (Pease 1999).

Criminal activity is concentrated at or near specific places or blocks (Eck and Weisburd 1995).

Streetlight campaigns have often led to scattering placement without plan.

Totally *unplanned* lighting had little effect on crime. As a result, some analysts went to an extreme position, claiming that lighting cannot reduce crime. Ken Pease (1999) referred to these people as the "disciples of darkness."

Yet Painter and Farrington (1997) produced a rigorous study, with victim surveys showing a 41 percent reduction in crime in the lighting-enhanced area, compared to a 15 percent reduction in the control area. We have to conclude that lighting has a major possible contribution to reducing crime.

At the same time, lighting can *increase* crime in some cases. Lights can help a burglar see what he or she is doing. Lights can draw students back to school for after-hours vandalism. Lights can glare in the eyes of victims or guardians. Lights can make a better hangout for getting drunk and becoming disorderly. So do not place lights without thinking. Lighting can be highly effective in reducing crime when it is clearly focused on the problem at hand (Painter and Farrington 1997; Painter and Tilley 1999; Pease 1999).

In an excellent intellectual and factual review of the topic, Pease (1999) noted that a number of cities with strategic improvement of lighting clearly showed decreased crime rates. He also worked out how to think about lighting and to disaggregate the mechanisms whereby it might affect crime. Figure 8.1 shows his seventeen different ways in which lighting can affect crime. The figure explains why lighting can lead to either more crime or less. It also shows that lighting can, surprisingly, affect crime in the daytime. For example, lights can give cues, even in daytime, that the area is not good for crime. It can keep people from moving out of the area, with fewer "For Sale" signs to assist burglars in finding empty places to break into. After reading Exhibit 8.1, I defy anyone to defend the position that the relationship between street lighting and crime is not a sophisticated enough topic for those of us in higher education to study.

8.3.9 Lighting Affects Crime in Many Ways (Adapted from Pease 1999)

Pease's contention is set forth in Exhibit 8.1 below:

Exhibit 8.1 Impact of Lighting on Crime

How More Lights Might Reduce Crimes after Dark

- Get people to spend late time in the yard or garden, serving as guardians.
- Encourage people to walk more after dark, serving as guardians.
- Make offenders more visible to guardians.
- Make police on patrol more visible to offenders.

How More Lights Might Increase Crimes after Dark

- Draw people away from home, assisting burglars.
- Give offenders a better look at potential targets of crime.
- Assist offenders in checking for potential guardians against crime.
- Get nearby areas to seem darker, helping offenders to escape into them.

How More Lights Might Reduce Crimes in Daytime

- Put new guardians on the street, those installing and maintaining lights.
- Show official commitment; local citizens then cooperate in crime prevention.
- Give cues—even in daytime—that the area is not good for crime.

- Provide a talking point for citizens, who then get to know one another.
- Keep people from moving out, with fewer "For Sale" signs to assist burglars.
- Apprehend more offenders after dark, with fewer left for daytime offending.

How More Lights Might Increase Crimes in Daytime

- Make it easy to pretend to be an electrical or maintenance employee.
- Provide more nighttime fun that carries over to daytime drunkenness.
- Set up new nighttime hangouts that might spill over as daytime trouble spots.

8.3.10 Music and Control

People are not only influenced by what they see but also by what they hear. Young people generally do not like classical music and will go away when it is played. That's far better than nightsticks and imprisonment. Music is also suitable for calming people down, as wise disc jockeys well know. When the music stops, crowds in bars are rowdiest. The type of dancing also has a major influence on their behavior, with wilder dancing making people bump and, sometimes, fight. Yet the topic of music and crime has been little studied. Psychology students with expertise in perception and human factors are especially likely to break new ground in explaining how music provides cues that affect criminal behavior.

8.3.11 Situational Degeneration

Crime institutions not only can be improved, but they can also be exacerbated. Thus, a store manager can remove crime control measures and cause shoplifting to rise. A homeowner can let well-trimmed bushes grow up, to the benefit of local burglars. A car manufacturer can cut costs by putting in cheaper steering wheel locks. One of the challenges of crime science is to put situational prevention and situational degeneration within the same intellectual framework. There is no better place to start the study of violence.

8.4 Preventing Violent Crime

It is quite a mistake to think that situational prevention applies only to property crime. Understanding of situational features of violence has grown considerably in recent years. The greatest source of progress stems from recognizing that violence is goal oriented and responds to cues from physical settings. A book by James Tedeschi and my brother, Richard Felson (1994), showed us that all violence is goal oriented. A person might use violence (1) to get others to comply with wishes, (2) to restore justice as he or she perceives it, or (3) to assert and protect his or her self-image or identity. (As we shall see, these goals often make violence highly amenable to situational prevention as well.) A simple robbery starts out with the robber demanding your money and using or threatening force to get it. The robber is simply getting you to comply with his or her wishes—receiving your money without an argument. But if you challenge the robber in front of a co-offender, they may harm you to assert and protect their own identity (the third reason for violence). That is why it is best not to have a big mouth when someone is pointing a gun at you (see "Situational Degeneration," above). It's also best not to go around giving people grievances against you; they may decide to restore justice. Fights between drunken young males usually occur as attempts to assert and protect identity. Road rage is often an effort to meet the second goal, restoring justice. Domestic violence can meet all three purposes (Felson in press).

Even with predatory violence, although generally oriented toward the first purpose—gaining compliance—-offenders will sometimes seek to protect identity or restore justice. For example, youths angry at the store owner who yelled at them may rob him not only for loot but also to retaliate and punish. Remember, all these evaluations are based on the offender's viewpoint. To understand violent or nonviolent crime, we cannot be distracted by our own moral outrage, or by the legal code, or by objective facts about what a person ought to think of others. If the guy in the bar hit you because he thinks you insulted him, the fact he heard you wrong is entirely beside the point.

You might readily guess that alcohol plays a major role in violence. It gives people big mouths and big ears. Big mouths help people make aggressive statements that provoke counterattacks and restoration of justice. Big mouths also help people to provoke others into fights. Alcohol makes bigger ears by getting people to hear things that were not said. Managing alcohol is part of preventing violence.

8.4.1   Sport Events and Revelry

Speaking of alcohol, British football (soccer) has an unfortunate pattern of serious—and sometimes fatal—violence. Many fans arrive hours before a game, get drunk, and then commit acts of violence, many against fans of the visiting team. Because most of those involved in the violence do not own cars and therefore take buses to the games, the government arranged for these buses to arrive at the game later than in the past, allowing only a few minutes to buy a ticket and no time to get drunk. The effect was a reduction in football violence (Clarke 1983).

Sweden also has a problem with alcohol-related violence, especially on one day each year. Midsummer's Eve (usually June 21) is the longest day of the year. In much of Sweden, this day has twenty-four hours of light. It is the most important holiday of the year. Swedes are usually reserved people, but they make an exception on Midsummer's Eve. A common behavior pattern is to get drunk and run wild. People also start bonfires, which sometimes get out of hand and burn more than intended. Moreover, many assaults occur on Midsummer's Eve. The crowds are far larger and wilder than anything police can handle, so deterrence loses its credibility. A more sensible policy was planned by Swedish authorities: They provided bonfires in designated and advertised locations and sought to channel the holiday spirit into these settings. Their efforts paid off by reducing assaults and other illegal behavior (see Bjor, Knutsson, and Kuhlhorn 1992).

Compared with events like football games in Britain, American sports venues usually are not bad. The probable reason is that American teams try to sell a lot of tickets to families and business groups. This results in people of mixed ages and both sexes. Even in hockey, with its violence on the ice, there is reasonable peace in the stands. We all know of exceptions, but the rule remains.

American sports venues try to prevent people from bringing in their own bottles. This probably is so that they can sell more drinks, but they also use security justifications. They generally sell soft drinks and beer to the larger crowd, with hard drinks sold only within the corporate boxes. Beer sales are cut off later in the game, when some fans are a bit too drunk. Security people with binoculars keep an eye on the crowd to see if there are fights or if fans are getting dangerous. They can cut off the beer sales in that section or even start watering down the beer. Because beer is highly profitable to management, cutting off beer sales reduces proceeds, but it clearly enhances safety. Watering the beer gets the heavy drinkers to complain, but management is glad to give them their money back and have the drinking dwindle.

To prevent conflicts and fights when people are going out of a stadium, the strategy is to keep people moving, whether in cars or on foot, so they have little time to linger or to get mad. A well-managed stadium looks for bottlenecks where crowds cannot move, relieving the traffic problem quickly as a service to customers and as a way to prevent trouble.

8.4.2   Cruising

In many European and Hispanic nations, young people walk around the center of town on weekend evenings. The United States version of this activity is cruising in cars. Cruising creates traffic jams and interferes with business. The automobile spreads adolescent activity over more space and makes it harder to prevent trouble; thus, vandalism and assaults become more serious (Felson et al. 1997; Wikstrom 1995). Many U.S. cities have enacted special cruising ordinances or enforce traffic and parking ordinances more heavily in trying to control cruising.

As explained by authors John Bell and Barbara Burke (1992), the city of Arlington, Texas, found that cruising by more than a thousand cars was creating a major traffic jam on its main street for hours at a time. Ambulances could not get to hospitals, and little else in the way of normal city business could happen. Conventional traffic control methods were doing little good.

City Councilman Ken Groves learned that teenagers wanted two things: an unstructured and unsupervised environment in which to mingle, and restrooms. He speculated that if these were provided, most teenagers would act reasonably. A "cruising committee" was formed to link local agencies, businesses, the University of Texas at Arlington, and teenage representatives.

The committee devised a plan for the city to lease a large parking lot from the university and open it to cruisers on weekend nights while providing unobtrusive police protection, portable restrooms, and cleanup the next morning. Within two weekends, the new cruise area was in use by a thousand parked or circling cars. The program channeled cruising into a smaller and safer area and pleased both teenagers and adults, while providing the gentle controls of a few police officers on the side.

The lesson of the program is that a crime problem may be related to another problem; solve the other problem, and the crime problem takes care of itself. In this case, the problem was to provide youths with an outlet for a social need in the context of the local situation. When this was done, the related crime problems dissipated.

8.4.3   Foul Play in College Water Polo

Many situational prevention measures emerge entirely by accident. An interesting example has to do not with a "crime" as such but with rule violations in the game of water polo. One of my former students was a water polo coach at the collegiate level and explained to me quite frankly how to cheat. When a member of the other team is about to get the ball or move toward the goal, simply put your hand inside their bathing suit, and they cannot proceed. This common form of foul play happens entirely under water, where the referees often fail to see it. The incentives to foul are strong and the controls are weak.

Water polo play got quite a bit cleaner some years ago. This did not happen because of more punishment or because players underwent moral regeneration; rather, now chemicals made the pool water less murky, so rule violations were easier to detect. As pools got clearer, water polo play got cleaner.

8.4.4   Barhopping and Bar Problems

On any given weekend night, more than 6,000 people from the surrounding towns and suburbs would go into Geelong, Australia, to socialize and drink alcohol. Some groups, drunk on the streets, would commit thefts or get into fights with one another. A typical pattern was this:

1. Go to a packaged liquor outlet to purchase beer.
2. Drink beer in the car for an initial effect.
3. Go to the nearest bar for special prices.
4. Move to the next bar for its specials.
5. Go back to the car and drink more.

At this point, some people would use empty bottles as missiles to throw at people or property. The bars not only involved males in these efforts but also gave free drinks to young females to attract males. As the situation got worse, there were attacks on pub personnel. Bars worried about the money they lost by offering so many specials.

The police decided to do something and got the bar owners or managers together with the liquor board. They formulated "The Accord," a set of policies to discourage barhopping and other alcohol-related problems. It had more than a dozen provisions, but the most important were these:

- Cover charges to enter bars after 11 P.M.
- Denial of free reentry after someone exits.
- No free drinks or promotions.
- A narrower drink price range.
- Enforcement against open containers on the street.

The Accord was a success in removing most of the street drinking and pubhopping, while reducing the violence and other crime problems in the central city. I evaluated The Accord with three Australian colleagues (Felson et al. 1997). We were very impressed by what it accomplished.

Other important insights are provided by Ross Homel and colleagues (1997) in their study on drunkenness and violence around nightclubs in Surfer's Paradise, an Australian tourist resort. Tourists generate a lot of crime victimization and offending alike (Pizam and Mansfield 1996; Stangeland 1995). The problems and policies that Homel's group discussed, however, can apply to any entertainment district. Among the alcohol policy features considered were

- Reduction of binge drinking incentives, such as happy hours.
- Low- and nonalcoholic drinks and lower prices for them.
- Staff policies to avoid admitting intoxicated persons.
- Food and snacks available more of the time.
- Varied clientele, not just hard drinkers.

- Smaller glasses or drinks not as strong.
- Strategies for dealing with problem customers.
- Security training.

The result was a substantial reduction in drunkenness and violence around the nightclubs.

Perhaps it is not surprising that a surgeon would be most aware of the ugly injuries from bar glasses. Jonathan Shepherd and his colleagues (1994) have written about the injuries reported by bar staff, classified by different types of glass.

A straight-sided 1-pint glass produced fifty-two of seventy-eight incidents. Only one of these injuries came from a splintered plastic glass. Tankards led to fewer injuries than straight-sided glasses. Half-pint glasses led to fewer injuries, but those drinking half a pint probably were not getting as drunk. Shepherd and colleagues (1993) also carried out an interesting experiment. By collecting samples of different glass types and smashing items, they learned how nasty a weapon each produced. They found clearly that tankards are more difficult to smash and that tempered beer glasses break into a pile of relatively harmless chunks.

Making sure that bars use safer glasses is an example of what Clarke (1997b) called "controlling crime facilitators." By paying close attention to what tools or weapon facilitate crime, we acquire more tools for preventing crime.

The general potential for regulating drinking environments to reduce crime has been discussed in an essay by Tim Stockwell (1997). In addition, Stuart Macintyre and Ross Homel (1997) offered a remarkable study titled "Danger on the Dance Floor." In examining behavior and accidents within discos and other nightclubs, they observed brushing, bumping, knocking, spilling drinks, pushing, shoving, hitting, and fighting. They found that density of activities within nightclubs and the indoor design—including the location of tables and stools, pillars, walls, and bars, as well as the presence of disc jockeys—was very important. This is a good example of how situational prevention and crime prevention through environmental design interact.

8.5 Preventing Drunk Driving

Liquor policies influence not only intentional violence but also drunk driving and any accidental damage to property or people. H. Laurence Ross offered a brilliant analysis (1992) of how liquor policies and abuse are linked to drunk driving and subsequent deaths in his book *Confronting Drunk Driving*. Ross offers many surprising facts:

Most drunk drivers involved in accidents or fatalities have never been arrested before for drunk driving. That means that "getting tough" on drunk drivers has its limits for preventing deaths.

Upping the punishment levels has not accomplished anything in the past and probably will not accomplish anything in the future.

Modern American society is organized so that it is natural to drive to the bar and back, and hence to drive with a blood alcohol level over the legal limit.

We can prevent drunk driving deaths and injuries only with more focused policies. These include making roads and cars safer to prevent accidents or reduce the injury from them, or to use the regulatory system to get bars to stop serving people who are already drunk.

Australian and Scandinavian efforts to reduce drunk driving have been quite successful in many cases. These include random breath tests on highways (Homel 1993). In New South Wales, they have learned to give dramatic publicity to their breath testing, not only with media coverage but also by placing at the side of the road a large testing vehicle with a big sign reading "Booze Bus." Even the license plates have these words, helping to get people talking and reminding one another not to mix drinking and driving. The public responds quite well to these efforts and tends to reduce its drunk driving, without many arrests and with no draconian punishment.

American efforts to raise drinking ages and make them consistent among states also have produced a major decline in drunk driving and related injuries and deaths. American society has long had in place rules or laws against drinking in the streets and serving alcohol to those already drunk, and limiting the size and conditions of bars. Of course, they are not always enforced.

8.6 Preventing Fraud

We are increasingly recognizing that situational prevention can help reduce fraud. Here are some important illustrations:

Bad checks. Knutsson and Kuhlhorn (1997) found that easy check cashing makes for easy check fraud. When rules were tightened, that crime declined significantly (just as Tremblay 1986 found in Canada). When banks refused to guarantee bad checks, the merchants stood to lose money and started to be careful before they would hand out cash.

Misleading information. Kuhlhorn (1997) studied how people cheat the government by filling in conflicting information on different forms. Computer comparisons were made to reveal fraud, and the public was told about this development. As a result, people cheated much less often.

Illicit refunds. Many people defraud retail stores by stealing goods, convincing the store they were bought there, then getting a cash refund. Challinger (1997) showed that new rules for refunds made this type of fraud more difficult to accomplish.

Employee falsification. Most organizations that reimburse employees require original receipts to discourage fraudulent medical claims or expense reimbursements.

Embezzling employees. Well-designed auditing and accounting systems make it harder for one person to steal money from an organization. For example, when more than one person signs each large check and when independent auditors go over the books, less fraud occurs. Some people still conspire to commit fraud, but the whole idea of designing out fraud is to require conspirators for a crime to be committed and hope one of them will lose his or her nerve.

Construction corruption. Racketeering in the New York City construction industry combines fraud with extortion, bribery, theft, sabotage, and bid rigging. The Organized Crime Task Force (OCTF), directed by Ron Goldstock, involved James Jacobs of New York University and several others to analyze organized crime's involvement in construction. Their recommendations were to change the structure and industry characteristics generating the motivation, ability, and opportunity to act corruptly. They invented the ugly term "racketeering susceptibility," but more important, they realized that the very structure of the industry was creating racketeering opportunities. By altering that structure, organized crime could be made less likely to succeed (Organized Crime Task Force 1988).

Even though the term "situational prevention" might not be used, business and government organizations are well aware that fraud and embezzlement are widespread and that it is possible to design management and procedures to prevent them.

8.7 Preventing Repeat Victimization

Queen Elizabeth bestowed the Order of the British Empire (O.B.E.) on criminologist Ken Pease for his contributions to crime prevention. Pease (1992) (see also Farrell 1995) had demonstrated that a very large share of crime victimizations were "repeats." People victimized once are especially likely to be victimized again.

Pease figured out how to focus prevention on those already victimized. When someone's home was burglarized a first time, a prevention team would zero in on that particular unit to prevent a repetition. The team enlisted the residents of the five or six homes nearest the burglarized unit to keep an eye on it, a "cocoon" neighborhood watch. The unit also helped improve locks and doors and otherwise reduce the risk of burglary. The unit's success was far greater than for the usual methods, such as the unfocused and ineffective neighborhood watch. Pease's focus on reducing repeat victimization is increasingly applied to other offenses (Anderson and Pease 1997; Farrell 1995). Its advantages include

- Efficiently reducing crime at low cost
- Avoiding the usual political controversies
- Assisting the worst victims
- Helping everyone think more clearly about crime

Students of crime should take note of major American efforts by the National Institute of Justice to prevent repeat victimization on this side of the Atlantic.

By this time this book is out, results of these studies might be available.

8.8 Preventing the Sale of Stolen Goods

Markets for stolen goods are extremely important. Mike Sutton (1998) elaborated the "market reduction" approach to prevent theft and burglary. Detectives have long known to watch pawnshops, jewelry stores, auto body shops, even flea markets. Crime prevention specialists are beginning to devise more elaborate efforts at market reduction. A careful department of motor vehicles can interfere with registration of stolen cars or with converting registrations of crashed cars to stolen cars of the same model.

The Internet offers a fast way to circulate pictures of stolen jewelry to merchants. Repair contracts for electronics goods could readily be used to trace their ownership and thus help defeat theft. Computers can handle a lot of this effort, but the reality is lagging behind the potential.

8.9 Conclusions

Situational prevention offers a broad repertoire for preventing crime here and now, rather than there and eventually. It is verifiable, clear, simple, and cheap. It is available to people of all income groups, seldom treading on civil liberties (Felson and Clarke 1997b).[2] Situational prevention bypasses

---

[2] Some people make moral and political attacks on situational prevention, but any techniques raising ethical controversies are greatly outnumbered by the ones that are innocuous but effective.

the hardliners and softheads. Its idealism is not utopian, because it has found practical ways to do the right thing. Most often, it applies to a narrow slice of crime, but sometimes it can be mass-produced effectively. Figure 8.2 shows how the process of control proceeds in six steps. First, we try to build human character. Then we design secure environments. Next, we use other means to remove crime situations, as this chapter considered. Then we make arrests and process suspects, try and convict offenders, and punish and rehabilitate. I have made it quite clear that our most realistic chance for reducing crime occurs during steps 2 and 3: designing secure environments and removing crime situations. In other words, situational prevention (broadly speaking) offers us our best chance to minimize crime, without interfering substantially or negatively with people's lives. As the repertoire of prevention methods continues to grow, we have a means for slicing away at crime.

8.9.1   Main Points

Situational crime prevention is highly focused on preventing crime here and now. It is practical, not utopian. It reduces the inducements to commit crime by making crime targets less rewarding while increasing the risks, efforts, and guilt associated with crime.

Situational prevention generally does not displace crime elsewhere. Indeed, crime prevention often leads to a "diffusion of benefits," reducing crime even beyond the immediate setting.

8.9.2   Projects and Challenges

Interview projects. (1) Talk to a security person in the retail field. Ask specific questions about each type of situational prevention. What does he or she prefer, use, or ignore? (2) During off-duty or slack hours, interview a bartender or barmaid about specific methods used to prevent conflict from developing and escalating. Ask about shutting off those drinking too much, how to refuse those who are underage, and how to calm people down. What does he or she do when someone spills a drink?

Media projects. (1) Check out the magazines in the security field. What products are advertised there, and what situational prevention methods are left out? (2) Find out whether any car manufacturer has made major efforts to reduce a certain model's vulnerability to theft. Then use the Highway Loss Data Institute pamphlets to see whether its theft rates really declined relative to other models.

Map project. Map out a shopping mall or mini-mall. Where are its weak spots and strong spots from a situational crime prevention viewpoint?

Photo project. Devise a low-cost situational crime prevention method to make a college dormitory more secure from crime. Cover as many types of situational prevention as you can, using photos to strengthen your argument.

Web project. Find the Web sites of several security companies. What do they sell? What is hard to find or neglected? Are they overselling their capabilities, in light of what you know about crime prevention? Is there a cheaper or simpler way to reduce the crime in question?

References

Anderson, D., and K. Pease. 1997. Biting back: Preventing repeat burglary and car crime in Huddersfield. In *Situational Crime Prevention: Successful Case Studies,* 2nd ed., ed. R. V. Clarke, 200-208. New York: Harrow and Heston.

Beck, A., and A. Willis. 1995. *Crime and Security: Managing the Risk to Safe Shopping.* Leicester, U.K.: Perpetuity Press.

Beck, A., and A. Willis. 1999. Context-specific measures of CCTV effectiveness in the retail sector. In *Surveillance of Public Space: CCTV, Street Lighting and Crime Prevention,* ed. K. Painter and N. Tilley, 251-269. Washington, DC: American Psychological Association.

Bell, J., and B. Burke. 1992. Cruising Cooper Street. In *Situational Crime Prevention: Successful Case Studies,* 2nd ed., ed. R. V. Clarke, 108-112. New York: Harrow and Heston.

Bichler, G., and R. V. Clarke. 1996. Eliminating pay phone toll fraud at the Port Authority Bus Terminal in Manhattan. In *Crime Prevention Studies: Preventing Mass Transit Crime,* vol. 6, ed. R. V. Clarke, 93-115. Monsey, NY: Criminal Justice Press.

Bjor, J., J. Knutsson, and E. Kuhlhorn. 1992. The celebration of Midsummer Eve in Sweden: A study in the art of preventing collective disorder. *Security Journal* 3(3), 169-174.

Brown, R. 1995. *The Nature and Extent of Heavy Goods Vehicle Theft.* Paper No. 66, Crime Detection and Prevention Series. London: British Home Office Research Publications.

Brown, R., and N. Billing. 1996. *Tackling Car Crime: An Evaluation of Sold Secure.* Paper No. 71, Crime Detection and Prevention Series. London: British Home Office Research Publications.

Challinger, D. 1997. Refund fraud in retail stores. In *Situational Crime Prevention: Successful Case Studies,* 2nd ed., ed. R. V. Clarke, 250-262. New York: Harrow and Heston.

Clarke, R. V. 1983. Situational crime prevention: Its theoretical basis and practical scope. In *Crime and Justice: An Annual Review of Research,* vol. 4, ed. M. Tonry and N. Morris, SS5-256. Chicago: University of Chicago Press.

Clarke, R. V. 1996. Introduction for "Crime Prevention in the Retail Environment" [Special issue]. *Security Journal* 7(1).

Clarke, R. V. 1997a. Deterring obscene phone callers. In *Situational Crime Prevention: Successful Case Studies*, 2nd ed., ed. R. V. Clarke, 90-97. New York: Harrow and Heston.

Clarke, R. V. 1997b. Introduction. In *Situational Crime Prevention: Successful Case Studies*, 2nd ed., ed. R. V. Clarke, 1-43. New York: Harrow and Heston.

Clarke, R. V., ed. 1997c. *Situational Crime Prevention: Successful Case Studies*, 2nd ed. New York: Harrow and Heston.

Clarke, R. V. 1999. *Hot Products: Understanding, Anticipating and Reducing Demand for Stolen Goods*. Paper No. 112, Police Research Series. London: British Home Office Research Publications.

Clarke, R. V., and P. M. Harris. 1992. Auto theft and its prevention. In *Crime and Justice: A Review of Research*, vol. 16, ed. M. Tonry, 1-54. Chicago: University of Chicago Press.

Clarke, R. V., R. Kemper, and L. Wyckoff. 2001. Controlling cell phone fraud in the U.S.: Lessons for the U.K. *Security Journal* 14(1), 7-22.

Conklin, J. 1994. *Art Crime*. Westport, CT: Praeger.

DiLonardo, R. L. 1997. The economic benefit of electronic article surveillance. In *Situational Crime Prevention: Successful Case Studies*, 2nd ed., ed. R. V. Clarke, 122-131. New York: Harrow and Heston.

Eck, J., and D. Weisburd. 1995. *Crime and Place*. Monsey, NY: Criminal Justice Press.

Farrell, G. 1995. Preventing repeat victimization. In *Crime and Justice: A Review of Research*, vol. 19, ed. M. Tonry and D. Farrington, 469-534. Chicago: University of Chicago Press.

Felson, M. 1997. Technology, business and crime. In *Business and Crime Prevention*, ed. M. Felson and R. V. Clarke, 81-96. Monsey, NY: Willow Tree Press.

Felson, M., R. Berends, B. Richardson, and A. Veno. 1997. Reducing pub hopping and related crime. In *Crime Prevention Studies: Reducing Crime, Public Intoxication and Injury*, vol. 7, ed. R. Homel, 115-132. Monsey, NY: Criminal Justice Press.

Felson, M., and R. V. Clarke. 1997a. *Business and Crime Prevention*. Monsey, NY: Willow Tree Press.

Felson, M., and R. V. Clarke. 1997b. The ethics of situational crime prevention. In *Rational Choice and Situational Crime Prevention: Theoretical Foundations*, ed. G. Newman, R. V. Clarke, and S. G. Shoham, 197-218. Dartmouth, U.K.: Ashgate.

Felson, M., and R. Peiser, ed. 1998. *Reducing Crime Through Real Estate Development and Management*. Washington, DC: Urban Land Institute.

Felson, R. B. In press. Blame analysis: Accounting for the behavior of protected groups. In *What's Wrong with Sociology*, ed. S. Cole. New Brunswick, NJ: Transaction Publications.

Gill, M., ed. 1994. *Crime at Work: Studies in Security and Crime Prevention*. Leicester, U.K.: Perpetuity Press.

Hayes, R. 1997a. Retail crime control: A new operational strategy. *Security Journal* 8(3), 225-232.

Hayes, R. 1997b. Retail theft: An analysis of apprehended shoplifters. *Security Journal* 8(3), 233-246.

Ho, T. N. 1998. Prevention of art theft at commercial art galleries. *Studies on Crime and Crime Prevention* 7(2), 213-219.

Homel, R. 1993. Drivers who drink and rational choice: Random breath testing and the process of deterrence. In *Routine Activity and Rational Choice: Advances in Criminological Theory*, vol. 5, ed. R. V. Clarke and M. Felson, 59-84. New Brunswick, NJ: Transaction Books.

Homel, R., M. Hauritz, G. McIlwain, R. Wortley, and R. Carvolth. 1997. Preventing drunkenness and violence around nightclubs in a tourist resort. In *Situational Crime Prevention: Successful Case Studies*, 2nd ed., ed. R. V. Clarke, 263-282. New York: Harrow and Heston.

Knutsson, J., and E. Kuhlhorn. 1997. Macro measures against crime: The example of check forgeries. In *Situational Crime Prevention: Successful Case Studies*, 2nd ed., ed. R. V. Clarke, 113-121. New York: Harrow and Heston.

Kuhlhorn, E. 1997. Housing allowances in a welfare society: Reducing the temptation to cheat. In *Situational Crime Prevention: Successful Case Studies*, 2nd ed., ed. R. V. Clarke, 253-241. New York: Harrow and Heston.

Macintyre, S., and R. Homel. 1997. Danger on the dance floor: A study of interior design, crowding and aggression in nightclubs. In *Crime Prevention Studies: Policing for Prevention: Reducing Crime, Public Intoxication and Injury*, vol. 7, ed. R. Homel, 91-113. Monsey, NY: Criminal Justice Press.

Masuda, B. 1993. Credit card fraud prevention: A successful retail strategy. In *Crime Prevention Studies*, vol. 1, ed. R. V. Clarke, 121-134. Monsey, NY: Criminal Justice Press.

Masuda, B. 1997. Reduction of employee theft in a retail environment: Displacement vs. diffusion of benefits. In *Situational Crime Prevention: Successful Case Studies*, 2nd ed., ed. R. V. Clarke, 183-190. New York: Harrow and Heston.

Mayhew, P., R. V. Clarke, and D. Eliot. 1989. Motorcycle theft, helmet legislation and displacement. *Howard Journal of Criminal Justice* 28(1), 1-8.

Natarajan, M., R. V. Clarke, and B. D. Johnson. 1995. Telephones as facilitators of drug dealing: A research agenda. *European Journal of Crime Policy and Research* 3(3), 137-154.

Painter, K., and D. P. Farrington. 1997. The crime reducing effect of improved street lighting: The Dudley Project. In *Situational Crime Prevention: Successful Case Studies*, 2nd ed., ed. R. V. Clarke, 206-226. New York: Harrow and Heston.

Painter, K., and N. Tilley. 1999. Editor's introduction: Seeing and being seen to prevent crime. In *Surveillance and Public Space: CCTV, Street Lighting and Crime Prevention*, ed. K. Painter and N. Tilley, 1-12. Monsey, NY: Criminal Justice Press.

Pease, K. 1992. Preventing burglary on a British public housing estate. In *Situational crime prevention: Successful case studies*, 2nd ed., ed. R. V. Clarke, 223-229. New York: Harrow and Heston.

Pease, K. 1999. A review of street lighting evaluation: Crime reduction efforts. In *Surveillance of Public Space: CCTV, Street Lighting and Crime Prevention*, ed. K. Painter and N. Tilley, 47-76. Monsey, NY: Criminal Justice Press.

Pizam, A., and Y. Mansfield, ed. 1996. *Tourism, Crime, and International Security Issues.* Chichester, U.K.: Wiley.

Ross, H. L. 1992. *Confronting Drunk Driving: Social Policy for Saving Lives.* New Haven, CT: Yale University Press.

Shepherd, J. P., M. R. Brickley, D. Gallagher, and R. V. Walker. 1994. Risk of occupational glass injury in bar staff. *Injury* 25, 219-220.

Shepherd, J. P., R. H. Hugget, and G. Kidner. 1993. Impact resistance of bar glasses. *Journal of Trauma* 35, 936-938.

Sloan-Howitt, M., and G. D. Kelling. 1997. Subway graffiti in New York City: "Gettin' up" vs. "meanin' it and cleanin' it." In *Situational Crime Prevention: Successful Case Studies,* 2nd ed., ed. R. V. Clarke, 242-249. New York: Harrow and Heston.

Stockwell, T. 1997. Regulation of the licensed drinking environment: A major opportunity for crime prevention. In *Crime Prevention Studies: Policing for Prevention: Reducing Crime, Public Intoxication and Injury,* vol. 7, ed. R. Homel, 7-33. Monsey, NY: Criminal Justice Press.

Strangeland, P. 1995. *The Crime Puzzle: Crime Patterns and Crime Displacement in Southern Spain.* Malaga, Spain: Andalusian Inter-University Institute of Criminology.

Southall, D., and P. Ekblom. 1985. *Designing for Car Security: Towards A Crime-Free Car.* Crime Prevention Unit Paper No. 204. London: British Home Office Research Publications.

Sullivan, R. R. 2000. *Liberalism and Crime: The British Experience.* Lanham, MD: Lexington.

Sutton, M. 1998. *Handling Stolen Goods and Theft: A Market Reduction Approach.* Home Office Research Study No. 178. London: British Home Office Research Publications.

Tedeschi, J., and R. B. Felson. 1994. *Violence, Aggression and Coercive Action.* Washington, DC: American Psychological Association.

Tremblay, P. 1986. Designing crime. *British Journal of Criminology* 26, 234-253.

von Hirsch, A., D. Garland, and A. Wakefield, ed. 2000. *Ethical and Social Issues in Situational Crime Prevention.* Oxford, U.K.: Hart.

Wikstrom, P. O. 1995. Preventing city-center street crimes. In *Crime and Justice: A Review of Research,* vol. 19, ed. M. Tonry and D. Farrington. Chicago: University of Chicago Press.

Early Developmental Crime Prevention[1]

9

DAVID P. FARRINGTON AND
BRANDON C. WELSH

Contents

[1] An earlier version of this chapter was presented at a conference on "Effective Methods in the Prevention of Juvenile Violence: Family and Community Interventions," at the Universidad Internacional Menéndez Pelayo in Valencia, Spain (September 2004).

9.1 Introduction

The main aim of this chapter is to summarize briefly some of the most effective programs for preventing delinquency and youth violence, whose effectiveness has been demonstrated in high-quality evaluation research. The focus is especially on programs evaluated in randomized experiments with reasonably large samples, because the effect of any intervention on delinquency or youth violence can be demonstrated most convincingly in such experiments (Farrington 1983; Farrington and Welsh 2006). The major methods of reducing crime can be classified as developmental, community, situational, and criminal justice prevention (Tonry and Farrington 1995).

Criminal justice prevention refers to traditional deterrent, incapacitative, and rehabilitative strategies operated by law enforcement and criminal justice system agencies. Community prevention refers to interventions designed to change the social conditions and institutions (e.g., families, peers, social norms, clubs, and organizations) that influence offending in residential communities (Hope 1995). These interventions target community risk factors and social conditions such as cohesiveness or disorganization. Situational prevention refers to interventions designed to prevent the occurrence of crimes by reducing opportunities and increasing the risk and difficulty of offending (Clarke 1995). Developmental prevention refers to interventions designed to prevent the development of criminal potential in individuals, especially those targeting risk and protective factors discovered in studies of human development (Tremblay and Craig 1995). The focus of this chapter is on developmental or risk-focused prevention.

Within the constraints of this chapter, it is not feasible to present an exhaustive or systematic review of interventions to prevent youth offending (Welsh and Farrington 2005). Systematic reviews are much more rigorous than more traditional narrative reviews of the literature. Whereas traditional reviews rarely include detailed information about why studies were included or excluded, systematic reviews provide explicit and transparent information about the criteria used for including or excluding studies. Systematic reviews focus on studies that have the highest methodological quality and use the most rigorous methods possible to combine results from different studies statistically to draw conclusions about what works. These reviews contain methods and results sections and are reported with the same level of detail that characterizes high-quality reports of original research. They include detailed summary tables of key features of studies such as design, sample sizes, and effect sizes. As mentioned, our aim is not to present a systematic review but rather to summarize some of the most effective programs.

9.2   Risk-Focused Prevention

The basic idea of developmental or risk-focused prevention is very simple: Identify the key risk factors for offending and implement prevention techniques designed to counteract them. There is often a related attempt to identify key protective factors against offending and to implement prevention techniques designed to enhance them. Longitudinal surveys are used to advance knowledge about risk and protective factors, and experimental and quasiexperimental methods are used to evaluate the impact of prevention and intervention programs.

Risk-focused prevention was imported into criminology from medicine and public health by pioneers such as Hawkins and Catalano (1992). This approach has been used successfully for many years to tackle illnesses such as cancer and heart disease. For example, the identified risk factors for heart disease include smoking, a fatty diet, and lack of exercise. These can be tackled by encouraging people to stop smoking, to have a healthier low-fat diet, and to take more exercise.

Risk-focused prevention links explanation and prevention; links fundamental and applied research; and links scholars, policymakers, and practitioners. The book *Serious and Violent Juvenile Offenders: Risk Factors and Successful Interventions* (Loeber and Farrington 1998) contains a detailed exposition of this approach as applied to serious and violent juvenile offenders. Importantly, risk-focused prevention is easy to understand and to communicate, and it is readily accepted by policymakers, practitioners, and the general public. Both risk factors and interventions are based on empirical research rather than on theories. This approach avoids difficult theoretical questions about which risk factors have causal effects.

By definition, a risk factor predicts an increased probability of later offending (Kazdin et al. 1997). For example, children who experience poor parental supervision have an increased risk of committing criminal acts later on. In the Cambridge Study in Delinquent Development, which is a prospective longitudinal survey of 400 London males beginning at age eight, 55 percent of those experiencing poor parental supervision at age eight were convicted up to age thirty-two, compared with 32 percent of the remainder, a significant difference (Farrington 1990). Because risk factors are defined by their ability to predict later offending, it follows that longitudinal studies are needed to establish them.

The most important risk factors for delinquency and youth violence are well known (Farrington 1998, 2001). They include individual factors such as high impulsiveness and low intelligence; family factors such as poor parental supervision and harsh or erratic parental discipline; peer factors such as hanging around with delinquent friends; school factors such as attending a high delinquency-rate school; socioeconomic factors such as low income and poor housing; and neighborhood or community factors such as living in a high-crime neighborhood. The focus here is on risk factors that can be changed by interventions. There is also a focus on protective factors that predict a low probability of offending, but less is known about them.

Risk factors tend to be similar for many different outcomes, including delinquency, violence, drug use, school failure, and unemployment. This is good news, because a program that is successful in reducing one of these outcomes is likely to be successful in reducing the others as well.

9.3 Cost-Benefit Analysis

This chapter describes some of the most important and best-evaluated programs, with special reference to programs that have carried out a cost-benefit analysis. The conclusion from the Perry Preschool project (discussed later), that for every dollar spent on the program, seven dollars were saved in the long term (Schweinhart, Barnes, and Weikart 1993), proved particularly convincing to policymakers. The monetary costs of crime are enormous. For example, Brand and Price (2000) estimated that they totaled £60 (approximately $120 billion) in England and Wales in 1999. There are tangible costs to victims, such as replacing stolen goods and repairing damage, and intangible costs that are harder to quantify, such as pain, suffering, and a reduced quality of life. There are costs to the government or taxpayer for police, courts, prisons, crime prevention activities, and so on. There are also costs to offenders, for example, those associated with being in prison or losing a job.

To the extent that crime prevention programs are successful in reducing crime, they will have benefits. These benefits can be quantified in monetary terms according to the reduction in the monetary costs of crime. Other benefits may accrue from reducing the costs of associated social problems such as unemployment, divorce, educational failure, drug addiction, welfare dependency, and so on. The fact that offending is part of a larger syndrome of antisocial behavior (West and Farrington 1977) is good news, because the benefits of a crime prevention program can be many and varied. The monetary benefits of a program can be compared with its monetary costs to determine the benefit-to-cost ratio. Surprisingly few cost-benefit analyses of crime prevention programs have ever been carried out (Welsh, Farrington, and Sherman 2001).

Cohen (1998) estimated that the monetary cost to American society of a high-risk youth was about $2 million. This took account of juvenile and adult crimes, drug use, and school failure. This high cost means that programs do not have to be very successful to have benefits outweighing their costs. For example, even if a program costs a thousand dollars per child and saved only one out of every thousand high-risk children, $1 million spent on treating a thousand children would save $2 million.

9.4 Family-Based Prevention

If poor parental supervision and inconsistent discipline are causes of delinquency, it is plausible that family-based prevention should succeed in reducing offending. The behavioral parent management training developed by Patterson (1982) is one of the most influential approaches. His careful observations of parent-child interaction showed that parents of antisocial children were deficient in their methods of child-rearing. These parents failed to tell their children how they were expected to behave, failed to state house rules consistently or monitor their behavior to ensure that it was desirable, and failed to enforce rules promptly and unambiguously with appropriate rewards and penalties. The parents of antisocial children used more punishment (such as scolding, shouting, or threatening), but failed to use it consistently or make it contingent on the child's behavior.

Patterson's technique involved linking antecedents, behaviors, and consequences. He attempted to train parents in effective child-rearing methods, namely noticing what a child is doing, monitoring the child's behavior over long periods, clearly stating house rules, making rewards and punishments consistent and contingent on the child's behavior, and negotiating disagreements so that conflicts and crises did not escalate.

His treatment was shown to be effective in reducing child stealing and antisocial behavior over short periods in small-scale studies (Dishion, Patterson, and Kavanagh 1992; Patterson, Reid, and Dishion 1992). However, the treatment worked best with children aged three to ten and less well with adolescents. Also, there were problems of achieving cooperation from the families experiencing the worst problems. In particular, single mothers on welfare were experiencing so many different stresses that they found it difficult to use consistent and contingent child-rearing methods.

We now review the most important types of family-based programs that have been evaluated. These are home visiting programs, day care programs, parent management training programs, home or community programs with older children, and multisystemic therapy (MST).

9.4.1 Home Visiting Programs

In the most famous intensive home visiting program, Olds and his colleagues (1986) in Elmira, New York, randomly allocated 400 mothers to receive home visits from nurses during pregnancy, to receive visits both during pregnancy and the first two years of life, or to a control group who received no visits. Each visit lasted about one and one-quarter hours, and the mothers were visited on average every two weeks. The home visitors gave advice about prenatal and postnatal care of the child, about infant development, and about the importance of proper nutrition and avoiding smoking and drinking during pregnancy. Hence, this was a general parent education program.

The results of this experiment showed that the postnatal home visits caused a decrease in recorded child physical abuse and neglect during the first two years of life, especially by poor unmarried teenage mothers; 4 percent of visited versus 19 percent of nonvisited mothers of this type were guilty of child abuse or neglect. This last result is important because children who are physically abused or neglected tend to become violent offenders later in life (Widom 1989). In a fifteen-year follow-up, the main focus was on lower class unmarried mothers. Among these mothers, those who received prenatal and postnatal home visits had fewer arrests than those who received just prenatal visits or no visits (Olds et al. 1997). Also, children of these mothers who received prenatal and/or postnatal home visits had less than half as many arrests as children of mothers who received no visits (Olds et al. 1998).

Several economic analyses show that the benefits of this program outweighed its costs for the lower class unmarried mothers. The most important are by Karoly and colleagues (1998) and Aos and his colleagues (2001). However, both measured only a limited range of benefits. Karoly measured only benefits to the government or taxpayer (in welfare, education, employment, and criminal justice), not benefits to crime victims consequent upon reduced crimes. Aos measured only benefits to crime victims (tangible and intangible) and in criminal justice savings, excluding other types of benefits (e.g., in welfare, education, and employment). Nevertheless, both reported a benefit-to-cost ratio greater than 1 for this program: 4.1 according to Karoly and 3.1 according to Aos. The benefit-to-cost ratio was less than 1 for the low-risk part of the sample. This study and other similar evaluations (Kitzman et al. 1997; Larson 1980; Stone et al. 1988) showed that intensive home visiting can help poor unmarried mothers and reduce later antisocial behavior of their children.

9.4.2 Day Care Programs

One of the very few prevention experiments beginning in pregnancy and collecting outcome data on delinquency was the Syracuse (New York) Family Development Research Program of Lally and his colleagues (1988). The researchers began with a sample of pregnant women (mostly poor African American single mothers) and gave them weekly help with child-rearing, health, nutrition, and other problems. In addition, their children received free full-time day care, designed to develop their intellectual abilities, up to age five. This was not a randomized experiment, but a matched control group was chosen when the children were aged three.

Ten years later, about 120 treated and control children were followed up to age fifteen. Significantly fewer of the treated children (2 percent as opposed to 17 percent) had been referred to the juvenile court for delinquency offenses, and the treated girls showed better school attendance and school performance. However, the benefit-to-cost ratio of this program was only 0.3, according to Aos et al. (1999). Therefore, the monetary benefits were much less than the costs. This was largely because of the cost of the program ($45,000 per child in 1998 dollars, compared with $14,000 for Perry—discussed later—and $7,000 for Elmira); providing free full-time day care up to age five was very expensive. Against this, it must be repeated that the Aos benefit-to-cost ratios are underestimates.

9.4.3 Parent Management Training

One of the most famous parent training programs was developed by Webster-Stratton (1998). She evaluated its success by randomly allocating 426 children aged four (most with single mothers on welfare) either to an experimental group that received parent training or to a control group that did not. The experimental mothers met in groups every week for eight or nine weeks, watched videotapes demonstrating parenting skills, and then took part in focused group discussions. The topics included how to play with your child, helping your child learn, using praise and encouragement to bring out the best in your child, effective setting of limits, handling misbehavior, how to teach your child to solve problems, and how to give and get support. Observations in the home showed that the experimental children behaved better than the control children.

Webster-Stratton and Hammond (1997) also evaluated the effectiveness of parent training and child skills training with about 100 Seattle children (average age five) referred to a clinic because of conduct problems. The children and their parents were randomly allocated either to receive (1) parent training, (2) child skills training, or (3) both parent and child training, or assigned to a control group. The skills training aimed to foster prosocial behavior and interpersonal skills using video modeling, whereas the parent training involved weekly meetings between parents and therapists for twenty-two to twenty-four weeks. Parent reports and home observations showed that children in all three experimental conditions had fewer behavior problems than control children, both in an immediate evaluation and in a one-year follow-up. There was little difference between the three experimental conditions, although the combined parent and child training condition produced the most significant improvements in child behavior at the one-year follow-up. There is a general finding that combined parent and child interventions are more effective than either one alone.

Scott and his colleagues (2001) evaluated the Webster-Stratton parent training program in London. About 140 children aged three to eight who were referred for antisocial behavior were allocated to receive parent training or to be in a control group. The program was successful. According to parent reports, the antisocial behavior of the experimental children decreased, while that of the control children did not change. Because this program is relatively cheap (only £571 ($1000) per child for a twelve-week program), it is likely to be cost-effective. Other studies also show that parent training is effective in reducing children's antisocial behavior (e.g., Kazdin, Siegel, and Bass 1992; Strayhorn and Weidman 1991).

Sanders and his colleagues (2000) in Brisbane, Australia, developed the Triple-P Parenting Program. This program can be either delivered to the whole community in primary prevention using the mass media or used in secondary prevention with high-risk or clinic samples. Sanders evaluated the success of Triple-P with high-risk children aged three by randomly allocating them either to receive Triple-P or to be in a control group. The Triple-P Program involves teaching parents seventeen child management strategies including talking with children, giving physical affection, praising, giving attention, setting a good example, setting rules, giving clear instructions, and using appropriate penalties for misbehavior ("time-out," or sending the child to his or her room). The evaluation showed that the Triple-P Program was successful in reducing children's antisocial behavior.

9.4.4   Other Parenting Interventions

Another parenting intervention, termed functional family therapy, was developed by James F. Alexander (Alexander and Parsons 1973; Alexander et al. 1976). This aimed to modify patterns of family interaction by modeling, prompting, and reinforcement; to encourage clear communication between family members of requests and solutions; and to minimize conflict. Essentially, all family members were trained to negotiate effectively, to set clear rules about privileges and responsibilities, and to use techniques of reciprocal reinforcement with each other. The program was evaluated by randomly allocating eighty-six delinquents to experimental or control conditions. The results showed that this technique halved the recidivism rate of minor delinquents in comparison with other approaches (client-centered or psychodynamic therapy). Its effectiveness with more serious offenders was confirmed in a replication study using matched groups (Barton et al. 1985).

Chamberlain and Reid (1998) evaluated treatment foster care (TFC), which was used as an alternative to custody for delinquents. Custodial sentences for delinquents were thought to have undesirable effects especially because of the bad influence of delinquent peers. In TFC, families in the community were recruited and trained to provide a placement for delinquent youths. The TFC youths were closely supervised at home, in the community, and in the school, and their contacts with delinquent peers were minimized. The foster parents provided a structured daily living environment, with clear rules and limits, consistent discipline for rule violations, and one-to-one monitoring. The youths were encouraged to develop academic skills and desirable work habits.

In the evaluation, seventy-nine chronic male delinquents were randomly assigned to treatment foster care or to regular group homes where they lived with other delinquents. A one-year follow-up showed that the TFC boys had fewer criminal referrals and lower self-reported delinquency. Hence, this program seemed to be an effective treatment for delinquency.

9.4.5 Multisystemic Therapy

Multisystemic therapy is an important multiple-component family preservation program that was developed by Henggeler and his colleagues (1993). The particular type of treatment is chosen according to the particular needs of the youth. Therefore, the nature of the treatment is different for each person. MST is delivered in the youth's home, school, and community settings. The treatment typically includes family intervention to promote the parent's ability to monitor and discipline the adolescent, peer intervention to encourage the choice of prosocial friends, and school intervention to enhance competence and school achievement.

In the evaluation by Henggeler and his colleagues (1993), eighty-four serious delinquents (with an average age of fifteen) were randomly assigned to receive either MST or the usual treatment (which mostly involved placing the juvenile outside home). The results showed that the MST group had fewer arrests and fewer self-reported crimes in a one-year follow-up.

In another evaluation, in Missouri, Borduin and his colleagues (1995) randomly assigned 176 juvenile offenders (with an average age of fourteen) either to MST or to individual therapy focusing on personal, family and academic issues. Four years later, only 29 percent of the MST offenders had been rearrested, compared with 74 percent of the individual therapy group. According to Aos and his colleagues (2001), the benefit-to-cost ratio for MST is very high (28.3), largely because of the potential crime and criminal justice savings from targeting chronic juvenile offenders.

Unfortunately, disappointing results were obtained in a large-scale independent evaluation of MST in Canada by Leschied and Cunningham (2002). Over 400 youths who were either offenders or at risk of offending were randomly assigned to receive either MST or the usual services (typically probation supervision). Six months after treatment, 28 percent of the MST group had been reconvicted, compared with 31 percent of the control group, a nonsignificant difference. Therefore, it is unclear how effective MST is when it is implemented independently.

9.4.6   Is Family-Based Intervention Effective?

Evaluations of the effectiveness of family-based intervention programs have produced both encouraging and discouraging results. In order to assess effectiveness according to a large number of evaluations, we reviewed forty evaluations of family-based programs, each involving at least fifty persons in experimental and control groups combined (Farrington and Welsh 2003). All of these had outcome measures of delinquency or antisocial child behavior. Of the nineteen studies with outcome measures of delinquency, ten found significantly beneficial effects of the intervention and nine found no significant effect. Happily, no study found a significantly harmful effect of family-based treatment.

Over all nineteen studies, the average effect size (d, the standardized mean difference) was .32. This was significantly greater than 0. When converted into the percentage reconvicted, a d value of .32 corresponds to a decrease in the percentage reconvicted from 50 percent to 34 percent. Therefore, we concluded that, taking all nineteen studies together, they showed that family-based intervention had substantial desirable effects.

9.5   School-Based Prevention

We now turn to school-based prevention programs, most of which also had a family-based component. First reviewed is the Perry Preschool program, which is perhaps the most influential early developmental prevention program, because it found that $7 were saved for every $1 expended. Next reviewed are the famous programs combining child skills training and parent training, implemented in Montreal by Tremblay and in Seattle by Hawkins, and the well-known anti-bullying programs by Olweus in Norway and Smith in England.

9.5.1   Preschool Programs

The most famous preschool intellectual enrichment program is the Perry project carried out in Ypsilanti, Michigan, by Schweinhart and Weikart (1980). This was essentially a Head Start program targeted on disadvantaged African American children. A small sample of 123 children was allocated (approximately at random) to experimental and control groups. The experimental children attended a daily preschool program, backed up by weekly home visits, usually lasting two years (covering ages three to four). The aim of the "plan-do-review" program was to provide intellectual stimulation, to increase thinking and reasoning abilities, and to increase later school achievement.

This program had long-term benefits. Berrueta-Clement and his colleagues (1984) showed that, at age nineteen, the experimental group was more likely to be employed, more likely to have graduated from high school, more likely to have received college or vocational training, and less likely to have been arrested. By age twenty-seven, the experimental group had accumulated only half as many arrests on average as the controls (Schweinhart, Barnes, and Weikart 1993). Also, they had significantly higher earnings and were more likely to be homeowners. More of the experimental women were married, and fewer of their children were born to unmarried mothers. By age forty, the most recent evaluation, experimental children had 35 percent fewer arrests and showed continued improvements in important life course outcomes (Schweinhart et al. 2005).

Several economic analyses show that the benefits of this program outweighed its costs. The benefit-to-cost ratio was 2.1, according to Karoly and colleagues (1998), and 1.5, according to Aos and colleagues (1999), but both of these figures are underestimates. The Perry project's own calculation (Barnett 1993) was more comprehensive, including crime and noncrime benefits, intangible costs to victims, and even projected benefits beyond age twenty-seven. This generated the famous benefit-to-cost ratio of 7.2. Most of the benefits (65 percent) were derived from savings to crime victims.

9.5.2 School Programs

The Montreal longitudinal-experimental study combined child skills training and parent training. Tremblay and his colleagues (1995) identified disruptive (aggressive or hyperactive) boys at age six, and randomly allocated over 300 of these to experimental or control conditions. Between ages seven and nine, the experimental group received training designed to foster social skills and self-control. Coaching, peer modeling, role playing, and reinforcement contingencies were used in small group sessions on such topics as how to help, what to do when you are angry, and how to react to teasing. Also, their parents were trained using the parent management training techniques developed by Patterson (1982).

This prevention program was successful. By age twelve, the experimental boys committed less burglary and theft, were less likely to get drunk, and were less likely to be involved in fights than the controls (according to self-reports). Also, the experimental boys had higher school achievement. At every age from ten to fifteen, the experimental boys had lower self-reported delinquency scores than the control boys. Interestingly, the differences in antisocial behavior between experimental and control boys increased as the follow-up progressed.

One of the most important school-based prevention experiments was carried out in Seattle by Hawkins and his colleagues (1991). They implemented a multiple-component program combining parent training, teacher training, and child skills training. About 500 first-grade children (aged six) in twenty-one classes in eight schools were randomly assigned to be in experimental or control classes. The children in the experimental classes received special treatment at home and school that was designed to increase their attachment to their parents and their bonding to the school. Also, they were trained in interpersonal cognitive problem-solving. Their parents were trained to notice and reinforce socially desirable behavior in a program called "Catch them being good." Their teachers were trained in classroom management, for example, to provide clear instructions and expectations to children, to reward children for participation in desired behavior, and to teach children prosocial (socially desirable) methods of solving problems.

This program had long-term benefits. By the sixth grade (age twelve), experimental boys were less likely to have initiated delinquency, while experimental girls were less likely to have initiated drug use (O'Donnell et al. 1995). In the latest follow-up, Hawkins and his colleagues (1999) found that, at age eighteen, the full intervention group (those who received the intervention from grades 1 to 6) admitted less violence, less alcohol abuse, and fewer sexual partners than the late intervention group (grades 5 to 6 only) or the control group. The benefit-to-cost ratio of this program, according to Aos and his colleagues (2001), was 4.3. Other school-based prevention experiments have also been successful in reducing antisocial behavior (Catalano et al. 1996).

9.5.3 Antibullying Programs

School bullying, of course, is a risk factor for offending (Farrington 1993). Several school-based programs have been effective in reducing bullying. The most famous of these was implemented by Olweus (1994) in Norway. The general principles of the program were to create an environment characterized by adult warmth, interest in children, and involvement with children; to use authoritative child-rearing (Steinberg et al. 1992), including warmth, firm guidance, and close supervision, because authoritarian child-rearing is related to child bullying (Baldry and Farrington 1998); to set firm limits on what is unacceptable bullying; to consistently apply nonphysical sanctions for rule violations; to improve monitoring and surveillance of child behavior, especially in the playground; and to decrease opportunities and rewards for bullying.

The Olweus program aimed to increase awareness and knowledge of teachers, parents, and children about bullying and to dispel myths about it. A thirty-page booklet was distributed to all schools in Norway describing what was known about bullying and recommending what steps schools and teachers could take to reduce it. Also, a twenty-five-minute video about bullying was made available to schools. Simultaneously, the schools distributed to all parents a four-page folder containing information and advice about bullying. In addition, anonymous self-report questionnaires about bullying were completed by all children.

Each school received feedback information from the questionnaire, about the prevalence of bullies and victims, in a specially arranged school conference day. Also, teachers were encouraged to develop explicit rules about bullying (e.g., do not bully, tell someone when bullying happens, bullying will not be tolerated, try to help victims, try to include children who are being left out) and to discuss bullying in class, using the video and role-playing exercises. Also, teachers were encouraged to improve monitoring and supervision of children, especially in the playground.

The effects of this antibullying program were evaluated in forty-two Bergen schools. Olweus measured the prevalence of bullying before and after the program using self-report questionnaires completed by the children. Because all schools received the program, there were no control schools. However, Olweus compared children of a certain age (e.g., thirteen) before the program with children of the same age after the program. Overall, the program was very successful because bullying decreased by half.

A similar program was implemented in twenty-three Sheffield schools by Smith and Sharp (1994). The core program involved establishing a "whole-school" antibullying policy, raising awareness of bullying, and clearly defining roles and responsibilities of teachers and students, so that everyone knew what bullying was and what they should do about it. In addition, there were optional interventions tailored to particular schools: curriculum work (e.g., reading books, watching videos), direct work with students (e.g., assertiveness training for those who were bullied), and playground work (e.g., training lunch-time supervisors). This program was successful in reducing bullying (by 15 percent) in primary schools, but had relatively small effects (a 5 percent reduction) in secondary schools. The effects of these antibullying programs on youth offending need to be investigated.

9.6 Multiple-Component Interventions

Many of the interventions described in this chapter have several different elements or components. It is generally true that the more risk factors that a young person has, the more likely he or she will become delinquent or violent. This encourages researchers to use multiple-component interventions that target multiple risk factors. Generally, multiple-component interventions are more effective than single-component ones (Wasserman and Miller 1998). However, the problem with multiple-component interventions is that, if they are effective, it is hard to know what the "active ingredients" were in order to decide which elements of the package were more or less effective. In turn, this makes it hard to learn from experience and to improve multiple-component interventions.

In the interests of maximizing effectiveness, what is needed is a multiple-component community-based program including several of the successful interventions listed above. Many of the programs reviewed in this chapter are of this type. However, Communities that Care (CTC) has many attractions (Farrington 1996). Perhaps more than any other program, it is evidence-based and systematic: The choice of interventions depends on empirical evidence about what are the important risk and protective factors in a particular community and on empirical evidence about "what works" (Sherman et al. 2006). It is currently being implemented in over twenty sites in England, Scotland, and Wales, and also in the Netherlands and Australia (Communities that Care 1997; Utting 1999; France and Crow 2001). Although the effectiveness of the overall CTC strategy has not yet been demonstrated, the effectiveness of its individual components is clear.

CTC was developed as a risk-focused prevention strategy by Hawkins and Catalano (1992) and is a core component of the U.S. Office of Juvenile Justice and Delinquency Prevention's (OJJDP's) Comprehensive Strategy for Serious, Violent and Chronic Juvenile Offenders (Wilson and Howell, 1993). CTC is based on a theory (the social development model) that organizes risk and protective factors. The intervention techniques are tailored to the needs of each particular community. The "community" could be a city, a county, a small town, or even a neighborhood or a housing estate. This program aims to reduce delinquency and drug use by implementing particular prevention strategies that have demonstrated effectiveness in reducing risk factors or enhancing protective factors. It is modeled on large-scale communitywide public health programs designed to reduce illnesses such as coronary heart disease by tackling key risk factors (e.g., Farquhar 1985; Perry, Klepp, and Sillers 1989). There is great emphasis in CTC on enhancing protective factors and building on strengths, partly because this is more attractive to communities than tackling risk factors. However, it is generally true that health promotion is more effective than disease prevention (Kaplan 2000).

CTC programs begin with community mobilization. Key community leaders (e.g., elected representatives, education officials, police chiefs, business leaders) are brought together, with the aim of getting them to agree on the goals of the prevention program and to implement CTC. The key leaders then set up a Community Board that is accountable to them, consisting of neighborhood residents and representatives from various agencies (e.g., school, police, social services, probation, health, parents, youth groups, business, church, media). The Community Board takes charge of prevention on behalf of the community.

The Community Board then carries out a risk and protective factor assessment, identifying key risk factors in that particular community that need to be tackled and key protective factors that need enhancing. This risk assessment might involve the use of police, school, social or census records, or local neighborhood or school surveys. After identifying key risk and protective factors, the Community Board assesses existing resources and develops a plan of intervention strategies. With specialist technical assistance and guidance, they choose programs from a menu of strategies that have been shown to be effective in well-designed evaluation research.

The menu of strategies listed by Hawkins and Catalano (1992) includes prenatal and postnatal home visiting programs, preschool intellectual enrichment programs, parent training, school organization and curriculum development, teacher training, and media campaigns. Other strategies include child skills training, antibullying programs in schools, situational prevention, and policing strategies. The choice of prevention strategies is based on empirical evidence about effective methods of tackling each particular risk factor, but it also depends on what are identified as the biggest problems in the community. Although this approach is not without its challenges and complexities (e.g., cost, implementation, establishing partnerships among diverse agencies), an evidence-based approach that brings together the most effective prevention programs across multiple domains offers the greatest promise for reducing crime and building safer communities.

9.7 Conclusions

High-quality evaluation research shows that many programs are effective in reducing delinquency and youth violence, and that in many cases the financial benefits of these programs outweigh their financial costs. The best programs include general parent education during home visiting, parent management training, preschool intellectual enrichment programs, child skills training, teacher training, antibullying programs, and multisystemic therapy.

High-quality experimental and quasiexperimental evaluations of the effectiveness of crime reduction programs are needed in all countries. Most knowledge about the effectiveness of prevention programs, such as cognitive-behavioral skills training, parent training, and preschool intellectual enrichment programs, is based on American research, but it is not clear how far American results can be replicated in other countries.

There have been many commendable British crime prevention initiatives in recent years. Following the review of research carried out as part of the

Comprehensive Spending Review in 1997 (Goldblatt and Lewis 1998), the Home Office Crime Reduction Program was established. The Crime and Disorder Act of 1988 required local authorities, police, and health, probation, and other agencies to form partnerships to produce a crime audit and to develop prevention strategies in each area. Unfortunately, most audits were based on available records (not on surveys of the population or of young people) and most interventions were situational (e.g., aiming to reduce burglary by improving physical security). However, the *On Track* program was launched at the end of 1999. This provided services for children aged four to twelve who were identified as at risk of being involved in crime in highly deprived communities.

The Youth Justice Board was established in 1998 and has been mainly concerned with providing services for offenders aged ten to seventeen, for example, through the Youth Offending Teams. However, it has established seventy Youth Inclusion Programs, each aimed at the fifty young people aged thirteen to sixteen who are most at risk in particularly deprived neighborhoods. The Department for Education and Skills established the *Sure Start* program for children up to age three in deprived neighborhoods, and *New Deal for Communities* and neighborhood renewal funds have been established by the Department for the Environment (Sutton, Utting, and Farrington 2004).

Although all of these initiatives are commendable, and all are being evaluated in some sense (at least by means of a process evaluation), what is largely missing in Great Britain at present is risk-focused primary prevention delivered at an early age and designed to reduce later offending and antisocial behavior. We think that consideration should be given to implementing a multiple-component risk-focused prevention program such as CTC more widely throughout Great Britain and in other countries. This integrated program could be implemented by existing Crime and Disorder Partnerships in Great Britain. However, they would need resources and technical assistance to conduct youth surveys and household surveys to identify key risk and protective factors for both people and places. They would also need resources and technical assistance to measure risk and protective factors, to choose effective intervention methods, and to carry out high-quality evaluations of the effectiveness of programs in reducing crime and disorder.

The focus should be on primary prevention (offering the program to all families living in specified areas), not on secondary prevention (targeting the program on individuals identified as at risk). Ideally, the program should be presented positively, as fostering safe and healthy communities by strengthening protective factors, rather than as a crime prevention program targeting risk factors.

Nationally and locally, there is no British agency whose primary mandate is the primary prevention of crime. For example, the very worthwhile intervention programs being implemented by Youth Offending Teams are overwhelmingly targeted on detected offenders. Therefore, a national agency should be established in Great Britain and in other countries with the mandate of fostering and funding the early prevention of crime.

This national agency could provide technical assistance, skills, and knowledge to local agencies in implementing prevention programs; could provide funding for such programs; and could ensure continuity, coordination, and monitoring of local programs. It could provide training in prevention science for people in local agencies and could maintain high standards for evaluation research. It could also act as a center for the discussion of how policy initiatives of different government agencies influence crime and associated social problems. It could set a national and local agenda for research and practice in the prevention of crime, drug and alcohol abuse, mental health problems, and associated social problems. National crime prevention agencies have been established in some countries, such as Sweden (Ministry of Justice 1997; Wikström and Torstensson 1999).

The national agency could also maintain a computerized register of evaluation research and, like the British National Institute of Clinical Excellence, could advise the government about effective and cost-effective crime prevention programs. Medical advice is often based on systematic reviews of the effectiveness of health care interventions organized by the Cochrane Collaboration and funded by the National Health Service. Systematic reviews of the evaluation literature on the effectiveness of criminological interventions should be commissioned and funded by all government agencies. Such reviews are currently being carried out by the Campbell Collaboration (Farrington and Petrosino 2001).

Crime prevention also needs to be organized locally. In each area, a local agency should be set up to take the lead in organizing risk-focused crime prevention. In Sweden, two-thirds of municipalities have local crime prevention councils. The local prevention agency could take the lead in measuring risk and protective factors and social problems in local areas, using archival records and local household and school surveys. It could then assess available resources and develop a plan of prevention strategies. With specialist technical assistance, prevention programs could be chosen from a menu of strategies that have been proved to be effective in reducing crime in well-designed evaluation research. This would be a good example of evidence-based practice.

The main conclusion of this chapter is that there is good evidence that early family and school interventions—such as general parent education, parent training, child skills training, teacher training, and antibullying programs—can be effective in reducing later delinquency and youth violence. The time is ripe to mount a large-scale evidence-based integrated national strategy for the reduction of crime and associated social problems, including rigorous evaluation requirements, in all countries. This should implement programs to tackle risk factors and strengthen protective factors, and it could be based on Communities that Care. Primary prevention has been effective in improving health, and it could be equally effective in reducing crime and violence in all countries.

References

Alexander, J. F., C. Barton, R. S. Schiavo, and S. V. Parsons. 1976. Systems-behavioral intervention with families of delinquents: Therapist characteristics, family behavior and outcome. *Journal of Consulting and Clinical Psychology* 44, 656-664.

Alexander, J. F., and B. V. Parsons. 1973. Short-term behavioral intervention with delinquent families: Impact on family process and recidivism. *Journal of Abnormal Psychology* 81, 219-225.

Aos, S., P. Phipps, R. Barnoski, and R. Lieb. 1999. *The Comparative Costs and Benefits of Programs to Reduce Crime* (version 3.0). Olympia: Washington State Institute for Public Policy.

Aos, S., P. Phipps, R. Barnoski, and R. Lieb. 2001. *The Comparative Costs and Benefits of Programs to Reduce Crime* (version 4.0). Olympia: Washington State Institute for Public Policy.

Baldry, A. C., and D. P. Farrington. 1998. Parenting influences on bullying and victimization. *Legal and Criminological Psychology* 3, 237-254.

Barnett, W. S. 1993. Cost-benefit analysis. In *Significant Benefits: The High/Scope Perry Preschool Study Through Age 27*, ed. L. J. Schweinhart, H. V. Barnes, and D. P. Weikart, 142-173. Ypsilanti, MI: High/Scope Press.

Barton, C., J. F. Alexander, H. Waldron, C. W. Turner, and J. Warburton. 1985. Generalizing treatment effects of functional family therapy: Three replications. *American Journal of Family Therapy* 13, 16-26.

Berrueta-Clement, J. R., L. J. Schweinhart, W. S. Barnett, A. S. Epstein, and D. P. Weikart. 1984. *Changed Lives: The Effects of the Perry Preschool Program on Youths Through Age 19.* Ypsilanti, MI: High/Scope Press.

Borduin, C. M., B. J. Mann, L. T. Cone, S. W. Henggeler, B. R. Fucci, D. M. Blaske, and R. A. Williams. 1995. Multisystemic treatment of serious juvenile offenders: Long-term prevention of criminality and violence. *Journal of Consulting and Clinical Psychology* 63, 569-587.

Brand, S., and R. Price. 2000. *The Economic and Social Costs of Crime.* Research Study No. 217. London: Home Office.

Catalano, R. F., M. W. Arthur, J. D. Hawkins, L. Berglund, and J. J. Olson. 1998. Comprehensive community and school based interventions to prevent antisocial behaviour. In *Serious and Violent Juvenile Offenders: Risk Factors and Successful Interventions*, ed. R. Loeber and D. P. Farrington, 248-283. Thousand Oaks, CA: Sage.

Chamberlain, P., and J. B. Reid. 1998. Comparison of two community alternatives to incarceration for chronic juvenile offenders. *Journal of Consulting and Clinical Psychology* 66, 624-633.

Clarke, R. V. 1995. Situational crime prevention. In *Building a Safer Society: Strategic Approaches to Crime Prevention*. ed. M. Tonry and D. P. Farrington, 91-150. Chicago: University of Chicago Press.

Cohen, M. A. 1998. The monetary value of saving a high-risk youth. *Journal of Quantitative Criminology* 14, 5-33.

Communities that Care. 1997. *Communities that Care (UK): A New Kind of Prevention Program.* London: Communities that Care.

Dishion, T. J., G. R. Patterson, and K. A. Kavanagh. 1992. An experimental test of the coercion model: Linking theory, measurement and intervention. In *Preventing Antisocial Behavior: Interventions from Birth through Adolescence*, ed. J. McCord and R. E. Tremblay, 253-282. New York: Guilford.

Farquhar, J. W. 1985. The Stanford five-city project: Design and methods. *American Journal of Epidemiology* 122, 323-334.

Farrington, D. P. 1983. Randomized experiments on crime and justice. In *Crime and Justice*, vol. 4, ed. M. Tonry and N. Morris, 257-308. Chicago: University of Chicago Press.

Farrington, D. P. 1990. Implications of criminal career research for the prevention of offending. *Journal of Adolescence* 13, 93-113.

Farrington, D. P. 1993. Understanding and preventing bullying. In *Crime and Justice*, vol. 17, ed. M. Tonry and N. Morris, 381-458. Chicago: University of Chicago Press.

Farrington, D. P. 1996. *Understanding and Preventing Youth Crime.* York, U.K.: Joseph Rowntree Foundation.

Farrington, D. P. 1998. Predictors, causes and correlates of male youth violence. In *Youth Violence*, ed. M. Tonry and M. H. Moore, 421-475. Chicago: University of Chicago Press.

Farrington, D. P. 2001. The causes and prevention of violence. In *Violence in Health Care*, 2nd ed., ed. J. P. Shepherd, 1-27. Oxford: Oxford University Press.

Farrington, D. P., and A. Petrosino. 2001. The Campbell Collaboration crime and justice group. *Annals of the American Academy of Political and Social Science*, 578, 35-49.

Farrington, D. P. and B. C. Welsh. 2003. Family-based prevention of offending: A meta-analysis. *Australian and New Zealand Journal of Criminology* 36, 127-151.

Farrington, D. P. and B. C. Welsh. 2005. Randomized experiments in criminology: What have we learned in the last two decades? *Journal of Experimental Criminology* 1, 9-38.

France, A., and I. Crow. 2001. *CTC—The Story So Far.* York, U.K.: Joseph Rowntree Foundation.

Goldblatt, P., and C. Lewis, eds. 1998. *Reducing Offending: An Assessment of Research Evidence on Ways of Dealing with Offending Behavior.* Research Study No. 187. London: Home Office.

Hawkins, J. D., and R. F. Catalano. 1992. *Communities that Care.* San Francisco: Jossey-Bass.

Hawkins, J. D., R. F. Catalano, R. Kosterman, R. Abbott, and K. G. Hill. 1999. Preventing adolescent health risk behaviors by strengthening protection during childhood. *Archives of Pediatrics and Adolescent Medicine* 153, 226-234.

Hawkins, J. D., E. von Cleve, and R. F. Catalano. 1991. Reducing early childhood aggression: Results of a primary prevention program. *Journal of the American Academy of Child and Adolescent Psychiatry* 30, 208-217.

Henggeler, S. W., G. B. Melton, L. A. Smith, S. K. Schoenwald, and J. H. Hanley. 1993. Family preservation using multisystematic treatment: Long-term follow-up to a clinical trial with serious juvenile offenders. *Journal of Child and Family Studies* 2, 283-293.

Hope, T. 1995. Community crime prevention. In *Building a Safer Society: Strategic Approaches to Crime Prevention*, ed. M. Tonry and D. P. Farrington, 21-89. Chicago: University of Chicago Press.

Kaplan, R. M. 2000. Two pathways to prevention. *American Psychologist* 55, 382-396.

Karoly, L. A., P. W. Greenwood, S. S. Everingham, J. Hoube, M. R. Kilburn, C. P. Rydell, M. Sanders, and J. Chiesa. 1998. *Investing in Our Children: What We Know and Don't Know about the Costs and Benefits of Early Childhood Interventions.* Santa Monica, CA: Rand Corporation.

Kazdin, A. E., H. C. Kraemer, R. C. Kessler, D. J. Kupfer, and D. R. Offord. 1997. Contributions of risk-factor research to developmental psychopathology. *Clinical Psychology Review* 17, 375-406.

Kazdin, A. E., T. C. Siegel, and D. Bass. 1992. Cognitive problem-solving skills training and parent management training in the treatment of antisocial behavior in children. *Journal of Consulting and Clinical Psychology* 60, 733-747.

Kitzman, H., D. L. Olds, C. R. Henderson, C. Hanks, R. Cole, R. Tatelbaum, K. M. McConnochie, K. Sidora, D. W. Luckey, D. Shaver, K. Engelhardt, D. James, and K. Barnard. 1997. Effect of prenatal and infancy home visitation by nurses on pregnancy outcomes, childhood injuries, and repeated childbearing: A randomized controlled trial. *Journal of the American Medical Association* 278, 644-652.

Lally, J. R., P. L. Mangione, and A. S. Honig. 1988. The Syracuse University Family Development Research Program: Long-range impact of an early intervention with low-income children and their families. In *Parent Education as Early Childhood Intervention: Emerging Directions in Theory, Research and Practice*, ed. D. R. Powell, 79-104. Norwood, NJ: Ablex.

Larson, C. P. 1980. Efficacy of prenatal and postpartum home visits on child health and development. *Pediatrics* 66, 191-197.

Leschied, A., and A. Cunningham. 2002. *Seeking Effective Interventions for Serious Young Offenders: Interim Results of a Four-Year Randomized Study of Multisystemic Therapy in Ontario, Canada.* London, Ontario, Canada: London Family Court Clinic.

Loeber, R., and D. P. Farrington, eds. 2001. *Serious and Violent Juvenile Offenders: Risk Factors and Successful Interventions.* Thousand Oaks, CA: Sage.

Ministry of Justice. 1997. *Our Collective Responsibility: A National Program for Crime Prevention.* Stockholm: National Council for Crime Prevention.

O'Donnell, J., J. D. Hawkins, R. F. Catalano, R. D. Abbott, and L. E. Day. 1995. Preventing school failure, drug use, and delinquency among low-income children: Long-term intervention in elementary schools. *American Journal of Orthopsychiatry* 65, 87-100.

Olds, D. L., J. Eckenrode, C. R. Henderson, H. Kitzman, J. Powers, R. Cole, K. Sidora, P. Morris, L. M. Pettitt, and D. Luckey, 1997. Long-term effects of home visitation on maternal life course and child abuse and neglect: Fifteen-year follow-up of a randomized trial. *Journal of the American Medical Association* 278, 637-643.

Olds, D. L., C. R. Henderson, R. Chamberlin, and R. Tatelbaum. 1986. Preventing child abuse and neglect: A randomized trial of nurse home visitation. *Pediatrics* 78, 65-78.

Olds, D. L., C. R. Henderson, R. Cole, J. Eckenrode, H. Kitzman, D. Luckey, L. Pettitt, K. Sidora, P. Morris, and J. Powers. 1998. Long-term effects of nurse home visitation on children's criminal and antisocial behavior: 15-year follow-up of a randomized controlled trial. *Journal of the American Medical Association* 280, 1238-1244.

Olweus, D. 1994. Bullying at school: Basic facts and effects of a school based intervention program. *Journal of Child Psychology and Psychiatry* 35, 1171-1190.

Patterson, G. R. 1982. *Coercive Family Process.* Eugene, OR: Castalia.

Patterson, G. R., J. B. Reid, and T. J. Dishion. 1992. *Antisocial Boys.* Eugene, OR: Castalia.

Perry, C. L., K.-I. Klepp, and C. Sillers. 1989. Community-wide strategies for cardiovascular health: The Minnesota Heart Health Program youth program. *Health Education and Research* 4, 87-101.

Sanders, M. R., C. Markie-Dadds, L. A. Tully, and W. Bor. 2000. The Triple P-Positive Parenting Program: A comparison of enhanced, standard and self-directed behavioral family intervention for parents of children with early onset conduct problems. *Journal of Consulting and Clinical Psychology* 68, 624-640.

Schweinhart, L. J., H. V. Barnes, and D. P. Weikart. 1993. *Significant Benefits: The High/Scope Perry Preschool Study Through Age 27.* Ypsilanti, MI: High/Scope Press.

Schweinhart, L. J., J. Montie, X. Zongping, W. S. Barnett, C. R. Belfield, and M. Nores. 2005. *Lifetime Effects: The High/Scope Perry Preschool Study Through Age 40.* Ypsilanti, MI: High/Scope Press.

Schweinhart, L. J., and D. P. Weikart. 1980. *Young Children Grow Up: The Effects of the Perry Preschool Program on Youths Through Age 15.* Ypsilanti, MI: High/Scope Press.

Scott, S., Q. Spender, M. Doolan, B. Jacobs, and H. Aspland. 2001. Multicentre controlled trial of parenting groups for child antisocial behavior in clinical practice. *British Medical Journal* 323, 194-196.

Sherman, L. W., D. P. Farrington, B. C. Welsh, and D. MacKenzie, eds. 2006 revised edition. *Evidence-Based Crime Prevention.* New York: Routledge.

Smith, P. K., and S. Sharp. 1994. *School Bullying.* London: Routledge.

Steinberg, L., S. D. Lamborn, S. M. Dornbusch, and N. Darling. 1992. Impact of parenting practices on adolescent achievement: Authoritative parenting, school involvement and encouragement to succeed. *Child Development* 63, 1266-1281.

Stone, W. L., R. D. Bendell, and T. M. Field. 1988. The impact of socio-economic status on teenage mothers and children who received early intervention. *Journal of Applied Developmental Psychology* 9, 391-408.

Strayhorn, J. M., and C. S. Weidman. 1991. Follow-up one year after parent-child interaction training: Effects on behavior of preschool children. *Journal of the American Academy of Child and Adolescent Psychiatry* 30, 138-143.

Sutton, C., D. Utting, and D. P. Farrington, eds. 2004. *Support from the Start: Working with Young Children and their Families to Reduce the Risks of Crime and Antisocial Behavior.* Research Report 524. London: Department for Education and Skills.

Tonry, M., and D. P. Farrington. 1995. Strategic approaches to crime prevention. In *Building a Safer Society: Strategic Approaches to Crime Prevention*, ed. M. Tonry and D. P. Farrington, 1-20. Chicago: University of Chicago Press.

Tremblay, R. E., and W. M. Craig. 1995. Developmental crime prevention. In *Building a Safer Society: Strategic Approaches to Crime Prevention,* ed. M. Tonry and D. P. Farrington, 151-236. Chicago: University of Chicago Press.

Tremblay, R. E., L. Pagani-Kurtz, L. C. Masse, F. Vitaro, and R. O. Pihl. 1995. A bimodal preventive intervention for disruptive kindergarten boys: Its impact through mid-adolescence. *Journal of Consulting and Clinical Psychology* 63, 560-568.

Utting, D., ed. 1999. *A Guide to Promising Approaches.* London: Communities that Care.

Wasserman, G. A., and L. S. Miller. 1998. The prevention of serious and violent juvenile offending. In *Serious and Violent Juvenile Offenders. Risk Factors and Successful Interventions*, ed. R. Loeber and D.P. Farrington, 197-247. Thousand Oaks, CA: Sage.

Webster-Stratton, C. 1998. Preventing conduct problems in Head Start children: Strengthening parenting competencies. *Journal of Consulting and Clinical Psychology* 66, 715-730.

Webster-Stratton, C., and M. Hammond. 1997. Treating children with early-onset conduct problems: A comparison of child and parent training interventions. *Journal of Consulting and Clinical Psychology* 65, 93-109.

Welsh, B. C., and D. P. Farrington, eds. 2006. *Preventing Crime: What Works for Children, Offenders, Victims and Places.* New York: Springer.

Welsh, B. C., D. P. Farrington, and L. W. Sherman. 2001. *Costs and Benefits of Preventing Crime.* Boulder, CO: Westview Press.

West, D. J., and D. P. Farrington. 1977. *The Delinquent Way of Life.* London: Heinemann.

Widom, C. S. 1989. The cycle of violence. *Science* 244, 160-166.

Wikström, P-O. H., and M. Torstensson. 1999. Local crime prevention and its national support: Organisation and direction. *European Journal on Criminal Policy and Research* 7, 459-481.

Wilson, J. J., and J. C. Howell. 1933. *A Comprehensive Strategy for Serious, Violent, and Chronic Juvenile Offenders.* Washington, DC: Office of Juvenile Justice and Delinquency Prevention.

Deterrence and Deterrence Experiences: Preventing Crime through the Threat of Punishment

10

PER-OLOF H. WIKSTRÖM

Contents

The immediate principal end of punishment is to control action.

Bentham ([1789] 1987)

It is better to prevent crimes than to punish them.

Beccaria ([1764] 1970)

10.1   Introduction

The questions "Why do people obey the law?" and "What is the role of
deterrence in making people comply with the law?" are crucial in thinking
about strategy and policies to deal with the problem of crime.

Law-making and its enforcement may be viewed as a main method of
social engineering. Social engineering may be defined as actions initiated by
political bodies with the aim of influencing social behavior through intervention in the social environment in which individuals develop and act. Laws
are made by political bodies, and law-making aims to influence people's
actions and interactions by stipulating rules about what is right or wrong,
backed up by criminal justice agencies enforcing compliance (policing) and
penalizing breaches of the rules of law (punishing). The complex of "the law,
its policing, and threats and administration of punishment" may therefore
be viewed as a key method of (attempted) social engineering. The two main
suggested mechanisms by which compliance is achieved through law-making
and its enforcement are (1) deterrence and (2) deterrence experiences (as
part of moral education).

The purpose of this chapter is to discuss the role of deterrence and
deterrence experiences in crime prevention.

10.2 Some Key Concepts and Their Relationships

A main characteristic of human beings is that they are rule-following agents. Rules that stipulate what is right or wrong to do (or not to do) may be called moral rules. Criminal law is a set of moral rules, but not all moral rules are criminal laws. What distinguishes a law from other moral rules is mainly the greater formality by which (generally) the rule is legislated and by which its breaches are policed and penalized. To explain why individuals obey the law, or why they commit acts of crime, is to explain why they follow or break moral rules defined in law. To explain why individuals commit crime is, in principle, the same as explaining why they break any moral rule (i.e., the basic causal mechanisms are the same).

To understand the role of deterrence in crime prevention is to understand its role in the causation of law abidance. Deterrence may be defined as the avoidance of breaking a moral rule (committing an act of crime) because of the fear of consequences,[1] the fear of consequences being dependent on the perceived risk of intervention (its certainty) and the associated risk of punishment (its severity) for breaking a particular moral rule (committing an act of crime) in a particular setting.

Punishment may be defined as the purposeful infliction by a third party of negative consequences, such as rebuke, pain, financial loss, or deprivation of freedom, motivated by and as a response to transgression of a moral rule. A major aim with the legal threat of punishment (e.g., fines or imprisonment) is to create compliance with moral rules defined in law through deterrence (fear of consequences).

Deterrence[2] may be viewed as a situational mechanism through which threats of punishment (cause) influence individual compliance with moral rules (effect) by creating fear of consequences (mechanism) when an individual considers breaching a moral rule in a particular setting (Figure 10.1). Only when an individual is motivated to break a moral rule and deliberates whether or not to break the rule can it be prevented through deterrence (fear of consequences). To prevent something is to make something not happen that otherwise would have happened (if we think we have prevented something, we have to assume—in a thought experiment—that if we had not done what we did to prevent it, it would have happened).

Effective crime deterrence is when an act of crime is prevented because an individual motivated to break a moral rule defined in law has refrained from

---

[1] For reasons of simplicity, I shall use fear of consequences throughout the chapter, although concepts like worry or anxiety may often better describe the active emotion in deterrence. The consequences are the pain or costs associated with being subjected to punishment.
[2] The only difference between deterrence and crime deterrence is whether the moral rule concerned is defined in law (crime deterrence) or not.

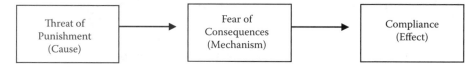

Figure 10.1   Deterrence as a situational mechanism.

doing so because of fear of consequences. To demonstrate effective crime deterrence is to show empirically that individuals have abstained from carrying out acts of crime they were motivated to do because they feared the consequences.

Although deterrence is a situational concept, an individual's deterrence experiences may be an important part of their moral education and as such have an impact on their current law abidance. Individuals acquire moral rules through being taught, by instruction or by observation, particular moral rules and by experiencing the monitoring of their (and others') compliance with those moral rules, of which deterrence experiences, that is, others' reactions to and punishing of any wrongdoing, are an important part of the process.

Moral education may be regarded as a developmental mechanism that (if successful) creates compliance with the particular moral rules (and laws) it aims to endorse. In other words, if an individual through moral education internalizes certain moral rules, and develops certain moral habits consistent with particular moral rules, he or she will be likely to comply with these moral rules (Figure 10.2). The extent to which these moral rules correspond to, and the moral habits are consistent with, the law, they will promote law-abiding behavior.[3] Moreover, if an individual's moral rules correspond to, and his or her moral habits are consistent with, the law, his or her compliance with the law is guided by his or her morality and moral habits rather than by fear of consequences. In other words, in these cases, deterrence is largely irrelevant for his or her choice of action.

Effective crime prevention through moral education occurs when acts of crime are prevented because individuals have internalized particular moral rules and developed particular moral habits that preclude them from engaging in particular acts of crime. To demonstrate effective crime prevention

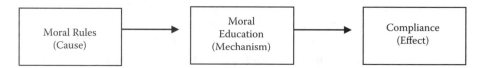

Figure 10.2   Moral education as a developmental mechanism.

---

[3] In this context, it is important to stress that individuals may sometimes break the law because they view the law as morally wrong; that is, the rules of law conflict with their own moral rules.

through moral education is to show empirically that individuals, through the process of moral education, have (1) internalized particular moral rules that prevent them from otherwise seeing particular moral rule breakings (acts of crime) as an action alternative, and (2) developed moral habits that do not involve breaking the rules of law. To demonstrate specifically the role of deterrence experiences in moral education is to show empirically that experience of negative reactions and the consequences of actions violating moral rules are an important part of the formation of an individual's morality and moral habits.[4]

To understand the role of deterrence in crime prevention, we need to understand its role (1) in the individual development of morality and (2) as a situational factor affecting decision-making.

10.3 Deterrence Theory

In discussing deterrence theory, I shall start with outlining a pure deterrence argument and then go on to develop it by introducing and assessing selected complicating themes (see also Bentham [1789] 1970; Beccaria [1764] 1963; Andenaes 1974; Zimring and Hawkins 1973). This discussion is a prelude to the next section, in which my aim is to place the role of deterrence in a broader theoretical framework dealing with through which factors, and through which mechanisms, people are influenced to abide by or break moral rules defined in law.

A pure deterrence argument is normally based on the idea that the driving force of human actions is to seek pleasure and avoid pain (motivations) and, furthermore, that choice of action is based upon a calculation of costs and benefits (decision-making) of potential actions. The role of the threat of punishment (the potential pain or costs it represents) is thus to outweigh the potential pleasures in an individual's decision-making about whether or not to commit an act of crime, and thereby cause him or her to refrain from committing an act of crime. "Nature has placed mankind under the governance of two sovereign masters, pain and pleasure. It is for them alone to point out what we ought to do, as well as determine what we shall do" (Bentham 1970:11).

A straightforward deterrence argument may read something like as follows: People obey the law because they fear the consequences (the pain or costs) more than they value the gain or satisfaction of breaching the rules of law; to make people obey the law is thus to make them fear the consequences

---

[4] It is a question of assessing the role and importance of threats of punishment, and punishments, and their interaction with other aspects that make up moral education (e.g., direct and indirect methods of moral teachings and rewards for compliance).

more than they value the gain or satisfaction of breaking the law; to make people fear the consequences is to make sure that any breach of the law is punished (certainty), and punished at a level where the pain or costs are high enough to outweigh the satisfaction or rewards (severity); if punishment for breaking the rules of law is certain and severe enough, people will refrain from committing acts of crime.

This requires commitment and adequate resources of policing to detect crime and apprehend offenders (certainty), as well as adequate resources and a commitment to effectively process and punish those apprehended at a level where the consequences are such they will be generally feared (severity). It also requires an effective communication to the population at large about (1) what is stated in the law, (2) the risk of getting caught if committing particular acts of crime (this must be perceived as high), and (3) the consequences of being caught if violating particular laws (this must be perceived as severe enough to instill fear of the consequences).

The crucial question here is, to what extent is human behavior in general, and law abidance in particular, an outcome of calculations of cost and benefit aiming to maximize pleasure and minimize pain?

Let's consider some important aspects of the problem of assessing the role of deterrence in crime prevention.

10.4   Actual and Perceived Risks

The first requirement for a threat of legal punishment to guide an individual's actions is that he or she be aware of the threat and that he or she regard it as credible and serious. The perceived risk of being caught and punished is, for obvious reasons, a more important factor in influencing an individual's actions than the actual risk (in cases where these two differ), although it is plausible to assume that the perceived risk is to some degree dependent on the actual risk. The preventive effect of threats of legal punishment on an individual's behavior is thus dependent on his or her perception of the risk of being caught and punished, were he or she to consider committing an act of crime (breaching a particular rule of law).

The crucial question here is, what is the link between the actual and the perceived risk of legal punishment, generally, and for different social groups (e.g., the mainstream population and active offenders)?

10.5   The Relevance of Threats of Punishment

A second requirement for a threat of legal punishment to guide an individual's actions is that he or she considers breaching a rule of law. Only when an individual considers breaching (deliberates over whether or not to breach) a rule of law can the perceived risk of punishment be a relevant factor in influencing his or her behavior. For individuals who do not see crime (or particular crimes) as an option, threats of punishment are irrelevant to their choice of action. In other words, the reason they comply with the law (or particular laws) is not that they fear the legal (or any other) consequences but rather that they do not see the act of breaching the law (or a particular law) as an option. Moreover, individuals may comply with or breach the law out of habit (that is, the action does not involve deliberation), in which case the threat of punishment does not enter as a factor influencing their actions. The fact that many individuals may comply with the law because (1) they do not see crime as an option or (2) they follow the rules of law, or breach them, out of habit, means that threats of legal punishment may have a more limited direct role in guiding human action than is implied by a pure deterrence argument.

The crucial question here is, when, for whom, and in what circumstances are individuals' actions guided by the threat of legal punishment?

10.6 Fear of Related Social Consequences

Fear of consequences may not be restricted only to the fear of legal punishments (e.g., fines or imprisonment). For example, Andenaes (1974:24) argued, "to the respectable cashier, fear of detection is more a fear of shame and scandal, and economic and social ruin, than it is fear of the punishment itself."

Fear of related social consequences, that is, social consequences that may be instigated by the fact that an individual is apprehended and/or convicted for a crime, may be regarded as an integral part of the perceived consequences. It may therefore be difficult to disentangle whether, for whom, and in what circumstances the risk of legal punishment (its certainty and severity) or the risk of related social consequences (their certainty and severity) has the most important deterrent effect.

The anticipated risk of the social costs of being caught and convicted for a crime may for some individuals, in certain circumstances, be an equally strong or even stronger feared consequence; for example, being publicly identified as an offender (particularly for certain types of crimes) with the risk of losing respect and social standing among significant others (and the added psychological costs such as feelings of guilt and shame), or being subjected to social sanctions (e.g., the risk of losing a job, a spouse, or friends).

The extent to which the risk of being identified as an offender (generally or for a particular type of crime) will act as a deterrent depends on the moral context in which an individual operates. In some cases, for individuals operating in certain moral contexts, being identified as an offender of a particular type of crime may not result in any negative reactions from significant others. On the contrary, it may even cause positive reactions. For others, it may be the reverse.

The extent to which social sanctions will act as a deterrent depends on an individual's social situation (e.g., does he or she have a job or family to lose?). For individuals who are poorly integrated in conventional society, the bite of potential social sanctions may be insignificant. That is, for these individuals, only legal threats of punishment may be relevant as a potential deterrent.

The crucial question here is, to what extent is fear of "related social consequences" an important part of crime deterrence, generally, and for particular individuals and social groups in particular circumstances?

10.7   General and Specific Deterrence

Deterrence is commonly discussed in terms of general and specific deterrence[5] (or prevention). Specific deterrence refers to the effects of a punishment on the punished person (e.g., the effects on his or her future actions), whereas general deterrence refers to the effects of the threat of punishment on the population at large. The main idea behind this division was well spelled out by Bentham (1970) when he distinguished between the effects of punishment in controlling action "by reformation" (special deterrence) and "in the way of example" (general deterrence). Together with incapacitation ("disablement"), these are, according to Bentham, the three main ways in which punishment may control action. "The immediate principal end of punishment is to control action. This action is either that of the offender, or of others: that of the offender it controls by its influence, either on his will, in which case it is said to operate by reformation; or on his physical powers, in which it is said to operate by disablement: that of others it can influence no otherwise than by its influence over their wills; in which case it is said to operate in the way of example" (Bentham 1970:158).

However, it is questionable whether the distinction between general and specific deterrence is analytically the most helpful in explaining and studying the role of deterrence in controlling human action. As observed by Zimring and Hawkins (1973:73), "Curiously enough, many who draw this distinction make no further use of it."

A particular problem with the concepts of general and specific deterrence is that they tend to analytically confuse the roles of developmental and situational processes in the understanding of compliance with the law. The concept of general deterrence tends to include both developmental and situational aspects of compliance, whereas the concept of specific deterrence

---

[5] Sometimes also referred to in the literature as special deterrence or individual prevention.

only refers to developmental aspects. Thus, developmental aspects are included under both concepts (i.e., influences on moral development and habit formation), whereas situational aspects are included only under the concept of general deterrence (i.e., the influence on decision-making by threats of punishment).

This problem is clearly illustrated in Andenaes' discussion of the two concepts:[6] "We can say that punishment has three sorts of general preventive affects: it may have a deterrent effect, it may strengthen moral inhibitions (moralizing effect), and it may stimulate habitual law-abiding conduct" (1974:8). The latter two effects are clearly developmental (influences on the formation of morality and moral habits), whereas the former is clearly a situational effect (the influence of perceived threats of punishment in decision-making whether or not to comply with a rule of law). That there is an important difference between situational and developmental aspects of the problem is, at least implicitly, acknowledged by Andenaes: "A deterrent effect can be achieved quickly; a moral effect takes longer" (Andenaes 1974:25).

When discussing individual prevention (specific deterrence), i.e., the effect of the punishment on the punished person, Andenaes stressed the developmental aspect. He argued that punishment "at best... results in genuine moral improvement or in the acquisition of pro-social habits" (ibid. p. 9) or an increased sensitivity to deterrence, that is, the punished individual will "be more careful next time" (ibid. p. 9) he or she considers a violation of the law. The fact that specific deterrence concerns developmental processes rather than situational mechanisms is also observed by Zimring and Hawkins (1973:73): "Insofar as [the] process [of specific deterrence] works by making, or attempting to make, individuals more sensitive to future threats of punishment because of present punishment, it is really not so much special or individual deterrence as it is a special effort to make individuals more sensitive to general deterrence."

10.8   Deterrence and Deterrence Experiences

I submit that when theorizing the role of deterrence in crime causation and prevention, a conceptually clearer (and more useful) distinction than that of general and specific deterrence is that between deterrence (as a situational mechanism) and deterrence experiences (as a part of a broader process of moral education). Although the former emphasizes the potential effect of threats of punishment (and related consequences) on an individual's decision-making (Figure 10.1 above), the latter stresses the role of an individual's

---

[6] Andenaes talks about general and individual prevention instead of general and specific deterrence.

experiences of, reactions to, and punishments for his or her own moral transgressions (and those of others) as part of the process in which his or her morality and moral habits develop and change (Figure 10.2 above). The distinction clearly highlights that we are talking about two important processes, one situational and one developmental, and that in order to understand the role played by deterrence in human compliance with the rules of the law, we fundamentally need to grasp how these two processes operate and interact. However, in order to do this, we first need to place the role of deterrence in crime causation and prevention in a wider theoretical context.

10.9   Deterrence and the Explanation of Crime

Human choice of action is only partly determined by fear of consequences (deterrence). An individual's morality, the moral habits he or she has developed, his or her capability to exercise self-control, and the characteristics of the moral context in which he or she operates, are all important factors in explaining why an individual abides by or breaks the rules of law (Wikström 2004; 2005; 2006).

Human action is an outcome of the interaction between an individual and the setting in which he or she takes part. At any given time, individuals vary in their morality, moral habits, and capability to exercise self-control. Individuals also vary in the kind of settings in which they take part, and settings vary in the opportunities and frictions they provide and in their moral context (i.e., the moral rules that apply to the setting, and their levels of enforcement and sanction).

Systemic factors (e.g., inequality and segregation) and individuals' life histories do not cause action but are important backgrounds to action in that they influence (1) why individuals come to have different characteristics and experiences and (2) why they come to operate in different behavioral contexts (see Wikström and Sampson 2003; Wikström 2006).

Which action alternatives an individual perceives, and what choices he or she makes (habitually or after deliberation), is ultimately dependent on who he or she is (his or her characteristics and experiences) and the features of the behavioral context in which he or she operates. An individual's moral actions (including acts of crime) can be viewed as an outcome of his or her moral engagement with the moral context of a particular setting. It is the interplay between an individual's moral values, capability to exercise self-control, and moral habits on the one hand, and the moral context in which he or she faces temptations and provocations on the other hand, which guide what alternatives for action he or she will see and what choices he or she will make, and consequently, what action he or she will take (including any acts of crime). Sometimes, individual characteristics and experiences, and at other times features of the behavioral context, are more important in guiding actions, but there is always an interaction between the two (see also Wikström 2006).

10.10 Moral Education and Deterrence Experiences

Deterrence experiences are an integral part of an individual's moral education and hence part of what forms his or her moral rules and moral habits. If an individual is taught moral rules that correspond to what is stated in the law, and the extent to which his or her compliance (and his or her observations of others' compliance) with these rules are rewarded and breaches punished,[7] he or she is likely to develop a morality and moral habits that promote law-abiding behavior. An individual who has internalized moral rules and developed moral habits that promote law-abiding behavior will tend not to see crime as an action alternative and will habitually act in accordance with the rules of law. For individuals who have developed a morality and moral habits that support law abidance, deterrence (fear of consequences) will, in most circumstances, play no (or only a marginal) role in guiding their choice of action.

I suggest that the reason why most people, most of the time, and in most places, comply with most of the rules of law is not because they choose not to commit acts of crime because they fear the consequences of violating the law,[8] but because they, as an outcome of their moral education, (1) do not generally see acts of crime as an action alternative, or (2) abide by the law out of habit. I submit that a moral education that (successfully) promotes the internalization of moral rules and the development of moral habits that

---

[7] It is out of the scope of this chapter to discuss what kinds of rewards and sanctions are the most effective in promoting internalization of particular moral rules and establishing particular moral habits, but it should be stressed that this is a key problem to address in evaluating the role of rewards and sanctions, particularly the role of legal "threats of punishment" and "punishments" in moral education.

[8] I find the sometimes voiced idea that individuals make "standing decisions" not to commit acts of crime in most cases less plausible (at least if one takes the word *decision* seriously). For example, Cook (1980:20) claimed, "Most of us have long ago adopted standing decisions to refrain from robbery and assault, no matter what the circumstances." I would rather argue that this is a question that most of us have never come to see, e.g., committing a robbery as an action alternative, and hence it is a question of which action alternatives we perceive rather than a question of our having have made a (standing) decision. I, for one, have never considered committing an act of robbery, and that is not because I at some point in my life made a (standing) decision not to commit robbery. It is just because I have never seen robbery as an action alternative.

correspond to the rules of law is the fundamental process through which compliance with the law is accomplished.

It is important to bear in mind that deterrence experiences (experiences of threats of punishment, and punishments) are only part of, and not necessarily the most central part of, what makes up an individual's moral education. Moreover, it is important to recall, particularly as regards the earlier formative ages, that in most cases the main source of an individual's deterrence experiences (threats of punishment, and punishments) may be actions taken by parents, teachers, and neighbors rather than actions taken by the police and the courts.

The crucial question here is, how important are the role of deterrence experiences (and specifically the role of law enforcement) in an individual's moral education, generally, and for specific groups?

10.11   Deterrence and Rational Choice

Although deterrence experiences are part of an individual's moral education and, as such, have an indirect influence on his or her current actions through their role in the development of his or her morality and moral habits, deterrence concerns the direct influence of perceived threats of punishment on an individual's choice of action in a particular circumstance.

It is reasonable to assume that when an individual deliberates over whether or not to commit an act of crime, he or she will aim to act rationally (that is, try to do what he or she judges to be the best thing to do).[9] However, if an individual does not see an act of crime as an option, or commits an act of crime out of habit, rational choice is not part of the process that guides his or her actions (i.e., part of the process that makes him or her comply with or breach a rule of law). It is only when an individual deliberates (makes a moral judgment) that rational choice comes into play in crime causation, because to make a rational choice (to choose what is judged best) requires a perception of different action alternatives to choose from (e.g., the alternatives to commit a particular act of crime or not to commit the particular act of crime).

The question of the role of rational choices in law abidance and law breaking is not a question of whether or not law abidance and law breaking is an outcome of rational choices, but rather a question of for whom and in what circumstances abiding by or breaching the law is an outcome of a rational choice. In other words, it is a question of trying to identify for whom and in what circumstances threats of punishment may be an effective way to influence their (rational) choice of action.

---

[9] Which is not necessarily the best alternative judged from some independent standard.

I submit that the main reason why most individuals most of the time comply with most of the laws is not because they have made "a standing decision" or "make repeated rational choices" to comply with the law (or particular laws) based on fear of consequences, but rather that their morality prevents them from seeing crime as an action alternative (no choice is made), and their moral habits do not include the commission of acts of crime (habits are expressions of "automatic" choices that do not involve any deliberation and therefore do not involve any rationality) (see Wikström 2006).

I also suspect that many acts of crime (particularly minor infractions like speeding or illicit drug use, but in some cases also more serious violations like assault) may be committed out of habit,[10] and hence for many acts of crime, deliberation and rational choice is not part of the process that causes an individual to violate the law.

The crucial questions here is, to what extent are crimes, and particular types of crime, committed out of habit or out of rational choice, and to what extent can changes in deterrence policies (changes in the risk of detection and the level of punishment) influence acts of crime that are committed out of habit and prevent habitual crime commission from developing in the first place?

10.12   Deterrence and Self-Control

Individuals vary not only in their morality and moral habits, but also in their capability to exercise self-control. An individual's capability to exercise self-control is a crucial factor when, but only when, he or she is making a (deliberate) choice between action alternatives that involve a conflict between his or her morality and motivation.[11] Self-control may be defined as the successful inhibition of a perceived action alternative or the interruption of a course of action that conflicts with an individual's morality.[12] An individual's capability to exercise self-control in a particular circumstance is based on the strength of his or her executive functions[13] interacting with momen-

[10] It is important in this context to stress that moral habits may not only promote law abidance but they may also promote law breaking. For a discussion of the difference between actions based on habit versus deliberation, see Wikström (2006).

[11] Please note the important difference between morality preventing an individual from seeing a particular crime as an option in the first place, and the conflict between a motivation to act in breach of the law and an individual's morality. Only in the latter case does the capability to exercise self-control come into play.

[12] Self-control is sometimes regarded as a trait (Gottfredson and Hirschi 1990), but I submit that self-control is better viewed as a situational concept (a mechanism): an individual's application of his or her executive functions (which is a trait) to the particularities of a setting (see further Wikström 2006).

[13] An individual's executive functions crucially involve his or her capability of gathering and holding, and effectively processing and evaluating, relevant information when deliberating over action alternatives.

tary factors such as stimuli or events causing strong emotions, and/or alcohol and drug intoxication (Wikström and Treiber 2007).

It appears plausible to assume that the role played by threats of punishment (deterrence) in a process of choice between action alternatives involving a conflict between motivation and morality is dependent on an individual's capability to exercise self-control. Poor executive functions, encounters with stimuli and events causing strong emotions, or being under the influence of alcohol and (certain) drugs may all be factors that promote impulsiveness in decision-making and a disregard for taking into account future consequence (i.e., cause a here-and-now orientation), thereby lessening the sensitivity to threats of future punishment as a factor guiding the choice of action. In other words, the threshold at which particular deterrent cues[14] influence an individual's choice of (deliberative) action may be dependent on his or her capability (generally and momentarily) to exercise self-control. I submit that for individuals with a poor capability to exercise self-control, only imminent and strong deterrent cues may influence their choice of action by overriding their motivational forces.

An individual's capability to exercise self-control may also be relevant for the role his or her deterrence experiences will play in his or her moral education. It seems plausible that individuals with poor executive capabilities, for the same reason that they may be less sensitive to deterrence in their choice of (deliberative) action, may also be less sensitive to the influence of deterrence experiences in their moral education.[15]

The crucial question here is, how important are differences in the capability to exercise self-control (generally and momentarily) as a factor in explaining individual and group variations in sensitivity to deterrence (in their deliberative actions) and sensitivity to deterrence experiences (in their moral education)?

10.13   Deterrence and Moral Contexts

A key aim of law-making and its enforcement should be to affect the moral context of the settings in which individuals develop and act. It is by influ-

---

[14] Deterrent cues may be defined as all those aspects of a setting that may influence an individual's perception of the risk of being caught and punished if breaching a rule of law. One may argue that "situational crime prevention" is mainly about influencing crime decision-making by providing deterrent cues (e.g., target hardening and surveillance).

[15] To argue that someone is less sensitive to deterrent cues is obviously not the same as to argue that they are insensitive to deterrent cues, just that stronger deterrents cues are needed before they have an influence.

encing the moral contexts in which individuals develop and act that law-making and its enforcement can influence human behavior.

Individuals do not develop and act in an environmental vacuum, a fact that is often overlooked in deterrence theory and research. Individuals' morality, their capability to exercise self-control, and their moral habits develop and change, and are expressed in response to their interaction with the environments in which they operate (i.e., their activity field). When dealing with moral actions like crime, understanding the role of the moral context of the settings in which an individual develops and acts is crucial in the explanation of why individuals comply with or breach the rules of law. The moral context of a setting may be defined as the moral rules that apply to the setting and their levels of enforcement and sanctioning.

Individuals develop and act in different moral contexts. One important consequence of this is that they differ in their deterrence experiences and the deterrent forces they encounter in their day-to-day life. Systemic factors (e.g., inequality and segregation) are important in the explanation of why individuals (or groups of individuals) vary in their (moral) context of development (their life histories) and their current (moral) context of action (Wikström 2005).

The fact that individuals develop and take action in different moral contexts is an important insight when devising crime prevention strategy and policies. Different measures may be needed, and the effectiveness of particular measures may vary, depending on the moral context in which they are applied. In other words, knowledge of how different deterrence policies work in different moral contexts may be essential for optimizing their effect on law abidance.

The crucial questions here are, to what extent do particular crime deterrence policies work equally well in different moral contexts, and to what extent, and by what means, is it possible to change particular existing moral contexts in a desired direction?

10.14   Crime Deterrence Policies

Deterrence as a tool for crime prevention does not work in isolation. The effectiveness of attempts to control action by introducing new laws (with their associated threats of punishment and enforcement) or by changes in the certainty and severity of punishment for violations of particular existing laws, is dependent on the social and moral contexts into which they are introduced.

I submit that the extent to which law- and public policymakers succeed in creating moral contexts (settings) that (developmentally and situationally) support law-abiding action is the extent to which their crime prevention strategy and policies will be effective. However, this does not only involve law-making and criminal justice measures, but crucially also extends to policies to influence the actions, and the capability to take action, by key agents of informal social control such as parents, teachers, and neighbors. It is a question of devising policies that make formal and informal social controls work together, recognizing (1) that processes of informal social controls often may be more fundamental to law abidance than those of formal social control, and (2) that the social conditions that support the emergence of effective informal social controls varies between segments of the society. For example, it appears generally more difficult to create strong informal social controls promoting law abidance in disadvantaged areas (e.g., Sampson and Wikström 2007).

Moreover, policies that aim to strengthen individuals' capability to exercise self-control (generally and momentarily) may be important in that they (if successful) contribute to an increased sensitivity in the population to deterrence experiences and deterrence. Such policies would crucially involve (1) measures to promote the early development of children's executive capabilities, (2) and alcohol and drug policies to reduce events in which an individual's capability to exercise self-control may be momentarily reduced.[16]

The success of a crime prevention policy (generally or for a particular type of crime) may be evaluated in terms of (1) the degree to which it succeeds in making citizens not even consider breaching the rules of law, or abiding by them out of habit, (2) the degree to which it can avert habitual offending from emerging, and (3) the degree to which the policy can make those who consider acting in breach of the law choose not to do so. The degree to which a crime prevention policy succeeds in the first goal is the degree to which the other two will be redundant. In other words, "to the lawmaker, the achievement of inhibition and habit is of greater value than mere deterrence." (Andenaes 1974:8).

10.15   Deterrence Research

In this chapter, I have so far mainly addressed the problem of the role of deterrence and deterrence experiences in crime prevention from a theoretical and analytical point of view. Although (strong) theory is crucial for understanding (and devising relevant research designs to test) the role of deterrence and deterrence experiences in crime prevention, the question that begs an answer is, to what extent are the presented analyses backed up by findings in deterrence research?

---

[16] In this context, it is also important to point out that alcohol and drug abuse may have long-term effects on an individual's executive functions and thereby also on their general capability to exercise self-control.

The overall answer to this question is a disappointing "Not that much." However, this is predominantly due to research gaps and the fact that some deterrence research has been methodologically weak, rather than a conflict between the findings of existing research and the presented theoretical propositions. In other words, it is not a question that key assumptions have been falsified, but rather a question that in many cases they have not been convincingly tested or tested at all. One can argue that the field of deterrence study is stronger analytically than empirically.

The main conclusions in assessments of the scope and quality of deterrence research made prior to 1980 are that the research is generally quite weak. Beyleveld stated, "Taking deterrence research as a whole, it must be concluded that... most studies are inconclusive, the main reason being methodologically defective designs or procedures and inadequate deterrence criteria" (1979:142). On a similar note, Cook observed that "deterrence research has enjoyed a revival during the 1970s, but so far has produced little more than a frame of reference, a variety of hypothesis and suppositions, and a scattering of empirical observations which are more anecdotal than systematic" (1980:212).

Although the situation has improved since these evaluations were made, whether or not one likes to agree with Nagin (1998:36) in his quite optimistic assessment that "our knowledge about deterrent effects is vastly greater than in 1980," is another matter.[17] I think it is fair to say that the research evidence relating to deterrence and its effectiveness as a crime prevention tool is still pretty meager in many areas, and this is particularly so if we consider (1) the role of (legal) deterrence experiences in moral education and (2) the role played by threats of (legal) punishment as a crime deterrent in different social and moral contexts (which are two almost totally neglected key areas of study in deterrence research).

10.16   Main Types of Deterrence Studies

Cook (1980:212) argued that "the core concern of deterrence research has been to develop a scientific understanding of the relationship between the crime rate and the threat of punishment generated by the criminal justice system." It is therefore no great surprise that studies of the association between different deterrence policies and crime rates (area variation studies), and studies of the relationship between changes in deterrence policies and

[17] It should be pointed out that Nagin qualified his assessment by saying, "The more we learn the more we come to appreciate that prior conceptions of the key questions were oversimplified" (1998:36), and he goes on to specify a number of important knowledge gaps that should be addressed.

crime rates (trend studies),[18] have been at the center of deterrence research. As Nagin (1998:2) pointed out, "Prior to 1980 these two kinds of studies were the mainstay of the deterrence literature."

More recently, these aggregate-level studies have been complemented with an increasing number of so–called perceptual studies on the individual level, focusing on "the relations of perceived sanction risk to either self-reported offending or intentions [as studied by scenarios]" (Nagin 1998:12). The great value of perceptual studies is that they begin to tap into the individual mechanisms that must be understood in order to explain any aggregate relationship between deterrence policy and crime rate.

Without an understanding of how (through which mechanisms) deterrence policies and their changes impact individual perceptions of certainty and severity, and how that, in turn, affects their behavior, we cannot really explain how deterrence policies affect individuals' crime involvement. I submit that without such an understanding, we lack the necessary knowledge to devise the most effective use of deterrence as a crime prevention tool.

10.17   Explaining Aggregate Relationships between Deterrence Policies and Crime Rate

To explain any aggregate relationship between deterrence policy and a crime rate,[19] it is necessary to show how (i.e., the processes by which) the macro and the micro levels are linked (Figure 10.3). This is basically so because there can be no direct causal relationship between a particular policy[20] (or anything else, for that matter) and a crime rate based on an aggregate of individual acts.

There are two main mechanisms that link deterrence policy to crime rates: One is how particular deterrence policies affect individual perceptions of certainty and severity (the macro-to-micro mechanism, marked in Figure 10.3 by a [2]); the other is how individual perceptions of certainty and severity affect decision-making on whether or not to engage in acts of crime

---

[18] It is not unusual that the main (policy) problem of deterrence is framed as one of understanding marginal deterrence, that is, the impact on the aggregate prevalence (or frequency) of a particular type of crime of changes in penal policy that alter the risk of detection (e.g., higher police presence) or the severity of punishment (e.g., longer sentences) for that particular type of crime.

[19] This obviously holds true regardless of whether it is a negative or a positive relationship between certainty and/or severity of punishment and crime rate that is the focus of explanation.

[20] For example, putting more police on the streets or increasing the length of sentences.

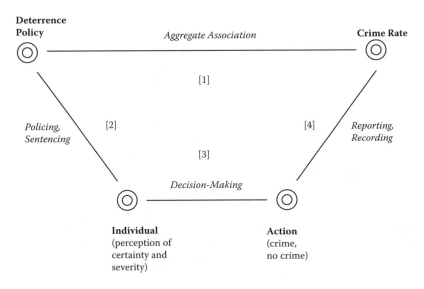

Figure 10.3 The aggregate relationship and its individual counterparts, illustrated in a so-called Boudon-Coleman diagram. (Boudon-Coleman diagram is a term introduced by Bunge (1999) to acknowledge that Boudon and Coleman pioneered this type of cross-level analysis [although they never applied it to deterrence].)

(the micro mechanism, marked by a [3]).[21] Knowledge about how these two mechanisms work, generally, and in particular social and moral contexts, and for individuals with different characteristics and experiences, will enable us to explain how the relationship between deterrence policies and aggregate crime rates are produced (the aggregate relationship, marked by a [1]). The key question then is, what have we learned from deterrence research about the processes indicated by numbers [2] and [3] in Figure 10.3?

10.18   The Link between Deterrence Policies and Individual Perceptions of Risk (Macro-to-Micro Mechanisms)

Nagin stated, "Knowledge about the relationship of sanction risk perceptions to actual policy is virtually nonexistent" (1998:36), and there is hardly any research on how particular deterrence policies (or changes in particular deterrence policies) affect individuals' perceptions (or changes in percep-

---

[21] There is also a third, more technical, "mechanism," the micro-to-macro mechanism [4], that deals with how individual acts of crime are aggregated into rates and involves questions such as how reporting and recording systems operate. However, although this is important knowledge when assessing "crime rates" (and their changes), it is out of the scope of this chapter to deal with this question. It should be noted that this problem also applies to cases in which the crime rate is based on survey data (e.g., victim survey data).

tion) of certainty and severity, that is, studies of the relationship between actual and perceived risk of detection and severity of punishment. Consequently, there is no research on (1) how the relationship between actual and perceived risks may vary between different social and moral contexts, and (2) how this relationship may differ among individuals with different characteristics and experiences.[22]

This is a central knowledge gap that needs to be addressed if we want to empirically advance our understanding of the (potential) effects of particular deterrence policies. The first step in establishing whether or not a particular deterrence policy is effective is to show that it actually succeeds in influencing individuals' perceptions of the certainty and severity of punishment. However, this is not enough because, crucially, we also need to know whether, and if so how, perceptions of certainty and severity affect an individual's law abidance, and whether, and if so how, this relationship varies depending on individual characteristics and experiences and the social and moral contexts in which they operate.

10.19   The Link between Individual Perceptions of Certainty and Severity of Punishment and Their Crime Involvement (Micro Mechanisms)

To demonstrate empirically that individuals' perceptions of certainty and severity of punishment influence their choice of whether or not to commit an act of crime ultimately requires a study of the role of deterrence in the process of decision-making. That is, it needs to be shown that individuals consider and take into account the risk of detection and/or the severity of punishment in making choices whether or not to commit an act of crime.

However, most so-called perceptual studies do not investigate the role of perceived threats of punishment in decision-making but rather the correlation between individuals' general assessments[23] of the certainty and/or sever-

---

[22] The only exception is some partial research that addresses individuals' knowledge of actual sentencing risk and policies, which indicate that the "general public" tends to underestimate the severity of sanctions imposed (Hough and Roberts 1998) and that those inexperienced in committing crime tend to "have unrealistically high expectations of sanction risks" (Nagin 1998:13, my emphasis). What this research potentially indicates is that those who are actively engaged in crime have a better knowledge about sanction risks and severity than those who are not. Which, of course, makes a lot of sense, although its value for understanding how deterrence policies influence individuals' perceptions of certainty and severity is limited.

[23] I submit that the term *general assessment* is a better and more accurate term than the commonly used word *perception* to describe what is actually investigated in these studies. The term perception has a clear situational meaning. That is, *perception* refers to what we can see, hear, and feel in a particular setting (concrete risk), whereas *general assessments* refer to evaluation of abstract risk.

ity of risk of punishment and self-reported offending. The crucial questions here are, (1) to what extent do an individual's abstract assessments of risk correspond to their concrete perceptions of risk (in their everyday decision-making), and (2) to what extent is an individual's abstract assessment of risk relevant in guiding their actions?

It seems reasonable to assume that an individual's general assessment of risk is somehow related to their perception of risk in real-life settings, and therefore the correlation between general assessment of risk of punishment and offending would tell us something about the association between perception of risk of punishment and offending. However, using general assessments of risk as a measure of how deterrence influences actions totally ignores the importance of the deterrent qualities of the environment (the social and moral context) in which an individual operates. In fact, I submit that general assessments of risk may be a measure of an individual's generalized sensitivity to deterrence rather than a measure of how deterrence influences his or her actions (which is an outcome of the interplay between an individual's sensitivity to deterrence and the deterrent cues in the settings in which he or she takes part).

Moreover, the interpretation of the correlation between a general assessment of risk of punishment and offending is complicated by the fact that many individuals will rarely or never consider breaching the law (particular laws) and, therefore, rarely or never have to make real-life decisions in which they take into account the perception of risk of punishment. For this group of respondents, their general assessment of risk of punishment will not be based on their own experiences of real-life decision-making and, crucially, will not be relevant for (i.e., a cause of) their law abidance. In other words, for this subset of respondents, the correlation between their general assessment of the risk of punishment and their (lack of) offending will not represent a causal relationship because their law abidance is more a question of their morality preventing them from seeing crime as an option than a consequence of their decision to refrain from crime due to a fear of consequences.[24] Regardless of whether (and for whatever reason) they assess the risk of punishment as high or low, this assessment is largely irrelevant in guiding their actions.

The main implication of all this is that it is only for those who (with some regularity) consider committing acts of crime that a study of the relationship between their perception of risk of punishment (as measured by their general assessment of the risk of punishment) and their offending will say something about the role of deterrence for law abidance. The fact that most studies of the correlation between general assessments of the risk of

---

[24] The fact that some individuals may commit acts of crime out of habit also contributes to the problem of making causal interpretations of the correlation between general assessments of the risk of punishment and offending.

punishment (certainty and/or severity) and offending are (1) studies of general assessments rather than perceptions, and (2) likely to include subjects that rarely or never consider committing acts of crime,[25] makes it difficult to draw straightforward conclusions from this research about the role of deterrence for law abidance (that is, conclusions about the role of perceptions of risk of punishment in crime decision-making).

The research into the correlation between general assessments of risk of punishment and offending commonly show a (weak to modest) negative bivariate relationship between certainty and offending, whereas the findings of the relationship between severity and offending are more inconclusive, e.g., some reported results even show a positive association (Paternoster 1987).[26] However, as I have argued above, the extent to which forthright conclusions about the role (and importance) of deterrence in crime prevention can be drawn from these findings (despite what the findings show) is questionable.[27] I submit that this argument holds true regardless of whether or not "controls" for other variables are included in the model,[28] perhaps with the exception of the inclusion of controls (measures) that tap into whether or not the respondents, on a more regular basis, consider breaching the law (committing the particular crime or crimes under study).[29]

One main approach in current research to overcome some of the methodological problems encountered in the study of the association between general assessments of punishment risk and offending is to address the role

---

[25] And the fact that some individuals may predominantly offend out of habit.

[26] Grasmick and Bryjak (1980) have argued that this may be a consequence of problems of measurement and analysis. They convincingly criticize the way in which *severity* of punishment has been *measured* in most studies. They also point out the importance of studying the *interaction* between certainty and severity in addressing their effects on crime involvement. Although valid points that should be addressed, taking them into account does not solve the fundamental problem faced by most of these studies, namely, the inclusion of those who may never or rarely consider committing the act(s) of crime(s) under study.

[27] It appears to me that a particular problem in some discussions of the relative importance of perceived certainty and severity of punishment is that they ignore the fact that (in most cases) it is unlikely that certainty would have any effect were it not for the perceived associated risk of negative consequences.

[28] That is, controlling for other potential influences on an individual's decision whether or not to offend does not solve this particular problem.

[29] If one can validate the assumption that for those individuals who, on a regular basis, consider committing acts of crime, "general assessments of risk" are a good indictor of "the perception of risk," and if control for (a measure of) the extent to which individuals consider breaching the law are included in the model, it may be justifiable to argue that the findings of such study could be a rough approximation of the influence of the perception of the risk of punishment on an individual's crime decision-making. Alternatively, one can aim to screen a sample for those who regularly consider committing acts of crime (if one has access to a valid measure of this) and then specifically study the relationship between general assessment of risk of punishment and offending for this subset of respondents. However, this still requires making the assumption that (for this group) their "general assessment" is a good indictor of their (everyday life) "perceptions."

of deterrence in decision-making by using scenario techniques (e.g., Klepper and Nagin 1989a, 1989b; Nagin and Paternoster 1993, 1994). In these studies, subjects are typically presented with hypothetical settings (mostly in written scenarios) with particular deterrent cues (referring to risks of detection and/or severity of punishment) and asked (1) to assess the risk of being caught and punished if carrying out a particular act in the particular setting,[30] and/or (2) to state whether or not (or how likely it is) they would commit a particular act of crime in the particular setting. At best, the scenario approach can create experimentlike conditions if (in a random sample) the deterrent cues in the scenario are systematically varied and randomly allocated to subjects.[31]

By and large, the findings of scenario-based studies give some support to the proposition that (at least some) people tend to consider deterrent cues in their "decisions" whether or not to offend. "Scenario-based research has consistently found deterrent-like relationships in the data" (Nagin 1998:15).

However, one potential problem with scenario studies is that the outcome is measured by intentions rather than actual behavior (one has to make the assumptions that intentions reflect behavior and that hypothetical intentions reflect real-life intentions);[32] another potential problem is to what extent the deterrent qualities presented in an abstract scenario can capture the complexities of deterrent forces and their influence in a real-life situation (one has to make the assumption that stated deterrent cues in a scenario would resemble influences an individual would experience and take into account in their real-life decision-making).

A further problem with current scenario studies (similar to that encountered in most general assessment studies) has to do with the inclusion of subjects that would never be motivated to or consider committing the crime(s) in question.[33] The problem here is, when these subjects respond to the scenario conditions, they are "forced" to react to a situation that would

[30] Often "the risk" refers to a "hypothetical" person, for example, "the plumber" in Klepper and Nagin's scenarios (1989a, 1989b).

[31] That is, subjects are randomly assigned scenarios that signify different risks of detection and/or severity of punishment. However, some scenario studies do not randomly vary the deterrent cues among the studied subjects but present the same scenario to all subjects. In these cases, the main objective is often to study individual differences in the response to a particular scenario.

[32] One way to explore whether there is a connection between reported intentions in scenarios and real life behavior is to study the relationship between stated intentions in response to scenarios and measures of real-life offending (self-reported or recorded). However, this ignores the importance of the influence on an individual's actions by the social and moral context in which he or she operates (which ideally also should be taken into account).

[33] Nagin and Paternoster (1993:483) report that many of the subjects in their study stated "no chance" that they would commit the crimes under study. This was so for the majority of subjects as regards theft (63 percent) and sexual assault (85 percent), while the corresponding figure for drunken driving was much less (33 percent).

not normally emerge for them in real life. In other words, in real life, the deterrent cues of the setting would be irrelevant to their actions because they do not see the particular act of crime as an action alternative in the first place. I suspect that the inclusion of individuals who do not see the crime under study as an option may risk providing a biased estimate of the role of deterrence in crime decision-making (which is specific to those who are motivated and would consider committing the crime in question). For example, what can we learn about the role of deterrence in adolescent date rape decision-making from adolescents who are neither motivated to nor would ever consider raping another person?

Another approach to addressing the role of deterrence in decision-making is to interview active offenders about their decision-making process when they commit acts of crime (particular types of crime[34]) and try to assess whether, and to what degree, they take into account deterrent qualities of the setting in their decision-making (e.g., Bennett and Wright 1984; Feeney 1986, Wright and Decker 1994).

The advantage with this method over scenario techniques is that we deal with real-life situations and only with those who have actually committed a crime (or the particular type of crime under study) on a regular basis. The main problem with this approach is the retrospective nature of the questioning. To be valid, findings from this kind of research require that the subjects remember and correctly identify (and, crucially, are capable of identifying) the role deterrence played in any decisions they made whether or not to commit an act of crime, and that the acts of crime they report on actually involved a decision-making process (and were not habitually committed).

The findings from interview studies regarding the role of deterrence in active offenders' decision-making suggest that active offenders often take into account deterrent cues in their choice of crime target and during the course of the commission of an act of crime (see von Hirsch et al. 1999:35–37). For example, deterrent cues may play a part in the choice of which house to burgle and whether or not to abort an ongoing break-in. Given the fact that there are ample targets for crimes like burglary and robbery, this research tells us more about the role of deterrent cues in crime target selection and the carrying out of acts of crime than of the role of deterrence in the decision whether or not commit an act of crime.[35]

This research also suggests that deterrence experiences (which should not be confused with deterrence, which is a situational concept) may play a

---

[34] Most of these studies concern specific crimes like burglary or robbery.

[35] Incidentally, one of the major problems facing "situational crime prevention techniques" is that it is often unclear to what extent such measures (which are mostly based upon providing deterrent cues) only momentarily prevent an offender from committing a particular type of crime. That is, to what extent would the successful prevention of an offender's targeting of one object simply result in the displacement of the crime to another object?

role in active offenders' process of desisting from (or scaling down) a life of active criminality (e.g., Shover 1996). That is, experiences of (repeatedly) being caught and punished may eventually influence (some) active offenders' sensitivity to deterrence and may even have some effect on (cause changes in) their morality and moral habits. However, the process of desistance, and specifically the role of deterrence experiences in this process, is rather poorly researched and understood.

10.20 Individual Differences in the Role of Deterrence in Crime Prevention

I have already argued, on analytical grounds, that if individuals do not see a particular crime as an option (or act habitually in accordance with a particular law), deterrence cannot be a factor that guides whether or not they will engage in that particular crime. Moreover, I have argued that the inclusion of subjects who do not normally consider committing crime (or particular types of crime) in studies of the effect of the role of deterrence in crime prevention (or the prevention of particular types of crime) may risk producing biased findings. I have also put forward that (only) for those individuals who, on a more regular basis, consider committing acts of crime (or particular acts of crime), will their capability to exercise self-control have any greater impact on their offending through its influence on how sensitive they are to deterrent cues in their crime decision-making.[36]

10.21 The Role of the Capability to Exercise Self-Control

In my assessment, the current research evidence (although not overwhelming and clear-cut) lends some support to the notion that the impact of deterrence perceptions (or general assessments of risk of punishment) is dependent on an individual's capability to exercise self-control.

Nagin and Paternoster, in a scenario-based study[37] in which they, among other things, measured the influence on (hypothetical) crime decision-mak-

---

[36] For those who do not consider breaching the law, their capability to exercise self-control is irrelevant to their choice of actions. This implies that the inclusion of those who rarely or never consider committing crime (particular acts of crime) in a study of whether the impact of deterrence on offending is dependent on an individual's capability to exercise self-control may risk producing biased findings.

[37] The subjects were asked to assess the probability that they would commit the crime presented in the scenario. The general problems with scenario studies have already been discussed and will not be repeated here.

ing by "deterrence perception"[38] and generalized self-control,[39] concluded, "Persons low in self-control perceive the rewards of crime as more valuable and the cost of crimes as less aversive, are less likely to feel the 'pangs of conscience,' and are more likely to report that they would commit crime than those with more self-control" (1993:484). The finding that there was a tendency that the perceived cost of crime was regarded less aversive by those with low self-control[40] is in line with the assumption that stronger deterrent cues are needed for those with low self-control to influence their actions.[41]

Wright et al. (2004), using longitudinal data from the Dunedin study, aimed to explore whether the influence of deterrence (general assessments of the risk of getting caught and the severity of social sanctions[42]) on crime involvement is dependent on an individual's propensity to engage in crime. The measures of "propensity" were measures of (generalized) self-control[43] and self-perceived criminality.[44] They addressed two important questions: First, the question of whether deterrence is a relevant factor that influences

[38] This was a composite measure aiming to summarize a range of aspects of perceived certainty and severity of consequences if committing the particular scenario crime.

[39] I submit that the term "generalized self-control" better describes what is actually measured here than the term "self-control," because, as I have already argued, self-control is a situational concept while the measure used here predominantly asks the subjects to report on their (non-setting-specific) general tendencies to be impulsive or discount the future (for example, "I base my decisions on what will happen to me in the short run rather than in the long run" or "I act on the spur of the moment without stopping to think"). A problem with the used scale, which I shall not further discuss here, is that some items appears to tap into morality rather than generalized self-control (for example, "I don't care if the things I do upset people").

[40] They reported "significant inverse effects for self-control on both total sanctions and shame" (Nagin and Paternoster 1993:483). Total sanctions are their measure of deterrence perception.

[41] Nagin and Paternoster (1993:483, footnote 19) stated, "The amount of variance explained in each case was not... substantial (less than 10 percent), suggesting that factors other than self-control are affecting the choice relevant variables." I suspect that one such variable may be the extent to which subjects consider committing acts of crime because, as I have previously argued, an individual's capability to exercise self-control (and the deterrent cues he or she is confronted with) are irrelevant in cases where the subjects would not consider committing the particular act of crime.

[42] Social sanctions were measured as anticipated negative reactions from significant others and assessed the risk of negative influences on future job prospects and finding "an ideal partner." No measure of the general assessment of the risk of legal threats of punishment was included in the study.

[43] They use two very complex measures of generalized self-control, summarizing many different scales, measured at many different ages. For example, the measure of childhood self-control summarizes "167 separate measurement items" (p. 191) and the measure of adolescent self-control summarizes "76 measurement items" (p. 192).

[44] Self-perceived criminality is a measure in which the subjects are asked to evaluate their own level of criminality compared to most people their age. Whether or not this is a good measure of propensity can be discussed. However, because the reported findings are essentially the same whether self-control or self-perceived criminality is used as the propensity measure, I shall not dwell any more on the potential problems with using their measure of self-perceived criminality as a measure of propensity. Moreover, the authors' stated interest is "on self-control and how it conditions the effect of sanction threats" (Wright et al. 2004:206).

all people's decisions regarding whether or not they will commit an act of crime (a question to which they appear to first answer yes, then no). Second, the question of whether or not the relationship between deterrence and offending varies by an individual's capability to exercise self-control (here they present the counterintuitive finding that the weaker an individual's self-control, the more important deterrence is as a preventive factor). Let's consider these two questions in some detail.

Wright et al. claimed that their findings "provide some empirical support for the theoretical position that all persons consider the consequences of their behavior and that even those who are high in criminal propensity and impulsivity are capable of foresight" (2004:196). This conclusion is based on studying the distribution of deterrence assessments (risk of getting caught and severity of social sanctions) across levels of propensity (i.e., levels of self-control and self-perceived criminality), and finding that deterrence risk assessment varies across all levels of propensity. If correct, their interpretation of this finding would be at odds with my claim (on analytical grounds) that it is only for those who consider committing crime that their capability to exercise self-control will influence whether or not they engage in acts of crime.

However, showing that there is a variation in the general assessment of the risk of consequences (risk of getting caught, severity of social sanctions) across all levels of generalized self-control (or self-perceived criminality) is not showing that all subjects consider the consequences of their behavior. This is not a study of the role of deterrent cues and self-control in decision-making, but a study of how general assessments of the risk of consequences[45] vary by levels of generalized self-control. Rather, what the finding suggests is that there is individual variation in generalized sensitivity to deterrence across all levels of generalized self-control. In this context, it is interesting to note that in the conclusion of their paper, the authors appear to contradict their previous claim that "all subjects consider the consequences," maintaining instead that "at sufficient low levels of criminal propensity,... threatened punishments may have no deterrent effect at all," and they go on to claim (in line with what I have argued) that for this group, "the deterrent effect of sanctions are irrelevant" (Wright et al. 2004:206).

Moreover, and for the same reasons, the findings do not show that all subjects consider the consequences of their actions, nor do the findings show that "even those who are high in criminal propensity and impulsivity are capable of foresight." Rather, what the findings show is that "generalized

---

[45] Recall, as I have previously argued, that general assessments of certainty and severity are at best measures of generalized deterrence sensitivity, but not of deterrence, which is a situational concept.

deterrence sensitivity" varies among those who have the highest propensity (as measured by low self-control and high self-perceived criminality).

Perhaps the most counterintuitive reported finding of Wright et al.'s study is that "the deterrent effect of 'getting caught' (i.e., its negative effect) was greatest (i.e., even more negative) among study members low in self-control and high in self-perceived criminality" (2004:198). This finding was repeated using "social sanctions" as a measure of deterrence.[46] On analytical grounds, it appears highly implausible that the weaker an individual's self-control, the more he or she would be influenced by deterrent effects. Thus, this finding, at first sight, appears contrary to what would be expected on analytical grounds.

However, if one makes the assumption that deterrence is relevant for actors' crime involvement only to the extent that they consider breaching the law, and further assumes that there is a negative correlation between an individual's level of generalized self-control (self-perceived criminality[47]) and his or her likelihood to consider committing acts of crime, the presented relationships are just what is to be expected.[48] In other words, the findings may merely reflect the fact that the relevance of deterrence as a factor influencing offending is strongest for those who are most likely to consider committing acts of crime (and irrelevant for those who are unlikely to consider breaching the law). This interpretation is close to the one at which Wright et al. finally arrived in their concluding discussion, "when other inhibitions are strong (such as those provided by one's moral beliefs), the deterrent effect of sanction threats are irrelevant" (2004:206). It should be stressed that this is an interpretation because the effect of any "other inhibitors" was not included in their study.[49]

---

[46] Apart from a significant interaction term, the authors also show that the negative relationship between the assessments of the risk of getting caught (severity of social sanctions) gradually decreases in magnitude when analyzed by five categories of generalized self-control ranging from "very low self-control" to "very high self-control." For the last category, "very high self-control," the relationship is nonsignificant.

[47] In this case, a positive correlation with the likelihood of considering committing acts of crime.

[48] The interpretation of the findings is complicated by the fact that there are no separate measures of "capability to exercise self-control" and "propensity to consider engaging in acts of crime," and the fact that the former tends to be treated in discussion as a measure of the latter. Ideally, these two variables should be measured separately in a study of crime decision-making to unravel their joint and separate impact on an individual's engagement in acts of crime. As I have previously argued, the propensity to consider acts of crime is more a question of morality than of the capability to exercise self-control. The latter only comes into play when an individual considers committing an act of crime.

[49] They do control for sex and social class, but it is unclear why they do this, because there is no discussion of, or argument presented for, why the relationship between "self-control," "deterrence," and "offending" should be dependent on an individual's sex or social class.

10.22   The Role of Deterrence Experiences

The role of deterrence experiences has not figured much in deterrence research (and that is particularly so as regards the role of deterrence experiences in the formation of an individual's morality and moral habits relevant to his or her engagement in acts of crime[50]). The main exception appears to be research on the role of past experiences of detection and punishment and its influence on (1) the current perception (general assessment) of risks of detection and punishment (often referred to in the deterrence literature as "experiential effects") and (2) active offenders' sensitivity to deterrence.

Horney and Marshall (1992:576) stated, "It is reasonable to argue that a major determinant of risk perception would be an individual's experience with crime and punishment." The basic research finding is that those with a prior involvement with crime (a particular type of crime) generally have a lower perception of the risk of detection[51] (e.g., Carmichael et al. 2005:267). The main suggested explanation for this is that there is (for whatever reason) a tendency for those inexperienced with crime (a particular type of crime) to overestimate the risk of detection (certainty).[52]

However, of greater interest is the finding that shows that among active offenders, their general assessments of the risk of getting caught is dependent on their prior success in committing crime without being arrested. Horney and Marshall (1992:589) reported from their study of convicted males that "the data suggest, at least for certain crimes, that perceptions are formed in a rational manner, that is, the likelihood of arrest is judged on the basis of how many times a person has been able to commit the crime without being arrested."[53] Horney and Marshall also showed that active offenders more sensitive to deterrence (i.e., those who assessed the general risk of arrest as higher) tended to commit less crime (ibid, p. 582). In other words, for active offenders, their prior deterrence experiences (their successes and failures) seem to matter for their current sensitivity to deterrence, which, in turn, seems to have some influence on their current level of crime involvement.

There is some evidence that for individuals who, on a more regular basis, consider committing acts of crime, there are two important sources of their

---

[50] Deterrence research should probably benefit from a greater integration with more general research on moral development (see, e.g., Turiel 2002).

[51] The findings are more inconclusive as regards the severity of punishment.

[52] There is, of course, no necessity in that those more experienced with crime always would evaluate the risk of detection as lower than others (for example, it is fully possible that studies in other social contexts than Western societies may yield different findings).

[53] They included a number of "control variables" in their statistical analysis, like "age," "race," and "education," but never do explain why the relationship between "arrest ratio" and "perceived risk of arrest" should be dependent on age, race, and education.

sensitivity to deterrence: (1) their capability to exercise self-control, and (2) their prior deterrence experiences.[54]

10.23   Conclusion: Does Deterrence Work?

Although acknowledging the shortcomings of the empirical evidence, review papers assessing deterrence research nevertheless in most cases come to the conclusion that the legal threat of punishment, by and large, does help prevent crime.

Blumstein, Cohen, and Nagin (1978:47) argued, "The evidence certainly favors a proposition supporting [effects of] deterrence more than it favors one... [in which the effects of] deterrence is absent." Cook (1980:213) stated, "My assessment is that the criminal justice system, ineffective though it may seem in many areas, has an overall crime deterrent effect of great magnitude." Nagin (1998:3) said that he could "concur with Cook's... conclusion that the criminal justice system exerts a very substantial deterrent effect." Von Hirsch et al. (1999:1) argued that "there are good reasons for believing that the criminal justice system as a whole exercises a deterrent effect—that crime would be much more prevalent were almost all offences to go undetected and unpunished."

I think it is fair to say that the abovementioned general conclusions about the effect of deterrence tend to be more analytically based than grounded in strong empirical evidence. If one accepts that knowledge is partly analytical, and partly empirical, it may be justifiable to conclude that, on balance, the current state of knowledge supports the proposition that (legal) deterrence, by and large, helps prevent crime.

There is no question that human action at times is influenced by fear of consequence (deterrence) and that deterrence experiences may be an important part of an individual's moral education. However, it is equally true that most human actions are not guided by fear of consequences (deterrence) and that deterrence experiences, particularly those relating to actions taken by agents of law enforcement, are only part of a wider complex of interacting socializing forces that determine how individuals' morality and moral habits of relevance to law abidance develops.

Garland argued, "A policy which intends to promote disciplined conduct and social control will concentrate not upon punishing offenders but upon socializing and integrating young citizens—a work of social justice and moral

[54] Although we know little about how the capability to exercise self-control and deterrence experiences interact in influencing sensitivity to deterrence, I have previously argued (on analytical grounds) that it is plausible that those with a poorer capability to exercise self-control may be less influenced by their deterrence experiences.

education rather than penal policy" (1990:292). Although it is easy to agree with Garland in general terms, his statement seems to ignore (or at least downplay) the fact that threats of punishment, and punishments themselves (including legal threats of punishment, and punishments), are part of what constitutes a moral education.[55]

I have argued that law abidance is largely a question of an individual's moral education (of which their deterrence experiences are a part) through which they have developed moral rules and moral habits that preclude them from engaging in crime. I have also argued that individuals breach the law either out of habit, or by making a deliberate choice, and that only in the latter case is there a question of whether or not deterrence may influence their choice to abide by or breach the law. I have also maintained that rationality and an individual's capability to exercise self-control come into play as factors influencing choice of action only when an individual deliberates over action alternatives. This has the important implication that crime commission cannot solely be understood in terms of rational choices and (a poor) capability to exercise self-control. Crime is fundamentally a question of morality and moral habits. Rational choices and the capability to exercise self-control only play a direct part when an individual's morality allows him or her to see crime as an action alternative. I have further argued that individuals develop and operate in different social and moral contexts and that particular deterrence policies may be differently effective in different social and moral contexts,[56] and furthermore that individuals with different characteristics and experiences may be differently sensitive to particular deterrence policies. Finally, I have submitted that to devise effective crime prevention policies, one needs to better understand the role of deterrence and deterrence experiences (i.e., situational and developmental deterrence mechanisms) in the broader context of other individual and environmental factors that interact with threats of punishment (and experiences of threats of punishment, and punishments) in the causation of whether or not an individual abides by or breaches the law.

---

[55] Garland talks about legal punishments as a "backup" when other socializing processes fail in achieving an individual's compliance with the law. I would argue that an individual's experience of, and observations of others', experiences of legal threats of punishment, and punishments, are not a backup to but rather an integral part of the socializing process.

[56] There is not much research of direct relevance to this topic, although the deterrance experiments on domestic violence by Sherman (1992) are illustrative as regards the potential for different outcomes of a specific deterrence policy depending on the particular social and moral context in which the deterrence policy is applied.

References

Andenaes, J. 1974. *Punishment and Deterrence.* Ann Arbor. University of Michigan Press.

Beccaria, C. 1789, 1987. *On Crimes and Punishment.* New York: Macmillan Publishing.

Bennett, T., and R. Wright. 1984. *Burglars on Burglary.* Aldershot, U.K.: Gower.

Bentham, J. 1764, 1970. *An Introduction of the Principles of Morals and Legislation,* ed. H. L. A. Hart. London: Methuen.

Beyleveld, D. 1979. Identifying, explaining and predicting deterrence. *The British Journal of Criminology* 19, 205-224.

Blumstein, A., J. Cohen, and D. Nagin, eds. 1978. *Deterrence and Incapacitation.* Washington, DC: National Academy of Sciences.

Bunge, M. 1999. *The Sociology-Philosophy Connection.* New Brunswick, NJ: Transaction Publishers.

Carmichael, S., L. Langton, G. Pendell, J. D. Reitzel, and A. Piquero. 2005. Do the experiential and deterrent effects operate differently across gender? *Journal of Criminal Justice* 33, 267-276.

Cook, P. J. 1980. Research in criminal deterrence: Laying the groundwork for the second decade. *Crime and Justice: An Annual Review of Research* 2.

Ducasse, C. J. 1968. Philosophy and wisdom in punishment and reward. In *Philosophical Perspectives on Punishment,* ed. E. H. Madden, R. Handy, and M. Farber. Springfield, MA: Charles C. Thomas.

Feeney, F. 1986. Robbers as decision-makers. In *The Reasoning Criminal: Rational Choice Perspectives on Offending,* ed. D. B. Cornish and R. V. Clarke. New York: Springer Verlag.

Garland, D. 1990. *Punishment and Modern Society.* Oxford: Clarendon Press.

Gottfredson, M., and T. Hirchi. 1990. *A General Theory of Crime.* Stanford, CA: Stanford University Press.

Grasmick, H. G. and G. J. Bryak. 1980. The deterrent effect of perceived certainty of punishment. *Social Forces* 59, 471-491.

Von Hirsch, A., A. E. Bottoms, E. Burney, and P.-O. Wikström. 1999. *Criminal Deterrence and Sentence Severity, An Analysis of Recent Research.* Oxford: Hart Publishing.

Horney, J., and L. H. Marshall. 1992. Risk perceptions among serious offenders: The role of crime and punishment. *Criminology* 30, 575-594.

Hough, M., and J. Roberts. 1998. *Attitudes to Punishment. Findings from the British Crime Survey.* Home Office Research Study No. 179. London: HMSO.

Klepper, S., and D. S. Nagin. 1989a. Tax compliance and perceptions of the risk of detection and criminal prosecution. *Law and Society Review* 23, 209-240.

Klepper, S., and D. S. Nagin. 1989b. The deterrent effect of perceived certainty and severity of punishment revisited. *Criminology* 27, 721-746.

Nagin, D. S., 1998. Criminal deterrence research at the outset of the twenty-first century. *Crime and Justice, An Annual Review of Research* 23.

Nagin, D. S., and R. Paternoster. 1993. Enduring individual differences and rational choice theories of crime. *Law and Society Review* 27, 467-496.

Nagin, D. S., and R. Paternoster. 1994. Personal capital and social control: The deterrence implications of a theory of individual differences in criminal offending. *Criminology* 32, 581-603.

Paternoster, R. 1987. The deterrent effect of the perceived certainty and severity of punishment: A review of the evidence and issues. *Justice Quarterly* 4, 173-217.

Sampson, R. J., and P.-O. Wikström. 2006. The social order of violence in Chicago and Stockholm neighborhoods: A comparative inquiry. In *Order, Conflict and Violence*, ed. I. Shapiro and S. Kalyvas. Cambridge: Cambridge University Press.

Sherman, L. W. 1992. *Policing Domestic Violence: Experiments and Dilemmas.* New York: The Free Press.

Shover, N. 1996. *Great Pretenders: Pursuits and Careers of Persistent Thieves.* Boulder, CO: Westview Press.

Turiel, E. 2002. *The Culture of Morality: Social Development, Context, and Conflict.* Cambridge: Cambridge University Press.

Wikström, P.-O. 2004. Crime as alternative: Towards a cross-level situational action theory of crime causation. In *Beyond empiricism: Institutions and Intentions in the Study of Crime, Advances in Criminological Theory* 13 ed. J. McCord. New Brunswick, NJ: Transaction.

Wikström, P.-O. 2005. The social origins of pathways in crime: Towards a developmental ecological action theory of crime involvement and its changes. In *Integrated Developmental and Life Course Theories of Offending, Advances in Criminological Theory* 14, ed. D. P. Farrington. New Brunswick, NJ: Transaction.

Wikström, P.-O. 2007. Linking individual, setting and acts of crime: Situational mechanisms and the explanation of crime. In *Explaining Crime: Contexts, Mechanisms and Development*, ed. P.-O. Wikström and R. J. Sampson. Cambridge: Cambridge University Press, 2006.

Wikström, P.-O., and R. J. Sampson. 2003. Social mechanisms of community influences on crime and pathways in criminality. In *Causes of Conduct Disorder and Juvenile Delinquency*, ed. B. B. Lahey, T. E. Moffitt, and A. Caspi. New York: The Guilford Press.

Wikström, P-O., and Treiber K. 2007. The Role of Self-Control in Crime Causation. Beyond Gottfredson and Hirschi's General Theory of Crime. *European Journal of Criminology*, 4, 237-264.

Wright, R. T., and S. H. Decker. 1994. *Burglars on the Job. Streetlife and Residential Break-ins.* Boston: Northeastern University Press.

Wright, B. R. E., A. Caspi, T. Moffitt, and R. Paternoster. 2004. Does the perceived risk of punishment deter criminally prone individuals? Rational choice, self-control and crime. *Journal of Research in Crime and Delinquency* 41, 180-213.

Zimring, F. E., and G. J. Hawkins. 1973. *Deterrence: The Legal Threat in Crime Control.* Chicago: University of Chicago Press.

Retribution and Retaliation

11

JOHN PRATT

Contents

When people commit some sort of harmful act against others, they can usually expect their victims to retaliate against them, although what this might be will vary in each case. In some, like may be visited on those who commit the original harmful act; in others, the response may vastly exceed what was originally done; in others still, there may be only the mildest of rebukes. When harms become classifiable as crimes, however, the position changes somewhat. The state, through its criminal justice system, will make a response to the harm—the crime—on behalf of the victim. This is really as far as the principle of retaliation is then allowed to proceed here. This is because what then happens is that the punishment for the crime will be imposed according to a range of aims and objectives that essentially preclude the arbitrary, unspecific, and unpredictable nature of retaliation. In this chapter, we will be examining one such aim and objective: retribution. What I want to do is provide, first, an overview of what this principle entails; second, an examination of its historical development in modern society and its reformulation in the post-1970s period into what is known as "desserts"; third, an examination of how an array of penal sanctions variously fit or do not fit this concept; fourth, an examination of the main arguments both for and against retribution; and fifth, returning to the subject of retaliation, an examination of the particular circumstances in which we can still find this taking place outside of the formal justice system and the reasons for this.

11.1   Retribution: What Is It?

The essence of retribution is that those who break the law—and only those who break the law—should be punished. They should then be punished according to their desserts, that is, punished according to how much wrong they have done. So far, retribution might sound quite similar to retaliation, and a number of its critics make this point, but there are important differences between the two. For retributivists, only those who break the law must be punished; Hart (1968) referred to this as retribution in distribution: The crime they have committed is a matter between them and the state, and the punishment will be specifically inflicted on them and only them. Although Mathiesen (1990) argued that criminal sanctions, particularly imprisonment, affect many more than just the criminal, the point here is that this at least is the formal intent. In contrast, retaliation to harm, including crime, can often extend far beyond the individual harm-doer—their families might also be shamed or excluded from particular social arrangements, for example. In retribution as well, a penalty must be imposed—it cannot be waived, as in a decision not to retaliate. Victims' views are irrelevant, whether they wish more punishment to be imposed or even none at all (Cross and Ashworth 1981: 130). This is because, for retributivists, there is a duty to punish: "Those who commit crimes deserve to be punished for the same reason that those who commit civil wrongs deserve to be made to pay for damages: there is a fundamental intuitive connection between crime and punishment" (von Hirsch and Ashworth 1998: 141).

How much punishment should then be imposed? For retributivists, criminals should be punished neither infinitely nor leniently (retaliation might allow for either) but in proportion to or commensurate with their crime. To use contemporary vernacular, they should be punished according to their "just desserts," neither more nor less (von Hirsch 1976). There is thus a fixed relationship between the seriousness of the crime committed and the punishment to be inflicted. On this basis, then, there is a clear distinction between retribution and the untrammelled, unspecific vengeance that retaliation allows to take place. Retaliation puts no limits to punishment, whereas retribution inflicted by appropriate public authorities is carefully circumscribed.

According to Ashworth (1989), modern retributivists believe that there is a twofold purpose to punishment. First, it restores the "balance" by eliminating the unfair advantage an offender gains through their crime(s) over nonoffenders. Second, punishment contributes to overall levels of crime control: In the knowledge that any such advantages would be removed, potential offenders are likely to desist. As von Hirsch, another very important contemporary retributivist, explained, "The blaming element in the criminal sanction conveys that the conduct is wrong; and the hard treatment element [that is, the punishment] supplies a person with a supplementary prudential reason for refraining from the conduct" (von Hirsch 1993: 41). In these respects, it is as if desistance from crime is some sort of inadvertent consequence of retributivism, the primary function of which is to punish, proportionately, the crime that had been committed (even if this sounds suspiciously like retributivists flirting with utilitarian-based deterrence). There would also seem to be a third purpose for retributive punishment. The idea of matching punishment to crime (in a figurative, not literal, sense) may help to satisfy the victim's need for vengeance and thereby offset any likelihood of informal retaliation. The notion of just desserts, which is what, for all intents and purposes, retribution is best understood as today, thereby has a commonsense appeal to it (Honderich 1984).

These restrictions—of punishment to lawbreakers only and to the gravity of the harm done and no more than that—also illustrate that retribution is essentially a *limiting* principle (something that is sometimes forgotten by its critics), and in essence, at least, it has strong humanitarian undertones. Unlike utilitarian reductivist aims and objectives of punishment, those who break the law are regarded as subjects with rights and responsibilities—not as deficient or inadequate subjects unable to help themselves (thus in need of treatment or rehabilitation) or as irredeemably wicked subjects (who thus have to be incapacitated). At the same time, it also places safeguards on individuals by limiting the amount of state power to be exercised over them through punishment.

11.2   Where Did it Come From?

Retribution, originally meaning paying back a debt or tax, has a long history and was characteristic of the talionic codes of ancient societies (Walker 1991), as well as being incorporated into the Scriptures (see, for example, Deuteronomy 19). However, it really emerged as a significant determining feature of sentencing during the Enlightenment. Up to that time, punishment in the premodern era was uncertain and unpredictable, with minimal regard for due process of law. It was essentially the property of local potentates, to be exercised arbitrarily with appalling force and brutality on a few, while being used minimally on a much greater number of lawbreakers (Foucault 1979). Aside from the theatricality of public executions (the death penalty could be imposed for the most minor indiscretion all the way through to murder—indeed, the eighteenth-century "Bloody Code" in England had over two hundred capital offenses), other public punishments such as the stocks and pillory were entirely unpredictable in the amount of punishment that would be inflicted on those sentenced to them. They might be pelted with rocks and die as a result, or alternatively, they might be garlanded with flowers (Weisser 1979). However, in the post-Enlightenment period, punishment began to obey a different set of rules. In Foucault's *Discipline and Punish*, we read of the following late-eighteenth-century reform proposals: "Those who abuse public liberty will be deprived of their own; those who abuse the benefits of law and the privileges of public office will be deprived of their civil rights; speculation and usury will be punished by fines; theft will be punished by confiscation; 'vainglory' by humiliation; murder by death; fire-raising by the stake" (Foucault 1979: 105). In contrast to the premodern era, we now read of punishment being matched with a remarkable exactitude to crimes.

These proposals were characteristic of a penal interregnum then in existence between the spectacular excesses of punishment in the premodern era and the more utilitarian correctionalism whereby punishments were matched to criminals rather than their crimes, which began to emerge in the mid-nineteenth century. In this interregnum, however, there was meant to be an exactitude, or at least an equivalence, between crime and punishment: neither too much, nor too little, nor any consideration of the kind of person the criminal was thought to be—they were to be known and identified only in relation to the crimes they had committed. Hence the significance of the rather clumsy and theatrical attempts to match punishment to crime above, with easily understandable signifiers of its gravity. Where, though, did these ideas come from?

11.2.1 Cesare Beccaria and Penal Reform in the Enlightenment

They reflect the influence of, first, the penal reformer, Cesare Beccaria ([1764] 1963). Some of the key themes of his remarkably influential *On Crimes and Punishments* were the need for fixed and immutable laws and equality before them. In such ways, it would be possible to wrest legal power and authority away from potentates and to invest them in the civic body as a whole: "Laws which surely are, or ought to be, compacts of free men, have been, for the most part, a mere tool of the passions of some, or have arisen from an accidental and temporary need. Never have they been dictated by a dispassionate student of human nature who might, by bringing the actions of a multitude of men into focus, consider them from this single point of view: *the greatest happiness for the greatest number*" (Beccaria 8). Obviously Beccaria, by virtue of this last comment, is showing himself to be a utilitarian—the criminal law serves a purpose other than punishing a particular individual's conduct. Nonetheless, it is clear that he did help to provide the intellectual force through which it would be possible to develop a fully fledged retributivism. For him, law reflected a social contract between all citizens in a given society. To prevent the arbitrary excesses of the pre-Enlightenment period, it should now be made certain and knowable to all through codification: "When a fixed code of laws, which must be observed to the letter, leaves no further care to the judge than to examine the acts of citizens and to decide whether or not they conform to the law as written: when the standard of the just or the unjust, which is to be the norm of conduct for all; then only are citizens not subject to the petty tyrannies of the many which are the more cruel as the distance between the oppressed and the oppressor is less, and which are far more fatal than that of a single man, for the despotism of many can only be corrected by the despotism of one; the cruelty of a single despot is proportional, not to his might, but to the obstacles he encounters" (Beccaria 16). As Edward Livingston wrote in 1822, in the United States (which also shows the spread of these ideas in this period), "laws, to be obeyed and administered, must be well-known; to be known they must be read; to be administered they must be studied and compared. To know them is the right of the people" (Friedman 1993: 63).

He also argued for a reduction in the level of intensity of punishment for breaches of the criminal law—again, he wanted penal arrangements to rid themselves of fruitless excess: "For a punishment to be just it should consist of only such gradations of intensity as suffice to deter men from committing crimes" (Beccaria 47). Equally, if law was now to be made on a secular basis (Beccaria 6), there was no need for the dramatic displays of punishment characteristic of societies where law is thought to be made by God (as befits a society where it was thought that crimes were committed not just against other individuals but against God himself). Instead, Beccaria argued for proportionality in punishment, or more specifically an *equivalence* between crime and punishment—the more serious the crime, the more serious the penalty it should attract: "For a punishment to attain its end, the evil which it inflicts has only to exceed *the advantage derivable from crime*" (Beccaria 43; my italics). On this basis, he proposed that "crimes against the person should always receive corporal punishment … injuries to honour should be punished with disgrace … thefts not involving violence should be punished by a fine" (Beccaria 68, 74). For smuggling, "Seizure of both the prescribed goods and whatever accompanies it is a very just punishment" (Beccaria 74). At the same time, Beccaria was opposed to the death penalty ("it cannot be useful, because of the example of barbarity it gives men") (Beccaria 50). If this seems to contradict Beccaria's (119) comments that "the penalty must be made to conform as closely as possible to the nature of the offence"—then this perhaps reveals a more fundamental conflict between the embryonic forms of utilitarianism and retributivism he was developing in his work (Beccaria 119).

11.2.2 Philosophical Influences—Kant and Hegel

This new formula for the quantity of punishment to be imposed on a given criminal was then removed from any utilitarian objectives that Beccaria was prepared to consider and set down in a more clearly retributive context in Kant's *Metaphysical Elements of Justice*: "Punishment can never be administered merely as a means for promoting another Good, either with regard to the Criminal himself or to Civil Society, but must in all cases be imposed only because the individual on whom it is inflicted *has committed a crime*" (331). Kant thus firmly prohibited punishment of the innocent as well as making punishment of the guilty an end in itself. The reason why he wanted the punishment fixed to the crime that had been committed and that alone was that "one man ought never to be dealt with merely as a means subservient to the purpose of another" (Kant 332). What seems apparent here, and again in the context of the Enlightenment, is an important qualifier, that utilitarianism might allow further excesses if punishment was allowed to become a means to something else rather than an end in itself: "What, then, is to be said of such a proposal as to keep a Criminal alive who had been condemned to death, on his being given to understand that if he agreed to certain dangerous experiments being formed on him, he would be allowed to survive if he came happily through them?" (Kant 332).

The epistemological basis of these arguments is that, for Kant, all moral concepts have their seat and origin wholly *a priori* in reason—they have an existence other than through experience: They are absolutes that should guide us all. Moral worth therefore exists only when a man or woman acts from an inbuilt sense of duty, whereas utilitarianism gave to morality a purpose outside of itself—for example, punishing an individual in such a way that others might be deterred from committing crime. Instead, for Kant, a criminal should be punished according to his or her desserts and not for any other means, giving the well-known example in justification of a people inhabiting an island resolving to separate and scatter themselves through the world: "The least Murderer lying in the prisons ought to be executed before the resolution was carried out" (333). This ought to be done because the criminal had deserved it—he or she would thus receive his or her desserts. Failure to punish, though, would mean that the rest of society would be complicit in this breach of the law: There is a categorical obligation to impose a penalty—it is an absolute value.

In practical terms, the emphasis on desserts led to the belief that the punishment should fit the crime. However, it is important to note that Kant was not arguing for some sort of reciprocity between punishment and crime: Such punishments would either be impossible in themselves or would be punishable as crimes against humanity in general. Punishments in fact should be banned either if they represented a direct assault on the dignity of human beings, or if they were radically disproportionate to the seriousness of the crimes committed. What he had in mind, again, was something like equivalence in punishment, as far as this would be allowed, and insofar as it did not constitute an affront to human dignity: "The state should never do anything to a criminal that humiliates and degrades his dignity as a man" (Kant 335). However, for rape and pederasty, he felt that imprisonment was not sufficient punishment: Instead, such criminals should be met with castration, whereas bestiality deserved expulsion (Kant 363). On the other hand, the death penalty must be "kept entirely free from any maltreatment that would make an abomination of the humanity residing in the person suffering it" (Kant 332). Other than this, and unlike Beccaria, Kant has no qualms about its place within a given sentencing framework.

Hegel, too, emphasized the rationality of the criminal who, by the same token, must be held responsible for his or her actions. As he put the matter, "Punishment is the right of the criminal. It is an act of his own will. The violation of right has been proclaimed by the criminal as his own right. His crime is the negation of right. Punishment is the negation of the negation and consequently an affirmation of right, solicited and forced upon the criminal himself" (Hegel 69). What Hegel seems to have had in mind here is that crimes violate the rights of others; if these rights are to be recognized, then it is important that the behavior that violated them is met with punishment, because without this, there could be no rights (Cooper 163). By inflicting punishment, then, the rights of others are thereby affirmed. It is, therefore, in this sense that Hegel wrote of the "annulment" of crime through its punishment (p. 69). Similarly, Bradley wrote that "punishment is the denial of wrong by the assertion of right, and the wrong exists in the self, or will, of the criminal; his self is a wrongful self, and is realized in his person and possessions; he has asserted in them his wrongful will, the incarnate denial of right; and in denying that assertion, and annihilating, whether wholly or partially, that incarnation by fine, or imprisonment, or even by death, we annihilate the wrong and manifest the right" (1876: 27). In addition, it is as if the act of punishment expiates criminals and then allows for the opportunity of their own moral transformation (Duff 1986). At the same time, as Bosanquet suggested, by punishing, misbehavior is not allowed to set a precedent: Punishment effectively annuls it (1918: 189). In a further extension of these ideas, we might also add that the criminal may well have a right to break the law, but so too there is a right for punishment to be delivered to him or her for breach of it (Honderich 1984: 48).

What level of punishment should then be imposed? Hegel, like Kant, wrote of the need for equivalence between crime and punishment, and of an exactitude in the level of pain to be inflicted: "Injustice is done at once if there is one lash too many, or one dollar or one cent, one week in prisons, or one day, too many or too few" (Hegel 71). He recognized as well, though, that there were obvious difficulties in devising punishments that exactly replicated the crime committed: "It is easy enough from this point of view to exhibit the retributive character of punishment as an absurdity (theft for theft, robbery for robbery, an eye for an eye, a tooth for a tooth—and then you can go on to suppose that the criminal has only one eye or no teeth) ... In crime, as that which is characterized at bottom by the infinite aspect of the deed, the purely external specific character vanishes all the more obviously and equality remains the fundamental regulator of the essential thing, to wit the desserts of the criminal, though not for the specific external form which the payment of those desserts may take. It is only in respect of that form that there is a plain inequality between theft and robbery on the one hand, and fines, imprisonment etc. on the other. In respect of their 'value' however, i.e., in respect of their universal property of being injuries, they are comparable" (Hegel 71–72). In other words, there should be a *conceptual similarity* between punishment and crime rather than some direct physical correspondence.

It was out of this combination of classical penal reform and post-Enlightenment philosophy that the concept of retribution was introduced to modern penal arrangements and sentencing frameworks around the beginning of the nineteenth century. It was these influences that lay behind the remarkable diversity of sanctions and proposals designed to match punishment to crime that came into existence around this time.

11.3　What Happened to Retribution?

Retributivism was initially a very significant influence on sentencing policy in the early nineteenth century. In the United States, up to the beginning of the Civil War, the criminal law consisted mainly of statutes prescribing fixed sentences for specific offenses. Thereafter, however, utilitarian thought systematically eroded early modern retributivist principles. Sentencing and penal policy began to be developed in such a way that punishments became more tailored to fit criminals rather than crimes.

This was a lengthy historical process that began in the early nineteenth century and then reached its high-water mark in the post-1945 period. Its roots lie within the sanction of imprisonment itself, developed as a penalty that could be applied to virtually all offenses—it broke the classical specificity of the relationship of punishment to crime. In most cases, suffering would now take the form of how long one was to spend in prison. During the second half of the nineteenth century, prison began to change its purpose as a result of the impact of significant penal reformers—Maconochie in Australia, Crofton in Ireland, and Wines in the United States. Prison regimes increasingly embraced rehabilitative ideas and became an area that lent themselves to the reform of the criminal: Time in prisons allowed for their study and classification to see what had caused them to commit crime in the first place and how their variety of problems and deficiencies that such study revealed might now be remedied. Modern penal systems increasingly began to look to the insights and techniques of what Foucault (1979) referred to as "the human sciences." In these ways, punishment now lost its equivalence to crime and began to be used instead to bring about change in the behavior of criminals, who also lost something as a result—their own rationality and responsibility, which retributivism had assumed they had. They were now seen as deficient citizens, below the norm, the exact nature of which was being specified in a succession of criminological discourses: the biological throwbacks of Lombroso; the mesomorphs of Sheldon; the psychological misfits of Burt; or the socially deprived, ghettoized beings of modern urban life that Chicago sociologists identified in the 1920s and 1930s.

By this time, a new group of penal philosophers had become very influential in changing the aims and objectives of punishment. For Saleilles, for example, "the legitimate purpose of punishment is to make of the criminal an honest man if that be possible; or, if not, to deprive him of the chance of doing further harm … punishment has thus a social end directed to the future, while hitherto it was regarded only as a necessary consequence of a past act … punishment for each individual case should be so adjusted to its purpose as to produce the largest possible return" (1911: 8).

Punishments based around this assumption now included the indeterminate prison sentence—particularly in the United States—which was the antipathy of retribution. This sentence then had to be accompanied by parole, to determine as an administrative procedure a release date, based on the prisoner's progress, response to treatment, and so on (and which formally at least bore no relation to their crime). Similar sanctions elsewhere in the Anglophone world included preventive detention, an indefinite prison sentence usually given to recidivist offenders; that is, they were being sentenced for their past record, not their present crime. Other provisions included special sentences for alcoholic offenders, and the use of probation, initially for first offenders but by the 1920s available to virtually all but the most serious criminals. Here was an order of the court, not a punishment, designed to "advise, assist, and befriend" (Prevention of Crime Act 1908). Indeed, in the provisions of the English 1948 Criminal Justice Act, it was not to count (along with absolute and conditional discharges) as a criminal conviction.

Modern penal arrangements began to be increasingly preoccupied with the treatment of the criminal—trying to explore their underlying psychology—while becoming further and further removed from the criminal act. Thus it was claimed that "the actual acts performed are not as important as the motives underlying the acts and the psychological state of the individual performing [them]" (Pollens 1938: 36). In these respects, the desire for individualized sentencing significantly undercuts the concept of individual responsibility and rationality. The primacy of juridical standards in the criminal court came to be significantly weakened—certainly in the United States, where the drive towards individualized sentencing was at its strongest—and the input of psychiatric and psychological knowledge at its greatest. As Dession put the matter, "Just as the political ideology of industrialization has produced a widening of the regulatory spheres assigned to penal control, so the seeping of psychological and psychiatric conceptions into everyday thought provoked a comparable expansion of penological expectations ... this shift of emphasis from the legal category of the offence to the personality of the offender ... is, of course, integrally tied up with what is gradually becoming the general approach to problems of human conduct and personality" (1937–8: 336). This certainly continued in the postwar period. Indeed, with the growing ascendancy of state welfarism, it was as if criminals, in the eyes of at least some commentators, were absolved from any responsibility at all for their crimes: As the British psychiatrist Edwin Glover observed, "They have certainly injured their fellows, but perhaps society has unwittingly injured them" (1956: 267).

Retribution still had its defenders, most notably, perhaps, H. L. A. Hart. He took the view that "both reform and individualized punishment have run counter to the customary morality of punishment" (1968: 26). That is, these new objectives and practices qualified or displaced altogether principles of justice or proportionality in determining the amount of punishment to be imposed in a particular case. For him, retribution remained a crucial aim, because it meant that only those who had actually broken the law should be punished (his retribution in distribution principle): "This is shown by the fact that we attach importance to the restrictive principle that only offenders may be punished, even where breach of this law might not be thought immoral" (Hart 1968: p. 12). He then goes on to write, "Indeed, even where the laws themselves are hideously immoral as in Nazi Germany ... the absence of the principle restricting punishment to the offender will be a further *special* iniquity; whereas admission of this principle would represent some individual respect for justice shown in the administration of morally bad laws" (Hart 1968: p. 12).

Ultimately, as modern penal systems came under the influence of ideas of correction, treatment, and rehabilitation, then the idea of matching punishment to crime seemed obsolete, indeed a relic of a more inhumane era, and one that had little place in a modern civilized world. Mabbott (1956: 301) claimed that "retributive punishment is only a polite name for revenge; it is vindictive, inhumane, barbarous and immoral." The only possible moral justification of punishment is to reform the criminal and/or deter others from committing similar crimes." Similarly, if less forthrightly, Nigel Walker wrote that "the relationship between penal retribution and humanitarianism is not easy to analyse logically. It would be unfair to point to the fact that in other centuries or other countries retributivists have supported punishments which here and now would be labelled 'inhuman' or even 'sadistic'" (1968: 20). Furthermore (sarcastically indicating his antipathy to the concept), "One of the least sophisticated reactions to offensive behaviour is the infliction of loss or suffering on offenders .... When inflicted by the aggrieved person without invoking the law it is called 'retaliation'; when applied according to law called 'retribution'" (Walker 1968: 128).

11.4   The Return of Retribution

Whatever the humanitarian ethos underpinning utilitarian reforms and thinking, by the early 1970s it was clear that these could also lead to manifest injustices. Individualized sentencing brought about great inconsistencies in the punishments given to two or more offenders for the same offense. At the same time, there was growing concern about being "sentenced to treatment." In the United States, the Model Penal Code 1962 specified that a court may choose to sentence to prison rather than probation "if an offender was in need of correctional treatment that can be provided more effectively by his commitment to an institution" (von Hirsch 1976: 12). In such cases, the sentence of imprisonment would be based on the extent of an individual's problems rather than their culpability for the crime they had committed. The courts had also begun to sentence on the basis of future conduct rather than current crime. The Model Penal Code 1972 specified that "an offender may be confined if the judge finds there is undue risk that during the period of a suspended sentence or probation the defendant will commit another crime" (von Hirsch 1993: p. 18).

Allied to these trends, there were concerns about the secret justice that the administration of parole represented. Decisions about release could seem

purely arbitrary with no redress or appeal. This, in conjunction with grievances brought about by the insecurity and anxiety associated with indeterminate sentences, helped to generate major prison riots (Mitford 1974). By
now, concepts such as treatment and rehabilitation were being treated with
considerable scepticism, particularly in the aftermath of Martinson (1974).
In answer to his question "What works?" he found that virtually "nothing
works" and that most of those involved in the criminal justice system had
no idea how to rehabilitate offenders. Notwithstanding his own subsequent
qualifications to his earlier position, this phrase came to dominate penal
thought and policy at a pivotal time (Martinson 1978). The "nothing works"
philosophy also coincided with the critique of the supposed benevolence of
psychiatric and other forms of state intervention in people's lives, set out
particularly in Szasz (1971).

In the light of such criticisms, we find the emergence of demands for
rights-based rather than welfare-based forms of governance across a range
of social fields: in particular, the right to be treated as a rational, responsible,
equal citizen rather than as deficient and dependent in some way or other.
Criminal justice should lead to "social justice," it was claimed; that is, a basic
standard of human rights that would lead to a more equitable and thereby
"just" society (American Friends Service Committee 1971). There was also
a demand for rights-based justice movement in prisons and the abolition of
parole in the work of David Fogel (1975).

It was out of these concerns that retribution began to make a comeback
to sentencing, albeit in something of a new guise. It underpinned the emergence of what became known as the "justice model" and just desserts theory,
which appeared as new ways of thinking about sentencing and punishment
in the mid-1970s, ultimately leading to the reinstatement of retribution as
an authentic response to crime. The most significant contribution to this
move was contained in the work of the Committee for the Study of Incarceration, which was published as Andrew von Hirsch's *Doing Justice* (1976).
As Gaylin and Rothman stated in their introduction, "Dessert has for some
time been in disrepute for many dismissed it as nothing but a polite term
for vengeance. This book distinguishes between vengeance and dessert ...
[but] dessert is a rich and important concept, grounded in ideas of fairness"
(xxix). What also concerned them was the apparent void in the sentencing
framework left by the collapse of the rehabilitative ideal: What should fill
this? This group chose to embrace "the seemingly harsh principle of 'just
desserts' ... certain things are simply wrong and ought to be punished"
(Gaylin and Rothman 1976: xxxvii). In the text itself, von Hirsch attempted
to find a legitimate place for punishment in modern penal arrangements,
thereby raising doubts about his and other desserts theorists' liberal creden-
tials among their critics (see, for example, Paternoster and Bynum 1982;

Orland 1978, many of whom conflated retribution/desserts with ven-geance/retaliation). Von Hirsch, however, made clear that although the "use of the old-fashioned word 'punishment' should be a reminder of the painful nature of criminal sanctions, whatever the claimed objectives are," there were important *limits* to the extent to which an offender might be punished (1976: 36). Not only should the length of prison sentences be "stringently rationed," but at the same time, "we favour minimum interference with confined offend-ers" (von Hirsch 1976: 113). The sanction should consist only of the depri-vation of the freedom to leave, and the rules governing inmates' behavior within institutions "should be limited to those necessary to secure their safe presence" (von Hirsch 1976: 115).

In effect, and in ideal type form, the just desserts model was a minimalist response to crime, not an overtly punitive one in the sense of harsher sen-tencing. Von Hirsch restated the retributivist position as follows: "The liberty of each individual, we assume, is to be protected so long as it is consistent with the liberty of others. We assume also that the state is obligated to observe strict parsimony in intervening in convicted offenders' lives" (1976: 5). What he was putting forward was a fairly orthodox Kantian position that justice had been satisfied once a convicted offender was convicted and punished according to these principles: The punishment was intended to be the end, and not a means to an end. He thus added, "We assume that the requirements of *justice* ought to constrain the pursuit of crime prevention" (von Hirsch 1976: 5). In opposition to the utilitarian argument that punishment should be used as a form of social defence, "a free society should recognize that an individual's rights are *prima facie* entitled to priority over collective interests" (von Hirsch 1976: 51; Rawls 1971).

Nonetheless, he rejected the term "retribution": In its present under-standing, it was thought to be both too narrow and too pejorative in terms of the way in which it had come to be thought. That is, it seemed to be locked into Biblical connotations of payback for wrong done in equal amounts. Instead, "desserts" was preferred, the term being "less emotionally loaded than retribution" (von Hirsch 1976: 46). It lent itself to a more straightfor-ward understanding: "The principle has its counterpart in common-sense notions of equity which people apply in their everyday lives. Sanctions dis-proportionate to the wrong are seen as manifestly unfair" (von Hirsch 1976: 69). In these respects, although the concepts of retribution and just desserts are largely synonymous, the latter term now becomes much more widely used than the former in penological discourse.

As to penalties themselves, these should be distributed or made com-mensurate with the seriousness of the offense and the number and serious-ness of previous convictions. The seriousness of the crime was to be judged on notions of harm and culpability. For example, "armed robbery is so much more serious than a burglary because the threatened harm is so much greater" (von Hirsch 1976: 79). As to the level of the penalty, this would depend on the internal composition of the scale of punishments—how offenses were to be punished in relation to each other (what von Hirsch and other desserts theorists refer to as the ordinal level of punishment); and its magnitude or cardinal level—that is, the scale's overall dimensions. In what is probably the weakest section of the book (just over six pages long), these very complex issues are dealt with in little more than commonsense terms; relying on a few opinion surveys of mainly criminal justice professionals, von Hirsch concluded, "Whatever the complexities in the concept of seriousness, such studies suggest that people from widely different walks of life can make common-sense judgments on the comparative gravity of offences and come to fairly similar conclusions" (1976). A further more plausible attempt was made to quantify "seriousness" in von Hirsch and Jareborg (1989): For them, crimes should be rated according to their effects on the victim's "living standard": The penalty would thus be imposed with reference to this quality-of-life assessment, but with a discount for a clean record prior to that point.

Although the punishment was to be tailored to the criminal act, the most significant concessions to this principle were in relation to the degree of the offender's culpability. Prior criminal record, rather than personality assessment, would be the yardstick of this, the idea being that the more extensive the criminal record, particularly for the same type of offense, the more the level of punishment should be intensified. On the other hand, the absence of a criminal record would serve to act as a restraint on the level of punishment to be imposed. Although some desserts theorists have argued that criminal record should not be considered at all (Singer 1979), here von Hirsch claimed to be recognizing human fallibility: "The reason for treating the first offence as less serious is that repetition alerts the degree of culpability that may be ascribed to the offender. In assessing a first offender's culpability, it ought to be borne in mind that he was ... only one of a large audience to whom the law impersonally addressed its prohibitions. His first caution, however, should call dramatically and personally to his attention that the behaviour is condemned" (1976: 66).

Such rigorous principles and consistency would necessitate a curtailment of judicial discretion, seen as having a large part to play in the widespread inconsistencies in sentencing then in existence. As such, von Hirsch proposed the development of general guidelines that would be able to define "the comparative gravity of different categories of crimes and specify the punishments which ordinarily apply to them" (1976: 99). Each crime category would be given a "presumptive sentence," that is, a specific penalty based on the crime's characteristic seriousness, with judges being authorized—within specified limits—to depart from the presumptive sentence if they found aggravating or mitigating circumstances. What we have here is the embryonic idea of sentencing guidelines, which were to become highly influential in the United States in particular (von Hirsch and Hanrahan 1981); von Hirsch and Ashworth (1998) wrote of twenty-three states that had some form of sentencing guidelines and, by implication, some injection of desserts thinking. These were later influential in Canada (Canadian Sentencing Commission 1987) and some European countries such as Sweden (von Hirsch and Jareborg 1989) and England (in relation to its Criminal Justice Act 1991). Just desserts theory was also influential in various initiatives to go "back to justice" in the juvenile justice arena in Britain and the United States in the late 1970s and early 1980s.

Yet at the same time, it was as if the idea was being put forward that sentencing could be developed in some kind of ideological vacuum; social influences on criminal behavior—deprivation, inequality, and so on—would be excluded from consideration: "A sentencing system may simply not be capable of compensating for the social ills of the wider society ... as long as a substantial segment of the population is denied adequate opportunities for a livelihood, any scheme for punishing must be morally flawed. At least under desserts, impoverished defendants would be punished no more than affluent defendants" (von Hirsch 1976: 147–8). The important point, then, was the intention that defendants would now be punished for the offense they had committed and not for their background.

As to the form punishment should take, there was certainly a preoccupation in this text (which was to have unforeseen consequences, as will be discussed later) with the place of prison in the sentencing process. At that time, of course, this institution was the source of major conflict in the United States (and elsewhere), justifying the focus of attention given to it. However, von Hirsch also argued for alternatives to custody, including "warnings," "unconditional release," and "intermittent confinement" (1976: 119). Probation was rejected because this dealt with future conduct rather than past crime. He was ambivalent about fines, because it would be difficult to impose them even-handedly: Inevitably, a fine on one offender would impose more or less pain on another.

Doing Justice proved to have a wide-ranging influence. In the United States, a number of states moved almost immediately from indeterminate sentencing to some version of the justice model. For example, in California, the Uniform Determinate Sentencing Law of 1976 prescribed fixed prison terms for felonies and abolished parole; the offender was to serve the full sentence of imprisonment with "good time" deductions up to one-third the sentence; the length of imprisonment was to be proportionate to the seriousness of the crime. In Minnesota, the research that von Hirsch, Knapp, and Tonry (1987) undertook found that judges' sentencing up to that point had been based more on prior record than the current offense. To replace it, the Minnesota Sentencing Committee devised its guidelines so that those convicted of serious offenses would go to prison (even without a prior record); relatively minor offenders, even with a lengthy record, would not.

Just desserts was clearly an idea whose time had come. It was greeted eagerly by many policymakers, legislators, and academic commentators searching for new ways of justifying punishment, necessitated by the collapse of faith in the rehabilitative ideal. In these respects, and whatever their philosophical differences, the retributive just desserts now sat alongside deterrence and incapacitation, without too much discomfort, it seemed, at least according to contemporary critics: Punishment was at the core of these three differing aims and objectives. Von Hirsch and other desserts theorists were (mistakenly) categorized with incapacitation theorists such as James Q. Wilson (1975) and deterrence theorists such as Ernest van den Haag (1975) on the basis of their common interest (Orland 1978: 32). In contrast to these other two philosophies, however, von Hirsch and other retributivists were concerned primarily with "making penalties more just" (von Hirsch and Hanrahan 1981: 29). On this basis, and in contrast to deterrence and incapacitation, where punishment beyond the gravity of the offense would be used as a means to achieve other ends, the severity of punishment "should comport with the blameworthiness of the offender's criminal conduct" (von Hirsch and Hanrahan 1981: 29).

The distinction between retributivist just desserts and utilitarian incapacitation was further addressed by von Hirsch (1985). By this juncture, incapacitation had gathered momentum, fuelled by new claims about the power to predict dangerousness (Monahan 1982). Indeed, Morris and Miller (1985) argued for the place of predictive assessments of dangerousness within a desserts framework, with such a judgment being allowed to intensify or extend the punishment. However, von Hirsch (1985) was firmly opposed to any intrusion of prediction on the just desserts principle, for both what he claimed was the lack of scientific validity for such predictions and also the ethical concerns regarding punishment for future crimes that the concept of incapacitation entailed. At the same time, in a modification to his own work on retributive desserts, he was now prepared to abandon the idea of desserts as "righting" the moral imbalance brought about by criminal conduct, as if the commission of a crime represented some kind of unfair advantage that the offender had gained over law-abiding citizens. Obviously, not all crime does lead to this. Instead, he now favored the idea of "censure" to justify punishment: "Penalties should comport with the seriousness of crimes, so that the reprobation visited on an offender through the penalty fairly reflects the blameworthiness of the conduct" (von Hirsch 1985: 59).

The concept of censure was further expanded by von Hirsch (1993). He again emphasized that a penal sanction is meant to convey disapproval of crime: For this to happen, it must impose some deprivation on the offender as a way of expressing this. Now, however, punishment is not seen solely as an issue between the state and the offender. The concept of censure also addresses victims, by acknowledging that they have been wronged through another person's culpable acts (von Hirsch 1993: 10). In these respects, some deterrent and, therefore, utilitarian purpose to penal law is admitted: "The criminal sanction announces in advance that specified categories of conduct are punishable ... censure embodied in the prescribed sanction serves to appeal to people's sense of conduct's wrongfulness, as a reason for desistance" (von Hirsch 1993: 11). Penal law can thus provide both normative and prudential reasons for conformity. Ultimately, though, for retributivists, punishment's "blaming function" should have primacy (von Hirsch 1993: 13).

Overall, perhaps the clearest statement of the retributivist/desserts position is set out in von Hirsch and Ashworth: "A dessert theorist is someone who claims that the seriousness of crimes should, on the grounds of justice, be the chief determinant of the quantum of punishment" (1998: 141).

11.5   How Do Retributive Sanctions Serve a Retributive Purpose?

As we have seen, retributivism has long been associated not simply with the *lex talionis* "eye for an eye" concept, but also with punishments that convey outright vengeance—that is to say, they may take a retaliatory form that far exceeds the harm caused by the crime itself. What has also been suggested, though, is that this is a very mistaken understanding of retribution. Retribution is essentially a *limiting* principle. Extrapolating from this, we can argue that retributivism does not allow for "cruel and unusual punishments" and punishments that are radically disproportionate to the seriousness of the conduct criminalized. In these respects, retributivist arguments helped to bring about a moratorium on the death penalty in the United States. In *Furman v. Georgia* (1972: 296–7), the Supreme Court, finding that this sanction was being used in an arbitrary and capricious way, declared it unconstitutional.

By the same token, other punishments to the human body would be offensive to retributivist principles because of their "direct assault on dignity" (cf. Kant)—the degrading spectacle of corporal punishment, for example, now prohibited under the European Convention on Human Rights and under the provisions of the British Human Rights Act 1998. At the same time, retributivists have been highly critical of current utilitarian incapacitatory penal trends. Von Hirsch and Ashworth argued that "measures which most clearly call for tougher sanctions tend to utilize criteria inconsistent with proportionality: mandatory sentences ... select particular offence categories of harsh treatment without regard to the gravity of the offence, or penalties for other offences" (1998: 142). On this basis, retributivists could have no truck with the U.S. "three strikes" laws, which are directed exclusively at the cumulative effect of a past record and may be out of all proportion to the particular offense that achieved the third strike; hence, the consternation that sentencing to a mandatory twenty-five-year minimum term for such crimes as stealing a slice of pizza—a third strike—have brought about. By the same token, the sexual predator laws in the United States could have no place in a retributivist's penal repertoire. These laws provide for indefinite confinement in a mental institution on completion of a finite term of imprisonment for the initial offense if one is judged to be a sexual predator. They are clearly based on one's likely future conduct in addition to the crime that has been committed.

What sanctions, then, are thought appropriate by today's retributivists, and how should they be ranked in terms of severity on any sentencing tariff? Retributivists recognize that imprisonment is almost certainly going to be more severe than noncustodial penalties and that its severity can be assessed by its duration (von Hirsch 1985: 209). As Wasik and von Hirsch suggested, "A punishment is ranked as more severe when it is characteristically experienced as being more onerous by its recipients" (1988: 564). Indeed, they propose a "discomfort index" to assess the severity of punishments—doubtless to run in parallel with the standard of living index, against which levels of victimization can be assessed. Nonetheless, imprisonment should not only be the maximum penalty, but for most retributivists, with their emphasis on parsimony, it should also be a punishment of last resort (Singer 1979).

At the same time, the determination of both imprisonment and nonincarcerative sanctions should be short so as to minimize the pain inflicted, because, for retributivists, unnecessary pain is to be avoided. It should be emphasized as well that there should be no indeterminate prison sentences and, similarly, no open-ended community-based orders. On noncustodial penalties, Singer wrote that these "must be punitive; if they are not, there will be a loss of proportionality between those who receive imprisonment and those who do not, and there will be a loss of public support when those who have committed offences are essentially released to the community without punishment" (1979: 48). Indeed, this is what happened to many noncustodial sanctions in the English criminal justice system in the 1980s (Pratt 1987). They then developed a tendency to have their own built-in sanctions for transgressions, which led to a huge growth in administrative (and secret) justice. Although this would no doubt be anathema to retributivists, such developments are perhaps an inevitable by-product of the attempt to make noncustodial sanctions more punitive. They represent some of the problems that exist in the space between the theory of just desserts and the practical realities of implementing appropriate penalties.

For the purposes of current sentencing, however, community service is judged to be the most serious noncustodial penalty: "It is now settled by appellate decision [in England] that community service is primarily an alternative to a sentence of immediate custody and hence assumes a high place in the tariff" (Wasik and von Hirsch 1988: 569). This can be followed by periodic and intermittent confinement; for example, attendance center orders, as these are halfway between noncustody and full custody. Where would home detention fit on this range? There is some ambiguity about this. On the one hand, it could be argued that because this can be extremely controlling and provide effective incarceration within the home, it should be the next most serious penalty after imprisonment. On the other, because offenders are not deprived of home comforts, it might be thought it should come below periodic detention and intermittent confinement. In most jurisdictions, however, it is high on the tariff as an alternative to custody sentence (although there also seems to be a growing tendency for it to be used administratively as a form of early release from prison).

In this ideal retributivist scale of punishments, the next place on the tariff would be the fine, midrange in seriousness. Wasik and von Hirsch argued that unit fines should be computed as a percentage of disposable income, thereby ensuring that the intended amount of pain to be delivered would be equally felt by its recipients (1988: 566). In effect, those with a high income should pay more than those with a lower, to ensure a similar distribution of pain through punishment. This idea was introduced to the desserts-influenced English Criminal Justice Act 1991, with disastrous consequences and outraged criticism from the mass media, judges, and magistrates. What was expected was one level of fine for all (Moxon 1997). The provision was quickly abandoned (as were two further retributivist components of the act: one that limited the number of current convictions to be taken into account in ordering punishment, and another that limited the relevance of prior records to when sentences were being considered) (Wasik 1997).

Wasik and von Hirsch (1988) argued for the place of absolute discharges for the least serious offenses. They are ambivalent about the role of probation in their model, arguing that the various conditions of a probation order might be able to constitute the offender's penalty ("it seems clear to us that probation may be more or less severe depending on the regime imposed") (Wasik and von Hirsch 1988: 569). What they seem to be suggesting, then, is that probation would primarily be a penalty of surveillance and coercion. It would presumably be stripped of what still remains of its traditional "advise, assist, and befriend" role, because this is meant to benefit offenders, not censure and punish them (the essence of retributivism and just desserts). There are also contemporary penalties that do not fit their model. These include the suspended sentence of imprisonment. Although this certainly has a high place on the penal tariff in the jurisdictions where it has been introduced, for retributivists it is impossible to justify. Not only does the offender suffer no special immediate deprivations, but the sentence itself is hinged around how the offender will behave in the future—which should not feature in the sanction. The same might also be said for conditional discharges.

What do retributivists make of restorative justice? Andrew Ashworth (2002) has provided one of the most cogent critical examinations of this phenomenon. He made the point that it is important not to deprive offenders of safeguards and rights that should be assured in any processes that impose obligations as a consequence of crime. Of course, in restorative justice, there seems to be an emphasis on blurring the legal requirements and principles necessary in the formal criminal justice system in nonlegal settings. As such, it would seem that rights, safeguards, and certainly proportionality in punishments would seem to be greatly at risk: Many restorative justice theorists prefer not to talk of crime and punishment, but instead of harms and redress. Inevitably, it would seem that retributivism and restorative justice are simply not compatible.

11.6   The Advantages and Disadvantages of Retribution and Just Desserts

Ashworth (1989) provided a general overview of the advantages of this approach to sentencing. First, it provides coherence in the sentencing system. The rise of just desserts has undoubtedly served to focus attention on systematic structuring as an integral part of sentencing. It thus represents a challenge to the "cafeteria" approach, whereby judges could choose any one of a range of options then available on the menu—as if sentences could be awarded according to the personal predilection of the judge. In these respects, it has the potential to significantly curtail judicial discretion, or at least ensure that it is exercised in a principled manner. Second, retributivism/just desserts promotes certainty and consistency. This not only recognizes the right of each offender to equal concern and respect, but also tends to enhance public acceptability of a sentencing system, as compared with one that seems to be a lottery, or which is very opaque and leads to the manifest unfairness frequently associated with individualized sentencing. At the same time, although mitigating and aggravating factors might be allowed in determining the punishment to be imposed (for example, presence or absence of a prior record), what are excluded from this model are discriminatory factors: So long as they can be shown to possess the requisite *mens rea*, all will be treated equally—they will receive the punishment their crime deserves. Third, retribution/just desserts provides a coherent rationale for punishment in opposition to current emphases on deterrence and incapacitation. And we might add that, fourth, rather than view criminals as sick or deficient citizens, or completely beyond redemption, as incapacitation theorists would argue, they are regarded as rational, competent subjects with rights and responsibilities by desserts scholars. Nonetheless, modern retributivists are prepared to recognize their own shortcomings. In particular, in setting cardinal levels of punishment, there is no clear notion as to how this might be achieved—save for the fact that von Hirsch and others have always argued in favor of reductions in the severity of penal sanctions.

However, critical scholarship extraneous to retributivism/desserts theory has raised four main concerns. First, as Cullen and Gilbert (1982) and also Hudson (1987) have argued, the impact of these ideas was to effectively remove a treatment ethos in the sentencing framework that had never really been practiced, or had never been given sufficient resources in which it could be put into effect. Whatever the merits and demerits of rehabilitation, whatever the extent it was practiced, the retributivist critique of it helped to limit the scope of humanitarianism and leniency that was associated with it. The just desserts-influenced critique largely focused on its coercive possibilities. In reality, some of the sanctions that rehabilitation fostered, such as probation, may often have meant very little other than cursory visits and meandering conversations between probation officer and client (Cicourel 1968). A strong argument could undoubtedly be made against this—it brings the sentencing system into disrepute and so on—but it could also have helped to legitimate a very lenient approach to crime. Given what is known about the dangers of over-reacting to it, courtesy of labelling theorists, this would seem to be no bad thing. However, just desserts signalled an end not just to treatment but also to the "romantic tolerance extended to deviants in a society" (Hudson 1987: 59). Instead of tolerance, treatment, and rehabilitation, we were meant to have proportionality and determinacy, with the liberal intent of limiting and restricting the scope and quantity of punishment. Instead, as just desserts began to make its impact in the United States in the early 1980s, "this coincided with the biggest single year rise [in 1981] in the prison population since 1925" (Hudson 1987: 63). And, of course, the prison population has continued to rise exponentially since then. As Cullen and Gilbert warned, "The 'barebones' of determinacy and desserts are as easily adaptable to the program of 'getting tough on crime' [as] to one of doing justice" (1982: 200).

Although it is certainly mistaken to conflate just desserts with incapacitation and deterrence, there seems little doubt, as Greenberg and Humphrey

(1980) noted, that "the state simply employs the vocabulary of just desserts to legitimate traditional sentencing patterns." What now seems clear is that rehabilitation has at least been able to provide a barrier to political debate on sentencing: It was populated by human sciences experts whose knowledge occluded the whole subject (Davies 1985). Although desserts theorists helped to demystify this with their critique, and render sentencing more accessible to the general public, it also laid it open to political influences. Davies thus wrote that in California, "even before determinate sentencing law reforms were introduced in 1977 there were amendments to them. The tendency to amend the determinate sentencing legislation has been continuous and mainly in one direction, towards tougher sentencing involving both longer and more mandatory prison terms" (1985: 16).

More generally, it would seem that unless there is a sentencing commission (which then, for all intents and purposes, hands back this arena to a new set of experts), principles of proportionality are hard to achieve, as ad hoc prison terms will be determined politically, with no overall coordination of the relevant seriousness of all offenses. More generally, it would appear that desserts-inspired reforms have a tendency to be incorporated into incapacitatory and deterrent sentencing policies. Even von Hirsch and Ashworth conceded that as the desserts principle has become adulterated as a result of the renewed popularity of deterrence and incapacitation, the model has lost its ideological prominence (1998). Hudson thus argued that desserts ideas have become just one component of neoconservative drives towards a minimalist state, with its responsibilities and obligations greatly pared down (1987: 58). Von Hirsch (1993) countered, however, by illustrating that desserts theory is not confined to societies where the political right has held sway. It has been influential in Sweden and Finland, two countries still strongly committed to welfarism (despite some retraction of this in the former). That may be so. There is no inevitability to the link between desserts and the political Right—but at the same time, and certainly as regards the United States, this may well eventuate.

Second, if there is to be proportionality between crime and punishment, then how can the prison be used in this way, given that the pains of crime and the pains of imprisonment (which do not feature at all in just desserts discourse—instead, it is as if the formal aims and objectives of imprisonment are seen as its reality) are simply not comparable (Mathieson 1990)? Is there any proportionality, for example, between the crime of murder and the punishment of a life sentence without parole in a maximum security prison? Is such a living death proportionate to the killing that preceded it? Indeed, it is now acknowledged by desserts theorists that initially their work paid too much attention to the sanction of imprisonment and neglected to explore how community-based sanctions could be used retributively (Wasik and von

Hirsch 1988). Although this is understandable, given the context out of which just desserts emerged, it also ensured that in subsequent developments of just desserts theory, particularly in the United States, much of the ensuing discussions were centered around the prison, thereby legitimizing it rather than fostering alternatives to it.

Third, desserts theory has been criticized because it has little to say about upper-class crimes, which may often not come to formal attention because of in-built class biases within the criminal justice system, while it sanctions the overpunishment of lower-class criminals (Greenberg and Humphries 1980). Equally, race and gender issues are ignored in favor of abstract moral preoccupations with the conduct of individual offenders (Hudson 1987). Indeed, it is as if retributivism is itself based on a "gentleman's club picture of the relationship between man and society" (Braithwaite 1982). The rules of criminal justice are treated as the rules of such an establishment (indeed, the same people probably make both sets!). There is an assumption that there is a consensus that all agree to, and that all are rational, responsible citizens who would normally be committed to these rules, having been given the same opportunities on life's supposedly level playing field. And yet if retributivists were able to consider the personal circumstances of most criminal justice rule breakers (which they are not able to do), then it would quickly become apparent that there is no level playing field.

Such matters have been taken further by Braithwaite (1982) and Braithwaite and Pettit (1990). If punishment is to be proportionate to the gravity of crime, then it is clear that there should be more white-collar criminals in prison than "common criminals." Not only, Braithwaite argued, is the harm of white-collar crime usually incalculably greater than common crime, but in addition, relying on survey evidence, many people think that this is the most serious type of crime (1982). But the courts are then left with the dilemma of whom to prosecute—the individual or the corporation. To make individuals responsible might be unfair (and they may not have the necessary *mens rea*). And yet if the corporation is prosecuted, the effects of sanctions (such as closure of the firm) will be felt much further afield. The dilemma is resolved, he argued, by regulators employing "extra-legal muscle flexing" (that is, instead of prosecuting, they issue warnings, make follow-up visits, and so on). This gives the public protection from white-collar crime. What this means, however, is that where dessert is greatest, punishment will be the least. In these respects, "Kantian retribution is a philosophical theory which may be formally correct, but materially incorrect" (Braithwaite 1982: 756). Furthermore, because the most serious types of crime are dealt with the most leniently, then "retribution is incapable of dealing with the [crime] complexities of modern society" (Braithwaite and Petit 1990: 182). In this latter text, the authors pressed the case for more utilitarian approaches to all types of crime, based on the selective enforcement principle that regulates the prosecution of corporate crime. They went on to criticize the way in which public intolerance of such activities is effectively thwarted because "dessert theorists rely on sentencing commissions of jurisprudence experts rather than public opinion." In other words, retributivists are both elitist and in collaboration with powerful forces that keep control of the criminal justice system in such a way that it suits the interests of the wealthy and punishes the poor. There should thus be more "community values" reflected in criminal justice and sentencing because "when the community comes to believe that criminal justice is something best left to experts, there is a risk they will neglect denunciatory obligations which are in their hands as citizens" (Braithwaite and Petit 1990: 162).

Against this, von Hirsch and Ashworth (1992) argued that it is because of a shared sense that typical crimes are wrong that a response is called for that testifies to their wrongfulness. The formal criminal justice system is thus a way of unifying otherwise fragmented communities and affirming moral values against crime. (It might be added that one of the reasons why there is so much white-collar crime is surely that its perpetrators think that, under current enforcement processes, nothing much is going to happen to them even if they get caught.) Furthermore, proportionality would seem to be an implicit requirement of justice in sentencing. When penalties are substantial, usually on utilitarian grounds of deterrence or incapacitation, then, far from condoning severe punishments, the idea of dessert becomes a particularly important constraint. Does the criminal justice system punish the poor, but not the rich? Retributivists focus on punishing crime, not the criminal: Sentencing cannot compensate for social ills (von Hirsch 1993). As to the unequal-playing-field argument that is raised against retribution, then simply "a modern state should be capable of alleviating poverty and social disorganization" (von Hirsch 1993: 97).

However, it could no doubt be argued that, over the last twenty years or so, many modern states have been in the business of actually creating such problems, and that to continue to proclaim the political neutrality of sentencing while this has taken place is akin to Nero fiddling while Rome burns. On the other hand, it may well be that the proof is in the pudding, so to speak. In the United States, one of states with a relatively low rate of incarceration—Minnesota at 300 per 100,000 of population, when the national rate is 737—is the one that seems to have bought most strongly into desserts theory and sentencing commissions (von Hirsch 1993). From this example, sentencing commissions may well provide a barrier to public opinion and influence in this area—an extremely punitive public, not the benevolent, vigilant-against-social-injustices one that seems to inform the work of Braithwaite, and a public whose sentiments are not themselves value free but which are shaped and fuelled by the mass media. For anyone with liberal values, such sentiments are best kept out of the sentencing process, rather than allowed to influence it.

Finally, many critical criminologists and Marxist criminologists level a fourth major criticism of retributivism and desserts theory. That is to say, how is it possible to have justice—which is what retributivists and desserts theorists purport to bring—in an unjust society? In an unjust society, there can only ever be unjust, not just, desserts (Clarke 1978). As Murphy put the matter, "If we think that institutions of punishment are necessary and desirable, and if we are morally sensitive enough to want to be sure that we have the moral right to punish before we inflict it, then we had better first make sure that we have restructured society in such a way that criminals genuinely do correspond to the only model that will render punishment permissible—i.e., make sure that they are autonomous and that they do benefit in the requisite sense" (1979: 110).

How, though, are we meant to respond to criminality in the meantime? And which society has—indeed has ever had—a sufficient quantum of justice within it to prevent it from being classified as an unjust society? For Marxists, the answer to this question would no doubt be Marxist societies, notwithstanding the collapse of at least the Eastern bloc version of this doctrine in Europe in the 1990s, and the manifest injustices that Marxism allowed to be carried out in the criminal justice systems of those countries. However, there really does not seem to be much point in indulging in such utopian niceties. At least, in the manner of Durkheim, retributivism can offer a necessary and proportionate response to law-breaking meantime, and is one that has the potential, at least, to provide respect for law and encourage conformity to it. By the same token, at present, retributivism/desserts theory offers a viable counterweight to the utilitarian forces of deterrence and incapacitation that have become so influential in formal criminal justice systems over the last decade or so and help guard against the erosion of fundamental rights of due process and proportionate punishment that restorative justice threatens to bring about in the informal criminal justice system.

11.7 Retaliation

As has been implied, retaliation as a kind of vengeance for crime largely disappeared during the development of modern society. Whatever vengeful feelings and desires to retaliate that victims might have had against those who offended against them, these, were meant to be assuaged and sublimated by the state's criminal justice system. Before the nineteenth century, of course, retaliation, whether by individuals or whole communities, was a frequent occurrence. Although it might take the form of violent revenge, it could also take the form of one of a range of activities (for example, carnivalesque parades known as *chari-vari*) designed to shame and drive away local offenders and troublemakers. Nor would retaliation be confined to law-breaking. Among upper-class men, duelling was a way of resolving disputes, particularly if aspersions had been cast upon one's honor. This would then be played out according to an elaborate and highly codified etiquette (Andrew 1980). Essentially, however, the challenge to a duel *had to be* taken up, otherwise one risked being "posted"—labeled a coward in the press or in some other form of community notice, with one's reputation forever shamed and ruined.

By mid-nineteenth century, however, such activities had more or less disappeared from modern societies. There are a number of reasons for this. First, the role played by middle-class elites in changing public attitudes towards retaliatory conduct (public shaming punishments and other public displays of violence, cruelty, excessive celebration, and so on had become increasingly distasteful to prominent opinion formers such as Charles Dickens and John Stuart Mill); second, social structural changes such as industrialization and changing labor practices made informal retaliatory practices impractical and impotent; third, the growth of the central state's monopolistic power to punish and its channelling of punitive sentiment through its bureaucratic organizations of government hastened the decline in informal retaliatory responses to crime.

The only significant exception to this pattern, at least in the modern English-speaking world, was to be found in the Deep South of the United States. Until the 1950s, extreme forms of retaliatory punishments were made in that region almost exclusively by whites on blacks. These could include the most horrific lynchings or other kinds of vigilante activities, most notably by the Ku Klux Klan (Southern Commission on the Study of Lynching 1931). Although ostensibly such retaliation was directed at individual black offenders, lynchings and vigilantism were not dependent on an offense having been committed, but could be directed against troublesome or seemingly truculent blacks or just happen spontaneously. Most usually, entire white communities would be involved in these activities—they were not practices confined to a deviant few. What was it, though, that allowed such activities to happen in that region but nowhere else in the English-speaking world? First, the absence of a strong state authority (in numerous lynchings, sheriffs would often hand over victims to a clamoring mob for fear of their own lives) seemingly gave free rein to these outpourings of local community sentiments. Second, such activities reaffirmed white solidarity and were a demonstration of its residual power and the possibilities of resistance to a central state authority that seemed to have no legitimacy in that region in the postbellum period. Third, the extraordinary brutality that the retaliation took not only locked the participants together in their anger but, at the same time, the more brutal the occasion became, the stronger the symbol of defiance it seemed against the despised central state authority.

By mid-twentieth century, though, such activities had largely disappeared, and the Deep South, like the rest of the modern English-speaking world, had no place for retaliation in its responses to crime. The reasons for its cessation had been, first, growing power of the central state authorities and a dilution of homogeneous Southern cultural values brought about by modernization and industrialization. Second, local elites, as in the nineteenth century in other regions, began to speak out about such offensive behavior and gained publicity and a wide audience through modern communication processes. Here too, then, the formal criminal justice system of the state began to act as a funnel through which retaliatory tendencies would be channelled (as lynchings declined in the 1930s, so state executions increased).

More generally, if the commitment to retribution as the dominant aim of sentencing for part of the nineteenth century had seemed to convey some common ground between the state and community sentiment about punishment, by the mid-twentieth, the trend towards rehabilitation and individualized punishment brought about a cleavage between bureaucratic expertise through which penal policy was now largely developed, and commonsensical and emotive public opinion excluded from it. As has been seen, however, this bubble burst in the early 1970s. Retribution re-emerged alongside deterrence and incapacitation as the main competing aims and objectives of sentencing. They have been joined in recent years, however, by a renewal of retaliatory activities outside of the formal criminal justice system (Johnston 1996; West 1998).

Most typically, this takes the form of vigilante-type activities, targeting and then inflicting punishment (usually of a shaming and humiliating nature) on known or suspected offenders (Girling, Loader, and Sparks 1998). One of the most widespread outbreaks (egged on by a section of the mass media) took place in England in the summer of 2000 (Pratt 2001). A brutal child-murder provided the spark for what became a conflagration, as vigilante groups up and down the country targeted suspected pedophiles, or even in some cases pediatricians: A similarity in the suffix was enough to brand them. Here again, then, such retaliatory activities can have a far wider orbit than retributive sanctions against a given offender. In these actions, no new offense had been committed by the targets of the vigilante groups. Indeed, many had committed no offense at all. However, there are no fixed parameters to retaliation (unlike retribution), no limits to the forms it might take.

11.8   Conclusions

Why is it, though, that at the present time, we should see such a resurgence of these practices, long since thought to have disappeared from modern societies? To understand this, we need to go back to the reasons for the disappearance of retaliatory punishments in the nineteenth century. The factors that brought this about now seem to be unravelling. First, we are currently living through a period when the authority of the central state has been in sharp decline, allied to the collapse of faith in its bureaucratic organizations of government: in criminal justice, no less than elsewhere (Garland 1996). Second, the dramatic social structural changes of the post-1970s period, which have weakened some of the foundational arrangements of modern society itself, have generated a profound sense of anxiety and insecurity (Bauman 2001). Third, these sentiments find outlet through the mass media and help to engender a new culture of penal intolerance and demands for greater public involvement in sentencing (Garland 2001).

In many English-speaking countries, there have been a range of measures introduced that provide for more community involvement in penal affairs—plebiscites, for example, in the United States, and community notification procedures regarding the release of sex offenders from prison. Even so, such measures may still not be enough to contain the public mood, disillusioned as it is by the state's self-divestment of authority and acknowledgment that its own bureaucracies were never particularly effective anyway.

Under such circumstances, it may well be that some citizens look towards their own forms of retaliation for perceived harms rather than putting their trust in the criminal justice system of the state to address them. Thus, whereas retributivists struggle to contain inflammatory penal trends in the formal criminal justice system at the present time, retaliation against perceived harms and wrongs breaks out beyond it. Retributions comeback seems to have faded. It has been outflanked by the shifts towards deterrence and incapacitation, by restorative justice and vigilante attacks. Nonetheless, what it represents is the last stand of jucidical expertise and rationality in an era when emotive forces and intolerance have become influential on sentencing processes.

References

American Friends Service Committee. 1971. *Struggle for Justice: A Report on Crime and Punishment in America*. New York: Hill & Wang.

Andrew, D. 1980. The code of honour and its critics: The opposition to duelling in England 1700-1850. *Social History* 5, 409.

Ashworth, A. 1989. Criminal justice and deserved sentences. *The Criminal Law Review* 340.

Ashworth, A. 2002. Responsibilities, rights and restorative justice. *British Journal of Criminology* 42, 578.

Bauman, Z. 2001. *Liquid Modernity*. Cambridge: Sage.

Beccaria, C. 1764, 1963. *On Crimes and Punishments.*, trans. H. Paolucci. Indianapolis: Bobbs-Merrill.

Bosanquet, B. 1918. *Some Suggestions in Ethics.* London: Macmillan and Co., 189.

Bradley, F. 1876. *Ethical Studies.* London: Oxford University Press, 27.

Braithwaite, J. 1982. Challenging just desserts: punishing white-collar criminals. *The Journal of Criminal Law & Criminology* 73, 723.

Braithwaite, J., and P. Pettit. 1990. *Not Just Desserts: A Republican Theory of Criminal Justice.* Oxford: Clarendon Press.

Canadian Sentencing Commission. 1987 *Sentencing Reform: A Canadian Approach.* Ottawa: Ministry of Supply and Services.

Cicourel, A. 1968. *The Social Organization of Juvenile Justice.* New York: Wiley.

Clarke, D. H. 1978. Marxism, justice and the justice model. *Contemporary Crises* 2, 27.

Cooper, D. E. 1971. Hegel's Theory of Punishment. In *Hegel's Political Philosophy Problems and Perspectives*, ed. Z. A. Pelczynski. Cambridge: Cambridge University Press, 163.

Cross, R., and A. Ashworth. 1981. *The English Sentencing System*, 3rd ed. London: Butterworths, 130.

Cullen, F. T., and K. E. Gilbert. 1982. *Reaffirming Rehabilitation.* Cincinnati: Anderson.

Davies, M. 1985. Determinate sentencing reform in California and its impact on the penal system. *The British Journal of Criminology* 25, 1.

Dession, G. 1937-38. Psychiatry and the conditioning of criminal justice. *Yale Law Journal* 47, 319.

Duff, R. A. 1986. *Trials and Punishments.* Cambridge: Cambridge University Press.

Fogel, D. 1975. *We Are the Living Proof: The Justice Model for Corrections.* Cincinnati: Anderson.

Foucault, M. 1979. *Discipline and Punish: The Birth of the Prison*, trans. A. Sheridan. Harmondsworth, U.K.: Penguin Books.

Friedman, L. 1972. *Crime and Punishment in American History.* New York: Basic Books, 63.

Furman v. Georgia. 1972. 408 US 238, 296-7.

Garland, D. 1996. The limits of the sovereign state: Strategies of crime control on contemporary society. *British Journal of Criminology* 36, 445.

Garland, D. 2001. *The Culture of Control.* Oxford: Oxford University Press.

Gaylin, W., and D. Rothman. 1976. Introduction. In *Doing Justice: The Choice of Punishments*, ed. A. von Hirsch. New York: A. Hill and Wang, xxix.

Girling, E., I. Loader, and R. Sparks. 1998. A telling tale: A case of vigilantism and its aftermath in an English town. *British Journal of Sociology* 49, 474.

Glover, E. 1956. *Probation and Re-education.* London: Routledge & Paul, 267.

Greenberg, D., and D. Humphries. 1980. The cooptation of fixed sentencing. *Crime & Delinquency* 26, 206.

Hart, H. L. A. 1968. *Punishment and Responsibility: Essays in the Philosophy of Law.* Clarendon: Clarendon Press.

Hegel, G. 1821, 1952. *Philosophy of Right*, trans. T. M. Knox. Oxford: Clarendon Press, 69.

Honderich, T. 1984. *Punishment: The Supposed Justifications.* Harmondsworth, U.K.: Penguin Books.

Hudson, B. 1987. *Justice Through Punishment: A Critique of the Justice Model of Corrections.* New York: St. Martin's Press.

Johnston, L. 1996. What is vigilantism? *British Journal of Criminology* 40, 127.

Kant, I. 1797, 1965. *The Metaphysical Elements of Justice*, trans. J. Ladd. Indianapolis: Bobbs-Merrill, 331.

Mabbott, J. D. 1956. Freewill and punishment. In *Contemporary British Philosophy*, ed. H. D. Lewis, 301. London: George Allen & Unwin.

Martinson, R. 1974. What works? Questions and answers about prison reform. *The Public Interest* 35, 22.

Martinson, R. 1978. New findings, new views: A note of caution regarding sentencing reform. *Hofstra Law Review* 7, 242.

Mathieson, T. 1990. *Prison on Trial: A Critical Assessment.* London: Sage.

Mitford, J. 1974. *Kind and Usual Punishment: The Prison Business.* New York: Vintage Books.

Monahan, J. 1982. The case for prediction in the modified dessert model of criminal sentencing. *International Journal of Law and Psychiatry* 5, 103.

Morris, N., and M. Miller. 1985. Predictions of dangerousness. *Crime and Justice: A Review of Research* 6, 1.

Moxon, D. 1997. England abandons unit fines. In *Sentencing Reform in Overcrowded Times: A Comparative Perspective*, ed. M. Tonry and K. Hatlestad. Oxford: Oxford University Press.

Murphy, J. 1979. *Retribution, Justice, and Therapy.* Boston: D. Reidel, 110.

Orland, L. 1978. From vengeance to vengeance: Sentencing reform and the demise of rehabilitation. *Hofstra Law Review* 7, 29.

Paternoster, R., and T. Bynum. 1982. The justice model as ideology: A critical look at the impetus for sentencing reform. *Contemporary Crises* 6, 7.

Pollens, B. 1938. *The Sex Criminal.* New York: The Macaulay Company, 36.

Pratt, J. 1987. Dilemmas of the alternative to custody concept. *Australian and New Zealand Journal of Criminology* 20, 148.

Pratt, J. 2001. Beyond "Gulags Westernstyle"? A reconsideration of Nils Christie's crime control as industry. *Theoretical Criminology* 5, 283.

Rawls, J. 1971. *A Theory of Justice.* Cambridge: Harvard University Press.

Saleilles, R. 1911. *Individualisation of Punishment*, trans. R. S. Jastrow. Boston: Little Brown, 8.

Singer, R. 1979. *Just Desserts: Sentencing Based on Equality and Dessert*. Cambridge: Ballinger.

Southern Commission on the Study of Lynching. 1931. *Lynchings and What They Mean: General Findings of the Southern Commission on the Study of Lynching*. Atlanta: The Commission.

Szasz, T. 1971. *The Manufacture of Madness: A Comparative Study of the Inquisition and the Mental Health Movement*. London: Routledge and Kegan Paul.

van den Haag, E. 1975. *Punishing Criminals: Concerning a Very Old and Painful Question*. New York: Basic Books.

von Hirsch, A. 1976. *Doing Justice: The Choice of Punishments*. New York: Hill and Wang.

von Hirsch, A. 1985. *Past or Future Crimes: Deservedness and Dangerousness in the Sentencing of Criminals*. New Brunswick, NJ: Rutgers University Press.

von Hirsch, A. 1993. *Censure and Sanctions*. Oxford: Clarendon Press.

von Hirsch, A., and A. Ashworth. 1992. Not just desserts: A response to Braithwaite and Petit. Oxford Journal of Legal Studies 12, 83.

von Hirsch, A., and A. Ashworth. 1998. *Principled Sentencing*, 2nd ed. Oxford: Hart Publishing, 141.

von Hirsch, A., and K. Hanrahan. 1981. Determinate penalty systems in America: An overview. *Crime & Delinquency* 27, 289.

von Hirsch, A., and N. Jareborg. 1989. Sweden's sentencing statute enacted. *The Criminal Law Review* 275.

von Hirsch, A., K. A. Knapp, and M. Tonry, M. 1987. *The Sentencing Commission and its Guidelines*. Boston: Northeastern University Press.

Walker, N. 1968. *Crime and Punishment in Britain: An Analysis of the Penal System in Theory, Law and Practice*. Edinburgh: Edinburgh University Press, 20.

Walker, N. 1991. *Why Punish?* Oxford: Oxford University Press.

Wasik, M. 1997. England repeals key 1991 sentencing reforms. In *Sentencing Reform in Overcrowded Times: A Comparative Perspective*, ed. M. Tonry and K. Hatlestad. Oxford: Oxford University Press.

Wasik, M., and A. von Hirsch. 1988. Non-custodial penalties and the principles of dessert. *The Criminal Law Review* 555, 564.

Weisser, M. 1979. *Crime and Punishment in Early Modern Europe*. Hassocks, U.K.: Harvestor Press.

West, A. 1998. Contemporary vigilantism: Do-it-yourself justice in the 1990s. Unpublished honors essay. Victoria University of Wellington.

Wilson, J.Q. 1975. *Thinking about Crime*. New York: Basic Books.

Reparation, Compensation, and Restitution: Our Best Explanations

12

CHARLES F. ABEL

Contents

12.1 Introduction

It is our social practice to suppress certain behaviors. Toward this end, we enjoin the state to visit particular consequences upon the unruly. Although this seems a natural course, there is in fact a gap between the occurrence of abjured behavior and the visiting of consequences. Given that people are agents, the option of not punishing is always at hand, and this option is exercised remarkably often. For example, deserving offenders are often spared for reasons of social or political policy (e.g., the pardon of President Nixon for covering up the Watergate conspiracy), or because the "crimes" were committed under extraordinary circumstances (e.g., as in *The Queen v. Dud-*

ley and Stevens, where crew members, shipwrecked for an extended period, were pardoned for killing and eating one of their number). Similarly, we afford state officials broad discretionary powers to mitigate or forego punishment whenever efficiency (e.g., a quick conviction in lieu of a trial), utility (e.g., turning state's evidence), or mercy (e.g., the age or infirmity of the offender, or the suffering of third parties) militates against the infliction of the standard sanction.

It appears that leaping the gap between offense and punishment requires some explanation. As neither punishment itself nor the nature of the sanction imposed are inevitable, reasoning people must ground both the decision to punish and the nature of the punishment imposed in something other than the fact of bad behavior itself. Likewise, the decision to vest the state with both the power to punish and the power to decide the nature and severity of the punishment must be explained. There is in fact no necessity that the state assumes this role. In fact, throughout "most of history in the West … the state's role in prosecution was quite minimal and it was considered the business of the community to solve its own disputes" (Zehr 1990:6).

It appears that we must explain in all of its particulars our practice of enjoining the state to punish certain behaviors. Of course, if we want to explain this social practice in any meaningful way, we cannot cleanse it of all normative content. Norms are fused into our explanations of social practice and cannot be removed without "radically changing their meaning and rendering them useless for those who study social life" (McKenzie 1967). Why, then, do we punish? Why do we inflict the punishments that we do? Why do we enjoin the state to act on our behalf in these endeavors? And is there any explanation for doing all of this that we can say is good in the normative sense?

Broadly, this chapter argues that we cannot give good explanations for either punishment itself or any form of punishment other than the forced transfer of money that is earned by the wrongdoer's labor, a labor that is specifically identified by a court to be performed in order to make reparation and that is recompensed at minimum wage regardless of its nature. As we can only give good explanations for this form of punishment, it constitutes the best social practice with regard to those who exhibit the behaviors we seek to suppress. More specifically, the argument will be that (1) the only forms of punishment that can be satisfactorily explained are those based upon a demonstration of the concrete social advantages that they secure and the concrete social disadvantages that they seek to repair, (2) such a demonstration cannot be based satisfactorily upon doctrinal integrity, intellectual elegance, or affect, but only upon "a realistic, empirically informed, unsentimental, preferably quantitative comparison of costs and benefits (not limited to monetary costs and benefits, however)" (Luban 1996), and (3) of the explanations and forms of punishment currently employed, only reparation (paid either in restitution or in compensation) meets these criteria. Further, to address pragmatically the nonpecuniary and nonmaterial damages that may be involved in a criminal violation, all recompense must include "expressive damages" (money paid to symbolize the vindication of immaterial damages to legal rights and in recognition of the fear, humiliation, mental distress, or harm to a person's reputation or dignity engendered by a crime), pecuniary damages (intended to represent the closest possible financial equivalent of the loss or harm suffered), and punitive damages intended to deter.

The question of whether forced reparation is punishment will not be considered at length. It will be taken as sufficient to note that forced reparation is required only of those upon whom blame has been fixed for engaging in behavior that is forbidden by law (Hart 1968). Hence, it is "inflicted on an offender because of an offence he has committed, and [it is] deliberately imposed, not just the natural consequence of a person's action (like a hangover)" (Benn 1967:29). Moreover, the offender is subjected to the discomfort and shame of being arrested, charged, put on trial, and forced into working and turning over the fruits of his or her labor. Hence coercion, censure, deprivation "and other consequences normally considered unpleasant" (Hart 1968) are all inflicted upon the wrongdoer "not [as] an accidental accompaniment to some other treatment (like the pain of the dentist's drill)" (Benn 1967:29), but because "the person upon whom it is being imposed should thereby be made to suffer and in that respect be worse off than before" (Wasserstrom 1982:476).

12.2   Clarifications

As a first step in the argument, it is important to note that we cannot use words whimsically. It is of course true that words have no necessary meaning and that social practices described by a common word need have no common essence (Wittgenstein 1953). However, if we are to be understood, the uses that we make of any particular word must bear reasonable "family resemblances" to uses that others have made of it already. Thus it is with "restitution," "compensation," and "reparation." Their meanings depend upon their uses and their uses depend upon our purposes. However, if we are to be understood, we cannot use them interchangeably. Instead, we must rely upon those differential uses that we can find consistently and reasonably employed for distinct purposes.

Now it appears that the bulk of thinking on these terms has in fact settled upon some fairly consistent usages and that the most reasonable among these usages argue strongly for defining "reparation," "compensation," and "restitution" in monetary terms alone. "Reparation," for example, is generally employed as an inclusive term, "restitution" and "compensation" being reserved for different forms that reparation may take (United Nations 2001a; van Boven 1993). Under this usage, "compensation" includes only those monetary reparations made for specific losses or specific damages to life or property (United Nations 2001a; van Boven 1993; Downey Jr. 1951; D'Orso 1996). "Restitution" includes any and all other payments or undertakings necessary to both re-establish the *status quo ante* and mitigate the consequences of the violation (United Nations 2001b; Crawford 2002; Factory at Chorzow Case 1928; Martini Case 1930). Although this much seems settled, there is still a fair amount of negotiation going on about exactly what constitutes the proper use "reparation" and therefore what must be done in addition to compensation by way of "restitution."

Some, for example, separate the consequences of an offense into "material harm" and "moral harm," employing "reparation" as a term addressing only the material harm done to the victim (Garvey 1999). To rectify the moral harm, offenders must undertake a "penance," defined as some "self-imposed hardship or suffering" (Garvey 1999). Others expand "reparation" to include not only "what the offender gives back to the victim in the form of money," but whatever else is felt necessary by way of "making amends" for the violation of the victim's rights, needs, wants, and desires (van Boven 1993; Wright 1985). Those of this persuasion are convinced that "reparation is not just about money, it is not even mostly about money; in fact, money is not even one percent of what reparation is about" (Wright 1996). Instead, they insist that reparation is "a fundamental stage in the progressive rehabilitation of the ... victim" and provides "the tools for mending a victim ... to a whole and integrated person (Chinweizu 1993)." Hence, the tendency of criminal justice systems "to declare victims' rights, without necessarily knowing what victims want or being able to ensure that they receive it" (Arcel, Christiansen, and Roque 2000), is lamentable.

Something other than (or in addition to) compensatory or restitutionary payments is necessary, such as an admission of wrongdoing, an apology, or a performance of some other kind (e.g., laboring or doing community service) (Wright 1996; Shapland 1984; Rock 1990). A still more expansive concept of reparation is suggested by those maintaining that the term should include "restoring the situation in a way that allows the offender to be legitimately reinstated in society" (Gaus 1991:45). Those of this persuasion are convinced that both "material reparation" and "moral reparation" are required to effect a proper reconciliation among the offender, the victim, and everyone else (Sayre-McCord 2001). Hence, the offender should be required to make "a symbolic public apology" of some sort in addition to any payments made by way of compensation and restitution (Duff 2000). Others feel that this is going entirely too far and suggest that such behavior should not be called "reparation" but "restoration" (Duff 2000).

In addition to the resistance of the "restorationists," there is resistance by many to the use of "reparation" beyond anything more than monetary compensation for material loss on the one hand, and monetary restitution "to make amends for more general wrongs and injuries," including affronts to rights and morals (D'Orso 1996). This seems the most reasonable approach for several reasons. First, it is unlikely that any measures of reparation in any of the broader senses could assist in meeting even some of the particularized needs and wants that individual victims might evince. Moreover, to the extent that we prefer "a government of laws and not of men," the forms that reparation should take cannot be grounded in either personal desires or personal needs. Rather, they should be grounded in public and objective conditions, deliberations, and determinations of what is proper and sufficient (Williams 1991). To meet this requirement, punishments cannot be based upon doctrinal integrity, intellectual elegance, or personal affect. They can only be based upon "a realistic, empirically informed, unsentimental, preferably quantitative comparison of costs and benefits" that, although not limited to monetary costs and benefits alone, must nevertheless remain concrete and calculable in some objective sense (Luban 1996).

Second, the more expansive uses of the term seem to confuse criminal justice with therapy or to confound the discourses of rights and criminal responsibility with the discourses of wants, needs, and religion. Speaking religiously, for example, "reparation" is employed with reference to atonement, forgiveness, redemption, and making amends for one's sins against god. Admissions of wrongdoing and apologies in this context are rituals whereby the "sinner" confesses, repents, and is purified. This sort of metaphysical vocabulary does not comport comfortably with the modern discourse of rights, speaking as it does of the legal and performative accountability of those in authority for securing and advancing the safety, security, and freedom of the individuals they rule in pragmatic and tangible ways (Cohen 1995), and of the tangible privileges and immunities that individuals enjoy either because of their particular status (e.g., child, property owner, licensed professional, citizen, victim) or because such privileges and immunities are necessary to the proper functioning of the societies they inhabit (e.g., freedom of association, press, and speech to a democracy).

Similarly, the language of psychotherapy bespeaks a concern with a specific person's inner world, with the unique struggle of each individual to maintain a sense of self-worth and to deal with a private sense of vulnerability while coping with social and cultural norms. In contradistinction, the discourse on rights and criminal responsibility bespeaks a concern with the safety, security, and freedom of the general population in a shared and public world. Within the latter discourse, therapy might be employed usefully as a metaphor, at least insofar as it is helpful to analogize social disruption to personal trauma and repairing concrete damage to helping people to cope. Beyond this, it is difficult to imagine that individuals have a right to any particular inner world or that the state has a duty to secure either a person's sense of self-worth or an individual's ability to deal with his or her social and cultural situation. Moreover, even if we decide that the state has some duty in these regards, there is no reason to believe that forced monetary reparation will not suffice to help ameliorate psychological trauma in both material and symbolic ways.

Finally, those arguing that "reparation" should include restoring "the situation in a way that allows the offender to be legitimately reinstated in society" (Sayre-McCord 2001) generally advocate replacing the formal criminal justice procedures with highly participative (preferably communitywide) processes whereby victims communicate with offenders, offenders repent and accept responsibility, and everybody works to re-establish a (once again) harmonious community (Zehr 1990; Braithwaite 1994). These ideas are akin to the "human relation" theories once popular in organization theory. Both argue, for example, that top-down management approaches (e.g., the control of criminal justice institutions and processes by judges and attorneys) deny the flexibility and responsiveness necessary to effect positive outcomes; both propose to solve this problem through such participatory devices as democratic decision making and flatter hierarchies (Kanter 1985; Womack and Jones 1990). With regard to criminal justice organizations, in particular, there is an assumption that highly participative, dialogue-oriented restorative justice forums will effect more meaningful, rational, and restorative outcomes (Zimring, Hawkins, and Kamin 2001).

Of course, several problems with broadly inclusive participatory processes come to mind. First, there is the problem of unattractive and overly attractive wrongdoers. Not only might familiarity breed contempt, but more subtle forms of partiality may arise within any group when it reacts to beauty, personality, celebrity status, racial or ethnic background, socioeconomic status, political ideology, or the fears of the moment. "Bottom-up" decision-making processes, therefore, offer fewer protections against biased sentencing decisions and may have greater difficulty achieving standards of proportionality that fit the burden to the offense (von Hirsch and Ashworth 1992). Thus it seems prudent to many that it "remain the responsibility of the state towards its citizens to ensure that justice is administered by independent and impartial tribunals, and that there are proportionality limits ... [enforced] to ensure some similarity in the treatment of equally situated offenders" (Ashworth 2002:591). Although failures of impartiality and proportionality nevertheless occur in mainstream criminal justice, there are procedures provided for their rectification (Ashworth 2002).

Moreover, there is little empirical evidence that participatory approaches deliver what they promise. Positive outcomes, for example, have not been empirically linked to expanded participatory decision making within organizations, and when the studies based upon these theories are taken as a whole, "the evidence is typically inconclusive, and the interpretations often contradictory" (Wilensky 1957:34). More generally, reviews of the literature on participatory decision making generally conclude that "strong participatory processes can never displace the need for hierarchical public and private bureaucracies [e.g., courts and formal procedures] ... [and that] those who claim that these participatory methodologies can fundamentally alter the nature of the power structures that sustain complex societies are simply ignoring the well-established insights of modern social science" (Brett 2003:1).

To best accord with the most reasonable and pragmatic usage of the terms, the prudent course seems to be that of characterizing "restitution" and "compensation" as monetary forms of "reparation." In accord with this usage, "compensation" should be employed when talking about monetary reparation for damages to property or injury to persons, and "restitution" should be used when talking about monetary forms of redress that must be added to compensation in order to both restore the *status quo ante* and mitigate the consequences of the wrong. Furthermore, "reparation" should not employ "the wishes of the victim" as a benchmark. With these clarifications in mind, we may proceed with the argument that as we cannot give any other good explanation for leaping the gap between offense and punishment, reparation constitutes the best social practice with regard to those who exhibit the behaviors we seek to suppress.

12.3   Leaping the Gap with Universal Standards

There are a limited number of ways to explain a social practice. One is to hold it as required by some standard that is accepted as both universal and everlasting. The problem with this approach is that there is some disagreement over what this standard might be. Suggestions include, for example, human nature (Aristotle), natural law (all of science), dialectical necessity (Hegel), certain categorical principles of rationality (Kant), and the social contract adopted by everyone upon leaving the state of nature (Hobbes, Locke, and Rousseau). Besides their diversity, one problem with such standards is that they tend to be highly abstract. Most would agree with Aristotle, for example, that we ought to treat equals equally, but what exactly does this suggest that we do (Aristotle, translated by Ross 1925)? First of all, no two people can be equal in all respects. That would constitute an identity with one another, and that is a simple impossibility. So which of the many aspects of human beings are to be the benchmark of equality? Aristotle suggests that "virtue" is the benchmark. However, one aspect of Aristotle's virtue is "justice," which he defines as treating equals equally. In brief, such standards are "empty vessels" that by themselves leave us without substantive direction in concrete situations (Alexander 1993).

A certain rendition of this Aristotelian idea is popular today. Retribution theories explain both punishment and the forms that it takes as rendering offenders equal to their victims by making the punishment fit the crime (von Hirsch 1976). Nietzsche, for example, explained punishment in terms of universally shared "feelings of anger and vengeance, in the desire to hurt those who have hurt us." Uncomfortable with sheer vengeance as an explanation, Hegel explained that by engaging in forbidden behaviors the criminal "lays down a law which he has explicitly recognized in his action and under which in consequence he should be brought under as his right" (Hegel, translated by Ross 1952:100) and Kant explained retribution as "willed" universally by wrongdoers because those who willingly engage in forbidden behavior thereby will that their acts redound upon themselves. As he put it, "If you insult him, you insult yourself; if you steal from him, you steal from yourself; if you strike him, you strike yourself; if you kill him, you kill yourself" (Kant, translated by Gregor 1991). Equalizing consequences then, follow as matters of universal desire, categorical imperative, or dialectical necessity.

But these are highly problematic explanations. They are problematic first of all because just as with Aristotle's explanation of how we should treat equals, the retributivist's explanation that the punishment should be equal to the crime leaves us without substantive guidance as to how much or exactly what kind of punishment should be visited upon an offender in a particular situation. This in turn leaves certain actors (prosecutors, judges, juries) free to exercise an immense and relatively unchecked discretion. Moreover, liberated from all considerations of context and consequence, the "tit-for-tat" standard of retribution allows these actors to "explain away" any problematic or previously inconsistent judgments by either resorting to *ad hoc* auxiliary explanations (e.g., this murder was particularly heinous or this murderer was particularly evil) or insisting that alternative approaches that may have avoided such difficulties are based upon "irrelevant" considerations (Lerman 2000; Butler 1999; Dolinko 1992).

Retributivist explanations are problematic for other reasons as well. For example, they seem hypothetical. That is, they seem to be saying that *if* a person is willing a consequence, laying down a law, free-riding, or asserting superiority by engaging in forbidden behavior, *then* certain consequences should be visited upon that person. Also, as the consequences do not occur absent human agency, we might ask in what sense they are "necessary." Why must we carry out the violator's will? Or, why should we bring offenders under the law that they themselves have "laid down"? Once again, the generally given responses to these questions seem hypothetical. For example, responses to the effect that "it is morally right" or that "it is our duty" seem to involve hypothetical claims that it *is* morally right, or that it *is* our duty. Finally, the attainment of "equality" between offender and victim seems hypothetical as well. Murder, for example, often calls forth either the death penalty or life imprisonment. Hence the offender is "equal" to the victim in being either actually dead or at least dead to society at large. But how exactly does this hold offenders accountable for their behaviors in any meaningful way (Braithwaite and Roche 2001), give sufficient attention to the actual harm inflicted upon the victim (Lerman 2000), or instill confidence that the punishment is in fact commensurable to the offense (Sharp 1908)? In response to these questions, retributivists seem to assert that *if* offenders value their biological or social life as much as the victims did, *if* all victims suffered equally at the hands of offenders, or if an offender's responsibilities are discharged in all cases by the passivity of either incarceration or death, *then* they should be imprisoned or killed.

Equally problematic is the fact that retributivist explanations seem to remove all reason from the practice of punishment. By narrowing the question of punishment to one of what the offending behavior alone calls forth, retributivists effectively "dumb down" the practice of punishment by removing from consideration all questions of consequence. Banished are all questions of practicality; all questions of social impact; all questions of deterrence; and all questions of what social, political, or economic good might be accomplished by choosing nonretributive responses. One particularly notable result of this narrowed field of vision is the neat way in which it removes the question of rights from consideration. Rights in this context have largely to do with protecting human dignity. They are recognitions that "even the worst criminals are worthy of basic human respect" (Margalit 1996:70), primarily because they enjoy the "capacity of re-evaluating one's life at any given moment [and] the ability to change one's life from that moment on" (Margalit 1996:70). As such, they are impositions upon those in the criminal justice system, one of which involves refraining from the arbitrary or unnecessary infliction of suffering and humiliation. Hence a person may deserve a punishment that would violate his or her human dignity were it to be imposed. However, as retributivists ground punishment in the wrongful act alone (i.e., without regard to any discernable benefit to the victim or society), they discount the human dignity of the offender, thereby allowing them to be reduced to means that may serve the ends of others (e.g., the desire for vengeance, the need for "closure," the symbolic assertion of the law's dignity, the "education" of society in general as to how citizens should behave).

This discounting of rights has bothered some retributivists. As an ameliorative, they have taken to turning the rights argument on its head by suggesting that offenders have a human right to be punished and that this right ought to be acknowledged even in the face of a pardon (Morris 1968). Of course, the roots of this idea can be traced to no greater a mind than Hegel, who insisted that "punishment is regarded as containing the criminal's right and hence by being punished he is honored as a rational being" (Hegel, translated by Knox 1952:100). And this sentiment was echoed by C. S. Lewis, when he admonished us to remember that "when we cease to consider what the criminal deserves and consider only what will cure him or deter others, we have tacitly removed him from the sphere of justice altogether; instead of a person, a subject of rights, we now have a mere object, a patient, a 'case'" (Lewis 1970:646).

But this seems a bit odd. First, it suggests that the human rights of offenders are violated whenever their offending behavior goes undetected, or whenever the evidence of an offense cannot be traced to them, or whenever they are not apprehended. It also suggests that the offender is due an apology and perhaps reparations for society's failure to secure his or her rights. Although a logically coherent argument can be made to these effects, the logical conclusions seem alien to how we otherwise employ the word "right." That term, it seems, is employed just in reference to some advantage, privilege, or immunity that is due an individual. It is odd, then, to employ it in contexts of disadvantage and liability. It seems to make more sense in these contexts to speak of an offender having breached his or her duties, and as a consequence of the breach we might speak of the offender's consequent duty to repair. Moreover, many argue that, setting aside such difficulties, the fact that so many offenders come from socially deprived backgrounds "weakens the contention that they have, in a sufficiently clear way, voluntarily forfeited rights or that they have done so as competent moral and prudential agents" (Lippke 2003:459). Those of this persuasion are convinced that "it seems absurd to portray socially deprived offenders as beings who enjoy a full array of rights and privileges, understand the benefits of their doing so, and who, in spite of this, simply chose to act in ways flouting the rules of civil society" (Lippke 2003:459).

Finally, retributivist explanations seem incoherent (Christopher 2002). Consider as an example the "right" to be punished in the face of a pardon.

If we assume that rational (nonarbitrary, noncapricious) agents are granting a pardon, that pardon must be deserved. If it is deserved, then deserving offenders must have at least as much a right to the pardon as to a punishment. But isn't it the case that a right to a pardon is the right not to be punished? Similarly, a moment's reflection will reveal that retributivist explanations allow for the punishment of both legally innocent but morally guilty acts, legally guilty but morally innocent acts (Christopher 2002), and morally culpable intentions regardless of whether they involve any acts at all (i.e., as intent reveals moral culpability, "just deserts" requires that an individual be punished for the intent to offend should the occasion arise, no matter how improbable that occasion might be).

To get around this difficulty, retributivists resort to a series of auxiliary and somewhat *ad hoc* explanations. Some, for example, explain that whereas "the distinctive aspect of retributivism is that the moral desert of an offender is a sufficient reason to punish," retributivists are not "monomaniacal" (Moore 1997). Consequently, punishing offenders is "subject to being overridden by other goods that outweigh the good of achieving retributive justice," one such good being an adherence to the principle that only those guilty of breaking the law should be punished (Moore 1997). But this improvisation abandons retributivism in favor of a consequentialist explanation; it explains punishment as an affirmation of the laws seeking to suppress certain behaviors. To get around *this* difficulty, retributivists improvise once again by explaining that we must combine the moral with the legal and explain punishment as the visiting of just deserts upon morally culpable people who are also legally guilty (Mundle 1954). But this does not explain the punishment of the legally guilty but morally righteous (e.g., the punishment of civil rights activists who intentionally violated "Jim Crow" laws).

In the end, retributivist explanations seem more dogmatic than explanatory. For this reason, many feel that "what pass for retributivist justifications of punishment in general, can be shown to be either denials of the need to justify it, or mere reiterations of the principle to be justified, or disguised utilitarianism" (Benn 1958:325). Thus, retributivist arguments seem to fail both as explanations of why we visit certain consequences upon offenders and as explanations that are good in the normative sense.

12.4 Leaping the Gap with Traditional Social Standards

An alternative approach to explaining why we punish and why we punish as we do is to hold both as required by some explicit standard that a society or a community traditionally accepts as proper. The problem here is that such standards are clearly contingent. They are grounded in a single group's history and experience and hence unlikely to prove convincing across time and across the board. Of course, such standards may be adhered to for political or pragmatic reasons; but then we are likely to consider such adherence "bad" for just those reasons. In fact, we often consider it a good thing when legal institutions adopt a nontraditional course (e.g., lower courts that followed and enforced *Brown v. Board of Education*) or persevere in traditional courses despite their resistance to the "politically correct." The problem here is that such traditional standards may not comport well with new experiences; or with the history and experience of minority communities within a society; or with the history and experiences of other societies with which we must or wish to interact; or with still more broadly accepted standards of reason, morality, or science.

Some retributivists have jumped on the "traditional standards" bandwagon by explaining punishment as a "proportionate" disadvantage visited upon any person who takes advantage of whatever system of social restraints has been traditionally established though mutual agreement. By renouncing their duties under this system, and by free-riding on the benefits gained by the fact that others are still acting under constraint, offenders are thought to behave culpably and so deserve punishment (Davis 1985; von Hirsch 1990). Certain forms of retribution, it is felt, restore a fair balance by imposing a proportionate burden to counter the advantage gained (Anderson 1997). Others taking this tack argue that by engaging in proscribed behavior, offenders claim an exalted place for themselves and that certain punishments are necessary as a repudiation of the offender's claim of superiority over both the victim and society. Still others explain proportionate punishment as a reconfirmation of the moral worth of both the victim and the society that seeks the protection of its citizens (Hampton 1992). In all cases, however, punishment is still explained as the universally necessary desert of moral culpability (Duff 1996) and is therefore still as hypothetical, unreasonable, incoherent, and dogmatic as ever.

12.5   Leaping the Gap with a "Reflexive Equilibrium"

One way out of this quandary produced by explanations of punishment as required by contingent traditional standards on the one hand and explanations of punishment as required by universal standards on the other is to point out that as societies customarily wish to survive and to flourish, they are quite likely to respond to what they perceive to be the realities of their situation. In fact, it is plausible to assume that societies will govern their beliefs and practices by the norm of responsiveness to the realities about them (Velleman 1996). Given that societies are thus committed to both understanding the truth about their situation and to changing their social practices in response to what they believe to be true, they must also be committed to changing their contingent standards if they turn out to be based on false understandings. They must, in other words, be committed to reaching a "wide reflective equilibrium" that grounds social practices in an ongoing assessment, integration, and harmonizing of (1) generally accepted moral principles; (2) community- and societywide attitudes, values, and beliefs; (3) the pragmatic dictates of experience; and (4) the evidence of scientific investigations (Rawls 1993). In this equilibrium, then, might be grounded an explanation for the social practice of punishment.

Early on in the development of criminal theory, for example, Blackstone explained both the leap from forbidden act to punishment and the particular practices that should constitute punishment, as rational means to the end of cultivating that certain security for the individual that is conducive to the flourishing of civilization (Lieberman 2002). It was his opinion that the requisite security could be attained by both the deterrent effect of threatened discomfort and the demonstration that the threat would be carried out. To further insure the desired effect, Blackstone opined that the nature and measure of punishment for any particular offense should not be determined by any invariable rule (e.g., just deserts). Rather, the nature and measure of the discomfort should in each case be those "as appear to be the best calculated to answer the end of precaution against future offences," whether that end might be served by rehabilitation, incapacitation, or general deterrence (Blackstone 1769). In any event, the discomfort was "by no means to exceed" that which was required to deter and thereby promote the flourishing of civilization (Blackstone 1769). Of course, any "want or defect of will" in the offender blocked the leap, as a "vitious will" and "an unlawful act consequent upon such vitious will" were necessary if deterrence were to work (Blackstone 1769). At the same time, however, "if a man be doing anything unlawful," he must be discomfited for "whatever consequence" followed regardless of whether or not it was a consequence that "he did not foresee or intend" (Blackstone 1769:11–12). True to this line of thinking, modern "individualists" argue that bad behavior is the result of either the wrongdoer's failure to cultivate adequately a good character or a failure by him or her to understand exactly what constitutes wrongdoing. Those holding to the prior conviction explain punishment as a last-ditch attempt to inculcate the recalcitrant with the necessary self-discipline (Haney 1982), whereas those of the latter conviction explain punishment as a last-ditch attempt to guide and inform (Horder 2002).

This seems a tidy explanation except to those harboring doubts about whether the "vitious will" is actually what accounts for the persistence of criminalized behavior. Some, for example, attribute criminal behavior to a withdrawal of god's grace or to a human nature corrupted by original sin; and these thinkers explain punishment as a ritual intended to remind community members that they are always on the verge of damnation and should therefore be especially careful (Halttunen 1998). Behavioral scientists, being of a more secular bent, also call into question the notion of free will and explain punishment as either an incapacitation of those who must offend, or as a purely deterring or "sublimating" factor in the environment (Green 1995). Along these lines, for example, "environmentalists" argue that bad behavior results from the interaction of the human genome and the social, political, or economic situation of the offender, and they explain different punishments as ways and means of "managing" the attendant risks (e.g., removing, rehabilitating, or repressing the individuals whose behaviors exhibit a native inability or congenital disinclination to adapt) (Wiener 1990). Finally, social scientists, being of a worldly bent, explain illegal behavior as socially determined.

To those of these persuasions, then, the explanation of punishment as a means to establishing a broad "reflexive equilibrium" is discounted. Whether for spiritual, behavioral, social, environmental, or genetic reasons, offenders (if not whole societies) are considered ultimately devoid of the "free will" required to instigate and maintain the equilibrium. The problem with these explanations is that they seem to go too far in suggesting that individual choice is largely predetermined. Although there is a certain bittersweet appeal to the idea that that our intersubjective experience of agency is a mere illusion that arises from our ignorance of the biological, chemical, physical, and mechanical "laws" that necessitate our behavior (Harré and Madden 1975; Locke [1690] 1978), these arguments seem only to demonstrate that we *can* analytically reduce our volition to chemical, physical, mechanical, or sociological "causes" if we choose to do so. They do not demonstrate, however, that any theory of agency must collapse as a result.

It is a simple matter to note that determinists do not know that our "voluntary" acts are necessitated any more than others know that they are freely chosen. It is ultimately a question of sufficient reasons for concluding that people are agents, and as we have intersubjective experiences of both volition and determination, and as these experiences are as real (as nonillusionary) as our intersubjective experiences of physical, chemical, and sociological processes, we must conclude not only that human agency is as ontologically grounded as the theory of determinism, but that it accounts for more as well. Determinism, that is, simply denies the reality of experiences that do not fit its view that, "all of the surface features of the world are entirely caused by and realized in systems of micro-elements, [and that] the behavior of micro-elements is sufficient to determine everything that happens" (Searle 1984:94). The idea of "free will," however, confirms both sorts of intersubjective experience, accepts their equal ontological status, and concludes that people are so ontologically constituted as to enjoy the properties of both volition and determination. As we thus have sufficient reason for accepting "free will," we can discount determinism as an obstacle to society's ability to instigate and maintain a "reflexive equilibrium" wherein an explanation of punishment and its particular forms might be grounded.

Many, of course, have come to this conclusion. Uncomfortable with not only the deterministic implications of spiritualist and behaviorist explanations, but the idea that a "vitious will" alone accounts for offending behavior as well, many thinkers insist that although our will is in fact free, it is inclined by nature to impulsive acts against the common good and that our ability to reason things out is more often employed toward serving personal rather than societal interests. Those of this persuasion either explain punishment as a device for building moral character and self-control (Wiener 1990), or give up on punishment altogether and call for treatment instead (Glueck 1928). In either event, these thinkers lend some hope to the idea of grounding an explanation of punishment in a "reflexive equilibrium" that promotes the flourishing of civilization.

Unfortunately, there is a more telling critique of the idea that a "wide reflective equilibrium" might be established. The hope for an equilibrium is founded in the idea that people will respond to the realities about them in a pragmatic way, and that they will do so by assessing, integrating, or balancing off against one another the moral principles of the broader society; the dictates of experience; the objective findings of science; the realities of any given moment; and the particular attitudes, values, and beliefs of any particular community. Critical theory, however, points out that many of the values, attitudes, and beliefs that societies accept, and many of the facts, concepts, and principles that science regards as "givens," are actually constructed socially in order to serve certain interests (Horkheimer 1972). At bottom, these interests include an interest in dealing advantageously with the natural world, an interest in communicating with one another so as to coordinate our activities, and an interest in freeing ourselves from any unnecessary dependencies (Habermas 1984).

Toward serving these interests, power relationships are constructed within groups, communities, and societies, and there is a tendency for these relationships to persevere even when they begin, due to changing internal and external circumstances, to work against the interests that account for their construction. This tendency results from an inclination by those in leadership positions to explain their dominance (perhaps quite sincerely or perhaps out of an interest in maintaining their pre-eminent position) as a "divine right," or as "natural," or as just the way things work out most practically (Veblen 1934; Horkheimer and Adorno 1947; Marcuse 1964), and it is bolstered by an uncertainty on the part of the community in general as to whether the leaders are correct (Veblen 1932, 1934). Unfortunately, it is too often the case that when constructed relationships are taken as ontological givens, social practice divorces from reality. Relationships of advantage and disadvantage become institutionalized, organizations and bureaucracies based upon them are established, these organizations begin to evolve values and goals contrary to the actual interests of many groups within the society, and disadvantaged groups become subjugated, marginalized, and alienated (i.e., "criminalized").

With regard to grounding an explanation of punishment in a "broad reflexive equilibrium," then, there isn't any independent reality to strike equilibrium with. There is only a socially constructed reality, the assessment of which may only reveal such "truths" as are determined to be correct according to the ideological commitments of the socially, politically, and economically dominant. Consequently, any "reflexive equilibrium" is suspect. It is very likely to be not so much an actual integration and balancing of of divergent values, needs, and interests as a reflection of the interests of the dominant social, economic, and political forces in any given society, as well as a mechanism for establishing and reinforcing their particular ways of seeing and thinking.

Now one might think that science would act as a corrective. Science might, for example, reveal when and how certain social practices and the values, attitudes, beliefs, and epistemologies of dominant groups actually subjugate, marginalize, alienate, and work against the advance of civilization. It might then suggest ways of establishing a truly "wide and reflexive equilibrium." However, many have pointed out that although science *can* operate as such a positive force (Foucault 1997), it may also be employed to conceal the dynamics of dominance and resistance that work against such an equilibrium. This was of central concern to Foucault, for example, as he elucidated how scientific practices and discourses are currently used by specific disciplines that exhibit what he called questionable "scientificity" (1972). These are disciplines such as criminal justice, political science, sociology, and organization studies that focus on the ever-shifting and dynamic sphere of human interactions rather than the relatively stable spheres of the natural world (Kritzman 1988). Scientific practices and discourses in these disciplines work against societal interests in these spheres because they tend to operate by delineating, organizing, and interpreting some fragment of reality with prescriptive intent. That is, they claim to reveal the exclusive practices and norms requisite to a strong and successful society, and proceed to ignore, explain away, or distort anomalies so that they accord with the accepted revelations. The success of such claims by these disciplines rests, in Foucault's view, on "a power which the West since medieval times has attributed to science and has reserved for those engaged in scientific discourse" (1994:24).

According to this way of thinking, then, neither the prevention of activities that preclude the flourishing of civilization nor the visiting of morally deserved retribution on the corrupt explains punishment. Rather, punishment and its different forms is a mechanism for vindicating and reinforcing certain social hierarchies, certain structures of authority, and certain "political economies of power" (i.e., certain ways of getting things done), regardless of their moral stature or their tendency to advance or retard the march of civilization. The institutions that punish are loci of domination as their goals, interests, preferences, and desired outcomes mediate the underlying power distribution ultimately founded upon societywide structural, ideological, and discursive domination (Benson 1977). By transmitting sets of decision premises and cognitive expectations that constrain choices to those prepatterned by the dominate ideology and discourses, punishing institutions exercise a discipline over both perception and understanding that induces individuals to perpetuate relationships of advantage and disadvantage in their day-to-day "rational" decision making (Deetz 1998). In Habermasian (1984) terms, criminal laws, courts, prosecutors, and prisons induce coordinated action outside of the individual's "life world," developing by themselves a structure of expectations, cognitions, and epistemologies (reflecting societywide relationships of domination) beyond the interests of the individuals and groups to whom they are addressed. Thus, the exercise of domination through the power of such punishing agencies inhibits the capacity of individuals to act as creative, reflective agents free of misconceptions about their own interests and therefore incapable of contributing to a truly "reflexive equilibrium" within which we might ground an explanation of punishment that truly advances civilization and is good in the normative sense.

12.6   Leaping the Gap with Veils of Ignorance, Inclusiveness, and the Ideal Speech Situation

The problem, then, is how to achieve a "wide reflexive equilibrium" that is genuine and pragmatic rather than reflective of some largely abstract ideal that secures the interests of certain social, political, and economic groups by enforcing particular relationships of advantage and disadvantage (Dunn 1990; for example, see Rawls 1971 and Hamlin and Pettit 1989). As we have seen, we cannot accomplish this equilibrium by doing as legal idealists propose. We cannot explain punishment meaningfully as required by a universal standard applied through the imaginative manipulation of legal precedents and contextual facts by judicial philosopher kings. Nor can we explain punishment as legal rationalists propose and explain the practices of punishment as required by socially constructed standards derived from the sort of reflective equilibrium critiqued by critical theory. "As often as not, [such theories] substitute for the articulate idealism of the theories which they fight an inarticulate idealism of their own, which is presented as a scientific fact based on observations" (Friedmann 1953:150). In both cases, a large amount of punishment is at bottom explicable only as an attempt to suppress deviant lifestyles or to secure the interests of those whose interests are best served by the dominant ideology.

To remedy these ills, some argue that we ought to suppress only those behaviors that citizens, reasoning together behind a "veil of ignorance," can agree upon as inimical to realizing their personal interests and to living their individually chosen lifestyles (Rawls 1971). A veil that blanks out their positions in society, it is thought, will allow everyone to arrive at a truly "wide and reflexive equilibrium," not only about what should be suppressed but how those abjured behaviors ought to be dealt with as well. Others argue that a common understanding of how to deal with properly abjured behaviors can develop without domination when the broadest possible array of individuals are drawn out of the private realm through incentives to participate in public (political) life (Barber 1984). In both cases, the proposed remedy involves the development of a thoroughgoing and highly inclusive participatory democracy as a check on dominant ideologies and upon the suppression of behaviors that contravene extent relationships of advantage and disadvantage.

Elaborating upon this idea of an inclusive public sphere, critical theorists argue that a common understanding of properly abjured behavior and proper reaction to them might be reached through "immanent critique" and honest debate within an "ideal speech situation." This remedy would proceed by first pointing out how certain social practices and their outcomes depart from the foundational norms and ideals of a given social order. It would then critique the foundational norms and values themselves by revealing the extent to which they fail to reflect a genuinely "wide reflexive equilibrium" (Horkheimer 1972, 1974). Once this is accomplished, progress toward such an equilibrium would be made by establishing and maintaining a public sphere that operates according to the principles of the "ideal speech situation," a situation wherein every competent individual and group is allowed to take part in a nonmanipulative and reasoned discourse that recognizes everyone's personal dignity (Honneth 1994); is genuinely aimed at reaching mutual understanding; and is dedicated to thoroughly considering all genuine expressions of desires, needs, and attitudes toward both generally accepted and generally abjured values, viewpoints, and lifestyles (Habermas 1984). As applied to the question of how we might best explain the social practices that we call punishment, the important point is that the proposed remedy would not only examine the concepts, principles, theories, and values at their foundation, but would "unfold [their] implications and consequences ... [and then] re-examine and reassess the [practice] ... in light of these implications and consequences" for everyone, including those marginalized, alienated, and suppressed by the dominant ideology (Held 1980).

Unfortunately, these remedies prove unsatisfactory. First, reasoning together behind a "veil of ignorance" is probably impossible. Reasoning, it seems, requires more than simply a clear head and the proper situation. The very ability to reason and to respond to reasoned argument appears to be both possible and limited in its breadth and depth by one's "cultural identity" (Fay 1987). Consequently, people who are removed from their historical and cultural milieu would be freed not only from certain ways of thinking, but from anything upon which to ground any thinking at all. Second, drawing people into a broadly inclusive public sphere tends to result not in a shared idea of what constitutes a good social practice but in little more than "the ... combining of preferences, all of which are counted equally" (Kymlicka 1990:206). Finally, any claim that a single legitimized set of social practices will result from participation in public life (no matter how ignorantly) implies that any society currently valuing interpersonal choice in such matters ought to be replaced by the rule of some authority embodying the revealed truth (e.g., philosopher kings, again) (Kymlicka 1990).

Regardless of the objections just raised, the arguments made by both "veil of ignorance" proponents and those critical theorists advocating immanent critique within an "ideal speech situation" seem compelling. It seems that a genuinely "wide reflexive equilibrium" requires something of the sort to both secure its emergence and exercise its influence. Something of the sort seems necessary to emancipate us from the epistemological and ideological effects of dominating power relationships. However, institutionalizing "veils of ignorance" or "ideal speech situations" requires encompassing the individual in a set of power relationships that flow if not from the center then from the group. Assuming, then, that everyone shares some interests and that everyone (even the most marginalized) would agree to certain practices that might then be fashioned legitimately into law and reflected back upon everyone as norms of proper behavior, practices and interests that are not so universally agreeable must remain unsatisfied at best and illegal at worst. These practices and norms may be challenged in courts and perhaps in future discourses in the ideal situation, but there is no reason to suspect that they will fare any better unless they happen to become shared by everyone. Some, then, must remain unemancipated.

Moreover, such practices invite frustration. The proffered emancipatory mechanisms recognize rational discourse in deliberative democracies as the only engine of legitimate collective will formation. History suggests, to the contrary, that collective will may be formed irrationally as a matter of taste or religious belief, that interests shared by everyone may be met nondemocratically, and that there is no reason to believe *a priori* that the same may not be true in the future. One might argue, for example, that an ideal authoritarian government could act as a corrective for the problem of those unemancipated by the communicative power of the ideal speech situation. Similarly, coercive power employed to meet and legitimize both shared and unshared interests and practices would seem as effective at emancipation as communicative power. Under certain circumstances (broadly shared extreme racial bias), it may even seem necessary (e.g., busing to achieve school integration). Arguably, such problems are remediable through courts and continued sincere discourse (though it seems that courts might need to resort to coercion as a remedy), but this seems an act of faith engendered by an ultimate dedication not to emancipation but to a particular societal and governmental form.

12.7 Leaping the Gap with Money

It appears, then, that we cannot explain satisfactorily either punishment or the particular things that we do to punish. The most important and popular explanations either are grounded in hypothesis, incoherence, and dogmatism or reflect the interests of dominant social, political, and economic groups. But perhaps we are reasoning in the wrong direction. Perhaps, rather than looking to the explanations to leap the gap between the occurrence of abjured behavior and punishment, we ought to take both punishment and its explanations as primary social facts, and then figure out some way of making sense of the whole lot. After all, "Why do we punish criminals? Is it from a desire for revenge? Is it in order to prevent a repetition of the crime? And so on. The truth is there is no one reason. There is the institution of punishing criminals. Different people support this for different reasons and for different reasons in different cases and at different times ... And so punishment is carried out" (Wittgenstein 1953:131).

In other words, perhaps we must simply accept the fact that punishment is one of the particular activities that together construct our "way of living" (Wittgenstein 1980, 1993) or "form of life." As such, it would not really be subject to explanation. Rather than being a product of our reasoning together, it would be one of those ultimate bases upon which we construct our explanations of the other things that we do (e.g., the particular ways that we punish) (Wittgenstein 1969). In other words, punishing in certain circumstances is simply what we do, and *because we punish*, we execute, or we imprison, or we fine. Punishment in particular cases, then, may occupy one of those points in our thinking where "the chain of reasons comes to an end" (Wittgenstein 1953:131), but "the end is not certain propositions striking us immediately as true, i.e., it is not a kind of seeing on our part; it is our acting [i.e., the simple fact that we punish] that is at the bottom," at the foundation or the beginning of our explanations for why we do certain things we call punishment (Wittgenstein 1969). We agree to punish because it is a constituent of our form of life, and it is our form of life that must change if we decide not to punish.

However, though we agree to punish, the analysis so far indicates that there are certain limits to the consensus that we have. Those limits have to do with *how* we punish. Regarding that issue, there is a clash of principles or foundational values that are also constituent of our "form of life." Life, liberty, equality, and utility, for example, are all foundational values, and it is a foundational principle that we all act in ways that secure and promote these values. Yet different people prioritize them differently. Some respect life above all else and would exclude it from our choice of punishments. Others prize utility and would take another's life if it served to deter. Still others prize liberty and consider its deprivation sufficient punishment regardless of the crime. And of course, debate rages over what sorts of punishments are most consistent with the dignity of both offenders and victims. Hence we find ourselves at that point "where principles really do meet which cannot be reconciled with one another, [and] each man declares the other a fool and a heretic" (Wittgenstein 1969:81).

The problem undoubtedly lies in the fact that human values are in all cases plural and diverse. This plurality certainly reflects the disparate theories of valuation that operate within different groups of people at different positions in our socioeconomic structure. But it also reflects the different ways that different relationships and things are valued by the individuals within the same group as they operate within the different spheres of their lives. Behaviors affecting things and relationships in the same or reasonably equivalent ways within families, markets, politics, religious organizations, and educational institutions, for example, call forth different valuations reflecting the different concerns, goals, desires, and affections that are at stake in those disparate spheres. Finally, even within the same spheres of human activity, one encounters objective and subjective valuation, instrumental and intrinsic valuation, mercy and "tough love." Consequently, the particular punishments that we inflict for abjured behaviors within those different spheres are valued in ways that are not reducible to some larger, more encompassing explanation regardless of how we seek to identify it (universally, traditionally, or reflexively). Hence it appears that none of the explanations considered so far can hope to explain adequately why we punish, and none of the particular punishments that they suggest that we visit upon the recalcitrant can be explained satisfactorily either.

Given these plural and disparate valuations, then, there appears at first glance to be three ways of punishing that can be satisfactorily explained. First, we might say that if people value the same things and relationships in different ways, the state should allow them to sort things out as they choose. Historically, as already mentioned, this is not an uncommon tack to take (Zehr 1990). However, in highly complex and interdependent societies, much more is a stake than the interests of those immediately involved or the interests of their immediate communities. Consider securities fraud or insider trading, for example. Certainly a primary concern is the unwarranted advantage that such behavior gives to a few and the consequent damage it wreaks upon those planning for retirement or their children's education. But these behaviors also entail statewide effects and collective action problems. A broad distrust of markets would cripple industry, medicine, science, and, in fact, nearly every aspect of life as it is currently known. Additionally, the ways that Hence there is a clear role for the state to play. Shelton (1999) said, to have effects beyond the individual plaintiff, "remedies for public wrongs must be seen ... as serving not only private redress but public policy" (52).

Alternatively, then, we might direct the state to punish a given offender in a variety of different ways simultaneously. In this way, we might hope to satisfy at least some of the different kinds of wrong that are experienced because of the different ways that different people value the different things and relationships that have been disturbed because of the offender's particular wrong. Along this line, some argue that "wronging is not simply harming; consequently, undoing the harm does not undo the wrong. One cannot undo wrongs in the way one can repay debts" (Gaus 1991:45). Consequently, to think that restitution, compensation, or even thorough and complete reparation might right the wrong is to mistake the nature of offense. These thinkers generally go on to suggest that the common spate of punishments be added to and enforced in order to right the wrong and "restore the equality" the crime dislodged.

Others argue, more expansively, that we should consider more than just the state, the offender, and the victim in fashioning our response to bad behavior. To focus on these alone, it is argued, removes the crime from its social context and calls forth a response that neglects other interested parties (e.g., families, community members, social relationships) (Strang and Sherman 2003). To "recontextualize" the crime and to fashion the most socially conscious result, a "restorative" approach should be taken. Offenders, victims, families, and representatives of both the state and the community should actively participate in a public deliberation over the causes and consequences of the particular offense that brings them together. The objective of this deliberation should be to "amend" and not to punish. However, as crime creates positive obligations, argue restorativists, it is the offender who must make amends. This requires not only doing what they can to amend whatever things and social relationships were harmed, but a public expression of remorse for admittedly bad conduct as well (Braithwaite 2000).

Unfortunately, there are problems with both narrow and expansive version of this explanation. Regarding the narrow version, it is difficult to see exactly why restitution, compensation, and reparation don't serve as well as other impositions to atone for wrongs. In fact, forced labor to earn money for the payments seems in many ways a more satisfying atonement than, say, sitting in prison or suffering the restrictions of parole. Regarding the more expansive version, for this to work (setting aside the logistical impracticalities) it seems that something like a veil of ignorance or an ideal speech situation is required. And as argued above, these are impossible.

The third alternative is to require the forced transfer of money. This choice recommends itself primarily because any chosen form of punishment must cease at some moment to be contemplative and become in a true sense practical. That is, we must at some moment actually do something that works to realize the punishment in the material world, and it is at such a moment that its degree of practicality becomes evident. Its degree of practicality, of course, lies in its efficacy. Does it accomplish its purposes within both the material world and the world of social practice? Can we rely upon it to secure concrete advantages and to repair concrete disadvantages? The problem, as demonstrated above, is that of diverse valuation. We cannot develop a proper form of punishment that corresponds to external reality if by that we mean hooking it up in a precise correspondence with every evil we might imagine has occurred or every evil that is subjectively experienced.

Given the diverse valuations that individuals and groups make of things and relationships, it would seem most efficacious to give people money and let them spend it in ways that they feel affords them the best satisfaction for whatever the wrongs they feel they have suffered. Money, after all, is a tool of social practice. As such, the same piece of currency, like the same tool, can be used in a wide array of contexts and to do very different things. Most importantly for the argument here, money is one constituent of our "form of life" that because of its homogeneity and nearly unconditional interchangeability turns all values commensurable (at least to the extent that it is humanly possible to do so). But what is equally important, money is a social tool without an essential nature or singular use. It may be used as a means of efficient exchange in markets, but also as a decoration, or as historical artifact, or as symbolic reward, or as a social bonding device. Consequently, it may be used as individual victims determine is necessary to meet their needs and interests regarding their individual things and relationships. Markets, after all, are employed to transfer goods that are not valued simply for market value. People purchase music, whether for the objective value to others or because they personally experience wonder or awe as they listen to it. They buy human care for their children. They trade money for the right to see beautiful areas. They purchase pets for which they feel affection or even love, and not solely for human exploitation and use.

12.8   The Charge of "Commodification"

The most noteworthy arguments against reparation as the most explainable form of punishment revolve around the notion of "commodification." Some things are priceless or sacred, so the argument goes, and so they should not be thought of as commodities, the loss of which might be compensated for monetarily. With regard to the social practice of punishment, the idea is that society, the victim, and the perpetrator are all denigrated ("turned into" commodities) when money is exacted for a criminal wrong. Money is impersonal and thus demeaning in certain contexts. It objectifies and thereby destroys the nuance and beauty of meaningful relationships, undermining nonpecuniary values. Money invades and changes social life for the worse.

As is the case with retribution, this argument seems hypothetical. It seems to propose that if making monetary reparation denies human dignity, then it is wrong. So how, exactly, does the exchange of money for the harm done deny the dignity and worth of human beings? It is significant in this regard to note that it is the understanding that people have of a social practice that determines to a very great extent their attitude toward it. For example, if reparation is understood as payment under a social contract for being a good citizen under extraordinary circumstances (i.e., victimization), such payment seems an affirmation of both personal dignity and the value of a good citizen. Similarly, if restitution is understood as a kind of endowment or grant in appreciation for good citizenship under extraordinary circumstances, its award does not seem to denigrate the individual. It does not generally occur to us, for example, that the money given for information leading to arrests, or the money given to the families of fallen soldiers, or the money we give to the bereaved at funerals, or that the money that we give in support of those experiencing "national disasters" (floods, hurricanes, etc.), might diminish the dignity or value of either the recipients or the people lost. Neither providing nor accepting money as reparation for all such losses or acts of good citizenship is thought to cause a loss of dignity.

The arguments against giving monetary reparation, then, stand on weak rational and sociological grounds. They do not account for different types of monetary transactions, nor are they sufficiently grounded in reality to be rationally convincing. They reason in the wrong direction when they suggest that people are used by money.

12.9 Conclusions

To summarize, the argument to this point has affirmed (1) that "reparation" is generally employed as an inclusive term, "restitution" and "compensation" being reserved for different forms that reparation may take, (2) that "compensation" includes only those monetary reparations made for specific losses or specific damages to life or property, (3) that "restitution" includes any and all other payments or undertakings necessary to both re-establish the *status quo ante* and mitigate the consequences of the violation, and (4) that to best accord with the most reasonable and pragmatic usage of the terms, the prudent course is to restrict the terms "restitution" and "compensation" to monetary forms of "reparation."

With this explication in mind, the argument proceeded to affirm that punishment is one of those particular activities that together constructs our "form of life," and that the only forms of punishment that can be explained satisfactorily are those that require reparation through a state–enforced transfer of money. This conclusion was bolstered by two contentions. The first contention was that the most important and popular alternative explanations are either grounded in hypothesis, incoherence, and dogmatism, or are normatively amiss in that they reflect the interests of dominant social, political, and economic groups. The second was that the disagreements over how to punish reflect the disparate theories of valuation operating among and within different groups of people at different positions in our socioeconomic structure, and that given these plural and disparate valuations, not only must the state take up the role of punisher, but the most efficacious form of punishment is to give people money and let them spend it in ways that they feel afford them the best satisfaction for whatever wrongs they feel they have suffered.

It remains to argue that in order to address pragmatically the nonpecuniary and nonmaterial damages that may be involved in a criminal violation, reparation must include "expressive damages" (money paid to symbolize the vindication of immaterial damages to legal rights and in recognition of the fear, humiliation, mental distress, or harm to a person's reputation or dignity engendered by a crime); pecuniary damages (intended to represent the closest possible financial equivalent of the loss or harm suffered); and punitive damages (intended to both deter and revenge the wrong).

The argument for these addenda is purely pragmatic. As Adam Smith observed, it is a simple fact of human judgment that an unfortunate experience prompts resentment (Smith 1853), and in the criminal justice context, resentment prompts retribution. A number of reasons have been identified for this judgment. One empirically based explanation is that people are motivated to make "defensive attributions" (Robbennolt 2000). That is, when we learn of harm to another, we feel threatened by the possibility that a similar harm may befall us as well. As we find it discomforting to believe that we cannot control the harms that may befall us, we hope to reduce the threat by locating the cause of harm in a single agent and controlling that agent and other potential agents of harm through punishment or the fear of punishment. Another explanation suggests that socially acceptable responses to crime involve necessarily some form of negative feedback that helps citizens to recognize the boundaries of acceptable behavior. As Durkheim reasoned, criminal acts arouse collective sentiments against the infringement of societal norms and elicit retribution as a means strengthening the society's normative consensus (1961).

References

Alexander, L. 1993. Liberalism, religion and the unity of epistemology. *San Diego Law Review* 30, 776.

Anderson, J. L. 1997. Reciprocity as a justification for retributivism. *Criminal Justice Ethics* Winter/Spring.

Arcel, L. T., M. Christiansen, and E. Roque. 2000. Reparation for victims of torture: Some definitions and questions. *Torture* 10, 3, 89.

Aristotle. 1925. *Nichomachian Ethics,* trans. D. Ross. New York: Oxford University Press.

Ashworth, A. 2002. Responsibilities, rights and restorative justice. *British Journal of Criminology* 42, 591.

Barber, B. R. 1984. *Strong Democracy: Participation in Politics for a New Age.* Berkeley: University of California Press.

Benn, S. I. 1958. An approach to the problems of punishment. *Philosophy* 33, 325.

Benn, S. I. 1967. Punishment. *The Encyclopaedia of Philosophy,* vol. 7 and 8. New York: Macmillan, 29.

Benson, K. J. 1977. Innovation and crisis in organizational analysis. In *Organizational Analysis,* ed. K. J. Benson. London: Sage.

Blackstone, W. 1769. *Commentaries on the Laws of England Volume 4.* Chicago: University Chicago Press, 11-12.

Braithwaite, J. 2000. Repentance rituals and restorative justice. *The Journal of Political Philosophy* 8.

Braithwaite, J., and P. Pettit. 1994. Republican criminology and victim advocacy. *Law and Society Review* 28, 770.

Braithwaite, J., and D. Roche. 2001. Responsibility and restorative justice. In *Restorative Community Justice: Repairing Harm and Transforming Community*, ed. G. Bazemore, G. S. Bazemore, and M. Schiffe. Cincinnati: Anderson.

Brett, E. A. 2003. Participation and accountability in development management. *Journal of Development Studies* 2, 40, 1.

Butler, P. 1999. Retribution, for liberals. *UCLA Law Review* 46, 1873.

Chinweizu. 1993. Reparations and a new global order: A comparative overview. Presented at the second Plenary Session of the First Pan-African Conference on Reparations, Abuja, Nigeria. Available at http://www.arm.arc.co.uk/New-GlobalOrder.html

Christopher, R. L. 2002. Deterring retributivism: The injustice of "just" punishment. *Northwestern University Law Review* 96 843.

Cohen, S. 1995. State crimes of previous regimes: Knowledge, accountability, and the policing of the past. *Law and Social Inquiry* 20, 7.

Crawford, J. 2002. *The International Law Commission's Articles on State Responsibility.* Cambridge: Cambridge University Press, 209.

D'Orso, M. 1996. *Like Judgment Day: The Ruin and Redemption of a Town Called Rosewood.* New York: G.P. Putnam's Sons, 206.

Davis, M. 1985. Just deserts for recidivists. *Criminal Justice Ethics* 4, 29.

Deetz, S. 1998. Discursive formations, strategized subordination and self-surveillance. In *Foucault, Management and Organization Theory*, ed. A. McKinlay and K. Starkey. London: Sage.

Dolinko, D. 1992. Three mistakes of retributivism. *UCLA Law Review* 39, 1623.

Downey, Jr., W. G. 1951. Claims for reparations and damages resulting from violation of neutral rights. *Law and Contemporary Problems: Duke University School of Law Journal* 16, 3, 487.

Duff, R. A. 1996. Penal communications: Recent work in the philosophy of punishment. *Crime and Justice* 1, 6, 20.

Duff, R. A. 2000. In defence of one type of retributivism: A reply to Bagaric and Amarasekara. *Melbourne University Law Review* 24, 411, 413.

Dunn, J., ed. 1990. *The Economic Limits to Modern Politics.* Cambridge: Cambridge University Press, 6.

Durkheim, E. 1961. On the normality of crime. In *Theories of Society*, ed. T. Parsons, E. Shils, K. D. Naegele, and J. R. Pitts. New York: Free Press, 872.

Factory at Chorzow Case (*F.R.G. v. Pol.*). 1928. P.C.I.J. (ser. A) No. 17, at 48.

Fay, B. 1987. *Critical Social Science.* Cambridge, U.K.: Polity Press.

Foucault, M. 1972. *The Archaeology of Knowledge and the Discourse of Language.* New York: Pantheon, 187.

Foucault, M. 1994. *Two lectures: Critique and Power: Recasting the Foucault/Habermas Debate*, ed. M. Kelly. Cambridge and London: The MIT Press, 24.

Foucault, M. 1997. *The Birth of the Clinic: An Archaeology of Medical Perception.* London: Routledge, 136.

Friedmann, W. 1953. *Legal Theory,* 3rd ed. London: Stevens, 150.

Garvey, S. P. 1999. Punishment as atonement. *UCLA Law Review* 46, 1801.

Gaus, G. 1991. Does compensation restore equality? In *Nomos XXXIII: Compensatory Justice,* ed. J. W. Chapman. New York: New York University Press, 45.

Glueck, S. 1928. Principles of a rational penal code. *Harvard Law Review* 41, 453.

Green, T. A. 1915, 1995. Freedom and criminal responsibility in the age of pound. *Michigan Law Review* 93.

Habermas, J. 1984. *The Theory of Communicative Action.* Boston: Beacon.

Halttunen, K. 1998. *Murder Most Foul: The Killer and the American Gothic Imagination.* Cambridge: Harvard University Press, 7.

Hamlin, A., and P. Pettit, eds. *The Good Polity: Normative Analysis of the State.* Oxford: Basil Blackwell.

Hampton, J. 1992. Correcting harms versus righting wrongs: The goal of retribution. *UCLA Law Review* 39, 1659.

Haney, C. 1982. Criminal justice and the nineteenth-century paradigm. *Law and Human Behavior* 6, 193.

Harré, R., and E. Madden. 1975. *Causal Powers: A Theory of Natural Necessity.* Oxford: Basil Blackwell.

Hart, H. L. A. 1968. Prolegomenon for the principles of punishment. In *Punishment and Responsibility,* ed. H. L. A. Hart. Oxford: Clarendon Press.

Hegel, G. 1952. *Hegel's Philosophy of Right,* trans. T. M. Knox. Chicago: University of Chicago Press, 100.

Held, D. 1980. *Introduction to Critical Theory: Horkheimer to Habermas.* Berkeley: University of California Press, 184.

Honneth, A. 1994. *The Struggle for Recognition.* Cambridge, U.K.: Polity Press.

Horder, J. 2002. Criminal law and legal positivism. *Legal Theory* 8, 221.

Horkheimer, M. 1972. Traditional and critical theory. In *Critical Theory,* ed. M. Horkheimer. New York: Herder and Herder.

Horkheimer, M. 1974. *Eclipse of Reason.* New York: Seabury Press, 182.

Horkheimer, M., and T. Adorno. 1947. *The Dialectics of Enlightenment.* London: Verso.

Kant, I. 1991. *Metaphysical First Principles of the Doctrine of Right,* trans. M. J. Gregor. Cambridge: Cambridge University Press.

Kanter, R. 1985. The *Change Masters: Corporate Entrepreneurs at Work.* London: Routledge.

Kritzman, L. D., ed. 1988. *Michel Foucault, Politics, Philosophy, and Culture: Interviews and Other Writings.* New York: Routledge, Chapman, & Hall, 108.

Kymlicka, W. 1990. *Contemporary Political Philosophy.* New York: Oxford University Press, 206.

Lerman, D. M. 2000. Forgiveness in the criminal justice system: If it belongs, then why is it so hard to find? *Fordham Urban Law Journal* 27, 1663.

Lewis, C. S. 1970. The humanitarian theory of punishment. *res judicatae* 6, 1954, reprinted in *Readings in Ethical Theory*, 2nd ed., ed. W. Sellars and J. Hospers. New York: Appleton-Century-Crofts, 646.

Lieberman, D. 2002. Mapping criminal law: Blackstone and the categories of English jurisprudence. In *Law, Crime and English Society 1660-1830*, ed. N. Landau. Cambridge: Cambridge University Press, 155.

Lippke, R. L. 2003. Diminished opportunities, diminished capacities: social deprivation and punishment. *Social Theory and Practice* 29, 3, 459, 2003.

Locke, J. 1978. *Two Treatises of Government.* New York: E. P. Dutton.

Luban, D. 1996. The Posner variations: Twenty-seven variations on a theme by Holmes. *Stanford Law Review* 48, 1001.

Marcuse, H. 1964. *One Dimensional Man.* Boston: Beacon.

Margalit, A. 1996. *The Decent Society.* Cambridge: Harvard University Press, 70.

Martini Case (*Italy v. Venez.*). 1930. 2 R.I.A.A. 975.

McKenzie, P. T. 1967. Fact and value. *Mind, New Series* 76, 302, 228.

Moore, M. 1997. *Placing Blame: A Theory of Criminal Law.* Oxford: Oxford University Press, 186.

Morris, H. 1968. Persons and punishment. *The Monist 52.*

Mundle, C. W. K. 1954. Punishment and desert. *Philosophy Quarterly* 4, 216.

Rawls, J. 1971. *A Theory of Justice.* Cambridge: Harvard University Press, 253.

Rawls, J. 1993. *Political Liberalism.* New York: Columbia University Press.

Robbennolt, J. K. 2000. Outcome severity and judgments of responsibility: A meta-analytic review. *Journal of Applied Social Psychology* 30, 2575.

Rock, P. E. 1990. *Helping Victims of Crime: The Home Office and the Rise of Victim Support in England and Wales.* Oxford: Clarendon.

Sayre-McCord, G. 2001. Criminal justice and legal reparations as an alternative to punishment. *Philosophical Issues, Vol. 11.* Oxford: Blackwell.

Searle, J. 1984. *Minds, Brains, and Science.* Cambridge: Harvard University Press, 94.

Shapland, J. 1984. Victims, the criminal justice system and compensation. *British Journal of Criminology*, 24, 131.

Sharp, F. C. 1908. The objectivity of the moral judgment. *The Philosophical Review* 17, 3, 249.

Smith, A. 1853. *The Theory Of Moral Sentiments.* London: Harrison & Sons, 152.

Strang, H., and L. W. Sherman. 2003. Repairing the harm: Victims and restorative justice. *Utah Law Review* 15, 16.

United Nations. 2001a. Article 34, Draft Articles on Responsibility of States for Internationally Wrongful Acts. In *Report of the International Law Commission on the Work of Its Fifty-third Session.* U.N. GAOR, 56th Sess., Supp. No. 10, art. 30, UN Doc. A/56/10, http://www.un.org/law/ilc/texts/State responsibility/responsibilityfra.htm

United Nations. 2001b. Article 35, Draft Articles on Responsibility of States for Internationally Wrongful Acts. In *Report of the International Law Commission on the Work of Its Fifty-third Session.* UN GAOR, 56th Sess., Supp. No. 10, art. 30, UN Doc. A/56/10, http://www.un.org/law/ilc/texts/State responsibility/responsibilityfra.htm

van Boven, T., and United Nations. 1993. *Study Concerning the Right to Restitution, Compensation and Rehabilitation for Victims of Gross Violations of Human Rights and Fundamental Freedoms, Final Report.* U.N. Doc. E/CN.4/Sub.2/1993, paragraph 137.

Veblen, T. 1932. *The Place of Science in Modern Civilization.* New York: Random House, 74.

Veblen, T. 1934. *The Theory of the Leisure Class.* New York: Random House, 198.

Velleman, D. 1996. The possibility of practical reason. *Ethics* 106, 694.

von Hirsch, A. 1976. *Doing Justice: The Choice of Punishments.* New York: Hill and Wang.

von Hirsch, A. 1990. The politics of just deserts. *Canadian Journal of Criminology* 32, 397.

von Hirsch, A., and A. J. Ashworth. 1992. Not just deserts: A response to Braithwaite and Pettit. *Oxford Journal of Legal Studies* 12, 83.

Wasserstrom, R. 1982. Capital punishment as punishment: Some theoretical issues and objections. *Midwest Studies in Philosophy* 7, 476.

Wiener, M. J. 1990. *Reconstructing the Criminal: Culture, Law, and Policy in England, 1830-1914.* Cambridge: Cambridge University Press.

Wilensky, H. L. 1957. Human relations in the workplace. In *Research in Industrial Human Relations: A Critical Appraisal,* ed. C. Arensberg et al. New York: Harper & Row, 34.

Williams, W. E. 1991. False civil rights vision and contempt for rule of law. *Georgetown Law Journal* 79, 1777.

Wittgenstein, L. 1953. *Philosophical Investigations.* Oxford: Oxford University Press, 131.

Wittgenstein, L. 1969. *On Certainty.* New York: Harper Torchbooks, 81.

Wittgenstein, L. 1980. *Remarks on the Philosophy of Psychology, Vol. 1,* trans. by G. E. M. Anscombe. Chicago: University of Chicago Press.

Wittgenstein, L. 1993. *Philosophical Occasions, 1912-1951,* ed. J. Klagge and A. Nordmann. Indianapolis: Hackett.

Womack, J. P., and D. T. Jones. 1990. *The Machine that Changed the World: ... the Future of the Automobile.* New York: Rawson.

Wright, M. 1985. The impact of victim/offender mediation on the victim. *Victimology* 10, 631.

Wright, M. 1996. *Justice for Victims and Offenders: A Restorative Response to Crime,* 2nd ed. Winchester, U.K.: Waterside Press, 47.

Zehr, H. 1990. *Changing Lenses: A New Focus for Crime and Justice.* Scottsdale, PA: Herald Press, 6.

Zimring, F. E., G. Hawkins, and S. Kamin. 2001. *Punishment and Democracy: Three Strikes and You're Out in California.* New York: Oxford.

The Police

JOSEPH A. SCHAFER AND CLEMENS BARTOLLAS

13

Contents

The police role in contemporary society raises several basic questions. For example, for what social purpose do the police exist (Skolnick 1994)? What does society want the police to do? How does society want the police to do these things? How do the police balance "to protect and serve" with "to enforce the law?" (Walker and Katz 2002). Are views of and experiences with the police uniform across members of the public? What aspects of modern policing generate controversy and conflict? Who will control the controllers? This chapter considers these questions central to developing a basic understanding of contemporary police and policing.

An examination of policing in a society must take place within the historical, legal, social, political, cultural, and economic contexts of that society. In the United States, policing takes place in a free and democratic society, including open, equal, and accountable governance. What this means is that the police must operate in accordance with democratic principles. The highest priority of the police in such a society is the protection of life. As recipients of public trust, the police are mandated to treat others with dignity and respect and are held accountable to the community they serve. Finally, the police are expected to discharge their duties in a nondiscriminatory manner (Langworthy and Travis 2003). Despite such lofty visions of the police, history is replete with situations in which officers and agencies have failed to live up to their mandate.

When there is clear evidence in the United States that the police have overstepped their authority, such as using force in an excessive manner, profiling or other forms of racial discrimination of minorities, or being involved in corruption, there is a public outcry and some forms of restrictions are usually placed on the police. Offending police departments have been the focus of public and political protest, cause for legal action, and, in recent years, subject to intervention and oversight by the federal government. Offending police officers have been terminated from their jobs, have been sued successfully in civil courts, and have been convicted in criminal courts and sent to prison. Despite these consequences, police officers and organizations continue to breach the public's trust, though the degree to which this is a problem is subject to some debate (Kappler, Sluder, and Alpert 1998).

Policing remains controversial because officers are granted wide discretionary authority and operate within an environment exemplified by openness and low levels of direct supervision. For reasons discussed below, police officers routinely make decisions from a range of options, including deciding whether to invoke the legal system through arresting or citing violators. The nature of police work allows officers to frequently make these weighty decisions with few witnesses; those who do observe police actions often lack credibility due to their lifestyle and criminal record. The discretionary choices of the police include decisions that invoke the criminal justice process. With an arrest, the criminal justice system swings into action. In various court processes, decisions will be made that will ultimately determine the defendant's guilt; if guilt is determined, the court pronounces a sentence. Depending upon the jurisdiction and sentencing structure, this defendant may be sentenced to prison or a community-based placement. As the "gatekeepers" of the justice system, the police play a pivotal role in shaping when and how laws are actually enforced; based on their enforcement choices, they have the capacity to influence who ends up in court and corrections systems.

This chapter begins with an overview of the history and development of modern policing systems; understanding the police of the twenty-first century requires that we look back more than one thousand years. Consideration is then given to the general structure of police organizations, followed by a discussion of the role of the police in contemporary society. Next, we explore police culture and how it affects police officers and the relationship between the police and the public they serve. This leads to an examination of police operations and community relations, including overviews of community policing and problem-oriented policing (POP). Finally, we describe four contemporary problems that shape the world of modern policing and police officers.

13.1   History and Development of the Police

The study of the history of the police helps us understand modern policing in the United States. For example, an examination of the history of the police can help explain the origins and impact of community policing, and it can also be useful in viewing the long history of corruption and why it has been so difficult to eliminate (Walker and Katz 2002). If we are to appreciate the structure and operation of contemporary policing, we must have an understanding of the successes and failures evident in earlier eras. To begin this brief review of policing, we will examine six periods in the development of policing in the United States: (1) early European origins, 1000–1700 c.e.; (2) policing England in the 1700s; (3) Peelian reforms; (4) colonial police; (5) the development of municipal police; and (6) twentieth- and twentieth-first-century police.

13.1.1   European Origins, 1000-1700 c.e.

The birth of modern policing can be traced to the reign of Alfred the Great, who ruled England from 871 to 900 c.e. Alfred instituted a system of mutual pledge in order to provide a defense against an impending Danish invasion. Designed to create internal stability, this system organized England from the smallest level to that of counties. The smallest level of this community-based police system was called a *tithing,* made up of ten families who assumed responsibility for each other. One man from each tithing was appointed to be the *tithingman* with the duty to make certain all members obeyed the law. When a crime occurred (a relatively rare phenomenon), the tithingman was responsible for bringing the offender before the court. The next level was the *hundred,* made up of ten tithings or 100 families. A constable was appointed to be in charge of the hundred. Within a specific geographic area, hundreds were combined to form *shires.* To maintain order in the shires, the king appointed a *shire-reeve* (later to be called a sheriff) to be the chief law enforcement officer. The sheriff traveled on horseback throughout the shire, keeping peace, holding court, and investigating crimes (Emsley 1996).

During the reign of Edward I (1272–1307), the first official police agency was created in an English town. Groups of men were appointed to patrol the streets at night with the twin function of maintaining a fire watch and arresting those committing crimes. This became known as the watch and ward system. The office of justice of the peace was created during the reign of Edward II to assist the mutual pledge system. The justice of the peace soon took over the role of magistrate and eventually asserted control over the sheriff and constables (Critchley 1978). Under these systems, every able-bodied man had a duty to lend aid in the pursuit of offenders. A man pursuing an offender was to raise the "hue and cry," alerting others to the presence of a threat to the community's safety and security. Other men were obligated to render aid to ensure the capture of the offender; failure to lend aid was a punishable criminal offense (Pringle 1955). Under these early systems, policing was not a full-time occupation; rather, it was a part-time civic duty that most men would eventually fulfill. Even when they were not the appointed police authority, all men were bound to take actions and lend aid to protect the community.

13.1.2   Policing England in the 1700s

The watch and ward system worked well while England was an agrarian society, with most people living in small villages. People knew one another and had few material possessions, so the opportunities for criminal behavior were limited, and informal social networks persuaded most residents to obey the law. In the 1700s, England began to undergo a social and economic transformation, partly caused by the start of the Industrial Revolution. People began to leave the countryside to pursue employment in factories located in urban centers; unfortunately, workers were more plentiful than jobs. Around this same time, legal and technological changes resulted in the wide availability of cheap distilled spirits. The result of these (and other) forces was a rise in urban centers marked by unemployment, alcoholism, vice, unsanitary living environments, and increasing levels of crime (Reith 1948). The social and legal systems that had been successful when England was an agricultural nation did not work well to quell this rising tide of crime and disorder.

For example, by the 1630s, London had instituted a system of watchmen, or *Charlies*, who were responsible for patrolling the streets at night, lighting lamps, and reporting unsanitary conditions (Critchley 1978). The poorly paid watchmen were frequently aging and sickly persons who were untrained, ill-equipped, and not inclined to risk harm in the pursuit of criminals. This era also witnessed the rise of corruption in the ranks of the police and legal systems; constables and watchmen often took bribes to ignore criminal behavior (Pringle 1955). The ineffectiveness of the magistrate, constable, and watchman arrangements led to the development of a private detective system as a supplement. The "thief taker" was one such system, in which private individuals would apprehend criminals for a fee or reward; although widely praised at the time, some evidence suggests that these private groups were often closely aligned with the criminals they "pursued" (Reith 1948; Pringle 1955). Through this convergence of circumstances, crime and disorder were rapidly rising in urban centers, yet citizens lacked confidence in the protective abilities of the existing police and court systems. Despite recognizing this situation, it was a number of decades before political reformers could craft an alternative justice system that British citizens would support.

13.1.3   Peelian Reforms

Sir Robert Peel, who was appointed England's Home Secretary in 1822, responded to the public mandate for greater order by proposing a bill to reorganize the police system. Initially, his recommendations were rejected by Parliament, but a bill entitled "An Act Improving the Police In and Near the Metropolis" was passed on July 19, 1829. Known as the Metropolitan Police Act, the measure set up two justices of the peace, called commissioners, to establish regulations for the hiring, training, and supervision of police officers to serve the greater London region (Emsley 1996). The act dissolved London's patchwork of existing constable and watch systems, replacing it with one large force, "the Met." The intent was to purge London of corrupt police authorities, replacing them with a trained and well-controlled force that could be effective and could regain public confidence.

Peel's foresight, along with strong leadership exhibited by the first commissioners, Charles Rowan and Richard Mayen, enabled the police to overcome distrust and hatred from the citizens and to develop the approach to law enforcement that became dominant in England and later the United States (although to a lesser extent). There were twelve principles developed during the period, including the following:

1. The police must be stable, efficient, and organized along military lines.
2. The police must be under government control.
3. The selection and training of proper persons are at the root of efficient law enforcement.
4. The keeping of crime records by police is necessary to determine the best distraction of police strength. (Adams 1973).

In order to be effective, officers of the Met were told they had to earn and maintain the public's respect. This was achieved by demanding that officers be professional, courteous, well mannered, and even-tempered.

The early Met implemented the first systematic attempt to link the police and the community they served. The beat was an important feature of this police system in that police constables were assigned relatively permanent posts and were expected to be familiar with them. The virtue of the beat system was that it provided for the continuing presence of a police officer as a part of the community or neighborhood. It was reasoned that the public would know the constable and that citizens with information about potential criminality would be more likely to convey it to a familiar figure than a stranger. By the end of the eighteenth century, the calm, courteous, and restrained "bobby" had become a national symbol and was given credit for making London a relatively safe city (Ramsay 1928).

13.1.4   Colonial Police

The origins of modern policing in the United States can be linked directly to their English heritage. Prior to the American Revolution, the colonies used a form of policing quite similar to the parish constable system. In seventeenth-century colonial America, the settlers occupied themselves with erecting homes and planting crops. Violations of the law most often involved individuals who ran afoul of community obligations or morals. Accordingly, policing typically concentrated on ordinary people's behaviors. Historian David R. Johnson wrote, "Colonists found themselves in court for such conduct as working on the Sabbath, failing to pen animals properly, begetting a bastard child, and cursing in public places" (1981: 4). Police officers and judges were rarely full-time positions; rather, these were part-time duties carried out by members of the community.

The sheriff, the constable, the watch, and the slave patrol were the principal forms of law enforcement in colonial America. The sheriff had the authority to protect life and property, enforce laws, and execute the wishes of the courts. The constable, whose duties varied from place to place, usually sealed weights and measures, announced marriages, surveyed land, and executed all warrants. Watchmen were charged to patrol the city, guarding against fires, crimes, and disorder; this eventually evolved into a paid professional position (Reppetto 1978). Created in the Southern states and an egregious form of American law enforcement, the slave patrol's purpose was to guard against slave revolts and to capture runaway slaves (Reichel 1988). These rudimentary systems worked well so long as the colonies consisted of small groups of people living off the land; familiarity was high and informal social control served as an effective regulator over undesirable behavior. The social changes that swept across Europe in the 1700s reached America's shores in the early 1800s, bringing comparable changes to crime, urban conditions, and the efficacy of prevailing justice systems.

13.1.5 Development of Municipal Policing

As the Industrial Revolution reached America's shores, the nation's social and economic systems underwent changes similar to those witnessed in England. Further complicating the associated crime and disorder problems in America was a constant inflow of immigrants, who fueled additional tensions among various economic, political, cultural, and religious groups. By the middle of the 1830s, riots were occurring in Boston, New York, and Philadelphia. The cities found it difficult to deal with this civil disorder because they had no force of social control available other than the military. Members of existing public safety systems were not trained, equipped, or staffed to deal with large-scale urban conflict.

In 1833, the city of Philadelphia separated the watch system into a paid day watch and night watch, but New York City is credited with organizing the first police force patterned to some extent after the British model. In 1844, the New York State Legislature gave cities and towns in that state the power to organize police forces, and the city of New York then consolidated its day and night watches under the leadership of an appointed chief of police. Similar police systems were soon adopted in Baltimore, Chicago, Cincinnati, Newark, New Orleans, and Philadelphia (Richardson 1974). In the 1840s and 1850s, major American cities began to implement a policing system loosely based on the London Met. Later, ideas such as crime prevention, community policing, sheriffs, and the posse were developed from English law enforcement.

Although rooted in many of the same ideas, early "modern" police systems were very different in England and American (Miller 1977). That

American policing divorced itself in many ways from its English heritage is largely a function of important differences in the social and legal contexts of these nations (Kappler, Sluder, and Alpert 1998). The most striking difference between the English and American models was in the area of control. In England, the strong central leadership in the Metropolitan Police was able to deal immediately with police problems. The English police had clear lines of authority leading up to the commissioner, who in turn answered to the Home Secretary in Parliament. In contrast, the American system was disorganized, with unclear lines of authority. A police officer in any given city could be at the command of the chief of police, the mayor, an elected alderman, or all three. Favors were rewarded and scores settled through the hiring and firing of police officers, who served at the will of elected city officials. In England, policing was a technical task with some political aspects, while policing became in the United States a political task with some technical aspects.

Initially, the police and the community had good relations, but the fact that nineteenth-century police were primarily tools of local politicians eventually affected their public relations. This political control led to widespread corruption and brutality and made the police ineffective in preventing crime or providing equitable services. This rampant corruption and abuse of office in nineteenth-century policing reflected a widespread condition in American municipal politics; the problems with policing systems were no different than the problems in other municipal government and regulatory systems. The passage of the Pendleton Act of 1833 finally brought some control to corrupt government systems. This act established and set rules for civil service commissions, governed entrance examinations and promotions, and provided means by which grievances could be resolved. Civil service rules did not solve all the problems of hiring and promotion, but they did remove much of the serious political interference that had adversely affected police forces in the United States (Johnson 1981).

13.1.6　Twentieth-Century Policing

In the twentieth century, policing went through a reform and professional movement, a fighting crime movement, and a public relations and community policing movement. These stages of police history did not follow each other in a sequential pattern but often took place at the same time.

13.1.7　Reform and Police Administration

The Progressives spearheaded a broad reform movement that began to develop during the final decades of the nineteenth century. These reforms focused on improving the quality and equity of government services to ensure that all citizens had equal access and protection. As part of their social and political movement, the Progressives supported upgrading the quality of police personnel and held that the police should be selected, deployed, and promoted on the basis of personal ability, rather than on the basis of partisan politics (Fogelson 1977). Three of the most noted reform leaders were Chiefs Augustus Vollmer, O. W. Wilson, and William H. Parker. All three believed strongly that a police officer must be carefully selected, well trained, free from political interference, and provided with the most up-to-date technology and hardware. The Reformers contributed a great deal to the firm establishment of professional policing, a movement that persists even today. In the 1970s, minority hiring, more extensive training, utilization of private sector management techniques, and evaluation of police operations, including patrol, were some of the approaches used to advance professionalism in policing. Contemporarily, there is still ongoing discussion of what new training, education, policies, technologies, and ideas can be applied to further the professionalism exhibited by police officers and agencies.

13.1.8 Crime Fighters

In the 1920s and early 1930s, the prohibition of liquor sales in the United States set the backdrop for the rise of the violent gangster and led police to see themselves as "crime fighters." For the first time, the American public began to associate the police with the large-scale enforcement of the law, and the police began to claim this role in society. Even today, people are familiar with the folklore images rooted in this era, such as federal agent Elliot Ness and his "Untouchables" relentlessly pursuing underworld figures such as Al Capone, George "Baby Face" Nelson, and Charles "Pretty Boy" Floyd. In the 1930s, the Federal Bureau of Investigation began to oversee the Uniform Crime Report, which provided police departments with a benchmark based on the level of crime in their community. Popular media images in the intervening decades cast the police as the "thin blue line" between order and chaos. Although rarely discussed prior to the 1930s, it is impossible to separate contemporary police from the crime fighter/law enforcer image.

In both the 1968 and 1972 presidential elections, Richard Nixon declared a war on crime, lamenting what crime in the streets was doing to the quality of American life. During his terms in office, President Nixon advocated a law-and-order approach to crime. Gerald Ford continued the war on crime from the White House, but President Ronald Reagan fought the war with even greater diligence. His emphasis was on violent street crime during his first term in office, but during his second term, he focused on violent crime, drug trafficking, and organized crime. President George Bush also continued the war on crime but his primary concern was with waging the war on drugs. President Bill Clinton did not abandon the war on crime and drugs during his two administrations. Nor has President George W. Bush chosen to abandon this unwinnable war on crime during his two administrations. Extending this crime-fighting tone set by national leaders, police continue to focus on their role as enforcers of the law, despite questionable evidence supporting their ability to fulfill this mandate (see chapter 14 by Weisburd and Eck).

13.1.9   Public Relations and Community Policing

In the 1960s and early 1970s, America underwent another era of social transformation as a result of Vietnam War protests, the Civil Rights movement, and the push for equal rights for women. From this came the belief that the government needed to be more responsive to the public, including reconsidering how the police and the public interacted. The reform, professionalism, and crime-fighting movements had reduced the emphasis on community contacts and relations. In the 1970s, the pendulum swung back to some degree as a number of community-based programs were developed and implemented in police departments across the nation. As discussed later in the chapter, one of the key ideas resulting from this reformulation of police operations was the idea of community-oriented policing (COP). Community policing envisions the police collaborating with the public to identify community problems, set local priorities, design and implement solutions, and reclaim troubled areas. Although it is tenuous to say community policing reduces crime (Cordner 1997), the idea has radically transformed the rhetoric of policing.

13.2   The Structure of Police Organizations

The organization of American policing is often labeled as "fragmented" because there are over 17,000 local, state, federal, and special police forces. This large number of agencies makes it difficult to describe policing in America; for every observation made, there are several hundred agencies that deviate. This chapter focuses on what is generally true about American police agencies; however, the reader should note that there are exceptions to every generalization made by the authors. Despite this caveat, police departments in the United States are similar in terms of organizational structure and administrative style. All but very small police departments are complex bureaucracies, with an authoritarian management style and a hierarchical structure. In addition, all but the smallest agencies are governed by civil service rules that regulate personnel policies. Furthermore, many departments are bound by collective bargaining agreements with unions representing rank-and-file officers (Walker and Katz 2002).

13.2.1 Police Departments as Bureaucratic Organizations

Historically, the idea of structuring organizations as bureaucracies was developed to make money, but many of the principles used to make profits are now used to manage people-oriented organizations. The purpose behind bureaucracies is to ensure efficient and methodical social organization. Bureaucracies are based on the principle of rationalism, the same principle that has been so vital to the rise of science and the mastery of the physical and biological worlds. If human social organization could approach the efficiency of a machine, theorists reasoned, profits and the acquisition of capital could be maximized.

Accordingly, bureaucracies were to be so organized that nothing was left to chance. Max Weber, the German sociologist who provided the theoretical basis for bureaucracies, wrote: "The decisive reason for the advance of a bureaucratic organization has always been its purely technical superiority over any other form of organization. The fully developed bureaucratic mechanism compares with other organizations exactly as does the machine with the nonmechanical model of production" (Gerth and Mills 1958: 214). In other words, bureaucracies were supposed to be more efficient, dependable, and accurate than other ways of structuring people and organizations.

Weber, in a now-classic statement, analyzed the basic components of rules of bureaucracies:

1. There is the principle of fixed and official jurisdictional areas, which are generally ordered by rules, that is, by laws or administrative regulations.
2. The principle of office hierarchy and of levels of graded authority means a firmly ordered system of super- and subordination in which there is a supervision of the lower offices by the higher ones.
3. The management of the modern office is based upon written documents ("the files"), which are preserved in their original or draft form.
4. Office management, at least all specialized office management—and such management is distinctly modern—usually presupposes thorough and expert training.
5. When the office is fully developed, official activity demands the full working capacity of the official, irrespective of the fact that his obligatory time in the bureau may be firmly delimited.
6. The management of the office follows general rules, which are more or less stable, more or less exhaustive, and which can be learned (Gerth and Mills 1958: 196-198).

As a reflection of its bureaucratic nature, an organizational chart of a large police department shows the complexity of the organization. In police agencies, a hierarchy exists, in which chiefs are at the top, generally followed by assistant chiefs, captains, lieutenants, sergeants, and line officers. In this paramilitary bureaucracy, officers are centrally commanded, owe allegiance to a commander, and execute orders originating from above. A central communication center directs how and where officers are to be deployed. The police, according to this bureaucratic model, are to be "professional," cool, and autonomous (Manning 1997).

A positive contribution of bureaucracy within police organizations can be seen through the lens of history. For example, bureaucratic principles have been useful in the control of police discretion and in the reduction of misconduct and excessive use of form (Schafer 2002). Yet there have been problems with the bureaucratic movement within policing. Police departments have been accused of failing to respond creatively to a changing social environment, being unresponsive and closed to the citizens they serve, and failing to develop the talents of the rank-and-file police officer. Police departments fall short of true bureaucracies, because despite having many written rules, they fail to control the behavior, or discretion, of officers on the streets in making routine decisions (Walker and Katz 2002).

13.2.2 Formal Patterns of Organizational Operations

Police organizations have a number of formal features that are reflective of their bureaucratic roots. First, police departments are organized along quasimilitary lines. Similar to the military, police officers wear uniforms, follow a hierarchical command structure, use military rank designations, and carry weapons with the legal authority to use physical and deadly force. Communication, information, and authority flow up and down the hierarchy; requests are processed through the "chain of command." Police organizations and their leaders tend toward authoritarian organizational styles, with stiff penalties for failing to follow orders.

Second, police departments are part of other organizational systems. The police do not exist in a vacuum. Other police, criminal justice, and social service agencies, as well as the communities they serve, affect them. The police are affiliated with various levels of government. They do not have direct control over the size of their budget, and legislative, executive, and judicial rulings all shape what and how they do. Police organizations and their leaders are also a part of the political system, making them somewhat susceptible to public demands and pressures. Although most police executives are not elected, they typically serve at the pleasure of elected government executive officers. Consequently, these police executives must be conscious of community and political pressures; by extension, this affects the organization and employees at all levels. Managers who fail to acknowledge the interconnected nature of policing tend to approach organizations as aggregates of components, each of which are separate from and managed independently of the other. The result is a fragmented approach to the management of the total organization.

Third, effective planning is vital for successful police operations. Planning is concerned with formulating and constructing the design of the organization and deciding on goals and priorities (Sheehan and Cordner 1995). The planning process is involved in the operation of every aspect of the department. Specifically, it involves staff supervision of planning activities; development of long-range capabilities; analysis of departmental subsystems, policies, and procedures; analysis of crime and accident patterns, service needs, and personnel deployment; and development of contingency plans for operational activities, crowd control and riots, and natural disasters. Planning further takes place in establishing intra- and intercity roadblock plans to intercept fleeing felons, in studying the feasibility of developing regional police services, in selecting electronic processing systems to streamline record keeping, and in developing a fiscal planning capability for future support of police services. Finally, planning is involved in evaluating current plans and services (Sheehan and Cordner 1995).

Fourth, staffing is an important consideration in respect to all work that takes place in a police department. Although the police executive usually delegates staffing responsibilities to others, he or she is still ultimately responsible for all the decisions that are made. The emphasis on standards and liability in police work encourages departments to spend more money on recruiting and testing police candidates and on upgrading training procedures. Staffing takes place in phases comprised of recruitment, hiring, retention, promotion, and ongoing training. Some departments recruit locally and others, such as the Dallas Police Department, have full-time recruiters who travel across the United States soliciting prospective candidates for employment.

Finally, supervising is an important dimension of police work. In the complex organization of police departments, the performance of police officers depends to a large extent on the first-line supervisor. The nature of police work makes it difficult to effectively and directly supervise front-line police officers. Patrol officers are mobile, work large geographic areas, and often conduct their job with few witnesses. Even if they have a small number of officers to monitor, front-line supervisors cannot observe all the actions of their subordinates. Too often, departments give promotions to people who have been "good" employees in their previous position. Unfortunately, the skill sets associated with being a good patrol officer may differ from those associated with being a good police officer. This problem is compounded because newly promoted supervisors are rarely given structured training to understand how to effectively supervise. Given the increased spectra of liability, it is not surprising that some supervisors are hesitant about the role they are supposed to assume. Lacking any clear indication of what they are supposed to do or not having adequate training to prepare them for their jobs, some supervisors withdraw from active supervision. The assumption of this passive orientation has the potential to create further liability and conduct problems due to inadequate supervision of front-line personnel.

13.3   The Role of the Police in Society

The police serve a variety of roles in contemporary society, a situation that is both desirable and the source of conflict and controversy (Roberg 1976). We want the police to serve various roles because we have a number of goals we expect them to achieve. For example, although the enforcement of criminal law is a central expectation we may have of the police, most citizens want the police to deal with additional matters that are not crimes. At the same time, there are a number of situations in which our expectations of the police are in conflict; if one expectation is fulfilled, another might be violated. In addition, our general vision of the role of the police in society may not be consistent with how officers actually spend their time.

13.3.1   Common Roles of the Police

One consequence of the move to professionalize the police is that officers have assumed the role of front-line representatives of criminal law. Through their power to investigate crimes and identify offenders for prosecution, they are the gatekeepers of the criminal justice system. When officers issue a citation or make an arrest, they are fulfilling the role of *crime fighter/law enforcer*. The public readily identifies the crime fighter role with the police, although it comprises a modest proportion of the duties officers actually perform. The police are responsible for ensuring that laws are followed by members of the public and taking actions when violations are noted. Whether their enforcement actions actually impact the crime rate is subject to some debate (see chapter 14 by Weisburd and Eck); society expects the police to spearhead crime-fighting efforts. Despite the general expectation that they will invoke the law when violations are detected, in many situations the police enjoy the discretion to choose what laws they will enforce and when. This situation, discussed later in this chapter, generates a great deal of controversy.

Police officers are also called upon to handle a wide range of matters that are not criminal in nature, but relate to *preserving order/keeping the peace*. For example, the police may be called to mediate for two neighbors arguing over removing a tree sitting on their property line. Society expects the police to diffuse personal disputes, regulate the flow of traffic, control rowdy crowds, and deal with a range of other behaviors that, while legal, are chaotic and/or socially undesirable. Because they are readily available (usually all day, every day) and because modern communications technology makes them easy to reach, "calling the cops" is an easy way for the public to generate an official response to a host of problems and conflicts (Bittner 1990). When a situation arises that is dangerous, objectionable, or annoying, the police are often called upon to restore the status quo.

The police also *provide services* within the community that are not related to crime or order. Officers assist disabled motorists, provide emergency medical care, check on the welfare of persons in need, and provide various forms of general assistance and information to the public. In a classic essay on the police, Egon Bittner discussed police work as dealing with "something-that-ought-not-to-be-happening-and-about-which-someone-had-better-do-something-now " (1990: 249). Because of their ready availability relative to most other government and social service agencies (which often only provide services during normal business hours), the public is conditioned to call the police, and they know the police will respond to most requests for service. The result is that police officers spend a considerable amount of time performing duties outside of society's popular vision of police work.

13.3.2 Conflict and Controversy in the Roles of the Police

The three roles discussed above likely seem acceptable to most citizens. They are not, however, always compatible with one another. One of the problems emerging from the historical evolution of Western policing (particularly in America) is the expectation that police simultaneously serve these three roles. Although their relative weight has varied across time, American police have been and are still expected to be law enforcers, peacekeepers, and service providers. It is desirable that police fulfill these roles, but doing so is not always a simple process. For example, consider an officer responding to a report of a rowdy party in a residential neighborhood. Upon arriving, the officer discovers that a recent college graduate is celebrating with forty close friends, including several partygoers who are standing in the street (a public area) drinking beer. In this community, it is illegal to possess open containers of alcohol on public property. The officer could fulfill the role of law enforcer and issue citations to those violators. In doing so, however, the officer might devote significant time away from other activities; is the enforcement of a minor alcohol crime more important than other law enforcement activities the officer might pursue? What if the crowd becomes unruly in response to the officer's enforcement action, creating a violent public disturbance? Although the latter possibility may not be sufficient cause for the officer to overlook the legal violations, it would mean enforcing the law occurred at the expense of public order.

In confronting these types of situations (which are common in policing), officers have little guidance as to which role they ought to pursue and in what ways. Officers are told to fulfill all three roles, but are not explicitly told how to decide which role is most important in a given situation or what to do when the roles are in conflict. Rather than being uniformly trained on this matter, officers develop individual styles based on their personality, experiences, informal peer influences, and organizational expectations. The result is that officers differ in how they interpret and prioritize these three roles. Similar offenders are often treated in different ways based upon the role orientation of the responding officer; in the scenario above, one officer might issue citations, whereas another may prefer warning the violators. Allowing officers to develop their own style is not inherently bad, but it does result in variation in how communities are policed and which laws are enforced.

Variation occurs not only across officers, but also across agencies. Some agencies encourage officers to place one role above the others. This is reflected in a classic work by James Q. Wilson that described three different "styles" of police organizations (legalistic, watchmen, and service) that reflect the three roles (1968). On the one hand, varieties in policing styles (across both officer and agencies) are desirable. Different communities have different local values, crime problems, and financial resources for policing efforts. A legal response to the public drinking scenario may be preferred and feasible in a small college community with little serious crime. In a major urban area with a drug and gang problem, however, we might prefer the police spend time and resources focusing on more serious offenses. Variety in the overall "style" of a police agency is desirable, but once again, it creates inconsistencies in how communities are policed. Public drinking in community A might result in a warning, whereas next door in community B it results in an arrest.

13.3.3   What the Police Do

Common public perceptions of police work tend to derive from myths and misleading media images. The bulk of activities officers handle are not criminal in nature; when criminal matters are encountered, they are rarely violent in nature. For example, an analysis of public calls to the police in a sample of major American cities found that only one-fifth involved crime; only 10 percent of these calls (2 percent of all calls) involved violent criminal offenses (Scott 1981). When citizens called the police, it was typically to request information or assistance, to report disorderly or nuisance behavior, or to report traffic problems. This is not to say that the crime fighter role is unimportant; rather, it is only a part of the role police actually fulfill in society.

Police patrol officers also spend large amounts of time outside of direct contact with the public. Observational studies of patrol officers in two major American communities suggested that officers only spent about one-quarter of their working hours in contact with the public; in an eight-hour shift, officers had contact with about ten citizens (Parks et al. 1999). Officers spent the majority of their shifts engaging in random patrol, traveling to/from calls for service, doing paperwork, and attending to tasks that did not place them in direct contact with the public. Although past policing eras involved more interaction with members of the public, technological developments such as automobiles, telephones, and computers have contributed to a reduction in direct police-citizen contact.

For most officers, the day-to-day reality of police work is routine, largely predictable, and fairly safe. This is not to say that police work is not a dangerous occupation and that officers do not confront violent and serious criminal offenders. The challenge most officers face is not the volume of danger and criminality, but the unpredictability with which they encounter these forces. Officers know that the average citizen they encounter poses no harm to the officer's safety; the problem, however, is that predicting who is dangerous is difficult. Consequently, officers become conditioned to treat citizens and situations as dangerous (see the discussion of police culture below). Officers are socialized to treat all situations as risky, because failing to do so once can have dire consequences. Such an orientation serves to protect the safety of officers, while contributing to strained relations between the police and the public (especially minority, youth, and male citizens).

13.4 Police Culture

Police officers have long been known to have a culture, one that frequently separates themselves from other citizens and groups in the community (Skolnick 1994). It is common to see occupational and social groups form a common culture in which they share values, beliefs, norms, and behaviors. Police officers are, in many ways, similar to soldiers, construction workers, teachers, accountants, and members of clubs and social organizations. Their culture creates an identity for the individual that closely links them with their occupation and their coworkers. What makes police culture worthy of consideration is that it defines many aspects of how police officers view the world, their job, their employing organizations, their family and friends, and the community they serve (Barker 1999). The police culture is characterized by secrecy, clannishness, and isolation from those outside their group. Accordingly, police officers often socialize together after work and on days off; this frequently involves discussions about their jobs (Dempsey and Forst 2005). Culture ties officers together, while creating a wedge between the police and the public; it creates safety and solidarity within the agency, while creating conflict and tension between officers and average citizens.

Michael K. Brown's *Working the Streets* explained that police officers create their own culture to deal with the recurring anxiety and emotional stress that is common with policing. Brown claimed that the police subculture is based on the major principles of honor, loyalty, and individuality (1981). Honor is extended to officers who engage in risk-taking behavior. For example, the officer who is the first one in the door to challenge an armed adversary receives honor. Loyalty, a major component of the police subculture, is defined by those who assist other officers in emergency situations and who come to their aid when they are challenged, criticized, or even charged with wrongdoing. This can mean that officers overlook or actively conceal the misdeeds of their peers (Reuss-Ianni 1983). Individuality has to do with an officer being able to handle any situation in the way this individual feels is appropriate (Brown 1981).

One veteran police officer, in making a statement about becoming a police officer, provides some insight about why such a culture exists in policing:

> How does one explain the raw excitement of being a cop? This is an excitement so powerful that it consumes and changes the officer's personality. For the officer all five senses are involved, especially in dangerous situations. They are stirred in a soup of emotions and adrenaline and provide an adrenaline rush that surpasses anything felt before. You are stronger and more agile; your mind functions on a higher level of quickness and alertness. Afterwards, the grass seems greener; the air fresher; food tastes better; and the spouse and children are even more precious. It is an addictive feeling that makes the runner's high in comparison feel like a hangover. Police work gets into the blood and possesses the spirit. You become the job and the job becomes you, until the day you die (Bartollas and Hahn 1999: 53).

This police officer is suggesting that policing becomes a calling; you become the job and the job becomes you. Similar to the mental patient and criminal who take the labels of ex-patient and ex-offender with them, the cop who leaves policing is always the ex-cop.

Jerome Skolnick's classic typology defines the police personality as having the three key elements of danger, authority, and efficiency (1994). Danger is ever-present and may be only a few seconds away. On average, a police officer is killed somewhere in the United States every 53 hours. Samuel Chapman noted that human errors are of concern in any occupation, but the results of those errors can be more profound for some groups of workers. Although officers know that lethal danger is rare, they must only err once by being too relaxed in order to generate serious consequences (Chapman

1986). New officers are conditioned to read their environment for signs of danger at all times and to keep themselves safe from potential harm (Barker 1999), though this means in most situations officers are overly cautious. Skolnick contended this element of danger socially isolates police officers from the segment of the citizenry that they regard as symbolically dangerous (usually minorities, males, younger citizens, and the poor) and also from conventional citizenry. Because police officers are operating in dangerous situations, Skolnick suggested, they become suspicious, constantly seeking indications that a crime is about to be committed or that they may become targets of lawbreakers (1994).

One of the ways officers handle potential dangers is to exert their authority in order to control citizens. Rookie officers are taught to exert a "command presence" (Barker 1999: 69) in the face of chaotic and potentially dangerous encounters with the public. Officers use forceful voice, maintain a dominant stance, and use other body cues to coerce citizens into compliance with the officers' directives. A paradox emerges from this situation because although authority helps keep an officer safe from danger, it tends to generate negative responses from citizens. Many citizens deny police authority by failing to comply with police commands (Skolnick 1994). This can escalate confrontations between the police and citizens, possibly resulting in the use of force. Even where force is not used, citizens may develop negative views of officers by seeing them as overbearing, authoritarian, rude, terse, and unprofessional. Despite this paradox, training officers and coworkers are also quick to remind rookies that they need to exert authority and to take charge of each situation which they face (Barker 1999).

Finally, Skolnick saw efficiency as another core aspect of the culture of the police (Skolnick 1994). This is rooted in the professional movement in American policing, which forced the police to define performance indicators for evaluating officers. One of the ideas emerging from this process was the notion that "good" officers handle their duties in a quick fashion. Although it is difficult to argue with the notion that officers should be efficient in performing their duties, efficiency can leave citizens dissatisfied with police services they receive. A crime victim who is upset about their experience and is looking for reassurance from the police may instead find the officer treating them in a manner that is curt, disinterested, distant, and unsympathetic.

Police officers tend to believe that civilians simply are unable to understand what it is like to be a police officer because officers face unique experiences. In another part of the interview that opened this section, the officer claimed that "it is hopeless to attempt to describe what it is like to be a police officer to one who has never experienced it" (Bartollas and Hahn 1999: 53). The reason for this is that "there is a brotherhood and a sisterhood that goes beyond words. It is an emotion, a psychic communication, a shared experience that brings officers from hundreds of miles around to offer emotional support for the family and co-workers of a fallen colleague" (Bartollas and Hahn 1999: 53). The police culture brings together officers (even officers who do not know one another), yet in so doing, it creates a psychological distance between the police and the public.

13.4.1 Informal System and Police Culture

Culture is important because it defines the worldview of police officers but also because it fills the void that the formal system of regulations, rules, policies, and procedures does not cover (Barker 1999). Criminal justice actors, including the police, are typically faced with job-related stressors and organizational pressures, lack of appreciation from the community and sometimes even from those who supervise them, and role conflict and ambiguity. When their job-related needs are unmet, these personnel feel varying degrees of frustration and anger, feel devalued, and feel marginal to the organizational goals and purposes. A choice is to resign, to withdraw emotionally from their jobs, or to join together and develop a subculture that better understands and meets their needs. This informal system develops its own norms of how a task should be properly performed and what are acceptable and nonacceptable behaviors.

The informal system is the human side of a police agency. It is what takes place behind the scenes, where no formal agents of social control can observe. The informal system varies from one police agency to another, and often within the same agency, there will be reflected different norms and values for the informal system. For example, what is defined as acceptable practice in a police vice squad in a high-crime area might be quite different from what police officers find acceptable in that same department in a low-crime area. The informal system helps us to better appreciate the freedom and ability of the police to affect the quality of law enforcement in their local communities.

The informal system, of course, is affected by its wider social context. Police personnel come to their jobs with experiences and values shaped from their growing up in communities. If they have grown up in communities in which drug use and violence are prevalent, these social contexts may affect their attitudes quite differently from those officers exposed to middle-class backgrounds and college educations. The social context also affects the law enforcement officer because communities define proper and improper behaviors differently. The police officer may find that drug trafficking is tolerated among many in a community, including even among some in the department. Faced with the large amounts of cash involved in drug translations, as well as the fact that some other officers may be involved in corrupt behaviors related to drugs, the officer may be tempted to compromise his or her values and to begin to reap some of the benefits of these drug transactions.

The socialization process is what exposes the police officer to the informal system. The informal system is taught to young recruits through a variety of socializing experience—at the academy, riding with a training officer, and interacting with peers on a daily basis. The values of the police culture, such as loyalty and individualism, are reinforced because of the feeling that the formal system does not adequately provide for the needs of the officer. This informal system provides both status and social satisfaction. Unlike the formal system, the informal system provides a sense of brotherhood and sisterhood that supposedly transverses gender, racial, and jurisdictional boundaries as represented by the slogan the thin blue line. The solidarity is most evident when officers travel across state lines to share emotions at the funeral of a fallen officer.

The actual content of these informal rules varies among departments. Elizabeth Reuss-Ianni found that the police culture of the New York Police Department included such maxims as "watch out for your partner," "don't give up another cop," and "getting the job done" (themes of solidarity), and "protect your ass," don't trust a guy until you have him checked out," "don't trust bosses to look out for your interests," "be aggressive when you have to, but don't be too eager," and "civilians never command police" (1983: 13). Malcolm K. Sparrow, Mark H. Moore, and David M. Kennedy suggest that police culture includes at least six beliefs:

- The police are the only real crime fighters.
- No one understands the work of a police officer.
- Loyalty counts more than anything.
- It is impossible to win the war on crime without bending the rules.
- The public is demanding and nonsupportive.
- Working in patrol is the least desirable job in policing (1990).

Officers who violate these informal rules risk having difficulties with fellow officers.

These difficulties range from being the brunt of wisecracks and derogatory comments, to being ignored by fellow officers, to being transferred to another district or area of assignment. These informal norms serve to protect those who become involved in corruption or the use of unnecessary force. The "blue curtain" or "code of silence" can be a firm barrier against administrative knowledge. It can also be exceptionally effective if it is or is perceived to be largely silent in regard to an act that promises to tarnish all the good work that police officers do.

The police have been concerned about the wide criticism that they have received from citizens, politicians in the community, and the media. They have reacted to the bombardment of criticism erupting from the media and the community when a particular officer or two or three officers become involved in inappropriate use of force. They retort that the police should not be judged by one or even a few "bad apples." Yet the police themselves must acknowledge how, in turning to a culture within a culture, they have created norms encouraging and protecting silence and loyalty at all cost, which is sadly misguided. It promotes engaging in outrageous behavior and defending those who engage in such behaviors.

The problem is that the policy of suppression within corrupt departments may mean that breaking the code of silence will, in one way or the other, probably mean walking away from a police career. It is certainly a career-ending move to take legal action against the department. Even if an officer wins in court, the "troublemaker" status follows whenever he or she applies for another law enforcement position. A major emphasis in policing in the United States today is pursuing integrity as a basic mission of their agencies in order to reduce wrongdoing in police departments. As applied to police services, integrity "provides structure to an agency's operation and officers' professional and personal ethics. These concepts and beliefs include, but are not limited to, honesty, honor, morality, allegiance, principled behavior, and dedication to mission" (Gaffigan and McDonald 1997: 86).

There are many unanswered questions that will determine whether and how much integrity will provide a renewal of police agencies and will help regain respect for these agencies. Can leaders supporting integrity overcome a police culture that supports a code of silence or a "blue flu"? Can it overcome the belief that it is impossible to win the war on crime without bending rules and regulations? How aggressive can police chiefs be in weeding out corruption and instilling and maintaining integrity? Is it possible to speak about integrity in departments with long histories and cultures of corruption and wrongdoing? Do ends ever justify the means; that is, is there a difference between wrongdoing and doing wrong for a noble cause? How would the incorporation of integrity into a department's beliefs and practices actually affect the police performance of its basic role of crime control? Perhaps, the most telling question is: Is it possible to create a culture in which genuine trust is present in law enforcement agencies (Bartollas and Hahn 1999)?

13.5   Police Operations and Policing Communities

Entire books can be and have been devoted to discussing what police officers do, how they perform their duties, the challenges they confront, and the nature of their relationship with the public. How policing occurs and how the police interact with the communities they serve are pivotal issues in understanding this social institution. This chapter's broad focus precludes in-depth consideration of these issues, but in this section a few major issues are examined. In particular, we discuss police discretion and decision making, problem- and community-oriented policing, and police-community inter-actions and relations.

13.5.1 Discretion and Decision Making

A defining aspect of American criminal justice is discretion; those working within the justice system are granted the power to choose from various courses of action in the performance of their duties. Granting discretion to officers is both desirable and necessary, although it generates concerns and controversies (Klockars 1985). The discretion to not enforce the law is desir-able because "justice" sometimes means that a person violating the law does not deserve punishment. A mother's choice to exceed the speed limit to transport a sick child to the hospital, while ill-advised, is something most of us would understand and forgive. Certainly, if we are pulled over by an officer, we want that officer to have the option to not issue a citation. Discretion is necessary because law and policy cannot define all facets of an officer's behavior; the social world is too complex. Furthermore, officers cannot take enforcement action against every offender they observe because criminal violations (especially minor offenses and traffic violations) are so common. When you drive to the grocery store, how many people do you see exceeding the speed limit by the slightest margin, failing to come to a complete stop at a traffic light, or in some other way violating traffic laws? If police officers issued citations for every traffic offense they observed, they would not have time to handle more serious matters. If officers cited and arrested every offender they encountered, the rest of the criminal justice system would be flooded with even more cases. Discretion is necessary because most of us support its existence, and it is a practical necessity.

At the same time, the fact that officers have discretion is the root of many public concerns about policing. In similar situations, a given officer may or may not use force, grant a citizen's request, take enforcement action, file a report, or provide assistance. The question that arises from this reality is whether the officer's decision was based upon "legitimate" factors, such as public notions of "justice," evidence related to the situation, and the totality of circumstances at hand. By its very existence in any context, discretion leads people to wonder whether choices were appropriate or based on bias, retal-iation, laziness, or some other "illegitimate" factor. Consequently, discretion creates a paradox for the police (Perez 1997). The nature of organized society necessitates its existence, but also means that people will sometimes view the police as racist, sexist, homophobic, ill-tempered, uneducated, vengeful, or bigoted in some other way. Unfortunately, these perceptions will arise even in situations where officers make choices based on legitimate factors.

13.5.2 Problem-Oriented Policing and Community-Oriented Policing

The traditional structure and function of American policing emerged in the early decades of the twentieth century through the movement to profession-alize the police. Although other visions of police organizations have evolved, the traditional model is still dominant in twenty-first-century policing. Offic-ers and agencies operating in a traditional orientation are seen as being distant and detached from the community. The traditional orientation is largely reactive; much of what officers do is in response to citizen reports that a crime had already occurred. The model advocates that officers should be deployed to maximize the amount of time spent on random patrol (in the hope that officers will intercept and deter crime) and to minimize the time it takes them to respond to calls for service. These priorities persist, despite research that suggests they do not yield tangible results (Kelling et al. 1974; Spelman and Brown 1981).

Under the traditional model, police are seen as having exclusive control over dealing with crime and disorder. They do not fully trust the public and tend to keep information to themselves. Traditional police organizations are very rigid and bureaucratic; they exemplify the term "red tape." There are dense and cumbersome policies and procedures designed to control and restrict how officers do their job. When this traditional style emerged, it seemed like a good idea. After decades of corrupt and politicized policing, the reformers of the early twentieth century wanted to control police officers and restrict police discretion. Over time, however, this system became too confining. American urban disorder in the 1960s has been partly attributed to police forces that were too rigid and too distant from the public (Skolnick 1969; Winslow 1969). A number of ideas emerged out of these realizations, including the notions of problem-oriented policing and community-ori-ented policing.

Problem-oriented policing was designed to remedy the highly reactive and disjointed nature of police responses to crime and disorder (Goldstein 1990). Research suggests that a small number of citizens and locations gen-erate large demands on police services. Using a POP orientation, police seek to identify and understand where and why pockets of crime and disorder occur in a community. This is often achieved through a four-phase model in which officers: *scan* their environment to identify problematic circum-stances; engage in an *analysis* of the cause and nature of the problem to understand why and how it occurs; *respond* in a manner that removes the causes of the problem in the context of a particular community; and *assess* the situation to ensure that the response was successfully and effectively implemented. Using this "SARA" model, police identify problematic people, areas, and conditions in their community; study why those areas are problematic; develop solutions for those conditions; and attempt to correct the concern once and for all (Spelman and Eck 1989). Agencies operating under a POP approach still respond to citizen calls for service. At the same time, officers are trained be mindful of the "big picture" of public safety problems in their jurisdiction. POP is predicated on the belief that police do have the capacity to impact the quality of the community, but doing so requires thought and analysis so that problems are understood and effective solutions are put into place.

One of the most popular and enduring ideas to emerge from the American Civil Rights movement was community policing. Unlike POP, which is a strategy intended to be used in select situations, community policing is a philosophy; it is a belief system intended to impact all levels of policing and police organizations. Community policing seeks to reinvolve the public in ensuring community safety and security (recall the level of public involvement seen in the parish constable systems of England and colonial America). Under a COP orientation, police seek to involve the public in identifying community problems, prioritizing what needs attention/resources, and developing solutions to remedy these situations. As Cordner noted, "Community policing simply argues that neighborhood-level norms and values should be added to the mix of legal, professional, and organizational considerations that influences decision making about policies, programs, and resources at the execution level as well as enforcement-level decisions on the street" (1997: 451). COP is similar to POP, as both seek to develop lasting solutions to community concerns; a key difference involves the role of the public in these processes. Both approaches rely on the same problem-solving models. Solely, the police can carry out POP, whereas COP, by definition, must involve the public in these processes (Trojanowicz, Kappler, and Gaines 2002). COP also seeks to re-establish two-way trust and communication between the police and the public, redefines how police organizations are structured and operate, and seeks to make both police and agencies more directly accessible and accountable to the public they serve.

13.5.3 Police-Community Interactions and Perceptions

Although modern officers may have less direct interaction with the public than their predecessors, policing is still squarely focused upon the public. When officers investigate offenses and enforce laws, restore public order, and provide public services, they are doing so to benefit the citizens who live and work in their assigned community. In order to understand police and police work, it is necessary to consider how police and citizens interact and relate. The relationship between the police and the public influences the efficacy of policing efforts within a community. Despite often believing the public does not like and support them, citizens generally offer positive evaluations of the police.

The notion that public perceptions shape the outcome of policing efforts can be traced to the British ideal of "policing by consent" (Carter 2002). Simply stated, this belief holds that the police can only achieve their goals and objectives when they enjoy the support and cooperation of the citizenry they serve. Although British police have reflected this belief since the establishment of modern policing systems in 1829, it is only in more recent decades that America has turned its attention to this nexus. In the 1960s and 1970s, violent conflicts between the police and the public reinforced that the police needed the support of the public if they were to serve citizens in an efficient and effective fashion (Decker 1981). Sporadic incidents in the present day continue to remind us that the public must consent to be policed; in the absence of consent, police struggle to maintain order. The emergence of community policing places additional focus on the importance of the public's support and attitudes toward the police in determining the outcome of police efforts.

The Kerner Commission conducted one of the earliest national studies of public perceptions of the police (Campbell and Schuman 1972). Data from fifteen communities suggested that African Americans were more likely to be critical of, and to have had negative interactions with, their local police. Since the Kerner Commission researched their findings, social scientists have worked to develop a better understanding of public attitudes toward the police and police services. On the whole, citizens express positive attitudes toward the police (Huang and Vaughn 1996), although variation is often noted based upon citizen demographics (race/ethnicity, gender, age, socioeconomic status), the context and culture of their neighborhood (perceptions of crime and safety), and their experiences with the police (nature of and satisfaction with contact) (Schafer, Huebner, and Bynum 2003).

13.6   Contemporary Problems

In considering modern police and policing systems, a number of problems emerge. These problems create legal hazards, hamper relations with the public, impede effective organizational performance, generate frustration and cynicism among officers, and may ultimately reduce the efficacy of policing efforts. In this section, we consider four such problems: bias and profiling, use of force, misconduct, and citizen oversight of police. At the onset, it must be noted that entire books are devoted to contemporary problems; our discussion here is far from exhaustive.

13.6.1   Bias and Profiling

Racial profiling has been the target of considerable public, political, and media attention since the mid-1990s. At its core, concern of this alleged police practice is simply the latest manifestation of apprehension regarding bias in policing; these bias concerns are rooted in the paradox of police discretion discussed earlier in this chapter. The term *racial profiling* has been used to describe different forms of police behavior, including an officer's decision to initiate a traffic stop and subsequent decisions (e.g., to conduct a search, to sanction) made during the course of that encounter. Racial profiling is an extension of an older police practice referred to as criminal profiling, which is based on social and geographic sciences (Harris 2002). For several decades, police have attempted to use criminal profiling to identify personal, behavioral, and spatial characteristics of offenders and offenses; this practice has been glamorized in media portrayals, such as the movie *The Silence of the Lambs*. Criminal profiling is an inexact science that is intended to help police focus their attention on places and people who are thought to be associated with criminal behavior. In their efforts to identify and apprehend drug couriers, the Drug Enforcement Administration has employed criminal profiling, including Operation Pipeline. This training program, which the DEA has administered to thousands of state and local police officers, educates officers about situational and behavioral cues that might indicate a motorist (particularly those on interstate highways) is transporting illicit substances.

The profile officers were given in Operation Pipeline training focused on several dozen factors thought to be associated with drug couriering. Although never systematically assessed for its accuracy or actual application, concerns over racial profiling emerged from Operation Pipeline's drug courier profile. Anecdotal evidence suggests that in some jurisdictions, officers streamlined the courier profile down to a handful of characteristics, particularly the age, gender, and race/ethnicity of the motorist (Carter 2002). Although Operation Pipeline training did not create racial profiling as a police behavior, it did focus attention on how race influences police decision making. The extent to which profiling actually occurs is very difficult to determine. Some jurisdictions present clear evidence of officer bias; for example, in the late 1990s minority motorists along parts of the New Jersey Turnpike were drastically more likely to be stopped, searched, and ticketed than were white motorists. In most communities, however, evidence concerning the extent to which profiling is a problem has been far more ambiguous. This is partly because "racial profiling" is not a well-defined concept, and it is very difficult to understand what actually motivates police behavior.

In response to the racial profiling debate, a number of state and local legislative bodies have mandated that officers collect data on the people they stop, the circumstances surrounding those contacts, and the choices officers make during the encounter. Additionally, a number of agencies have voluntarily initiated these types of data collection efforts in the hope of protecting themselves from possible legal action and/or public scrutiny. Unfortunately, such data are limited in their ability to inform us about the nature of profiling in a given community (Carter 2002). Evidence that some motorists are more likely to receive a ticket does not, in and of itself, prove that profiling behavior is occurring. If there is also variation in who commits traffic offenses, we would expect that the police would issue more tickets to some categories of motorists. The racial profiling debate will continue for the foreseeable future, whether it occurs or not and whether it is a new form of behavior or not. Public scrutiny of police discretion is healthy in a democratic society, but the complexities of understanding police behavior create the risk that the officer's actions will be misunderstood.

13.6.2   Use of Force

It is an unfortunate reality that contemporary societies need to entrust someone with the right to use physical force and coercion to ensure public safety and order. Since their modern inception, the police have been granted the authority to use violence (within the limits of the law) to overcome public resistance in the performance of their duties, a right that is not granted to any other agents of the government (Kobler 1975). Societies need to have the capacity to respond to violent situations that threaten public safety; within reasonable parameters, governments need to have the ability to use force and coercion to ensure compliance with lawful directives. The police are the mechanisms of coercion and force that are entrusted with these powers to keep society safe and orderly, to protect citizens from harm, and, at times, to protect citizens from themselves (Bittner 1990). The use of force is similar to discretion; it is a necessary right we must grant the police, but it also generates controversy, mistrust, anger, and ill-will. The law can define when and how much force officers are allowed to use, but these guidelines are not always consistent with public notions of justice and propriety.

For example, on February 4, 1999, four New York City police officers were searching for a serial rape suspect when they observed Amadou Diallo in the vestibule of an apartment building. The officers, who were working a plainclothes assignment, called out to Diallo, identifying themselves as police and instructing Diallo to "freeze." Diallo allegedly reached into his pants pocket, pulling out a shiny object. One of the officers believed this object to be a weapon and fired his sidearm at Diallo. The other officers, believing Diallo had fired the shot, also shot at Diallo. In four seconds, the officers fired forty-one rounds; Diallo was mortally wounded after being struck by nineteen of these bullets. The shooting generated tremendous public outcry, particularly from local minority and civil rights groups. After a thorough police investigation and a trial on charges of manslaughter, the four officers were absolved of any wrongdoing. The Diallo shooting is an example of how legal definitions of police use of force do not always satisfy public opinions. The force used by the four officers was found to be within the parameters of law and policy, yet the public remained vocally concerned about the officers' behavior. The shooting remains a source of tension between the New York City Police Department and some segments of the community.

The use of force is not only problematic when it is employed within the letter of the law; the American police have a long history of generating public outcry as a result of their use of force that is considered excessive. Because of their close affiliation with local political corruption, early police officers were typically not seen as representing a legitimate institution, such as the law. In order to ensure public cooperation, officers frequently had to resort to physical violence to assert their authority (Miller 1977). As discussed earlier, one of the key objectives of reform efforts was the root out corruption, incompetence, and violence from police departments. The use of force is also problematic because of the ambiguous standards used to determine whether a particular incident of force was appropriate within the letter of the law (Bartollas and Hahn 1999). The Diallo shooting was determined to be lawful, yet it generated considerable public outcry and negative attention directed at the New York City Police Department and its officers. Although many would contend that excessive force by the police is much less prevalent than it was in the past, this legacy of violence still haunts modern police. The situation is fueled by high-profile violent encounters, such as the Diallo shooting.

13.6.3 Misconduct

In late 1997, the Los Angeles Police Department (LAPD) was once again the subject of public scrutiny for the behavior of its officers. A series of criminal incidents came to light, all involving officers who were or had been assigned to the Rampart Area within LAPD. A subsequent investigation found that a number of officers working within the Rampart Area (including a number of officers assigned to an elite antigang squad) had committed numerous acts of perjury, corruption, evidence-planting, attempted murder, and physical assault (Rampart Independent Review Panel 2000). The Rampart Area investigation suggested that although the misdeeds were committed by a small proportion of officers, many others (including supervisors) likely knew of the situation and failed to report or correct the problem (the earlier discussion of police culture suggests why an officer might be reluctant to take action in response to the misdeeds of a coworker). Much like police use of force, it is difficult to accurately know the prevalence of misconduct beyond general observations. Although rampant in the early decades of modern American policing, misconduct seems less prevalent today. A national survey of officers indicated that misconduct was uncommon, but did occur; most officers did not support improper behavior, but some did agree that such acts were acceptable under some conditions (Weisburd et al. 2000).

Two different perspectives can be used to explain why officer misconduct remains a concern in contemporary policing. The *rotten apple* perspective holds that misconduct is rare behavior by a small number of people; much like the proverbial rotten apple that spoils the barrel, these rogue officers taint policing as an occupation, even though most officers are thought to be honest. This view suggests that some people in society make poor employees and will be problematic in any occupational setting; the key is to find better ways to avoid hiring these individuals as police officers. In contrast, the *rotten barrel* perspective sees the problem not in the individual, but in the environment. Through this perspective, police organizations and their culture are thought to facilitate misdeeds. The nature of police work grants officers ample opportunity to engage in illicit behavior with a low probability of detection. The nature of police culture and the "blue wall of silence" discourage even honest officers from taking action in response to the misdeeds of a peer. The true cause of misconduct is likely a combination of both perspectives. Many officers remain "clean" even in agencies that facilitate misconduct; some officers will be "dirty," even in agencies that take a very hard stand against misconduct.

Several different forms of misconduct need to be recognized, including gratuities (free goods and services), bribes (goods and service given so the law will not be enforced), internal corruption (stealing from an agency, such as taking drugs from a property room), abuse of authority (using one's position as a police officer for personal gain), excessive force (the conscious use of more force than is allowed under the law), and internal misconduct (violating policies and procedures, such as sleeping on the job). Although corruption often evokes images of officers committing illicit acts for their own benefit, much concern is also focused on "noble cause corruption" (Caldero and Crank 2004). Officers engaging in this type of misconduct are trying to fulfill crime control objectives, rather than seeking personal gain. For example, an officer stopping a vehicle driven by a known gang member may conduct an unauthorized search, locate an illegal firearm, and file an arrest report claiming the gun was in plain view. Another example might involve officers lying in court in order to ensure the conviction of a person they "know" committed an illegal act; absent the officer's false statement, the accused might not be convicted. Some may see this form of conduct as being less serious because officers engage in wrongful behavior in an effort to control crime; others see this as equally or more serious because it violates the public's trust and expectation of honesty by the police.

13.6.4   Citizen Oversight

Because they are entrusted with extraordinary rights and powers, it is crucial to develop systems to effectively monitor police behavior and to respond to unacceptable acts. Further, principles of democratic government hold that all public institutions should operate in reasonably transparent manner and with necessary levels of citizen input. Despite accepting these ideas in the abstract, historically, few mechanisms have been in place to hold the police accountable to the public (Walker and Katz 2002). Ample evidence can be seen in earlier eras of American policing; although abuses of authority and misconduct have improved, these problems continue to generate discussion and concern (Kappeler, Sluder, and Alpert 1998). Many of the mechanisms put into place to monitor and regulate the police (internal investigations, direct supervision, performance reviews) are under the direct control of police organizations. Some still see reason to be concerned with "who polices the police."

A wide range of monitoring mechanisms has been developed under the umbrella of citizen oversight. Walker organized these mechanisms into four classes (Walker and Katz 2002). Class I oversight systems empower select citizens with the right to investigate complaints and make disposition recommendations to police officials. These systems operate independently of police departments. Citizens, not the police, are responsible for investigating and resolving complaints that have been made against police officers. In Class II systems, police investigate allegations; investigations are reviewed by select citizens, who recommend whether the findings should be accepted. In Class III, mechanisms empower citizens to serve as an appellate body. Police personnel receive, investigate, and dispose of complaints; if the complainant is dissatisfied with the outcome, a citizen group reviews the matter and makes a recommendation to the agency. Class IV oversight systems serve as auditors that monitor the procedures police organizations use to receive, investigate, and dispose of complaints.

Little is known about the extent to which citizen oversight actually curbs problematic police behavior. Police officers and unions tend to vigorously oppose involving citizens in the investigation and adjudication of complaints against officers (Walker and Katz 2002; Wells and Schafer 2005). The main complaint issued is that citizens do not have the knowledge and expertise to effectively understand and evaluate police behavior. Additionally, although oversight bodies do shed light on the investigation and adjudication of complaints brought against officers, they are reactive in nature. Oversight bodies are dependent on citizens to bring situations to their attention. Given the low levels of direct supervision and diffuse nature of police work previously discussed, it is likely that citizen oversight will have a limited deterrent effect in reducing undesirable police behavior.

13.7 Conclusions

The police are one of the most visible branches of the government and remain a focus of public awe, respect, vitriol, and scorn. It is common for citizens to have mixed feelings about the police, but few are neutral in their views. The world of the police is, then, a mixed lot. They receive our trust, support, and respect, but also our fear, apprehension, and anger. They routinely confront danger, uncertainty, fear, excitement, revulsion, humor, and boredom. We recognize that they are a needed social institution, that they must have discretion, that they must use force, and that they must assert their authority. At the same time, these dimensions of policing create conflict, ill will, and animosity. Although many problematic aspects of policing have improved in the past century and a half, concern still abounds regarding misconduct, abuse of authority, excessive force, and corruption. This is tempered by the positive feelings people have toward the police, particularly in the aftermath of critical incidents in which police are viewed as heroes and saviors, such as the September 11, 2001, terror attacks.

Egon Bittner suggested the police will always be viewed in a mixed manner (1990). On the one hand, they are the thin blue line that separates "good citizens" from the "criminal element" in society. They are paid to handle nasty and messy social problems (sexual assault, domestic battery, the mentally ill, drunks, the homeless, child molesters) that the average citizen prefers to ignore. At the same time, they own a historical legacy of corruption and abuse, and they deal with the dark side of humanity. An old adage warns that there is a bit of the dragon in the dragon-slayer; is the same true of police? The fact that they have discretion further complicates public views of police because most citizens do not understand limits on police power and do not know what to expect when they have contact with an officer. Finally, media images of the police often portray them in extreme manners, under- or overplaying the violence, stress, bureaucracy, boredom, and comraderie that define the world of police officers.

References

Adams, T. F. 1973. *Law Enforcement*. Englewood Cliffs, CA: Prentice-Hall.

Barker, J. C. 1999. *Danger, Duty, and Disillusion: The Worldview of Los Angeles Police Officers*. Prospect Heights, IL: Waveland.

Bartollas, C., and L. D. Hahn. 1999. *Policing in America.* Boston: Allyn & Bacon.

Bittner, E. 1990. *Aspects of Police Work.* Boston: Northeastern University Press.

Brown, M. K. 1981. *Working the Street: Police Discretion and the Dilemmas of Reform.* New York: Russell Sage Foundation.

Caldero, M. A., and J. P. Crank. 2004. *Police Ethics: The Corruption of Noble Causes,* 2nd ed. Cincinnati, OH: Anderson.

Campbell, A., and H. Schuman. 1972. A comparison of black and white experiences in the city. In *The End of Innocence: A Suburban Reader,* ed. C. M. Haar. Glenview, IL: Scott Foresman, chap. 4.

Carter, D. L. *The Police and the Community,* 7th ed. Upper Saddle River, NJ: Prentice-Hall.

Chapman, S. G. 1986. *Cops, Killers and Staying Alive.* Springfield, IL: Charles C. Thomas.

Cordner, G. W. 1997. Community policing: Elements and effect. In *Critical Issues in Policing,* 3rd ed., ed. R. G. Dunham and G. P. Alpert. Prospect Heights, IL: Waveland, chap. 26.

Critchley, T. A. 1978. *A History of Police in England and Wales,* rev. ed. London: Constable and Company.

Decker, S. 1981. Citizen attitudes toward the police. *Journal of Police Science and Administration* 9, 80-87.

Dempsey, J. S., and L. S. Forst. 2005. *An Introduction to Policing.* Belmont, CA: Thompson Wadsworth.

Emsley, C. 1996. *The English Police: A Political and Social History,* 2nd ed. London: Longman.

Fogelson, R.M. *Big-City Police.* Cambridge, MA: Harvard University Press.

Gaffigan, S.J., and P. P. McDonald. 1997. *Police Integrity: Public Service with Honor.* Washington, DC: National Institute of Justice.

Gerth, H. H., and C. W. Mills. 1958. *From Max Weber: Essays in Sociology.* New York: Oxford.

Goldstein, H. 1990. *Problem-Oriented Policing.* New York: McGraw-Hill.

Harris, D. A. 2002. *Profiles in Injustice: Why Racial Profiling Cannot Work.* New York: New Press.

Huang, W. S. W., and M. S. Vaughn. 1996. Support and confidence: Public attitudes toward the police. In *Americans View Crime and Justice,* ed. T. J. Flanagan and D. R. Longmire. Thousand Oaks, CA: Sage, chap. 3.

Johnson, D. R. 1981. *American Law Enforcement: A History.* St. Louis: Forum.

Kappeler, V. E., R. D. Sluder, and G. P. Alpert. 1998. *Forces Of Deviance: Understanding the Dark Side of Policing,* 2nd ed. Prospect Heights, IL: Waveland.

Kelling, G. L., T. Pate, D. Dieckman, and E. E. Brown. 1974. *The Kansas City Preventive Patrol Experiment: A Summary Report.* Washington, DC: The Police Foundation.

Klockars, C. B. 1985. *The Idea of Police.* Newbury Park, CA: Sage.

Kobler, A. 1975. Police homicide in a democracy. *Journal of Social Issues* 31, 1, 163-184.

Langworthy, R. H., and L. F. Travis. 2003. *Policing in America,* 3rd ed. Upper Saddle River, NJ: Prentice-Hall.

Manning, P. K. 1997. *Police Work,* 2nd ed. Prospect Heights, IL: Waveland.

Miller, W. 1977. *Cops and Bobbies: Police Authority in New York and London, 1830-1870.* Chicago: University of Chicago.

Parks, R. B., S. D. Mastrofski, C. DeJong, and M. K. Gray. 1999. How officers spend their time with the community. *Justice Quarterly* 16, 483-518.

Perez, D. W. 1997. *The Paradoxes of Police Work: Walking the Thin Blue Line.* Incline Village, NV: Copperhouse.

Pringle, P. 1955. *Hue and Cry: The Birth of the British Police.* London: Museum Press.

Rampart Independent Review Panel. 2000. *Report of the Rampart Independent Review Panel: Executive Summary.* Los Angeles: Los Angeles Board of Police Commissioners.

Ramsay, A. A. V. 1928. *Sir Robert Peel.* New York: Dodd, Mead.

Reichel, P. L., 1988. Southern slave patrols as a transitional police style. *American Journal of Police* 7, 2, 51-77.

Reith, C. 1948. *A Short History of the British Police.* London: Oxford University.

Reppetto, T. 1978. *The Blue Parade.* New York: The Free Press.

Reuss-Ianni, E. 1983. *Two Cultures of Policing: Street Cops and Management Cops.* New Brunswick, NJ: Transaction.

Richardson, J. F. 1974. *Urban Police in the United States.* Port Washington, NY: Kennikat.

Roberg, R. 1976. *Changing Police Role: New Dimensions and New Issues.* San Jose: Justice Systems Development.

Schafer, J. A. 2002. Community policing and police corruption. In *Policing and Misconduct,* ed. K. M. Lersch. Upper Saddle River, NJ: Prentice-Hall, chap. 8.

Schafer, J. A., B. M. Huebner, and T. S. Bynum. 2003. Citizen perceptions of police services: Race, neighborhood context, and community policing. *Police Quarterly* 6, 440-468.

Scott, E. J. 1981. *Calls for Service: Citizen Demand and Initial Police Response.* Washington, DC: National Institute of Justice.

Sheehan, R., and G. W. Cordner. 1995. *Police Administration,* 3rd ed. Cincinnati: Anderson.

Skolnick, J. H. 1969. *The Politics of Protest.* New York: Ballantine.

Skolnick, J. H. 1994. *Justice without Trial: Law Enforcement in a Democratic Society,* 4th ed. New York: Macmillan.

Sparrow, M. K., M. H. Moore, and D. K. Kennedy. 1990. *Beyond 911: A New Era for Policing.* New York: Basic Books.

Spelman, W., and Eck, J. E. 1989. Sitting ducks, ravenous wolves, and helping hands: New approaches to urban policing. *Public Affairs Comment* 35 2, 1-9.

Spelman, W. G, and D. K. Brown. 1981. *Calling the Police.* Washington, DC: Police Executive Research Forum.

Trojanowicz, R., V. E. Kappeler, and L. K. Gaines. 2002. *Community Policing: A Contemporary Perspective,* 3rd ed. Cincinnati: Anderson.

Walker, S., and C. M. Katz. 2002. *The Police in America: An Introduction,* 4th ed. New York: McGraw-Hill.

Weisburd, D., R. Greenspan, E. E. Hamilton, H. Williams, and K. A. Bryant. 2000. Police Attitudes Toward Abuse of Authority: Findings from a National Study. Washington, DC: National Institute of Justice.

Wells, W. M., and J. A. Schafer. 2005. Officer Perceptions of Citizen Oversight. Carbondale, IL: Center for the Study of Crime, Delinquency, & Corrections, Southern Illinois University.

Wilson, J. Q. 1968. *Varieties of Police Behavior.* Cambridge, MA: Harvard University Press.

Winslow, R. W. 1969. *Crime in a Free Society.* Belmont, CA: Dickenson.

What Can Police Do to Reduce Crime, Disorder, and Fear?[1]

14

DAVID WEISBURD AND
JOHN E. ECK

Contents

[1] This chapter is a condensed version of a paper that appeared in the *Annals of the American Academy of Political and Social Science* in May of 2004 (volume 593, pp. 42-65). More generally, our review of police practices derives from a subcommittee report on police effectiveness that was part of a larger examination of police research and practices undertaken by the National Academy of Sciences and chaired by Wesley Skogan. We cochaired the subcommittee charged with police effectiveness, which also included David Bayley, Ruth Peterson, and Lawrence Sherman. While we draw heavily from that review, our analysis also extends the critique and represents our interpretation of the findings.

14.1   Introduction

The decade of the 1990s was one of the most innovative periods in American policing. Such approaches as community policing, problem-oriented policing, hot spots policing, and broken windows policing either emerged in the 1990s or came to be widely adopted by police agencies at that time. The changes in American policing were dramatic. From an institution known for its conservatism and resistance to change, policing suddenly stood out as a leader in criminal justice innovation. This new openness to innovation and widespread experimentation in new practices were part of a renewed confidence in American policing that could be found not only among police professionals but also among scholars and the general public. Although there is much debate over what caused the crime drop of the 1990s, many police executives, police scholars, and laypeople looked to new policing practices as a primary explanation (Bratton 1998a; Eck and MaGuire 2000; Kelling and Sousa 2001).

At the same time that many in the United States touted the new policing as an explanation for improvements in community safety, many scholars and police professionals identified the dominant policing practices of earlier decades as wasteful and ineffective. This criticism of the "standard model" of policing was part of a more general critique of the criminal justice system that emerged as early as the mid-1970s (e.g., Martinson 1974). As in other parts of the criminal justice system, a series of studies seemed to suggest that such standard practices as random preventive patrol or rapid response to police calls for service had little impact on crime or fear of crime in American communities (e.g., Kelling et al. 1974; Spelman and Brown 1981). By the 1990s, the assumption that police practices were ineffective in combating crime was widespread (Bayley 1994; Gottfredson and Hirschi 1990), a factor that certainly helped to spawn rapid police innovation at that time.

In this chapter, we revisit the central assumptions that are at the root of recent American police innovation. Does the research evidence support the view that standard models of policing are ineffective in combating crime and disorder? Are there elements of the standard model that deserve more careful study before they are abandoned as methods of reducing crime or disorder? Do recent police innovations hold greater promise of increasing community safety? Or does the research evidence suggest that they are popular but actually ineffective? What lessons can we draw from research about police innovation in reducing crime, disorder, and fear over the last two decades? Does such research lead to a more general set of recommendations for American policing or for police researchers?

Our chapter examines these questions in the context of a careful review of the research evidence about what works in policing. Our focus is on specific elements of community safety: crime, fear, and disorder. We begin by developing a typology of police practices that is used in our chapter to organize and assess the evidence about police effectiveness. We then turn to a discussion of how that evidence was evaluated and assessed. What criteria did we use for distinguishing the value of studies for coming to conclusions about the effectiveness of police practices? How did we decide when the evidence was persuasive enough to draw more general statements about specific programs or strategies? Our review of the evidence follows. Our approach is to identify what existing studies say about the effects of core police practices. Having summarized the research literature in this way, we conclude with a more general synthesis of the evidence reviewed and a discussion of their implications for police practice and research on policing.

14.2   The Standard Model of Policing and Recent Police Innovation: A Typology of Police Practices

Over the past three decades, there has been increasing criticism of what has come to be considered the standard model of police practices (Goldstein 1990; Bayley 1994; Visher and Weisburd 1998). This model relies generally on a "one size fits all" application of reactive strategies to suppress crime and continues to be the dominant form of police practices in the United States. The standard model is based on the assumption that generic strategies for crime reduction can be applied throughout a jurisdiction regardless of the level of crime, the nature of crime, or other variations. Such strategies as increasing the size of police agencies, random patrol across all parts of the community, rapid response to calls for service, generally applied follow-up investigations, and generally applied intensive enforcement and arrest policies are all examples of this standard model of policing.

Because the standard model seeks to provide a generalized level of police service, it has often been criticized as focused more on the means of policing or the resources that police bring to bear than on the effectiveness of policing in reducing crime, disorder, or fear (Goldstein 1979). Accordingly, in the application of preventive patrol in a city, police agencies following the standard model will often measure success in terms of whether a certain number of patrol cars are on the street at certain times. In agencies that seek to reduce police response times to citizen calls for service, improvements in the average time of response often becomes a primary measure of police agency success. In this sense, using the standard model can lead police agencies to become more concerned with how police services are allocated than whether they have an impact on public safety.

This model has also been criticized because of its reliance on the traditional law enforcement powers of police in preventing crime (Goldstein 1987). Police agencies relying upon the standard model generally employ a limited range of approaches, overwhelmingly oriented toward enforcement, and make relatively little use of institutions outside of policing (with the notable exception of other parts of the criminal justice system). "Enforcing the law" is a central element of the standard model of policing, suggesting that the main tools available to the police, or legitimate for their use, are found in their law enforcement powers. It is no coincidence that police departments are commonly referred to as "law enforcement agencies." In the standard model of policing, the threat of arrest and punishment forms the core of police practices in preventing and controlling crime.

Recent innovations in policing have tended to expand beyond the standard model of policing along two dimensions. Figure 14.1 depicts this relationship. The vertical axis of the figure, "the diversity of approaches," represents the content of the practices employed. Strategies that rely primarily on traditional law enforcement are low on this dimension. The horizontal axis, "the level of focus," represents the extent of focus or targeting of police

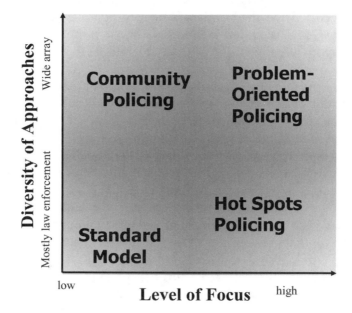

Figure 14.1   Dimensions of policing strategies.

activities. Strategies that are generalized and applied uniformly across places or offenders score low on this dimension. Innovations in policing over the last decade have moved outward along one or both of these dimensions. This point can be illustrated in terms of three of the dominant trends in innovation over the last two decades: community policing, hot spots policing, and problem-oriented policing. We note at the outset that in emphasizing specific components of these innovations, we are trying to illustrate our typology, though in practice the boundaries between approaches are seldom clear and they often overlap in their application in real police settings. We will discuss this point in fuller detail in our examination of specific strategies later in our chapter.

Community policing, perhaps the most widely adopted police innovation of the last decade, is extremely difficult to define, and its definition has varied over time and among police agencies (Greene and Mastrofski 1988; Eck and Rosenbaum 1994). However, one of the principal assumptions of community policing is that the police can draw from a much broader array of resources in carrying out the police function than is found in the traditional law enforcement powers of the police. For example, most scholars agree that community policing should entail greater community involvement in the definition of crime problems and in police activities to prevent and control crime (Skolnick and Bayley 1986; Weisburd, McElroy, and Hardyman 1988; Goldstein 1990). Community policing suggests a reliance on a more community-based crime control that draws on the resources of the public as well as the police, and thus it is placed in our typology high on the dimension of "diversity of approaches." It lies to the left on the dimension of "level of focus," because when community policing is employed without problem solving (see later), it provides a common set of services throughout a jurisdiction.

Hot spots policing (Sherman and Weisburd 1995; Braga 2001; Weisburd and Braga 2003) represents an important new approach to crime control that illustrates innovation on our second dimension, "level of focus." It demands that the police identify specific places in their jurisdictions where crime is concentrated and then focus resources at those locations. When only traditional law enforcement approaches such as directed patrol are used in bringing attention to such hot spots, hot spots policing is high on the dimension of level of focus but low on that of "diversity of approaches."

Problem-oriented policing (Goldstein 1990) expands beyond the standard model both in terms of focus and the tools used. Problem-oriented policing, as its name suggests, calls for the police to focus on specific problems and to fit their strategies to the problems identified. It thus departs from the generalized "one size fits all" approach of the standard model and calls for "tailor-made" and focused police practices. But in defining those practices, problem-oriented policing also demands that the police look beyond their traditional law enforcement powers and draw upon a host of other possible methods for addressing the problems they define. In problem-oriented policing, the toolbox of policing might include community resources or the powers of other government agencies.

14.3   Evaluating the Evidence

Before we turn to what our review tells us about the standard model of policing and recent police innovation, it is important to lay out the criteria we used in assessing the evidence we reviewed. There is no hard rule for determining when studies provide more reliable or valid results, or any clear line to indicate when there is enough evidence to come to an unambiguous conclusion. Nonetheless, social scientists generally agree on some basic guidelines for assessing the strength of the evidence available. Perhaps the most widely agreed-on criterion relates to what is often referred to as internal validity (Weisburd, Lum, and Petrosino 2001; Sherman et al. 2002). Research designs that allow the researcher to make a stronger link between the interventions or programs examined and the outcomes observed are generally considered to provide more valid evidence than designs that provide for a more ambiguous connection between cause and effect. In formal terms, the former designs are considered to have higher internal validity. In reviewing studies, we used internal validity as a primary criterion for assessing the strength of the evidence provided.

It is generally agreed that randomized experiments provide a higher level of internal validity than do nonexperimental studies (e.g., Campbell and Boruch 1975; Cook and Campbell 1979; Farrington 1983; Boruch, Victor, and Cecil 2000; Feder and Boruch 2000; Shadish, Cook, and Campbell 2002; Weisburd 2003). Another class of studies, referred to here as quasiexperiments, typically allow for less confidence in making a link between the programs or strategies examined and the outcomes observed (Cook and Campbell 1979). Finally, studies that rely only on statistical controls—generally termed nonexperimental or observational designs—are often seen to lead to the weakest level of internal validity (Cook and Campbell 1979; Sherman et al. 1997).

In our review, we rely strongly on these general assessments of the ability of research to make statements of high internal validity regarding the practices evaluated. However, we also recognize that other criteria are important in assessing the strength of research. Although it is generally recognized that randomized experiments have higher internal validity than nonrandomized studies, a number of scholars have suggested the results of randomized field experiments can be compromised by the difficulty of implementing such designs (Cornish and Clarke 1972; Pawson and Tilley 1997; Eck 2002). Accordingly, in assessing the evidence, we also took into account the quality of both the measures identified and the implementation of the research design.

Even if a researcher can make a very strong link between the practices examined in a specific study and their influence on crime, disorder, or fear, if one cannot make inferences from that study to other jurisdictions or police practices more generally, then the findings will not be very useful. Moreover, most social scientists agree that caution should be used in drawing strong policy conclusions from a single study, no matter how well designed (Weisburd and Taxman 2000; Manski 2003) For these reasons, we took into account such additional factors related to our ability to generalize from study findings in drawing our conclusions.

14.4 What Works in Policing Crime, Disorder, and Fear of Crime

Below, we review the evidence on what works in policing using the criteria outlined above. In organizing our review, we rely on our typology of police practices and thus divide our discussion into four sections, representing the four broad types of police approaches suggested in our discussion of Figure 14.1. For each type, we begin with a general proposition that summarizes what the research literature tells us about the effectiveness of that approach in reducing crime, disorder, and fear of crime.

14.4.1 Proposition 1

The standard model of policing has relied on the uniform provision of police resources and the law enforcement powers of the police to prevent crime and disorder across a wide array of crimes and across all parts of the jurisdictions that police serve. Despite the continued reliance of many police agencies on these standard practices, there is little evidence that such approaches are effective in controlling crime and disorder or reducing fear of crime.

In our review of the standard model of policing, we identified four broad strategies that have been the focus of systematic research over the last three decades: (1) increasing the size of police agencies, (2) random patrol across all parts of the community, (3) rapid response to calls for service, and (4) generally applied intensive enforcement and arrest policies.

14.4.1.1 *Increasing the Size of Police Agencies*

Evidence from case studies in which police have suddenly left duty (e.g., police strikes) shows that the absence of police is likely to lead to an increase in crime (Sherman and Eck 2002). Although these studies are generally not very strong in their design, their conclusions are consistent. But the finding that removing all police will lead to more crime does not answer the primary question that most scholars and policymakers are concerned with, that is, will marginal increases in the number of police officers lead to reductions in crime, disorder, or fear? The evidence in this case is contradictory, and the study designs generally cannot distinguish between the effects of police strength and factors that ordinarily are associated with police hiring such as changes in tactics or organizational structures. Most studies have concluded that variations in police strength over time do not affect crime rates (van Tulder 1992; Chamlin and Langworthy 1996; Eck and Maguire 2000; Niskanen 1994). However, two recent studies using more sophisticated statistical designs suggest that marginal increases in the number of police are related to decreases in crime rates (Marvell and Moody 1996; Levitt 1997).

14.4.1.2   Random Patrol across All Parts of the Community
Random preventive patrol across police jurisdictions has continued to be one of the most enduring of standard police practices. Despite the continued use of random preventive patrol by many police agencies, the evidence supporting this practice is very weak and the studies reviewed are more than a quarter century old (Press 1971; Kelling et al. 1974; Dahmann 1975; Minneapolis Medical Research Foundation 1976; Larson and Cahn 1985; Sherman and Weisburd 1995).

14.4.1.3   Rapid Response to Calls for Service
A third component of the standard model of policing, rapid response to calls for service, has also not been shown to reduce crime or even lead to increased chances of arrest in most situations (Kansas City Police Department 1977; Spelman and Brown 1981). The crime reduction assumption behind rapid response is that if the police get to crime scenes rapidly, they will apprehend offenders, thus providing a general deterrent against crime.

14.4.1.4   Generally Applied Intensive Enforcement and Arrests
Tough law enforcement strategies have long been a staple of police crime-fighting. We reviewed three broad areas of intensive enforcement within the standard model: disorder policing, generalized field interrogations and traffic enforcement, and mandatory and preferred arrest policies in domestic violence.

Disorder Policing: The model of intensive enforcement applied broadly to incivilities and other types of disorder has been described recently as "broken windows policing" (Kelling and Coles 1996; Kelling and Sousa 2001) or "zero tolerance policing" (Cordner 1998; Dennis and Mallon 1998; Bowling 1999; Manning 2001). Although there is a common perception that enforcement strategies (primarily arrest) applied broadly against offenders committing minor offenses lead to reductions in serious crime, research does not provide strong support for this proposition (e.g., Skogan 1990, 1992). More recent claims of the effects of disorder policing based on crime declines in New York City have also been strongly challenged because they are confounded with other organizational changes in New York (notably Compstat; e.g., Bratton 1998; Silverman 1999; Weisburd et al. 2003), other changes such as the crack epidemic (see Blumstein 1995; Bowling 1999), or more general crime trends (Eck and McGuire 2000; Karmen 2000). One observational study by Kelling and Sousa (2001) found a direct link between misdemeanor arrests and more serious crime in New York, though limitations in the data available raise questions about the validity of these conclusions.

Generalized Field Interrogations and Traffic Enforcement: There is limited evidence supporting the effectiveness of field interrogations in reducing specific types of crime, though the number of studies available are small and the findings mixed (Boydstum 1975; Wilson and Boland 1979; Whitaker 1985; Sampson and Cohen 1988; Weiss and Freels 1996).

Mandatory Arrest Policies for Domestic Violence: Mandatory arrest in misdemeanor cases of domestic violence is now required by law in many states. Consistent with the standard model of policing, these laws apply to all cities in a state, in all areas of the cities, for all kinds of offenders and situations. Research and public interest in mandatory arrest policies for domestic violence was encouraged by an important experimental study in Minneapolis (Sherman and Berk 1984a, 1984b), which found reductions in repeat offending among offenders who were arrested as opposed to those who were counseled or separated from their partners. This study led to a series of replications supported by the National Institute of Justice. These experiments found deterrent effects of arrest in two cities and no effect of arrest in three other cities (Dunford 1990; Dunford, Huizinga, and Elliot 1990; Sherman et al. 1991; Berk et al. 1992; Hirschel and Hutchinson 1992; Pate and Hamilton 1992), suggesting that the effects of arrest will vary by city, neighborhood, and offender characteristics (e.g., Sherman 1992; Maxwell, Garner, and Fagan 2001, 2002).

14.4.2 Proposition 2

Over the past two decades, there has been a major investment on the part of the police and the public in community policing. Because community policing involves so many different tactics, its effect as a general strategy cannot be evaluated. Overall, the evidence does not provide strong support for the position that community policing approaches impact strongly on crime or disorder. Stronger support is found for the ability of community policing tactics to reduce fear of crime.

Police practices associated with community policing have been particularly broad, and the strategies associated with community policing have sometimes changed over time. Foot patrol, for example, was considered an important element of community policing in the 1980s, but has not been a core component of more recent community policing programs. Consequently, it is often difficult to determine if researchers studying community policing in different agencies at different times are studying the same phenomena. One recent observational study that attempted to assess the overall impact of federal government investment for community policing found a positive crime control effect of "hiring and innovative grant programs" (Zhao, Scheider, and Thurman 2002); however, a review of this work by the U.S. General Accounting Office (2003) has raised strong questions regarding the validity of the findings.

Studies do not support the view that community meetings (Wycoff and Skogan 1993), neighborhood watch (Rosenbaum 1989), storefront offices (Skogan 1990; Uchida, Forst, and Annan 1992), or newsletters (Pate and Annan 1989) reduce crime, though Skogan and Hartnett (1995) found that such tactics reduce community perceptions of disorder. Door-to-door visits have been found to reduce both crime (e.g., Sherman et al. 1997) and disorder (Skogan 1992). However, simply providing information about crime to the public does not have crime prevention benefits (Sherman et al. 1997).

As noted above, foot patrol was an important component of early community policing efforts. An early uncontrolled evaluation of foot patrol in Flint, Michigan, concluded that foot patrol reduced reported crime (Trojanowicz 1986). However, Bowers and Hirsch (1987) found no discernable reduction in crime or disorder due to foot patrols in Boston. A more rigorous evaluation of foot patrol in Newark also found that it did not reduce criminal victimizations (Police Foundation 1981). Nonetheless, the same study found that foot patrol reduced residents' fear of crime.

There is additional evidence that community policing lowers the community's level of fear when programs are focused on increasing community-police interaction. A series of quasiexperimental studies show that policing strategies characterized by more direct involvement of police and citizens, such as citizen contract patrol, police community stations, and coordinated community policing, have a negative effect on fear of crime among individuals and on individual level of concern about crime in the neighborhood (Pate and Skogan 1985; Wycoff and Skogan 1986; Brown and Wycoff 1987).

An aspect of community policing that has only recently received systematic research attention concerns the influences of police officer behavior toward citizens. Citizen noncompliance with requests from police officers can be considered a form of disorder. Does officer demeanor influence citizen compliance? Based on systematic observations of police-citizen encounters in three cities, researchers found that when officers were disrespectful toward citizens, citizens were less likely to comply with their requests (Mastrofski, Snipes, and Supina 1996; McCluskey, Mastrofski, and Parks 1999).

14.4.3 Proposition 3

There has been increasing interest over the past two decades in police practices that target very specific types of criminals and crime places. In particular, policing crime hot spots has become a common police strategy for addressing public safety problems. Although there is only weak evidence suggesting the effectiveness of targeting specific types of offenders, a strong body of evidence suggests that taking a focused geographic approach to crime problems can increase policing effectiveness in reducing crime and disorder.

Although the standard model of policing suggested that police activities should be spread in a highly uniform pattern across urban communities and applied uniformly across the individuals subject to police attention, a growing number of police practices focus on allocating police resources in a focused way. We reviewed research in three specific areas: (1) police crackdowns, (2) hot spots policing, and (3) focus on repeat offenders.

14.4.3.1 Police Crackdowns

There is a long history of police crackdowns that target particularly troublesome locations or problems. Such tactics can be distinguished from more recent hot spots policing approaches (described below) in that they are temporary concentrations of police resources that are not widely applied. Reviewing eighteen case studies, Sherman (1990) found strong evidence that crackdowns produce short-term deterrent effects, though research is not uniformly in support of this proposition (see, e.g., Barber 1969; Kleiman 1988; Annan and Skogan 1993). Sherman (1990) also reported that crackdowns did not lead to spatial displacement of crime to nearby areas in the majority of studies he reviewed.

14.4.3.2 Hot Spots Policing

Although there is a long history of efforts to focus police patrols (Wilson 1967; Gay, Schell, and Schack 1977), the emergence of what is often termed hot spots policing is generally traced to theoretical, empirical, and technological innovations in the 1980s and 1990s (Braga 2001; Sherman and Rogan 1995; Sherman and Weisburd 1995). A series of randomized field trials shows that policing that is focused on hot spots can result in meaningful reductions in crime and disorder (see Sherman and Rogan 1995; Sherman and Weisburd 1995; Eck and Wartell 1996; Braga et al. 1999; Braga 2001).

There is strong empirical support for the hot spots policing approach. However, such approaches would be much less useful if they simply displaced crime to other nearby places. Although measurement of crime displacement is complex and a matter of debate (see, e.g., Weisburd and Green 1995a), in a number of the studies, immediate geographic displacement was examined (e.g., see Weisburd and Green 1995b; Green-Mazerolle and Rohl 1998; Braga et al. 1999). In each of these studies, no displacement of crime was reported, and some improvement in the surrounding areas was found.

14.4.3.3 *Focusing on Repeat Offenders*

Two randomized trials suggest that covert investigation of high-risk, previously convicted offenders has a high yield in arrests and incarceration per officer-hour, relative to other investments of police resources (Martin and Sherman 1986; Abrahamse and Ebener 1991). It is important to note, however, that these evaluations examined the apprehension effectiveness of repeat offender programs, not the direct effects of such policies on crime. However, a recent study—The Boston Ceasefire Project (Kennedy, Braga, and Piehl 1996)—which used a multiagency and problem-oriented approach (referred to as a "pulling levers" strategy) found a reduction in gang-related killings as well as declines in other gun-related events when focusing on youth gangs (Kennedy et al. 2001).

Another method for identifying and apprehending repeat offenders is "antifencing" or property sting operations, where police pose as receivers of stolen property and then arrest offenders who sell them stolen items (see Criminal Conspiracies Division 1979; Pennell 1979; Weiner, Chelst, and Hart 1984). Though a number of evaluations were conducted of this practice, most employed weak research designs, thus making it difficult to determine if such sting operations reduce crime.

14.4.4 Proposition 4

Problem-oriented policing emerged in the 1990s as a central police strategy for solving crime and disorder problems. There is a growing body of research evidence that problem-oriented policing is an effective approach for reducing crime, disorder, and fear.

Research is consistently supportive of the capability of problem solving to reduce crime and disorder. There are a number of quasiexperiments going back to the mid-1980s that consistently demonstrate that problem solving can reduce fear of crime (Cordner 1986), violent and property crime (Clarke and Goldstein 2002; Eck and Spelman 1987; Mazerolle et al. 2000), firearm-related youth homicide (Kennedy et al. 2001), and various forms of disorder, including prostitution and drug dealing (Eck and Spelman 1987; Capowich and Roehl 1994; Hope 1994). Two experimental evaluations of applications of problem solving in hot spots also suggest its effectiveness in reducing crime and disorder (Braga et al. 1999; Weisburd and Green 1995b).

Evidence of the effectiveness of situational and opportunity-blocking strategies, although not necessarily police-based, provides indirect support for the effectiveness of problem solving in reducing crime and disorder. Problem-oriented policing has been linked to routine activity, rational choice perspectives, and situational crime prevention (Eck and Spelman 1987; Clarke 1992a, 1992b). Recent review of prevention programs designed to block crime and disorder opportunities in small places noted that most of the studies report reductions in target crime and disorder events (Poyner 1981; Weisburd 1997; Eck 2002). Furthermore, many of these efforts were the results of police problem-solving efforts. We note that many of the studies reviewed employed relatively weak designs (Clarke 1997; Weisburd 1997; Eck 2002).

14.5 Discussion

We began our chapter with a series of questions about what we have learned from research on police effectiveness over the last three decades. In Table 14.1, we summarize our overall findings using the typology of police practices we presented earlier. One of the most striking observations in our review is

Table 14.1 Synthesis of Findings on Police Effectiveness Research

Police Strategies that ...	Are Unfocused	Are Focused
Apply a diverse array of approaches, including law enforcement sanctions.	**Inconsistent or weak evidence of effectiveness** Impersonal community policing, e.g., newsletters	**Moderate evidence of effectiveness** Problem-oriented policing
	Weak to moderate evidence of effectiveness Personal contacts in community policing Respectful police-citizen contacts Improving legitimacy of police Foot patrols (fear reduction)	**Strong evidence of effectiveness** Problem solving in hot spots
Rely almost exclusively on law-enforcement sanctions	**Inconsistent or weak evidence of effectiveness** -Adding more police -General patrol -Rapid response -Follow-up investigations -Undifferentiated arrest for domestic violence	**Inconsistent or weak evidence of effectiveness** -Repeat offender investigations **Moderate to strong evidence of effectiveness** -Focused intensive enforcement -Hot spots patrols

the relatively weak evidence there is in support of the standard model of policing—defined as low on both of our dimensions of innovation. Although this approach remains in many police agencies the dominant model for combating crime and disorder, we find little empirical evidence for the position that generally applied tactics that are based primarily on the law enforcement powers of the police are effective. Whether the strategy examined was generalized preventive patrol, efforts to reduce response time to citizen calls, increases in numbers of police officers, or the introduction of generalized follow-up investigations or undifferentiated intensive enforcement activities, studies fail to show consistent or meaningful crime or disorder prevention benefits or evidence of reductions in citizen fear of crime.

Of course, a conclusion that there is not sufficient research evidence to support a policy does not necessarily mean that the policy is not effective. Given the continued importance of the standard model in American policing, it is surprising that so little substantive research has been conducted on many of its key components. Preventive patrol, for example, remains a staple of American police tactics. Yet, our knowledge about preventive patrol is based on just a few studies more than two decades old and that have been the subject of substantial criticism. Even in cases where a larger number of studies are available, like that of the effects of adding more police, the nonexperimental designs used for evaluating outcomes generally make it difficult to draw strong conclusions.

This raises a more general question about our ability to come to strong conclusions regarding central components of the standard model of policing. With the exception of mandatory arrest for domestic violence, the evidence we review is drawn from nonexperimental evaluations. These studies are generally confounded in one way or another by threats to the validity of the findings presented. Indeed, many of the studies in such areas as the effects of police hiring are observational studies using existing data from official sources. Some economists have argued that the use of econometric statistical designs can provide a level of confidence that is almost as high as randomized experiments (Heckman and Smith 1995). We think that this confidence is not warranted in police studies, primarily because of the lack of very strong theoretical models for understanding policing outcomes and questions of validity and reliability that can be raised about official police data. But what does this mean for our ability to come to strong conclusions about police practices that are difficult to evaluate using randomized designs, such as increasing the numbers of police or decreasing response time?

A simple answer to this question is to argue that our task is to improve our methods and data over time, with the goal of improving the validity of our findings. In this regard, some recent research on police strength has tried to advance methods in ways likely to improve on prior conclusions (e.g., see

Levitt 1997). We think this approach important for coming to strong conclusions not only about the effectiveness of the standard model of policing but also about recent police innovation. But more generally, we think experimental methods can be applied much more broadly in this area, as in other areas of policing. For example, we see no reason why the addition of police officers in federal government programs that offer financial assistance to local police agencies could not be implemented experimentally. Although the use of experimental methods might be controversial in such cases, the fact that we do not know whether marginal increases in police strength are effective at reducing crime, disorder, or fear suggests the importance and legitimacy of such methods.

Although we have little evidence indicating the effectiveness of standard models of policing in reducing crime, disorder, or fear of crime, the strongest evidence of police effectiveness in our review is found in the cell of our table that represents focused policing efforts. Studies that focused police resources on crime hot spots provide the strongest collective evidence of police effectiveness that is now available. A series of randomized experimental studies suggest that hot spots policing is effective in reducing crime and disorder and can achieve these reductions without significant displacement of crime control benefits. Indeed, the research evidence suggests that the diffusion of crime control benefits to areas surrounding treated hot spots is stronger than any displacement outcome.

The two remaining cells of the table indicate the promise of new directions for policing in the United States; however, they also illustrate once more the tendency for widely adopted police practices to escape systematic or high-quality investigation. Community policing has become one of the most widely implemented approaches in American policing and has received unprecedented federal government support in the creation of the Office of Community-Oriented Policing Services and its grant program for police agencies. Yet, in reviewing existing studies, we could find no consistent research agenda that would allow us to assess with strong confidence the effectiveness of community policing. Given the importance of community policing, we were surprised that more systematic study was not available. As in the case of many components of the standard model, research designs of the studies we examined were often weak, and we found no randomized experiments evaluating community policing approaches.

The evidence available does not allow for definitive conclusions regarding community policing strategies. Nonetheless, we do not find consistent evidence that community policing (when it is implemented without problem-oriented policing) affects either crime or disorder. However, the research available suggests that when the police partner more generally with the public, levels of citizen fear will decline. Moreover, when the police are able to gain wider legitimacy among citizens and offenders, there is growing evidence that the likelihood of offending will be reduced.

There is greater and more consistent evidence that focused strategies drawing on a wide array of non–law enforcement tactics can also be effective in reducing crime and disorder. These strategies, found in the upper right of the table, may be classed more generally within the model of problem-oriented policing. Although many problem-oriented policing programs employ traditional law enforcement practices, many also draw on a wider group of strategies and approaches. The research available suggests that such tools can be effective when they are combined with a tactical philosophy that emphasizes the tailoring of policing practices to the specific characteristics of the problems or places that are the focus of intervention. Although the primary evidence in support of the effectiveness of problem-oriented policing is nonexperimental, initial experimental studies in this area confirm the effectiveness of problem-solving approaches and suggest that the expansion of the toolbox of policing practices in combination with greater focus can increase effectiveness overall.

14.6   Conclusions

Reviewing the broad array of research on police effectiveness in reducing crime, disorder, and fear, rather than focusing in on any particular approach or tactic, provides an opportunity to consider policing research in context and to assess what the cumulative body of knowledge we have suggests for policing practices in the coming decades. Perhaps the most disturbing conclusion of our review is that knowledge of many of the core practices of American policing remains uncertain. Many tactics that are applied broadly throughout the United States have not been the subject of systematic police research, or have been examined in the context of research designs that do not allow practitioners or policymakers to draw very strong conclusions. We think this fact is particularly troubling when considering the vast public expenditures on such strategies and the implications of their effectiveness for public safety. American police research must become more systematic and more experimental if it is to provide solid answers to important questions of practice and policy.

But what should the police do, given existing knowledge about police effectiveness? Police practice has been centered on standard strategies that rely primarily on the coercive powers of the police. There is little evidence to suggest that this standard model of policing will lead to communities that feel and are safer. Although police agencies may support such approaches for other reasons, there is not consistent scientific evidence that such tactics lead to crime or disorder control or reductions in fear. In contrast, research evidence does support continued investment in police innovations that call for greater focus and tailoring of police efforts, and for the expansion of the toolbox of policing beyond simple law enforcement. The strongest evidence is in regard to focus and surrounds such tactics as hot spots policing. Police agencies now routinely rely on such approaches (Weisburd and Lum 2005), and the research suggests that such reliance is warranted. Should police agencies continue to encourage community and problem-oriented policing? Our review suggests that community policing (when it is not combined with problem-oriented approaches) will make citizens feel safer but will not necessarily impact upon crime and disorder. In contrast, what is known about the effects of problem-oriented policing suggests its promise for reducing crime, disorder, and fear.

References

Abrahamse, A. F., and P. A. Ebener. 1991. An experimental evaluation of the Phoenix repeat offender program. *Justice Quarterly* 8(2), 141.

Annan, S. O., and W. G. Skogan. 1993. *Drug Enforcement in Public Housing: Signs of Success in Denver.* Washington, DC: Police Foundation.

Barber, R. N. 1969. Prostitution and the increasing number of convictions for rape in Queensland. *Australian and New Zealand Journal of Criminology* 2(3), 169.

Bayley, D. H. 1994. *Police for the Future.* New York: Oxford University Press.

Berk, R. A., et al. 1992. Bayesian analysis of the Colorado Springs spouse abuse experiment. *Journal of Criminal Law and Criminology* 83(1), 170.

Blumstein, A. 1995. Youth violence, guns, and the illicit-drug industry. *Journal of Criminal Law and Criminality* 86, 10.

Boruch, R., T. Victor, and J. Cecil. 2000. Resolving ethical and legal problems in randomized studies. *Crime and Delinquency* 46(3), 330.

Bowers, W., and J. H. Hirsch. 1987. The impact of foot patrol staffing on crime and disorder in Boston: An unmet promise. *American Journal of Policing* 6(1), 17.

Bowling, B. 1999. The rise and fall of New York murder. *British Journal of Criminology* 39(4), 531.

Boydstum, J. 1975. *The San Diego Field Interrogation Experiment.* Washington, DC: Police Foundation.

Braga, A. 2001. The effects of hot spots policing on crime. *The Annals of American Political and Social Science* 578, 104.

Braga, A. A., et al. 1999. Problem-oriented policing in violent crime/places: A randomized controlled experiment. *Criminology* 37(3), 541.

Bratton, W. J. 1998. Crime is down in New York City: Blame the police. In *Zero Tolerance: Policing a Free Society,* ed. J. B. Williams and D. Norman. London: Institute of Economic Affairs Health and Welfare Unit, 29-42.

Bratton, W. J. 1998. *Turnaround: How America's Top Cop Reversed the Crime Epidemic.* New York: Random House.

Brown, L. P., and M. A. Wycoff. 1987. Policing Houston: Reducing fear and improving service. *Crime and Delinquency* 33, 71.

Campbell, D. T., and R. Boruch. 1975. Making the case for randomized assignment to treatments by considering the alternatives: Six ways in which quasi-experimental evaluations in compensatory education tend to underestimate effects. In *Evaluation and Experiment: Some Critical Issues in Assessing Social Programs,* ed. C. A. Bennett and A. A. Lumsdaine. New York: Academic Press, 195-296.

Capowich, G. E., and J. A. Roehl. 1994. Problem-oriented policing: Actions and effectiveness in San Diego. In *The Challenge of Community Policing: Testing the Promises,* ed. D. P. Rosenbaum. Thousand Oaks, CA: Sage, 127-146.

Chamlin, M. B., and R. Langworthy. 1996. The police, crime, and economic theory: A replication and extension. *American Journal of Criminal Justice* 20(2), 165.

Clarke, R.V. 1992a. *Situational Crime Prevention: Successful Case Studies.* Albany, NY: Harrow and Heston.

Clarke, R. V. 1992b. Situational crime prevention: Theory and practice. *British Journal of Criminology* 20, 136.

Clarke, R.V. 1997. *Situational Crime Prevention: Successful Case Studies,* 2nd ed. New York: Harrow and Heston.

Clarke, R. V., and H. Goldstein. 2002. Reducing theft at construction sites: Lessons from a problem-oriented project. In *Analysis for Crime Prevention,* ed. N. Tilley. New York: Criminal Justice Press.

Cook, T., and D. Campbell. 1979. *Quasi-Experimentation: Design and Analysis Issues.* Chicago: Rand McNally College Publishing Company.

Cordner, G. W. 1986. Fear of crime and the police: An evaluation of a fear-reduction strategy. *Journal of Police Science and Administration.* 14(3), 223.

Cordner, G. W. 1998. Problem-oriented policing vs. Zero-Tolerance. In *Problem-Oriented Policing,* ed. T. O. Shelly and A. C. Grant. Washington, DC: Police Executive Research Forum.

Cornish, D. B., and R. V. G. Clarke. 1972. *The Controlled Trial in Institutional Research: Paradigm or Pitfall for Penal Evaluators?* London: Her Majesty's Stationery Office (HMSO).

Criminal Conspiracies Division. 1979. *What Happened: An Examination of Recently Terminated Anti-Fencing Operations: A Special Report to the Administrator.* Washington, DC: U.S. Department of Justice, Law Enforcement Assistance Administration.

Dahmann, J. S. 1975. *Examination of Police Patrol Effectiveness.* McLean, VA: Mitre Corporation.

Dennis, N., and R. Mallon. 1998. Confident policing in Hartlepool. In *Zero Tolerance: Policing a Free Society*, ed. N. Dennis. London: Institute of Economic Affairs Heath and Welfare Unit, 62-87.

Dunford, F. W., D. Huizinga, and D. S. Elliot. 1990. Role of arrest in domestic assault: The Omaha police experiment. *Criminology* 28(2), 183.

Dunford, F. W. 1990. System-initiated warrants for suspects of misdemeanor domestic assault: A pilot study. *Justice Quarterly* 7(1), 631.

Eck, J. E. 2002. Preventing crime at places. In *Evidence-Based Crime Prevention*, ed. L. W. Sherman, D. Farrington, B. Welsh, and D. L. MacKenzie. New York: Routledge, 241-294.

Eck, J. E., and E. McGuire. 2000. Have changes in policing reduced violent crime? An assessment of the evidence. In *The Crime Drop in America*, ed. A. Blumstein, and J. Wallman. New York: Cambridge University Press, 207-265.

Eck, J. E., and D. Rosenbaum. 1994. The new police order: Effectiveness, equity and efficiency. In *The Challenge of Community Policing: Testing the Promises*, ed. D. P. Rosenbaum. Thousand Oaks, CA: Sage, 3-23.

Eck, J. E., and W. Spelman. 1987. *Problem Solving: Problem Oriented Policing in Newport News*. Washington, DC: Police Executive Research Forum.

Eck, J. E., and J. Wartell. 1996. *Reducing Crime and Drug Dealing by Improving Place Management: A Randomized Experiment*. Report to the San Diego Police Department. Washington, DC: Crime Control Institute.

Farrington, D. 1983. Randomized experiments on crime and justice. In *Crime and Justice: An Annual Review of Research*, ed. M. H. Tonry and N. Morris. Chicago: University of Chicago Press, 4, 257-308.

Feder, L., and R. Boruch. 2000. The need for randomized experimental designs in criminal justice settings. *Crime and Delinquency* 46(3), 291.

Gay, W. G., T. H. Schell, and S. Schack. 1977. *Prescriptive Package: Improving Patrol Productivity, Volume I Routine Patrol*. Washington, DC: Office of Technology Transfer, Law Enforcement Assistance Administration.

Goldstein, H. 1979. Improving policing: A problem oriented approach. *Crime and Delinquency* 24, 236.

Goldstein, H. 1987. Toward community-oriented policing: Potential, basic requirements and threshold questions. *Crime and Delinquency* 33(1), 6.

Goldstein, H. 1990. *Problem-Oriented Policing*. New York: McGraw-Hill.

Gottfredson, M., and T. Hirschi. 1990. *A General Theory of Crime*. Stanford, CA: Stanford University Press.

Greene, J. R., and S. D. Mastrofski. 1988. *Community Policing: Rhetoric or Reality*. New York: Praeger.

Green-Mazerolle, L., and J. Rohl. 1998. *Civil Remedies and Crime Prevention*. Monsey, NY: Criminal Justice Press.

Heckman, J., and J. A. Smith. 1995. Assessing the case for social experimentation. *Journal of Economic Perspectives* 9(2), 85.

Hirschel, D. J., and I. W. Hutchinson. 1992. Female spouse abuse and the police response: The Charlotte, North Carolina experiment. *Journal of Criminal Law and Criminology* 83(1), 73.

Hope, T. 1994. Problem-oriented policing and drug market locations: Three case studies. In *Crime Prevention Studies,* ed. R. V. Clarke. Monsey, NY: Criminal Justice Press, 2, 5-31.

Kansas City Police Department. 1977. *Response Time Analysis.* Kansas City, MO: Kansas City Police Department.

Karmen, A. 2000. *New York Murder Mystery: The True Story behind the Crime Crash of the 1990's.* New York: New York University Press.

Kelling, G., and C. M. Coles. 1996. *Fixing Broken Windows: Restoring Order and Reducing Crime in Our Communities.* New York: Free Press.

Kelling, G., et al. 1974. *The Kansas City Preventive Patrol Experiment: Technical Report.* Washington, DC: Police Foundation.

Kelling, G. L., and W. H. Sousa, Jr. 2001. *Do Police Matter? An Analysis of the Impact of New York City's Police Reforms, Civic Report No. 22.* New York: Manhattan Institute.

Kennedy, D. M., A. A. Braga, and A. M. Piehl. 1996. *Youth Gun Violence in Boston: Gun Markets, Serious Youth Offenders, and a Use Reduction Strategy.* Boston: John F. Kennedy School of Government, Harvard University.

Kennedy, D. M., et al. 2001. *Reducing gun violence: The Boston Gun Project's Operation Ceasefire.* Washington, DC: National Institute of Justice.

Kleiman, M. 1988. Crackdowns: The effects of intensive enforcement on retail heroin dealing. In *Street-Level Drug Enforcement: Examining the Issues,* ed. M. Chaiken. Washington, DC: National Institute of Justice, 3-34.

Larson, R. C., and M. F. Cahn. 1985. *Synthesizing and Extending the Results of Police Patrols.* Washington, DC: U.S. Government Printing Office.

Levitt, S. D. 1997. Using election cycles in police hiring to estimate the effect of police on crime. *American Economic Review* 87(3), 270.

Manning, P. K. 2001. Theorizing policing: The drama and myth of crime control in the NYPD. *Theoretical Criminology* 5(3), 315.

Manski, C. F. 2003. Credible research practices to inform drug law enforcement. *Criminology and Public Policy* 2(3), 543.

Martin, S. E., and L. W. Sherman. 1986. Selective apprehension: A police strategy for repeat offenders. *Criminology* 24(1), 155.

Martinson, R. 1974. What works? Questions and answers about prison reform. *Public Interest* 35, 22.

Marvell, T. B., and C. E. Moody. 1996. Specification problems, police levels, and crime rates. *Criminology* 34(4), 609.

Mastrofski, S. D., J. B. Snipes, and A. E. Supina. 2001. Compliance on demand: The public response to specific police requests. *Journal of Research in Crime and Delinquency* 3, 269.

Maxwell, C. D., J. D. Garner, and J. A. Fagan. 2001. *The Effects of Arrest on Intimate Partner Violence: New Evidence from the Spouse Assault Replication Program.* Research in Brief NCJ 188199. Washington, DC: National Institute of Justice.

Maxwell, C. D., J. D. Garner, and J. A. Fagan. 2002. The preventive effects of arrest on intimate partner violence: Research, policy, and theory. *Criminology and Public Policy* 2(1), 51.

Mazerolle, L. G., et al. 2000. Problem-oriented policing in public housing: The Jersey City evaluation. *Justice Quarterly* 17(1), 129.

McCluskey, J.D., S. D. Mastrofski, and R. B. Parks. 1999. To acquiesce or rebel: Predicting citizen compliance with police requests. *Police Quarterly* 2, 389.

Minneapolis Medical Research Foundation, Inc. 1976. Critiques and commentaries on evaluation research activities: Russell Sage reports. *Evaluation* 3(1-2), 115.

Niskanen, W. A. 1994. *Crime, Police, and Root Causes, Policy Analysis no. 218.* Washington, DC: Cato Institute.

Pate, A. M., and S. O. Annan. 1989. *The Baltimore Community Policing Experiment: Technical Report.* Washington, DC: Police Foundation.

Pate, A. M., and E. E. Hamilton. 1992. Formal and informal deterrents to domestic violence: The Dade County Spouse Assault experiment. *American Sociological Review* 57, 691.

Pate, A. M., and W. G. Skogan. 1985. *Coordinated Community Policing. The Newark Experience Technical Report.* Washington, DC: Police Foundation.

Pawson, R., and N. Tilley. 1997. *Realistic Evaluation.* Beverly Hills, CA: Sage Publications.

Pennell, S. 1979. Fencing activity and police strategy. *Police Chief* 71-75, September.

Police Foundation. 1981. *The Newark Foot Patrol Experiment.* Washington, DC: Police Foundation.

Poyner, B. 1981. Crime prevention and the environment—street attacks in city centers. *Police Research Bulletin* 37, 10.

Press, S. J. 1971. *Some Effects of an Increase in Police Manpower in the 20th Precinct of New York City.* New York: New York City Rand Institute.

Rosenbaum, D. 1989. Community crime prevention: A review and synthesis of the literature. *Justice Quarterly* 5(3), 323.

Sampson, R. J., and J. Cohen. 1988. Deterrent effects of the police on crime: A replication and theoretical extension. *Law and Society Review,* 22(1), 163.

Shadish, W. R., T. Cook, and D. Campbell. 2002. *Experimental and Quasi-Experimental Designs.* Boston: Houghton Mifflin.

Sherman, L. W. 1990. Police crackdowns: Initial and residual deterrence. In *Crime and Justice: A Review of Research, Vol. 12*, ed. M. H. Tonry and N. Morris. Chicago: University of Chicago Press, 1-48.

Sherman, L. W. 1992. *Policing Domestic Violence: Experiments and Dilemmas.* New York: Free Press.

Sherman, L. W., and R. A. Berk. 1984a. Specific deterrent effects of arrest for domestic assault. *American Sociological Review* 49(2), 261.

Sherman, L. W., and R. A. Berk. 1984b. *Specific Deterrent Effects of Arrest for Domestic Assault: Minneapolis.* Washington, DC: National Institute of Justice.

Sherman, L. W., and J. E. Eck. 2002. Policing for crime prevention. In *Evidence Based Crime Prevention*, ed. L. W. Sherman, D. Farrington, and B. Welsh. New York: Routledge, 295-329.

Sherman, L. W., and D. P. Rogan. 1995. Deterrent effects of police raids on crack houses: A randomized, controlled experiment. *Justice Quarterly* 12(4), 755.

Sherman, L. W., and D. Weisburd. 1995. General deterrent effects of police patrol in crime "hot spots": A randomized controlled trial. *Justice Quarterly* 12(4), 625.

Sherman, L. W., et al. 1991. From initial deterrence to long-term escalation: Short custody arrest for poverty ghetto domestic violence. *Criminology* 29(4), 1101.

Sherman, L. W., et al. 1997. *Preventing Crime: What Works, What Doesn't, What's Promising?* A report to the Attorney General of the United States. Washington, DC: United States Department of Justice, Office of Justice Programs.

Sherman, L. W., et al. 2002. *Evidence-Based Crime Prevention.* New York: Routledge.

Silverman, E. B. 1999. *NYPD Battles Crime: Innovative Strategies in Policing.* Boston: Northeastern University Press.

Skogan, W. G., and S. M. Hartnett. 1995. *Community Policing Chicago Style: Year Two.* Chicago: Illinois Criminal Justice Information Authority.

Skogan, W. G. 1990. *Disorder and Decline.* New York: Free Press.

Skogan, W. G. 1992. *Impact of Policing on Social Disorder: Summary of Findings.* Washington, DC: Office of Justice Programs, U.S. Department of Justice.

Skolnick, J. H., and D. H. Bayley. 1986. *The New Blue Line: Police Innovation in Six American Cities.* New York: Free Press.

Spelman, W., and D. K. Brown. 1981. *Calling the Police: A Replication of the Citizen Reporting Component of the Kansas City Response Time Analysis.* Washington, DC: Police Executive Research Forum.

Trojanowicz, R. C. 1986. Evaluating a neighborhood foot patrol program: The Flint, Michigan project. In *Community Crime Prevention: Does It Work?* ed. D. P. Rosenbaum and M. F. Cahn. Beverly Hills, CA: Sage, 157-178.

Uchida, C., B. Forst, and S. O. Annan. 1992. *Modern Policing and the Control of Illegal Drugs: Testing New Strategies in Two American Cities.* Washington, DC: National Institute of Justice.

U.S. General Accounting Office (GAO). 2003. *Technical Assessment of Zhao and Thurman's 2001 Evaluation of the Effects of COPS Grants on Crime.* Washington, DC: GAO. *http://www.gao.gov/new.items/d03867r.pdf*

van Tulder, F. 1992. Crime, detection rate, and the police: A macro approach. *Journal of Quantitative Criminology* 8(1), 113.

Visher, C., and D. Weisburd. 1989. Identifying what works: Recent trends in crime. *Crime, Law and Social Change* 28, 223.

Weiner, K., K. Chelst, and W. Hart. 1984. Stinging the Detroit criminal: A total system perspective. *Journal of Criminal Justice* 12, 289.

Weisburd, D. 1997. *Reorienting Crime Prevention Research and Policy: From the Causes of Criminality to the Context of Crime.* Research report. Washington, DC: U.S. Government Printing Office.

Weisburd, D. 2003. Randomized ethical practice and evaluation of interventions in crime and justice: The moral imperative for randomized trials. *Evaluation Review* 27, 336.

Weisburd, D., and A. Braga. 2003. Hot spots policing. In *Crime Prevention: New Approaches,* ed. H. Kury and J. Obergfell-Fuchs. Mainz: Weisner Ring, 337-354.

Weisburd, D., and L. Green. 1995a. Assessing immediate spatial displacement: Insights from the Minneapolis hot spot experiment. In *Crime and Place: Crime Prevention Studies,* Vol. 4, ed. J. E. Eck and D. Weisburd. Monsey, NY: Willow Tree Press.

Weisburd, D., and L. Green. 1995b. Policing drug hot spots: The Jersey City drug market analysis experiment. *Justice Quarterly* 12(4), 711.

Weisburd, D., and C. Lum. 2005. The diffusion of computerized crime mapping in policing: Linking research and practice. *Police Practice and Research* 6(5), 419.

Weisburd, D., and F. Taxman. 2000. Developing a multi-center randomized trial in criminology: The case of HIDTA. *Journal of Quantitative Criminology,* 16 (3), 315.

Weisburd, D., C. Lum, and A. Petrosino. 2001. Does research design affect study outcomes in criminal justice? *Annals of American Political and Social Science* 578, 50.

Weisburd, D., J. McElroy, and P. Hardyman. 1988. Challenges to supervision in community policing: Observations on a pilot project. *American Journal of Police* 7(2), 29.

Weisburd, D., et al. 2003. Reforming to preserve: Compstat and strategic problem solving in American policing. *Criminology and Public Policy* 3, 425.

Weiss, A., and S. Freels. 1996. Effects of aggressive policing: The Dyton traffic enforcement experiment. *American Journal of Police* 15(3), 45.

Whitaker, G. P. 1985. Aggressive policing and the deterrence of crime. *Law and Policy* 7(3), 395.

Wilson, J. Q., and B. Boland. 1979. The effect of police on crime. *Law and Society Review* 12(3), 367.

Wilson, O. W. 1967. *Crime Prevention—Whose Responsibility?* Washington, DC: Thompson Books.

Wycoff, M. A., and W. G. Skogan. 1993. *Community Policing in Madison: Quality from the Inside Out.* Washington, DC: Police Foundation.

Wycoff, M. A., and W. G. Skogan. 1986. Storefront police offices: The Houston field test. In *Community Crime Prevention: Does It Work?* ed. D. P. Rosenbaum and M. F. Cahn. Beverly Hills, CA: Sage, 179-201.

Zhao, J., M. C. Scheider, and Q. Thurman. 200S. Funding community policing to reduce crime: Have COPS grants made a difference. *Criminology and Public Policy* 2(1), 7.

When States Do Not Extradite: Gaps in the Global Web of Formal Social Control

15

WILLIAM F. MCDONALD

Contents

On April 29, 2002, Los Angeles County Deputy Sheriff David March pulled over a vehicle in Irwindale, California. While attempting to pat down the driver, Armando Garcia, he was shot in the chest by Garcia, who then fled to Mexico. Garcia had been deported three times for drug charges and was wanted for two other murder charges. Because California has the death penalty, Mexico refused to extradite him. In her plea before a Congressional committee examining the extradition process, Deputy March's widow, Teri, expressed her frustration and outrage that Garcia was known to be living freely in Mexico. She wanted justice to be done. Remarkably, she alluded to a well-known alternative to extradition, abduction by bounty hunters, and suggested that it was worth considering (March 2003).[1]

Teri March's grief and desperation represent normal human responses to egregious wrongs inflicted by others. The hunger for justice is a powerful and legitimate one. It is felt keenly not just by the immediate family but by the larger community as well—whose sense of security and righteousness have been violated. Bringing offenders to justice cannot undo the harm but it does serve many important functions. It restores a sense of balance to victims and to the community; it reaffirms the value of the norms and the individuals who have been violated; it deters potential future offenders; and it relieves those who feel a special sense of responsibility for the well-being of the victim—whether they are spouses, parents, fellow police officers, or others—of the felt duty to vindicate the wrong.

Bringing norm violators to account for their wrongdoing is a challenging task with an ancient history. The task is more difficult when offenders flee to other lands. In the nineteenth century, the responsibility for this task was fully assumed by the state. However, nation states have been far more successful in bringing domestic offenders to justice than transnational fugitives.

15.1   Historical Background: From Private to Public Wrongs

Historically, the responsibility and the authority to bring wrongdoers to justice passed from private to public hands. This transition is regarded as the "birth of criminal law" (Bonner and Smith 1930; Ehrenberg 1968). Wrongs that once had been regarded as private matters came to be considered public wrongs. That transition happened at different times and to varying degrees in different places. Even after the shift occurred, for a long time the individual victim or his or her relatives bore much of the burden of bringing criminals to justice.

The blood feud in England, for example, was replaced by the king's court as the legitimate means for settling disputes as early as the twelfth century (Jeffrey 1969). Yet, until 1829 when the Metropolitan Police of London was established, crime victims bore the cost of prosecuting their victimizers. For centuries, the English system for the administration of criminal justice relied upon self-help. During the era of sedentary village

---

[1] Her comments about bounty hunters were made during her live testimony, which I observed.

life in agrarian communities, victims could call upon their neighbors for help in apprehending a criminal by raising the hue and cry. With the growth of towns and the increasing presence of foreigners, especially those involved in international commerce, that option declined and other institutions emerged to replace it. People who could afford to do so formed "prosecution societies," a kind of insurance system to spread the costs of prosecution (Little and Sheffield 1983). Also, a system of rewards to encourage the private prosecution of offenders was created. It led to the development of the infamous system of "thief taking." Professional thief-takers colluded with thieves to rob people and then return stolen goods to collect rewards and then split the take (Pringle 1958).

15.2 Nationalism and the Limits of Modern Policing

The establishment of the modern police in the early nineteenth century resolved many but not all of the problems with the system of self-help. The tasks of investigating, arresting, and prosecuting criminals were assumed by the state—which by then held the monopoly on the use of force. In principal at least, no criminal could expect impunity, and even poor victims could expect justice to be done in their cases (McDonald 1976). In theory, agents of the state would track down all offenders and bring them to justice. There was, however, a major limitation to the new system of professionally administered and publicly supported criminal justice. Its reach stopped at national borders. It did not encompass the problem of the mobile criminal who fled the jurisdiction to avoid prosecution.

As historians of police and policing have stressed, the concept of the police agency as we understand it today is "intimately bound up with the imposition of the nation-state system and the state." (Sheptycki 1998; Bayley 1975). Even using the broader, seventeenth- and eighteenth-century sense of the term, "police," historians of social power stress that the idea of good "police" was inextricably linked to the "governmentalization" of the state, not to the international system of states (Foucault 1991; Pasquino 1991). Indeed, it was the international system of states itself that produced major obstacles to reliable prosecution of criminals abroad. The sentiment of nationalism and the lack of a higher authority with a monopoly on the legitimate use of force have left the world with a mottled patchwork of international agreements whereby some states do some things about some fugitives some of the time. Today, the limitations and inadequacies of this international arrangement are coming under increasing pressure to improve, and indeed, some improvements are happening. But major gaps remain.

15.3 Developments in Transnational Law Enforcement Cooperation

There are two aspects of the task of bringing the transnational fugitive to justice, both of which were responded to by states in the nineteenth century (but not with equal success). One has to do with getting foreign law enforcement agencies to cooperate in locating, investigating, and capturing fugitives. The other has to do with getting foreign states to surrender fugitives to the states of origin. Halting, partial steps toward addressing these matters were taken.

Developments regarding transnational law enforcement cooperation have gone further than those regarding the rendition of fugitives. States have not yet succeeded in achieving at the external, international level what they were able to do internally. They have not eliminated safe havens where fugitives can live with impunity, and they have not raised the value of doing justice above political considerations and state interests. Criminal justice at the international level is not treated by officials responsible for international relations as the highest value. It is just another bargaining chip in international politics. It continues to be "politicized" in ways long since regarded as intolerable if done at the domestic level (Sullivan 2004).[2]

Transnational law enforcement cooperation in the form of regional cooperative agreements began to be developed in Europe and North America at approximately the middle of the nineteenth century (Nadelmann 1993; Deflem 2002; McDonald 1976). Developments proceeded slowly at first. In order to stop agitations by liberal revolutionaries, assassinations of political leaders, and the counterfeiting of national specie, central and eastern European states convened several unsuccessful international conferences intended to establish an international network of police cooperation. Finally, in the wake of World War I, the organization that has come to be known as Interpol was established. The United States did not join it until 1933 and did not begin to participate in major way until the late 1970s (Nadelmann 1993; McDonald 2004).

Substantial developments in the building of a broad regional and increasingly global system of law enforcement cooperation began happening in the 1960s and 1970s in response to two crises that transcended national borders: drug abuse and terrorism. Even before the September 11, 2001, and March

---

[2] Using the administration of criminal justice to achieve political ends is widely regarded as a corruption of justice. For example, when President Vincente Fox's administration sought to charge the former president, Luis Echeverria, with genocide for a massacre of thirty protestors in 1971, David Penchyna, the secretary of the national council of the Institutional Revolutionary Party, which ruled Mexico for seventy-one years before Fox's election, condemned the Fox administration for "politicizing justice" (Sullivan 2004, A1, A16).

11, 2004, terrorist attacks, major steps had been taken with regard to modernizing the institutions for effective transnational cooperation among police agencies and criminal justice systems among Western states. An increasing number of states had posted police liaison officers at their foreign embassies (Bigo 2000; Vise 2000; Statewatch 2001, 2002). Europol, a new regional police institution, was established, and its remit was continually expanded (European Union 1995). The slow and cumbersome old system of *letters rogatory* for obtaining legal assistance in criminal matters from another state was replaced by agreements allowing direct communication among law enforcement agencies without going through diplomatic channels (United Nations 1990; Fijnaut 1993; Muller-Rappard and Bassiouni 1993). New and powerful databases and linkages for the electronic exchange of information had been constructed and were awaiting greater integration (O'Harrow 2003; Hsu 2003; European Commission 2004) Investigative techniques (such as "controlled buys" of drugs) developed in some countries were transplanted to others, requiring adjustments in legal concepts (Nadelmann 1992). Advanced states were competing with each other to train the police of the newly emerging democratic states—diffusing their practices and police cultures as widely as possible. Bilateral anti-organized crime task forces were in use (Martin 1990–1991; Martin 1998). Economically advanced states agreed that more of the above should be done to further perfect the nascent institutions of cross-border cooperation (G7.P8. 1996).

Today, the cooperation among some states regarding the surveillance, investigation, and apprehension of criminals abroad is substantial. The transnationalization of policing is well under way. Nevertheless, the long arm of the law does not yet reach everywhere equally well. Moreover, nationalism and international politics mixed together in some places with corruption and unprofessional policing have left gaping holes in the web of formal, transnational social controls. The unwillingness or inability of some states to surrender wanted persons to states or to international institutions, such as the International Criminal Court, or other states seeking to hold them accountable for harms done has been a major source of lacunae in the global coverage of the forces of order. Victims of crime or their family or friends as well as states themselves often find themselves facing the choice of allowing wrongs to go unrighted or taking extralegal and internationally provocative action.

15.4   The Grand Compromise: Extradite or Prosecute

In the geography of international law enforcement and criminal justice, there are still frontier areas. Moreover, as President George W. Bush reminded us with his allusion to wanting Osama Bin Laden "dead or alive," the kind of justice that is expected and even condoned for dealing with wrongdoers in these geographic, legal, and social frontiers has a Wild West quality about it—although often at the expense of amicability among states. It would not be this way if legal theorists and states had succeeded in bringing the same kind of governmentability to the international system of states that they managed to establish within their own national boundaries by the end of the nineteenth century.

Instead, a grand compromise was struck regarding the obligation of states to ensure that foreign fugitives be brought to justice. The compromise was draped in the language of eliminating impunity, but in truth it laid the groundwork for the haphazard system that prevails today. States could choose to extradite fugitives or prosecute them at home. The compromise allowed states to choose the type of justice they were willing to see done. Extradition means that the fugitive is tried in the jurisdiction where the crime occurred; the evidence and witnesses are more accessible; and the community and victims are able to experience justice being rendered. But it also means that the fugitive may be subject to prejudice against his nationality, to weaker standards of judicial process, and to harsher penalties.

On the other hand, prosecuting the fugitive domestically means that the fugitive is unlikely to be discriminated against—at least on the basis of nationality. He or she will be subject to justice equal to that which his or her fellow citizens would experience under similar circumstances. But, it also means that access to evidence and witnesses is more costly and less forth-coming; that the community and the victims are less likely to experience the cathartic, deterrent, and reconciling influences of the public ritual of a trial; that there is less urgency about the prosecution and possibly a prejudice against the state where the crime occurred; and a greater likelihood that the case will be ignored or will fail.

In competition with churches, local communities, and other organiza-tions for the loyalties of the people within their national boundaries, many nation states decided to embellish the attractions of citizenship by guaran-teeing that their citizens would not be extradited. Nationals would be subject only to the criminal justice institutions of their own nation administered by their fellow citizens. In any event, in the absence of a higher power, all states retained the prerogative of doing nothing about crimes committed by their citizens abroad.

The grand compromise has been sustainable until now. In an era when the scale of international travel was small and international fugitives were rare, the failure to bring the occasional fugitive to justice was not likely to produce much public outrage. But in this "century of migration" where an estimated 100 million people (2 percent of the world's population) live out-side their homelands; international borders are crossed at the rate of 7 million times a day (Schmid 1996); and a fugitive with only a few hundred dollars can catch a flight to another continent, the failures and loopholes in the international system for rendering cross-border fugitives are producing a rising chorus of complaints about its inadequacies.

Legal agreements addressing the problem of international fugitives have existed since ancient times. Indeed, purportedly the oldest document in diplomatic history—the peace treaty between Rameses II of Egypt and the Hittite prince Hattusili signed in 1280 B.C.—contained a provision authorizing the return of criminal fugitives from the other regime's territory (Nadelmann 1992). However, it was not until the seventeenth century that Grotius, the Dutch legal theorist, advanced the argument that all states had the duty to either extradite or prosecute fugitive criminals. He derived this principle from the assumption that a common moral order exists and that all states shared a common interest in suppressing all forms of crime. Therefore, each state had an obligation owing to other states (Bassiouni and Wise 1995).

This principle, *aut dedere aut judicare,* came to be regarded as a rule of customary international law and has been incorporated into many treaties and international conventions. But it has not produced a reliable international system for bringing fugitives to justice. After the first quarter of the nineteenth century, virtually all states of continental Europe uniformly adopted the policy of not extraditing their nationals. Although this practice can be traced back to the Brabantine Bull of 1355, until the nineteenth century, states had been inconsistent and contradictory about it. Robert Rafuse concluded that the uniform adoption of the policy of nonextradition of nationals by the continental states represented an expression of nationalism. "Before the rise of national states it was non-existent," he wrote. "It emerged along with, and grew along with, the growth of national sentiment and national solidarity" (1939).

Rafuse noted that England and the United States did not adopt the policy of nonextradition of nationals. Moreover, in 1939 it appeared to him as if the world were moving away from the nonextradition policy as an absolute position. Various committees of experts tried to formulate an acceptable rule by which governments that did not normally extradite their nationals might do so under certain conditions. He predicted that the nonextradition of nationals would gradually break down as world unity grew stronger (Rafuse 1939). His prediction has yet to come true (Labarini 2001).[3]

---

[3] Among the countries that are prohibited today by their constitution, legislation, or policy from extraditing nationals are France, Germany, Austria, and Belgium; Brazil, Ecuador, Panama, and Venezuela (Labarini 2001, fn. 19).

15.5   Four Rationales for Not Extraditing

Two common rationales for not extraditing fugitives, whether or not they are nationals, have been offered: (1) that justice would not be done fairly and lawfully by the foreign government or (2) that the punishments in the requesting country were inhumane. At the turn of the eighteenth century, learned thinkers like Thomas Jefferson held in great disdain the quality of justice administered in countries other than their own. They preferred to allow the most heinous criminals to walk free rather than surrender them to a foreign power—a position not unlike that of today, whereby states refuse to extradite fugitives to the United States because it practices capital punishment.

In denying a French request for extradition, Thomas Jefferson, as secretary of state, put the argument as follows:

> The laws of this country take no notice of crimes committed out of their jurisdiction. The most atrocious offender coming within their pale is received by them as an innocent man, and they have authorized no one to seize and deliver him. The evil of protecting malefactors of every dye is sensibly felt here as in other countries, but until a reformation of the criminal codes of most nations, to deliver fugitives from them would be to become their accomplices. The former, therefore, is viewed as the lesser evil (Nadelmann 1992).

None other than the father of modern criminal jurisprudence himself, Cesare Beccaria, refused to endorse the concept of extradition because of the dubious standards of justice found in many countries. He wrote:

> But, whether international agreements for the reciprocal exchange of criminals be useful, I would not dare to decide until laws more in conformity with the needs of humanity, until milder punishments and an end to dependence on arbitrary power and opinion, have provided security for oppressed innocence and hated virtue—until universal reason, which ever tends to unite the interests of throne and subjects, has confined tyranny forever to the vast plains of Asia, though, undoubtedly, the persuasion that there is not a foot of soil upon which real crimes are pardoned would be a most efficacious means of preventing them ([1764] 1963).

Two additional reasons for not extraditing are that the offense with which the fugitive is charged is either (3) a "political crime" or (4) not crime at all in the state harboring the fugitive. The latter was the source of the first of many conflicts in the troubled relationship between Mexico and the United

States over extradition. Between 1825 and 1832, the newly independent Mexicans, who abolished slavery in 1829, refused to ratify the proposed Treaty of Amity, Commerce and Navigation with the United States until the Americans finally removed the provision for the arrest and surrender of fugitive slaves (Nadelmann 1993).

15.6   Foreign Prosecution and Its Discontents

Under Grotius's principle, nations that do not extradite are expected to prosecute the crime on behalf of the state where the crime occurred. Known as "foreign prosecution" (or "vicarious prosecution"), this procedure is provided for by the laws of many of those states that refuse to extradite. For example, Article 4 of the Mexican Federal Penal Code provides as follows:

> Crimes committed in a foreign country, by a Mexican citizen against Mexican citizens or against a foreign citizen, or by a foreign citizen against Mexican citizens, shall be punishable in the Republic, in accordance with the federal laws, if the following requirements are met: (1) that the defendant is found in the Republic; (2) the defendant must not have been definitively judged in the country where the crime was committed; and (3) the offense being charged must be a crime in the country in which it was committed and in the Republic of Mexico (Briones 1996).

There are many problems with the foreign prosecution option in both theory and practice. Cesare Beccaria was opposed to the theory. He argued:

> Some people have maintained that punishment may be meted out for a crime, that is, for an action contrary to the laws, regardless of where it is committed.... Some believe also, that a cruel act done, for example, in Constantinople, may be punished in Paris, for the abstract reason that one who offends humanity merits the collective enmity of mankind and universal execration—as if judges were the vindicators of the universal sensibility of men, rather than of the pacts that bind them to one another.... The place of punishment is the place of the crime, because only there and not elsewhere are men under constraint to injure a private person in order to prevent public injury. A wretch who has not broken the pacts of a society of which he was not a member may be feared and, therefore, by the superior force of society exiled and excluded; but he should not be punished with the formality of the laws,

which are vindicators of social compacts, not of the intrinsic malice of human actions ([1764] 1963).

In a lecture on transnational law enforcement and criminal justice delivered two weeks before the end of her second term as attorney general (January 2001), Janet Reno weighed in against foreign prosecution and in favor of extradition. Justice should be done in the community where the crime occurred, she argued, so that the community that suffered the crime can experience the functional benefits of justice done (Reno 2001). Attorney General Reno was voicing the traditional American policy with regard to extradition, which it inherited from England. It is a policy based on adherence to the principle of territorial jurisdiction, which entails the rule that persons accused of crimes should be tried in the *forum delicti commissi* (at or near the place where the crime was committed) (Rafuse 1939).

Beyond the theoretical arguments against foreign prosecution, there is a practical one. It does not work. At least, it did not work in most places other than along the U.S.-Mexican border since the mid-1980s. European states may no longer face this problem because they are building a new judicial space within the borders of the European Union (EU), which will allow fugitives from one EU state to be extradited to other EU states almost as easily as American states extradite offenders among themselves (Statewatch 2001).[4] But before the integration of European states began, the reality was that foreign prosecution failed as an effective alternative to extradition.

According to one official with direct responsibility for these matters, foreign prosecution cases had a low priority for the governments being requested to prosecute, and even the requesting governments would lose incentives to pursue the matter. Witnesses and investigating magistrates had to be persuaded to travel to another country, statements had to be translated, and other hurdles had to be jumped. As a result, most requests for foreign prosecutions went unanswered. The major exceptions to this were cases in

---

[4] Following the Tampere Summit in 1999, Spain and Italy took the lead in creating a "European area of justice." For cases involving "serious crime" (including terrorism, drug trafficking, people trafficking, arms dealing, and sexual abuse of minors) with maximum penalties of no less than four years, the two countries are replacing extradition procedures with administrative transfers. Additionally, the two countries agreed to other procedures and criteria related to transnationalizing their respective criminal justice systems including "mutual recognition of criminal judgments, formal procedures for requesting custody, demanding arrests and the transfer of persons facing judicial sentences or proceedings, and for dealing with extradition requests from third countries." Moreover, they restricted the possibility of political considerations determining the decision to extradite by limiting the valid reasons for refusing to surrender a suspected or convicted criminal to two: (1) inadequate documentation relating to the extradition request and (2) cases in which the requested person is granted immunity by legislation in the requested state (Statewatch 2002).

which high-level officials from a powerful foreign country made their interest in a case very clear (Wilkitzki 1988).

In the U.S.–Mexican relationship, until the mid-1980s, the situation was similar. Mexican law provided for the possibility of foreign prosecution but it was rarely used and was largely unknown to law enforcement and judicial officials on either side of the border (McDonald 1976). Combined with the fact that Mexico refused to extradite, the absence of the foreign prosecution option meant that for much of its history, Mexico was a virtual safe haven for fugitives—as were many other states in a similar situation.

15.7 Legal Vacuums and Alternatives to the Extradite-or-Prosecute Choice

Around the globe, states that lack extradition treaties, or have them but refuse to extradite while also not prosecuting fugitives, constitute the last frontier for global criminal justice. They create legal vacuums in which justice gets done, if at all, by other means: either by self-help on the part of victims, or through ruses by law enforcement officials who lure the fugitive back to jurisdiction where the crime occurred, or through blatant violations of sovereignty. If the fugitive is not a citizen of the state of destination, there is another legal option. If the fugitive is a foreigner, the state of destination might be persuaded to expel him on immigration grounds. This usually depends upon either the political climate between the two states or the venality of the officials.

Even nations that are willing to extradite—like the United States—become safe havens for criminals from countries with whom no extradition treaty exists (Lathem 2001).[5] The police in major American cities can usually point out gangsters from certain countries known to be wanted for brutal crimes back home but who are untouchable in the United States for their foreign crimes because of the absence of an extradition agreement.

More than two centuries after Beccaria and Jefferson expressed their disdain, the criminal justice systems of the world still vary widely in the quality of fairness, legality, and humanity they exercise. Torture, corruption, and abuse are still commonplace (Lakshmi 2004). Many of the old objections to surrendering fugitives to foreign justice systems remain. Although international renditions have been more frequent, many fugitives still go unpunished. Victims like Teri March and law enforcement officials are left with difficult choices: accepting that justice will not be done; hiring a bounty

---

[5] Additionally, there are as many as 800 war criminals, torturers, and human rights abusers from foreign countries living comfortably in the United States thanks to loopholes in the immigration laws (Lathem 2001).

hunter; trying to persuade or bribe the foreign government to expel the fugitive (if not a national); waiting for the fugitive to return and get caught again; luring the fugitive back to the jurisdiction; or taking matters into their own hands.

15.8   International Migration and Fugitives

With international migration being what it is today, more and more countries of the developed world are facing this choice. Increasingly, they are faced with foreigners, particularly illegal immigrants (*clandestini*, undocumented immigrants), who get involved in crimes and flee home to avoid prosecution.

The United States, for example, is undergoing a demographic revolution that is Latinizing the population (Camarota and McArdle 2003; Schmitt 2001; U.S. Census Bureau 2001; Camarota 2002; Center for Immigration Studies 2003, 2004; Bunis 2002).[6] Although the vast majority (70 percent) of all immigrants settle in only six states (U.S. Census Bureau 2001),[7] many others have been settling in new locations (U.S. Census Bureau 2001; Passel and Zimmerman 2004). Law enforcement agencies far removed from the Southwest border have begun to confront the problem of international fugitives. It was not too surprising in 1984 when the Los Angeles Police Department reviewed its list of outstanding murder warrants and found that 100 of the 237 open cases involved Mexican nationals presumed to have fled to Mexico (Gates and Ross 1990). Nor was it surprising to find that of the nienty-seven outstanding murder warrants in Orange County, California, eighty-seven of them were for Mexican nationals or Mexican Americans, and that half of them were believed to have fled to Mexico (Eaton 1993). But it was stunning to learn in 1998 that almost two-thirds of the thirty-seven outstanding murder warrants of the District of Columbia police were Salvadorans believed to have fled to El Salvador (Thomas-Lester 1998).[8]

---

[6] By March 2000, there were 28.4 million foreign-born persons in the United States, a 43 percent increase since 1990 and a tripling of the number in 1970. Half (51 percent) of the immigrants were from Latin America. Mexico contributed by far the largest share of all immigrants, accounting for 25 percent of the total (Bunis 2002; Schmitt 2001; U.S. Census Bureau 2001; Camarota 2002).

As of January 2000, there were an estimated 7 million unauthorized immigrants in the United States (U.S. Immigration and Naturalization Service, Office of Policy and Planning, 2003). (For higher, more recent estimates, see Center for Immigration Studies 2004.) About 4.8 million of them were from Mexico. More than 100,000 of them came El Salvador, Guatemala, and Honduras each. An estimated additional 350,000 unauthorized residents were being added each year. Mexico's share of the unauthorized population increased from 58 percent in 1990 to 69 percent in 2000. Mexico accounted for 43 percent of the growth in the total of foreign born population (Camarota and McArdle 2003).

[7] California (8.8 million); New York (3.6 million); Florida (2.8 million); Texas (2.4 million); New Jersey (1.2 million); and Illinois (1.2 million) (U.S. Census Bureau 2001).

[8] Thomas-Lester 1998, A1, A12.

Medium to small jurisdictions across the country, which have rarely been involved in international criminal matters in the past, are now dealing with international fugitives (ABC 20/20 1999).[9] The Congressional inquiry into the problem of extradition from Mexico, for instance, was driven by the concerns of local prosecutors from Georgia experiencing their first brush with Mexican murder suspects who had fled back to Mexico (Porter 2003; Warren 2003). Georgia prosecutors were frustrated and angered by their experience with Mexican justice—unlike the favorable experiences they had had with Canada and the Cayman Islands. In October 2001, the Mexican Supreme Court stepped back from its new willingness to extradite fugitives (Labarini 2001; Sullivan and Jordan 2001; Rice 2003; Kocherga 2004).[10] It ruled that Mexican residents could not be extradited to a jurisdiction where they might receive a "life sentence" (Stevenson 2000; Lezon 2001).[11]

[9] Perhaps most surprising of all was story of a Fairfax County, Virginia, police detective, Rich Perez, who was outraged by the federal government's failure to get custody of a Salvadoran man who allegedly committed a murder in Fairfax and then fled to Salvador. Perez decided to take matters into his own hands and to show the country how easy it would be to find this fugitive. He invited the television journalism program, ABC 20/20, to accompany him to Salvador while he tracked down the alleged killer. The broadcast aired complete with a face-to-face interview in which Perez told the fugitive he wanted him to return to Fairfax to stand trial for murder. The fugitive simply stood up and walked out of the interview (ABC 20/20, 1999).

[10] For a century and a half, the United States and Mexico were locked in a virtual standoff regarding the rending of fugitives. In 1980, a new extradition treaty between the two countries went into effect. For the next fifteen years, however, the extraditions between the country averaged only one per year (Mexico extradited eight, the United States thirty). Then in 1996, against the background of the North American Free Trade Agreement, cooperation began happening regarding the rendering of fugitives either through extradition or by expulsion (for violations of immigration law). From 1995 through 2000, there was average of more than twenty extraditions per year. Mexico extradited a total of sixty-one fugitives to the United States, and the United States delivered a total of eighty-six individuals (Labarini 2001).

In addition, the United States and Mexico established the Fugitive Identification and Alert Program, through which information is exchanged regarding fugitives residing in the other country in violation of immigration laws. The program led to the expulsion of ten fugitives during six months of 1997 and of over thirty U.S. citizens in 1998 (Labarini 2001). The election of Vincente Fox, international "neighbor" of former Texas governor, President George W. Bush, in December 2000 to the Mexican presidency brought even greater cooperation. Fox's directive to the Mexican federal judicial police help locate U.S. fugitives and yielded record numbers of fugitives being captured (thirty-nine in five months vs. seventeen in the preceding year) (Sullivan and Jordan 2001). In 2002, Mexico captured 200 fugitives (up from 160 in 2001) for expulsion for immigration violations (90 percent to the United States). Only twenty-five fugitives were formally extradited in 2002 (up from nine in 2000 and four in 1995) (Rice 2003; Kocherga 2004).

In January 2001, the Mexican Supreme Court had reached a momentous decision. It ruled that it was constitutional to extradite Mexican nationals (Labarini 2001). Until the court's decision of October 2001 prohibiting the extradition to jurisdictions with life sentences, American officials thought the road was clear to an era of robust cooperation.

[11] This decision put at risk the rending of 55 U.S. fugitives being held in Mexican jails and another 700 believed to be living there (Lezon 2001, A1; Stevenson 2000).

For many American jurisdictions, this ruling created an untenable situation for prosecutors. Their laws often provided sentences of capital punishment or life for all homicides. Their penal codes did not permit the judge or the prosecutor the discretion necessary to give the assurance that a life sentence would not be imposed—a condition for extraditing required by Mexico. American prosecutors would have to drop the murder charge to something lower in order to be able to give the guarantees Mexico demanded (Zavala and Marlow 2002). This would mean that murderers who fled to Mexico and were caught would be guaranteed a lower penalty than those caught in the United States (Cowan 2004).[12]

15.9   Criminal Justice Vacuums, Desperate Victims, and Self-Help

Despite improvements in the transnational administration of criminal justice, there are still victims like Teri March who find themselves in situations akin to that of victims before the establishment of the modern police. To get justice, they have to rely upon self-help. Some bereaved victims put their lives on hold while they personally track down their offenders. Others hire bounty hunters or bribe foreign police to bring offenders to them. Still others are assisted by well-meaning law enforcement officers who arrange for the offenders to be brought back by bounties or through personal favors from foreign officials or who kidnap the offenders themselves and bring them back.

[12] The Mexican Supreme Court's decision illustrates the kind of problem that happens when officials of one system do not understand the real meaning of the terminology used by the other system. The Mexican Supreme Court's logic in this case rested on Mexico's philosophy of punishment. Mexico has abolished capital punishment and has a maximum sentence of sixty years. Its penal philosophy emphasizes inmate rehabilitation. "In a life sentence, it would be absurd to hope to rehabilitate the criminal if there will be no chance he will return to society," Justice Roman Palacios stated in the decision (Lezon 2001).

The Mexican court assumed that American legal language should be taken at face value. It seems to be unaware that "life sentence" in America is very likely to be substantially shorter than sixty years. Some American officials recognized this language problem and began negotiating with Mexico for extradition of their cases with the intention of explaining to Mexican officials that the phrase, "life sentence," is not being taken literally.

Addressing this cultural misunderstanding may remove the obstacle (when the political will is there). Wharton County (Texas) District Attorney Josh Cowan had agreed to waive the death penalty in an extradition request involving a murder. In addition, he overcame the Mexican Supreme Court's prohibition of "life sentences" by explaining that a life sentence in Texas actually was shorter than Mexico's sixty-year sentence. Whether this clarification carried the day or not, however, is unclear. He had just about given up on the extradition when he was stunned by a call "from out of the blue" from the Mexican consulate saying "he [the fugitive] will be delivered tomorrow." Cowan believes it is no coincidence that the call came while President Vincente Fox was in Texas visiting with then-Governor George W. Bush. "It was as much politics was it was anything," he said (phone interview, July 27, 2004).

Occasional stories of self-help can be found in the news from along the U.S.-Mexico border (Cowan 2004).[13] An example is Mario Girela's three-year quest to bring Nicolas Mauro Gutierrez to justice for killing Gutierrez's common law wife, Margaret, Girela's daughter (Black 2000; Eaton 1993).[14] Ignoring advice from Texas law enforcement officials about the dangers of searching for a fugitive in Mexico on his own, Girela repeatedly traveled south of the border (Eaton 1993). Driven in part by a sense of guilt that he could have prevented the killing if he had responded to the letter he received from his daughter three days before the killing, telling him for the first time of the problems she was having, he pursued the case on his own, following tips regarding where Gutierrez was living. On one occasion, he spent a fruitless six weeks in Monterrey and four days and nights staking out a house where Gutierrez was supposedly staying. Finally, he got a tip that Gutierrez was living in Gomez Palacios, Mexico.

Not waiting for the Texas attorney general's office to return his call notifying them of the tip, Girela went alone to Gomez Palacios, changed his appearance so as not to be recognized, and contacted the head of the local penitentiary where Gutierrez was supposed to be serving time. Luckily, the prison commandant recognized the photo of Gutierrez and said he was living under an alias in Cevallos, a small place three hours away. Girela then went to the Gomez Palacios police, showed them all the paperwork he had—news clippings, police reports, and the prison mug shot—and asked for their help. When the police responded that they had no authority to detain Gutierrez, he decided to go after Gutierrez himself. The police accompanied him with four police officers carrying submachine guns.

In Cevallos, Girela and his escort made contact with two undercover police officers. When shown Gutierrez's mug shot, they said they had just seen him. The officers went off on their own, returning later with Gutierrez in handcuffs. Gutierrez was transported to the police station in Gomez Palacios, where he was held awaiting official action. Girela and his other daughter contacted several American law enforcement agencies, which contacted the Mexican officials who activated a provisional arrest warrant. The warrant was based upon a request filed in the case years earlier by the Texas

---

[13] There are no statistics on how often transnational self-help activities happen but Texas District Attorney Josh Cowan believes they are becoming less common. In addition to the one in which he was personally involved, he remembers hearing details of another case mentioned over drinks with a prosecutor from West Texas, who described how someone had gone across the border and brought back a fugitive. "That was the way it used to be done but I don't hear much about it anymore" (phone interview, July 27, 2004).

[14] This account is based on the story by reporter Jonathan Black and the recollection of David Garza, who at the time was head of the Foreign Prosecution Unit, Texas Attorney General's Office (interviewed by phone on July 27, 2004) (Black 2000, A1, A5). For a sense of the danger for families of searching for people in Mexico, see Eaton 1993.

attorney general. In the end, however, Gutierrez hung himself while await-ing extradition.

Another successful apprehension of a fugitive as a result of self-help by victims is the capture of Romeo Lopez, who shot his wife, Lori, and dumped her body along Highway 59 on his way to Laredo, where he abandoned his car and walked into Mexico (Schutze 1989; Hegstrom 2000; Rendon 2003).[15] The hunt for Lopez would have ended at the border in typical fashion if it were not for some luck and the extra efforts of Lori Lopez's family. Her father and brother searched for her body for two weeks along the highway they assumed he had taken, finding it on a side road bloated and partially devoured by animals. They also went searching for Romeo in his family's hometown in Mexico. They posted pictures of Romeo and a notice of a reward for $10,000 along the border on bulletin boards and public spaces at crossings.

Heeding the warnings of Texas law enforcement about the dangers of such forays, they discontinued searching in Mexico. But their posters paid off seventeen months later. Romeo Lopez had gotten a construction job in Monterrey. His boss saw one of the posters and contacted the Texas district attorney, Josh Cowan, whose telephone number was given. Cowan wanted a positive identification. So the boss secretly photographed Romeo at work and sent the photo to the Cowan and later sent fingerprints. Romeo was arrested and held for extradition, which he fought for three years but even-tually lost after extensive negotiations between Cowan and Mexican officials, regarding waiving of the death penalty and satisfying the no-life-imprison-ment standard (see *infra*).

Sometimes, the prospect of the legal systems not getting justice done drives aggrieved families to extremely desperate measures. In 1985, Jose Preciado Renteria allegedly killed his brother-in-law in Placentia, California. He was later found murdered and tied to a tree in Jalisco, Mexico. The Placentia police believed it was a revenge killing by the family (Eaton 1993).

15.10   Rewards, Bounty Hunting, and International Relations

An alternative to the direct involvement of victims in pursuing offenders is the ancient system of bounty hunting. The victim—who may be an individ-ual, a family, a law enforcement agency, a community, or a state—pays a fee

---

[15] This account is based on two news reports and interviews on July 27, 2004, one with David Garza, former head of the Foreign Prosecution Unit, Texas Attorney General's Office, the other with Josh Cowan, Wharton County (Texas) district attorney (Hegstrom 2000, A:1; Rendon 2003, A:25). For yet another account of a father's desperate search for his son in Mexico, which unearthed the gruesome, ritual (santaria) killings of his son and others, see Schutze 1989.

or establishes a reward for having the fugitive either killed ("wanted dead or alive") or returned to the jurisdiction where the offense occurred. The fee/reward might be paid to a professional bounty hunter or to corrupt police officials in the country of destination or to others.

Professional bounty hunting is still a legitimate, albeit dicey, occupation (http://www.scapecast.com/bho/index.html; http://www.dogthebounty-hunter.com; Barbee 2001). As long as there are bail bonds, rewards for apprehending offenders, and territories without the reliable enforcement of law, there will be bounty hunters. International terrorism and the establishment of the International Criminal Court have breathed new life into this ancient institution. The hunt for today's international terrorists has spawned the largest and most publicized rewards ever. Multimillion-dollar rewards have been offered for Osama Bin Laden and Saddam Hussein and were paid for help locating Hussein's sons (Tierney 2002; Haskell 2004; http://www.reward-sforjustice.net/).[16] It has been argued that the International Criminal Court needs to rely upon private bounty hunters in the absence of other mechanisms for the rendition of war criminals (Izes 1997; Supernor 2001).

Transnational bounty hunting in which the hunter kidnaps the wanted fugitive and returns him to the jurisdiction of origin may involve violations of the domestic laws of the state where the fugitive was hiding (Weiner 2003; Weilminster 2003).[17] Nevertheless, it is regarded as fair play by many victims, law enforcement agents, and the hunters themselves. The justification is axiomatic. Justice must be done. The state harboring the fugitive refuses or is too corrupt or inept to do it. Therefore, the unlawful acts are justified.

Perhaps this was the thinking of the U.S. Drug Enforcement Administration (DEA) when it paid bounty hunters $20,000 to kidnap Humberto Alvarez-Machain, a Mexican doctor, in connection with the 1985 torture-killing of DEA agent Enrique Camarena (Zagaris and Padierna Peralta 1997). Unable to get the Mexican government to solve the case, the DEA finally took

---

[16] In the mid-1980s, the U.S. State Department initiated its Rewards for Justice program. By December 2002, it had paid $9.5 million to twenty-three informants and was offering $25 million for the capture of Osama Bin Laden. The $2 million bounty it paid for the nabbing of Mir Amal Kansi, who went on a shooting rampage outside the CIA's Virginia headquarters in 1993, was critical to solving the case (Tierney 2002, 4; Haskell 2004). For the State Department's Rewards for Justice Web site, go to http://www.rewardsforjustice.net/.

[17] When Duane (Dog) Chapman, the self-proclaimed "greatest bounty hunter in the world," maced and subdued Arthur Luster, heir to the Max Factor fortune and fugitive convicted rapist, outside a taco stand in Puerto Vallarta and hauled him off in a van towards the airport in June 2003, the Mexican police quickly arrested him, his son, his cameraman, and his publicity agent. The four were charged with kidnapping and jailed (Weiner 2003, 9); Weilminster 2003, 14A).

Some advocates of the use of bounty hunters to render war criminals to the International Criminal Court urge the granting of legal immunity to hunters for violations of domestic laws in fulfilling their tasks (Supernor 2001).

matters into its own hands (Golden 1992).[18] In April 1990, a half-dozen men abducted Dr. Alvarez from his office in Guadalajara; drove him to Nuevo Leon, Mexico; and flew him to El Paso, Texas. There, he was arrested by DEA agents and brought to Los Angeles to stand trial. He was charged with administering stimulants to Camarena so he could withstand torture with a red-hot pipe while being interrogated, before being killed (Eaton 1993).[19] The abduction provoked howls of protest from Mexico and other countries, which accused the United States of violating Mexican sovereignty (Zagaris and Padierna Peralta 1997).

An even louder outcry was heard two years later when the U.S. Supreme Court held that Dr. Alvarez could be brought to trial despite the kidnapping (Lewis 1992). The United States and Mexico had an extradition treaty. The United States had not requested the extradition of Dr. Alvarez because Mexico had a policy of refusing to extradite its nationals. The extradition treaty did not specifically prohibit kidnapping. Therefore, kidnapping did not void the legality of the trial.

Within hours of the Supreme Court's ruling, the Mexican Foreign Ministry suspended all DEA activities within Mexico. However, after threats of retaliation from the United States and assurances from high-level officials that the United States would not kidnap again, Mexico retracted its suspension and gave DEA agents "temporary" permission to remain (Golden 1992; Holmes 1993). Mexico's willingness to cooperate with extraditions and expulsions, however, cooled.

15.11 Terrorism, Extraordinary Rendition, and Torture

Transnational rendition of individuals has assumed a new dimension in this new era of counterterrorism. The American response to the September 11 atrocity has been to shift law enforcement priorities from prosecution to prevention. Today's highest priority is to pre-empt future attacks, now seen as potentially catastrophic. Bringing terrorists to trial is a secondary matter or, even, something to be avoided in order to prevent terrorists from communicating with anyone (Bravin 2001; Eggen 2001; Fainaru 2002).

On the other hand, kidnapping and transporting them across international borders so that they can be interrogated (some say "tortured") has become a key weapon in the American fight against terrorism. The U.S. Central Intelligence Agency (CIA) refers to these cases as "extraordinary

[18] American officials suspect the reason for Mexico's inaction was the identities of two of the Mexicans eventually indicted in the case: the brother-in-law of a former president and a former head of the federal investigations police (Golden 1992, 4).
[19] After being held for nearly three years in U.S. prisons, Alvarez was acquitted for lack of evidence and released (Eaton 1993).

renditions"—described by the *Washington Post* as "the fast and forcible transfer of foreign terrorism suspects to other countries, often their places of
origin, where they can be detained or interrogated more freely, often without
all the legal protections available in the country they left" (Whitlock 2004).
George Tenet, then-director of the CIA, testified to the 9/11 Commission
that even before September 11, the CIA had conducted about seventy such
renditions. Since then, their use has increased substantially, according to
security analysts (Whitlock 2004).

The details of extraordinary renditions are mostly unknown. Some
insights have emerged from cases that have come to light. Individuals have
been transported either to one of the secret prisons the United States operates
abroad (e.g., at the Bargram Air Base north of Kabul) or handed over to the
intelligence services of their native countries, where allegedly they were tortured. Critics have condemned the practice as "torture out-sourcing," by
which the United States government was able to get around restrictions on
torture by having other countries do it. The United States and other countries
involved deny the charge, claiming they had assurances from the countries
to which these individuals were rendered that they would not be tortured
(Murphy 2004; Slevin 2004; Obsidian Wings 2004; Meek 2005).

The legality of the procedure is less problematic than its political and
moral aspects. The state doing the rending may have legal grounds for its
action and/or may have the cooperation of both the state from which the
person is abducted and the state to which he or she is rendered. For example,
on the way home to Canada from a holiday, Marher Arar, who holds both
Canadian and Syrian citizenship, was taken into custody by U.S. immigration
officials while changing planes at Kennedy Airport. He was deported to Syria
for alleged terrorist ties. There he was held for almost a year, allegedly tortured, and released after the Syrian government's interrogators found no
direct ties to Al Qaeda (Higgins 2002).

On December 18, 2001, two Egyptian nationals who had applied for
refugee status in Sweden were whisked off the streets of Stockholm, escorted
to the airport by hooded security officials who did not speak Swedish, and
flown to Cairo on a U.S.-registered Gulfstream jet. There, according to credible evidence produced by their friends and attorneys, they were tortured
and imprisoned: one after a six-hour trial, the other held without charges.
The Swedish officials say they had been given assurances by Cairo that torture
would not be used. Embarrassed, the Swedish government now says the
deportation was a mistake and has called for an international inquiry (Whitlock 2004).

Khaled el-Masri, a German citizen born in Lebanon, was on a vacation
in Macedonia where, he claimed, Macedonian authorities took him into
custody for several weeks, questioned him about being a member of Al Qaeda,

and turned him over to officials (whom he believes were American). They flew him to a prison in Afghanistan, where he says he was beaten, drugged, and asked about Al Qaeda. After five months in captivity, he was blindfolded, put on a flight then a bus ride, and finally released on a deserted mountain road in northern Albania. Around the bend, he met three men in uniforms at a border crossing. He told one of them his story of captivity. "The man was laughing at me," he said. "Don't tell that story to anyone because no one will believe it. Everyone will laugh" (van Natta and Mekhennet 2005). German authorities have begun an investigation into the matter.

The United States has not renounced the use of extraordinary renditions. However, in the wake of the Abu Ghraib scandal as well as allegations of torture of the prisoners held at Guantanamo and the suspicion that torture was supported by then-White House counsel (now Attorney General) Alberto Gonzalez, the Bush administration finally pledged to not use torture against terrorists (Slevin 2004).

15.12   Conclusions

By the end of the nineteenth century, nation states had abolished impunity for criminal behavior within their borders. States assumed full responsibility for investigating, apprehending, bringing to trial, and punishing individuals who violated the criminal law. Publicly funded police agencies were tasked with bringing all criminals to justice. Victims of crime were reduced to witnesses. They no longer bore the risks and costs of apprehending and prosecuting criminals. The state tried to guarantee that justice would be done. But that guarantee was only good for cases that stayed within the national territory. If the offender fled abroad, the state's ability and will to bring the offender to justice diminished dramatically.

Beyond the national borders lies the international system of states, some of which do not have the institutional or legal structures or the political will to try to abolish impunity for transnational criminals and fugitives worldwide. Although major steps have been taken in building institutions of transnational cooperation in law enforcement and criminal justice, many gaps in the web of transnational formal social controls still exist. Under the principles of international law, states harboring fugitives or transnational criminals are obliged to extradite or prosecute them. But there are many reasons why this principle does not serve to eliminate safe havens. The obligation does not apply if there is no treaty between the two states. In many cases where states refuse to extradite, the case is not prosecuted for various reasons including a lack of interest in the prosecution and the many disincentives for the jurisdiction of origin to pursue the prosecution (costs of travel and translation; lack of knowledge of how to make or prepare the case; political objection to a foreign trial; and more).

When states neither extradite nor prosecute, there are alternatives: some legal, others not. If the political relations between the two states are favorable and if the fugitive is a foreigner, then the state of destination might agree to use its immigration laws to expel the fugitive. Otherwise, victims seeking justice are left with the choice between impunity for their offender or problematic strategies such as relying upon kidnapping by bounty hunters, or upon doing their own investigation, or taking justice into their own hands. These options do indeed get exercised occasionally. With the high rate of international migration, especially of illegal immigrants, developed countries are likely to see an increase in the use of these alternatives.

The terrorism of the past decade has added a new and surreal dimension to the transnational rendition of individuals associated with serious social harm. Terrorists and their supporters are being taken into custody by state agents, sometimes by abduction off the streets, and flown to foreign lands for interrogation. They alleged that they have been drugged, beaten, tortured, and held against their wills without due process of law for months at time and then released without ever being charged with a crime.

In sum, looking at the status of law enforcement and the administration of criminal justice from the perspective of globalization, one sees a patchwork of agreements and tensions among contending geopolitical and legal entities. Although the institutions of transnational cooperation in law enforcement and criminal justice assistance have developed substantially in the recent past, impunity for criminals is a serious reality. For the prosecution of transnational fugitives, many victims today are like victims before the development of the modern police. If they want justice, they have to make their own arrangements. Governmental institutions cannot be relied upon to render justice. Even the states themselves are forced to rely upon heavy-handed, questionable, and politically costly methods to get evidence and to bring offenders to justice.

The power to refuse extradition has always been a political weapon with which states can try to inflict political damage to rival states; to assert the moral superiority of their system; and/or to try to leverage other states to conform their penal practices to higher standards of justice. The power to whisk terrorists off to foreign lands to be interrogated under intimidating circumstances, if not torture, is threatening the traditional respect for human dignity and due process of law maintained by liberal states. The development of effective global institutions of criminal justice that would assure victims that offenders would be brought to trial in a lawful and fair way is not yet on the horizon. Terrorism is having a contradictory impact, prompting greater cooperation but spawning new and questionable tactics.

In short, the system of international states represents today's frontier, today's Wild West where badlands exist and the justice can be rough. The governmentability achieved within states by the nineteenth century has yet to be achieved among states.

References

ABC 20/20. 1999. A journey for justice. Television broadcast. *20/20*, June 9.

Agence France Presse. 2002. Mexico justice system corrupt and needs change: UN rights expert. http://www.thenewsmexico.com/printedformat.asp?id=23080. *The News* (Mexico City), April 9.

Barbee, D. 2001. Bounty hunters leery of tracking escapees: $300,000 reward not worth risk, some say. *Fort Worth Star-Telegram*, January 13, 1.

Bassiouni, M. C., and E. M. Wise. 1995. *Aut Dedere Aut Judicare: The Duty to Extradite or Prosecute in International Law*. Dordrecht, Boston: M. Nijhoff.

Bayley, D. H. 1975. The police and political development in Europe. In *The Formation of Nation States in Western Europe*, ed. C. Tilly, 328-79. Princeton, NJ: Princeton University Press.

Beccaria, C. 1764, 1963. *On Crimes and Punishments*. Trans. H. Paolucci. Indianapolis: Bobbs-Merrill.

Bigo, D. 2000. Liaison officers in Europe: New officers in the European security field. In *Issues in Transnational Policing*, ed. J. W. E. Sheptycki. London, New York: Routledge.

Black, J. 2000. Murder suspect possibly dead: Father's three-year quest ends with fugitive's arrest. *Laredo Morning Times*, May 2, A1, A5.

Bonner, R. J., and G. Smith. 1930. *The Administration of Justice from Homer to Aristotle*. Chicago: University of Chicago Press.

Bravin, J. 2001. New rules allow U.S. to indefinitely detain illegal aliens who are suspected terrorists. *The Wall Street Journal*, November 15.

Briones, J. J. 1996. *International Liaison Unit (San Diego District Attorney's Office)*. Internal document. San Diego: San Diego District Attorney's Office.

Bunis, D. 2002. Foreign-born in U.S. soars 60 percent since '90: 1 in 11 people weren't born here. *The Orange County Register* (CA), June 5. http://www.ocregister.com/nation_world/census00606cci3.shtml

Camarota, S. A. 2002. *Immigrants in the United States—2000: A Snapshot of America's Foreign-Born*. Report by the Center for Immigration Studies. http://www.cis.org/articles/2001/back101release.html

Camarota, S. A., and N. McArdle, N. 2003. Where immigrants live. Center for Immigration Studies, September. http://www.cis.org/articles/2003/back1203.html, accessed August 2, 2004.

Center for Immigration Studies. 2004. Current Numbers. Center for Immigration Studies. August 2. http://www.cis.org/topics/currentnumbers.html. Cowan, J. 2004. Telephone interview. July 27.

Deflem, M. 2002. *Policing World Society: Historical Foundations of International Police Cooperation.* New York: Oxford University Press.

Eaton, T. 1993. Wanted for murder: Many find haven in Mexico. *Orange County (CA) Register,* February 14.

Eggen, D. 2001. Ashcroft plans to reorganize Justice, curtail programs. *The Washington Post,* November 11, A17.

Ehrenberg, V. 1968. *From Solon to Socrates.* London: Methuen.

European Commission. 2004. Towards enhancing access to information by law enforcement agencies. In Statewatch. Communication from the Commission to the Council and the European Parliament, COM 429/4. July 22. http://www.statewatch.org/news/2004/jul/08-com-lea-access.htm

European Union. 1995. *The Europol Convention.* 020801, July 26. http://www.sci.fi/~haki/europole.html

Fainaru, S. 2002. N.J. Appeals Court upholds secret detentions: Judges rule U.S. may withhold names of people jailed in Sept. 11 investigation. *The Washington Post,* Jun. 13, A18.

Fijnaut, C. 1993. Police co-operation within Western Europe. In *Crime In Europe,* ed. F. Heidenshon and M. Farrell, 108-20. London: Routledge.

Foucault, M. 1991. Governmentality. In *The Foucault Effect: Studies in Governmentality,* ed. G. Burchell, C. Gordon, and P. Miller, 87-104. Chicago: University of Chicago.

G7. P8. 1996. Senior Experts on Transnational Organized Crime ('Lyons Group'). Senior Experts Group Recommendations. Presented at the Meeting of Senior Experts' Group on Transnational Organized Crime, Lyons, France. http://www.library.utoronto.ca/g7/meetings.html

Gates, D. F., and K. E. Ross. 1990. Foreign prosecution liaison unit helps apprehend suspects across the border. *The Police Chief,* April, 153-54.

Golden, T. 1992. Mexicans mollified over drug ruling. *The New York Times,* June 18, A03.

Haskell, K. 2004. Turning in terrorists: Take the money and run, *The New York Times,* Mar. 28, 4.5.

Hegstrom, E. 2000. Line of elusion: Father's bid to ensnare accused killer spotlights old story of border escapes. *The Houston Chronicle,* July 22, A1.

Higgins, M. 2002. Ottawa issues rare U.S. travel advisory: Sees risk to citizens born in security threat nations. *The National Post.* October 7. http://nationalpost.com/search/site/story.asp?id=A71526DC-80B7-4C75-8498-B23F70B23FEE, accessed October 30, 2002.

Holmes, S. A. 1993. U.S. gives Mexico abduction pledge. *The New York Times,* June 22, A11.

Hsu, S. S. 2003. Crossing lines to fight terrorism: D.C., four states to share law enforcement, other records. *The Washington Post*, August 6, Metro: B02.

Izes, B. 1997. Drawing lines in the sand: When state-sanctioned abductions of war criminals should be permitted. *Columbia Journal of Law and Social Problems* 31 (Fall), 1.

Jeffery, C. R. 1969. The development of crime in early English society. In *Crime and the Legal Process*, ed. W. J. Chambliss, 12-32. New York: McGraw-Hill.

Kocherga, A. 2004. Crossing the border no longer means a criminal is home free. KHOU TV 11 News, October 8. http://www.khou.com/news/mexico/ stories/khou031008_ds_MexicoFugitives.204441e.html, accessed July 27, 2004.

Krauss, C. 2003. Qaeda pawn, U.S. calls him. Victim, he calls himself. *The New York Times*, November 15, late edition (East Coast), A4.

Labarini, R. 2001. Mexico's Supreme Court allows the extradition of Mexican nationals. *International Enforcement Law Reporter* 17, 3.

Lakshmi, R. 2004. In India, torture by police is frequent and often deadly. *The Washington Post*, August 5, A11.

Langdon, S., and A. H. Gardner. 1920. Treaty between Hatusili and Ramses II. *Journal of Egyptian Archeology* 6, 181.

Lathem, N. 2001. War-crime fiends flock to U.S. *The New York Post*, May 14.

Lewis, N. A. 1992. U.S. tries to quiet storm abroad over high court's right-to-kidnap ruling. *New York Times*, June 17, late edition (East Coast), A8.

Lezon, D. 2001. Mexican high court ruling may benefit U.S. fugitives. *The Houston Chronicle*, October 16, A1.

Little, C. B., and C. P. Sheffield. 1983. Frontiers and criminal justice: English private prosecution societies and American vigilantism in the eighteenth and nineteenth centuries. *American Sociological Review*, December.

McDonald, W. F. 1976. Criminal justice and the victim: An introduction. In *Criminal Justice and the Victim*, ed. W. F. McDonald, 17-55. Beverly Hills, CA: Sage.

———. 1999. *The Changing Boundaries of Law Enforcement: State and Local Law Enforcement, Illegal Immigration and Transnational Crime Control: Final Report*, Unpublished report available from author. Washington, DC: National Institute of Justice.

———. 2004. American and European Paths to International Law Enforcement Cooperation: McDonalidization, Implosion and Terrorism. *International Journal of Comparative Criminology* 4(1), 127-171.

Malone, J. 2002. Tide of immigration surges in America. *The Atlanta Journal-Constitution*, June 5. http://www.accessatlanta.com/ajc/epaper/editions/ wednesday/news_c3dfca63f66cc08f00e1.html

March, T. 2003. Widow of Los Angeles County Deputy Sheriff, David March. Testimony. In *Committee on Government Reform. Subcommittee on Criminal Justice, Drug Policy and Human Relations.* Hearing: Strengthening the Long Arm of the Law: How Are Fugitives Avoiding Extradition, and How Can We Bring Them to Justice. Washington, DC: U.S. House of Representatives.

Marenin, O., ed. 1996. *Policing Change, Changing Police: International Perspectives.* New York: Garland Press.

Martin, R. A. 1990-1991. Problems in international law enforcement. *Fordham International Law Journal* 14, 519.

Meek, J. 2005. They beat me from all sides. *The Guardian.* January 14, 2005. http://www.guardian.co.uk/print/0%2C3858%2C5103186-103680%2C00 .html, accessed January 31.

Moore, J. B. 1891, 1996. *A Treatise on Extradition and Interstate Rendition Vol. I.* Littleton, CO: F. B. Rothman & Co.

Moore, M. 1996. Lynch law the rule in Mexican towns. *The Washington Post*, September 7, A1, A8.

Muller-Rappard, E., and M. C. Bassiouni. 1993. *European Inter-State Cooperation in Criminal Matters: The Council of Europe's Legal Instruments*, Rev. 2nd ed. Dordrecht, Boston, Norwell, MA: M. Nijhoff; in U.S., Kluwer Academic Publishers.

Murphy, C. 2004. Va. couple files lawsuit to free their son held in Saudi Arabia. *The Washington Post*, July 29, A1.

Nadelmann, E. A. 1992. *Criminalization and Crime Control in International Society.* Unpublished manuscript cited with permission.

——. 1993. *Cops Across Borders: The Internationalization of U.S. Criminal Law Enforcement.* University Park: The Pennsylvania State University Press.

Obsidian Wings. 2004. *Legalizing Torture.* September 29. http://obsidianwings. blogs.com/obsidian_wings/2004/09/legalizing_tort.html, accessed January 31, 2005.

O'Harrow, Jr., R. 2003. U.S. backs Florida's new counterterrorism database: 'Matrix' offers law agencies faster access to Americans' personal records. *The Washington Post*, August 6, A01.

Pasquino, P. 1991. Theatrum Politicum: The genealogy of capital—police and the state of prosperity. In *The Foucault Effect: Studies in Governmentality*, ed. G. Burchell, C. Gordon, and P. Miller, 105-18. Chicago: University of Chicago.

Passel, J. S., and W. Zimmerman. 2001. Are immigrants leaving California: Settlement patterns of immigrants in the late 1990s. Urban Institute. April 01. http:// www.urban.org/urlprint.cfm?ID=7307, accessed August 2, 2004.

Porter, D. J. 2003. District Attorney. Gwinnett Judicial Circuit. Lawrenceville, GA. Testimony. In *Committee on Government Reform. Subcommittee on Criminal Justice, Drug Policy and Human Relations.* Hearing: Strengthening the Long Arm of the Law: How Are Fugitives Avoiding Extradition, and How Can We Bring Them to Justice. Washington, DC: U.S. House of Representatives.

Pringle, P. 1958. *The Thief-takers*. London: Museum Press.

Rafuse, R. W. 1939. *The Extradition of Nationals*. Urbana: University of Illinois Press.

Rendon, R. 2003. Mexico sends back fugitive sought in slaying of ex-wife: Government agrees to rare extradition in 1999 case. *The Houston Chronicle*, November 6, A25.

Reno, J. 2001. Global partners: International co-operation against crime. U.S. Attorney General presented at the Council on Foreign Relations, General Meeting, Washington, DC.

Rice, J. 2003. Expulsions on the rise in Mexico: 90 percent of fugitives returned to U.S. *The Arizona Republic*, June 26, http://www.azcentral.com/arizonarepublc/news/articles/0626fugitives26.html. Accessed June 28, 2003.

Schmid, A. P. 1996. Migration and crime: A framework for discussion. In *Migration and Crime*, ed. A. P. Schmid. Milan: International Scientific and Professional Advisory Council of the United Nations Crime Prevention and Criminal Justice Program.

Schmitt, E. 2001. Census shows big gain for Mexican-Americans. *The New York Times*, May 10.

Schutze, J. 1989. *Cauldron of Blood: The Matamoros Cult Killings*. New York: Avon Books.

Schwartz, R. 1975. *Across the Rio to Freedom*. El Paso: Texas Western Press.

Shearer, I. A. 1971. *Extradition in International Law*. Dobbs Ferry, NY: Oceana Publications.

Sheptycki, J. W. E. 1998. The global cops cometh: Reflections on transnationalism, knowledge work and policing subculture. *The British Journal of Sociology* 49, 1, 57-74.

Slevin, P. 2004. U.S. pledges not to torture terror suspects. *The Washington Post*, June 27, A01.

Statewatch. 2001. EU liaison officers to combat illegal immigration in the Balkans. http://www.statewatch.org/semdoc. Accessed July 2, 2002.

Statewatch. 2002. Spain and Italy pioneer a common area of security and justice. Semdoc Summary. October 14. http://www.statewatch.org/semdoc, accessed by subscription October 18, 2002.

Stevenson, M. 2000. Run for the border now a bad idea for U.S. fugitives. *The News* (Mexico City), June 15.

Sullivan, K. 2004. Mexico prepares to charge ex-president. *The Washington Post*, July 24, A1, A16.

Sullivan, K., and M. Jordan. 2001. Fugitive's haven no longer: Efforts by Mexico bring Americans to justice. *The Washington Post*, May 22, A1.

Supernor, C. M. 2001. International bounty hunters for war criminals: Privatizing the enforcement of justice. *The Air Force Law Review* 50, 215.

The Italian American Working Group against the Mafia. 1998. Presentation at Executive Leadership Seminar: Georgetown University, presented at the Strategic Approaches to Transnational Crime and Civil Society, Washington, DC.

The New York Times. 1992. To Mexico, high court sounds like a bully. June 21, 4, 3.

The Washington Post. 1998. Corruption—A hard act to follow: Mexico City's new government finds the old one stripped its offices bare. February 25, A19.

Thomas-Lester, A. 1998. Salvadoran fugitives frustrate D.C. Police suspects fleeing U.S., officials say. *The Washington Post,* July 18, A1, A12.

Tierney, J. 2002. Even for $25 million, still no Osama Bin Laden. *The New York Times,* December 1, 4.

United Nations General Assembly. 1990. *Model Treaty on Mutual Legal Assistance in Criminal Matters Adopted by the General Assembly as resolution 45/117 on the recommendation of the Eighth Congress on the Prevention of Crime and the Treatment of Offenders on 14 December 1990.*

U.S. Census Bureau. 2001. *Profile of the Foreign-Born Population in the United States: 2000.* Washington, DC: U.S. Government Printing Office. Current Population Report: Special Studies, P23-206. U.S. Census Bureau. December 2001. http://www.census.gov/prod/2002pubs/p23-206.pdf, accessed August 10, 2004.

U.S. Immigration and Naturalization Service, Office of Policy and Planning. 2003. Estimates of the unauthorized immigrant population residing in the United States: 1990-2000. Office of Policy and Planning, U.S. Immigration and Naturalization Service. U.S. Citizenship and Immigration Service. http://uscis.gov/graphics/shared/aboutus/statistics/Ill_Report_1211.pdf, accessed August 2, 2004.

van Natta, Jr., D., and S. Mekhennet. 2005. German's claim of kidnapping brings investigation of U.S. link. *The New York Times,* January 9, late edition (East Coast), A1.

Vise, D. A. 2000. New global role puts FBI in unsavory company. *The Washington Post,* October 29, A1.

Warren, B. 2003. DA to testify in Washington Gwinnett's. *The Atlanta Journal–Constitution* (GA), October 1, C3.

Weilminster, D. 2003. Bounty hunter may face prison time. *Rocky Mountain News* (Denver), June 24, 14A.

Weiner, T. 2003. Bounty hunting for fame. *The New York Times,* June 22, 9.

Whitlock, C. 2004. A secret deportation of terror suspects: 2 men reportedly tortured in Egypt. *The Washington Post,* July 24, A1.

Wilkitzki, P. 1988. Director, Office of International Criminal Law Enforcement Matters, Federal Ministry of Justice, Bonn, Germany. Unpublished remarks. *Conference on International Cooperation in Criminal Matters.* Cambridge, MA: Harvard University Law School. Reported by E. Nadelmann, *Cops Across Borders: The Internationalization of U.S. Criminal Law Enforcement,* 1993, 434.

Zagaris, B., and J. Padierna Peralta. 1997. Mexico-United States extradition and alternatives: From fugitive slaves to drug traffickers—150 Years and Beyond the Rio Grande's Winding Courses. *American University Journal of International Law and Policy* 12, 4, 519-621.

Zavala, V., and J. Marlow. 2002. Life and Times Tonight. *Life and Times Tonight: Transcript Archives.* LC020531. http://www.kcet.org/life_times/transcripts/200205/20020531.htm, May 31, accessed August 7, 2002.

A Comparative Look at the Roles and Functions of the Prosecution and Defense in Western Trial Systems

WILLIAM T. PIZZI

Contents

16.1 The Structure of Common Law and Civil Law Trial Systems

In discussing criminal trial traditions, legal scholars often distinguish trials that take place in countries within the common law tradition and those that take place in countries that have a legal system based on the civil law tradition. Common law countries include the major English-speaking countries such as the United States, Canada, England, and Australia. Continental countries such as France, Germany, the Netherlands, and Denmark share the civil law tradition.

Common law countries structure their trial systems on an adversarial basis in which the prosecutor must present sufficient evidence to convict the defendant of the crime with which he or she has been charged, and if the prosecutor has done so, the defense may present evidence to challenge the prosecutor's evidence (Merryman 1985). The trial is structured as a two-sided battle (hence the term *adversarial*) between the prosecution and the defense, in which the trial judge serves as a neutral referee who ensures that both sides comply with the rules. In all serious criminal cases in common law countries, a jury of ordinary citizens, usually twelve in number, will listen to the evidence and then decide at the end of the trial whether the prosecution has proven the defendant guilty beyond a reasonable doubt. On those charges that the jury decides were proven beyond a reasonable doubt, the jury will announce a verdict of "guilty," and on those charges for which the prosecution has not met that standard, the jury will return a verdict of "not guilty." There is no formal opinion issued by the jury that explains how and why the jury reached its decisions.

By contrast with the adversarial structure of common law trials, judges in inquisitorial systems play a more active role in the production of evidence and in questioning witnesses. The reason is that the trial is not conceptualized as a battle between two adversaries, but it is more an official inquiry (hence the term *inquisitorial*) aimed at determining the truth about the charges, and in this inquiry the judges have a responsibility for determining the truth that cannot be deferred to the parties. Another way of expressing the responsibility of the judges in inquisitorial systems is that they are not bound by the submissions of the parties; if the charges are inaccurate or the evidence is incomplete, the judges have an obligation to correct such problems.

Because judges in civil law countries will decide the defendant's guilt and also the sentence that will be imposed if the defendant is found guilty, most trials in civil law countries take place before more than one judge. Usually, there is a panel of at least three judges hearing any serious criminal cases. Sometimes the panel is a mixed panel that combines a professional judge or professional judges with so-called "lay judges." Lay judges are ordinary citizens who are appointed for a term of years to participate occasionally in criminal trials along with professional judges. They will sit on the main bench in the courtroom with the professional judges and will deliberate with their professional colleagues at the end of the trial. Unlike jury verdicts in common law systems, when the panel of judges reaches a decision, the presiding judge will carefully explain how the panel reached its decision and, if the defendant is convicted, why the panel decided to impose the particular sentence. Shortly after the trial has been completed, there will usually be a carefully written judgment issued that explains in detail the nature of the charges and the evidence that was presented, how legal issues were resolved at the trial, and why the judges reached their decisions (Langbein 1977).

Sometimes in inquisitorial trial systems, the presiding judge on the panel, who is usually very experienced, will take the main responsibility for deciding the witnesses who will testify and for questioning the witnesses at trial. In such a system, the state's attorney or the defense attorney can always suggest additional witnesses and will certainly have a chance to question each witness, but the main responsibility belongs to the presiding judge. The reason that the presiding judge can carry out this responsibility is that the presiding judge has access before trial to the full investigative file containing all police reports, witness statements, ballistics test, and other materials.

There is an important caveat to the above descriptions of adversarial and inquisitorial trial systems, and that is that there is no litmus test for determining which trial features show a system to be adversarial and which make such a system inquisitorial. Today, trial systems increasingly seem to blend features from both trial traditions (van den Wyngaert 1993). For example, although England uses juries for serious criminal cases, the vast majority of criminal cases in that country are heard by a panel of three lay magistrates, who are not that different from lay judges in continental systems. The lay magistrates have been appointed to their position for a term of years and sit several weeks each year, hearing burglary cases, minor drug cases, theft cases, simple assaults, and the like.

The same blending of features occurs in continental countries. In some continental countries, such as Norway, the presiding judge plays a more passive role at trial, and instead, the state's attorney and the defense attorney present the evidence as one might expect in an adversarial system, with the state's attorney presenting one side of the evidence and the defense then calling witnesses.

This tendency to blend features from the two trial traditions means increasingly that trial systems are best viewed not as sharply divided between adversarial and inquisitorial systems, but rather as existing along a spectrum with extremely adversarial trial systems at one end and very inquisitorial trial systems at the other. But there will be many systems between these extremes.

16.2   An Initial Problem—Who Is the "Prosecutor"?

If one were to attend criminal trials in different Western countries, on the surface there would seem to be lawyers for the state and lawyers for the defense doing much the same work. But beneath the surface are major differences in the way they see their position and in their responsibilities. A starting point for understanding these differences is the fact that there is no word for *prosecutor* in some languages, such as Italian or French. The reason is that the "prosecutor" in those legal traditions is a "magistrate" who is a member of the judiciary, just like the professional judges who may be deciding the case.

This is not just a problem that divides common law countries from civil law countries; the same terminological problem exists among common law countries. For example, in the United States, a prosecutor is typically a full-time public employee of a prosecutorial office and, if the case is a serious one, the prosecutor will often be involved in all stages of the case starting with the investigation and continuing through charging and the trial. But it is not a "prosecutor" in this sense who presents the evidence at Crown Court in England (where the most serious crimes are tried). Rather, it is usually a "prosecuting barrister," meaning a lawyer trained in trial advocacy, who is hired in this particular case to present the evidence at trial against the defendant. But that is the extent of his or her involvement in the case—the prosecuting barrister will not have advised the police during the investigation of the crime, will not have filed the charges in the case, and is not employed full-time by the government. Even more surprising from a U.S. perspective, barristers, who have their own private law practices, often "switch sides" in England, meaning that they may represent the prosecution in one trial, but are then hired to represent a defendant in a different criminal case (Tague 1996). In most other countries, this would not be possible as a structural matter. In the United States, this would be ethically improper because it would be seen as compromising the defense lawyer's duty to the client if the defense lawyer knew that he or she would be representing the prosecution in a case the following week. (This is a nice example of the fact that usually the U.S. trial system tends to be more adversarial than other trial systems, even those within the common law tradition.)

16.3   Politics and Prosecutorial Discretion

One difficulty any criminal justice system faces is that of ensuring that prosecutors (or state's attorneys or prosecuting magistrates) as well as judges, police officers, and others who work in the system) do their job properly and professionally. One way in which continental countries do this is by making sure there are internal controls within the system to prevent abuse or misuse of power. Comparatists speak of continental justice systems as being "hierarchical" in their organizational structure (Damaska 1986). Obviously, courts within any legal system are organized hierarchically, with decisions at the trial being reviewed for correctness at a higher level. But continental systems are hierarchically organized in the broader sense that the decisions of those in the system as well as the general performance of those in the system are subject to evaluation and review at a higher level. There is typically a national civil service bureaucracy that evaluates the work individuals are doing and that makes sure that only those who are doing the best work advance to more desirable positions within the system.

In a continental system, the decision of the state's attorney not to file charges is subject to review. If the state's attorney believes that there is evidence of a crime, but the state's attorney does not think that the case merits prosecution for some reason, the state's attorney must usually seek judicial approval not to file charges. There will also usually be departmental procedures through which members of the public, such as a crime victim, can seek review of decisions of the state's attorney or other functionaries in the system.

These internal procedures are needed because the state's attorneys, like other members of the judiciary, are career civil servants who are insulated from direct political pressure, and thus there needs to be some way to make sure that decisions are made properly, according to the law.

In the United States, the position of prosecutor is quite different, in part because the political heritage is very different (Pizzi 1993). The typical prosecutor in the United States is usually referred to as an "assistant district attorney" because the assistant works in the office under the direction of the district attorney. The district attorney is usually a lawyer with considerable practical experience, perhaps some as a prosecutor or defense attorney, who runs for the position of district attorney in an election. Districts will vary in size, but often a district will consist of a county, or in very rural parts of a state, a district might encompass a few counties. A very large city will often have its own district attorney or even several district attorneys, depending on the way political power is divided in that state.

The election of district attorneys on a local basis rather than a statewide basis is reflective of the strong preference for local control over political power in the U.S. political tradition. Obviously, district attorneys need to cooperate on common issues and work together on some investigations and prosecutions. But at the same time, district attorneys are free to make determinations of prosecutorial policy based on what they believe to be the priorities of their district. Thus, it would not be unusual within a single state for a district attorney elected in a rural district to take a stricter view on the enforcement of drug laws, to give one example, than a district attorney in a heavily urban area. This difference in the way the same criminal statute is enforced in a state would seem unfair and improper in many continental countries, but it is part of the political tradition in the United States to tolerate local differences.

In individual cases, broad prosecutorial discretion in charging is an accepted feature of the U.S. criminal justice system. Obviously, there are ethical restraints of prosecutors, and no prosecutor can ethically charge someone with a crime if the prosecutor does not believe that the person committed the crime or if there is not sufficient evidence to support the charges. But as long as the prosecutor has sufficient evidence, it is accepted that a prosecutor has discretion over the crime to be charged or the number of crimes to be charged. If a prosecutor chooses not to charge someone with a crime even though there is sufficient evidence, perhaps because the prosecutor does not think the case worth the effort and the costs to prosecute it, there is no formal mechanism for compelling the prosecutor to file the charges. This is part of the adversarial tradition—it is up to the prosecutor within ethical limits to decide whether to bring charges and what charges to bring. In the case of a child who is kidnapped and sexually abused, a prosecutor may decide only to charge the kidnapping because the prosecutor does not wish to put the young victim through the psychological strain that testifying about the sexual assault would entail at trial.

Notice that the political position of the prosecutor is very different from that of the state's attorney, who is a judicial figure and who has responsibilities to the presiding judge to see that the charges brought are correct, complete, and proper. There is not the same relationship between prosecutor and judge in the United States. As mentioned above, the judge in the adversarial tradition is more analogous to a neutral referee at a sporting contest. Just as it would be out of place for the referee in a sporting event to get involved in determining one team's offensive strategy and then go back to a neutral position during the contest, it would be awkward for a trial judge to get involved in a prosecutor's charging decisions, unless it were a very unusual situation, such as the claim that charges violated the constitutional rights of the defendant in some way. This might occur if a defendant alleged that the charges were motivated by racial bias. But short of such an extreme situation, prosecutors have broad prosecutorial discretion.

16.4 The Work of Defense Attorneys—Factual Investigations

Criminal law can be very complicated, and not surprisingly, defendants charged with a crime usually need the assistance of counsel to help them understand the charges and to help them through the various stages in the process. All Western countries provide defense counsel for indigent defendants unless the crime involved is very minor. But the amount of work that defense attorneys must do in preparation for trial varies tremendously between adversarial trial systems and inquisitorial trial systems. It is common in adversarial trial systems in serious criminal cases for the defense lawyer to do some investigative work about the charges prior to trial. This may involve hiring a defense investigator to try to locate certain witnesses or to interview people known to have information about the crime. The defense may also decide to hire an expert, such as a ballistics expert or a psychiatric expert, depending on the nature of the case, to help with the defense.

This is different from continental trial systems, where defense attorneys do not usually get involved in factual investigations about the case. It is the job of the police to do a complete and thorough investigation, not the defense attorney. This means that if a defense attorney feels there is a deficiency in the investigation, the proper avenue would be to ask the police or the state's attorney to supplement the investigation and correct the deficiency. Just as the state's attorney is supposed to be a judicial figure who brings out at trial not just strengths of the case against the defendant, but also possible weaknesses or even defenses, the police are supposed to be thorough and neutral in their investigation.

The adversarial tradition is generally more skeptical of claims of "neutrality"—one rarely sees "neutral" experts in court; rather, there will be experts for the prosecution and experts for the defense. The police are viewed similarly. Although the police have obligations of fairness and professionalism in the way they investigate crimes, the police are viewed as aligned on the side of the prosecution. Thus, to provide competent representation for a defendant, the defense attorney will often need to undertake some independent investigation into the facts of the case to assess the strength of the evidence against the defendant and to prepare for trial.

A related reason for the need for some independent investigation by the defense is that evidence gathered by the police is not as readily available to defense attorneys in adversarial trial systems as it is in continental countries. In inquisitorial systems, there usually is an official file or "dossier" that contains all of the information that the police and other state agencies have developed during the investigation. Statements from witnesses, descriptions of the physical evidence seized, crime scene photographs, results of tests, reports of experts, and so on will be available to the state's attorney, the defense attorney, and the judge prior to trial. In a sense, they are all working from the same bank of information.

But there is no equivalent to the dossier in common law trial systems. The prosecutor will have the information gathered by the police, but the defense does not generally have ready access to this information (nor will the trial judge have access to this information). This is not to say that defense attorneys are expected to prepare for trial with no information about the case the prosecution will present at trial. But there are rules governing the sharing of information by the prosecutor with the defense attorney (and also rules requiring the defense attorney to share certain information with the prosecutor in advance of trial). In short, even the sharing of basic information about the case can get complicated in adversarial trial systems.

16.5 The Work of Defense Attorneys—Legal Preparations for Trial

Another major difference between adversarial trial systems and inquisitorial trial systems has to do with the amount of legal preparation that must be undertaken before trial. Part of the problem stems from the very different approach that the two traditions take to the admissibility of evidence. In adversarial systems, the rules of evidence are complicated and they tend to be enforced strictly. One way to understand how different the approaches to evidence are in the two systems is to consider the way the systems view narrative evidence. At continental trials, after a few preliminary questions to identify the witness who has been called to give evidence, it is common for the presiding judge to encourage the witness to speak freely about events or issues relating to the crime. Sometimes, the judge will tell the witness to try to be as complete as possible and not to leave anything out of his or her account. If the witness is a crime victim, it is not unusual to hear the victim speak for twenty or thirty minutes about the events leading up the crime, the crime, and what happened after the crime (Pizzi 1996).

At trials in adversarial systems, this sort of narrative testimony by an important witness would not be allowed. The testimony of the witness must be filtered through rules of evidence, and to do that, the information from the witness must be elicited piece by piece by the party calling the witness so that objections by the opposing party to the proposed testimony can be raised. For example, a crime victim describing the crime from her point of view may very well talk about what she was thinking at the time of the crime and what she later told others about the crime. This sort of information is problematic in an adversarial trial system and might not be admissible under the rules of evidence. With respect to the victim's thoughts or fears at the time of the crime, a defense lawyer might object that such testimony is irrelevant and possibly prejudicial. As for statements of the victim to others about the crime, there would be hearsay objections to this retelling of what she had told others.

How these evidentiary issues would be resolved in a particular case would depend on exactly what the victim says, on the particular rules of evidence in the jurisdiction, and on court interpretations of those rules. A good defense lawyer in an adversarial trial system needs to think about these issues before trial, especially if the evidentiary issue is important.

Another sort of evidentiary issue that a defense lawyer in an adversarial trial system will need to anticipate concerns a defendant's prior criminal convictions. If a defendant is on trial for robbery with a knife and the defendant had a prior conviction a few years earlier for aggravated assault with a knife, it would be a concern of the defense lawyer whether the jury will be told about the prior assault. Even though the defendant was convicted of the prior assault, the admissibility of this conviction is complicated issue in common law trial systems, and a defense lawyer (as well as the prosecutor) will want to have researched before trial whether this conviction can be mentioned at trial and whether, if the judge allows the conviction to be mentioned to the jury, the judge will usually give an instruction about the way such a conviction can and cannot be used by the jury.

Some of these evidentiary issues are a reflection of the fact that most important trials in adversarial trial systems usually take place in front of a jury of laypersons who are assembled for this particular trial and may never have been in a courtroom previously. There is naturally a worry that jurors may overvalue or misunderstand some types of evidence.

But the different approaches to evidence in the two trial traditions run deeper than simply worries about the jury. There seems to be a different attitude in the two traditions about the efficacy of elaborate sets of rules, with adversarial systems putting more faith in systems of rules whereas inquisitorial systems seem more confident that trial judges will be able to sort the evidentiary wheat from the chaff (Pizzi 1999). More proof of this confidence that trial judges will use items of evidence for the right purpose and not for improper purposes is the fact that continental trials often decide both guilt and sentence in the same proceeding. There would be serious doubts were it proposed that a jury decide both issues at the same hearing.

Whatever explains the differences in evidentiary rules, the amount of pretrial preparation that a good defense lawyer in an adversarial system will need to devote to trial preparation will be significantly more than a defense lawyer would spend to prepare for a similar trial in a continental trial system. This is partly a reflection of the differences in rules, but also a reflection of the fact that in many continental systems, the presiding judge will do the sort of careful preparation normally done by attorneys for the parties in adversarial systems.

When this difference in the hours that a defense attorney needs to spend preparing for trial is translated into the funds that will be needed to provide attorneys to indigent defendants, an adversarial system cannot afford to provide trials to the vast majority of defendants, and as will be discussed below, usually there are "plea bargaining" mechanisms to persuade defendants to admit guilt and avoid trial.

16.6   Ethical Issues for Defense Lawyers and Prosecutors

Ethical issues for prosecutors and defense lawyers are somewhat different in adversarial and inquisitorial systems because of the different structures of the two systems. For example, in the United States, where the prosecutor is an elected public official, the political pressure on a prosecutor to file charges against a suspect in a high-publicity murder case may be very strong, even though the evidence is not strong. There will be pressure to file charges in such cases in continental countries, too, but the prosecutorial equivalent—the state's attorney or the prosecuting magistrate—is better insulated from that pressure due to the civil service nature of the position.

To help prosecutors resist such pressures in the United States, there is an important body of ethical standards, developed by the American Bar Association, that tell prosecutors what they may or may not do (American Bar Association 1992). For example, with respect to filing charges, those standards state that a prosecutor should give no weight to the political advantages or disadvantages that might ensue from a decision to file charges or not to file charges. As a licensed attorney, a prosecutor (as well as a defense lawyer) can be disciplined for violating the jurisdiction's ethics standards.

Another important ethical issue (and a constitutional issue) that occurs in adversarial systems stems from the fact that prosecutors and defense lawyers do not usually work from a single dossier containing all the investigative material relating to the case. Although there are rules governing the exchange of information between the prosecutor and the defense attorney, there is the worry that a defense attorney may not get access to information that would help the defense attorney show weaknesses in the prosecution's evidence at trial.

To help protect against wrongful convictions, there is a constitutional obligation on prosecutors as well as an ethical obligation that requires prosecutors to give to the defense all information that tends in any degree to negate the defendant's guilt or otherwise mitigates the defendant's culpability. This is one way in which the adversarial model is tempered—even if the defense lawyer has not asked for such information, the prosecution must make sure this exculpatory evidence has been given to the defense in a timely fashion so it can be used at trial if the defense wishes.

There is no direct analog of this obligation in continental trial systems because investigative material is freely shared by the state's attorney and the defense attorney. But the obligation on the state's attorney to make sure that justice is done is stronger in continental systems and would even extend to making the judges aware of any possible defense the defendant might have, whether or not raised by the defense attorney. This would not be required of a prosecutor unless there was the possibility of serious injustice.

As for defense lawyers, there are pronounced differences in the sorts of ethics issues that arise between adversarial systems and inquisitorial systems due to way the defendant is treated in the trial structures of the two systems. In common law systems, the defendant does not directly participate at the trial. The defendant may give advice to his or her lawyer about questions that the lawyer might ask of witnesses, but even this can be difficult in some systems. For example, in England, the defendant is required to sit in the back or side of the courtroom in a small enclosed area called "the dock," which is usually some distance from his or her barrister. This makes it difficult for the defendant to give advice to the barrister.

The issue that raises the most difficult ethical issues for defense lawyers in adversarial trial systems concerns the proper response where the defendant wishes to testify, but the lawyer knows that the client will testify falsely (*Nix v. Whiteside* 1986). Among the questions that come up when the defendant insists on testifying are, Should the lawyer try to withdraw from the case (even though it is usually the middle of the trial)? Would it be ethical for the lawyer to assist the client in the giving of false testimony by asking questions to develop the testimony? Would it be ethical for a lawyer, knowing the defendant has committed perjury, to argue the merits of this testimony to the jury at the end of the trial?

The ethical tensions between the defendant and the defense lawyer over tactics are not nearly as strong in continental trial systems because defendants are treated more as participants at the trial rather than spectators. It is often the case, for example, that after the defense lawyer has finished asking questions, the defendant is asked if he or she wishes to ask any additional questions. The trial structure is more relaxed, and testimony is not as sharply divided between direct and cross-examination as it is in adversarial systems. In this more flexible structure, where rules of evidence are also more relaxed, defendants, as well as lay judges or sometimes even experts, may ask questions if it will help assist in understanding the testimony.

Another aspect of the defendant's ability to participate at trial has to do with the way the defendant is invited to speak about the charges against him or her. In adversarial systems, the defendant gives testimony under oath only after the prosecution has finished presenting its evidence. But at continental trials, the defendant is invited to respond to the charges at the start of the trial. After the state's attorney has read the charges against the defendant (which usually provide most of the details of the crime), the defendant is always asked if he or she wishes to speak about the charges. The defendant is not forced to speak about the charges, but most defendants choose to talk about the charges—about what is correct and what is not correct about them. From the common law perspective, this seems strange and even improper—"The defendant testifies at the start of the trial before the evidence against him has been presented?" But this is not "testifying" in the common law sense. There is no concern about perjury, because the defendant is never put under oath. It can best be understood as part of the defendant's right to participate at the trial if he or she wishes to do so.

When it is recalled that continental trials usually concern both guilt and sentencing, it is not surprising that most defendants will want to speak about the charges.

16.7 The Role of Victims at Criminal Trials

There is not a single Western country that has not been affected by the victims' movement and its struggle for better treatment of crime victims within criminal justice systems. This movement has achieved a great deal, especially in the treatment of crime victims in the immediate aftermath of the crime. For example, many urban police departments have established specialized units for sensitive crimes, such as sexual assault and child abuse, where the investigators have specialized training in the handling of victims.

But difficulties arise for adversarial trial systems when the question is asked: Is there not some way to improve the treatment of crime victims at trial, especially in those cases where the integrity and character of the victim are likely to be the major focus of the trial? The obvious example of such cases are those rape cases in which the defendant argues that the victim consented to the intercourse and the victim vehemently insists she was forcible raped. To reach a verdict in such a case, the fact-finders need to make some judgments about the veracity of the victim and the defendant.

The problem is made worse in adversarial trial systems by the fact that most of these cases will be tried in front of a jury, and the only formal result if the defendant is not convicted is a verdict of "not guilty." This is often interpreted by the defense and the press as a verdict indicating that the jury found the victim not credible (in continental systems, where the verdict is explained and justified, a victim can draw consolation from judgment that found the victim entirely credible, even if there was insufficient evidence to convict).

But in a trial system that conceptualizes the contest as two-sided, it is difficult to accommodate victims in the courtroom without the feeling that the balance between the state and the defendant has been altered unfairly against the defendant. So victims who are going to testify at trial in common law systems are usually treated like other witnesses. They are excluded from the courtroom until they are called to testify. As for victims who are not going to testify at the trial, they are treated like other members of the public and they can watch the trial, but they cannot participate.

Unable to accommodate victims at trial, some adversarial trial systems, like that in the United States, allow victims to participate at sentencing hearings. Sentencing in most adversarial trial systems takes place in front of a judge, not a jury, and the evidentiary rules for sentencing are more relaxed than they are at trial. It has thus been thought appropriate to allow victims to testify or give a written report to the judge that describes the crime from the victim's perspective and the impact that the crime has had on the victim's life. (These written reports are usually referred to as "victim impact statements.")

The participation of victims at sentencing is controversial because it is often not clear how the impact of the crime on a victim or the victim's family relates to the punishment the defendant should receive (*Booth v. Maryland* 1987; *Payne v. Tennessee* 1991).[1] For example, if a victim who was killed in a convenience store robbery was a much-beloved parent of young children, should the defendant receive a greater sentence than if the victim was a loner with drug problems and a criminal record? Because it is often felt that this sort of distinction should not bear at all on the sentence that should be imposed, some adversarial trial systems do not permit judges to consider victim impact statements at sentencing.

The conceptual difficulty of allowing victims to participate at trial does not arise to the same extent in inquisitorial trial systems. Because the judges have the responsibility to determine the accuracy of the charges, and often the presiding judge will take the lead in calling witnesses and questioning them, it is easier to accommodate victims at trial. Not all systems allow victims to participate at trial through counsel, but many continental systems do permit such representation. It is not unusual to see victims of serious crimes sitting in the front of the courtroom, much like the defendant, and participating through counsel on a rather equal basis with the defense attorney and the state's attorney. In some countries, victims may even ask for civil damages as part of the judgment at the criminal trial.

---

[1] Some indication of how controversial victim impact testimony has proven is the fact that the U.S. Supreme Court has had trouble deciding the relevance of this information for sentencing purposes. Initially, the court held that it was unconstitutional to allow juries in death penalty cases to hear victim impact testimony. See *Booth v. Maryland* 1987. But a few years after this decision, the court reversed itself and allowed juries to hear victim impact evidence. See *Payne v. Tennessee* 1991.

16.8 The Pressure to Resolve Criminal Cases without Full Trials

Trials are expensive, and government budgets everywhere are under strain, so there is a lot of pressure to try to resolve criminal cases short of full-blown trials. Sometimes this can be achieved by decriminalizing categories of minor crimes, so they can be handled administratively. Another alternative is to minimize the punishment for certain offenses, so simpler trial procedures can be used.

But even these alternatives leave too many serious cases to be tried. The way in which countries with adversarial trial systems resolve the vast majority of criminal cases is through plea bargaining. The term refers to the fact that in exchange for an admission of guilt by the defendant—a guilty plea—the defendant receives a bargain in the form of a sentence that is shorter than he or she would likely have received after trial.

Plea bargaining comes in many different forms. Often the bargain involves a "sentence bargain," meaning that the defendant agrees to plead guilty to the crime in exchange for an agreement that a sentence will not exceed a certain specified sentence. But some countries also permit "charge bargains," in which a prosecutor agrees to reduce the charges filed against the defendant (and lower the sentencing range) if the defendant pleads guilty to the reduced charge. Thus, for example, a prosecutor may agree to reduce an armed robbery charge to simple robbery if the defendant pleads guilty to the latter offense (Alschuler 1983).

Not every country with an adversarial trial system permits all forms of plea bargaining. In England, for example, there is a fixed discount of roughly 30 percent from the sentence the defendant would have received after trial for defendants who choose to plead guilty instead of going to trial. The sorts of extreme sentence bargains one sees in the United States, where defendants receive sentence discounts far in excess of 30 percent or where defendants are given charge bargains that achieve the same result, are not permitted.

Plea bargaining of any type presents philosophical problems because the idea of "bargaining justice" seems to clash with what should be the goal of a strong trial system, namely, to see if the defendant is guilty of the crime and that, if guilty, he or she receives the sentence he or she deserves. Why should a defendant who is guilty of a crime be allowed to "bargain" in order to receive a shorter sentence than someone who has committed the same crime just because the latter defendant chose to exercise the right to trial? The system seems to be punishing those who go to trial and exercise their right to have the evidence against them evaluated and weighed.

There is also the problem that plea bargaining can put tremendous pressure on an innocent defendant to admit guilt, even though he or she has a strong defense. If the discount is steep enough, the pressure to admit guilt can be overwhelming. At the same time, plea bargaining encourages prosecutors to be aggressive in charging defendants with particular crimes so as to increase the leverage on defendants to plead to less serious crimes.

But despite these serious concerns, it is easy to understand why adversarial trial systems have an easier time, from a philosophical perspective, accepting the idea of some forms of plea bargaining. If a trial is conceptualized as a "battle" between adversaries and if the adversaries can reach an agreement short of trial, it is hard for a judge to reject such an agreement. More specifically, if the adversary for the state thinks that the public interest supports the agreement and if the defendant, assuming competent representation, wants to enter into such an agreement, in a trial system driven by the parties, under what circumstances should the judge override the wishes of the parties?

On the continent, there is also pressure on trial systems caused by having too many criminal cases to be able to afford a complete trial for each case. But plea bargaining is much more difficult to accept in an inquisitorial system. If the state's attorney and the defense attorney wish to resolve the criminal case in some compromise, this does not relieve the trial judges of their responsibility to determine the truth of the allegations and to sentence the defendant to a fair sentence if he or she is found guilty. For this reason, continental countries do not have plea bargaining as such in which a defendant's formal admission of guilt avoids a trial.

But some countries have a form of negotiated justice that bears some resemblance to plea bargaining. In Germany, for example, there sometimes occurs discussion in advance of trial between the defense attorney and the presiding judge about the length of the sentence the defendant is likely to receive if convicted (Hermann 1992), the understanding being that if the judge indicates a likely sentence that would be consistent with the expectations of the defense, the trial can be shortened considerably because the defendant would admit to the crime and the defense would not contest the evidence necessary to confirm that confession. In short, the defense would allow a much-shortened trial to establish the defendant's guilt.

This sort of negotiated justice clashes with the basic assumptions of continental legal systems, but it is a growing reality, and efforts to try to limit the practice so that it would not be allowed for serious crimes have not been effective in Germany.

16.9 The Blending of Trial Features from Both the Adversarial and Inquisitorial Traditions at International Criminal Tribunals

From a comparative perspective, one of the most interesting and important experiments in the blending of trial features has been the experience of the

International Criminal Tribunal for the former Yugoslavia (ICTY) and the International Criminal Tribunal for Rwanda (ICTR). These tribunals were set up to deal with the most heinous crimes any criminal justice system can face—genocide, war crimes, and crimes against humanity. The trials are not only very important due to the enormity of the crimes, but they are very complicated, often involving hundreds of witnesses and thousands of exhibits. For example, the trial of Dario Kordic—a trial that was not unusual among the cases that have been tried at the ICTY—involved 241 witnesses and 4,665 exhibits, and it lasted twenty months.

On top of the complexity of these trials, the tribunals have had to face enormous logistical problems that no national system would face because the tribunals sit in locations at considerable distances from the places where the crimes occurred. This has slowed the investigation of crimes and added to the difficulties the tribunals have locating witnesses to these tragic events (Amoury Combs 2002).

The judges appointed to the tribunals come from countries with different trial traditions, so they have had to reach compromises and work under procedures that are different from what any of them had been accustomed to in courtrooms in their home countries.

One clear compromise between the two trial traditions described above concerns the right of the defense to access the materials in the prosecution's files to prepare for trial. The tribunals do not give defendants an automatic right of access to the prosecutor's dossier, as would be the case in continental trial systems. Instead, the tribunals have worked out a rather complete list of the items that the prosecutor must make available to the defense to prepare for trial, and this list is more generous than would be required in most adversarial trial systems. The result is a compromise that places the rules somewhere in between the two trial traditions.

With respect to the way that evidence is presented and developed at trial, the tribunals have also compromised. The tribunals use an adversarial structure for the presentation of evidence, with the prosecution first presenting its case and then the defense presenting its case to the court. Witnesses are questioned along the adversarial model, with the party calling the witness allowed to question first, and then the other party is permitted to cross-examine the witness.

But when it comes to the admission of evidence, the tribunals take an approach to evidence that is decidedly inquisitorial. The evidence rules are far more permissive than one would find at trials in common law countries. The judges, like judges in inquisitorial trial systems, are free to consider any relevant evidence if they think it has probative value. This is very important because it means that hearsay evidence can often be considered without the necessity of calling the witness to testify.

It would be nice to say that the procedures at the ICTY and ICTR have worked well, but the experience of this blended trial system has been that trials have been more lengthy (and expensive) than anticipated. Some of this is just the result of the terrible logistical problems the tribunals face. For example, the tribunals have no power to compel witnesses to come to the tribunals and sometimes have had to rely on national legal systems to obtain an important witness, and this has slowed trials considerably.

But as the years have gone by, there has been increasing pressure on the tribunals to expedite the procedures as much as possible. (This is particularly a problem with the Rwandan tribunal because there are so many potential defendants in jail awaiting trial.)

In an attempt to expedite procedures, the tribunals have shifted their procedures to make them more inquisitorial. Judges now are taking a much more active role in the pretrial phase. They supervise the attorneys more closely, and they study for themselves the evidence the parties want to present to see if there are ways to avoid the need for some of the evidence. Sometimes, the judges can avoid the need for certain witnesses by taking judicial notice of the point those witnesses would have been called to establish. In other situations, the judges may decide to rely on the statements the witness gave to investigators rather than requiring the live testimony of the witnesses. In short, judges are exerting more control over the trials, and the trial procedures have become more inquisitorial as time goes on.

But that is not the whole story, because the tribunals have started to employ, on occasion, a decidedly adversarial technique for achieving greater efficiency, namely, plea bargaining in which defendants who admit their guilt and agree to cooperate with the investigators and provide evidence for use in other trials receive some sentencing consideration in return. This is a difficult issue for the tribunals because the crimes being prosecuted are so serious that any sort of a bargain seems unthinkable. But the reality is that these tribunals are having trouble completing their work, and so practical necessity has driven them to accept negotiated bargains that substantially shorten the proceedings and strengthen other prosecutions.

What has happened procedurally at the ICTY and the ICTR will have a strong influence on what happens in other international forums, such as the International Criminal Court as well as the tribunals starting to work on crimes committed in Sierra Leone and East Timor. The ICTY and the ICTR show dramatically just how difficult it is to prosecute even the worst crimes when the trials must take place outside the country in which the crimes took place. These tribunals also show the need to be flexible and pragmatic about procedure. It may well prove to be the case that blended systems on the model of these international tribunals can work more efficiently and effectively than a system that is more purely adversarial or inquisitorial.

16.10   Conclusions

This chapter has provided an overview of some of major differences between trial systems that are adversarial, putting much of the responsibility for the production of evidence in the hands of the parties, and those that are more inquisitorial in structure, where the presiding judge controls the production of evidence at trial. These structural differences often reflect different political values. The heavy use of juries of laypeople in adversarial systems reflects a deep distrust of governmental power and, at the same time, a willingness to tolerate the occasional problems that occur when fact-finding is left to citizens who have usually done nothing similar previously.

On the other hand, inquisitorial systems are less concerned about the possible misuse of governmental power and place a higher value on the accurate application of the law to the facts of the case. To provide protection against aberrant decisions by a trial judge, inquisitorial systems build into their systems protections that restrain the power of the individual trial judge through devices such as the use of panels of judges (and sometimes laypeople), the requirement of reasoned verdicts that explain how the evidence was evaluated and how the judge reached their decisions, and generous appellate review, often even of important factual issues.

But although it continues to make sense to divide Western trial systems into those that are more adversarial in nature as distinguished from those that are more inquisitorial in nature, this chapter has discussed the way that trial systems today often blend features of the two trial traditions. Sometimes, as with international criminal courts, the blending occurs because the judges and lawyers who come to work at such courts come from the two trial traditions, and some blending is needed to accommodate their skills and backgrounds.

But, in addition to the experience at international tribunals, individual countries are starting to adopt features from other trial traditions in an effort to improve their domestic trial system. Sometimes, the particular feature is legislatively adopted after a period of study and debate. Italy, for example, passed a new code of criminal procedure and also amended its constitution to try to make its trial system more adversarial (Pizzi and Montagna 2004).

Sometimes, the change is not formally adopted but simply evolves from practical reasons. An example of this is the emergence of the type of negotiated settlement on the continent. Though often formally forbidden under the law, the practice has emerged as a way of expediting the handling of cases (Damaska 2004).

Although the differences in the priorities and the values in the two trial traditions are significant, it is safe to predict that there will continue to be more examples of cross-fertilizations between the two trial traditions in the future.

References

Alschuler, A. 1983. Implementing the criminal defendant's right to trial: Alternatives to the plea bargaining system. *U. Chi. L. Rev.* 50, 931.

American Bar Association. 1992. *Standards Relating to the Administration of Criminal Justice.* Washington, DC: American Bar Association, chapters 3, 4.

Amoury Combs, N. 2002. Copping a plea to genocide: The plea bargaining of international crimes. *U. Pa. L. Rev.* 151, 1.

Booth v. Maryland. 1987. 482, U.S., 496.

Damaska, M. R. 1986. *The Faces of Justice and State Authority.* New Haven, CT: Yale University Press, 18-23.

Damaska, M. 2004. Negotiated justice in international criminal courts. *J. Int. Crim. J.* 2, 1018, 1023-30.

Hermann, J. 1992. Bargaining justice—a bargain for German criminal justice? *U. Pitt. L. Rev.* 53, 755.

Langbein, J. H. 1977. *Comparative Criminal Procedure: Germany.* West Publishing Company American Casebook Series, 61-86.

Merryman, J. H. 1985. *The Civil Law Tradition*, 2nd ed. Stanford, CA: Stanford University Press, 124-32.

Nix v. Whiteside. 1986. 475 U.S., 157.

Payne v. Tennessee. 1991. 501 U.S., 808.

Pizzi, W. T. 1993. Understanding prosecutorial discretion in the United States: The limits of comparative criminal procedure as an instrument of reform. *Ohio S.L.J.*, 54, 1324.

Pizzi, W. T. 1996. Crime victims in German courtrooms: A comparative perspective on American problems. *Stan. J. Int. L.* 32, 37.

Pizzi, W. T. 1999. *Trials Without Truth: Why Our System of Criminal Trials Has Become an Expensive Failure and What We Need to Do to Rebuild It.* New York: New York University Press.

Pizzi, W. T., and M. Montagna. 2004. The battle to establish as adversarial trial system in Italy. *Mich. J. Int. L.*, 24, 429.

Tague, P. W. 1996. *Effective Advocacy for the Criminal Defendant: The Barrister vs. The Lawyer.* Buffalo: W. S. Hein.

van Den Wyngaert, C. 1993. *Criminal Procedure Systems in the European Community.* London: Butterworth.

Sentencing Structure and Reform in Common Law Jurisdictions

17

JULIAN V. ROBERTS AND
ESTELLA BAKER

Contents

17.1   Introduction

In many respects, sentencing represents the apex of the criminal process. The community looks to sentencing to affirm social values as well as to protect them from offenders who may represent a threat to public safety. Members of the public are keenly interested in the sentencing of offenders and hold strong opinions about individual cases. The high degree of public interest in the sentence imposed in a case helps to explain the intense media interest in the subject. Determining sentence represents one of the most challenging tasks confronting a judge.

The judiciary in most common law jurisdictions exercises considerable discretion when imposing sentence. Although the law specifies maximum penalties for all offenses, practice at the trial court level is usually to impose sentences that are far less severe than the statutory maxima (Roberts 1999).[1] Furthermore, the maximum penalties tend to lack theoretical coherence; they do not necessarily reflect in severity the seriousness of the crimes for which they may be imposed. Penalties for some long-standing offenses may not have been updated since the nineteenth century, whereas those for more recently created crimes have been determined piecemeal, according to the timing of their introduction. Consequently, not only do maximum penalties provide little guidance as to the typical sentence for common crimes, they

---

[1] Canadian data illustrate the problem well. Burglary of a private dwelling carries a maximum penalty of life imprisonment, although the median sentence of imprisonment imposed for this offense at the trial court level is well under six months (see Roberts 1999).

also provide an inadequate indication of the relative seriousness of the offenses for which they may be imposed.[2]

The purposes and some principles of sentencing are usually codified or placed on a statutory footing. Little guidance is offered as to which objectives are paramount for which kinds of cases. In most countries—the United States being an important exception—only a small number of crimes carry a minimum sentence. In recent years, however, legislatures in most Western nations have also created mandatory sentences of imprisonment for a number of serious offenses such as crimes committed with a firearm or burglary. Beyond these legal parameters on the exercise of their sentencing powers, judges generally receive submissions from counsel to the parties,[3] as well as direction from courts of appeal.

Taken together, these constraints leave sentencers with much residual discretion for most offenses. This discretion, in practice, is left substantially unchecked by the process of appellate review. Few offenders appeal against their sentences on the grounds that they are overharsh, and the Crown right of appeal against the imposition of unduly lenient punishments is a relatively new feature of sentencing in some jurisdictions and may be circumscribed (Shute 1994, 1999).[4] Furthermore, in most jurisdictions, the standard of review for courts of appeal is relatively high: Appeal courts interfere with the sentence imposed at the trial court level only rarely, where compelling circumstances justify intervention. The exception to this picture of wide discretion at sentencing is the United States, where numerical sentencing guidelines restrict judicial discretion to a much greater degree. However, as will be seen, some other common law jurisdictions such as England and Wales are currently engaged in introducing more detailed sentencing guidelines for sentencers than have traditionally been provided.

This contribution reviews the principal sentencing structures that exist in common law countries. Clearly, no single chapter can provide an exhaustive review of all sentencing systems. Considerable variance exists between jurisdictions that nevertheless also share a number of common elements. Instead, we explore a limited number of issues as well as the most important challenges confronting many countries. We illustrate the variability regarding sentencing with examples from around the world. The chapter begins with

---

[2] Again, the Canadian experience illustrates the problem: The maximum penalty for sexual assault (including crimes prosecuted elsewhere as rape) carries a much lower maximum penalty than burglary (ten years compared to life imprisonment).

[3] In England and Wales, prosecutors simply identify any relevant aggravating factors before the court at the sentencing hearing. Elsewhere, prosecutors play a more active role, suggesting specific dispositions for the court to consider.

[4] In England and Wales, for example, the Crown does not have a general right of appeal but is restricted to sentences for a statutory list of offenses (for discussion see Shute 1994, 1999).

a brief outline of sentencing purposes that draws attention to their inherently conflicting nature. Although it is possible to reconcile some combinations of purposes within the confines of a single sentence, it is certainly not possible simultaneously to reconcile all of them. This fundamental fact is closely connected to the issue of sentencing discretion because it means that, in principle, on every occasion that an offender appears for sentencing, the sentencer must exercise a choice as to which goal to pursue. Therefore, by its very nature, sentencing is liable to prove problematic.

However, the difficulties do not stop there. Not only does the decision as to which sentencing goal to pursue generate a number of further problems, but as the remainder of this initial section will show, it is also necessary to take account of a wider set of issues that complicate the task still further. Thereafter, the chapter will focus on judicial discretion, considering its nature and appropriate scope before proceeding to review a range of methods that states have adopted in an attempt to structure its exercise. These will then be evaluated in terms of their capacity to address problematic issues, and some other solutions will be identified. Finally, we will briefly examine whether the growing popularity of restorative justice as an alternative approach to more conventional models of criminal justice might be a reflection of its superiority in dealing successfully with these issues. The chapter focuses on the sentencing of adult offenders; most jurisdictions have separate statutory regimes for young offenders, for whom different penal priorities are appropriate (Duff 2002).[5] We do not deal with the issue of parole, although the existence of discretionary release programs has an important impact on sentences of imprisonment.[6] Finally, we do not deal with the contentious issue of capital punishment, as that sanction is relevant to only a small number of countries.

17.2　The Inherently Problematic Nature of Sentencing

17.2.1　Sentencing Purposes and their Incompatible Nature

Some sentencing objectives are utilitarian in nature; that is, they seek to achieve an explicitly measurable goal, usually preventing crime. For example,

---

[5] It is worth noting that all jurisdictions impose mitigated punishments on most juvenile offenders. A small proportion of these offenders are subject to "adult" penalties, usually after having been transferred from juvenile to criminal court.

[6] Common law countries generally permit almost all prisoners to serve part of their sentences under supervision in the community, although the nature of these programs and the proportion of the sentence that may be served on parole vary considerably. In the United States, many states have abolished parole or adopted "truth in sentencing" laws that require offenders to serve at least 85 percent of the sentence in prison.

deterrence, rehabilitation, and incapacitation are all intended to prevent further offending, although by different means. Deterrence seeks to prevent crime by means of the threat of punishment. General deterrence provides a threat to potential offenders; individual or special deterrence is aimed at the specific offender being sentenced. According to the deterrence model, the sentence imposed should be sufficiently severe as to deter the person from future criminal acts. Rehabilitation also attempts to prevent crime in the future, but by reforming rather than by promoting a message of fear to the offender. Incapacitation is the most punitive sentencing objective, the one that is usually reserved for offenders who represent a clear threat to the community. Incapacitation usually means preventing offenders from committing further crimes (against society at least) by incarcerating them in a correctional facility.

In contrast to the utilitarian purposes of sentencing, retributive sentencing aims to express censure of the criminal conduct for which a sentence is imposed. Retributive sentencing is more concerned with the seriousness of the crime, and the offender's level of culpability, than the likelihood that he or she will reoffend. This is sometimes referred to as "just deserts" sentencing: Offenders are being punished because they deserve punishment, and to the extent that they deserve it; not because punishment will lower their risk to society or make them more law-abiding individuals. Deserts-based sentencing is a communicative theory of sentencing: The state is communicating a message of censure to offenders for their conduct. The degree of censure is measured by the severity of the sentence imposed (von Hirsch 1993). An alternative communicative theory is proposed by Duff (2001), who emphasized the importance of reintegrating offenders through repentance, self-reform, reparation, and reconciliation. According to Duff, "Criminal punishment should be conceived of as a communicative enterprise that aims to communicate to offenders the censure they deserve for their crimes, and thus bring them to repent their crimes, to reform themselves, and to reconcile themselves with those they have wronged" (2001: 129).

No consensus exists regarding which of the above purposes or objectives should underlie the sentencing process (von Hirsch and Ashworth 1998; Walker 1991; Miethe and Lu 2005). However, although they may vary from country to country, they generally include a core of common goals. Most common law jurisdictions, for example, provide judges with a list of possible objectives. England and Wales provides one illustration. Section 142(1) of the Criminal Justice Act 2003 identifies the following: punishment; the reduction of crime; rehabilitation; protection of the public; and reparation. In Canada, section 718 of the Criminal Code identifies the objectives of sentencing as denunciation; deterrence; incapacitation; rehabilitation; reparation; and promotion of a sense of responsibility in offenders. In the United

States, the federal sentencing guidelines identify "the basic purposes of criminal punishment, i.e., deterring crime, incapacitating the offender, providing just punishment, and rehabilitating the offender" (U.S. Sentencing Guidelines Commission 2004: 2).

Merely legislating a list of sentencing objectives, however, does little to assist judges in exercising sentencing discretion because it does not alleviate the problem of the various purposes coming into conflict. A court that is interested in pursuing rehabilitation as a sentencing goal, for example, will be reviewing alternatives to custody, the simple reason being that it is harder to achieve reformation if the offender is imprisoned. By contrast, the objective of deterrence may call for a lengthy prison term, in order to deter other potential offenders. Judges must weigh the relevance of different sentencing purposes in each particular case. For this reason, simply providing judges with a list of sentencing purposes in the absence of any further guidance as to how to select between them will do little to promote uniformity of sentencing; different judges will simply select different objectives. This, together with a number of other problems that stem from the exercise of sentencing discretion, will be discussed in the next section.

17.3   Problems in Sentencing

17.3.1   The Role of Previous Convictions (the Recidivist Premium)

General agreement exists across a wide range of jurisdictions that the seriousness of the offense should be the primary determinant of the severity of imposed sentence. This explains much of the popular appeal of proportional sentencing. Surveys have shown widespread public support for proportionality in sentencing (Roberts and Hough 2005). After crime seriousness, the next most important determinant of sentence severity is usually the offender's criminal record (Roberts 1997). All sentencing systems impose less severe sanctions on offenders who have been convicted for the first time; this is known as the "first offender discount." The treatment of recidivist or repeat offenders follows a different path, known as the "progressive loss of mitigation" (Ashworth 2005).

According to the principle of the progressive loss of mitigation, first offenders and people who have only two or three prior convictions should receive a discount, but this mitigation is progressively withdrawn, so that once offenders have accumulated perhaps three or four convictions, they can no longer plausibly argue that their offending was an aberration, a temporary lapse. At this point, they should receive the full sentence that is deserved for the offense of conviction. However, thereafter, previous convictions become largely irrelevant; the focus is almost exclusively on the crime and any relevant mitigating or aggravating factors. In theory, jurisdictions such as Canada, South Africa, and New Zealand follow the progressive loss of mitigation model (Roberts 1997).[7] Although England and Wales has traditionally been associated with this approach to the use of criminal history, section 143(2) of the Criminal Justice Act 2003 directs the courts to "treat each previous conviction as an aggravating factor if (in the case of that conviction) the court considers that it can reasonably be so treated." This suggests that English sentencing law is moving towards an alternative model, known as "cumulative sentencing."

According to this model, the severity of sentence should increase continuously to reflect the extent of the offender's record. Thus both models assign less severe penalties to first offenders, but under the cumulative model, sentences continue to rise in severity. An offender with ten previous convictions will be punished more harshly than another with five priors; according to the progressive loss of mitigation doctrine, these two individuals should receive the same penalty (assuming the other circumstances are the same). Critics of the cumulative sentencing approach to the use of previous convictions argue that offenders are being punished a second time for the same offense (e.g., Bagaric 2001). Proponents of the "recidivist premium" in sentencing might respond that harsher penalties are necessary for repeat offenders in order to provide additional deterrence. Some also suggest that harsher sentences for recidivists can be justified in terms of the offender's failure to learn from previous sentences and the element of contempt for the criminal justice system that the failure implies.

The U.S. sentencing guideline systems (which will be discussed below) follow the cumulative sentencing model: Sentences become progressively more severe to reflect the number and seriousness of the offender's previous convictions. In some states, an offender's criminal history counts for more at sentencing than the seriousness of the offense of current conviction (see Roberts 1997). As Bagaric aptly noted: "The U.S. is the least pleasant place for an offender with prior convictions to be" (2001: 234). The "three strikes" sentencing laws represent the most extreme version of a recidivist premium. Under some three strikes statutes, the third offense triggers a very long period of custody, even if it involves a relatively minor offense. Thus, offenders in the United States have been sentenced to many years in prison for crimes such as stealing a pizza or a bicycle, simply because they had two violent felony convictions in their criminal history.

---

[7] We use the phrase "in theory" advisedly, for sentencing statistics in these jurisdictions reveal that sentences tend to rise in severity to match the offender's criminal history. In other words, the courts do not necessarily adhere to the progressive loss of mitigation model, even if that is the theoretical model found in the case law (see discussion in Roberts 1997).

Consideration of an offender's previous convictions at sentencing requires more than simply counting the number of prior offenses. Judges will consider many aspects of the offender's record, including the following: the time elapsed since the last conviction; the relationship between the previous and the current offense; whether there is a pattern of escalating seriousness in the record; as well as many other variables (Roberts 1997). In the American guideline schemes, these considerations are spelled out in accompanying sentencing guidelines manuals. In other jurisdictions, such as has formerly been the position in England and Wales, judicial interpretation of an offender's record for the purposes of sentencing is regulated by case law (Ashworth 2000).

17.3.2 Disparity

There is a clear relation between the degree of judicial discretion and the extent of variability in sentencing outcomes. If judges are allowed much discretion, and provided with little guidance regarding the exercise of that discretion, disparity will result. Indeed, the movement to curtail judicial discretion in the United States arose as a result of general recognition that sentencing patterns were unpredictable, with a consequent loss of fairness for offenders. Researchers in a number of jurisdictions going back many years (Gaudet 1932) have documented the existence of unwarranted sentencing disparity, using a variety of methodologies. For example, in Canada, Hogarth (1971) and Roberts (1999) explored actual sentencing decisions of judges, whereas Austin and Willams (1977) and Palys and Divorski (1986) employed a sentencing simulation paradigm, in which a group of judges were all asked to sentence the same description of a criminal case (Palys and Divorski 1986).[8] The research findings from different methodologies converged on the same conclusion: Sentencing outcomes vary according to the individual sentencing philosophies of the judges (Lawrence 1994).[9] Concern about disparate outcomes at sentencing was responsible for the sentencing reform initiatives launched across the United States in the 1970s and 1980s,

[8] In the Palys and Divorski study, a sample of judges was given the same case descriptions to read and was then asked to impose sentence. The sentences varied considerably; in one case of armed robbery, the range of sentences imposed ran from a suspended sentence to thirteen years in prison (Palys and Divorski 1986).
[9] More fundamentally still, research conducted in Australia suggests that a further cause of disparity in sentencing outcomes lies in the differential interpretations that individual judges place on particular pieces of information and which then in turn influence them in the sentencing philosophy to apply. For example, faced with a wealthy shoplifter, some will regard the offender's lack of need as suggesting a psychological "cry for help" that justifies a mitigated treatment response, whereas others will see it as indicative of the offender's greed and thus as a clear aggravating factor that calls for an additional quantum of punishment (Lawrence 1994).

Table 17.1   Recent Prison Population Trends, Selected Nations

Jurisdiction	Percentage increase in prison population, 1990-2000
Netherlands	101
United States	68
Germany	56
Australia	52
England and Wales	44
Portugal	39
Ireland	37
Spain	37
New Zealand	37
Belgium	30
Canada	19
Norway	17

Source: Barclay and Tavares (2002).

and it has also influenced successive attempts at reforming sentencing law in England and Wales over the last fifteen years (Home Office 1990, 1996, 2001, 2002).

17.3.3   Reliance on Incarceration as a Sanction

In recent years, many countries have struggled to constrain their prison populations. For example, in 1991, the average daily prison population in England and Wales was 45,897. A decade later, the number of prisoners had increased by more than half to 73,012 (Hough, Jacobson, and Millie 2003). Similar trends, which are not confined to common law jurisdictions, have been observed in a number of other countries. Table 17.1 provides a summary of imprisonment trends in a selection of Western nations over the period 1990–2000, some of which have common law systems and some civil law. As can be seen, prison populations increased in a number of countries, despite the fact that crime rates declined during most of this decade. One cause of the high rates of incarceration in common law countries has been the traditional judicial reliance on imprisonment as a sanction. This has led many jurisdictions to adopt sentencing reforms to reduce the use of custody as a sanction (these are reviewed in section 17.4.3).

17.3.4   Public Pressure on Sentencers

A considerable volume of research has now accumulated on the views of the public in this area. This research has demonstrated that most people know little about the sentencing process, but nevertheless hold strong opinions regarding the severity of the courts. Representative polls conducted in developed and developing nations show that a clear majority of the public perceives their judges to respond with excessive leniency when sentencing (Roberts and Hough 2005). This view can be attributed in large measure to media coverage of crime and justice: Sentencing stories reported in the news media seldom contain information about the judicial reasoning underlying the sanction, or the range of sentence usually imposed for the crime in question. As well, the cases that are selected for coverage are often unusual in some respect: generally, the sentence imposed is often seen as lenient. Coverage of this kind gives the public the impression that judges are often lenient and capricious in their sentencing decisions.

This negative perception of the courts explains why judges receive low performance ratings from the public, and why confidence levels are lower for the courts than for the institutions that operate at most other stages of the criminal justice system. For example, a representative survey of the British public conducted in 2003 found that over three-quarters of respondents were "very" or "fairly" confident in the police, whereas only half the sample expressed this level of confidence in the courts[10] (Hough and Roberts 2004).

Low levels of public confidence are cause enough for concern. A sentencing system that is subject to continual public criticism will ultimately lose legitimacy. However, public opinion may exercise a powerful indirect influence on sentencing policy and practice. There is ample evidence that judges are to some unknown degree affected by public attitudes, or what they perceive the attitudes of the public to be (Roberts 2002; Hough, Jacobson, and Millie 2003). In addition, politicians in a number of countries have responded to opinion poll trends by proposing or legislating specific sentencing reforms. These are usually punitive in nature, reflecting the misperceptions of the politicians themselves. For example, mandatory sentencing laws are often introduced in response to a perceived public dissatisfaction with sentencing trends. In reality, members of the public have complex views about punishment, and when given an adequate amount of time to reflect, or an adequate amount of information on which to base an opinion, they often choose sentences in line with actual sentencing practices (Roberts and Hough 2005).

17.3.5　Plea Bargaining

Plea bargaining (or plea negotiations, to use a more appropriate term) is a daily and, for some, controversial feature of criminal justice systems in common law countries. A number of different forms of plea negotiations exist,

---

[10] Levels of public confidence were even lower for the prisons and the youth courts.

with charge bargaining being the most common:[11] The accused pleads guilty to a lesser but included offense, or agrees to plead guilty to one of a number of offenses with which he or she is charged. In return, the prosecutor may stay or discontinue proceedings on certain others. In many cases, a joint sentencing submission is placed before the sentencing court. There is a strong presumption that the court will adopt this joint submission, otherwise predictability would suffer, and plea negotiations would cease, as the parties would have little confidence that their agreement would result in the mutually desired outcome. In some countries such as Canada, plea bargaining is an unregulated, informal practice. Elsewhere, the United States, for example, plea agreements require judicial approval.

Given that the presumption of innocence is meant to be a fundamental tenet of criminal proceedings, so that an accused is innocent until proven guilty beyond reasonable doubt, it seems strange that those facing criminal charges might elect to plead guilty. By doing so, they are in effect waiving the right to have the case against them tested in court. Moreover, in at least some jurisdictions, defendants opt to do so in startling numbers. For example, recent statistics for England and Wales record that guilty pleas occur in approximately 95 percent of cases in the magistrates' court (lower tier criminal court) and 74 percent of cases in the Crown court (upper tier criminal court) (Home Office 2002). No doubt some of these defendants are motivated by the knowledge that the prosecuting authorities have a cast-iron case against them and others by a remorse-driven desire to confess, but such high figures cannot be accounted for satisfactorily on these grounds. In order to understand the high rate at which defendants enter guilty pleas, it is necessary to consider the interaction between plea negotiations and another prevalent, and at least as controversial, practice: that of offering a defendant a sentence discount in return for entering a guilty plea. Why is this discount offered?

17.3.5.1   Guilty Plea Discount

A number of grounds exist, some principled, some pragmatic in nature, that lead proponents of plea negotiation to maintain that it can profit all parties to a criminal proceeding. First, a guilty plea spares the crime victim in particular—but also other witnesses—from having to testify and from being subject to cross-examination. For some of these individuals, reliving the offense in a public forum, particularly in the context of hostile questioning from defense counsel, can be very traumatic. Consequently, it is argued that offenders should receive some credit for sparing victims and witnesses from having to go through this ordeal. Second, it is suggested that offenders who accept responsibility for their offending should be rewarded for such a step,

---

[11] The other forms include sentence bargaining and fact bargaining.

which may represent the first movement towards rehabilitation and a return to a law-abiding lifestyle. Third, the resolution of a high proportion of cases without a contested trial allows the state to conserve valuable court resources by avoiding a great deal of time and expense.

That a high premium is placed on extracting these benefits can be seen from the magnitude of the discount that is offered. In England and Wales, for example, the offender can expect a reduction of 33 percent of the sentence that would otherwise have been imposed unless there are good reasons for a lower amount (Sentencing Guidelines Council 2007). This is a significant decrease. However, because the reduction that is awarded for the plea diminishes the further that the proceedings advance towards trial, in order for the offender to gain the maximum advantage, the plea must be entered at an early stage. The sentence discount is likely to be lower in cases where there is a delay, and a sudden change of plea at the start of a trial will bring little change in the severity of the sentence ultimately imposed. English law also takes account of the probability that the offender would be convicted if the case were contested. If the prosecution case is strong, and the offender is virtually certain to be convicted, then he or she will receive little credit for bowing to the inevitable by pleading guilty. Conversely, the greater the contribution that the plea makes to the chances of a successful prosecution, the greater the sentence discount that the offender is likely to receive for entering it.

But if the grounds for offering the discount are as soundly based as its advocates claim, why is the practice of negotiation condemned by many? Its critics argue that a catalogue of negative consequences ensues (Sanders and Young 2006). For present purposes, the most important are as follows: First, the practice can distort the sentencing process by divorcing the actual criminal conduct from the offense of conviction. An accused charged with murder may plead guilty to the lesser and included offense of manslaughter and be sentenced for the latter crime. This decision by the accused will result in a much more lenient disposition. For example, in Canada, a conviction for first-degree murder carries a mandatory sentence of imprisonment for life, with no possibility of parole until at least twenty-five years have been served in prison. Manslaughter, however, carries no mandatory sentence, and the average sentence is in the range of three to four years in prison, with eligibility for release on parole at the one-third point of the sentence. Offenders convicted of first-degree murder will spend twenty-five years in prison; if they plead guilty to manslaughter, they may well be released on parole after one year. Thus, by engaging in plea negotiation, offenders stand to receive a doubly reduced punishment. In the first place, they are able to reap the benefit of the sentence discount that is offered in return for a guilty plea, and in the second, the sentence that is discounted is likely to be significantly lower anyway because it relates to a less serious offense (Baker 2004). Members of the public or criminal justice professionals may see the offender as being guilty of the more serious charge (Cohen and Doob 1989)[12] and interpret this outcome as further evidence of a lenient judicial system.

17.3.6   Third Parties: The Role of the Victim in Sentencing

A second problem with plea bargaining touches upon an issue that is of wider concern; namely, how, and to what extent, sentencing decisions should take account of the interests of the crime victim. Regarding plea bargaining itself, the concern is that if the prosecution accepts a guilty plea to the offense of manslaughter in the type of case that we have been discussing, the victim may feel that justice has not been done. The offender has avoided the exceptionally stigmatizing label of "murderer" as well as the correspondingly "appropriate" level of punishment. In addition, guilty pleas often result in an immediate sentencing hearing, leaving the victim little or possibly no opportunity to submit a victim impact statement or to attend the sentencing hearing. Although judges have the power to put the matter over until the victim has been apprised of developments, this is rarely done, particularly if the offender is in custody.

More generally, the problem is that there is little room under a traditional adversarial system of criminal justice to accommodate the interests of third parties such as crime victims. The crime is seen as a purely public wrong, committed against and prosecuted by the state. To allow victims to express an opinion at sentencing would appear to undermine the bipartite nature of the proceeding by introducing a third party. Allowing victims to speak at sentencing may, it is argued, also introduce a degree of emotion that may sway the court and result in further disparity of treatment. Whatever the merits of this position, it has largely been rejected, as almost all jurisdictions allow the victim to provide limited input into sentencing. Over the past decade, there has been increased attention paid to the role of the victim at all stages of the criminal process, including sentencing. Victims clearly have needs throughout the criminal justice system, but it is at the stage of sentencing that their input is, from their perspective, vital and, from other perspectives, controversial.

Faced to a greater or lesser degree with the sorts of serious problems that have just been discussed, a number of countries have taken steps to adopt a more rigid approach to structuring sentencing discretion, usually by means of some form of formal sentencing guidelines. Before discussing the different approaches that have been taken, however, it is important first to say something about the nature of judicial discretion in sentencing, because in a number of jurisdictions it has proved to be a controversial topic in its own right.

---

[12] This explains why members of the public hold a negative view of plea bargaining, which is perceived to be simply a means for the offender to avoid punishment (see Cohen and Doob 1989).

17.4   Judicial Discretion

17.4.1   The Nature and Parameters of Judicial Discretion in Relation to Sentencing

Given that the task of passing sentence is one that falls to judges and magistrates, it is an unavoidable consequence of any remotely successful attempt to structure sentencing discretion that it must necessarily involve circumscribing the powers of the judiciary. Potentially, this raises some important constitutional questions concerning the operation of the doctrine of separation of powers with respect to sentencing; that is, the appropriate division of power between the three branches of government (executive, legislature, and judiciary), and the importance of preserving judicial independence with respect to the exercise of sentencing functions. These issues have surfaced in particularly acute form in those jurisdictions where there has been little legislative intervention in the sentencing sphere until very recently. England and Wales provides a good example.

For a prolonged period before the Criminal Justice Act 1991 came into force, most aspects of sentencing had been left in the hands of the judiciary. In practical terms, this meant that punishments were generally tariff based (proportional to the offense), but judges were free to adopt an alternative rationale (deterrence, rehabilitation, or incapacitation) in those cases where they felt that it was appropriate to do so (*Regina v. Sargeant* 1974)). However, because it generated many of the problems that were outlined at the beginning of this chapter, the 1991 act sought to replace this "cafeteria" model with a bifurcatory, statutory sentencing scheme.

This scheme was substantially founded in the philosophy of just deserts and provided that for virtually all categories of offender, both the type of punishment (custodial, community based, financial) that was imposed and its duration should be commensurate with the seriousness of the offense. The exception concerned dangerous offenders who had been convicted of a violent or sexual offense. For these offenders only, the courts retained the power to impose an incapacitative custodial sentence in the interests of public protection. Sentences that were underpinned by other penal aims, particularly by deterrence, were apparently thus rendered unlawful (*Regina v. Cunningham* 1993; Ashworth 2005).[13]

---

[13] Nevertheless, in an early decision on the interpretation of the act, the court of appeal held that the purposes of a custodial sentence "must primarily be to punish *and to deter*" and that the phrase "commensurate with the seriousness of the offense," which was used in relevant provisions, "must mean commensurate with the punishment *and deterrence* which the seriousness of the offense requires": *Regina v. Cunningham* (1993) p. 447, emphasis added. For discussion see Ashworth 2005, pp. 99-101.

The act proved highly controversial for a variety of reasons (Dunbar and Langdon 1998), among them being the way that it purported to curb the powers of the judiciary to sentence offenders as they saw fit. It was suggested both that the act constituted a threat to judicial independence and that, by legislating in the sentencing field, Parliament had trespassed into a sphere in which it was constitutionally inappropriate for it to intervene. Similar allegations were also subsequently made in relation to the Crime (Sentences) Act 1997, which introduced a small number of mandatory sentences (Baker 1996). Despite the fact that further pieces of sentencing legislation have followed, however, arguments over these issues have died away and no longer seem to surface in public debate. This seems to reflect a more mature appreciation of the constitutional position.

There is increasingly widespread acceptance that the task of passing sentence in individual cases is truly a judicial function and that neither the legislature nor the executive should interfere therein (van Zyl Smit 2002).[14] However, although it might fall to the judiciary by default, the position with respect to determining sentencing policy is different. As a general proposition, the legislature is free to intervene in all realms of public policy, and sentencing does not have any identifiably distinct features that mark it out for exceptional treatment. Therefore, provided always that relevant constitutional constraints such as the need to comply with human rights guarantees are respected, there is no constitutional bar that prevents the legislature from acting in this policy sphere any more than in any other (Ashworth 2005). Nor does the fact that it chooses to do so pose a threat to judicial independence.

In view of the comprehensive problems that arise from allowing judges to exercise sentencing discretion in the absence of some form of guidance, it is not surprising that legislative intervention in sentencing matters has become commonplace across many jurisdictions. However, there has been a proliferation of such interventions during the past decade or so. Therefore, some brief consideration should be given to the factors that underlie this trend, and its timing. Apart from the growing body of international research that attests to the ills that result from permitting judges to exercise discretion unimpeded, these relate in substantial part to the way that the prevailing political and social climate has shaped attitudes to punishment and its control.

---

[14] An important impetus in the achievement of this understanding has been the increasing prominence that has been given over recent years to the development of human rights doctrine and the willingness of human rights courts to insist that sentencing in individual cases should be the sole preserve of the judiciary. Thus, for example, in the United Kingdom, an entirely new scheme for the granting of parole to life sentence prisoners has had to be created in recent years because, in a series of cases, the former arrangements were held to violate the European Convention on Human Rights, owing to the degree of executive involvement (see further van Zyl Smit 2002).

The 1980s was notable as a decade in which political parties of the new Right met with electoral success. A key aspect of the policies with which these parties were associated was the introduction of a new "managerialist" philosophy towards the delivery of public services that promoted privatization and recast voters as "consumers" (Lacey 1994). Consistent with the connotations of the latter label, individuals were encouraged to question the claims of experts and professionals, rather than implicitly to take their judgments on trust, as had previously been the case. That included the judgments of judges and other professionals involved in the delivery of criminal justice, including those carrying out the tasks of sentencing and punishment.[15] As a result, sentencing decisions were criticized for lacking transparency and sentencers for their lack of accountability and unresponsiveness in reacting to public opinion. Therefore, leaving aside the substantive reasons for legislative intervention to structure sentencing discretion, politicians were able to point to a popular mandate to bring sentencers under democratic control (see further Morgan 1999).

17.4.2 Guiding Judicial Discretion

A number of ways exist to structure judicial discretion, including codifying the purposes of sentencing, creating mandatory or voluntary sentencing guidelines, and establishing mandatory sentences for most crimes. A number of jurisdictions have moved to restrict judicial discretion by placing the purposes and principles of sentencing on a statutory footing, the idea being that greater consistency with respect to sentencing purposes will result in greater uniformity of outcome.

17.4.3 Guidance by Words: Purposes and Principles

The least intrusive method by which states have attempted to structure the exercise of judicial discretion in sentencing is to adopt an approach that may be termed "guidance by words." Apart from setting the maximum permitted penalties for offenses, legislatures do not prescribe specific ranges of punishment for offenses but only intervene to the extent of articulating the purposes of sentencing and identifying a number of critical principles. Judges are then left to interpret and apply these purposes and principles. This approach to sentencing has been embraced by most common law jurisdictions such as Australia, Canada, New Zealand, and South Africa

---

[15] The implications of this cultural change were not lost on judges, certain of whom were alert to its potential to undermine their relationship with the public. Thus, when the government decided to introduce a small number of mandatory sentences of the three strikes type in England and Wales in 1996, a senior member of the judiciary complained that its proposals sent out a loud and clear message that the courts could not be trusted to protect the public adequately.

(Freiberg 2001; Roberts and Cole 1999; Roberts 2003; Terreblanche 1999). The specific principles placed on a statutory footing vary from country to country; however, two important principles emerge in all of these jurisdictions: proportionality and restraint.

17.4.3.1   Proportionality

According to the principle of proportionality, the severity of the sentence imposed should be proportionate to the seriousness of the crime and, to a lesser degree, the offender's level of culpability as evidenced by his or her degree of responsibility for the crime. In practical terms, the principle means that the more serious offenses should attract a more severe punishment. For example, murder should be punished more severely than rape on the grounds that it is more serious. The principle of proportionality is central to, and derives from, the just deserts or retributive sentencing perspective (von Hirsch 1993). Many jurisdictions have codified this principle, thereby elevating it to a level above other principles. For example, in Canada, proportionality is identified in section 718.1 as the "fundamental principle" of sentencing.[16]

17.4.3.2   Restraint

Most jurisdictions have embraced the principle of restraint or parsimony regarding the use of imprisonment; judges are directed to use imprisonment only when no other sanction will achieve the statutory objectives of sentencing. This is part of a broader principle that argues that the state should invoke the criminal law only when no other remedy is sufficient. The principle of restraint states that imprisonment should be used only as a sanction of last resort, to be imposed when all other sentences are inappropriate. Most jurisdictions have placed this principle on a statutory footing.

For example, in Canada, sections 718.2(d) and (e) of the Criminal Code stipulate that "an offender should not be deprived of liberty, if less restrictive alternatives may be appropriate in the circumstances; and all available sanctions other than imprisonment that are reasonable in the circumstances should be considered for all offenders." In New Zealand, the principle is worded in a rather different way. Section 16(1) of the Sentencing Act 2002 states: "When considering the imposition of a sentence of imprisonment for any particular offense, the court must have regard to the desirability of keeping offenders in the community as far as that is practicable and consonant with the safety of the community." And section 16(2) further provides: "The court must not impose a sentence of imprisonment unless it is satisfied that: (a) the sentence is being imposed for all or any of the [sentencing]

---

[16] The exact wording is: "A sentence must be proportionate to the gravity of the offense and the degree of responsibility of the offender."

Box 17.1   Section 8 of the Sentencing Act, New Zealand

In sentencing or otherwise dealing with an offender, the court:

(a) must take into account the gravity of the offending in the particular case, including the degree of culpability of the offender; and

(b) must take into account the seriousness of the type of offense in comparison with other types of offenses, as indicated by the maximum penalties prescribed for the offenses; and

(c) must impose the maximum penalty prescribed for the offense if the offending is within the most serious of cases for which that penalty is prescribed, unless circumstances relating to the offender make that inappropriate; and

(d) must impose a penalty near to the maximum prescribed for the offense if the offending is near to the most serious of cases for which that penalty is prescribed unless circumstances relating to the offender make that inappropriate; and

(e) must take into account the general desirability of consistency with appropriate sentencing levels and other means of dealing with offenders in respect of similar offenders committing similar offenses in similar circumstances.

---

purposes ... (b) those purposes cannot be achieved by a sentence other than imprisonment...." In addition, as Box 17.1 illustrates, judges are provided with a detailed set of directions that are designed to guide them in the exercise of their discretion. This is a similar approach to that used in a number of other jurisdictions.

Before turning to consider other methods that states have adopted in the quest to restrain judicial sentencing discretion, it is worth pausing briefly to examine recent developments in England and Wales. A conscious decision was made to adopt the guidance by words model in the controversial Criminal Justice Act 1991 (Home Office 1990). Despite further piecemeal reforms and amendments, as already indicated, that legislation was widely seen to be unsuccessful in achieving its objectives (Ashworth 2005; Dunbar and Langdon 1998). Consequently, Parliament enacted a universal sentencing scheme — the Criminal Justice Act 2003.

The legislation retains a number of features that are consistent with the guidance by words approach, several of which, such as the inclusion of a statutory list of sentencing principles, are highlighted elsewhere in this chapter. On the face of it, this might suggest that it leaves very considerable room for judicial interpretation and discretion in its application. However, the act also provides for the establishment of a Sentencing Guidelines Council. This body has a majority, but not exclusively, judicial membership and is afforded the responsibility that its name suggests. Under section 170 of the act, the Council is mandated to draw up guidelines on the sentencing of offenders. Section 172(1) of the act goes on to provide that "every court must ... have regard to any guidelines which are relevant to the offender's case" in sentencing him or her. Although this is not the language of compulsion, the wording appears sufficiently forceful to ensure that the guidelines cannot be written off as merely symbolic. The legislation sets up a clear presumption that they will be followed in all cases other than those involving exceptional circumstances.

The sentencing scheme involving the Council represents an interesting interim model between traditional guidance by words and the more formalized methods of controlling judicial discretion in sentencing that are about to be discussed. It has now been in existence for some time and has started the complex and time-consuming process of issuing guidelines (Sentencing Guidelines Council 2004). Unfortunately, however, these developments are too recent to make it possible to judge how successful this latest endeavor at structuring sentencing discretion is likely to prove.

17.4.4 Numerical Sentencing Guidelines

The principal alternative to guidance by words is the adoption of formal numerical sentencing guidelines. Found in a variety of jurisdictions in the United States, this is an approach that is responsible for the fact that sentencing is more closely regulated there than elsewhere. Many states employ a two-dimensional sentencing grid, in which the vertical axis usually represents the seriousness of the offense, while the horizontal axis reflects the number and nature of the offender's previous convictions. Offenders are assigned points for each previous conviction, and the total number of points determines the appropriate column in the sentencing grid. Appendix 17.A provides an example of a sentencing grid; in this case the one used in the state of Minnesota. Offenses are assigned to one of eleven categories of seriousness. The nature and seriousness of the offender's criminal history is computed by means of a number of calculations, and the final score will fall into one of seven criminal history categories.[17] An example illustrates the use of the grid in Minnesota. An offender with a criminal history score of 4 (fourth column), who is convicted of residential burglary (an offense at seriousness level V) is liable to a term of imprisonment of not less than thirty-six and not more that forty months (see Appendix 17.A).

The schemes that have been adopted have assumed either a voluntary or presumptive nature. When the guidelines are voluntary, judges may follow

---

[17] The criminal history score is not simply the sum of all prior convictions. Points are assigned for each conviction, but additional points are assigned if certain conditions exist. For example, offenders acquire an extra point if the current offense was committed while on parole for a previous conviction, or if the current offense is in the same category as the previous convictions. Detailed scoring rules are provided in the *Guidelines Manual*.

or depart from the prescribed sentences, as they see fit, and without consequences. Unsurprisingly, when no more rigorous constraint than this is imposed, the guidelines are relatively ineffective in changing judicial practice (Tonry 1996). By contrast, under a presumptive guideline scheme, courts are bound to impose the sentence prescribed by guidelines. If they choose to impose a sentence outside the range (e.g., a term of custody in excess of, or below, the prescribed range, or an alternate sentence), this is classified as a "departure" outcome, and usually all such departures must be justified by the provision of reasons. In practice, the "departure rate"—the proportion of imposed sentences outside the range—is relatively low.

17.4.5   Mandatory Sentences of Imprisonment

Mandatory sentencing laws represent a third approach to controlling judicial discretion with respect to sentencing that is found in most jurisdictions. Mandatory sentences of imprisonment have long existed for the most serious crimes—usually planned and premeditated murder, or the murder of a correctional or police officer while on duty. However, during the 1990s, mandatory sentences of imprisonment proliferated as a number of countries adopted mandatory sentencing laws that affected large numbers of offenders. Politicians "sold" these measures to their electorates on the basis that they targeted crimes of particular concern at a given time (offenses involving firearms, for example) or that they were an apposite response to the problem of repeat offenders.

An important point to note, however, is that such measures do not just place strict restrictions on offenders; they also tie the hands of judges. In England and Wales, for example, the Crime (Sentences) Act 1997 introduced an automatic life sentence for offenders who were convicted of what the act identified as a "serious offense."[18] All such offenses carried a maximum sentence of life imprisonment in any case. Therefore, the effect of the legislation was to eliminate judges' discretion to impose that penalty and to force their hand to do so, regardless of whether such action would be justified according to established sentencing principles (Baker 2001; Thomas 1998).

The most visible example of recidivist mandatory sentences is the three strikes laws that originated in the United States, which mandate a long prison term or life imprisonment for offenders convicted for the third time of a serious felony. Table 17.2 provides some examples of mandatory sentencing laws in common law jurisdictions.

---

[18] This provision subsequently became the Powers of Criminal Courts (Sentencing) Act 2000, section 109 and has now been repealed by the Criminal Justice Act 2003. In the meantime, the measure had been substantially neutralized by the courts following a successful challenge under the Human Rights Act 1998: *Regina v. Offen and others* (2001).

Table 17.2   Examples of Mandatory Sentences of Imprisonment

Jurisdiction	Offense(s)/Offenders	Mandatory penalty
Canada	Ten serious violent crimes committed with a firearm (e.g., manslaughter)	Four to fourteen years imprisonment
England and Wales	Offenders convicted of certain firearms offenses	At least five years imprisonment
South Africa	Robbery when there are aggravating circumstances or involving the taking of a motor vehicle	First offender: at least fifteen years Second offender: at least twenty years Third or subsequent offender: at least twenty-five years

Mandatory sentences of imprisonment violate the two important principles of sentencing to which reference has been made (proportionality and restraint). Because a mandatory sentencing law imposes the same punishment for different offenders, it prevents judges from imposing sentences proportional to the crime and culpability level of the offender. Mandatory sentencing can result in highly punitive and disproportionate sentences. A good example can be found in the widely publicized sentence imposed on an offender in Utah in November 2004. The individual had been convicted of dealing in marijuana; there was agreement between the defense and prosecution that a sentence of approximately six years was appropriate. However, because he had three previous convictions for possessing (but not using or even displaying) a firearm, a federal statute[19] required the imposition of an additional fifty-five years in prison (five years for the first occasion, and twenty-five for each subsequent term).[20] Thus, although the offender's crime of conviction was not very serious (selling bags of marijuana to a police informant), mandatory sentence laws meant that the judge had to impose a very punitive sentence, in the light of the offender's previous convictions. In addition to creating disproportionately severe sentences, mandatory sentences of imprisonment also violate the principle of restraint, as there will undoubtedly be cases in which the sentence is not necessary and therefore should not be imposed.[21]

If mandatory sentences of imprisonment violate important sentencing principles common to many countries, why have they become so popular? Several explanations exist. First and foremost, these tough laws result from what has been called "penal populism" (Bottoms 1995; Roberts et al. 2003).

[19] 18 U.S.C. S. 924(c).
[20] See *New York Times* November 17, 2004. The judgment in *USA v. Weldon Angelos*. Case No. 2: 02-CR-00708PGC can be downloaded from www.famm.org.
[21] For a discussion of these issues in the context of human rights guarantees, see *Regina v. Offen and others* (2001).

This term refers to the tendency of politicians to pass legislation in order to enhance their standing in the eyes of the public, rather than to accomplish some penological goal. By "getting tough" with offenders (particularly violent offenders), some politicians hope to enhance their prospects for re-election. Mandatory sentences appeal to the punitive element of public opinion. The 1990s can be characterized as a decade in which such populist pressures were unprecedentedly intense, and offenders around the world are now serving long sentences of custody as a result of the laws that were passed in this time.

A second explanation for the mandatory sentencing laws is that some policymakers believe that crime rates for some specific offenses—importing drugs or armed robbery, for example—can be reduced by introducing a tough mandatory sentence. The hope is that potential offenders will "get the message" if the sentence is harsh enough. The problem with these severe mandatory sentencing laws, particularly in the United States, is that they affect large numbers of offenders and have little impact on the overall crime rate. The empirical research on the deterrent power of sentences suggests that deterrence is not an effective way of reducing aggregate crime rates. Thus, after reviewing the relevant research, Michael Tonry concluded: "There is little basis for believing that mandatory penalties have any significant effects on rates of serious crime" (1996: 141).[22] Reviews published since have sustained this conclusion (e.g., von Hirsch et al. 1999; Doob and Webster 2004).

17.5 How Effective Are these Methods as Responses to Sentencing Problems?

Not all of the methods of structuring judicial discretion that have just been discussed purport to address the full range of sentencing problems that were described in the opening section of this chapter. And, even where their proponents claim that they offer solutions to some or all of them, their effectiveness varies. Consequently, some jurisdictions have developed alternative or additional means to combat deficiencies in their sentencing systems.

17.5.1 Dealing with Previous Convictions

The decision as to whether previous convictions should be dealt with in accordance with the progressive loss of mitigation model or the cumulative sentencing model is linked to the broader question of which penal philosophy to adopt. Both are matters of policy and thus presumptively for the legislature to determine. With one notable exception, there is no connection between

---

[22] More plausibly, three strikes measures can be rationalized on the basis of general incapacitation.

the way that these policy choices are resolved and the decision as to which method of judicial guidance should be selected.

That exception is mandatory sentencing of the three strikes type. Here the offender's prior record simultaneously provides the underlying rationale for the particular approach to punishment (that offenders who have committed a series of offenses of a specified kind or level of severity should be punished more severely purely by dint of that fact) and the factual trigger for the three strikes measure through which that policy is executed. Leaving this special case aside, though, once the policy towards prior record has been set, the material issue is whether a particular technique for structuring judicial discretion is capable in principle of ensuring that judges follow the chosen policy, and what technical requirements must be incorporated into its design for that capability to be realized in practice. That this latter matter is of genuine practical concern can be illustrated by reference to experience in England and Wales.

Earlier in this discussion, it was noted that the traditional approach in dealing with criminal history was to adopt the progressive loss of mitigation model. Originally a policy that had been developed by the judiciary during the era in which there was little legislative regulation of sentencing, it was placed on a statutory footing by section 29 of the Criminal Justice Act 1991—or, at least, that was the intention. Unfortunately, however, the provision was so poorly drafted that even trained lawyers found its meaning opaque. As a result, the provision fell into disrepute so rapidly that within a year of being brought into force, it was repealed and replaced with a substitute section (Ashworth 2005; Baker 1996). Contrary to what might have been anticipated, the new provision did not clarify the original policy in clear and unequivocal terms. Rather, it was itself worded sufficiently ambiguously that it could be interpreted as providing authority for cumulative sentencing (Wasik and von Hirsch 1994). Given that the problem with the original section lay not in the depth of commitment to the progressive loss of mitigation approach but in the way that it was translated into legislation, this abrupt change was remarkable. It appears that the technical failings of the statute served to undermine confidence in the policy that it was meant to put into effect.

17.5.2 Responding to Sentencing Disparity

The numerical sentencing guidelines adopted in the United States clearly represent the most effective way to reduce disparity. However, when discretion is constrained to such a high degree, the system creates other problems. If the guidelines grid prescribes narrow ranges of sentence length, the problem of unwarranted uniformity arises. This can be defined as treating unlike cases in a similar way. Unwarranted uniformity may prevent judges from imposing a fit disposition on the offender. This may explain why numerical sentencing grids have not been adopted in other common law countries.

17.5.3 Restricting the Use of Custody

A useful comparison between the guidance by words and numerical guidelines approaches to structuring judicial discretion can be achieved by considering the decision to imprison offenders. As noted, many Western nations are confronted by rising prison populations. This is a common correctional problem to which many have responded by sentencing reforms. Under a numerical guidelines scheme, a court receives guidance on the appropriateness of custody from the offender's location on the grid; imprisonment is considered appropriate for offenses deep in the "custodial" zone. Constraining the number of admissions to prison is, or should be, a relatively simple task. It merely involves moving offenses out of the "imprisonment" zone of the grid. Reductions in the prison population can also be achieved by lowering the sentence lengths prescribed by the guidelines. The alternative approach adopted in jurisdictions without formal, numerical guidelines is to offer judges directions regarding the use of custody as a sanction. The principle of restraint (see above) is an important direction in this regard. An additional means of directing judges to restrict the use of custody is to prescribe specific criteria that must be met before an offender can be committed to custody. An example of this approach can be found in the youth sentencing law adopted in Canada in 2003. Under this sentencing regime, judges may not incarcerate a juvenile offender unless the case falls into one of four specific categories (Bala 2003).

17.5.3.1 Alternatives to Imprisonment

Finally, another way of reducing the flow of admissions to custody is simply to increase the number of alternative dispositions available to sentencing judges in the hope that they will be used in place of imprisonment. Most countries have expanded the range of intermediate sanctions (Tonry 1996; Morris and Tonry 1990). These are community sentences that are harsher than probation, but which do not involve the incarceration of the offender. Among the alternative sanctions found in many countries are the following: intensive supervision probation (an enhanced form of probation), day reporting centers, boot camps, community service, and an option that has become increasingly popular in recent years: home confinement.

The statutory regimes that govern this latter punishment differ (Roberts 2004), but the essential elements are the same: The offender is required to remain at home under house arrest or a strict curfew and is only permitted to leave the residence for court-authorized purposes (such as going to work or attending treatment). If the offender is found to have violated the conditions imposed, he or she will be committed to custody for the remaining time on the order. Verification of the offender's whereabouts is sometimes achieved through the use of electronic monitoring in jurisdictions in which the technology is available. Otherwise, surveillance is dependent upon calls or visits by supervising officers. Home confinement or community custody raises unique issues for the sentencing process. For example, some jurisdictions require the explicit consent of the offender's co-residents before the offender may be permitted to serve a term of home confinement. This requirement transfers some authority from the court to third parties (Roberts 2004).

17.5.4   Eliminating the Problems Associated with Plea Bargaining

Far from eliminating plea bargaining and the problems with which it is associated (particularly the more rigid methods of structuring judicial discretion), numerical sentencing guidelines that are presumptive in kind and mandatory sentencing are likely to induce it. Central to the aim of such schemes is that the scope for arguments at the time of sentencing that an offender should receive a mitigated punishment is drastically reduced, if not eliminated outright. That being so, it is natural that offenders who are faced with the almost certain prospect of what may be a very harsh sentence will turn their attention to those points earlier on in the criminal justice process, where there remains some residual discretion, in the hope that they can manipulate events in such a manner as to end up with a more lenient sentence. Striking some form of bargain with the prosecuting authorities would be an obvious example of such a tactic (Baker 1996).

There is a case for abolishing plea bargaining because of its adverse impact on the quality and impartiality of criminal justice. However, attempts by policymakers to restrict judicial discretion with respect to sentencing appear only to make the practice more entrenched and, consequently, to contribute further to the factors that appear to make its abolition inconceivable. However, there have been proposals in a number of countries to reform the practice. One such proposal involves holding the discussions before a judge, to promote greater accountability. It has also been suggested that victims be allowed greater input into the process, either by being given the right to be consulted regarding any possible agreement or, more controversially, by being accorded a veto over any agreement that may be reached between the offender and the prosecution.

17.5.5   Accommodating Victims and Third Parties in the Sentencing Process

The most popular vehicle for providing victim input is the victim impact statement (VIS). The use of these statements originated in the United States in the 1970s. Today, most jurisdictions provide victims with a form that allows them to state, in their own words, the impact that the crime had upon their life. With the exception of some parts of the United States, victims are discouraged from expressing an opinion about the sentence that should be imposed; the statement is restricted to the question of the impact of the crime.[23] In reality, victims often include recommendations with respect to sentencing. These are sometimes edited out by the prosecutor; if not, the court will disregard the victim's "submissions" on sentencing.

Allowing victims to express themselves at sentencing is consistent with a number of international conventions such as the U.N. Declaration on Basic Principles of Justice for Victims of Crime, which states that the responsiveness of judicial processes should be facilitated by "allowing the views and concerns of victims to be presented and considered at appropriate stages of the proceedings where their personal interests are affected."[24] In some jurisdictions (such as Canada), victims are allowed to deliver their statement orally at the sentencing hearing, provided the oral statement is in accordance with the form submitted to the court in advance.[25]

Although initially introduced to serve an "expressive" function—to allow victims to express themselves to the court and also to the offender—over the years, VISs have assumed a more instrumental purpose: Many victims see them as a potential vehicle to affect the sentence imposed (Roberts and Erez 2004). When this does not occur, victims can often be disappointed. Whether, and to what degree, victim impact statements serve the interests of justice remains controversial. Some researchers argue that allowing the victim to make a statement to the court about the impact of the crime benefits all parties. The victim may feel a sense of inclusion, or empowerment, as a result of speaking to the court. Judges may find the statements useful in determining the seriousness of the offense. There may even be a positive effect upon offenders, who may be sensitized to the true impact of their actions as a result of hearing from the crime victim. On the other hand, critics argue that victim impact statements add little to the sentencing process and may actually make matters worse for victims (Sanders et al. 2001).

17.5.5.1 Sources of Information for Courts

At sentencing, judges receive submissions from the prosecutor, representing the state, and counsel for the offender. As noted, these two parties sometimes place a joint submission before the court, as a result of plea negotiations. Otherwise, the court will consider the relative merit of the separate submissions. These will contain specific recommendations to assist the court and

---

[23] In England and Wales, this is the case even where the victim wishes to recommend that the offender's punishment should be lenient.

[24] This declaration was adopted in 1985.

[25] The reason for this is that victims sometimes extemporize and make inappropriate comments about the offender or the sentence that should be imposed.

will draw upon precedents similar to the case before the court. Another important source of information in many jurisdictions is the presentence report (PSR). This is a document prepared in advance by a probation officer. The PSR will contain a summary of the offender's personal situation and will identify important needs that may be addressed in the sentence to be imposed. Presentence reports do not often contain direct sentence recommendations, as this is seen as usurping the role of the court. However, the information contained in the report may sway a court towards or away from a particular disposition. For example, a probation officer may note that the offender is "not well suited for a community placement"—this is an indirect suggestion to the court that custody is the appropriate sanction to impose.

Finally, in some jurisdictions, a risk prediction device is completed. This is a scale with a number of items that are scored by the probation officer and provides the court with an indication of the risk level represented by the offender. Offenders who score high on a risk prediction scale represent—or are perceived to represent—a high risk of reoffending. A number of jurisdictions have shown an increased interest in risk-based sentencing in recent years. In Virginia, for example, judges employ a 71-point risk assessment scale (Virginia Criminal Sentencing Commission 2002). If the defendant scores 35 points or lower, the court receives a recommendation for an alternative to custody, such as probation or house arrest. Scores over 35 result in a recommendation for imprisonment. Basing sentencing decisions on risk prediction is a controversial practice. The utilitarian perspective on sentencing, which attempts to reduce future offending by means of deterrence or incapacitation, would approve of the use of this variable. However, desert-based theorists would have a different view: If the primary determinant of sentence severity is the seriousness of the offense and the offender's level of culpability, a risk-based prediction should not be considered at sentencing.

17.6   Restorative Justice: A Different Approach?

We end this review of sentencing by noting a recent development that has emerged around the world. Restorative justice has begun to challenge the traditional model of criminal justice. Defining restorative justice is far from easy, as it means different things to different people around the world (Dignan 2005). However, it can be said that restorative justice focuses on restoring the offender to the community and, where possible and appropriate, reconciling victims and offenders. This approach to justice also attempts to promote the interests of the victim to a greater degree (Braithwaite 1999). Restorative initiatives exist throughout the criminal process, from initial contact with a suspect through to the correctional stage. It is therefore not surprising that the sentencing process has been affected by this new paradigm of justice. Restorative justice has made greater inroads into sentencing at the juvenile level, but it has also affected adult sentencing in a number of jurisdictions.

One manifestation of the influence of restorative justice at sentencing has been a renewed interest in alternative sanctions, particularly those involving reparation to the victim. For many victims, obtaining reparation may be the most important purpose of sentencing. Indeed, like the public, many victims see greater merit in sanctions that oblige the offender to make reparation than they do in imprisonment. Victims receive no tangible benefit from the offender's incarceration. In Canada, two restorative sentencing objectives have been codified. Section 718(e) of the *Criminal Code* states that the sentencing objectives include "to provide reparations for harm done to victims or the community" and "to provide a sense of responsibility in offenders, and acknowledgement of the harm done to victims and to the community." These codified purposes of sentencing carry the same weight as deterrence, incapacitation, or rehabilitation (Roach 2000). Similar provisions exist in New Zealand's Sentencing Act (Roberts 2003).

Public support for restorative initiatives at sentencing is strong, at least for less serious offenses or offending by first offenders (Roberts and Stalans 2004). Members of the public are attracted by the benefits to the victim as well as the potential to save money, if the offender makes reparation in the community rather than being committed to prison. However, public support declines rapidly when people are asked to consider "restorative" sentencing options for offenders convicted of serious crimes of violence. For these individuals, the traditional retributive model is seen as being most appropriate. Another limitation on the restorative sentencing model is that many criminal justice professionals remain unconvinced of its merits. For these reasons, there seems little likelihood that restorative sentencing will replace the more traditional model in the near future.

17.7 Conclusions

As this chapter has illustrated, the task of sentencing offenders involves the need to resolve a complex set of issues. Some, such as the selection of which penal purposes should inform sentencing decisions and how an offender's criminal record should be treated, are fundamental matters of policy. There is no right or wrong answer to these. They are questions about which individuals are likely to have conflicting views, reflecting their own personal moral and political values about punishment; their perspective on criminal justice matters (whether as victim, offender, criminal justice professional, or nonparticipating observer); and their broader aspirations with regard to the type of society within which they wish to live. Sentencing has this multidimensional sociopolitical character, which helps to explain why it provokes such a keen interest in the general public; it also supplies a positive reason why constitutional authority over sentencing policy should properly reside in the legislature.

Even if the result of leaving decisions about such matters to the judiciary is to produce a rational and coherent sentencing policy (and experience demonstrates that such an outcome is unlikely), there is a danger that it will nevertheless be regarded as lacking in legitimacy by the public and thus fail to win their confidence. Although the courts play a vital role in ensuring the health of a democracy, they do not provide a suitable forum for settling fundamental disagreements over sociopolitical issues of this kind; that is the function of the legislature. In theory, therefore, it ought to be possible to use the democratic process to dissipate some of the public pressure that is exerted on sentencers to exercise their powers in accordance with what purports to be popular opinion because the policies to which they are giving effect will have achieved prior legitimacy.

Not all of the issues that have been considered in this chapter are of the same character, however. The drive that has been felt across jurisdictions to structure judicial discretion and guide its exercise is not concerned with which sentencing policy to follow, but how best to ensure that it is put into practice. As has been seen, a variety of techniques have been adopted, but none is ideal. If guidance is too lax, it will not have the desired effect because judges will simply ignore it or interpret it to accord with pre-existing practices. Of the methods that have been discussed, guidance by words, is probably the most prone to this type of problem, as is arguably illustrated by the unhappy history of the English Criminal Justice Act of 1991. On the other hand, if the guidance is too rigid, then there is a risk that both defendants and prosecutors will be encouraged to indulge in practices such as plea bargaining that circumvent the rules altogether and which create other difficulties in their wake. Numerical guidelines that are presumptive in nature and mandatory sentencing laws of the three strikes type are cases in point here. The effect of introducing such measures in some instances has been to create fresh problems that threaten to overshadow those that they solve.

It is hardly surprising that sentencing policies and practices have been evolving rapidly over the past twenty years, nor that they continue to evolve. There is evidence, for instance, that many American states are beginning to question the utility as well as the justice of the harsher mandatory sentencing laws, particularly those that apply to drug offenders. These laws have resulted in rising prison populations and have disproportionately affected African-American communities. Meanwhile, in other jurisdictions, there is evidence that sentencing is becoming more structured. For example, in England and Wales, the Criminal Justice Act 2003 is resulting in detailed sentencing guidelines for sentencers. Elsewhere, jurisdictions such as South Africa, where to date sentencing has been entirely "judge-driven," are contemplating creating a more structured statutory framework. In 2000, the South African Law Commission released a report containing an integrated package of proposals. The fact that sentencing reform remains high on the agenda in these as well as many other jurisdictions attests to the difficulty of the issues involved, their continuing political importance, and the lack of satisfaction with attempts that have been made to date to solve the problems that have been outlined in this chapter.

References

Ashworth, A. 2005. *Sentencing and Criminal Justice*, 4th ed. Cambridge: Cambridge University Press.

Austin, W., and T. Williams. 1977. A survey of judges' responses to simulated legal cases: Research note on sentencing disparity. *The Journal of Criminal Law and Criminology* 68, 306-310.

Bagaric, M. 2001. *Punishment and Sentencing. A Rational Approach*. Sydney: Cavendish Publishing.

Baker, E. 1996. From "making bad people worse" to "prison works": Sentencing policy in England and Wales in the 1990s. *Criminal Law Forum* 7(3), 639-671.

Baker, E. 2001. Mandatory sentences in England and Wales: A review. Paper in Criminology in the 21st Century: Public Good or Private Interest? The Annual Conference of the Australian and New Zealand Society of Criminology, Melbourne, Australia.

Baker, E. 2004. Guilty pleas, diversion and consensual disposition: England and Wales. In *Criminal Justice between Crime Control and Due Process*, ed. A. Eser and C. Rabenstein. Berlin: Duncker and Humblot.

Bala, N. 2003. *The Youth Criminal Justice Act*. Toronto: Irwin Law.

Barclay, G., and C. Tavares. 2002. *International Comparisons of Criminal Justice Statistics 2000*. London: Home Office, Research, Development, and Statistics.

Bottoms, A. E. 1995. The philosophy and politics of sentencing and punishment. In *The Politics of Sentencing Reform*, ed. C. M. V. Clarkson and R. Morgan. Oxford: Clarendon Press.

Braithwaite, J. 1999. Restorative justice: Assessing optimistic and pessimistic accounts. In *Crime and Justice. A Review of Research*, ed. M. Tonry. Chicago: University of Chicago Press.

Cohen, S., and A. N. Doob. 1989. Public attitudes to plea bargaining. *Criminal Law Quarterly* 32, 85-109.

Dignan, J. 2005. *Understanding Victims and Restorative Justice*. Maidenhead: Open University Press.

Doob, A. N., and C. Webster. 2004. Sentence severity and crime: Accepting the null hypothesis. In *Crime and Justice. A Review of Research*, ed. M. Tonry. Chicago: University of Chicago Press.

Duff, R. A. 2001. *Punishment, Communication, and Community*. Oxford: Oxford University Press.

Duff, R. A. 2002. Punishing the young. In *Punishing Juveniles*, ed. I. Weijers and A. Duff. Oxford: Hart Publishing.

Dunbar, I., and A. Langdon. 1998. *Tough Justice: Sentencing and Penal Policies in the 1990s*. London: Blackstone.

Freiberg, A. 2001. Three strikes and you're out—it's not cricket: Colonization and resistance in Australian sentencing. In *Sentencing and Sanctions in Western Countries*, ed. M. Tonry and R. Frase. New York: Oxford University Press.

Gaudet, F. 1932. Individual differences in the sentencing tendencies of judges. *International Journal of Criminal Law, Criminology and Political Science* 23, 811-818.

Hogarth, J. 1971. *Sentencing as a Human Process*. Toronto: University of Toronto Press.

Home Office. 1990. *Crime, Justice and Protecting the Public*. Cm 965. London: HMSO.

Home Office. 1996. *Protecting the Public*. Cm 3190. London: HMSO.

Home Office. 2001. *Making Punishments Work: Report of a Review of the Sentencing Framework in England and Wales*. London: Home Office.

Home Office. 2002. *Justice for All*. Cm 5563. London: HMSO.

Hough, M., and J. V. Roberts. 2004. *Public Confidence in Criminal Justice. An International Review*. ICPR Report No. 3. London: Kings College.

Hough, M., J. Jacobson, and A. Millie. 2003. *The Decision to Imprison. Sentencing and the Prison Population*. London: Prison Reform Trust.

Lacey, N. 1994. Government as manager, citizen as consumer: The case of the criminal justice act 1991. *Modern Law Review* 57, 534.

Lawrence, J. 1994. Sentencing and the criminal courts. Paper in Judging and Decision Making conference, held by the University of Sheffield Institute for the Study of the Legal Profession, Sheffield, U.K., September 8-9.

Miethe, T., and H. Lu. 2005. *Punishment. A Comparative Historical Perspective*. Cambridge: Cambridge University Press.

Morgan, N. 1999. Accountability, transparency and justice: Do we need a sentencing matrix? *Western Australian Law Review* 28, 259-292.

Morris, N., and M. Tonry. 1990. *Between Prison and Probation: Intermediate Punishments in a Rational Sentencing System*. New York: Oxford University Press.

Palys, T., and S. Divorski. 1986. Explaining sentence disparity. *Canadian Journal of Criminology* 28, 347-362.

Regina v. Cunningham. 1993. 14 Criminal Appeal Reports (Sentencing) 444.

Regina v. Offen and others. 2001. 2 Criminal Appeal Reports (Sentencing) 10.

Regina v. Sargeant. 1974. 60 Criminal Appeal Reports 74.

Roach, K. 2000. Changing punishment at the turn of the century: Restorative justice on the rise. *Canadian Journal of Criminology and Criminal Justice* 42, 249-280.

Roberts, J. V. 1997. Paying for the past: The role of criminal record in the sentencing process. In *Crime and Justice. A Review of Research,* ed. M. Tonry, 22. Chicago: University of Chicago Press.

Roberts, J. V. 1999. Sentencing patterns and sentencing disparity. In *Making Sense of Sentencing,* ed. J. V. Roberts and D. Cole. Toronto: University of Toronto Press.

Roberts, J. V. 2002. Public opinion and sentencing policy. In *Reform and Punishment: The Future of Sentencing,* ed. S. Rex and M. Tonry. Cullompton, U.K.: Willan Publishing.

Roberts, J. V. 2003. An analysis of the statutory statement of the purposes and principles of sentencing in New Zealand. *Australia and New Zealand Journal of Criminology* 36(3), 249-271.

Roberts, J. V. 2004. *The Virtual Prison. Community Custody and the Evolution of Imprisonment.* Cambridge: Cambridge University Press.

Roberts, J. V., and D. Cole, eds. 1999. *Making Sense of Sentencing.* Toronto: University of Toronto Press.

Roberts, J. V., and E. Erez. 2004. Communication in sentencing: Exploring the expressive and the impact model of victim impact statements. *International Review of Victimology* 10, 223-244.

Roberts, J. V., and M. Hough. 2005. *Understanding Public Attitudes to Criminal Justice.* Maidenhead, U.K.: Open University Press.

Roberts, J. V., and L. S. Stalans. 2004. *Restorative Justice and the Sentencing Process: Exploring the Views of the Public.* Social Justice Research, 17: 351-334.

Roberts, J. V., L. S. Stalans, D. Indermaur, and M. Hough. 2003. *Penal Populism and Public Opinion. Lessons from Five Countries.* Oxford: Oxford University Press.

Sanders, A., and R. Young. 2000. *Criminal Justice,* 3rd ed. Oxford: Oxford University Press.

Sanders, A., C. Hoyle, R. Morgan, and E. Cape. 2001. Victim impact statements: Don't work; can't work. *Criminal Law Review* 447-458.

Sentencing Guidelines Council. 2007. *Reduction in Sentencing for a Guilty Plea—Revised Guidelines.*

Shute, S. 1994. Prosecution appeals against sentence: The first five years. *Modern Law Review* 57, 745-772.

Shute, S. 1999. Who passes unduly lenient sentences? How were they listed? A survey of attorney-general's reference cases, 1989-1997. *Criminal Law Review* 603-626.

South African Law Commission. 2000. Sentencing (A New Sentencing Framework). Discussion Paper 91 (Project 82). Available at www.law.wits.ac.za/salc/discussion/proposal

Terreblanche, S. S. 1999. *The Guide to Sentencing in South Africa.* Capetown: Butterworths.

Thomas, D. A. 1998. The Crime (Sentences) Act 1997. *Criminal Law Review* 83-90.

Tonry, M. 1996. *Sentencing Matters.* New York: Oxford University Press.

U.S. Sentencing Guidelines Commission. 2004. *Guidelines Manual. November 1, 2004 version. Available at www.ussc.gov/2004guid*

van Zyl Smit, D. 2002. *Taking Life Imprisonment Seriously in National and International Law.* The Hague: Kluwer.

Virginia Criminal Sentencing Commission. 2002. Annual Report. Available at www.vcsc.state.va.us.

von Hirsch, A. 1993. *Censure and Sanctions.* Oxford: Clarendon Press.

von Hirsch, A., and A. J. Ashworth. 1998. *Principled Sentencing: Readings on Theory and Policy,* 2nd ed. Oxford: Hart Publishing.

von Hirsch, A., A. Bottoms, E. Burney, and P.O. Wikstrom. 1999. *Criminal Deterrence and Sentence Severity.* Oxford: Hart Publishing.

Walker, N. 1991. *Why Punish?* Oxford: Oxford University Press.

Wasik, M., and A. von Hirsch. 1994. Section 29 revised: Previous convictions in sentencing. *Criminal Law Review* 409.

Appendix 17.A

Table A17.1 Sentencing Grid Used in the State of Minnesota

CRIMINAL HISTORY SCORE

SEVERITY LEVEL OF CONVICTION OFFENSE (Common offenses listed in italics)		0	1	2	3	4	5	6 or more
Murder, 2nd Degree *(intentional murder; drive-by-shootings)*	XI	306 299- 313	326 319- 333	346 339- 353	366 359- 373	386 379- 393	406 399- 413	426 419- 433
Murder, 3rd Degree *Murder, 2nd Degree* *(unintentional murder)*	X	150 144- 156	165 159- 171	180 174- 186	195 189- 201	210 204- 216	225 219- 231	240 234- 246
Criminal Sexual Conduct, *1st Degree[2]* *Assault, 1st Degree*	IX	86 81-91	98 93- 103	110 105- 115	122 117- 127	134 129- 139	146 141- 151	158 153- 163
Aggravated Robbery 1st Degree *Criminal Sexual Conduct,* *2nd Degree (c),(d),(e),(f),(h)[2]*	VIII	48 44-52	58 54-62	68 64-72	78 74-82	88 84-92	98 94- 102	108 104- 112
Felony DWI	VII	36	42	48	54 51-57	60 57-63	66 63-69	72 69-75
Criminal Sexual Conduct, *2nd Degree (a) & (b)*	VI	21	27	33	39 37-41	45 43-47	51 49-53	57 55-59
Residential Burglary *Simple Robbery*	V	18	23	28	33 31-35	38 36-40	43 41-45	48 46-50
Nonresidential Burglary	IV	12[1]	15	18	21	24 23-25	27 26-28	30 29-31
Theft Crimes (Over $2,500)	III	12[1]	13	15	17	19 18-20	21 20-22	23 22-24
Theft Crimes ($2,500 or less) Check *Forgery ($200-$2,500)*	II	12[1]	12[1]	13	15	17	19	21 20-22
Sale of Simulated *Controlled Substance*	I	12[1]	12[1]	12[1]	13	15	17	19 18-20

Presumptive commitment to state imprisonment. First Degree Murder is excluded from the guidelines by law and continues to have a mandatory life sentence. See section II.E. Mandatory Sentences for policy regarding those sentences controlled by law, including minimum periods of supervision for sex offenders released from prison.

Presumptive stayed sentence; at the discretion of the judge, up to a year in jail and/or other non-jail sanctions can be imposed as conditions of probation. However, certain offenses in this section of the grid always carry a presumptive commitment to state prison. These offenses include Third Degree Controlled Substance Crimes when the offender has a prior felony drug conviction, Burglary of an Occupied Dwelling when the offender has a prior felony burglary conviction, second and subsequent Criminal Sexual Conduct offenses and offenses carrying a mandatory minimum prison term due to the use of a dangerous weapon (e.g., Second Degree Assault). See sections II.C. Presumptive Sentence and II.E. Mandatory Sentences.

[1]   One year and one day

[2]   Pursuant to M.S. § 609.342, subd. 2 and 609.343, subd. 2, the presumptive sentence for Criminal Sexual Conduct in the First Degree is a minimum of 144 months and the presumptive sentence for Criminal Sexual Conduct in the Second Degree – clauses c, d, e, f, and h is a minimum of 90 months (see II.C. Presumptive Sentence and II.G. Convictions for Attempts, Conspiracies, and Other Sentence Modifiers).

Victims and Victimization

18

KEN PEASE

Contents

"A rose is a rose is a rose" (Stein 1922) is a profoundly unfortunate statement. (I have no idea what the poet meant by the phrase, except that the poem from which it is taken appears to be about human identity.) Translating it into "a Jew is a Jew is a Jew" or "a woman is a woman is a woman" makes its perniciousness clearer. Each individual rose is subtly unique in coloration, petal structure, fragrance, and the like. Each individual Jew is a person subtly unique in appearance, personality, and experience. All categorization, however necessary, diminishes those categorized. It evokes perceptions of within-category similarities and submersion of within-category differences, not least through the manipulation of the self-perception of those so categorized. The readiness with which categorization can be translated into hostility and conflict has been demonstrated in the classic studies of Muzafer and Carolyn Sherif, including their classic "Robber's Cave" demonstration of the creation and removal of conflict (Sherif and Sherif 1956), by the work of Henri Tajfel (1982), repeatedly by other scholars, and movingly by William Shakespeare in *The Merchant of Venice*, with Shylock's plea not to be regarded as a Jew, rather as a person: "I am a Jew. Hath not a Jew eyes? Hath not a Jew hands, organs, dimensions, senses, affections, passions? Fed with the same food, hurt with the same weapons, subject to the same diseases, healed by the same means, warmed and cooled by the same winter and summer, as a Christian is?" Unidimensional categorization is perhaps especially insidious when the dimension involves gender, religion, or ethnicity. If a woman is seen as nothing but a woman, a Muslim nothing but a Muslim, and a person of color nothing but a person of color, the consequences are foreseeable and regrettable. The significance of our failures to make within-category distinctions lies at the core of much social psychology, not least psycholinguistics, wherein the inability to see or the tendency to discount within category distinctions underpins much of social cognition (Steinberg 1982). Individual differences in the tendency to tolerate within-category variation, the "tolerance of ambiguity," was central to the psychological investigations of Fascism after World War II (Adorno et al. 1951; Rokeach 1960). The failure to recognize within-category variation ("All Xs look the same to me") was linked specifically with anti-Semitism and more generally with fascistic leanings. Impoverishment by categorization is greatest where the category has pejorative overtones.

18.1   Victim Status as Strait-Jacket

One kind of unidimensional categorization is as a victim. This is understandable because it defines the "script" for police officers attending an incident. Yet categorization as a victim is no less regrettable than others, although ostensibly more sympathetic to the person so categorized. It is itself perhaps a form of victimization, even when the victim seeks such an attribution by others or needs such an attribution to gain access to the resources of criminal justice. Victim is certainly a category with pejorative connotations. It is dignified (or further impoverished) by its own "-ology," victimology, as a subdiscipline of criminology, which focuses on a particular set of concerns. The existence of that discipline differentiates victims from more powerful actors in crime and justice. It is hardly an accident that there is no discipline known as judgeology, and that those branches of psychology that deal with the powerful have more allusive titles (occupational psychology, forensic psychology) than those that deal with the less powerful (child psychology, criminal psychology). In short, victimology, founded with the best of motives, outraged by the marginalized status of those suffering crime within the criminal justice process, turns out to be a mixed blessing for crime victims.

Recognizing that categorization as victim brings with it overtones of passivity and powerlessness, interest groups—particularly those concerned about offenses against women and the gendered associations of victimhood—have sought to replace the term with that of survivor. This form of categorization also has its downside. First, the term remains essentially passive. Second, it has application to only some crime types. Used more generally, it invites ridicule. It sounds ridiculous to be said to have survived events that are not life-threatening or seriously traumatizing. For example, can people who have repeatedly suffered criminal damage, unpleasant as that is, be said to be survivors? Although the word *survivor* seems wrong, the informing spirit that gave rise to it is both understandable and laudable. It is poetically enshrined in Hamlet's most famous soliloquy in which he contemplates suicide and muses whether it is "nobler in the mind to suffer the slings and arrows of outrageous fortune, or to take arms against a sea of troubles, and by opposing, end them."

The choice identified by Hamlet is central to the selection of a term appropriate to be applied to those who suffer harm through crime. The designation survivor is an attempt to move people from the first (suffering) to the second (opposing) but stops halfway, at enduring. The orientation towards one or other pole (suffering versus opposing) is one that the psychologist would couch in terms of locus of control. This is the expression used to describe how people vary in the extent to which they believe they can bend the world to their will (Ajzen 2002). Depression is seen to be linked to a primarily external locus of control. The attempt to redesignate the victim as survivor is in essence a linguistic attempt to move the locus of control of those suffering crime to become more internal. Survival is something one achieves by endurance; victimhood is something one passively suffers.

The nexus between victim status and locus of control is important enough to discuss a little more fully. A fictional but stunningly insightful presentation of that nexus is to be found in one of Saul Bellow's less well-regarded novels, *The Victim* (1947). In most contexts, internal locus of control (within the range dictate by realism) is valued. It leads to questioning of the unreasonable status quo and to innovation in problem-solving, and is perhaps the central characteristic of those who transform society. Criminal justice, the armed forces, and some religious forms are the obvious contexts in which internal locus of control is least valued. In the armed forces, orders must be obeyed without question, control of one's actions being temporarily given over to those in command. In authoritarian religious variants, deviation from prescribed action is sinful. In an analogous way, criminal law is by definition the area in which the regulation of relations between citizens is given over by the citizen to the state. In civil law, conflicts are played out with the state as adjudicator. The distinctiveness of criminal justice in this respect has led to the charge that criminal law involves the "theft" of conflicts between citizens (Christie 1977) and that the scope of the criminal law should therefore be as narrowly circumscribed as possible. The literature covering the variety of ways in which harms are dealt with in other cultures and at other times is fascinating and dispels any notions of the inexorability of any route to resolution of those conflicts that Westerners are accustomed to think of in terms of criminal victimization.

18.2   The Political Attractions of the Passive and Fearful

There are some advantages to those set in authority for crime victims to be induced into a mind-set where there is external locus of control, just as there are advantages to be had for military and religious leaders to have compliant followers. External locus of control makes for passivity. Passivity is inimical to vigilantism (Morrissey and Pease 1982), vengeance, and protest. At the time of writing, prominent in the news is the murder in a Belfast bar of Robert McCartney, apparently by members of the Provisional Irish Republican Army (PIRA). The murder was brutal and the aftermath callous, in that the bar was cleaned, CCTV tape removed, and threats issued to prevent the seventy or so people in the bar from reporting what they saw to the police. PIRA has had a long-standing policy (Morrissey and Pease 1982) of not cooperating with the official agencies of crime and justice in Northern Ireland (despite the radical reform of the police service, including a change of name from Royal Ulster Constabulary to Police Service of Northern Ireland, to make it acceptable to the nationalist community). PIRA's political wing, Sinn Fein, in its public pronouncements, has pointedly not enjoined those responsible for the McCartney murder to give themselves up to the police. In a bizarre twist, PIRA offered to shoot the murderers! The sisters and fiancée of the murdered man declined that warped substitute for due process (*Irish News* 2005; *Glasgow Herald* 2005).

The reason for dwelling at some length on the McCartney case is that it illustrates the raison d'être of the state interposing itself between a person needing redress and the perpetrators of crimes against them. In the West Belfast context, most of the people with guns belong to PIRA. The power balance between PIRA and the McCartney family is so heavily weighted in favor of the former that fairness could not prevail when one inflicts hurt on the other. If the stronger harms the weaker, the weaker is left without redress. If the weaker harms the stronger, a parodic unofficial version of justice is meted out. The McCartneys need a criminal justice system to take up the cudgels on their behalf. The Ulster situation illustrates what happens when that system is not generally perceived to be legitimate or relevant. Such situations are not uncommon, as the prevalence of blood feuds attests. We thus recognize a trade-off between, on the one hand, the desirability of people believing that their fate is in their own hands (making internal locus of control a good thing) and the fact that in an unfair world, people are often powerless against their persecutors and need the state to intervene.[1]

The McCartney case illustrates the dynamics of individual-community links particularly starkly because of the armed strength of the relevant para-military groups, but does have wider applicability, for example, to the power of gangs and extended families to impact upon victimized communities. A particularly insightful account of the defensive propaganda that paramilitary groups dispense, and the harrowing individual stories that underlie such propaganda, is provided by Kirwan Sarma (2003). In the testimony of the murdered Eamon Collins, the dimension of power as central is evident. The man soon to be murdered observed: "Threats, exile, car burnings, house burnings, mass intimidation of one man in a housing area where hundreds of families live. How can it be explained? How can it be justified? It is justified by stigmatizing, by stereotyping, by demonizing, by depersonalizing .... Victims elect have been demonized, the rest of the community anaesthetized .... Strip people of their status as mothers, fathers, brothers, children, and what you are left with is the non-person, and with it justification for arson, murder, expulsion. Will I suffer further violence?" (Sarma 2003: 206).

Sadly, despite his articulate and insightful declarations, he was killed, and his murderer never brought to trial. One fears that this will be an all-too-exact precursor of the McCartney events. Although state intervention via criminal justice is an unhappy necessity for individuals harmed by crime, as noted above, it can also serve the state's interests as an opiate of the people for a secular age, limiting the extent to which people are minded to take matters into their own hands. The vested interest of the state in inducing an external locus of control in relation to citizen victimization by crime is more subtly illustrated in the pre-eminence of fear as the "official" emotion to be experienced in relation to crime victimization. Latterly, the politics of fear has emerged as an issue of massive interest and controversy, wherein social control and the curtailment of civil liberties are justified by the appeal to the purpose of public protection, currently stimulated by fears of terrorism. In the conclusion of a monumental cultural history of fear, we read: "Fear is manipulated by numerous organizations with a stake in creating fear while promising to eradicate it. Fear circulates within a wealthy economy of powerful interest groups dependent upon ensuring that we remain scared. Theologians, politicians, the media, physicians, and the psychological services depend on our fright. Despite the proliferation of discourses about fear, its eradication has never been seriously countenanced: substitution of fear-inspiring discourses, rather than its obliteration, has been the goal" (Bourke 2005: 385–386).

Looking at the holdings of the Criminal Justice Library at Rutgers University in New Jersey, entering the keyword *fear* brings up 1,954 refer-

---

[1] By extension, it also reflects the need for international law and an international justice process for circumstances where the nation state is itself the persecutor.

ences. Entering the keyword *anger* brings up a mere 469. Little would one know from this imbalance that anger is more often expressed as the emotion experienced by crime victims, and by other citizens, than fear (Ditton et al. 1999).

> The major planks of the victim movement cast the victim as essentially passive. The charity formed to aid victims came to be known as 'Victim Support'. This has overtones of victim tendency to wilt which the alternative expression 'victim help' does not. ... Fear is a seemly reaction by the passive. Anger is not. Anger is inconsistent with the victim role. Why do we prefer to characterize those who suffer crime as passive? It is expedient so to do. The passive accept gratefully such support as is given and such compensation as the state is prepared, however tardily, to provide. The angry victim is liable to vigilantism, informal punishments of the locally troublesome, and is likely to get uppity in the face of the inefficiencies and absurdities of the criminal justice process. The fearful victim is mercifully compliant. Angry victims are the ultimate silent majority, those whose reaction is not documented or attended to in policy. It is difficult to overstate the consequences of the lack of attention given to the angry victim, and the celebration of the fearful crime victim. It is time to redress the balance (Ditton et al. 1999: 52).

Victim emotional response is complex. Crime is associated not with a specific symptom profile but rather with a pervasive elevation of symptoms across domains. The emotional impact of crime varies with pre-existing personal characteristics and with *perceived* more-than-official support after the victimization (Norris, Kaniasty, and Thompson 1997; Shaw 2001).

The relation between fear and external locus of control is a close one. Joanna Bourke's cultural history of fear detailed how the sense of being able to do something to change a situation diminishes fear (2005). She noted, for example, how fighter pilots experienced less fear than bomber crews, and how anti-aircraft batteries were allowed to keep firing even when their targets had moved out of range, in the recognition that to do so would reduce anxiety.

> Whether male or female, officer or private, the fear engendered by modern warfare was less likely to be linked to the multiple threats to survival than to the crippling anxiety arising out of the stripping away of individual agency. Increasingly, coping with fear

on the battlefield was linked to the ability of combatants to strike out and kill the enemy (Bourke 2005: 208).

18.3   Locus of Control, Victim Blame, and Realism

Bourke wrote at length about the role of fear of sexual assault in gender relations and, in the same vein, emphasizing the importance for peace of mind of fostering internal locus of control. However, there is a complication here. How does one foster internal locus of control without engaging in victim blame? Some categories of victim are already prone to blame themselves for what happened to them, victims of sexual assault being one poignant category of self-blamer. How can one square a healthy movement towards internal locus of control with the avoidance of victim blame? Does not the internal locus of control suggest that avoidance of victimization was in one's own power, implying that the offense *was* at least in part the victim's fault? Certainly many victims see it this way. Some 10.2 percent of victims responding to the 1996 British Crime Survey answered in the affirmative to the question: "Apart from the offenders, would you say you or anyone else were responsible in any way for what happened, because of something you did or forgot to do?" Three-quarters of those answering yes blamed themselves; 13 percent of those blaming themselves said they had provoked the offender. The proportion of victims of violence and sexual crime saying they had "provoked the offender" was around 8 percent. To eliminate victim self-blame would appear to constitute a considerable enterprise.

Victim blame is a corrosive and common phenomenon. In a meta-analysis (Whatley 1996) of forty-nine experimental studies conducted between 1973 and 1995, the degree of responsibility assigned by third-party observers to female rape victims varied with

- The revealingness of the victim's clothing
- Victim personality
- Acquaintance with the attacker

The apparent continued salience of extralegal factors in blame attribution in rape cases is also evident in research (Finch and Munro 2005). Victims of sexual assault who sought help from formal support services were commonly faced with victim blame, stigmatization, and the controlling reactions of others (Filipas and Ullman 2001). Perhaps a clue is to be gleaned from their linkage of victim blame with the controlling reactions of others (the opposite of internal locus of control). As Rebecca and Russell Dobash opined in respect of domestic violence: "The idea of provocation ... is both naïve and insidious

.... the idea of provocation is a very powerful tool used in justifying the husband's dominance and control" (1979: 168).

The uncomfortable (or liberating) reality is that in many cases, had crime victims behaved differently, their victimization would not have occurred. In many circumstances and contexts, it is outrageous to suggest that any disapproval should attach to their choices or they should have behaved otherwise than they did. People should wear what they feel happy in. They should not be required to submit in domestic arguments to avoid being assaulted. On the other hand, leaving the keys in a vehicle ignition is an action that may be later regretted, where that degree of self-blame is not a major threat to mental well-being. Attribution theory may, it is controversially claimed, help to clarify victim self-blame in the clinical and research literature on child sexual abuse (Dalenberg and Jacobs 1994). Other-blame is often presented as the preferable attributional outcome for abuse victims, while the empirical evidence is held by the writers concerned to be less than supportive of this claim. Important differences in definition of self- and other-blame across studies are noted, and it is suggested that further research examine the attributions more broadly, assess their accuracy, and allow for the possibility of evaluating interactional hypotheses. This is a brave argument, not least because the researchers concerned chose the most emotive form of victimization, child sexual abuse, on which to focus.

Essentially the same argument is cast more widely, and expressed less provocatively, by others (Davis, Taylor, and Titus 1997), who consider that victims can be regarded as "agents" in their own victimization in three ways: by enduring personal characteristics that make them an attractive target, by virtue of the choices they make about places and company they choose, and by how they respond to the behavior of would-be perpetrators. Yet others go further by referring to the victim role in personal fraud in terms of cooperation and concluding that some victims exhibit "considerable cooperation" (Titus and Gover 2001), of types that can be paraphrased as follows:

- The victim either makes or facilitates the initial contact with the offender.
- The victim provides information about him- or herself that aids offenders in the crime.
- The victim allows the offender to convert what should be a business relationship into a personal relationship.
- The victim allows the offender to create a version of events that, when believed, enables fraud.
- The victim writes checks or gives personal details that enable the offender to access victim funds.

These elements have particular resonance in the years since they were written in reflecting common elements in fraud via the Internet.

One answer to the charge of colluding in victim blame is as follows:

"Surprisingly, rather than leading to denigration of victims, the view of the victim as an integral part of criminal incidents is proving to have significant benefits for victims. By understanding how their behavior or characteristics make them vulnerable, people can begin to shift the odds more in their favor" (Davis, Taylor, and Titus 1997: 169).

In the foregoing part of the chapter, the downside of categorization as crime victim was discussed at length. It masks differences among the experiences of those who suffer crime, it has overtones of passivity, and it invites simplistic notions of the interactions between perpetrators and victims. Nonetheless, the term *crime victim*, with some diffidence, has to be accepted as reflecting both common usage and the reality of the currently passive role which the crime victim typically occupies. The rationale for the content and structure of the remainder of this chapter is, however, that any crime event should trigger a process in which the victim is active, both in preventing the recurrence of crime against the self, intimates, colleagues, neighbors, or unknown others, and as an actor in the forums of criminal justice. Both because the victim will usually have the opportunity to be involved in the first, and only rarely to be involved in the second, the emphasis will be placed on the first. This will give the chapter a different focus from that usually given to reviews of the victim literature (Zedner 2002).

18.4   The Concentration of Victimization

Perhaps the most striking fact about crime victimization is how unevenly it is distributed across the "eligible" population. This will not be surprising to those with experience of schools, dysfunctional families, or abusive relationships where assault, verbal bullying, and intimidation are focused upon the same individual, often remorselessly. Looking beyond these well-understood special (and massively important) cases to volume crime generally, it is the case that in industrialized countries, crime victimization surveys find an average of 40 percent of crimes to have been committed against individuals and households are repeats against targets already victimized that year (Farrell and Bouloukos 2001). In one year:

- 16 percent of the U.K. population experience property crime but 2 percent of the population experience 41 percent of property crime.
- 8 percent of the U.K. population experience personal crime, but 1 percent of the population experience 59 percent of personal crime (Pease 1998).

With variation by crime type, time, and place, repeat victimization contributed disproportionately to all types of crimes adequately studied to date. A study by Soumyo Moitra and Suresh Konda, investigating network attacks on computer systems, demonstrated extensive repeat victimization (2004). The International Crime Victims Survey (ICVS) showed that:

- Patterns of repeat victimization are remarkably similar in the seventeen Western industrialized countries that were studied.
- Repeated sexual incidents against women are typically the crimes most likely to be repeated, with close to half of all incidents being repeats against the same women.
- Rates of repeat personal crimes were generally higher than those of repeat property crime. Rates of repeat "assault and theft" and robbery were particularly high.
- The ICVS findings on repeat victimization are remarkably consistent for survey sweeps covering more than a decade.

From the mid-1990s, there was a substantial increase in the number of studies examining repeat victimization. By the start of 2005, they numbered in the hundreds and documented the extent of repeat victimization for various crime types, using various methods and in many countries and contexts. It is clear from personal and vicarious experience, even if it were not intuitively obvious, that concentrated victimization is a feature of domestic violence, racial attacks, and bullying. However, concentration has been demonstrated for many types of crime and disorder. Property crimes include:

- Bank robbery
- Commercial burglary
- Computer network hacking
- Computer theft
- Credit card fraud
- Criminal damage and vandalism
- Fraud and other white-collar crimes
- Graffiti
- Property crime against schools
- Residential burglary
- Shoplifting
- Theft of and from vehicles
- Computer network attacks

Personal or violent crimes and disorder where extensive repeat victimization has been shown to date include:

- Common assault
- Domestic violence
- Elder abuse
- Neighbor disputes
- Robbery of shops and stores (commercial)
- Sexual victimization (including rape and other physical, verbal, and visual sexual victimizations)
- Serious assault
- Stalking
- Child abuse (physical, sexual, and emotional, including neglect as a repeated or ongoing crime of omission)
- Street robbery (including muggings, stick-ups, robbery at cash machines)
- Threats of violence (Farrell 2005b)

The list of crime types above is not exhaustive, but demonstrates some crime types where the prevention of repetition involves the prevention of all offending of the type. When contrasted with current evaluated practices discussed further below, it quickly becomes apparent that efforts to prevent repeat victimization are in their infancy. The theme underpinning this chapter is that the prevention of further offenses against the same and related targets is the best service that can be afforded to a crime victim, and that the involvement of the victim in that process is empowering. With this orientation, the crime event should be the starting point for remedial action, not a process of wrapping up an event by desultory police attendance and recording. Relatively few crime types have been tackled by prevention efforts (and when they have, they have seldom been evaluated, still less often adequately), but enough evidence exists that repetition can be reduced by postcrime action. If that were not the case, then internal locus of control is a myth and a delusion.

The significance of repeat victimization becomes ever clearer in relation to new and different types of crime as they come to be studied. Facts about repeat victimization other than the most obvious one, its apparent ubiquity, make it a good starting point of an attractive strategy for change in both individual and a real crime risk, the detection of prolific offenders and victim empowerment. These include the following:

- Second and subsequent victimizations against the same targets tend to occur quickly after the preceding one. The pattern is consistent across crime types, including those like bank robbery, where this is counterintuitive (Matthews, Pease, and Pease 2001).
- Rates of repeat victimization are disproportionately higher in high-crime areas for the relevant types of property and personal crime,

suggesting that crime-proneness is intimately linked to concentration at the individual household level.

- Repeat victimization often underlies, or disproportionately contributes to, geographical hot spots of crime.
- The same offenders are more likely to commit repeat victimization (after learning that a target is suitable for further crime). This means that the prevention of repeat victimization meshes with the detection of repeat offenders.
- The rate of repeat victimization varies by crime type and context, but high rates are typically found for personal crimes including domestic violence, sexual victimization, racial attacks, bullying, shoplifting, and assaults and threats.
- Among property crimes, high rates of repeat victimization are often found in crimes against businesses including commercial burglary, robbery, and shop theft.
- Rates of repeat victimization are generally higher for personal crime than property crime.
- When a house is burgled, nearby neighbors experience a heightened risk. The risk declines with time and distance from the crime site. This is crucially important in that the individual crime event provides an opportunity for action that extends beyond the individual crime victim.

The last point speaks to an issue not addressed in this chapter, but which must be alluded to, namely the notion of vicarious and secondary victimization. The effects of a crime event are not limited to those directly suffering it. They extend to those distressed by dealing with it or hearing about it (and the more intrinsically distressing a crime, the more people will get to hear about it), those who will have to pay for its consequence (through taxation payment for emergency and court services, and elevated insurance premiums), and opportunities forgone by having to make those payments. Discussions of secondary and vicarious victimization are available (Shichor 1989; Schneider 2001; Kenney 2002; Orth 2002). The reason for not going down this route in this chapter is that the least contentious means of addressing secondary and vicarious victimization is by reducing primary victimization. Trying to limit secondary victimization per se will be possible only by the manipulation of emergency and court services to primary victims, or by limiting media freedoms to report.

For the same reasons, the writer is hostile to fear-reduction programs. The emphasis will remain on direct victimization. That said, there is a wider political and cultural agenda to which secondary victimization is central. Seeking to change (for example) gender relations so that victims of sexual offenses do not suffer humiliation on the basis of rape myths is valuable in its own right. The role of anticipated victimization by terrorist crime, induced by governments for the purpose of social control, is one of the fundamental motifs of political debate in the early twentieth century. The position of crime victims, the designated topic of this chapter, is important. However, the way in which the threat of victimization by organized others is coming to hold citizens in thrall, and justify enhanced state powers, is fundamental.

All of the points made above about the concentration of direct victimization can inform decisions about where, when, and how to allocate crime prevention resources, and crucially how to foster internal locus of control among crime victims, whether individuals or communities. Attempting to use the crime event as a stimulus to action is the central informing principle. Several projects aiming to prevent repeat victimization have been evaluated. Some have proven more effective than others. Practical lessons have been learned. Of particular importance are those lessons relating to implementation. These include the following:

- Even if it is clear where and when preventive resources should be put in place, developing preventive tactics can still be difficult for many types of crime.
- Where well-tried prevention tactics exist, victims can be difficult to contact, and many do not want or have the means to adopt preventive measures. Reasons for this include alienation from the police and the power of insurance to leave those who have had property stolen in a materially better position than before.

It currently seems unarguable that the best predictor of crime victimization is crime victimization. If that is so, the task is of mobilizing victim motivation to prevent repetition, often in the face of severe obstacles. This would be aided by an understanding of why repeats occur. There are two general classes of explanation, referred to as event dependence and risk heterogeneity in the criminological literature, and colloquially (and here) as flag and boost accounts, respectively.

Flag accounts imply that targets have stable chances of victimization attributable to their enduring characteristics. To take an obvious example, the World Trade Center was repeatedly victimized because it was talismanic of U.S. economic power, as was the Pentagon (which remains a symbol of U.S. military power). On a more mundane level, fuel filling stations will reliably hold nontrivial amounts of cash and tobacco, and jewelers of jewelry. These stable attributes make and maintain them as attractive crime targets. *Boost* accounts contend that circumstances of a first attempt make repetition more likely, be it shocked passivity by the victim of domestic violence, fuller awareness of vulnerability, or knowledge that stolen goods will be replaced by more valuable new goods. Boring and obvious as the conclusion might seem, all but one of the relevant research studies suggest that both boost and flag accounts contribute materially to the phenomena of repeat victimization (Lauritsen and Davis-Quinet 1995; Osborn and Tseloni 1998; Wittebrood and Nieuwbeerta 2000; Tseloni and Pease 2003). These more conventional quantitative analyses are bedeviled by the fact that one cannot measure everything about a person or place, so that "unmeasured heterogeneity," that is, the existence of enduring differences that haven't been measured, makes conclusions difficult. Perhaps the most persuasive evidence that boost accounts cannot be overlooked comes from interviews with offenders (Ashton et al. 1998). The "slipperiness" of hot spots shown by the work of Shane Johnson and Kate Bowers (2004; discussed below) also argues for boost effects.

To rehearse the evidence, we know that crime is concentrated on particular victims, and that crime risk moves out from those already victimized to those living nearby or sharing attributes that make them vulnerable. We can be confident that the reason for this comprises both enduring differences (flags) and experience gained by offenders making similar actions likely (boost). All these things should be incorporated in prudent victim help and empowerment. The unit of count, that is, what is a victim, arguably should be that which works best to promote crime prevention. So, whether repeats are counted as occurring against, say, the owner or the vehicle (if it changes ownership) or the household or its occupants (if they relocate) should be determined by what best serves prevention of future crime.

Lest this sound vague, an example may be taken from an interview with a versatile burglar (Ashton et al. 1998). One of his activities was the burglary of gas stations. He noticed that one supplier, with outlets across the United Kingdom, had standard floor layouts and security features across the country. Thus wherever he found himself, he could find somewhere to burgle that was familiar to him, familiarity being the central attraction to the offender of repetition against the same target. Such events have come to be known as virtual repeats, that is, instances where targets are selected because offenders have already offended against similar or identical targets. For example, the same make and model of car offers similar prospects to offenders whatever the particular lump of metal to which it refers. If the car is parked in a similar location or situation, the virtual-repeat is all the more identical. Households with the same layout are prone to virtual repeats because, for the offender, there is a good chance that the same type of effort and skills are needed, and the risks and rewards are similar to those of the previous target. The four planes downed by terrorist action in the United States on September 11, 2001, are perhaps the most dramatic possible instance of virtual repeats. These virtual-repeats provide a useful angle for thinking about how one thinks about the crime victim, and what kinds of collaboration between victims and actions by the police on their behalf are most likely to result in reduced crime.

As noted earlier, the theme of this chapter is the involvement of victim agency after the crime event to mobilize action. Because some repeat crimes against the same person or household are different, and because, at least as far as burglary is concerned (and probably in respect of other offenses), risk "leaks" to nearby times and places, generating crime spates, meaning that crime reductive action should extend beyond the immediate victim. The term "near-repeat" was coined (obviously) to refer to the victimization of spatially and temporally close targets (Townsley, Homel, and Chaseling 2003; Johnson and Bowers 2004; Johnson, Bowers, and Pease 2004; Bowers, Johnson, and Pease 2004). The increased risk declines with distance from the initial target. Burglaries are "infectious"; that is, they can spread like a disease across an area, and interestingly their statistical analysis came from epidemiology. Infectious risk is greatest in areas with uniformly similar housing type and layout, with higher repeat rates in areas of more diverse housing type. The likely explanation is that many offenders prefer easy pickings, that is, more familiar targets where they have better knowledge of likely risk, effort, and rewards. Where housing type varies, the safe option is to go back to the home already burgled. Where one house is much like another, nearby homes are virtual repeats in the sense set out above. Shane Johnson and Kate Bowers (2004) invoked the ecological concept of the optimal forager, whereby just as (for example) a grazing animal minimizes effort while maximizing nutrition, so a burglar maximizes profit in relation to effort.

If the hand that helps is indeed holier than the voice that sympathizes, the existence of crime spates affords the prospect of help beyond the immediate victim to others at elevated risk. Although the same basic patterns are being established in relation to other crime types, the evidence and its implications are furthest advanced with respect to domestic burglary, and it is that work which will be discussed below. The key insight is that, whereas some areas have enduringly higher rates of crime than others, hot spots are surprisingly slippery, with crime spates meaning that deployment of resources according to rates of crime measured over long periods of time is going to be suboptimal when one looks at the immediate future (any immediate future). The smart way of thinking about this is to decide how events of the past are best combined to predict the future. Johnson and Bowers, thinking along these lines, have developed "prospective hot spotting," which utilizes near-repeats as the trigger for area-based preventive interventions. They demonstrated that "the risk of burglary is communicable, with properties within 400 meters of a burgled household being at a significantly elevated risk of victimization for up to two months after an initial event" (Johnson, Bowers, and Pease 2004: 641).

Prospective hot spotting can substantially increase the predictability of future crime compared to traditional hot spotting. In the popular press, the comparison was made between these crime analysis efforts and the futuristic prediction/prevention effort of a Hollywood blockbuster: "Every police force in the country has been ordered to develop hi-tech crime maps—as seen in the sci-fi blockbuster film *Minority Report*—to predict future offending .... In *Minority Report*, starring Tom Cruise, criminals are caught before the crimes they commit" (Roberts 2005).

Prospective hot spotting presents fewer ethical problems than its fictional counterpart and is consistent with the emphasis on the quest for internal locus of control among those victimized. Kate Bowers and Shane Johnson are currently examining the *modus operandi* of near-repeats to find similarities, suggesting they are committed by the same offenders.

Apart from obvious advantages of concentrating on those already victimized set out above, there are others, both tactical and principled. The first is equity. Western European countries in particular seek to limit the degree of misery that their citizens should endure by way of illness and poverty by providing a safety net of health care and welfare benefits. If the distribution of misery through crime victimization is likewise skewed, similar safety net logic should arguably prevail. Indeed, the historical separation of crime prevention and victim support can be seen to represent a notable failure to distribute help equitably (Farrell and Pease 1997).

Apart from reasons of principle, the prevention of repeats and near-repeats has tactical advantages. These include the following (Farrell 2001, 2005b):

- Preventing repeat victimization is apparently less likely to result in displacement than unfocused crime prevention efforts.
- Preventing repeat victimization is a form of "drip feeding" of prevention resources. Because all crime does not occur at once, police resources need only be allocated as victimizations occur from day to day.
- Preventing repeat victimization presents possibilities for preventing and detecting organized crime and terrorism that focuses on vulnerable and rewarding victims and targets—including protection rackets, forced prostitution, loan-sharking, repeat trafficking via certain low-risk locations, art and other high-value thefts and robberies, and terrorist bombings.
- Preventing repeat victimization can generate common goals and positive work between police and other agencies (such as housing, social services, and victim organizations), which may in turn facilitate broader cooperation.

- Focusing on repeat victimization empowers police officers to do something tangible and constructive to help crime victims and for policing to become more generally oriented towards victims, who are arguably its core consumers.
- Preventing repeat victimization is triggered by a crime being reported. Because victims can be asked about prior victimizations, a response does not necessarily require data analysis.

A review of evaluated efforts to prevent repeat residential burglary produced findings that are likely to apply to other types of crime (Farrell 2005b). The details of the review will not be given here. The evaluated projects were not all successful in reducing crime. Depending on how a "project evaluation" is defined, between half and two-thirds of the projects were assessed to have prevented burglary. Graham Farrell (2005b) carefully drew out the lessons to be learned. To paraphrase, he concluded that what works to prevent repeat victimization is the following:

1. *A strong preventive mechanism.* Specific prevention tactics need to be tailored to the context and household because the nature of residential burglary varies from one place to the next.
2. *Multiple tactics.* The currently available evidence suggests multiple tactics working together can produce a synergistic effect. Although there is little conclusive evidence regarding the effectiveness of particular tactics, opportunity-blocking security aimed at preventing repeat residential burglary by the same *modus operandi* seems the most likely candidate for effectiveness.
3. *Strong implementation.* Some prevention efforts failed because the preventive mechanism was not introduced.
4. *A focus on high-crime- and high-burglary-rate situations.* Those times and places where rates of repeat burglary rates are highest are the most appropriate focus for prevention efforts.

Although in most work, the prevention effort has centered on domestic burglary, efforts in which repeat victimization concepts have been central deal with commercial burglary (Tilley 1993; Taylor 1999; Bowers 2001), domestic violence (Farrell and Buckley 1999; Hanmer, Griffiths, and Jerwood 1999), family violence (Davis and Taylor 1997), elder abuse (Davis and Medina-Ariza 2001), and sexual victimization (Breitenbecher, Hanson, and Gidycz 1998). In some other work, the prevention of repeats has formed one element among others, or the tactic of preventing repeats is presented in other terms. For example, seeking to prevent domestic violence by arresting the perpetrator is essentially a single-tactic approach to the prevention of repetition (Sherman and Berk 1984; Sherman 1992). Because it is a single-tactic approach, it would be regarded by Graham Farrell as unlikely to succeed.[2]

There are a number of conditions that seem necessary for a successful (and successfully evaluated) enterprise seeking to reduce crime through the prevention of repeat attacks against the same target. These include the following:

- *The availability of defensible measures of repeat victimization*: Current police systems and practice do not always accurately represent the extent of repeat victimization. Paradoxically, during projects to reduce repeats, repetition comes to be salient to practitioners, leading them to record such events more assiduously, and leading to an illusory increase in the extent of repeat victimization. Where repeat victimization is poorly measured or increasingly well measured over the course of a project, an evaluation will not be precise enough to detect change. Some successful prevention efforts go without recognition because of measurement error. Victimization surveys are more likely to elicit more accurate measures of repeat victimization than recorded crime data and should be the measurement tool of choice where feasible. They are too expensive to be routine.[3]
- *A repertoire of tactics commensurate with the problem*: The existing repertoire to prevent many types of personal crime appears relatively limited relative to property crime and in particular burglary.
- *Implementation:* Antipathy to the police, antipathy of the police to victim-focused prevention, lack of coordination between preventing agencies, lack of resources to take preventive action, feelings of impotence, lack of clarity in what preventive action to take, and insurance-driven indifference to loss may all contribute to implementation failure. Given that many well-organized people and households will take preventive action without any external inducement, the burden of repeat victimization will disproportionately fall on the most vul-

[2] The reader impatient with the emphasis on repeat victimization and its prevention is referred to Farrell and Buckley (1999) for the clearest possible demonstration of the centrality of concentration of victimization to both the practice and evaluation of domestic violence reduction. To oversimplify, they demonstrated that a successful initiative involved no change in the number of calls for service but an increase in first-time callers and a reduction of repeat callers as word of the quality of the service got round, inducing victims who had hitherto not sought help to begin to do so.

[3] A particularly important instance of the measurement problem is manifest in the U.S. National Crime Victimization Survey (NCVS). The NCVS systematically undercounts repeat victimization, with the result that the national crime rate in the United States is significantly misrepresented.

nerable. A survey of U.K. police forces in 2000 found that, although all of them had written policies to prevent repeat victimization, there was relatively little evidence of thorough implementation of prevention efforts. Some crime prevention officers who responded to the survey appeared unable to distinguish tactics to prevent repeat victimization from more general crime prevention tactics (Farrell et al. 2000). One little-documented problem concerns police attitudes, which sometimes tend to label residents of areas as generally undeserving, so that victimization of residents of particular areas is a matter for wry humor rather than sympathy. Further, in many projects, officers are reluctant to extend the same support to those believed to be active criminals as to others.

- *Sustainability:* Many crime prevention evaluations or development projects receive funding from local or central government. The funding is typically for a fixed period of time in which the crime prevention effort is developed, implemented, and evaluated. The usual scenario is that funding then ceases, which, in turn, means that prevention efforts cease. More subtly, a crime reduction program has a champion (for example, a local police chief) whose movement onwards and upwards makes way for a replacement, usually strong-minded, who wants to implement his or her own cherished initiatives. A necessary (but not sufficient) condition for sustainability is the perception of the crime event as the starting point for coordinated action rather than (after the necessary paperwork is completed) the end-point of action. This involves a fundamental reorientation of traditional conceptions of policing.

Crime control and victim support policy and strategies are beginning to reflect the concentration of crime however considered—hot spots, prolific offenders, repeat victims, and "hot" products. Repeat offenders are the target of focused detection, special sentencing considerations, in-prison behavioral and other treatments regimes, and intensive probationary supervision. Hot products are gradually achieving attention from product designers as well as from legislators who realize that crime-free product design may pre-empt much crime. Hot spots draw police and other resources. The repeatedly victimized receive postvictimization advice and assistance. Which of these various strategies is the most cost-effective is probably not a question that should be asked, because the appropriate strategy should involve them all. Just as drug cocktails are often more effective than individual treatments, so multiple-stranded interventions may be preferable in the prevention of repeat crime. Certainly it would be bizarre if criminogenic products and services proliferated alongside programs to target the detection of the prolific offender. Specific strategies or combinations of strategies will be more appropriate at particular times and locations and must evolve and adapt to meet the constantly changing shape of crime.

18.5   The Victim and Criminal Justice

Although the bulk of this chapter has been given over to victims attempting to secure the prevention of repeat crime against the same target, some crimes are detected, so a modest account of victim involvement postdetection is necessary. When a perpetrator is found, what role should the victim play in the criminal justice process? One strand, the compensation of victims for harm caused, is now in principle uncontentious though complex in application. The second deals with the incorporation of victim concerns in the enforcement of law and administration of justice. The literature shows how services for crime victims have developed over the last three decades (Kelly and Erez 1997; Lurgio, Skogan, and Davis 1990ed), and how much of that can be credited to unfunded grassroots movements concerned primarily with violence against women (Friedman and Tucker 1997). There remains much cause for unease about the experiences that victims continue to have, although matters have improved. The failure to notify victims of the progress of cases (even when there is no progress to report), their vulnerability to witness intimidation, the failure to separate victims from other witnesses (including defense witnesses) in court waiting arrangements, the presumption that witness time is not valuable and that victims' lives can be reorganized at short notice to give priority to court requirements (and frequent lengthy waits when the court's needs are accommodated), the paucity of support services for victims, their preparation for the hostile questioning that is part of an adversarial process, the feelings of hurt and rejection that follow an acquittal (with the implicit suggestion that the victim was lying), or a sentence that seems derisory and makes the victim vulnerable to repeats through the imminent freedom of the perpetrator. Even the language is often insensitive. In England and Wales, cases may be discontinued by the Crown Prosecution Service for two primary reasons—evidentiary insufficiency and "in the interests of justice." For victims willing to testify, the first reason is demeaning. The second is tantamount to saying that the victim's experience did not matter enough for the state to become involved.

In the court setting, the victim impact statement (VIS) is the most usual form in which victim involvement is secured, with victim-offender reconciliation programs and their close relation restorative justice also having their champions. The most obvious reason for some involvement is that of fairness, which may be thought to require that injured parties should have a voice

(Sumner 1987), and that if they do not, the state has stolen their conflict. The realities of criminal justice process mean that such involvement comes at a price. These include the following:

- Variable victim involvement and variable verbal facility among victims introduce a source of unwarranted variation in sentencing (Grabosky 1987).
- Legal precept is that unforeseen consequences should not play a part in sentencing. If victim impact statements to the court reveal personal vulnerabilities (for example, a thin skull or hemophilia) that make the consequences of assault more severe, unfairness to the defendant follows (Ashworth 1993).
- Victim involvement creates expectations that, if unrealized, would amount to secondary victimization. If the court, having heard a victim account, proceeds to a sentence that seems lenient, the victim will feel that the court has placed a low price on his or her distress (Fattah 1986).

For some, the compensation for hurt, and the humane treatment of victims, does not exhaust the victim agenda. The recasting of justice as restorative, or in terms of reintegrative shaming, has latterly been in vogue (Braithwaite 1989, 1999; Umbreit 2001). Taking much of its inspiration from practices among the indigenous peoples of Australasia, it sits uneasily with a criminal justice system that is focused upon culpability as well as harm. Put oversimply, in the writer's view there is more in the practice of restorative justice for the perpetrator than for the victim, and the dangers of railroading well-intentioned and kindly victims into a process that is primarily for the benefit of the offender may, particularly in unskilled hands, become a form of secondary victimization. The empirical research on the topic shows mixed results, with strong stories of reconciliation in short supply (Daly 2002).

18.6   Conclusion

In brief, the argument of this chapter has been that stimulating into existence a realistic degree of internal locus of control among victims should be at the core of victim programs. This should be focused upon the prevention of repeated crimes against the prior victim or those linked to that victim by location or vulnerability. This emphasis requires a diminution of stress on the avoidance of victim blame. Victims sometimes recognize their contribution to crime events, and it serves internal locus of control that this should be so in certain circumstances (and emphatically not in others). The progress towards practical victim help and support in a criminal justice environment that is largely hostile to them must continue. The involvement of victims in schemes of restorative justice will require more and more persuasive evidence of benefit to be safely advocated.

References

Adorno, T. W., E. Frenkel-Brunswik, D. J. Levinson, and R. N. Sanford. 1951. *The Authoritarian Personality.* New York: Harper.

Ajzen, I. 2002. Perceived behavioural control, self-efficacy, locus of control, and the theory of planned behaviour. *Journal of Applied Social Psychology* 32, 665-683.

Ashton, J., et al. 1998. Repeat victimisation: Offender accounts. *International Journal of Risk, Security and Crime Prevention* 3, 269-280.

Ashworth, A. 1993. Victim impact statements and sentencing. *Criminal Law Review* 517-567.

Bellow, S. 1947. *The Victim.* New York: Vanguard.

Bourke, J. 2005. *Fear: A Cultural History.* London: Virago.

Bowers, K. 2001. Small business crime: The evaluation of a crime prevention initiative. *Crime Prevention and Community Safety: An International Journal* 3, 23-42.

Bowers, K., S. Johnson, and K. Pease. 2004. Prospective hot-spotting: The future of crime mapping? *British Journal of Criminology* 44, 641-658.

Braithwaite, J. 1989. *Crime, Shame and Reintegration.* Cambridge: Cambridge University Press.

Braithwaite, J. 1999. Restorative justice: assessing optimistic and pessimistic accounts. In *Crime and Justice 25*, ed. M. Tonry. Chicago: University of Chicago Press.

Breitenbecher, K., J. Hanson, and C. A. Gidycz. 1998. An empirical evaluation of a program designed to reduce the risk of multiple sexual victimization. *Journal of Interpersonal Violence* 13, 472-488.

Christie, N. 1977. Conflicts as property. *British Journal of Criminology* 17, 1-15.

Dalenberg, C. J., and D. A. Jacobs. 1994. Attributional analyses of child sexual abuse episodes: Empirical and clinical issues. *Journal of Child Sexual Abuse* 3, 37-50.

Daly, K. 2002. Restorative justice: The real story. *Punishment and Society* 4, 55-79.

Davis, R. C., and J. Medina-Ariza. 2001. Results from an elder abuse prevention experiment in New York City. *Research In Brief.* Washington, DC: National Institute of Justice.

Davis, R. C., and B. G. Taylor. 1997. A proactive response to family violence: The results of a randomized experiment. *Criminology* 35, 307-333.

Davis, R. C., B. G. Taylor, and R. M. Titus. 1997. Victims as agents: Implications for victim services and crime prevention. In *Victims of Crime*, 2nd ed., ed. R. C. Davis, A. J. Lurigio, and W. G. Skogan. London: Sage.

Ditton, J., S. Farrell, J. Bannister, E. Gilchrist, and K. Pease. 1999. Reactions to victimisation: Why has anger been ignored? *Crime Prevention and Community Safety: An International Journal* 1, 37-53.

Dobash, R. E., and R. Dobash. 1979. *Violence Against Wives.* New York: Free Press.

Farrell, G. 2001. How victim-oriented is policing? In *Tenth International Symposium on Victimology: Selected Symposium Proceedings*, ed. A. Gaudreault and I. Waller. Tenth International Symposium on Victimology, Montreal.

Farrell, G. 2005a. Preventing repeat residential burglary. In *Preventing Crime: What Works for Children, Offenders, Victims, and Places*, ed. B. C. Welsh and D. P. Farrington. London: Wadsworth Press.

Farrell, G. 2005b. Progress and prospects in the prevention of repeat victimization. In *Handbook of Crime Prevention and Community Safety*, ed. N. Tilley. Cullompton, U.K.: Willan.

Farrell, G., and A. C. Bouloukos. 2001. A cross-national comparative analysis of rates of repeat victimization. In *Repeat Victimization*, ed. G. Farrell and K. Pease. Monsey, NY: Criminal Justice Press.

Farrell, G., and A. Buckley. 1999. Evaluation of a U.K. police domestic violence unit using repeat victimization as a performance indicator. *The Howard Journal* 38, 42-53.

Farrell, G., and K. Pease. 1997. Repeat victim support. *British Journal of Social Work* 27, 103-113.

Farrell, G., et al. 2000. RV Snapshot: U.K. Policing and Repeat Victimization. Crime Reduction Research Series. Policing and Reducing Crime Unit Paper 5. London: Home Office.

Fattah, E. A., ed. 1986. *From Crime Policy to Victim Policy.* New York: Macmillan.

Filipas, H. H., and S. E. Ullman. 2001. Social reactions to sexual assault victims from various support services. *Violence and Victims* 16, 673-692.

Finch, E., and V. E. Munro. 2005. Juror stereotypes and blame attribution in rape cases involving intoxicants. *British Journal of Criminology* 45, 25-38.

Friedman, L. N., and S. B. Tucker. 2005. Violence prevention through victim assistance. In *Victims of Crime*, 2nd ed., ed. R. C. Davis, A. J. Lurigio, and W. Skogan. London: Sage.

Glasgow Herald. 2005. March 12, 12.

Grabosky, P. N. 1987. Victims. In *The Criminal Injustice System*, ed. J. Bastan et al. Sydney: Australia Press.

Hanmer, J., S. Griffiths, and D. Jerwood. 1999. *Arresting evidence: Domestic violence and repeat victimization.* Police Research Series Paper 104. London: Home Office.

Irish News. 2005. March 14, 8.

Johnson, S., and K. Bowers. 2004. The burglary as a clue to the future: The beginnings of prospective hot-spotting. *The European Journal of Criminology* 1, 237-255.

Johnson, S., K. Bowers, and K. Pease. 2004. Predicting the future or summarising the past? Crime mapping as anticipation. In *Launching Crime Science*, ed. M. Smith and N. Tilley. Cullompton, U.K.: Willan.

Kelly, D. P., and E. Erez. 1997. Victim participation in the criminal justice system. In *Victims of Crime*, 2nd ed., ed. R. C. Davis, A. J. Lurigio, and W. G. Skogan. London: Sage.

Kenney, J. S. 2002. Victims of crime and labelling theory: A parallel process? *Deviant Behaviour* 23, 235-265.

Lauritsen, J. L., and K. F. Davis-Quinet. 1995. Repeat victimisation among adolescents and young adults. *Journal of Quantitative Criminology* 11, 143-66.

Lurigio, A. J., W. G. Skogan, and R. C. Davis. 1990. *Victims of Crime: Problems, Policies and Programmes.* London: Sage.

Matthews, R., C. Pease, and K. Pease. 2001. Repeat victimisation of banks, building societies, betting shops, and jewelers: Theme and variations. In *Repeat Victimisation*, ed. G. Farrell and K. Pease. Monsey, NY: Criminal Justice Press.

Moitra, S. D., and S. L. Konda. 2004. An empirical investigation of network attacks on computer systems. *Computers and Security* 23, 43-51.

Morrissey, M., and K. Pease. 1982. The Black criminal justice system of West Belfast. *Howard Journal of Criminal Justice* 21, 133-136.

Norris, F. W., K. Kaniasty, and M. P. Thompson. 1997. The psychological consequences of crime: Findings from a longitudinal population-based study. In *Victims of Crime*, 2nd ed., ed. R. C. Davis, A. J. Lurigio, and W. G. Skogan. London: Sage.

Orth, U. 2002. Secondary victimization of crime victims by criminal proceedings. *Social Justice Research* 15, 313-325.

Osborn, D. R., and A. Tseloni. 1998. The distribution of household property crimes. *Journal of Quantitative Criminology* 14, 307-330.

Pease, K. 1998. Repeat victimisation: Taking stock. Crime Detection and Prevention Series Paper 90. London: Home Office.

Roberts, B. 2005. Computer maps "will beat crime." *Daily Mirror*, 12 February 2005. Available at http://www.mirror.co.uk/news/allnews/page.cfm?objectid=15129313andmethod=fullandsiteid=50143, accessed 15 February 2005.

Rokeach, M. 1960. *The Open and Closed Mind.* New York: Basic Books.

Sarma, K. 2003. Terrorist propaganda: The republican movement's use of propaganda in justifying attacks against their supportive community and discrediting their internal critics. Unpublished PhD thesis, University College, Cork, Ireland.

Schneider, H-J. 2001. Victimological developments in the world during the past 3 decades: A study of comparative victimology—Part 2. *International Journal of Offender Therapy and Comparative Criminology* 45, 539-555.

Shaw, M. 2001. Time Heals All Wounds? In *Repeat Victimisation*, ed. G. Farrell and K. Pease. Monsey, NY: Criminal Justice Press.

Sherif, M., and C. W. Sherif. 1956. *An Outline of Social Psychology*, Rev. ed. New York: Harper.

Sherman, L. W. 1992. *Policing Domestic Violence: Experiments and Dilemmas*. New York: Free Press.

Sherman, L. W., and R. A. Berk. 1984. The specific deterrent effects of arrest for domestic assault. *American Sociological Review* 49, 261-272.

Shichor, D. 1989. Corporate deviance and corporate victimization: A review and some elaborations. *International Review of Victimology* 1, 67-88.

Stein, G. 1922. *Geography and Plays*. Boston: Four Seas.

Steinberg, D. D. 1982. *Psycholinguistics*. London: Longman.

Sumner, C. J. 1987. Victim participation in the criminal justice system. *Australian and New Zealand Journal of Criminology* 20, 195-217.

Tajfel, H. 1982. Social psychology of inter-group relations. *Annual Review of Psychology* 33, 1-39.

Taylor, G. 1999. Using repeat victimization to counter commercial burglary: the Leicester experience. *Security Journal* 12, 41-52.

Tilley, N. 1993. The Prevention of Crime Against Small Businesses: The Safer Cities Experience. Crime Prevention Unit Series Paper 45. London: Home Office.

Titus, R. M., and A. R. Gover. 2001. Personal fraud: The victims and the scams. In *Repeat Victimisation*, ed. G. Farrell and K. Pease. Monsey, NY: Criminal Justice Press.

Townsley, M., R. Homel, and J. Chaseling. 2003. Infectious burglaries: A test of the near repeat hypothesis. *British Journal of Criminology* 43, 615-633.

Tseloni, A., and K. Pease. 2003. Repeat personal victimisation: Boosts or flags? *British Journal of Criminology* 43, 186-212.

Umbreit, M. 2001. *The Handbook of Victim-Offender Mediation: An Essential Guide to Practice and Research*. San Francisco: Jossey Bass.

Whatley, M. A. 1996. Victim characteristics influencing attributions of responsibility to rape victims: A meta-analysis. *Aggression and Violent Behavior* 1, 81-95.

Wittebrood, K., and P. Nieuwbeerta. 2000. Criminal victimisation during one's life-course: The effects of previous victimisation and patterns of routine activities. *Journal of Research in Crime and Delinquency* 37, 91-122.

Zedner, L. 2002. Victims. In *The Oxford Handbook of Criminology*, ed. M. Maguire, R. Morgan, and R. Reiner. Oxford: Clarendon.

Restorative Justice: An Alternative for Responding to Crime?

19

LODE WALGRAVE

Contents

All over the world, restorative justice is steadily gaining credibility as a powerful alternative in the response to crime. According to van Ness and Heetderks Strong, the phrase "restorative justice" was launched by Eglash in 1977 (van Ness and Heetderks Strong 2002). Some ideas and practices then circulated among a few practitioners and academics, who, for many, seemed to ground their vision on nostalgic and utopian visions and on a few experiments of anecdotical significance only. Much has changed since then. Restorative justice now has become a broad and still "widening river" (Zehr 2002) of renovating practices and empirical evaluation; a central issue in theoretical, juridical, and social ethical debates; and a ubiquitous theme in juvenile justice and criminal justice reforms worldwide.

Restorative practices have been inserted into most systems of responding to crime (Mier and Williams 2004), especially youth crime (Walgrave 2004). International organizations have delivered recommendations and statements to promote the implementation of restorative principles and practices in dealing with crime (United Nations Economic and Social Council 2002; Council of Europe 2004). In the maximalist ambition of some advocates, these are steps only toward a full-fledged systemic restorative response to crime. Others consider the maximalist option too ambitious. They see restorative justice as a basis for diversion or as alternate sanctions, but they do not believe that restorative practices are appropriate for serious crimes and are skeptical about the possible combination of restorative practices with legal safeguards.

This chapter presents the state of affairs of restorative justice, its options, achievements, and problems. But it must be clear by now that restorative justice is an unfinished product. It is a complex and lively realm of different and often opposite beliefs and options, renovating inspirations and practices in different contexts, scientific crossing swords over research methodology and outcomes. Restorative justice is at the same time a social movement with different degrees of self-criticism, and a scientific domain with different degrees of methodological adequacy. It is a field on its own, looking for constructive ways of dealing with the aftermath of crime, but also part of a larger socio-ethical and political agenda. As a consequence, my presentation cannot but include a number of personal views and options. Where necessary, I shall indicate my deviations from the restorative justice mainstream.

19.1   The Emergence of Restorative Justice in Modern Times

19.1.1   Ancient Wisdom

Restorative justice is not an invention of recent decades. For some authors, a reparative type of response to injustice committed was in fact the mainstream in earlier times (Zehr 1990; Weitekamp 1999; van Ness and Heetderks 2002). One can expect, indeed, that the original small communities could not afford exclusion or enduring conflict in their midst, because the struggle for life needed intensive cooperation and mutual support. They probably tried to find constructive solutions to internal conflicts and to avoid outcasting as much as possible. For a number of scholars, the centralizing of power gradually shifted the meaning of norm transgression from harming another and social life to breaking the king's or the pope's law. The settlement of the aftermath of a "crime" was taken away from its main proponents, and reparation for the victim became subsidiary to punishment to enforce law compliance. In that view, the state has done much damage to the quality of conflict resolution in communities. The state in fact stole the conflict from its owners (Christie 1977).

Other authors, however, reject this view as being mythical and based on an unscientific approach (Sylvester 2003). They suggest a history of escalating violence and revenge (Miller 1999). Experienced injustices and damages were responded to by counter actions to pay back, undertaken by the victims, their families, and clans. The emergence of central power then gradually blocked this violent private retaliation, to replace it by an increasingly sophisticated, legally ordered system of punishment. Violence in communities was reduced and monopolized more and more in the hands of the state (Elias 1994).

As an amateur historian, I draw two lessons from these contradictory positions. First, there may be a problem in "objective" historians' methodology. As it is based predominantly on written sources, it may lead to a relative underestimation of the amount of restitutive responses. Much compensation and negotiation about it were informal and occurred among illiterate people. No authorities or other literate agencies were involved, so that written indications of such resolutions may be scarce. On the contrary, violent settlements have probably come more to the central power's attention, entailing a powerful intervention to stop it. More written reports of such incidents can be expected.

Second, reality was probably not uniform, but mixed, and it must have developed differently in several communities and societies. It seems plausible that compensation and restitution have been important ways of responding to injustices, but also that violent settlements occurred, especially when deliberation appeared not to be possible, or no agreement was reached (Schafer 1977). Gradually, rules ordered compensations and other settlements, and they have originally contributed to reducing the endurance of conflicts and violence. The scale has tipped, however, by the rise of state power, when punishing the law breaking overruled repairing the harm. Apparently, restitution and compensation have always been practiced over time, but their scope and degree of prevalence in the past is uncertain and probably variable over communities and periods of time.

Restorative ideas have, however, been present over times as normative goods. Texts of all great spiritual traditions—Judaism, Christianism, Islam, Confucianism, Buddhism, Hinduism—promote crucial restorative values such as compensation, apology, and forgiveness.[1] Practices described in ancient Arab, Greek, Roman, German, Chinese, Hindu, and other societies witness adherence to restorative values (Braithwaite 2002). One can therefore claim that restorative justice is deeply rooted in ancient wisdom, even if its predominance in practice may be uncertain. This appears also through the recent emancipation of native peoples, especially in New Zealand and in North America. It has made their ancient traditions visible, which in many cases (but not all) are oriented towards objectives such as encounter, community involvement, and reparation (Zellerer and Cunneen 2001).

Restorative concerns never disappeared completely, but they were subordinated by the punitive mainstream over many centuries. In 1900, for example, Tallack wrote that "reparation as the chief, and often whole, element of punishment was wiser in principle, more reformatory in its influence, more deterrent in its tendency and more economic to the economy" (Weitekamp 1992). All this does not mean that the ancient or native practices can just be copied to be applied into our modern societies and cities (Johnstone 2002; Sylvester 2003).

19.1.2 Modern Roots

In its modern form, restorative justice reappeared in the late seventies, and it became an increasingly important factor in practice and policy in the 1990s.

---

[1] It is true, of course, that the same religions also have produced texts imbued by anger, vengeance, and severe punishments against the sinful.

Its re-emergence was based on multiple roots and tendencies, in which three bottom lines can be distinguished (Faget 1997; van Ness and Heetderks Strong 2002).

Victims' movements claimed an expanded role in criminal justice. Victims' rights movements were initially narrowly focused at promoting victims' rights in conflict with the offender and held a strict oppositional view on victims' and offenders' interests. In their "zero-sum" approach to justice (Strang 2002), the more attention is paid to the offender's rights and needs, the less space there is for the victim's. They strongly supported the punitive aspect in criminal justice. Today, most victims' advocates are oriented towards a broader scope of social, personal, and juridical needs of those victimized by crime. They now understand that simply making a coalition with the traditional criminal justice system is often counterproductive for the victims. More than boosting punishment on the offender, seeking reparation and compensation may result in deeper and continuing satisfaction. Deliberation, rather than enforcement, may contribute to mental peace (Peters and Aertsen 1995).[2]

Another source of restorative justice is communitarianism. As a reaction to the fragmentation of our postmodern Western societies, some propagate the revival of community as the organic resource of informal mutual support and control (Etzioni 1998). Communities are seen at the same time as a means and as an end for restorative justice. They are a means in that communities are needed as the "niches" wherein reintegrative shaming and restorative processes can take place (Braithwaite 1989); they are an end, because it is believed that achieving restorative processes in a community is constructive to the revival of community life (Bazemore and Schiff 2001). Within the communitarian agenda, restorative justice has been inspired by religious beliefs (Hadley 2001), as appears through the spiritual basis of the Victim Offender Reconciliation Program (VORP) in Kitchener, Ontario, Canada, mentioned often as the roots-projects of restorative practices (Coates 1990), and through the publications of one of the founders of the restorative body of ideas (Zehr 1990). The communitarian agenda has also been boosted by the emancipation of native people, especially in North America and New Zealand. Their community-based, peace-oriented, and deliberation-driven ways of dealing with conflicts and norm transgression deeply influenced restorative practice and thinking (Zellerer and Cunneen 2001).

Especially in the seventies and the eighties, critical criminology described convincingly the counterproductive effects of criminal justice and its incapacity to assure peace in social life. Abolitionists argued for scrapping or phasing out the criminal justice system, in order to replace it by a bottom-

---

[2] This is not to say that there are no problems between RJ and victims' advocates. We shall come back to this issue later in this chapter.

up deliberative model of dealing with conflicts (Christie 1994). Inheritors of this tendency proposed restorative justice-like alternatives (de Haan 1990), or have turned to restorative justice as the mainstream alternative to criminal justice (Blad 1996), or to youth justice (Walgrave 1995; Bazemore and Walgrave 1999a).

All these tendencies and movements and a multitude of isolated intuitive initiatives led to a realm of practices, empirical research, social movement, theory-formation, and ethical reflection that is now indicated as restorative justice. The application of its principles goes far beyond criminalizable matters. It is also increasingly penetrating the regulation of disputes and discipline problems in schools, neighborhood conflicts, and child welfare and protection matters, and even the resolution of conflicts including systematic political violence.

Given its diverse roots, broad field of implementation, and currently different forms, it is not surprising that restorative justice does not appear as a clearly defined set of thoughts and implementations, but as a rather confused, seemingly even incoherent assembly. Adding to the confusion are apparently similar movements under banners like transformative justice, relational justice, community justice, peacemaking justice, and others.

19.2   In Search of the Essentials

Only recently have practitioners and researchers recognized a fundamental commonality underlying most versions of mediation, conferencing, circles, and other reparative or compensatory practices. That is probably one of the reasons why no generally accepted definition of restorative justice exists, and different (sometimes even opposing) views exist (McCold and Wachtel 1998; Dignan 2002). But if the words *restoration* and *justice* do have a meaning, it should be possible to find the key characteristics of what can be called restorative justice.

19.2.1   Towards a Definition

Maybe the most quoted definition is by Tony Marshall: "Restorative justice is a process whereby all the parties with a stake in a particular offense come together to resolve collectively how to deal with the aftermath of the offense and its implications for the future" (1996). This definition has two problems. First, it does not include that the outcome of the process must be reparative or restorative. If the process leads, for example, to the offender's agreement to walk around in the shopping mall dressed in a T-shirt that reads "I am a thief" (Braithwaite 2002), it is difficult to call this a restorative practice. Or if the invited victim prefers not to assist in a conference, and the unique outcome is that the offender accepts a drug treatment, the degree of restorativeness is doubtful. Second, Marshall's definition excludes actions that may lead to reparative outcomes without "parties coming together." As we shall see, victim support, for example, or community service may, under certain conditions, have restorative value, even if the communication between the parties is very poor or absent.

Recently, Howard Zehr proposed another definition, which, more than Marshall's, orients the process towards restoration: "Restorative justice is a process to involve, to the extent possible, those who have a stake in a specific offense and to collectively identify and address harms, needs and obligations, in order to heal and put things right as possible" (Zehr 2002). This clearly remains a process-based definition, which may exclude (partly) reparative actions through imposed obligations.

While not proposing a one-sentence definition, others try to grasp the essentials of restorative justice in a few propositions and subpropositions. Zehr and Mika advanced three "critical components": "Crime is fundamentally a violation of people and interpersonal relationships," "violations create obligations and liabilities," and "restorative justice seeks to heal and put right the wrongs" (1997).

Dignan and Marsh applied the notion of restorative justice to any approach or program "that have the following characteristics: an emphasis on the offender's personal accountability to those harmed by an offence (which may include the community as well as the victim); an inclusive decision-making process that encourages participation by key participants; and the goal of putting right the harm that is caused by an offence" (2001).

Van Ness and Heetderks Strong wrote: "What is restorative justice? It is a different way of thinking about crime and our response to it. It focuses on the harm caused by crime: repairing the harm done to victims and reducing future harm by preventing crime. It requires offenders to take responsibility for their actions and for the harm they have caused. It seeks redress for victims, recompense by offenders, and reintegration of both within the community. It is achieved through a cooperative effort by communities and the government" (2002).

Although they all point to the essentials of restorative justice, they add elements that seem not necessary or confusing to understand restorative justice, or which exclude actions that also may have restorative value. That is why Bazemore and Walgrave have proposed a simple and essentialist definition: "Restorative justice is every action that is primarily oriented toward doing justice by repairing the harm that has been caused by a crime" (1999a). This definition is reduced to its most crucial characteristic, the aim of reparation, and does not mention underlying principles nor specific requirements or rights for parties. It also may include nondeliberative interventions, such as victim support, or imposed restitution or community service if it is intended as a symbolic compensation for the harm to social life.

This "maximalist"[3] version of restorative justice is controversial. McCold, for example, is strongly opposed to it and confronted it with his holistic "purist" version, based uniquely on voluntary cooperation by the stakeholders, rejecting any use of coercion under the restorative justice label (2000). He referred to Marshall's earlier definition, and therefore considered the deliberative and inclusionary process as the key characteristic of restorative justice. Both Walgrave and Bazemore replied that a purist vision would keep restorative justice at the margins of the social response to crime, leaving the mainstream to the traditional punitive criminal justice system (Walgrave 2000; Bazemore 2000).

The opposition between both visions is faded by the increasing awareness that restorativeness is not just a clear-cut feature. It is an option that may penetrate different actions in different degrees. Between fully restorative programs or systems and minimally restorative ones, graduations of partly or moderately restorative approaches exist (McCold 2000; van Ness 2002a; Zehr 2002).

I therefore suggest an adaptation of the earlier Bazemore and Walgrave definition and consider as restorative justice an option on doing justice after the occurrence of an offense that is primarily oriented towards repairing the individual, relational, and social harm that is caused by that offense.

In this version, the focus is shifted from "action" to "option." Restorative justice indeed is not a monopoly of certain fully restorative actions opposed to all the other nonrestorative actions. It is, on the contrary, an option, a vision, an intention that may inspire in different degrees a variety of initiatives, programs, and systems. "Restorative justice is a compass, not a map" (Zehr 2002). I also add three categories of harm, to make clear that the harm considered transcends the harm and suffering of the individual victim. But it remains a simple one-sentence definition, limiting restorative justice to a response to an offense[4] and, especially, defining restorative justice through its goal to repair.

---

[3] This version is called "maximalist" because it includes judicial sanctions in view of reparation as being partly restorative, and because it aims at a fully fledged restorative justice system, consequently oriented toward doing justice through reparation and restoration. In the longer term, it would replace the existing punitive a priorism in the criminal justice system.

[4] For reasons of clarity, I do not include in the definition of restorative justice the practices to resolve conflicts in neighborhoods, schools, labor, and elsewhere, though they are largely inspired by the same participatory and inclusionary philosophy. But they deal with different types of problems in different contexts and different mandates, with more mixed objectives and different stakeholders. We might call them restorative practices, but not restorative *justice* practices.

19.2.2 Two Additional Comments

19.2.2.1 *An Outcome-Based Definition*

The definition proposed clearly is outcome-based, whereas probably a majority of the "restorativists" are sympathetic to the process-based approach. As McCold clearly wrote: "The essence of restorative justice is not the end, but the means by which resolution is achieved" (2004). They all rightly promote informal voluntary settlements as being crucial for achieving restoration maximally. The communicative potentials of mediation and family group conferences, for example, indeed favor the authentic assessment of the harm suffered and may more easily lead to a genuine agreement on how it can be reasonably repaired or compensated. The offender's agreement to make up expresses his or her understanding of the wrongs committed and harms caused and his or her compliance with the social norms; the recognition of harm confirms the value and recognizes the rights of the victim. This is all much more restorative for the victim, for the community, and for the offender as well, than if the offender is simply imposed a sanction.

Nevertheless, restorative justice cannot be reduced to such a process, for two reasons. First, a process cannot be defined and valued without referring to the purpose it is undertaken for (van Ness 2002b). Defining a process without referring to its goal is like pedaling in the air. The process is valued not because of the deliberation on its own, but because of the outcomes it helps to achieve. A deliberative process is more "restorative" because the expressions of remorse, compassion, apology, and forgiveness that it facilitates may readily yield feelings of being respected, of peace, and of satisfaction. These feelings are outcomes, even if they are not explicitly written down in the resulting agreement.

Secondly, restricting restorative justice to voluntary deliberations would limit its scope drastically (Dignan 2002) and doom it to stay at the margins of the system, as a way of diversion. The mainstream response to crime would remain being coercive and punitive. The gatekeeping criminal justice system would probably refer a selection of the less serious cases only to deliberative restorative processes. Consequently, victims of serious crimes, who need restoration the most, would be excluded from it. Moreover, giving up the principled priority for restoration would hand over a category of citizens to the punitive a priorism, including its problems, to which we shall come back.

Therefore, restoration must be seen as the goal, and voluntary processes as means only, though very important ones. Process-based definitions confuse the means with the goal and limit the possible means to achieve (partial) restoration. Deliberative processes appear to hold the highest potentials for achieving restoration, but if voluntary agreements cannot be accomplished, coercive obligations in pursuit of (partial) reparation must be encompassed in the restorative justice model. I shall comment later on this, but possible examples of such reparative sanctions are formal restitution or compensation, a fine, doing work for the benefit of a victims' fund, or community service. Such sanctions, of course, do not achieve completely the potential of the restorative paradigm, but we are just reminded that restorative justice is not a simple black-and-white option. It can be achieved in different degrees.

This position is a challenge for restorative justice in its relation to traditional criminal justice thinking and legalizing. Possible coercive sanctions in view of restoration can indeed only be imposed by the judicial system. The questions will rise of how far possible sanctions still are distinct from punishment in view of reparation, and how the preference for informal processing can be related to the formal judicial system.

19.2.2.2 Another Paradigm

Restorative justice does not primarily ask what should be done to the offender, but how the harm can be repaired. That is what distinguishes it from punitive and rehabilitative justice approaches. That is why it is another paradigm (Zehr 1990; Bazemore and Walgrave 1999b; McCold 2000). It offers a distinctive "lens," in Zehr's term, for defining the problem caused by crime and for solving it. Crime is considered through the harm it causes and not by its mere transgression of a legal order. The primary function of the response is neither to punish nor to rehabilitate the offender but to set the conditions for repairing as much as possible the harm caused. Restorative justice thus can go a long way without an offender involved. If the offender is not caught, while the harm is assessed, (partial) justice can be done by repairing or compensating the victim and by restoring public assurance that the crime is not acceptable.

The authorities' action to involve the offender's responsibility in the response to the offense nevertheless remains crucial. Not in the first place because something must be done to him or her, but because his or her involvement will serve the goal of restoration. Influencing the offender is a secondary objective only, within the frame of the primary restorative goal. The kind and amount of obligation is decided by the needs of reasonable restoration, not by the needs for adequate treatment or proportionate punishment.

We now turn to the three main components of the definition: the harm, the way of restoration, and doing justice.

19.2.3 Harm

The harm considered for (partial) reparation includes the material damage, all forms of suffering inflicted on the victim and his or her proximate environment, social unrest and community indignation, uncertainty about legal order and about authorities' capacity for assuring public safety, and the social damage the offender has caused to him- or herself by the offense.

19.2.3.1 Crime Caused Harm

The only limitation is that the harm considered by the restorative process must be caused by the particular offense. Restorative justice indeed is a reactive option, "a way of responding to crimes which have been already committed" (Johnstone 2002). This is particularly important with regard to the offender's harm to be considered for possible reparation. It is limited to trying to avoid further stigmatization or social marginalization caused by the offense, not to cure the social exclusion or psychosocial problems that possibly existed already before the offense and might have caused the offending. Not all accept this limitation. Some believe that restorative processes should address the underlying causes of offending as well. However, I believe that this is a dangerous option. It would blur the distinction from the rehabilitative approach and risk a shift from a harm-focused to an offender-focused program (Braithwaite 1999). It would risk degrading the victim to being a tool for the offender's rehabilitation and not recognizing the victim as a party on his or her own.

The underlying problems and needs of the offender must be considered to keep the reparative effort within reasonable limits, but they are not the primary subject of the reparation itself. As we shall see, however, the restorative processes offer great opportunities for addressing these problems as well. But, strictly speaking, they are beneficiary side effects, not primary aims.

19.2.3.2 Public Harm

A particular problem is how to understand the public dimension of the crime in restorative terms. Restorative justice is not limited to settling a tort according to civil law, but deals with crimes, which are also public events, traditionally dealt with by criminal law. In traditional criminal justice, legal order is the public good to be preserved, but this is too abstract and too top-down a value for restorative justice.

What then makes an offense a collective or public event? A burglary, for example, is a private and a public affair. Restitution or compensation for the individual victim's losses could be private, to be arranged by civil law. But we all are concerned that authorities intervene and try to make things right. The particular victim stands as an example of risks all citizens face. If the authorities would do nothing, it may lead to private actions to "make things even," escalating in revenge, dragging down security in the community as a whole. It would also hurt all citizens' trust in public rules, in their right to privacy and property, and in the authorities' power and willingness to preserve order and justice in social life.

The public dimension of crime lies in the harm it causes to public trust in norms and norm enforcement. As we shall see later in this chapter, the concept of "dominion," as introduced by Braithwaite and Pettit, can help to understand this (1990). Dominion is a social concept of rights and freedoms, because it rests upon the assurance that fellow citizens and the state will take rights and freedoms seriously. Only then can the dominion fully be enjoyed.

Crime then is seen as an intrusion upon dominion and, more particularly, upon the assurance of rights and freedoms. The burglary does not diminish the actual legal rights of privacy and property, because they still are laid down in legal texts, but the extent to which the victim and the citizens are assured that these rights are respected and taken seriously. Public intervention after a crime is primarily needed to enhance assurance: It communicates the authorities' public disapproval of the norm transgression and it responds through an action in view of restoration. It makes clear that authorities take dominion seriously.

19.2.4   Restoration

A wide range of processes and procedures may lead to a reparative outcome. But not all processes are equally appropriate for it. The main distinction is between voluntary processes and coercive procedures.

19.2.4.1   Deliberative Restoration

Most suitable are processes that consist of voluntary deliberation between the victim and the offender, as the main stakeholders. Later in this chapter, I shall describe briefly the most typical processes known today (McCold 2001; van Ness, Morris, and Maxwell 2001): mediations between the individual victim and offender, various forms of conferencing including the victim and offender both supported by their communities of care, and sentencing circles in which the local indigenous community as a whole is a part of the meeting on the occasion of a crime in its midst.

Well-conducted restorative processes offer the opportunity for a powerful sequence of moral and social emotions and exchanges (Braithwaite and Mugford 1994; Morris 2002; van Stokkom 2002; Walgrave and Braithwaite 2004). This "encounter" (van Ness and Heetderks Strong 2002) may lead to a common understanding of the harm and suffering caused and to an agreement on how to make amends (van Ness and Heetderks 2002). It also can enhance the willingness of the offender to fulfill these agreements.

Agreements may include a wide range of actions like restitution, compensation, reparation, reconciliation, apologies, and forgiveness. They may be direct or indirect, concrete or symbolic. They are aimed at (partial) reparation of the victim's prejudices and at restoration of peace and order in social life. The degree of the offender's willingness to undertake such actions is crucial. It expresses his or her understanding of the wrong committed and his or her willingness to make up for it. For the victim, it means the restoration of his or her citizenship as a bearer of rights, and possibly also a partial material redress. For the larger community, it contributes to assurance that the offender takes rights and freedoms seriously and will respect them in the future. Even offenders' agreements to undergo a treatment can have a restorative meaning, because they express their recognition of a personal problem that they want to resolve in accordance with their social environment. All this may lead to satisfaction of the victim, reintegration of the offender, and restored assurance of security in community and of rights and freedoms in society.

Such a sequence is, of course, the ideal, which is often far from being fully achieved. However, we shall see that the reach of restorative processes is larger than is often supposed, and that even partial results in terms of satisfaction, procedural justice, and reoffending are generally significantly better than what the traditional criminal justice procedures can offer.

19.2.4.2 *Imposed Reparation*

When participatory processes cannot be achieved voluntarily or are judged to be insufficient, pressure or coercion on the offender must be considered. In a constitutional democracy, coercion may only be exerted through a judicial procedure. And here, some divergence exists among restorative justice advocates. In line with their process-based characterization (see above), a number of scholars exclude (judicial) coercion from restorative justice (McCold 2000).

Others believe that, even if judicial coercion towards the offender is considered to be necessary, the procedures should be oriented to obligations or sanctions that should primarily seek as much as possible reparation (Claassen 1995; Wright 1996; Walgrave 2002a, 2003). There is no reason to give up the principled priority for restoration when it is confronted with the offender's resistance. Concerns for the harm caused by the crime also apply if the offender is not cooperative. The social response must express that concern by aiming at the largest possible reparation. The reason for the possible use of coercion remains the harm caused, not "deterrence" on its own. Possible sanctions in view of reparation are, for example, material restitution or compensation to the victim, a contribution to a victims' fund, or community service (Dignan 2002; Walgrave 2002a). These judicially imposed obligations mostly yield a reduced reparative outcome, but, as mentioned here above, degrees of restorativeness exist between the fully restorative processes and the not-at-all-restorative reactions.

At several occasions later in this chapter, we shall come back to this difficult relation between restorative justice and legal coercion.

19.2.5 Doing Justice

Restorative justice not only is about restoration, it is also about justice. The notion of justice has two meanings.

19.2.5.1　Moral Justice

Justice is the outcome of an ethical evaluation. It means a feeling of equity, according to a moral balance of rights and wrongs, benefits, and burdens. Basically, the feeling is subjective, imbedded though in a social cultural dimension. In retributive justice, the balance is achieved by imposing suffering on the offender that is commensurate to the social harm caused by the crime. In restorative justice, the balance is restored by taking away or compensating the suffering and harm caused by the crime. Restorative justice aims at achieving "procedural fairness" (Tyler 1990) and satisfaction (van Ness and Schiff 2001) for all parties involved. Victims feel that their victimization has been taken seriously and that the compensation and support are reasonably in balance with their sufferings and losses. Offenders experience that their dignity has not unnecessarily been hurt and that they are given the opportunity to make up for their mistake in a constructive way. All participants, including the community, feel reassured that rights and freedoms are taken seriously by fellow citizens and the authorities.

The best way to guarantee that losses are well-understood and that the reparation is adequate is to leave the decision to those with a direct stake: victims, offenders, and others directly affected. Justice is what those concerned experience as such. This bottom-up approach is crucial in restorative justice and contrasts with the top-down approach of the criminal justice system. This does not, however, mean that the state should be excluded.

19.2.5.2　Legal Justice

Justice can also mean legality. Restorative justice processes and their outcomes must respect legal safeguards (Trépanier 1998; van Ness 1999; Walgrave 2000b; Dignan 2002). Legal safeguards protect citizens against illegitimate intrusions not only by fellow citizens but also by the state. This is obvious in coerced interventions, but it applies also in voluntary settlements. How to make sure rights are observed is a matter of debate among restorative justice proponents. Some rely fully on the potentials of communities and try to reduce state control over restorative processes to a strict minimum (Pranis 2001). They fear the state's power to invade the process and undo its informal, humane, and healing potentials. Others try to find a balanced social and institutional context, which allows maximum space for genuine deliberative processes but also offers full opportunities for all parties to appeal to judicial agencies if they feel not respected in the process.

In a coercive procedure, all legal guarantees must be observed. In a traditional criminal justice procedure, safeguards like legality, due process, and proportionality are evident. The rights that they protect should be protected in coercive restorative interventions as well (Ashworth 1993; Warner 1994). However, as these principles are meant for a punishment-oriented system, it is not obvious that they should be applied unchanged in a system premised on restoration (Walgrave 2000b). It is a crucial assignment for restorative justice advocates to rethink the traditional legal safeguards so that they respect the restorative justice philosophy.

One of the most important criticisms of traditional criminal justice is that its procedures and outcomes may lead to legal justice, but they very often (or even mostly) have lost track with the subjective justice experiences. "The right punishment, according to some retributive theory, will almost always be the wrong solution to the problem. By wrong I mean less just" (Braithwaite 2000). It must be the restorative justice ambition to make both justice concepts coincide as much as possible.

19.3   From Options to Practice

Restorative justice is not an invention by academics or by enlightened policymakers. It is deeply rooted in the lively field of conflict resolution and responding to crime, where creative practitioners tried to find more satisfying alternatives to the predominant administrative or judicial routine. Currently, a broad range of different practices exists, which all may express the restorative justice philosophy.

19.3.1   Restorative Practices

Through the diversity, some basic restorative justice models can be indicated.

19.3.1.1   Victim Support

Victim support is not always listed in the series of restorative practices. However, a comprehensive restorative justice model must include victim service and support, available regardless of whether the offender is apprehended and collaborative or not (van Ness 2002b). That is a consequence of the paradigm shift in restorative justice, where the main focus is not anymore on punishing or rehabilitating the offender, but on repairing as much as possible the harm caused. Support of the victim, then, is the first and most important action in doing justice through reparation. Basically, restorative justice can thus be applied without an offender arrested. The occurrence of a crime demonstrates that society and community have failed in protecting the victim's security to which he or she is entitled, so that they must grant as much as possible the compensation or reparation of the harm suffered. If the offender is not known, not arrested, unwilling, or unable to contribute to the reparation, the authorities must contribute themselves directly to the reparation. Victims' funds help to repair or compensate materially. Support schemes help to make the mental sufferings livable and advise victims in their trajectory through the justice procedures. If the offender is arrested, authorities must try to involve him or her in the restorative action, as designed in the next restorative practices, and still grant the accompanying support and/or additional compensation to the victim.

Currently, almost all victim support agencies are located at the margins of the mainstream justice system and only deal with welfare problems linked to the victimization. This is important, of course, but a consequent restorative way of thinking must position victim support in the heart and at the first line of the system, not at its margins. It is the first concern of the public intervention after a crime occurs, not an ornamental addendum.

19.3.1.2 Victim-Offender Mediation

In victim-offender mediation (VOM), an impartial mediator invites both most evident protagonists in the aftermath of an offense to communicate with each other, in search of finding an appropriate restitution, compensation, or reparation for the harm caused by that offense (Umbreit 1994; European Forum for Victim-Offender 2000). Mediation can occur through a face-to-face meeting, or via a "shuttle process," in which the mediator acts as a go-between for both participants. Sometimes the mediation process includes members of the communities of care, which brings it close to the conferencing model described in the next section. In the 1980s, the Victim-Offender Reconciliation Program in Kitchener, Ontario, was presented as the original archetype in the re-emergence of restorative justice. It based the spread of VORP and VOM, especially in Canada and the United States.

At the beginning, mediation was often identified with restorative justice as a whole. It is partly understandable, because in mediation, the restorative aspect speaks for itself. Most communication is about the harm and suffering incurred; the outcome aims at restitution, reparation, or compensation. All this can be observed and controlled evidently.

However, as the restorative justice philosophy and other practices developed, mediation appeared too reduced in scope. Victim-offender mediation indeed deals with the contention between the victim and the offender only, whereas settling the aftermath of a crime should also include concern for its public dimensions. Another limitation of mediation is that its scope is reduced to voluntary processes. Mediation thus can happen only if both opponents are willing to cooperate, which reduces its reach drastically to a form of diversion for good willing cases. This is not congruent with the increasing ambition to see restorative justice as a comprehensive alternative to the traditional punitive responses to crime.

19.3.1.3 Restorative Conferencing

Literature often advances conferencing as the "most restorative practice" (McCold 2000). In general, a restorative conference is facilitated by an impartial facilitator and consists of an inclusionary process that brings together the victim and the offender, both with their communities of care, in order to find a socially constructive solution to the problems and harms caused by the offense (Hudson et al. 1996; Masters and Roberts 2000; Conferencing in Australia and New Zealand 2001). The majority of conferencing practices are working with youth offenders.

Its original version, Family Group Conference (FGC), was included in 1989 in the New Zealand Children, Young Persons and their Families Act. According to this act, the youth court cannot impose any sanction to any youth offender unless an FGC has been tried. The only exceptions are murder and manslaughter, which are referred to adults' court. The success of FGC has provoked a boost in conferencing practices all over the world, in different versions and reaches (Umbreit and Zehr 1996; Prichard 2003; Dignan 2005). They are also known as "diversionary conferences," "youth justice conferences," "real justice conferences," "community conferences," or the like. All these versions and labels are often grouped under a common denomination: "restorative conferences." Most conferences are organized as a form of diversion at the police or public prosecutor's level; sometimes, they are facilitated by a police officer as a kind of cautioning to the young offender; some conferences do address the welfare problems of the young offender more than the victims' genuine needs. One could consider most of these versions as extended mediations, including also the communities of care in the deliberation. They more or less keep the same limitations as in mediation.

In my view, the original New Zealand model transcends most of these limitations and can be seen as a more complete alternative response to crime. First, it is procedurally located at the heart of the public response to crime, closer to courts, so that it is not just a diversionary offer. Second, police are present in the conference in their typical role of informant and safeguarder of public order (and not as facilitator), so that the public dimension of the crime is explicitly represented in the deliberation. Third, the presence of the lawyers offers an additional guarantee for legal safeguards. This is especially important for FGC with serious cases, because they may lead to intensive deprivations of liberties.

These peculiar characteristics enable the original FGC model to deal with serious cases also. Moreover, FGC can proceed in the absence of the victim. Indeed, the police and the other participants can draw the attention to the victimization aspects better than can a single mediation. In fact, the New Zealand practice has proven its capacity to deal successfully with serious cases, so that it seems to hold more potential for a more general alternative.

19.3.1.4 Peacemaking Courts and Circles

The emancipation of native communities in North America has revitalized a number of circle models to deal with injustices and conflicts in local contexts, which are deeply rooted in indigenous traditions in the United States and in Canada (Stuart 1996; Lilles 2001; Winfree 2002). By and large, healing circles are meant especially to restore peace within the affected native community. Sentencing circles are a kind of community cojudgment in the criminal justice procedure and take place in the presence of an official judge. Both involve the local community as a whole in dealing with the aftermath of a crime in its midst. The deliberative process is very intensive and may require several meetings or even a series of meetings. Both are deeply community based and aim at restoring peace through reparation and healing (McCold 2001; van Ness and Heetderks 2002).

Such circles come very close to the genuine restorative ideals and have influenced intensely current restorative justice philosophy. However, their expansion in modern urban contexts is difficult. The protagonists in many urban crimes transcend by far the local community; the circles presuppose the availability of an active and dense community to be involved in the circle process, which is more than doubtful in many urban areas; and the circles require an intensive time investment from the participants, which is not evident in modern managerialist environments.

19.3.1.5 *Community Service*

From a restorative justice perspective, community service is unpaid labor done by the offender for the benefit of a community or its institutions, meant as (symbolic) compensation for the harm caused by the offense to that community. It can be imposed by a court or it may also be a part of the agreement after a restorative conferencing, when the offender agrees voluntarily to carry out a task.

Community service is not accepted by all scholars as a restorative justice action. It indeed is often imposed in a nonrestorative sense. Some criminal justice practices use community service as a punishment, imposing a task that is deliberately unpleasant and even humiliating. In other contexts, the service is part of a treatment or educative program, in order to influence the offender's attitudes and competencies. In both, the compensatory dimension is secondary or even absent. Another problem is that "compensating harm to social life" may be too vague and too expansive a notion, which would supersede the immediate and concrete victims' needs. It is feared then that accepting the community (or even society) as a fully fledged separate stakeholder in the restorative process or procedure would cause a shift back towards the initial position in criminal justice, overruling again the interests and needs of the concrete victim.

However, as we have seen, restorative justice is not limited to a specific kind of actions but is a philosophy, an option on doing justice. The harm caused by crime surpasses the concrete victims' sufferings and losses, and includes also harm to the larger community. A credible restorative response to offending should therefore also address the needs of community. Community service is advanced as the prototype of a compensating or restoring gesture towards community (Bazemore and Maloney 1994; Bazemore and Walgrave 1999b; Dignan 2002). Mediation, restorative conferencing, and community service, then, have the following in common:

- A definition of crime as an injury to victims (concrete and societal), which is quite different from the retributive definition considering crime as a transgression of a general juridical-ethical rule.
- An intervention primarily oriented towards restoration of that injury, which is unlike the predominantly punitive a priorism.
- A concept of an accountable offender, involving him or her actively and directly in the restorative action, whereas the retributive or rehabilitative responses reduce the offender to being a passive object of retribution or treatment.

But it must be accepted that imposed community service does not have the same restorative value as conferences, for example.

19.3.1.6   Citizen Boards

The state of Vermont often stands as an example for including in its Reparative Probation Program (1995) so-called community boards composed of citizens (Karp and Walther 2001). They meet with local offenders convicted of minor offenses to negotiate a "reparative" contract, which may include letters of apology, community service, or a treatment. A comparable board is the Youth Offender Panel in the English Youth Justice and Criminal Evidence Act (1999), which meets with young offenders appearing for the first time at court and pleading guilty. Two of its three members are volunteering citizens. Its task is to conclude a contract with the offender in a nonadversarial way, according to the principles of restorative justice (Crawford and Newburn 2003). The proponents of such boards do believe that this formula will involve the community more than if professional judges or probation officers would decide, and that the principles underlying restorative justice philosophy will be implemented.

In practice, however, this is far from evident. It is not because the members of the boards are nonprofessionals that they really represent community. The composition of most boards does not reflect the heterogeneity of the community they are supposed to represent. The plan resulting from the meeting is very often not at all primarily oriented towards reparation. Finally, such boards are not really deliberative, as they keep the ultimate decision in their own hands (McCold 2004; Dignan 2005).

Of course, the comments on the restorativity of the several types of possible actions must not be taken too strictly. They only regard what the formal model as such facilitates or not, but do not address the huge diversity in practices within the models. For example, although restorative conferencing is often presented as the most genuinely restorative process, concrete conferences can be catastrophic for the participants because they are monitored very poorly. Some community services may be used in a punitive way, but they also can have a highly restorative caliber if the community really understands it as an expression of the offender's compliance and his or her willingness to contribute constructively to social life. Citizens' boards may have a deep restorative significance if they succeed in involving the victim and the offender in a constructive dialogue and to commit the participants in the plan concluded. Let us not forget: Restorative justice is not a detailed set of practices, but a philosophy that can penetrate different practices to a different degree.

19.3.2 Evaluating the Practice

Restorative practices are being implemented for an increasingly wider range of crimes, including the most serious ones, all over the world, and they are extending to noncriminalizable matters; a growing number of countries and states provide in their legislations dispositions that favor responses in view of reparation; international organizations have recently issued statements and recommendations to endorse a restorative approach to offending (van Ness, Morris, and Maxwell 2001). Simplistically, this boosting expansion alone might lead to the conclusion that restorative justice practices actually are feasible in the response to crime, and that they obviously are attractive to justice and policymakers.

But of course, more nuance and specification is needed. There is a large and still growing amount of empirical research to assess restorative practices empirically. Several surveys and meta-analyses have recently been published, including especially victim-offender mediation and conferences (Schiff 1999; Latimer, Dowden, and Muise 2001; Braithwaite 2002; Kurki 2003; McCold 2003; Sherman 2003). They all mention serious methodological shortcomings[5] (Parker 2005). That is why McCold concluded that "research on restorative justice practice is a mile wide, but only an inch deep" (2003). The most serious problem is that evaluation programs comparing adequately random assigned experimental and control groups are not abundant. Latimer, Dowden, and Muise (2001) meta-analyzed thirteen studies with a control

---

[5] Evaluation research of interventions always is precarious and seldom yields generalizable conclusions. That is not only true for research on restorative justice practices, but also in assessing traditional punishment or treatment programs.

group, and Sherman counted fourteen such programs in 2003 and still seven more in progress (Sherman 2003). A provisional document by the Jerry Lee Program in randomized controlled trials of restorative justice provided additional data on police-led conferencing (Sherman and Strang 2004). Another problem is that many evaluated programs are in fact "demonstration projects" (Dignan 2005), meaning experimental initiatives undertaken in privileged circumstances, of which the generalizability is doubtful. Despite these shortcomings, some general conclusions can be drawn.

19.3.2.1 Victims

Victims' willingness to participate in mediation or conferencing processes varies between 20 percent and more than 80 percent. Most programs score over half. Participation depends partly, but certainly not totally, on the nature and the seriousness of the offense. Surviving family members also participate after the most serious crimes (Umbreit et al. 2003). Participation rates are higher with juvenile offenders than with adults. Crucially decisive is the process by which the victims are invited. Reasons mentioned for nonparticipation are fear for being confronted with the offender (and his or her family), apprehension for losing control over one's own anger, and an unwillingness to spend more time on the case. Principled rejection of the restorative approach is found rather seldomly. Maxwell and Morris (1996) found only 4 percent of the victims who explicitly wanted a punitive judicial procedure. In a sample of forty-five victims, only one refused to participate in a conference, because he wanted the (juvenile) offender to be punished (Vanfraechem 2003).

Satisfaction of those who participated is one of the most general and stable findings in restorative justice research (Strang 2002). Victims who participated in a mediation or conferencing are significantly more satisfied than those who have gone through a traditional judicial procedure. They feel high degrees of procedural justice, appreciate the communicative value of the encounters, and find the outcomes more just than a traditional judicial sanction. Victims also suffer less post-traumatic stress after a conference and score lower in fear and anger, and higher in sympathy for the offender (Sherman and Strang 2004; Strang and Sherman 2005). However, not all victims are equally satisfied (Daly 2005a), and a small percentage are even more in distress after the process than they were before (Maxwell et al. 2004). But still, this amount is significantly lower than in those who went to court. Most of the dissatisfied victims had been involved in poorly monitored conferences (Strang 2002), which draws attention to the need for ensuring the intrinsic technical quality of mediation or conferencing.

Of course, the high satisfaction rates are found in a selected group: those who were prepared to participate. One can expect that they would be lower with those not participating. Moreover, victims in conferencing have to deal with an offender who already has admitted guilt, which is certainly not always so in court sessions. The admission of the offender is crucially important for the victim (Daly 2005a). Our conclusion must therefore remain cautious and can only be that those victims who are willing to participate are not deceived. And probably, many of those who did not participate would have been more satisfied if they had (Vanfraechem 2003). These findings are crucial for restorative justice, as it is focused first of all on repairing the harm. They also are important in the debate on victims' position in restorative justice.

19.3.2.2 Offenders

Also among offenders, the willingness to participate in a restorative process is very high. Their motivation is not clear. Probably, a great part of them simply hope to come off better that way than if they went to court. That is not necessarily a problem. As long as it does not lead to secondary victimization for the victims, one can realistically expect and accept that the offender begins a meeting with some calculation. As we shall see, it is the process during the meeting itself that makes offenders understand what they caused and become increasingly more emotionally involved and less rationally calculating.

Satisfaction rates among offenders are very high. The expressions of experienced fairness in the process and satisfaction with the outcome vary between 80 and 97 percent (Braithwaite 2002). McCold distinguished the programs according to the degree of stakeholder participation and found higher fairness and satisfaction in the most participative programs (2003).

The question on reoffending is classical, but it is in fact not the first concern of restorative justice. Restorative interventions are not a new treatment program; they express another paradigm, in which repairing the harm is the first concern. But, of course, the bottom line is that restorative justice interventions may not provoke more recidivism than traditional interventions would do. If it would, it would yield very negative consequences for public safety, and thus cause additional harm to peace and safety in community. Moreover, systematically increased reoffending after restorative processes would be detrimental for the restorative justice acceptability in public and politics. That is why reliable indications on reoffending are needed.

It is methodologically a difficult issue (Hayes and Daly 2003). Like for evaluating reoffending after punishment or treatment programs, methodological problems also subsist in restorative justice evaluations with regard to composing adequate control groups, finding reliable measurements, and so on. All in all, data on reoffending after restorative processes do not lead to triumphant conclusions. Mediation and conferencing yield no or only slight decreasing effects in recidivism: "While restorative justice programs do not involve a consistent guarantee of reducing offending, even badly managed restorative justice programs are most unlikely to make re-offending worse" (Braithwaite 2002). However, the Reintegrative Shaming Experiment found conferences with drunk drivers to result in a small number of reoffending, compared to court proceedings (Sherman, Strang, and Woods 2000). One possible explanation could be the absence of a concrete victim. The Jerry Lee Program found so far four randomized control trials resulting in lower recidivism, but the Canberra project appeared to produce more repeat offending for property offenses. The project also yielded more reoffending in aboriginal offenders (Sherman and Strang 2004). The authors are puzzled with that result, which is probably because they in fact evaluated only police-led conferences and unjustly concluded about restorative justice in general. Aboriginals may have bad relations to police in general, and police-led conferences may therefore provoke more defiance than compliance.

There is thus a need of refining the research, according to the type of conferencing, its technical quality, the type of crimes and of criminals, and other variables. Compared with the outcomes of court procedures, conferences with juveniles appear to lower reoffending most in violent offenders (Sherman, Strang, and Woods 2000) or after serious crimes (Sherman 2003). This is paradoxical when one observes that conferences are applied the most to divert rather benign youth offending from court appearances. Not all conferences have equal impact. When the offender expresses remorse and a consensus is reached, the conferences are more effectual (Maxwell et al. 2003). It is not always certain whether remorse really is provoked by the quality of the conference, or expresses the more compliant attitude of the offender. Younger offenders desisted more after conference than older ones (Hayes and Daly 2004).

Parker (2005) was very critical towards the available restorative justice assessments and concluded that there is no proof at all that restorative justice works in reducing recidivism. He pointed to the so-called What Works research[6] to indicate what should be done (Andrews 2001). But the way restorative justice actually functions may be less contradictory to the What Works principles than Parker suggested. According to What Works surveys, for example, behavioral-cognitive programs that appeal to the active responsibility of the offender in a "no-nonsense," well-structured way would be more effective than other treatment or punitive approaches (McGuire and Priestly 1995). Well-conducted conferences do respond to these requirements: They go straight to the crime problem and appeal to the offender's active responsibility in a way that is perfectly understandable for all participants.

---

[6] "What Works" mainly refers to a series of meta-analyses of earlier evaluations of treatment programs, with the ambition to methodologically filter out the characteristics that might be effective in reducing recidivism.

Another conclusion of the What Works meta-analyses is that the duration of the intervention matters. And that is a lesson for restorative justice evaluation. Most of it has so far measured the reoffending outcome of the restorative meeting but isolated it from its "after care." It may have been somewhat naïve to expect that a conference of one or a few hours would make up for a life course that sometimes went wrong from birth. General living conditions and perspectives are better predictors for reoffending than having a conference or not (Maxwell et al. 2004; Hayes and Daley 2004). What we can assume, however, is that a conference, if it is well conducted, may offer a better opportunity for reflection and turning the page than the traditional judicial procedures. At the occasion of the conference, the offender and his or her family become aware that things are really going wrong and that this must be stopped. They may more ready to accept treatment afterwards. Daly (2005b), for example, found that offenders who participated in a conference are more likely to accept voluntary treatment afterwards than those who were subjected to court. Maxwell et al. (2004) found that juveniles who were well monitored after the conference did better than the others, but the conference itself may provide an excellent occasion to start the monitoring. The quality of the follow-up is thus at least as important as the conference itself, and that should be included in the evaluation studies.

Restitution programs seem to have predominantly better reoffending rates than traditional sanctions (Schiff 1999). Schiff concluded that "when community service is imposed as a restorative sanction ... the possibility that community service will benefit offenders, victims and the community is considerably increased" (1999). We also found significantly less reoffending in young offenders after a community service than in a comparable group of offenders who were imposed a traditional juvenile justice sanction (Walgrave and Geudens 1997).

But still, having an impact on the offender is not the primary aim of restorative justice programs, though impact on the offender can be a part of the "balanced" reparative goal (Bazemore and O'Brien 2002). Our main conclusion can be that, compared to traditional judicial procedures and sanctions, reoffending rates after restorative processes certainly are not worse, and they produce greater satisfaction and fairness experiences among victims and offenders.

19.3.2.3 Explaining the Results

"Research on restorative decision-making must be viewed as in the stages of relative infancy" (Bazemore and Schiff 2005). So far, evaluative research has tried to find out whether such processes do work, but not why it possibly works. The process itself is mostly considered as a black box (Bazemore and Schiff 2005). Several possible explanations may be advanced on why restorative justice processes perform generally better than traditional criminal justice responses (Braithwaite 2002; Bazemore and O'Brien 2002; Bazemore and Schiff 2005). The simplest explanation could be that restorative justice processes avoid some deficiencies inherent in penal justice, such as the scarcity of communication, defiance in the offender under the threat of punishment, and so on. But there are also positive reasons why restorative justice might be more satisfactory.

Sherman (2003) linked restorative justice to two other empirically sustained theories: desistance theory and procedural justice. Research shows that desistance from further criminality depends most of all from the occasion to construct a new, more socially conformable identity (Maruna 2001). External events may provoke a relatively sudden awareness that life can and must be changed (Laub and Sampson 2001). Sherman suggested that restorative encounters may facilitate such "epiphanies" (as Sherman calls them) and that the offer to make up is a possibility to rebuild a new identity. This theory, of course, only applies to possible desistance of offenders. The procedural justice theory could explain the stable findings with regard to satisfaction in both the victim and the offender. Procedural justice theory and its research show that "clients" of the police and justice system are more concerned with the way they have been treated than with the outcome of the procedure (Tyler and Huo 2001). Being treated with respect and equity, being taken seriously, being listened to are crucial for citizens' beliefs in the system's legitimacy, in both victims and offenders. "The manners and emotional overtones of justice officials affect future offending rates as much [as] or more than the formal decisions and severity of punishment" (Sherman 2003). The characteristics of a restorative justice meeting probably offer better conditions for the stakeholders to feel such procedural justice than traditional court proceedings.

Braithwaite's theory on reintegrative shaming has been fundamental in developing insight into what happens emotionally in a restorative justice process (1989). The theory suggests that shame in the offender for the offense committed is a crucial emotion for his or her further conduct. If the shaming is stigmatizing, as in most court interventions, the risk is psychosocial identification with nonconformism and further offending. If, on the contrary, shaming is focused on the behavior and not on the person, and is followed by gestures of reacceptance, it is a powerful emotion to provoke desistance from reoffending. This theoretical approach has been predominant in explaining restorative processes, especially conferencing (Braithwaite and Mugford 1994). Since then, the centrality of the shame emotion is increasingly being nuanced and completed by emotions like guilt, remorse, empathy, and others (Walgrave and Aertsen 1996; Morris 2002; Karstedt 2002; van Stokkom 2002). Moreover, reintegrative shaming only tries to explain what happens to the offender, whereas restorative processes are focused at least as much on the emotional and other benefits for the victim.

19.3.2.4   A Sequence of Moral Emotions

Based on these criticisms, on new research, and on observations, Harris, Walgrave, and Braithwaite (2004) have proposed a possible sequence of moral emotions that may typically happen to victims and offenders in restorative conferences.

We think that most offenders will begin the session with feelings of embarrassment, as they are exposed as being nonconforming. This embarrassment is unpleasant and disempowering and may provoke defiance (Sherman 1993). Many offenders feel at the beginning probably some vague shame and guilt: They disappointed their parents, they committed a legally prohibited act, and they caused trouble and/or harm. Most offenders hope to get away in the least possible uncomfortable way. Victims' beginning emotions are linked directly to their victimization: The offense has caused harm and was humiliating. They feel shame (and embarrassment) for the humiliation they have undergone (Strang 2002), but also want this suffering made right, because they know the intrusion was unjust. Victims probably will hover between two ways of making things right: the retributive way, which would consist of inflicting an equal humiliation and suffering upon the offender, or the restorative way, which would diminish or compensate their own suffering caused by the offense.

These emotional starting points can orient the rest of the conference. An unremorseful or defiant offender can immediately cause greater anger in the victim and others, leading to a possible escalation of the conflict in more stigmatization and secondary victimization. It is therefore crucial to create a secure, respectful, and supportive climate, so that the offender may feel able to take a vulnerable position and accept responsibility, and that the victim may understand that the conference cannot respond from the very beginning to his or her expectations.

And then the victim tells his or her story of harm and suffering, fear, and anger. Confronted with that, most offenders will be touched by compassion. We do believe indeed that most humans, including offenders, have a potential to feel a sense of empathy for other humans, and especially compassion for other humans who are suffering. It can be observed in daily life, when people selflessly help each other in distress; it is illustrated by the spontaneous compassion when mass media show the miserable situations of fugitives, victims of war, crimes, or natural disasters. Not all have the same degree of empathy, the empathy may be very selective, and circumstances may diminish or block the potential for empathy. In our expectation, most offenders will not remain indifferent to the suffering of their victims, even if they were indifferent initially. Victims appear to be more than "an object with a handbag" or some anonymous owner of a car, but a concrete human being with needs and feelings. If the conference goes well, the offenders now understand the suffering. But it is not only sadness they feel. They know that their own behavior has caused the suffering. The wrongfulness of the behavior appears clearer now. Guilt may emerge and its grounds become more concrete than at the beginning: The reason of the norm is clear now and even emotionally felt. Moreover, offenders also feel shame, especially because their wrongfulness is exposed in the eyes of those who care for them and for whom they care.

It should be noticed at this point that the sequence relies very much on empathy to induce remorse or guilt and shame. As a consequence, it is crucial to activate the potential for compassion in the offender by ensuring a conference climate wherein the offender him- or herself experiences respect and empathy.

Shame-guilt is a very unpleasant feeling, which one wants to be relieved of. At this point again, it can go wrong. The direct confrontation may provoke in the offender a defensive reaction by denying the suffering or rejecting the responsibility for it. But shame-guilt may also be accepted and resolved through acknowledgment and reparation. If the offender experiences support and "gestures of reacceptance," he or she is more likely to risk a weak position and accept responsibility for what happened. To be relieved of the unpleasant feelings, the offender then will be inclined to make positive gestures in a restorative sense and seek apology.

In an apology, the offender recognizes guilt. He or she expresses an understanding of the wrongfulness of the norm transgression and confirms the offender's recognition of the victim as a bearer of rights. While recognizing guilt, the apologizing offender asks the victim to "excuse," literally to "de-accuse," to undo him or her from guilt. The offender takes the vulnerable position by placing his or her fate in the hands of the victim. The victim may refuse or accept the apology, possibly under certain conditions. The roles are reversed now. Whereas the offender exercised power over the victim in the offense, it is now the victim who has the more decisive power. The willingness of offenders to undertake material actions to secure restoration underlines the truthfulness of the apology and makes their recognition of the harm they have caused concrete.

In a successful sequence, most victims feel restored in dignity and in citizenship. Emotions of revenge in the victim fade. Whereas revenge emotions are a drive to respond to humiliation by a counter-humiliation, there is no object for this any more: The offender has, in fact, removed the humiliation through his or her apology. Moreover, we must bear in mind that a conference does not consist of a dialogue between victim and offender only.

The offender's apology is amplified by the other participants' support, which still additionally satisfies the victim's vindication. The basic empathy between all humans is activated also in the other sense so that the victim can feel some sympathy, which opens the way to forgiveness and the dialogue towards a constructive solution.

The offender's public expressions of remorse and apology, and his or her offer to make reparation, may also lead to respect for the offender, because he or she had the courage to face responsibility and be willing to make up. The acceptance of the offer by the victim and the approval by the beloved ones are expected to have an impact on his or her ethical identity as being basically a respectable person. There is a real chance that he or she is able to leave the offense and its consequences behind (after meeting the conditions), and that he or she is not fixed in the role of "irredeemable criminal" (Maruna 2001).

Moreover, the whole process, in a nonadversarial climate, may facilitate the offender's and his or her family's awareness that things are going wrong, and that something must be done to stop the negative development. It may be the occasion to search actively for treatment or help, or to accept such an offer.

This outline of the emotional dynamics that might be expected in a restorative justice conference is an ideal typical sketch. Reality is, of course, much more complicated. There are differences and nuances in each conference, depending on the nature of the crime and of those with a stake in its aftermath, and on many specific circumstances and conditions. However, the outline points to the central importance of empathy as the gate opener to the process. Therefore, the context in which it should occur is crucial. Respectful and reintegrative processes enable offenders to feel empathy. This climate is probably the key to understand the communicational and interactional plus value of restorative processes. It is as an experienced conferencing facilitator said: "Conferences bring the good in the people out" (Macrae 2000).

19.3.2.5   Public Dimensions of Restorative Justice

As crime is also a public event, the public dimensions of the restorative justice impact are also important. Restorative justice theory says that implementing restorative practices is beneficial for building stronger communities (McCold 2004b). A direct influence is expected by the decrease of reoffending in the offenders who have been involved in restorative programs. As we have just seen, this expectation is only partially confirmed by the empirical data. Indirectly, impact of restorative justice on community is anticipated by the increasing community involvement in restorative practices. That would be beneficial for cohesion within community, which in turn would improve informal social control and decrease feelings of insecurity. Counterarguments are made by those who consider restorative practices as being too soft on crime and, therefore, not deterring enough for the offenders. They fear that a systematic restorative approach would provoke an increase in crime. However, the real impact on community has not yet been documented strongly by empirical data (Kurki 2003). Reasons for that may be (1) the difficulty to define what a community is, and the consequent difficulty to measure empirically its development, and (2) the lack of systematic implementation of restorative practices in given communities, so that its impact on social life at large is hard to observe. So, we must do with partial data only.

Braithwaite supposed that "restorative justice practices restore and satisfy communities better than existing criminal justice practices" (2002). He therefore pointed to the satisfaction rates among community members participating in conferences, the increased community orientation and decreased reoffending rates among offenders, the benefits for school communities and for workplaces that implement restorative responses to norm transgressions in their midst, and also the few historical moments in which restorative-like processes have influenced peacemaking in macro-communities. Guarino-Ghezzi and Klein (1999) described two local restorative justice programs that involve the public and seem to enhance public safety.

Data are available to suggest that public acceptance of restorative responses to crime is high. First of all, careful and nuanced research of public attitudes to crime and justice clearly suggest that the public is not as straightforwardly punitive as is sometimes simplistically suggested. In a survey of public attitudes to punishments, Roberts and Hough found that "the public is unlikely soon to abandon the notion of punishment," but they also found dissatisfaction with the traditional punitive system and support for "more creative, non-carceral alternatives" (2002). They also wrote that "restorative (non-punitive) responses carry considerable appeal for the public, particularly for the young and non-violent offenders" (ibid.). Roberts and Hough suggested that public opinion cannot be considered as being cut-and-dried, but can be changed. In a research project in London and the East of England, Maruna and King found one-third of the 941 respondents who could be considered punitive, and a similar one-third who take an opposing view (2004).

Samples of lay respondents have been presented options on how to respond to crime in New Zealand (Galaway 1984), Great Britain (Wright 1989), Germany (Sessar 1999), Canada (Doob et al. 1998), and the United States (Bae 1992). If reparative alternatives are included and presented in a realistic way, a majority prefers responses that allow for reparation. As could be expected, the type of crime codefines the degree of preference. One of the most significant studies is by Sessar (1995). To a large sample of inhabitants in Hamburg, he presented thirty-eight dummy cases, ranging from theft in cars to armed robbery and rape. Respondents could choose among five possible alternative responses:

- Voluntary victim offender regulation without any official intervention.
- Victim offender regulation monitored by an official mediator.
- Possible reparative agreements to be prepared and confirmed by criminal justice system.
- Criminal punishment may be diminished if offender is willing to make amends.
- Criminal punishment, not at all influenced by possible reparation.

A majority always chooses the restitutive options, mostly outside the system (41 percent), but sometimes also inside the system (17 percent). Of those who opted for punishment by principle, only 21 percent chose the latter purely punitive response. The outside-juridical modalities were seldom chosen for burglary and for rape, but even then, a large majority preferred reparative possibilities under judicial supervision. Noticeably, possible reoffending did not change anything In regard to these preferences.

Despite the reduced availability of reliable empirical data on the subject, a tentative conclusion can be drawn. The communitarian rhetoric of much of the restorative justice advocates are not falsified so far. The data suggest that many communities and the public at large might find benefits in implementing more systematically restorative responses to crime. There is no reason to believe that it would be detrimental for safety and safety feelings. Rather the contrary. While simplistic repressive outcries may sound the loudest, it is far from evident that they are the mainstream. There is no empirical indication that the restorative justice option would be blocked by a so called general public punitiveness. Such attitude seems rather to be a myth, boosted by simplistic media and extreme right politics. Kurki writes: "Restorative justice processes carry great potential to turn incidents of crime into positive opportunities of creating new relationships, building communities, and strengthening grass roots democracy. The potential is as yet unrecognized by most criminal justice agencies and researchers, and as a result, largely unrealized and unstudied" (Kurki 2003).

19.3.3   Intermediate Conclusions

Successful restorative justice practices are spreading quickly, and in increasingly differentiated versions, all over the world. Its potential reaches a much broader scope than was originally supposed. Consequently, a growing number of scholars see restorative justice as another paradigm, which may on the longer term offer a fully fledged alternative to the traditional responses to crime. Empirical research so far brings no reason to scale down these ambitions. It is rather the contrary. But the results must be read with care. Methodological inadequacies make a great part of the research data illustrative, but not decisive. Practices evaluated are reduced in size and in scope, and are implemented often in privileged circumstances.

Restorative justice is a promising track to be further explored. Extension of practices towards more serious and more difficult crime cases is needed, and the intrinsic quality of the facilitating procedures must be monitored continuously. Sound methodology must improve research. One of the most urgent challenges is to find an adequate relation of restorative justice to the other approaches to crime, and especially to the traditional and still predominant punitive criminal justice model. As long as restorative practices were carried out in the margins of the system, and were mostly applied to less serious (juvenile) crime, they were seen as forms of diversion that would not challenge the hard core of how crime was tackled. But as the restorative justice ambitions grow, its relation to the existing criminal law and criminal justice system comes under pressure.

To examine this pressure, two functions of criminal law must be distinguished: (1) delivering a response to law breaking by an appropriate punishment, to express public disapproval of the behavior and/or to promote future law abiding by the offender and citizens; and (2) safeguarding in the course of these actions the legal and human rights of all those concerned. These functions are uncoupled, because there is no principled reason to believe that only a punitive system has the monopoly of safeguarding legal rights. Therefore, section 19.4 will first question whether punishing crime is as evident as is mostly suggested, and whether restorative responses would not be a better option. Although the choice is made mainly on social ethical grounds, section 19.5 will develop the social ethical foundations. Section 19.6, finally, will seek a political and law theory to find a legal frame that would position restorative justice into the principles of a democratic constitutional state.

19.4 Restorative Justice and Criminal Punishment

Restorative justice is not a soft option. For the offenders, being confronted directly with the suffering and harm caused and with the disapproval of the beloved persons (as in family group conferences) is a deeply touching burden. Apologizing in front of others may be felt hard and humiliating. The agreements after the mediation often require serious and unpleasant commitments and demanding investments of time. When imposed by a court order, community service is experienced as being serious sanctions, also when it is imposed in a restorative perspective (Schiff 1999).

The obvious unpleasantness of being involved as an offender in a restorative process has led several scholars to consider restorative justice as another version of punishment. Restorative justice interventions are then not called "alternatives to punishment" but "alternative punishments" (Duff 1992). For Duff, criminal mediation is a kind of punitive mediation, a special species of penal hard treatment, which is not purely retributive, but also future oriented (Duff 2001). Daly (2000, 2002) also is of the opinion that restorative justice is a punishment, because it leads to unpleasant obligations for the offender. In Duff's and Daly's view, all hard burdens imposed or accepted under pressure as a response to a wrong committed before are punishments. This is for them no reason to reject restorative approaches to crime. On the contrary, it includes restorative justice in what they consider to be indispensable in the reaction to crime: hard treatment.

From another point of view, McCold (2000) criticized the maximalist version of restorative justice, because the inclusion of coercive judicial sanctions as being potentially reparative would shift restorative justice back to being punitive. For McCold, all coercive interventions are punishments. He therefore rejects coerciveness in restorative justice.

Much depends, of course, on how punishment is understood. If every painful obligation that follows after committing a wrong is called a punishment, then most initiatives in view of reparation may be viewed as punishments. However, such a position overlooks some, in my view, critical differences between punishment and restoration, which I shall develop now.

19.4.1   Intentional Pain Infliction versus Awareness of Painfulness

"Punishing someone consists of visiting a deprivation (hard treatment) on him, because he supposedly has committed a wrong" (von Hirsch 1993).[7] Three elements are distinguished: hard treatment, the intention of inflicting it, and the link with the wrong committed before. If one of these elements is lacking, there is no punishment. Painful obligations that are not imposed with the intention to cause suffering are not punishments. That is the key difference between a fine and taxes. "Pain in punishment is inflicted for the sake of pain" (Fatic 1995).

The crux lies in the intention (Wright 2003). Equating every painful obligation after a wrong done before with punishment is based on a mistaken "psychological location" of the painfulness. The key lies in the intention of the punisher, not in the perception of the punished. It is the punisher who

[7] Contrary to von Hirsch, I do not add disapprobation as another characteristic. Punishment is often administered routinely and experienced as a "prize" to be paid, without any moral reflection at all.

considers an action to be wrong and who wants the wrongdoer to suffer for it. Even if a juvenile sees the punishment as a reason for pride in his or her peer group, it will remain a punishment. Conversely, if he or she feels the obligation to repair as hard and calls it "a punishment," it actually is no punishment if the intention of the judge was not to make the juvenile suffer, but to request from him or her a reasonable reparative contribution.

But the relation between a restorative action and pain is more complicated. Not taking the hardship of a reparative obligation into account could lead to draconian results. Obliging a deprived juvenile who stole and crashed a Jaguar to pay back the full amount of the car would condemn him or her to a lifetime of repaying and poverty. Even if there is no intention to inflict pain, there must be an awareness of the painful effects, which must be taken into account. The offender has to contribute to reparation. It will probably transcend the material repayment, which will be reduced to a small amount, in view of the offender's financial, mental, and social capacities, and the offender's future. The remaining material damage should be repaid by the insurance or by a victims' fund.

Knowing that something will hurt, and taking the hardship into account, is not the same as intentionally inflicting pain. Pain in restorative justice is only a reason to possibly reduce the obligation, never to augment it. In retributive punishment, on the contrary, the painfulness is the principal yardstick, and its amount can be increased or decreased in order to achieve proportionality. In restoration, a relation may be sought between the nature and seriousness of the harm and the restorative effort; painfulness can lead to its decrease, not to its increase.

19.4.2   Punishment as a Means, Restoration as a Goal

Punishment is a means used to enforce any legal and political system, in truly democratic societies, as well as in the most dictatorial regimes. It is an act of power to express disapproval, possibly to enforce compliance, but it is neutral about the value system it enforces. Restoration, on the contrary, is not a means, but a potential outcome. Restorative justice is indisputably a consequentionalist approach. It is characterized by the aim of doing justice through restoration. The broad scope of harm in view for possible reparation inherently demonstrates its orientation to the quality of social life, as a normative beacon. Restorative justice is not morally neutral.

Traditional criminal justice conceives of punishment as the a priori means of the intervention, in view of achieving a variety of possible goals. The long tradition of criminological research on the effectiveness of criminal punishment leads to the overall conclusion that punishment is socially not really effective (Tonry 1995; Sherman 2003). In the actuarial vision, criminal punishment would not even function adequately as a moral agent, and thus not as an authoritative censurer (Feeley and Simon 1992).

In contrast, restorative justice advances restoration in the broader sense as the objective and chooses among a diversity of social and legal means in view of this objective. Punishment is not an appropriate means for achieving restoration. On the contrary, the a priori option for punishment is a serious obstruction. Priority for the procedure in view of determining a proportionate punishment is an often decisive interference with the attention for the harm and suffering done to victims; the threat of punishment makes genuine communication about harm and possible reparation almost impossible; the penalty itself seriously hampers the offender's effort for reparation and compensation.

19.4.3   Punishment, Communication, and Restoration

Especially counterproductive is the communicative scarceness of the a priori option for punishment. The most important function of criminal justice is to be a beacon of social disapproval, to show clear limits that are observable to all. After a crime has been committed, disapproval must be expressed in such a way that it is generally understood and accepted. Society at large must see the norm being reconfirmed and perceive the authorities' determination to enforce the norm and to protect citizens from victimization. The victim must feel support in his or her victimization and assured in his or her citizenship. It should be made clear to the offender that his or her behavior is unacceptable and must change in the future.

19.4.3.1   The Communicative Poverty of Punishment

The a priori option for punishment in criminal justice interferes with effective communication. Disapproval expressed by the criminal sentence may communicate a clear message to the public at large, but it fails to communicate adequately to the other key actors: the victim and the offender. Good communication needs adequate settings. This is not the case in court, where confrontation prevails over communication, in front of the judge who will at the end decide upon the kind and degree of hard treatment (Wright 2003). The offender does not listen to the moralizing message, but tries to get away with as lenient a punishment as possible. He or she does not hear the invitation, but merely experiences the threat. It is the a priori option for inflicting hard treatment that is the major obstruction for good communication.

Although censure is needed, hard treatment is not the only way to express it. In daily life, in families and in schools, disapproval is routinely expressed without punishment. Morally authoritative persons without any power to punish are more effective in influencing moral thinking and behavior than punishment. After a crime has occurred, the settings in view of restoration are more appropriate for communicating moral disapproval and provoking repentance than are the traditional punitive procedures and sanctions. Victim-offender mediation or family group conferences intensely disapprove of the act through those who care for the offender and for whom the offender cares. Most offenders are open for communication if they themselves experience respect and elementary understanding. They can feel empathy for the suffering of their victims. Restorative settings position the harm and suffering centrally, presenting victimization as the focal concern in the norm, and this provides huge communicative potential.

19.4.3.2 Punishment, Censure, and Repentance

Understanding the traditional courts' poor communicative potentials, Duff tried to combine his retributivist position with a punitive communication through mediation (Duff 2002): "a kind of censure that aims to bring offenders to face up to and recognize the wrongs they have done; ... of burdensome reparation that expresses such an apologetic and repentant recognition; ... of a reconciliation, mediated by such recognition and reparation, between victim and offender" (Duff 2001). Duff clearly remained within the retributivist line of thinking, as he stated that "punishment is the proper response to criminal wrongdoing," or "punishment should bring them to suffer what they deserve to suffer" (Duff 2002). Traditional punishments are rejected. Ways are searched of "constructive punishing," which favor communication with the offender. "Criminal mediation" and a combination of probation with community service are advanced as prototypes. Duff projected a sequence "censure → recognition of wrongfulness → painful repentance → willingness to repair," which seems to combine retributivist standpoints with restorative concerns. But three crucial problems subsist from a restorative standpoint.

First, Duff referred to wrongfulness, as opposed to harmfulness, to consider hard treatment after a crime as necessary. It is, however, not clear how wrongfulness can be understood separately from harmfulness. Religious systems conceive of wrongfulness that is not evidently harmful for others, but such wrongs are not acceptable as reasons for public intrusions upon our liberties. It would express an ethical absolutism that would lead to a kind of Talibanization of our societies. The only justification for the authorities' interventions in our lives is sanctioning and preventing harm done to fellow citizens or to social life (von Hirsch and Jareborg 1991).

Second, the sequence just mentioned is important indeed, but it may be more difficult to achieve by the a priorism that it must be burdensome for the offender. As argued already, confirmation of the norm and disapproval of the norm transgression does not necessarily need the willing imposition of hard treatment. On the contrary, instead of promoting repentance, it may provoke defiance (Sherman 1993). The already repentant offender does not need punishment to comply with apologies and willingness to make up, and the defiant offender might become more defiant under the threat of punishment.

Finally, Antony Duff's retributive approach cannot be reconciled with the restorative one. The approach focuses on what should be done to the offender, whereas restorative justice primarily focuses on how harm can be restored. His main concern is not how the harm and suffering may be repaired, but how the "wrong" can be undone. This wrong and the way to respond to it are given, not socially debatable categories. "The reactions of others [including the victim], and of the wrongdoer, are ... subject to normative appraisal: we must ask not just what they in fact feel, but what they should feel" (Duff 2002). It clearly remains a top-down approach, as opposed to the bottom-up perspective that, as we shall see, is fundamental to restorative justice.

I have argued so far that punishment is a means, based on intentional infliction of pain, whereas restorative justice is an objective for which intentional infliction of pain is an obstacle. More crucial still is that the a priorism that crime should be responded to by an intentional infliction of pain poses serious social ethical problems.

19.4.4   Ethical Problems with Punishment

Penal theory provides justifications of why crime must be punished (von Hirsch 1998). I have commented on them more extensively elsewhere (Walgrave 2001). In the rich and complex variety of propositions, consequentionalist and retributivist arguments can be distinguished. According to consequentionalist reasoning, the evil of punishment is needed to achieve a greater social good: social order and peace. It is assumed that the public at large is learned about the social wrongfulness of certain behavior, that possible offenders are deterred by the threat of punishment, and that the individual offender is reformed, or at least incapacitated during incarceration. Besides principled difficulties to limit consequentionalist interventions, empirical research clearly shows that the instrumentalist ambitions are not fulfilled (Braithwaite 1989; Sherman 2003). On the contrary, there is an increasing awareness that relying on punishment for dealing with crime leads to more imprisonment, more human and financial costs, less ethics, and less public safety (Skolnick 1995; Tonry 1995).

The several versions of retributivism all basically go back to the Kantian principle that punishing the wrong is a categorical imperative. It is inherent in morality that wrongdoing must be responded to by imposing hard treatment on the wrongdoer. Because of the wrongdoing, the offender intrinsically deserves to be punished. The offender even has the right to be punished, because it considers him or her as a morally responsible person. Contrary to consequentionalism, retributivism primarily does not ask questions about possible targets or effects of punishment. Reasons for pain infliction are sought in a conception of equality (by rectifying the illegitimate advantage, obtained by the crime) or in the expression of blame. The amount of pain to be inflicted depends on the amount of illegitimate advantage or the degree of blameworthiness of the crime (von Hirsch 1993). By referring uniquely to the crime already committed, retributivists base the sentencing on retrospective considerations and find therein the stakes for assuring proportionality.

The censuring aspect in retributivism is easy to accept. No community can survive without norms, which are to be enforced. Clear reprobation of norm transgression is a minimum. But does censuring require punishment, i.e., intentional infliction of pain? This is an important question, because most ethical systems consider deliberately and coercively imposing suffering on another person as unethical and socially destructive. Punishment "involves actions that are generally considered to be morally wrong or evil were they not described and justified as punishments" (de Keijser 2000). Punishment of offenses by criminal justice is considered as evidence, while leaving unanswered why the general ethical rule not to inflict pain on others does not apply when responding to offenses (Fatic 1995). "Punishing today is a deeply problematic and barely understood aspect of social life, the rationale for which is by no means clear," Garland wrote (1990). What arguments do retributivists advance to except the punitive pain infliction from the general disapproval of pain infliction?

19.4.4.1 A Human Need

It is often pretended that punishing the evil is a deep human need, to overcome our resentment (Moore 1995) or to express our adherence to the good. However, the evil is not an abstract moral category, opposed to another abstract category, the good. Since Freud and Durkheim, we know that morality and social norms are basically pragmatic, to preserve self-interest and social life. The evil then is what threatens me, or already has hurt me in my human dignity, my social and material territory, my physical integrity (Maxwel 1914). Anger is basically a self-interested emotion. Fortunately, self-interest is mostly well understood in terms of being integrated into a peaceful community (Putnam 2000). Anger is understandable in victimized or threatened humans and can provoke actions of revenge. But this is no reason for anger to ground the well-reflected, rational, systemic punishment, organized by the state. Civilization is a process of increasing control over spontaneous violence and of bringing violence under state monopoly (Elias 1994). Maybe the next step in civilization is to reduce state violence itself, by not taking for granted pain infliction after a crime.

Moreover, the earlier mentioned historical studies and data from public surveys suggest that responding to law breaking by revenge is at least not as predominant in social life, as the punishment-as-general-human-need position presupposes.

19.4.4.2   A Moral Obligation

Although retributive arguments are basically grounded on the ethical categorical imperative that norm transgressions must be responded to by punishment, retributivism does hardly question the ethical value of the norm system itself, which punishment is supposed to enforce (Fatic 1995). Most retributivists seem to accept that legal order is the same as moral order.

That is not evident at all. Why, for example, is penal law predominantly geared to public order, individual security, and property, and not, for example, to social peace, solidarity, and social and economic equity? As mentioned here above, punishments can be used in any regime, to enforce any legal rule, including the most immoral ones. Leaving the use of pain infliction open to all these possible options is a very dangerous game, as daily practice overwhelmingly demonstrates.

19.4.4.3   Proportionality

Retribution refers to the wrong committed in the past, which provides a controllable yardstick for constructing proportionality in the degree of pain delivery (von Hirsch 1993). This proportionality issue is one of the main reasons for skepticism about restorative justice, which would not offer satisfying grounds for it (von Hirsch 1993).

Indeed, the response to crime must be kept within just and reasonable limits. However, the construction of proportionality in punishment is itself highly debatable (Wright 2003). There is no reason to suppose that only punitive retributivism can provide retrospective yardsticks for the intervention: Instead of linking the wrongfulness of a behavior to the degree of pain inflicted, the seriousness of harm caused might be related to the intensity of reparative effort required (Walgrave and Geudens 1997). Deliberative processes might be more appropriate to assess the reasonable and just balance than traditional criminal justice is (Braithwaite 2002).

19.4.4.4   Censure

The only remaining argument to keep a retributivist response to crime is censure. Good societies guarantee that rights and freedoms are assured and taken seriously. They therefore must issue clear norms, enforce them, and unambiguously disapprove of law breaking, so as to keep the norm well understood by all citizens and to reduce as much as possible law breaking in the future. But does censure necessarily include intentional pain infliction?

Even authoritative punitive retributivists such as von Hirsch (1993) agree that censure can also be expressed in other ways. He chose the punitive way, because of its (supposed) preventive (deterrent) impact, and because he considered its retrospective dimension as the best way to construct proportionality in the response to crime. Throughout this chapter, we have documented our position that restorative processes offer far better ways for delivering serious and effective censure than hard treatment does.

To conclude, punishment as an intentional infliction of suffering causes serious social ethical problems, which are not resolved by penal theories. The a priori position that crime must be punished is a typical top-down approach, based on an imposed rule of law, and does not consider genuinely the social context of possible solutions. For society at large, penal criminal justice intervention offers a strong confirmation of legal order, but public safety is badly served. Pure punishment carries the seeds of more social discord and un-well-being, and thus of more crime and criminalization (Braithwaite 1989). Victims are principally used as witnesses, but then left alone to deal with their losses and grievances (Dignan and Cavadino 1998). The priority given to the penal procedure and the penal sanction hinders the chances for victims to be compensated and/or restored. For the offender, the sanction is a senseless infliction of suffering, which does not contribute to public safety, or to the victim's interests. It is a counterproductive, ethically highly doubtful intrusion on the offender's freedom.

In fact, the evidence of accepting punishment as the mainstream response to crime is in itself ethically doubtful. That is why the possible ways of expressing blame without punishment must thoroughly be explored. That brings us to the question whether restorative justice really is grounded on a different, and more satisfying, social ethical basis. That is what we are going to explore in the next section.

19.5   The Socio-Ethical Foundations of Restorative Justice

Restorative justice recalls the fundamental raison d'être of the criminal justice system. Why is it forbidden to steal and to commit private violence? Because if it were not forbidden, severe victimizations would occur all the time, provoke counter actions to make things even, and lead to an escalation in mutual victimizations. Constructive social life would be impossible, because it would be dominated by abuse of power and fear. Therefore, if a crime occurs nevertheless, what should logically be the first concern of the social reaction to it? It should be to repair as much as possible, and in an orderly way, the harm to the victimized citizen, and the damage to social life.

Restorative justice (re)positions the quality of social relations and of social life in general, and not the abstract legal order, as the ground reason for criminalizing certain behavior. Its aim is to restore this quality, and not primarily to enforce an abstract legal rule.

To achieve this goal, the restorative approach relies mainly on cooperation among the citizens, and not primarily on coercive intervention by the state. The trust is that, if appropriate conditions are shaped, opponents in a conflict are able to meet each other in mutual understanding and respect, and find a constructive solution. Restorative justice philosophy as a whole rests upon the earlier mentioned belief that almost all humans feel a deeply rooted sense of empathy for other humans, and that they can understand their common interest in living together in harmony and peace.

Consequently, restorative practice tends to give back to the "owners of the conflict" the search for a solution, through deliberation (Christie 1977). It is those with a direct stake in the aftermath of the crime who should be given priority to define what the problem is and how it can best be resolved. The role of the state in the restorative philosophy is to serve the deliberative process, to complement them with coercion if deliberative processes appear not to be possible or do not lead to satisfying agreement, and to guard the public interests in the settlement of the crime (Declaration of Leuven 1998).

This clearly is a bottom-up approach to crime, giving priority to what can be achieved in the grassroots and considering the state-intervention as subsidiary to that. This is opposed to the top-down approach in traditional criminal justice, where abstract legal rules are imposed from above on the citizens, offenders, victims, and communities.

Although restorative justice has been developed most clearly for implementation in criminalizable matters, its participatory philosophy was developed also beyond criminal justice matters. Community mediation is used for settling disputes in the lifeworld of (increasingly multiethnic) urban neighborhoods (Merry and Milner 1993; Peper and Spierings 1999), conferencing is used for dealing with bullying and other discipline problems in schools (Ahmed 2001; Cameron and Thorsborne 2001; Nothafft 2003), restorative models are used to find solutions after corporate crime (Braithwaite 2003), and deliberative processes including parents and other family members have been developed in child welfare issues (Fraser and Norton 1996; Marsh and Crow 1996). In short, restorative principles are penetrating as an important dimension in everyday life (Watchel and McCold 2001). Principles of restorative justice appear increasingly in peacemaking initiatives after gross violations of human rights and collective armed violence, as in

Serbia, the Truth and Reconciliation commissions in South Africa, or the Gacaca regulations in Rwanda (Braithwaite 2002; Nikolic-Ristanovic 2003).

What is common in all these approaches is the belief in the grassroots potentials and the concern for the quality of social life, best expressed in the notion of communitarianism.

19.5.1 From Community to Communitarianism

Community occupies a focal position in restorative rhetoric (Bazemore and Schiff 2001). The priority given to restoring the harm caused by crime inevitably draws the attention to the social unrest suffered by community. The living community is more directly victimized by the occurrence of an offense than the state is. Moreover, restorative interventions require a minimum of community: victim and offender must feel a minimal common interest in constructively settling together the aftermath of the crime.

However, it is difficult to grasp the community notion and to insert it into a coherent theory. Three problems appear. First, even if it is not a territorial space (McCold and Watchel 1998), "community" suggests an area, distinguishing an inside community from an outside noncommunity. But it is impossible to delineate it mentally, socially, or territorially. It expands as far as the vague and drifting limits conceived by individual subjects (Crawford and Clear 2001). Community is a psychological entity, rather than a set of characteristics of given collectivities.

Second, building on communities for developing restorative responses to crime presupposes that communities really exist, which is far from evident (Braithwaite 1993; Crawford and Clear 2001). Crawford wrote: "Communities are not the heavens of reciprocity and mutuality nor are they the utopias of egalitarianism, that some might wish" (Crawford 2002). It is difficult to mobilize community in the resolution of a street robbery in which victim and offender live many miles from each other and belong to totally different social networks. Most crimes occur in non-community-like social settings, and the solution is to be found in the absence of such a setting.

Third, the community notion is vulnerable to possible misuses (Pavlich 2001). Communities are not good per se. The supposed *niche* of community may appear to be a hotbed of suffocating social control within the community, and exclusivism versus the outside world. In the name of community, people are subjected to unreasonable control and local stigmatization (Putnam 2000). Local communities support repressive police forces and judges and vote for exclusivist politicians. To the outside world, communities based on territory, ethnicity, or religion may develop exclusionary tendencies, provoking possibly violent conflicts. Community contains "the seeds of parochialism which can lead ... to atrocious totalitarian exclusions" (Pavlich 2001).

Skepticism about the community notion does not necessarily mean rejecting the ideals promoted by most communitarians: social unity, a form of harmonious living together, based on shared values and beliefs and mutual commitment. But do we need community for promoting such ideals? Must these socio-ethical attitudes and functions be limited to a given area defined by community? Most communitarians in fact promote social ethics and values, not areas. "Community" is a container for ethics and social values. The ethics and values must be unpacked from their container. Although I am hesitant about the appropriateness of community to characterize part of social reality, I believe that communitarianism may be a useful label for a socio-ethical movement.

19.5.2 Towards Communitarian Social Ethics for Restorative Justice

Restorative justice is more than a technical view on doing justice. It is an ideal of justice in a utopian ideal of society. In the communitarian utopia, the distinction between society and community is meaningless, because collectivity is governed in view of individual and collective emancipation, in which autonomy and solidarity are not seen as opposed, but as mutually reinforcing principles. Collective life draws its strength not from threat, coercion, and fear, but from motivation, based on trust, participation, and support. Communitarianism can tend towards a suffocating collectivism. That is why it must be considered together with a political theory that combines social values with individual rights and freedoms. Later in this chapter, we shall look into the republican theory.

A collectivity aiming at this utopia promotes as "virtues" socio-ethical attitudes that serve it. I see three such virtues or behavioral guidelines: respect, solidarity, and taking responsibility. In respect, the intrinsic value of the other is recognized. The recognition may be broad. It is ethical to respect not only humans, but also nature and objects. Respect for humans recognizes the intrinsic value of a human being, made concrete through the Universal Declaration of Human Rights, for example. Respect for "human dignity" is a bottom-line obligation for all social institutions.

Solidarity is more specific than respect. It is not evident to feel solidarity with objects or with nature. Solidarity presupposes more commitment than respect, because solidarity includes a form of companionship and reciprocity of support. Companionship goes with empathy and mutual trust, which is most visible in the approach of those in trouble. Community rhetoric often locates solidarity within the scope of a given community, but as it is now unpacked from its "community container," solidarity is no longer limited by a given area but is a general ethical value. "This spirit of solidarity may be regarded as a forever-elusive promise of unpremeditated collective togetherness" (Pavlich 2001).

Responsibility links the person to his or her acts and their consequences. It confronts the self with its own actions. In passive responsibility, one is confronted for one's actions by others. Active responsibility is an awareness of the link between the self and the actions and behaving accordingly (Braithwaite and Roche 2001; Braithwaite 2002). It is essential that members of a community, or citizens, take their responsibility and respond actively and autonomously to the obligations in social life, which in communitarian ethics are oriented towards solidarity.

Other ethical guidelines might be superfluous if members of the collectivity behaved according to these three. This also applies to "justice." As van Ness wrote: "Where there is sufficient community peace, there will be relatively little need for order. Where there is little peace, more order will be needed" (2002b). In Duff, we read: "If people are bound together by strong bonds of mutual affection or concern ... there may be less need and less proper room for contractual definitions of their respective rights and obligations" (2001). Justice is currently advanced as a separate ethical rule only because respect, solidarity, and responsibility are not achieved sufficiently.

19.5.3   Ethics in Restorative Justice and in Punitive Justice

At first glance, advancing respect, solidarity, and responsibility as basics in communitarian ethics may seem to be mere rhetoric. Don't we all value these virtues?

Do we really? Is respect an ethical guideline in retributivism? Respect for the victim is absent, because he or she is not included in the retributivist reflections. Retributivism is focused on the offender. Considering offenders as moral agents, and treating them in a just (deserts) way, recognizes them as human beings and as citizens with guaranteed rights. But the respect is not complete. The offenders are not respected as whole persons with personal interests and interpretations, including their possible willingness to make up for their misbehavior. In the end, the offender has to submit to a proportionate punishment. Once the crime has been committed, respect for the person is withdrawn. The offenders are judged as moral agents to be considered guilty, but not to contribute to finding a constructive response to the problems caused by their crimes (Duff 2001).

I do not see solidarity, the companionship including willingness for mutual support, in retributivism. The response does not support the victim, but merely punishes the offender, which often hampers possible reparation. In restorative justice, solidarity with the victim is evident, but solidarity with the offender is also present. The offender is not excluded but encouraged to make up for the conduct, in order to preserve his or her position as an integrated member of the collectivity.

Responsibility is central to retributivism. The offender is held responsible by having to respond to the obligation created by the misconduct, but again, the responsibility is incomplete. Responsibility only means accepting the negative consequences, but not searching for a constructive solution to the problems created. It is only a passive, retrospective form of responsibility. The victim is not considered responsible for anything except, maybe, to report the crime and to witness. Retributivism burdens the criminal justice system with the crucial responsibility to censure criminal behavior and to impose proportionate punishments. Restorative justice largely relies on active responsibility. The offender's active responsibility includes the obligation to contribute to the reparation of the harm. The victim is encouraged, but not obliged, to assume the general citizens' responsibility for trying to find peace-promoting solutions. Restorative justice also stands for responsible collectivities, bound by obligations to search for socially constructive responses within the rules of law.

This exercise of course needs more deepening and extension. It may, however, make clear that restorative justice promotes social ethical attitudes or virtues like respect, solidarity, and taking responsibility more than retributive justice does, and that it is, therefore, more likely to contribute constructively to social life and relations. The priority for the quality of social life, as expressed in the communitarian utopia, grounds the bottom-up approach in restorative justice, which appears through the preference for informal regulations, away from imposed procedures and outcomes. The point of departure for restorative justice, as in communitarianism, is that solutions primarily must be sought through the human and social resources in social life itself. This is opposed to the top-down approach in traditional criminal justice, where decisions are imposed according to strict rules, leaving restricted room, if any, for the views and interests of those directly concerned.

19.6   Communitarian Ethics, the Rule of Law, and Participatory Democracy

The communitarian utopia is far from being realized. Although "justice" was considered as a derivative value only in the "communitarian utopia," it must currently be seen as a value on its own in the nonideal societies. Often, agreed constructive solutions of the aftermath of a crime cannot be achieved, due to a lack of mutual respect, solidarity, or active responsibility. In free processes and agreements, respect and solidarity may be overruled by self-interest and abuse of power. It is, therefore, necessary to check processes and outcomes according to rights and duties. We are seeking a system that combines a large margin for informal processes in line with the "communitarian ethics," with rules of law and legal mechanisms of formal control. These rules and mechanisms should themselves express maximally the social-ethical guidelines described above.

19.6.1   Dominion

Earlier in this chapter, I mentioned "dominion" as a concept to understand better the public aspect of the harm caused by a crime. Dominion is the central notion in Braithwaite and Pettit's republican theory of criminal justice (Braithwaite and Pettit 1990), which offers an excellent basis for developing legal theory on restorative justice (Walgrave 2000b).

"Dominion" can be defined as the set of assured rights and freedoms. Dominion (or "freedom as nondomination")[8] is the ultimate criterion to evaluate restorative processes and values (Braithwaite 2000). It is the mental and social territory of which we freely dispose, as it is guaranteed by the state and the social environment. The assurance aspect of rights and freedoms is crucial in the theory (Putnam 1993). "I know that I have rights, I know that the others know it, and I trust that they will respect it." I am assured only if I trust my fellow citizens and the state that they will take my rights and freedoms seriously, based on respect and solidarity. It is only then that I will fully enjoy my mental and social domain.

The assurance element makes the crucial distinction between the social concept of "freedom as nondomination" and the liberal concept of "freedom as noninterference." In the latter, the rights and freedoms of the individual citizen end where the rights and freedoms of the other citizen begin. Rights and freedoms are conceived as a stable given, which must be distributed as justly as possible. All other citizens are possible interferers in my freedom and rivals in my struggle to expand my freedom. In the republican view, on the contrary, rights and freedoms are a collective good. Dominion is not a stable given but a value to be promoted and expanded by individual and collective action. The fellow citizens are allies in trying to extend and mutually assure dominion as a collective good.

19.6.1.1   Restoring Assurance in Dominion

A good state, Braithwaite and Pettit wrote, must promote dominion (1990). Dominion is thus not delineated, but a value to be promoted. One could see the republican theory as a formalization of the earlier described communi-

---

[8] In later publications, "dominion" has been renamed as "freedom as nondomination." It may make it easier to oppose it to the liberal concept typified as "freedom as noninterference," but I see no other advantage in complicating the wording. I will therefore stick to the old naming, "dominion."

tarian ideal into a political theory. This formalization is necessary to avoid communitarianism shifting downwards collectivism, extreme nationalism, or moral absolutism. The communitarian utopia of a collectivity driven by shared values, solidarity, and active responsibility can be achieved only so far as the state and the citizens mutually assure respect for rights and freedoms, as accorded in dominion. Inversely, the assurance of rights and freedoms is achieved only in the degree to which citizens take up their responsibilities in view of respect and solidarity.

The state seeks to extend and deepen dominion by promoting equality through more democracy, education, equitable socioeconomic policy, welfare policy, and the like. Criminal justice is the defensive institution. Crime is an intrusion upon dominion, and criminal justice must act to repair it (Walgrave 2000b).[9] The intrusion most hurts the assurance in dominion. In the example of the burglary, the restitution or compensation of the concrete victim's losses could strictly be private, to be arranged by civil law. But there is also a public side, which is the loss of assurance: The burglary not only hurts the victim's trust that his or her privacy and possessions will be respected by fellow citizens. The particular victim also stands as an example of what all citizens risk to undergo. If the authorities did nothing against the particular burglary, it would undermine citizens' trust in the right to privacy and possession.

Public intervention after a crime is, therefore, not primarily needed to put right the balance of benefits and burdens, nor to reconfirm the law. It is needed first of all to enhance assurance, by communicating the message that authorities do take dominion seriously. The intervention must reassure the victim and the public of their rights and freedoms, and restore these rights and freedoms into being an assured, fully fledged dominion. This happens by clearly censuring the intrusion and by involving, if possible, the offender in reparative actions. Voluntary cooperation of the offender is more effective to restore assurance, but only if it is backed by public institutions. The assurance indeed not only comes from the individual offender's repentance and apologies, but also from the authorities' determination to take the assured set of rights and freedoms seriously.

Earlier in this chapter, we defined restorative justice as an option on doing justice that is primarily oriented towards repairing the individual, relational, and social harm that is caused by an offense. We now make the social harm in the definition more focused and precise: The aim of restorative justice as a public intervention is to restore the assurance of rights and freedoms, which is essential for restoring the intruded dominion.

---

[9] The target of criminal justice must be repairing dominion, and not promoting it, as Braithwaite and Pettit suggest, because promotion of dominion is an insatiable target.

19.6.1.2 *Respecting Rights and Freedoms in Dominion*

Dominion is not only a value to be promoted; it also has a "hard core," consisting of actual rights and freedoms, which provides grounds for defining limits to (restorative) justice interventions. The intervention must be assuring for dominion by the respect it shows itself for rights and freedoms (Walgrave 2000b). Braithwaite and Pettit (1990, 2000) listed four constraints: parsimony, checking of authorities' use of power, reprobation of crime, and reintegration of victims and offenders.

The parsimony constraint is crucial to combine informal processes with the need for formal controls. In the republican theory, criminal justice is bound by the constraint of parsimony in using its coercive power. Parsimony is more restricting than the proportionality obligation in traditional criminal justice theories. Proportionality includes setting an upper limit and a lower limit in degree of punishment. In parsimony, there is no under limit. On the contrary, the parsimony constraint requires an active search for noncoercive ways to restore dominion. The more voluntary restorative processes can lead to satisfying and balanced outcomes, the less appeal to coercive judicial interventions is needed and, thus, the more the parsimony principle is achieved. A fully fledged restorative justice system should fulfill its parsimony obligation by leaving space for and diverting to voluntary processes, wherein victim, offender, and collectivity can seek together an agreed settlement of the aftermath of a crime that maximally restores dominion.

"Checking of power" as a constraint is derived from the assurance aspect in dominion. Citizens must be assured that they cannot be subjected to arbitrary power by the powerful and the authorities. Possible abuse of power is best avoided in two ways: (1) The top-down power of courtroom must be decentralized as much as possible towards bottom-up deliberative meetings with those most directly concerned. (2) Controllable rules must be provided to hold the authorities accountable (Roche 2003) and to check whether dominion has not been unnecessarily intruded for the offender, the victim, and other stakeholders. The traditional deontological principles guiding criminal justice can serve as a basis, but we shall see in short that they must be revised in view of restorative justice principles.

The constraint "reprobation" includes that the intervention must clearly reject the criminal offense, but the constraint "reintegration" means also that it may not unnecessarily be excluding. In the republican theory, indeed, the dominion must be maximized for all, including for victims and offenders. Both constraints thus lead together to responses to crimes that clearly reject the act, while avoiding as much as possible the exclusion of the actor, or even while favoring his or her reintegration. That is why traditional punitive a priorism is rejected and restorative possibilities are maximally explored.

19.6.2   A Pyramid of Restorative Law Enforcement

How restorative justice would be included more concretely in a republican system of criminal justice is proposed in Braithwaite's regulatory pyramid (2002). The bottom consists of participatory restorative processes, which, he assumed, will regulate the great majority of offenses. A more reduced space of punitive deterrence is located above the restorative space, to influence the offenders who cannot be motivated to participate in voluntary reparation, but who do calculate rationally the benefits and burdens of their behavior. On top of the pyramid is located a small triangle of incapacitation to deal with the incompetent or irrational offenders. Braithwaite wrote that "restorative justice will often fail … and in such cases the safety of the community requires escalation to more punitive approaches." He added, however, that "restorative justice values should be given as much space as possible within the punitive institution" (Braithwaite 2002). In Braithwaite's view, the longer term ambition is to enlarge the bottom, to reduce the top, and to include restorative values as much as possible within the punitive justice institution.

Dignan has adapted the proposal in his "enforcement pyramid" (2002, 2003). He mainly included the judicial sanctions in the middle space more explicitly into restorative justice. What Braithwaite called deterrent punishment is, in Dignan's option, replaced by two subparts, namely a larger part for court-imposed restoration orders, and a smaller one for court-imposed presumptive "restorative" punishments.

The pyramid in Figure 19.1 is largely inspired by both preceding designs.

19.6.2.1   Deliberative Conflict Resolution in Community

The enforcement pyramid is based on the potential to seek deliberative conflict resolution in community. We have seen that such models are being developed increasingly in schools, neighborhoods, welfare, labor, and other contexts. They are the niches to be extended for a generalized approach to conflict resolution, based on a philosophy of participation and inclusion into a community of mutual respect and solidarity. Expanding such core models helps to develop mental and social capacities to communicate, to listen with respect, and to seek consensus in a conflict resolution.

To further promote these schedules, agencies should be largely available and easily accessible in schools, neighborhoods, and other local community levels. They should be supported, but not steered, by authorities. Their availability would avoid the escalation of conflicts into criminalization of tensions and behavior. Moreover, they would contribute to a general mentality of deliberation and autonomous conflict resolution, and decrease improper appeal to societal institutions for trifles.

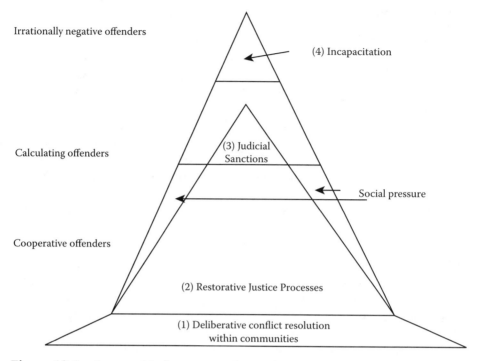

Figure 19.1 A pyramid of restorative law enforcement.

19.6.2.2 *Restorative Justice Processes*

When an offense has been committed, dominion is intruded. Public interest requires that something must happen. In the dominion concept, public interest is best served by giving priority to the less intrusive responses, steered by the most direct stakeholders. As in both Braithwaite's (2002) and Dignan's (2002, 2003) pyramid, I assume that a great part of the crimes can be resolved by voluntary processes involving the direct stakeholders in view of finding a restorative solution. It may be expected that this part will increase as the agencies to monitor such processes become more skilled and are more spread and available, and as the public gets more used to work that way.

However, even in such processes, the state cannot withdraw completely. If it did, it would give free way to possible uncontrollable abuses of power. Despite a high degree of "deliberative accountability" in conferences and other restorative processes, there is also a considerable risk that such meetings turn into serious abuses of power, and unreasonable and all-too-punitive outcomes (Dignan 2002; Roche 2003). Second, the complete absence of the state in the process would leave the parties alone to find a solution. State authorities would not guarantee respect for rights and freedoms and would thus not assure dominion. To give assurance, the state must guarantee that everything possible will be done to respect and restore the intruded-on dominion. In a voluntary restorative deliberation, the state must be present at least in the background to ensure that the deliberation takes place and results in an acceptable outcome, to guarantee the power balance in the deliberation, and to provide an opportunity for the parties to leave the deliberative process and turn to the traditional judicial response, if one of them feels that their interests are not adequately acknowledged in the deliberative process. Authorities demonstrate that they take dominion seriously not only with regard to the victim's rights and freedoms but also as a guarantor of the offender's rights and as a safeguard for the collectively assured set of rights and freedoms.

Though voluntariness is said to be crucial in restorative processes, one must not be naïve. Offenders do not ask to participate in a conference or to be involved in mediation. The expectation is that the great majority of them seek to get away with the least possible sanction. They agree to participate because they are pressured by the family, by other members of their community of care, or even by the threat to be referred to court (Boyes-Watson 2000). That is why restorative justice processes have a broad space for free choice and deliberation but also a broadening margin of social pressure. The more pressure is needed to bring the parties to meet, the closer is the eventuality to refer the case to court.

19.6.2.3 Judicial Sanctions

Several reasons may make an appeal to the public judicial system necessary. Often, the voluntary process cannot be achieved, because the victim or the offender refuses to step into the encounter, or because they do not find an agreement. Some particular offenses may provoke such public turmoil, because of their seriousness, repetitiveness, or other circumstances, that a public response is considered vital to restore social peace. Judicial interventions then may lead to imposing obligations and deprivations of liberties. As I have explained earlier, these sanctions should not be punitive, meaning intentionally inflicting pain, but they should serve as much as possible the restorative goal. Material restitution or compensation to the victim can be imposed, a fine may be paid as a contribution to a victims' fund or to another social agency, community service can be imposed and understood as a symbolic compensation for the harm caused to social life. These judicially imposed obligations have a primarily reparative ambition, though their restorative impact will almost never be as intense as after a deliberative process. But it must be reminded that giving priority to restoration does not mean that it will always completely be possible.

The space of free choice and deliberation is still present, but limited. The offender can try to negotiate with the judge and decide to comply or not. To enforce compliance with these primarily reparative sanctions, additional pressure may be exerted by (threatening with or carrying out) explicitly unpleasant deprivations of liberty like a curfew or forced stay in a closed facility. In principle, they would last only till the offender agrees to carry out the reparative sanction. A maximum is, however, needed to avoid very resistant or stubborn offenders undergoing a disproportionately long sentence, while not representing a serious threat to public safety (Dignan 2002; Walgrave 2002a).That needs further comments.

(1) As in the punitive approach, restorative justice procedures and sanctions must also be controllable by checks and balances. But the principles underpinning criminal punishment cannot evidently be copied for application to restorative justice procedures and sanctions. The main functions and goals, the actors, and the social and judicial context all are (partly) different. Contrary to the top-down approach in traditional justice, a restorative system should allow ample space for a bottom-up approach. Restorative justice must therefore rethink the traditional legal safeguards in a way that they respect the restorative justice philosophy. "Judges have an important role to play in monitoring restorative justice programs, but should approach this role in a new way" (Roche 2003). How that would look is only recently a subject of debate and research (Braithwaite 2002; Dignan 2002; Walgrave 2002b; von Hirsch et al. 2003; Roche 2003; van Ness 2004).

A justice system that is primarily oriented towards doing justice through restoration has some commonalities and crucial differences compared to the traditional criminal justice system. Both the criminal justice and the restorative justice systems express clear limits to social tolerance, hold the offender responsible for his or her behavior, tend to restore a kind of justice balance, and use, if necessary, coercion according to legal standards.

First, like in retributive punishment, restorative justice also clearly displays the limits to social tolerance, because the reason for the intervention explicitly refers to the wrong done before. Both retributive and restorative interventions are retrospective, which is crucial to deduce legal safeguards. In penal justice, the seriousness of the crime committed is the yardstick to decide upon the proportionate punishment. In restorative justice, the seriousness of the harm caused can be the criterion to gauge which maximum amount of restorative effort is reasonable (Walgrave and Geudens 1997).

Restorative interventions also clearly express disapproval of the wrong and therefore also provide censuring. What distinguishes restorative censuring from punitive censuring is that the reasons for the disapproval are rooted in social relations. The wrongfulness disapproved is the one that causes harm to another person and to social life. Restorative censuring does not refer to an abstract ethical or legal rule, but to the obligation to respect quality of social life.

Second, holding the offender responsible is essential in both punitive and restorative approaches to crime. Punitive retributivism is based on a passive concept of responsibility, wherein the offender is confronted with his or her responsibility by others and must submit to the consequences imposed by the criminal justice system. Restorative justice refers to an active responsibility concept, wherein the offender must take active responsibility, by contributing actively to repairing the negative consequences of the offense (Braithwaite and Roche 2001). Whereas passive responsibility is retrospective only, active responsibility is retrospective and prospective as well.

Both also can include personal and social circumstances in the sentencing. Not only crime seriousness defines the amount of punishment or obligation to compensate, but also the offender's mental capacities and material resources, the degree of premeditation, and his or her social and situational peculiarities. Such elements would evidently be considered more adequately and thoroughly in deliberative conditions like in the voluntary processes, but they are also crucial in judicial sentencing.

Both retrospectivity and (degree of) responsibility address the two crucial questions in traditional sentencing: Have the facts been established and has the (degree of) guilt been established (Ashworth 1986)?

But, third, sentencing in view of reparation ads a third question: How can the sanction contribute maximally to reparation? This question is not asked in punitive retributive justice, because of the a priori option for punishment, and because it is not prospective. Restorative justice, on the contrary, aims at repairing the harm and is, therefore, prospective also. Again, voluntary deliberative processes are more adequate to assess the harm and to consider possible reasonable reparation, but the question must also be central in judicial proceedings.

Retribuere, in Latin, literally means to pay back. In retributive punishment, the imbalance is supposed to be repaired by paying back to the offender the suffering and harm he or she has caused. It is supposed that things are even then: Both suffer equally much. The problem is, however, that "balancing the harm done by the offender with further harm inflicted on the offender … only adds to the total amount of harm in the world" (Wright 1992). The amount of suffering is doubled but equally spread.

The paying back principle is reversed in restorative justice and, therefore, even in a more genuine form than in punitive retributivism. The offender's passive role in punitive retributivism is reversed in an active role: He or she must pay back, by repairing as much as possible the harm and suffering caused. Instead of restoring the balance by doubling the total amount of suffering, it is now restored by taking suffering away. Retribution in its genuine meaning is achieved, in its constructive way, unlike in punitive retributivism. This reversed, restorative retributivism also may include a kind of proportionality, which, however, will not refer to "just deserts," but to "just due." Surprisingly, restorative justice thus appears as a form of inversed retributivism (Zehr 2002; Walgrave 2004b). It does not inflict pain as a punitive a priorism, but it creates, possibly even imposes, obligations in view of reparation, which may be painful.

(2) How would such principles concretely influence procedures and sanctions? It is difficult to develop this in detail, because thinking about it is only beginning, experience is reduced, and the practical consequences may be specific according the different legal systems and traditions in each country. However, some options may be advanced.

- Because coercive intervention must be used parsimoniously, restorative justice procedures should at all stages allow easy exits towards voluntary informal crime regulations. Diversion is obligatory wherever possible. The decision to prosecute in court must be justified with positive arguments, and not simply because the law has been broken. This is so because dominion must be intruded minimally, and because the restorative caliber of voluntary agreements is higher.
- Restorative justice procedures must allow large opportunities for input by victims and others affected by the crime. This input is crucial in defining the kind and amount of harm and in finding the best possible restorative outcome. But victims cannot be given decisive power in judicial sentencing, because such sentencing must transcend the victim's option and needs.
- Criminal investigation is focused not only on establishing the facts and guilt, but also on defining the harm, suffering, and social unrest caused by the offense. It will also explore the potentials for negotiation, and thus for "diversion," and for possible restorative sanctions if diversion would not be possible.
- As mentioned already, the sanction would not link the seriousness of crime to a proportionate punishment, but the seriousness and kind of harm to a maximum of reasonable restorative effort.

19.6.2.4 *Incapacitation*

Finally, some irrational or fanatic offenders clearly represent a serious threat to public safety. They have committed serious crimes, and the fear is justified that they will reoffend, causing new severe victimizations. Opportunities for deliberative restorative actions seem not to work or to be insufficient to reasonably expect that the threat will end. In such cases, restorative justice has reached its limits. Priority must then be given to incapacitation, to preserve dominion for the potential victims and for the offender as well, as he or she may be victimized by revenge or by vigilantism.

There is a difference between such incapacitation and punishment. In punishment, an offender is locked up because he or she has committed a crime; in incapacitation, the offender is locked up because we are afraid. Theoretically, the decision to incapacitate depends on the assumed dangerousness of the offender. And that is a dangerous option itself. How shall we assess the dangerousness? How long will the incapacitation last? On what basis? How to combine this practice with decent and controllable legal safeguards? In practice, we will probably see traditional punitive principles be applied to serious offenders who are unwilling to participate in deliberation and about whom justified fears exist that they will reoffend seriously.

Priority for security concerns does not exclude completely the tentative actions in view of reparation. If possible, mediation in detention can be tried; inmates may be encouraged to undertake reparative efforts or to work for a victims' fund, for example.

19.6.2.5 Conclusions

The pyramid of restorative law enforcement tries to design how restorative justice gives priority to voluntary deliberation with decisive participation by the stakeholders to resolve conflicts and the aftermath of crimes, but also how coercion and even public security are indispensable complements, and how a legal system needs to frame the entire construction. It must be clear by now that distinguishing restorative from punitive criminal justice, as I did before, does not mean rejecting coercion and legalism. In my view, restorative justice deals with a particular kind of problem behavior, because it has a formal public dimension, contrary to torts or improper behavior, for example. I therefore strongly believe in the necessity to keep a criminal justice system, but it must be oriented primarily towards doing justice through restoration, and not through punishment. On the longer term, the criminal justice system should evolve towards being a fully fledged restorative criminal justice system.

The pyramid provides for the possibility to increase pressure and coercion gradually. But it is important that even at the lowest level, possible coercion is implicitly present already. Understanding that even for a benign act of vandalism, for example, the community of care, the local community, the broader community, the public authorities, and finally the criminal justice system may expect, demand, and finally eventually enforce a gesture of reparation, has its influence on the most freely accepted deliberative level. For the victim, it is reassuring that the victimization is not tolerated and must be repaired. For offenders, it makes clear that they will in any case not escape taking their responsibility. For both, it is reassuring and moderating to know that the legal frame keeps the action within limits. In the pyramid, "the rights/procedural justice discourse percolates down into restorative justice conferences" (Braithwaite and Parker 1999). After all, such deliberation never is completely free of pressure, and it would be unworldly to expect that it could be.

But the most powerful and coercive intervention systems must be permeated by the parsimony constraint. Wherever and whenever favorable for restoration and possible in view of public security, "de-escalation back down the pyramid" is needed (Braithwaite 2002). When the offender after a while appears to represent a lesser danger for public security as he or she originally seemed to do, when he or she finally agrees to comply with reparative sanctions, when victim and offender agree to try to find a constructive agreement, each time, the case should be left or given back to the less coercive levels. That, of course, presupposes a moderated and reserved attitude in the more coercive agencies, and especially in the justice system. The rule of law must not only "percolate down into restorative justice," as stated above, but restorative justice concerns must also "bubble up the pyramid into legal discourse and procedures" (Braithwaite and Parker 1999).

All this presupposes both active and responsible citizens and authorities who respond positively to the grassroots in society. It, in fact, relies on an ideal typical vision of democracy.

19.6.3   Restorative Justice and Democracy

Roche said, "By bringing participatory deliberative democracy back into the centre of the criminal justice system, restorative justice offers a possible route for restoring not just victims and offenders, but also for restoring citizens' faith in governments perceived to be unresponsive to their concerns" (2003). Braithwaite advanced "responsive regulation" as the basso continuo to link restorative justice to a state model of justice and state institutions as a whole: "Law enforcers should be responsive to how effectively citizens or corporations are regulating themselves before deciding whether to escalate intervention" (2000). "What we want is a legal system where citizens learn that responsiveness is the way our legal institutions work. Once they see the legal system as a responsive regulatory system, they know there will be a chance to argue about unjust laws" (Braithwaite 2002).

Many restorative justice advocates have a broader agenda than just changing the way justice is done after a crime has occurred. They see restorative justice as a part of a larger ideological movement aiming at restoring the quality of our democracies as a whole. The promotion of the participatory philosophy throughout social and societal institutions may contribute to a more participatory and deliberative democracy, as opposed to what I call the current, predominantly consumerist democracies.

Putnam gave a compelling account of the decline of social capital in the United States. Social capital "refers to connections among individuals—social networks and the norms of reciprocity and trustworthiness that arise from them." Social capital, the "conceptual cousin" of community, is a private as well as a public good. "The touchstone of social capital is the principle of generalized reciprocity (Putnam 2000)." In reciprocity, we expect that if we do something for our neighbor, our neighbor will also do something for us. In generalized reciprocity, we do not necessarily expect that our neighbor will do something for us, but we believe that doing good in general will provide a return in the form of a peaceful and constructive social environment, from which we will draw many benefits. We abide by the law, not because we obey "some impossibly idealistic rule of selflessness, but rather because we pursued "self-interest rightly understood" (Putnam 2000). We are committed to social life in general, because we expect reciprocity from community and the society we are living in (Braithwaite and Pettit 1990).[10] This presupposes honesty and trust in the honesty of the others. Thick trust is attributed to those we have good personal experiences with, our family, good friends. Thin trust is given to the "generalized other." Thin trust is an attitude by which we give the other people, also foreigners, "the benefit of the doubt." Thin trust "lubricates" social life and makes democracy work smoothly (Putnam 1993).

Putnam described how social capital in the United States has declined drastically recently, as expressed in less mutual confidence in business and other relations, less political and civic participation, decreasing commitment in the workplace, declining volunteering, and other indications. This has consequences for the quality of politics. "Politics without social capital is politics at a distance" (Putnam 2000). Civic participation in democracy fades away. Commonsense bottom-up input from where life is really lived gets lost and gives way to extremist or professionalized options and decisions, making participation and control from the grassroots still more difficult.

There is no reason to believe that the United States has the monopoly on this process. The decline in participation in elections, in civic engagement, in mutual trust, and the rise of lawyers and other professional experts to rule social life and in welfare agencies are typical Western phenomena of recent decade(s). The distance between governments and citizens increases, the democratic deficit rises, and citizens' discontent grows.

What happened? One of the most fundamental causes may be capitalist globalization (Bauman 2000). Global economic, social, and safety developments, with direct impact on citizens' living conditions and opportunities, have by far transcended the decision margins of individual governments. The globality and complexity leads to an increasing appeal to expertise by economists, jurists, engineers, and criminologists, and to an increasing space for self-interested lobbying by powerful groups, beyond citizens' understanding and control. The democratic game has lost a great deal of its relevance for citizens' life. As citizens are aware that they lost grips on their

---

[10] As in the earlier described dominion concept (Braithwaite and Pettit 1990), Putnam also does not oppose individual self-interest to the obligations of social life, but, on the contrary, understands that social and individual interests are closely intertwined.

living conditions, and understand that the democratic institutions themselves have only marginal impact on social and political developments, their participatory commitment in democracy is decreasing also. Social capital is being lost. The citizen withdraws in an increasingly cynical self-interested position and is gradually less interested in the quality of social life as a whole. Social institutions are consumed: Rights are exploited maximally and obligations are avoided or circumvented as much as possible. We do not vote for the candidates who may have the best option for social life, but for the one who is supposed to defend best our own selfish interests. Democracy has become an arena of struggle for maximum possible consumption of rights and opportunities.

Because "unpredictable 'market forces' … are far beyond the reach of … territory bound governments" (Bauman 2000), they focus on local crime and safety problems. For the impotent governments, "doing something, or be[ing] seen to be doing something, about fighting the crime which threatens personal safety is a realistic option—and one containing a lot of electoral potential" (ibid.). The problem is, however, that the citizen behaves like a consumer here also. Authorities are requested to deliver maximum security at the lowest possible price. The means used for this end do not matter, as long as they do not hamper one's own personal short-term comfort. If the consuming citizen is involved in a criminal procedure, he or she tries to find the best lawyer to get the most possible personal benefits or the least possible sanction, not to find the most just, the most reasonable, or most peacemaking solution. All this results in a negative spiral of more discontentment with authorities, more cynicism with regard to social life, more political consumerism and extremism, less security.

Fortunately, social forces are at work to try to stop this spiral and to turn it over in a positive direction. They are found in the younger generation; in the other-globalists; and among intellectuals, artists, and enlightened politicians. Political philosophies, social sciences, and social practices try to develop other visions and alternative options on governing social life, which would be more constructive and emancipatory for individuals and for communities as well. I have extended slightly on a few examples, such as communitarianism, the republican theory and responsive regulation, and the social capital theory.

The restorative philosophy is closely linked to this movement. Promoting deliberation among responsible citizens to find socially constructive solutions to injustices or other conflicts promotes the understanding that participation definitely matters and may increase citizens' commitment to social life as a whole. Deliberative democracy comes closer, wherein citizens actively take up their responsibility and understand increasingly that they may have benefits in making peace, more than in trying to win a war.

19.7   Conclusions

19.7.1   Limits to Restorative Justice

Positioning restorative justice as another paradigm and opting for a maximalist view that would replace in the longer term the mainstream punitive criminal justice system raises questions as to the limits of restorative justice. Several possible limits must be considered.

19.7.1.1   Serious Crimes

Several arguments have been advanced to exclude serious crimes from restorative processes.

The position that actors of serious crimes cannot be involved beneficially in a restorative process witnesses a naïve view on the etiology of crime, as if seriousness of crime would express directly the social callousness of the offender. Evidence makes clear that serious criminals can be sensitive as well to calls from the social context, can feel deep remorse, and may be willing to make up for what they have done.

Retributivists call it a matter of principle that serious crimes must be responded to through punishment. Whereas mild misbehavior could possibly be left for restorative processes, severe offenses should be responded to by inflicting a proportionate hard treatment (von Hirsch 1993; Duff 2001). I have earlier already rejected the principled a priorism for punishment. Though offending, and a fortiori serious offending, must be responded to by a possibly coercive public reaction, these coercive interventions should be imposed primarily in view of reparation, and not for making the offender suffer.

Media, policymakers, justice professionals, and some victims' movements often refer to the feelings of the victims to justify (harsh) punishment on the offenders. However, there is no systematic research documenting that most victims of serious crimes really call for a punitive response. Practical experiences show, on the contrary, that many victims of serious crimes do agree to participate in restorative processes. Moreover, we know that victims, including victims of serious crimes, have more to benefit from participating in a restorative process than in a traditional penal justice procedure.

An important reflection is that fewer risks can be taken with those who committed a serious crime, because their possible reoffending could lead to serious revictimization. As we just wrote, one can indeed not run after restoration immoderately, while at the same time giving space for more harm, suffering, and social unrest. That is why the top of the earlier described pyramid provides the possibility to incapacitate "irrationally negative offenders" of serious crimes. The principled priority given to restoration is confronted with its limits when incapacitation is needed for preserving public security. As we described, possible reparation is reduced then, but not completely played out.

All in all, no principled or empirical arguments seem to hold out to exclude offenders and victims of serious crimes from restorative interventions. On the contrary, if the paradigm shift of restorative justice is taken seriously, the amount of harm and suffering caused by a crime is an argument to favor actions in view of restoration. Victims of serious crimes and communities wherein these crimes occurred are probably hurt more than after trivial offending. They are more in need of reparation. Even if it may sometimes seem more difficult in practice, it is contradictory to the restorative principles to a priori exclude victims of serious crimes from the possible benefits of restorative actions.

19.7.1.2   Respect for Victims' Interests and Needs

At first glance, it may seem evident that justice responses inspired by restorative principles do meet victims' needs more than traditional criminal justice does (Dignan 2005). It is, however, more complicated than that. Especially the rights-focused victim advocates strongly oppose victims' interests to those of the offenders (Strang 2002). In their view, the more offenders are approached in a constructive, respectful way, the less respect is shown for the victims. Such strong oppositional approach is losing its impact. Victims increasingly understand that they have much to lose in an uncritical coalition with the criminal justice system. Despite recent efforts to improve the victim's position and experience in traditional criminal justice, they still often risk secondary victimization (Dignan and Cavadino 1998; Dignan 2005). It is one of the main reasons for restorative justice to challenge the oppositional approach.

However, some victimists' concerns must be taken seriously. Restorative justice indeed considers a much broader concept of harm, which surpasses the individual victim, and includes broader unrest in social life and the prejudices caused to the offender him- or herself. Some fear that the concrete victim may lose in this broadened perspective on harm, and that respect for his or her interests and needs may be submitted to focus on other. This risk is especially considerable in juvenile justice context, with its strong rehabilitational tradition. Mediation or conferencing may in such context still be seen in a treatment perspective, and subordinate the victim's view (Davis, Boucherat, and Watson 1988). It happens that social pressure is exerted on the victim to obtain his or her participation, to be "moderate" in his or her claims, or to accept agreements that are primarily made up for the treatment needs of the offender. The victim's story may be used in the process as a "pedagogical means" in order to motivate the offender for treatment, rather than to understand genuinely the suffering in view of determining appropriate reparative actions. Obviously, secondary victimization is at hand when such pressure happens.

Taking these possible problems seriously is, however, no reason to abandon or delimit the restorative approach. After all, research clearly demonstrates the benefits victims may draw from restorative processes. It must be clear that abusing the victim as just mentioned is opposite to restorative justice principles. Such deviations must be prevented by strengthening the links between practices and principles. It is then simply obvious that restorative justice's purpose is to restore as much as possible, so that any risk of secondary victimization is unacceptable (Walgrave 2003b).

19.7.1.3   *Naïvety of Restorative Justice Presuppositions?*

Restorative justice philosophy rests upon a belief that, if the adequate conditions are fulfilled, humans are willing and able to encounter and to find constructive peacemaking solutions to crime and other conflicts. Despite their contrasting roles and originally contradictory views on the criminal incident, both victims and offenders will find their common interest in a constructive settlement and in the social peace it facilitates.

Some may consider these presuppositions naïve or simplistic. They find arguments for that in the increasing hardening of social life and in human relations, as visible through the shameless abuse of power in (international) politics, mercilessness in business, cynical exploitation of legal rights, loss of engagement in community, and selfishness in social relations and in daily life. They all express the above-mentioned loss of social capital and the development towards a consumerist attitude to democracies. These phenomena seem to be contradictory to the restorative justice advocates' belief in a basic human empathy.

At the other side of the coin, however, another image of humans is visible. We have witnessed recently the worldwide expression of deep interhuman empathy at the occasion of the tsunami in South Asia. The victims have not any connection with our living world, and there is no real interest in helping these people, but still, massive donations and support actions were set up, not only by governments and international organizations, but also by individuals and private groups. The only motive that provokes this huge movement is compassion with victimized humans. We spontaneously feel compassion when mass media show the miserable situations of refugees and victims of war, crimes, or natural disasters.

At first sight, this observation seems to confirm Rorty's statement that the basis of human solidarity rests upon the common wish to avoid suffering (1989). We all are moved by a wish to avoid suffering, and perceiving this in other humans is the basis for mutual understanding and solidarity. As a response to the "actuarial" developments in criminal justice, and largely inspired by Rorty, Boutellier (2000) proposed "victimalization" as the common moral minimum, to remoralize the fundamentals of criminal justice. Both Rorty and Boutellier develop the negative side only of interhuman understanding: avoiding suffering. However, if they suppose compassion with the sufferer, this compassion is only possible in case of empathy, which is more comprehensive than just negative. We also can enjoy the happiness of others, or the conclusion of a peaceful agreement in which we are ourselves not directly involved. Humans are aware of their common fate and can feel what other humans feel. It is the ground for their potential to understand and for solidarity, despite differences in options and immediate interests. Solidarity goes far beyond negatively avoiding suffering, but also aims at constructing a peaceful and emancipatory community.

For several reasons, the potential for mutual empathy is not always activated. It may be diminished or blocked through earlier experiences in childhood, for example, or by opposition in immediate interests. Living conditions and daily life stress may cause indifference for the other. War situations sometimes lead to dehumanizing the enemy. Intensity of empathy also depends on the degree of identification: We sympathize more easily with our family members, our fellow citizens, than with more distant people. The notion of psychopathy even refers to a psychological incapacity to feel empathy.

Actually, the human has both the Jekyll and Hyde side. The question is which one we give priority. According to its earlier described ideology, restorative justice opts for approaching the positive side of the human. Do we suffocate the potentials for sympathetic encounters beforehand through legal procedures and threats with punishments? Or do we give solidarity and interhuman sympathy its full chance by acting first as if they were able to encounter? Putnam mentioned experimental psychological evidence to show that if you treat people in an honest way, they are more likely to be honest themselves. If you act as if they were trustworthy, they will be more trustworthy. If you give people active responsibility, they will assume it constructively. If you approach people with positive sympathy, they will respond to it equally sympathetically. "In that sense, honesty, civic engagement, and social trust are mutually reinforcing" (Putnam 2000). Therefore, relying on interhuman empathy is not naïvety, but a well-reflected option. We have described earlier in this chapter how human sympathy may ground the positive emotional dynamics in a conference. The high participation rates and successful agreements demonstrate that also opposing people can look beyond immediate conflicts for mutually satisfying outcomes.

But sometimes, this approach will fail or appear to be impossible. It would witness naïvety if restorative justice was conceived as a totally isolated model. To a certain extent, restorative encounters will remain unachievable. "In a society of fallible humans, what kind of assurance can each of us have in the good faith of others? A legal system, complete with courts and law enforcement, provides a strong answer" (Putnam 2000). That is why restorative justice must be included in a formal system, as designed in the pyramid.

19.7.2   A Look in the Future

We have presented restorative justice, not as a diversionary addendum to penal justice, but as an ambitious renovative project, based on a new paradigm on doing justice after the occurrence of a crime. Since the *Défense Sociale* movement in the late nineteenth century, restorative justice is probably the most challenging development in criminal justice thinking and practice.

Like the several penal theories, the option for restorative justice also is primarily a normative theory on how justice should be done, a social ethically based choice, imbedded into a broader view on humans, human relations, and society. The option is not contradicted by systematic empirical research. On the contrary. Evidence available so far suggests that the victims are better off with restorative responses than with the rehabilitative or punitive approaches to crime, that it is more satisfying for both victims and offenders, and more effective even for reintegrating offenders. Moreover, restorative justice seems not to provoke destructive consequences for public safety, and it has good intrinsic potentials for public law enforcement. Its clear normative approach and its retrospective aspect offer adequate criteria for deducing legal safeguards.

No wonder that many countries increasingly insert restorative schemes in their criminal and juvenile justice systems. Probably, this development will still be going on for a while, but it is unclear how far it will go. There are good arguments to aim at "mainstreaming restorative justice solutions" (Dignan 2005), a position of restorative justice as the most evident, first considered way of responding to crime, also when it is channeled through the judicial system. But the restorative mainstream will never be the unique possible response. Offenders whose responsibility is considered to be very reduced, because of their age or their obvious psychosocial incapacity, will always be referred to mainly welfare-oriented responses. Offenders who committed severe offenses, and are considered as a risk for serious reoffending, will have to be imposed sanctions with a mixed rationale of incapacitation and punishment. The crucial question is how the three tracks will in the future relate to each other. The capacity of the restorative justice track will depend on several conditions.

19.7.2.1   *Improving the Technical and Practical Quality of Restorative Justice Practice*

Possible expansion of restorative principles strongly depends on the methodological quality of the practices. Not all restorative-called practices are carried out well. Research has made clear that the methodical quality of the way the process is monitored has an often-decisive impact on the outcome and on the general degree of restorativeness.

In recent years, restorative practice has improved drastically, leading to more confidence and broader implementation. This is, paradoxically, also a threat, as it may lead to routinized "fast food" practices (Umbreit 1999), with weak theoretical and methodological underpinnings. There is a need for ongoing attention to the quality of what is done under the label restorative justice. Continuous care for methodology of restorative practice is based on permanent interaction between advanced practitioners, evaluative research, and theoretical reflection. It can improve the processes and the outcomes, leading to more satisfaction among the participant victims, offenders, and communities of care; can extend the scope of restorative justice to more difficult and more serious cases; and can by that gain credibility among the criminal justice professionals and among the public.

19.7.2.2 *Exploring Thoroughly the Relation of Restorative Justice to the Law*

The more restorative justice is leaving its research and development phase, and evolves towards a kind of mainstream response, the more urgent is the reflection on how to insert it into an adequate legal frame. In this chapter, I have referred to several questions in that regard. Fundamentally, they all concern the relation between the bottom-up option that is crucial in restorative justice philosophy and practice, and the typically top-down formalizing procedures that seem to be essential for regulation in a democratic constitutional state. The concrete terms of the debate are partly different in the Anglo-Saxon-based common law countries and in the countries with centralized legalistic systems on the European continent, but the basic issues are the same: How to juxtapose informal processes with formal procedures, how to rely on communities while living in organized states, how to combine the creativity and richness of the bottom-up approach with the clarity and strictness of the top-down approach, how to complete priority for voluntariness and compliance with possible coercion? If the paradigm status of restorative justice is taken seriously, the legal safeguards of the punitive systems cannot just be reproduced. Due process, legality, equality, right of defense, presumption of innocence, proportionality may be irrelevant or be made concrete differently. Maybe other legal principles must be constructed, which would be more appropriate for the restorative perspective.

Restorative justice literature on these questions is not abundant but has recently increased. Skeptics do not believe that restorative justice can ever be combined with decent legal standards and, therefore, keep it at the margins of the mainstream of the social response to crime (Ashworth 1993;

von Hirsch 1998; Feld 1999). Among restorative justice proponents, different positions are held by so-called diversionists, maximalists, and purists (McCold 2000; Braithwaite 2002; von Hirsch et al. 2003; Dignan 2002; Walgrave 2002b; van Ness 2002b). It is one of the most important themes to decide how far restorative justice will succeed in penetrating the mainstream response to crime.

19.7.2.3 *Developing Normative and Explanatory Theory*

Currently, most restorative experiments take place in institutional contexts that are not based on restorative principles. Traditional juvenile justice or criminal justice deliver the mainstream responses and act as the gatekeepers to possible restorative practices, considered as exceptions, often even as favors. Success of these practices is judged by the gatekeepers along their criteria, which are not really restoration based. They value, for example, mediation because it may have deep influence on the offenders, or they accept conferencing because it may include the family in the reeductive action towards the offender, while appreciating that the "hard core justice business" is unburdened. The genuine restorative values are not recognized and not valorized.

Paradoxically, the greatest threat to restorative justice may be the thoughtless enthusiasm of policymakers, police, magistrates, judges, and social workers to integrate a few techniques in the traditional rehabilitative or punitive justice systems. A grasp of mediation, a bit of conferencing, a pinch of community service are added to the system, without questioning the fundamentals of the traditional functioning. Restorative justice practices then are stripped from their philosophy and deteriorate into being a pure technique, serving as ornaments of a system that essentially remains unchanged.

The crucial means to avoid such deterioration is permanent theorizing. The *technicité* of restorative justice may not be isolated from its theoretical and socio-ethical foundations. Together with developing methodology, ongoing theoretical and socio-ethical reflection must point to the essentials of restorative justice, bundle and interpret experience, and build reference models to comment and orient the practices, which all together form the best possible counterforce to avoid absorption into the traditional modes of responding to crime.

19.7.2.4 *Strategy*

Developments in criminal justice are a matter of criminal policy, which only partially are depending on practical and scientific qualities and options, but more still on the cultural and political climate. In almost all Western countries, crime problems are currently exploited commercially by dramatizing media and boosted through populist rhetoric by some politicians, which together may lead to a rather simplistic attitude among a great part of the public. Many observers typify the predominating social climate as being intolerant for deviancy and repressive against offending. If that is true, the chances for restorative responses to be generally accepted and promoted would be reduced.

However, reality is more nuanced. Media and the public represent different views and opinions. Simplistic repressive outcries may sound the loudest, but it is far from evident that they really are the mainstream (Roberts and Hough 2002). I have alluded to several scientific explorations of public attitudes that show results that are not at all unfavorable to restorative responses. Therefore, there is no reason to be too pessimistic about the future of restorative justice. Restorative justice advocates have a strong case. They may have deep impact on future developments, if the case is presented well. This is partly a matter of strategy (van Ness and Heetderks Strong 1997, 2002; Bazemore and Walgrave 1999; van Ness 2002b). First, the full potentials of restorative justice must be exploited as much as possible, by developing the three lines described above. It will improve the intrinsic quality of the restorative offer, which is in itself the most crucial trump in any strategy. But besides that, specific efforts must be done to make this quality visible to policymakers, leading professionals, the judiciary, and the public. One may expect that if these actors are informed realistically about what can be achieved by opting for actions in view of reparation, and what cannot, they will more easily agree to try out the restorative potentials as much as possible. But there may, of course, also be ideological objections, and that is another story.

References

Ahmed, E. 2001. Shame management: Regulating bullying. In *Shame Management through Reintegration*, ed. E. Ahmed, N. Harris, J. Braithwaite, and V. Braithwaite, 211. Cambridge: Cambridge University Press.

Andrews, D. 2001. Principles of effective correctional programs. In *Compendium 2000 on Effective Correctional Programming*, ed. L. Motiuk and R. Serin. Ottawa: Correctional Service Canada.

Ashworth, A. 1986. Punishment and compensation: Victims, offenders and the state. *Oxford Journal of Legal Studies* 6, 86.

Ashworth, A. 1993. Some doubts about restorative justice. *Criminal Law Forum* 4, 277.

Bae, I. 1992. A survey of public acceptance of restitution as an alternative to incarceration for property offenders in Hennepin County, Minnesota, USA. In *Restorative Justice on Trial. Pitfalls and Potentials of Victim-Offender Mediation*, ed. H. Messmer and H. U. Otto, 291. Dordrecht/Boston: Kluwer Academic Publishers.

Basic principles on the use of restorative justice programs in criminal matters. 1999. United Nations Economic and Social Council 2002. *Recommendation R (99) 19 of the Committee of Ministers to Member States Concerning Mediation in Penal Matters.* Council of Europe, Committee of Ministers.

Bauman, Z. 2000. Social uses of law and order. In *Criminology and Social Theory*, ed. D. Garland and R. Sparks, 23. Oxford: Oxford University Press.

Bazemore, G. 2000. Rock and roll, restorative justice, and the continuum or the real world: A response to "purism" in operationalizing restorative justice. *Contemporary Justice Review* 3, 4, 459.

Bazemore, G., and D. Maloney. 1994. Rehabilitating community service: Sanctions in a balanced justice system. *Federal Probation* 58, 2, 24.

Bazemore, G., and S. O'Brien. 2002. The quest for a restorative model of rehabilitation: Theory-for-practice and practice-for-theory. In *Restorative Justice and the Law*, ed. L. Walgrave, 31. Cullompton, U.K.: Willan Publishing.

Bazemore, G., and M. Schiff, eds. 2001. *Restorative Community Justice. Repairing Harm and Transforming Communities.* Cincinnati: Anderson, 245.

Bazemore, G., and Schiff, M. 2005. *Juvenile Justice Reform and Restorative Justice.* Cullompton, U.K.: Willan Publishing.

Bazemore, G., and L. Walgrave, eds. 1999. Restorative juvenile justice: In search of fundamentals and an outline for systemic reform. In *Restorative Justice for Juveniles. Repairing the Harm by Youth Crime*, ed. G. Bazemore and L. Walgrave, 45. Monsey, NY: Criminal Justice Press.

Bianchi, H. 1994. *Justice as a Sanctuary. Towards a New System of Crime Control.* Bloomington: Indiana University Press.

Blad, J. 1996. *Abolitionisme als Strafrechtstheorie* (Abolitionism as Penal Law Theory). Amsterdam: Gouda Quint.

Boutellier, H. 2000. *Crime and Morality. The Significance of Criminal Justice in Postmodern Culture.* Dordrecht: Kluwer Academic Publishers.

Boyes-Watson, C. 2000. Reflections on the purist and the maximalist models of restorative justice. *Contemporary Justice Review* 3, 4, 441.

Braithwaite, J. 1989. *Crime, Shame and Reintegration.* Cambridge: Cambridge University Press.

Braithwaite, J. 2000. Decomposing a holistic vision of restorative justice. *Contemporary Justice Review* 3, 4, 433.

Braithwaite, J. 2002. In search of restorative jurisprudence. In *Restorative Justice and the Law*, ed. L. Walgrave, 150. Cullompton, U.K.: Willan Publishing.

Braithwaite, J. 2003. Restorative justice and corporate regulation. In *Restorative Justice in Context. International Practice and Directions*, ed. E. Weitekamp and H. J. Kerner, 161. Cullompton, U.K.: Willan Publishing.

Braithwaite, J. 1993. Shame and modernity. *British Journal of Criminology* 33, 1.

Braithwaite, J., and S. Mugford. 1994. Conditions of successful reintegration ceremonies. *British Journal of Criminology* 34, 139.

Braithwaite, J. 1999. Restorative justice: Assessing optimistic and pessimistic accounts. In *Crime and Justice: A Review of Research*, ed. M. Tonry. Chicago: University of Chicago Press.

Braithwaite, J. 2002. *Restorative Justice and Responsive Regulation*. Oxford: Oxford University Press.

Braithwaite, J., and C. Parker. 1999. Restorative justice is republican justice. In *Restorative Justice for Juveniles. Repairing the Harm by Youth Crime*, ed. G. Bazemore and L. Walgrave, 103. Monsey, NY: Criminal Justice Press.

Braithwaite, J., and P. Pettit. 1990. *Not Just Desert. A Republican Theory of Criminal Justice*. Oxford: Oxford University Press.

Braithwaite, J., and P. Pettit. 2000. Republicanism and restorative justice: an explanatory and normative connection. In *Restorative Justice. Philosophy to Practice*, ed. H. Strang and J. Braithwaite, 145. Aldershot, U.K.: Dartmouth.

Braithwaite, J., and D. Roche. 2001. Responsibility and restorative justice. In *Restorative Community Justice. Repairing Harm and Transforming Communities*, ed. G. Bazemore and M. Schiff, 63. Cincinnati: Anderson.

Cameron, L., and M. Thorsborne. 2001. Restorative justice and school discipline: Mutually exclusive? In *Restorative Justice and Civil Society*, ed. H. Strang and J. Braithwaite, 180. Cambridge: Cambridge University Press, 180.

Christie, N. 1977. Conflicts as property. *British Journal of Criminology* 17, 1, 1.

Christie, N. 1981. *Limits to Pain*. Oxford: Martin Robertson.

Claassen, R. 1995. Restorative justice principles and evaluation continuums. Presented at National Center for Peacemaking and Conflict Resolution, Fresno, CA, May.

Coates, R. 1990. Victim-offender reconciliation programs in North America. An assessment. In *Criminal Justice, Restitution and Reconciliation*, ed. B. Galaway and J. Hudson, 125. Monsey, NY: Willow Tree Press.

Crawford, A. 2002. The state, community and restorative justice: Heresy, nostalgia and butterfly collecting. In *Restorative Justice and the Law*, ed. L. Walgrave, 101. Cullompton, U.K.: Willan Publishing.

Crawford, A., and T. Clear. 2001. Community justice: Transforming communities through restorative justice? In *Restorative Community Justice. Repairing Harm and Transforming Communities*, ed. G. Bazemore and M. Schiff, 127. Cincinnati: Anderson.

Crawford, A., and T. Newburn. 2003. *Youth Offending and Restorative Justice. Implementing Reform in Youth Justice*. Cullompton, U.K.: Willan Publishing.

Daly, K. 2000. Revisiting the relationship between retributive and restorative justice. In *Restorative Justice. Philosophy to Practice*, ed. H. Strang and J. Braithwaite, 33. Aldershot, U.K.: Dartmouth.

Daly, K. 2001. Conferencing in Australia and New Zealand: Variations, research findings and prospects. In *Justice for Juveniles. Conferencing, Mediation & Circles*, ed. A. Morris and G. Maxwell. Oxford: Hart.

Daly, K. 2002. Restorative justice: The real story. *Punishment & Society* 4, 1, 55.

Daly, K. 2005a. A tale of two studies: Restorative justice from a victim's perspective. In *Restorative Justice: Emerging Issues in Practice and Evaluation*, ed. E. Elliott and R. Gordon. Cullompton, U.K.: Willan Publishing.

Daly, K. 2005b. Restorative justice and sexual assault: An archival study of court and conference cases, unpublished paper.

Davis, G., J. Boucherat, and D. Watson. 1988. Reparation in the service of diversion: The subordination of a good idea. *The Howard Journal* 27, 127.

Debuyst, C. 1990. Pour introduire une histoire de la criminologie. Les Problématiques du départ. Déviance et Société 14, 4, 347.

De Haan, W. 1990. *The Politics of Redress*. London: Sage.

de Keijser, J. 2000. *Punishment and Purpose. From Moral Theory to Punishment in Action*. Ph. D. Thesis. Leyden, Netherlands: University of Leyden.

Declaration of Leuven on the advisability of promoting the restorative approach to juvenile delinquency. 1998. In *Restorative Justice for Juveniles. Potentials, Risks and Problems for Research*, ed. L. Walgrave, 403. Leuven, Belgium: Leuven University Press.

Dignan, J. 2002. Restorative justice and the law: The case for an integrated, systemic approach. In *Restorative Justice and the Law*, ed. L. Walgrave, 168. Cullompton, U.K.: Willan Publishing.

Dignan, J. 2003. Towards a systemic model of restorative justice: Reflections in the concept, its context, and the need for clear constraints. In *Restorative Justice and Criminal Justice: Competing or Reconcilable Paradigms*, ed. A. von Hirsch et al., 135. Oxford: Hart, Oxford.

Dignan, J. 2005. *Understanding victims and Restorative Justice*. Maidenhead, U.K.: McGraw-Hill, Open University Press, 167-178.

Dignan, J., and M. Cavadino. 1998. Which model of criminal justice offers the best scope for assisting victims of crime? In *Support for Crime Victims in a Comparartive Perspective*, ed. E. Fattah and T. Peters, 139. Leuven, Belgium: Leuven University Press.

Dignan, J., and P. Marsh. 2001. Restorative justice and family group conferences in England: current state and future prospects. In *Restorative Justice for Juveniles. Conferencing, Mediation & Circles*, ed. A. Morris and G. Maxwell, 85. Oxford: Hart.

Doob, A. J., et al. 1998. *An Exploration of Ontario Residents' View of Crime and the Criminal Justice System*. Toronto: University of Toronto, Centre of Criminology.

Duff, A. 1992. Alternatives to punishment or alternative punishment? In *Retributivism and its Critics*, ed. W. Cragg, 44. Stuttgart: Steinder.

Duff, A. 2001. *Punishment, Communication and Community.* Oxford: Oxford University Press.

Duff, A. 2002. Restorative punishment and punitive restoration. In *Restorative Justice and the Law*, ed. L. Walgrave. Cullompton, U.K.: Willan Publishing.

Elias, N. 1994. *The Civilizing Process.* Oxford: Blackwell.

Etzioni, A. 1998. *The Essential Communitarian Reader.* Lanham, MD: Rowman and Littlefield.

European Forum for Victim-Offender Mediation and Restorative Justice. 2000. *Victim-Offender Mediation in Europe. Making Restorative Justice Work.* Leuven, Belgium: Leuven University Press.

Faget, J. 1997. *La Médiation: Essai de politique pénale.* Ramonville Saint Agnes: Erès.

Fatic, A. 1995. *Punishment and Restorative Crime-Handling.* Aldershot, U.K.: Avebury.

Feeley, M., and J. Simon. 1992. The new penology: Notes on the emerging strategy of corrections and its implications. *Criminology* 30, 451.

Feld, B. 1999. Rehabilitation, retribution and restorative justice: Alternative conceptions of juvenile justice. In *Restorative Juvenile Justice: Repairing the Harm of Youth Crime*, ed. G. Bazemore and L. Walgrave. Monsey, NY: Criminal Justice Press.

Fraser, S., and J. Norton. 1996. Family group conferencing in New Zealand child protection work. In *Family Group Conferences. Perspectives on Policy and Practice*, ed. J. Hudson, 37. Leichhardt, NSW, Australia/Monsey, NY: The Federation Press/Willow Tree Press.

Galaway, B. 1984. A survey of public acceptance of restitution as an alternative for imprisonment for property offences. *Australian and New Zealand Journal of Criminology* 17, 2, 108.

Garland, D. 1990. *Punishment and Modern Society. A Study in Social Theory.* Oxford: Clarendon Press.

Guarino-Ghezzi, S., and A. Klein. 1999. Protecting community: The public safety role in a restorative juvenile justice. In *Restorative Justice for Juveniles. Repairing the Harm by Youth Crime*, ed. G. Bazemore and L. Walgrave, 195. Monsey, NY: Criminal Justice Press.

Hadley, M. 2001. *The Spiritual Roots of Restorative Justice.* Albany, NY: SUNY Press.

Harris, N., L. Walgrave, and J. Braithwaite. 2004. Emotional dynamics in restorative conferences. *Theoretical Criminology* 8, 2, 191.

Hayes, H. 2004. Assessing re-offending in restorative justice conferences. In *Australian and New Zealand Journal of Criminology* 38, 77.

Hayes, H., and K. Daly. 2003. Youth justice conferencing and re-offending. *Justice Quarterly* 20, 4, 725.

Hayes, H., and K. Daly. 2004. Conferencing and re-offending in Queensland. *Australian and New Zealand Journal of Criminology* 37, 2, 167.

Hudson, J., A. Morris, G. Maxwell, and B. Galaway, eds. 1996. *Family Group Conferences. Perspectives on Policy and Practice*. Annandale, Australia/Monsey, NY: The Federation Press/Willow Tree Press.

Johnstone, G. 2002. *Restorative Justice. Ideas, Values, Debates*. Cullompton, U.K.: Willan Publishing.

Karp, D., and L. Walther. 2001. Community reparative boards in Vermont: Theory and practice. In *Restorative Community Justice. Repairing Harm and Transforming Communities*, ed. G. Bazemore and M. Schiff, 199. Cincinnati: Anderson.

Karstedt, S. 2002. Emotions and criminal justice. *Theoretical Criminology* 6, 3, 299.

Kurki, L. 2003. Evaluating restorative practices. In *Restorative Justice and Criminal Justice: Competing or Reconcilable Paradigms*, ed. A. von Hirsch, 293. Oxford: Hart.

Latimer, J., C. Dowden, and D. Muise. 2001. *The Effectiveness of Restorative Justice Practices: A Meta Analysis*. Ottawa: Department of Justice.

Laub, J., and R. Sampson. 2001. Understanding desistance from crime. In *Crime and Justice. A Review of Research*, vol. 28, ed. M. Tonry. Chicago: Chicago University Press.

Lilles, H. 2001. Circle sentencing: Part of the restorative justice continuum. In *Restorative Justice for Juveniles. Conferencing, Mediation & Circles*, ed. A. Morris and G. Maxwell. Oxford: Hart.

Macrae, A. 2000. At that time a youth justice coordinator in Wellington, NZ.

Marsh, P., and G. Crow. 1996. Family group conferences in child welfare services in England and Wales. In *Family Group Conferences. Perspectives on Policy and Practice*, ed. J. Hudson et al., 152. Monsey, NY/Leichhardt, NSW, Australia: Willow Tree Press/The Federation Press.

Marshall, T. 1996. The evolution of restorative justice in Britain. *European Journal of Criminal Policy and Research* 4, 4, 21.

Maruna, S. 2001. *Making Good: How Ex-Convicts Reform and Rebuild their Lives*. Washington, DC: American Psychological Association Press.

Maruna, S., and A. King. 2004. Shame, materialism and moral indignation in the east of England. An empirical look at Ranulf's thesis. Presented at Workshop on Emotions, Crime and Justice, Onati, Spain, September 13-14.

Masters, G., and A. Roberts. 2000. Family group conferencing for victims, offenders and communities. In *Mediation in Context*, ed. M. Liebman. London: J. Kingsley.

Maxwell, G., and A. Morris. 1996. Research on family group conferences with young offenders in New Zealand. In *Family Group Conferences. Perspectives on Policy and Practice*, ed. J. Hudson, 88. Monsey, NY/Annandale, NSW, Australia: Willow Tree Press/Federation Press.

Maxwell, G., and A. Morris. 1999. *Understanding Re-offending. Final Report*. Wellington, New Zealand: Victoria University, Institute of Criminology.

Maxwell, G., et al. 2004. *Achieving Effective Outcomes in Youth Justice*. Wellington, New Zealand: Ministry of Social Development.

McCold, P. 2000. Toward a holistic vision of restorative juvenile justice: A reply to the maximalist model. *Contemporary Justice Review* 3, 4, 357.

McCold, P. 2001. Primary restorative practices. In *Restorative Justice for Juveniles. Conferencing, Mediation & Circles*, ed. A. Morris and G. Maxwell. Oxford: Hart.

McCold, P. 2003. A survey of assessment research on mediation and conferencing. In *Repositioning Restorative Justice*, ed. L. Walgrave, 67. Cullompton, U.K.: Willan Publishing.

McCold, P. 2004a. Paradigm muddle: The threat to restorative justice posed by its merger with community justice. *Contemporary Justice Review* 7, 1, 13.

McCold, P. 2004b. What is the role of community in restorative justice theory and practice? In *Critical Issues in Restorative Justice*, ed. H. Zehr and B. Toews, 155. Monsey, NY/Cullompton, U.K.: Criminal Justice Press/Willan Publishing.

McCold, P., and B. Wachtel. 1998. *Restorative Policing Experiment*. Pipersville, PA: Community Service Foundation.

McGuire, J., and P. Priestly. 1995. Reviewing "What works": Past, present and future. In *What Works: Reducing reoffending*, ed. J. McGuire. Chicester, U.K./New York: Wiley.

Merry, S., and N. Milner, eds. 1993. *The Possibility of Popular Justice: A Case Study of Community Mediation*. Ann Arbor: University of Michigan Press.

Miers, D., and J. Willemsens, eds. 2004. *Mapping Restorative Justice. Developments in European Countries*. Leuven, Belgium: European Forum for Victim-Offender Mediation and Restorative Justice.

Miller, W. 1999. In defence of revenge. In *Medieval Crime and Social Control*, ed. B. Hanawalt and D. Wallace, 70. Minneapolis: University of Minnesota Press.

Moore, M. 1995. The moral worth of retribution. In *Punishment and Rehabilitation*, ed. J. Murphy. Belmont, CA: Wadsworth.

Morris, A. 2002. Shame, guilt and remorse: Experiences from family group conferences in New Zealand. In *Punishing Juveniles. Principle and Critique*, ed. I. Weijers and A. Duff. Oxford: Hart.

Nikolic-Ristanovic, V. 2003. The possibilities for restorative justice in Serbia. In *Repositioning Restorative Justice*, ed. L. Walgrave, 239. Cullompton, U.K.: Willan Publishing.

Nothafft, S. 2003. Conflict resolution and peer mediation: A pilot programme in Munich secondary schools. In *Restorative Justice in Context. International Practice and Directions*, ed. E. Weitekamp and H. J. Kerner, 80. Cullompton, U.K.: Willan Publishing.

Parker, R. 2005. Restorative justice. Why doesn't it work in reducing recidivism? Presented at the 7th International Conference on Restorative Justice, Canberra, February 23-25.

Pavlich, G. 2001. The force of community. In *Restorative Justice and Civil Society*, ed. H. Strang and J. Braithwaite, 56. Cambridge: Cambridge University Press.

Peper, P., and F. Spierings. 1999. Settling disputes between neighbours in the life-world: An evaluation of experiments with community mediation in the Netherlands. *European Journal of Criminal Policy and Research* 7, 4, 483.

Peters, T., and I. Aertsen. 1995. Restorative justice. In search of new avenues in dealing with crime. In *Changes in Society, Crime and Criminal Justice in Europe* vol. 1, ed. C. Fijnaut et al., 311. The Hague, Netherlands: Kluwer Law International.

Pranis, K. 2001. Restorative justice, social justice, and the empowerment of marginalized populations. In *Restorative Community Justice. Repairing Harm and Transforming Communities*, ed. G. Bazemore and M. Schiff, 287. Cincinnati: Anderson.

Prichard, J. 2003. *Juvenile conferencing and restorative justice in Tasmania.* Unpublished Ph.D thesis, Faculty of Law, University of Tasmania.

Putnam, J. 2000. *Bowling Alone.* New York: Simon and Schuster.

Putnam, R. 1993. *Making Democracy Work. Civic Traditions in Modern Italy.* Princeton, NJ: Princeton University Press, 167.

Roberts, J., and M. Hough. 2002. Public attitudes to punishment: the context. In *Changing Attitudes to Punishment. Public Opinion, Crime and Justice*, ed. J. Roberts and M. Hough, 1. Cullompton, U.K.: Willan Publishing.

Roche, D. 2003. *Accountability in Restorative Justice.* Oxford: Oxford University Press.

Rorty, R. 1989. *Contingency, Irony and Solidarity.* Cambridge: Cambridge University Press.

Schafer, S. 1977. *Victimology. The Victim and His Criminal.* Reston, VA: Prentice Hall.

Schiff, M. 1999. The impact of restorative interventions on juvenile offenders. In *Restorative Justice for Juveniles. Repairing the Harm by Youth Crime*, ed. G. Bazemore and L. Walgrave, 327. Monsey, NY: Criminal Justice Press.

Schoeman, F., ed. 1987. *Responsibility, Character and Emotions.* Cambridge: Cambridge University Press.

Sessar, K. 1995. Restitution or punishment. An empirical study on attitudes of the public and the justice system in Hamburg. *Eurocriminology*, 8, 9, 199.

Sessar, K. 1999. Punitive attitudes of the public: Myth and reality. In *Restorative Justice for Juveniles. Repairing the Harm by Youth Crime*, ed. G. Bazemore and L. Walgrave, 287. Monsey, NY: Criminal Justice Press.

Sherman, L. 1993. Defiance, deterrence and irrelevance: A theory of the criminal sanction. *Journal of Research in Crime and Delinquency* 30, 445.

Sherman, L. 2003. Reason for emotion: Reinventing justice with theories, innovations, and research. *Criminology* 41, 1, 1.

Sherman, L., and H. Strang. 2004. Restorative justice: What we know and how we know it. ww.sas.upenn.edu/jerrylee/jlc-new/research/rj.htm.

Sherman, L., H. Strang, and D. Woods. 2000. *Recidivism Pattern in the Canberra Reintegrative Shaming Experiments (RISE).* Canberra: Center for Restorative Justice, Australian National University.

Skolnick, J. 1995. What not to do about crime. The American Society of Criminology 1994 Presidential Address. *Criminology* 33, 10, 1.

Strang, H. 2002. *Repair or Revenge: Victims and Restorative Justice.* Oxford: Clarendon, Oxford.

Strang, H., and L. Sherman. 2005. Effects of face-to-face justice on victims of crime in four randomized controlled trials. Presented at the 7th International Conference on Restorative Justice, Canberra, February 23-25.

Stuart, B. 1996. Circle sentencing: Turning swords into ploughshares. In *Restorative Justice: International Perspectives*, ed. B. Galaway and J. Hudson. Amsterdam/Monsey, NY: Kugler/Criminal Justice Press.

Sylvester, D. 2003. Myth in restorative justice history. *Utah Law Review* 1, 471.

Tonry, M. 1995. *Malign Neglect: Race, Crime and Punishment in America.* New York: Oxford University Press.

Trépanier, J. 1998. Restorative justice: A question of legitimacy. In *Restorative Justice for Juveniles. Potentials, Risks and Problems for Research*, ed. L. Walgrave, 55. Leuven, Belgium: Leuven University Press.

Tyler, T. 1990. *Why People Obey the Law.* New Haven, CT: Yale University Press.

Tyler, T., and Y. Huo. 2001. *Trust in the Law. Encouraging Public Cooperation with the Police and Courts.* New York: Russel Sage Foundation.

Umbreit, M. 1999. Avoiding the "McDonaldization" of victim-offender mediation: A case study in moving toward the mainstream. In *Restorative Juvenile Justice: Repairing the Harm of Youth Crime,* ed. G. Bazemore and L. Walgrave. Monsey, NY: Criminal Justice Press.

Umbreit, M., and H. Zehr. 1996. Restorative family group conferences: Differing models and guidelines for practice. *Federal Probation* 60, 3, 24.

Umbreit, M. et al. 2003. *Facing Violence.* Monsey, NY: Criminal Justice Press.

Umbreit, M. 1994. *Victim Meets Offender: The Impact of Restorative Justice and Mediation.* Monsey, NY: Criminal Justice Press.

van Ness, D. 1999. Legal issues of restorative justice. In *Restorative Juvenile Justice. Restoring the Harm by Youth Crime,* ed. G. Bazemore and L. Walgrave, 263. Monsey, NY: Criminal Justice Press.

van Ness, D. 2002a. Creating restorative systems. In *Restorative Justice and the Law,* ed. L. Walgrave, 142. Cullompton, U.K.: Willan Publishing.

van Ness, D. 2002b. The shape of things to come: A framework for thinking about a restorative justice system. In *Restorative Justice and the Law,* ed. L. Walgrave, 1. Cullompton, U.K.: Willan Publishing.

van Ness, D. 2004. *Restorative Justice City.* Available online at www.restorativejustice.org.

van Ness, D., and K. Heetderks Strong. 1997. *Restoring Justice.* Cincinnati: Anderson.

van Ness, D., and K. Heetderks Strong. 2002. *Restoring Justice,* 2nd ed. Cincinnati: Anderson.

van Ness, D., and M. Schiff. 2001. Satisfaction guaranteed? The meaning of satisfaction in restorative justice. In *Restorative Community Justice. Repairing Harm and Transforming Communities*, ed. G. Bazemore and M. Schiff, 47. Cincinnati: Anderson.

van Ness, D., A. Morris, and G. Maxwell. 2001. Introducing restorative justice. In *Restorative Justice for Juveniles. Conferencing, Mediation & Circles*, ed. A. Morris and G. Maxwell. Oxford: Hart.

van Stokkom, B. 2002. Moral emotions in restorative justice conferences: Managing shame, designing empathy. *Theoretical Criminology* 6, 3, 339.

Vanfraechem, I. 2003. *Hergo in Vlaanderen* (FGC in Flanders). Leuven, Belgium: Onderzoeksgroep Jeugdcriminologie K.U. Leuven. Unpublished research report.

von Hirsch, A., and N. Jareborg. 1991. Gauging criminal harm: A living-standard analysis. *Oxford Journal of Legal Studies* 11, 1.

von Hirsch, A. 1993. *Censure and Sanctions*. Oxford: Clarendon Press.

von Hirsch, A. 1998. Penal theories. In *The Handbook of Crime and Punishment*, ed. M. Tonry, 659. New York/Oxford: Oxford University Press.

von Hirsch, A., et al., eds. 2003. *Restorative Justice and Criminal Justice: Competing or Reconcilable Paradigms?* Oxford: Hart.

Wachtel, T., and P. McCold. 2001. Restorative justice and everyday life. In *Restorative Justice and Civil Society*, ed. H. Strang and J. Braithwaite, 114. Cambridge: Cambridge University Press.

Walgrave, L. 1995. Restorative justice for juveniles: Just a technique or a fully fledged alternative? *Howard Journal* 34, 3, 228.

Walgrave, L. 1999. Community service as a cornerstone of a systemic restorative response to (juvenile) crime. In *Restorative Juvenile Justice: Repairing the Harm of Youth Crime*, ed. G. Bazemore and L. Walgrave, 129. Monsey, NY: Criminal Justice Press.

Walgrave, L. 2000. How pure can a maximalist approach to restorative justice remain? Or can a purist model of restorative justice become maximalist? *Contemporary Justice Review* 3, 4, 415.

Walgrave, L. 2001. On restoration and punishment: Favorable similarities and fortunate differences. In *Restorative Justice for Juveniles. Conferencing, Mediation and Circles*, ed. A. Morris and G. Maxwell, 17. Oxford: Hart.

Walgrave, L. 2002a. Restorative justice and the law: Socio-ethical and juridical foundations for a systemic approach. In *Restorative Justice and the Law*, ed. L. Walgrave, 191. Cullompton, U.K.: Willan Publishing.

Walgrave, L. 2002b. Restorative justice and the republican theory of criminal justice: An exercise in normative theorizing on restorative justice. In *Restorative Justice. Philosophy to Practice*, ed. H. Strang and J. Braithwaite, 165. Aldershot, U.K.: Dartmouth.

Walgrave, L., ed. 2002. *Restorative Justice and the Law*. Cullompton, U.K.: Willan Publishing.

Walgrave, L. 2003a. Imposing restoration instead of inflicting pain: reflections on the judicial reaction to crime. In *Restorative Justice and Criminal Justice: Competing or Reconcilable Paradigms*, ed. A. von Hirsch et al., 61. Oxford: Hart.

Walgrave, L. 2003b. La justice restauratrice et les victims. *Journal International de Victimologie/International Journal of Victimology* 1, 4, 13. www.jidv.com.

Walgrave, L. 2004a. Has restorative justice appropriately responded to retribution theory and impulses? In *Critical Issues in Restorative Justice*, ed. H. Zehr and B. Toews, 47. Monsey, NY/Cullompton, U.K.: Criminal Justice Press/Willan Publishing.

Walgrave, L. 2004b. Restoration in youth justice. In *Youth Crime and Youth Justice. Comparative and Cross-national Perspectives*, ed. M. Tonry and A. Doob, 31, 543. Chicago: University of Chicago Press, Crime and Justice.

Walgrave, L., and I. Aertsen. 1996. Re-integrative shaming and restorative justice: Interchangeable, complementary or different? *European Journal of Criminal*, 4, 4, 67.

Walgrave, L., and H. Geudens. 1997. Restorative community service in Belgium. *Overcrowded Times* 8, 5, 3.

Warner, K. 1994. Family group conferences and the rights of the offender. In *Family Conferencing and Juvenile Justice. The Way Forward or Misplaced Optimism?* ed. C. Alder and J. Wundersitz, 141. Canberra: Australian Institute of Criminology.

Weitekamp, E. 1992. Can restitution serve as a reasonable alternative to imprisonment? In *Restorative Justice on Trial. Pitfalls and Potentials of Victim-Offender Mediation*, ed. H. Messmer and H. U. Otto, 81. Dordrecht/Boston: Kluwer Academic Publishers.

Weitekamp, E. 1999. History of restorative justice. In *Restorative Justice for Juveniles. Repairing the Harm by Youth Crime*, ed. G. Bazemore and L. Walgrave, 75. Monsey, NY: Criminal Justice Press.

Winfree, T. 2002. Peacemaking and community harmony: lessons (and admonitions) from the Navajo peacemaking courts. In *Restorative Justice: Theoretical Foundations*, ed. E. Weitekamp and H. J. Kerner, 285. Cullompton, U.K.: Willan Publishing.

Wright, M. 1989. What the public wants. In *Mediation and Criminal Justice: Victims, Offenders and Community*, ed. M. Wright and B. Galaway, 105. London: Sage.

Wright, M. 1992. Victim-offender mediation as a step towards a restorative system of justice. In *Restorative Justice on Trial*, ed. H. Messmer and H. U. Otto, 525. Dordrecht: Kluwer Academic Publishers.

Wright, M. 1996. *Justice for Victims and Offenders: A Restorative Response to Crime*, 2d ed. Winchester, U.K.: Waterside.

Wright, M. 2003. Is it time to question the concept of punishment? In *Repositioning Restorative Justice*, ed. L. Walgrave, 3. Cullompton, U.K.: Willan Publishing.

Zehr, H., and H. Mika. 1997. Fundamental principles of restorative justice. *The Contemporary Justice Review* 1, 1, 47.

Zehr, H. 1990. *Changing Lenses. A New Focus for Crime and Justice.* Scottsdale, PA: Herald.

Zehr, H. 2002. *The Little Book of Restorative Justice.* Intercourse, PA: Good Books.

Zellerer, E., and C. Cunneen. 2001. Restorative justice, indigenous justice and human rights. In *Restorative Community Justice. Repairing Harm and Transforming Communities*, ed. G. Bazemore and M. Schiff, 245. Cincinnati: Anderson.

The Practice of Victim Offender Mediation: A Look at the Evidence

20

MARK S. UMBREIT,
ROBERT B. COATES, AND
BETTY VOS

Contents

Restorative justice is a process to involve, to the extent possible, those who have a stake in a specific offense and to collectively identify and address harms, needs, and obligations, in order to heal and put things as right as possible.

Zehr (2002)

Victim offender mediation (VOM) is the oldest, most widely practiced, and most extensively studied form of restorative justice (Bazemore and Umbreit 1995; van Ness and Heetderks Strong 2002; Zehr 2002). VOM is a process that provides interested victims and offenders an opportunity to meet in a safe and structured setting with a trained mediator in order to hold offenders directly accountable for their behavior while also providing assistance and compensation to the victim (Umbreit 2001).

Most commonly, the crimes are property crimes and minor assaults, and the mediators are often community volunteers. With the assistance of a trained mediator, victims are able to let the offender know how the crime affected them, receive answers to questions they may have, and be directly involved in developing a restitution plan for the offender to be accountable for the losses incurred. Offenders are able to take direct responsibility for their behavior, learn the full impact of what they did, and develop a plan for making amends to the victim. VOM offers opportunities for both parties to come together in a safe and neutral setting to share the anger and pain of being victimized, as well as to answer questions of why and how. This personalization of the consequences of crime enhances satisfaction levels with the entire justice process.

More than 1,500 VOM programs in seventeen countries have been developed in the past three decades, and more than fifty empirical studies of VOM have been conducted in five different countries. In this chapter, we will provide an overview of the phases of VOM practice, followed with a summary of what has been learned from VOM research. Because the practice of VOM in cases of severe and violent crime differs significantly from more general VOM practice, it will be taken up separately.

20.1 The Practice of VOM

In contrast to many other types of mediation, which are largely "settlement driven," VOM is primarily "dialogue driven," with the emphasis upon victim healing, offender accountability, and restoration of losses. Therefore, the model for service delivery differs in significant ways from that of other dispute resolution models. Most VOM programs use a process that is based upon a humanistic model of mediation (Umbreit 1994, 1997, 2001). An especially important element of the humanistic model is preparation of participants prior to bringing them together for face-to-face dialogue. In preparatory sessions, mediators maintain a neutral stance, connect with the parties, focus on building rapport and trust, and identify the strengths of each party.

When the parties are brought together in dialogue, mediators use a nondirective style of mediation that creates a safe space for dialogue and accesses the strengths of participants. Mediators are also trained to recognize and use the power of silence. Mediators using a humanistic approach typically say very little in the mediation session and intentionally try to get out of the way so that the involved parties can speak directly with each other and be empowered to reach their own resolution.

Most VOM sessions result in a signed restitution agreement. Within VOM theory, however, reaching an agreement is secondary to the importance of the face-to-face dialogue between the parties that addresses emotional and informational needs of victims and holds offenders accountable. This dialogue is central to victim healing and to development of victim empathy in the offender, which can lead to reduced criminal behavior in the future.

20.1.1   Referral/Intake Phase

The typical VOM process begins when offenders are referred to a program by a criminal justice agency. Roughly one-third of VOM programs primarily take cases that are referred as diversion, prior to any formal finding of guilt; another 28 percent handle postadjudication or disposition referrals; and the remainder receive cases at many points in the justice process (Umbreit and Greenwood 1999).

The most common types of offenses that are referred for VOM include property offenses such as residential burglary, commercial burglary, theft, and vandalism, and those involving individuals or small businesses. Certain crimes against persons, such as common assault, are also referred for VOM. Most programs utilize a similar set of criteria determining which referrals to accept. They are most likely to consider a case appropriate for VOM if there is an identifiable loss with an accompanying need for restitution and if the offender has admitted guilt, has no more than two prior convictions, has no major mental-health problems, and has no major active substance abuse problems. The referral and intake steps are important to ensure that the type of cases entering the victim offender mediation process are appropriate for the service being offered and are likely to benefit from the opportunity for dialogue and conflict resolution.

20.1.2   Preparation Phase

Preparation for the mediation phase begins with the assignment of a case to a case manager or facilitator/mediator and ends with the beginning of the first joint mediation session. The quality of work done during this phase has a significant impact upon the actual mediation session. Unless rapport and trust is effectively established with both the victim and offender, it is difficult to proceed to a mediation session. Most problems that occur during mediation sessions result from a failure to complete this essential VOM phase thoroughly.

Careful preparation of participants is one of the hallmarks of the victim offender mediation movement. In general, preparation meetings consist of face-to-face contact with the participants, though meetings are sometimes carried out via telephone. In some programs, the offenders are more likely than the victims to have received their preparation in face-to-face meetings, although this practice is not encouraged.

Most programs begin their preparation process with offenders, to assess appropriateness and to elicit the offender's decision about participation. The major reason for this approach is to prevent the potential revictimization that could result from victims being invited to participate and then learning their offenders have not agreed to meet.

Preparing the offender begins with listening to the offender's story and explaining the program and potential benefits. If the offender is interested in participating, the conversation turns to potential repayment options; part of preparation includes assessing the offender's ability to pay restitution, perform work for the victim, or undertake community service.

The humanistic model strongly values voluntary participation for all parties, and the rhetoric of much of the literature implies that offender participation in the mediation process is voluntary. Actual practice in the field suggests something quite different. The state exercises a significant amount of coercion when offenders are referred to mediation by the court via probation or are diverted from prosecution on the condition that they complete the program. Most programs attempt to moderate this by trying to get referrals in the least coercive manner possible and by allowing offenders to choose not to participate if they are either strongly opposed to participation or deemed to be inappropriate candidates for VOM. Offenders who deny significant involvement in the crime are very likely to revictimize victims in a VOM meeting rather than contribute to their healing.

Once the offender has agreed to meet, the second task in the preparation phase is to interview victims to explore their interest in participating. This involves calling the victim to schedule an individual meeting, meeting with the victim to listen to his or her story, explaining the program and its potential benefits, encouraging the victim's participation, and making clear that participation in the program is voluntary. It can often be helpful for a mediator to share with the victim some of what has been learned about the offender during the initial meeting. The mediator makes every effort to avoid having to "sell" the program to the victim over the phone during the initial call.

Rather, the mediator attempts to obtain a commitment from the victim to meet in order to listen to the victim's version of the offense and the concerns he or she may have about VOM. At that meeting, the victim will decide if he or she wants to participate in VOM.

Preparation usually gets high marks from both offenders and victims. Across six empirical studies, the proportion of victims feeling adequately prepared to meet the offender ranged from 68 to 98 percent (Collins 1984; Fercello and Umbreit 1999; Roberts 1998; Strode 1997; Umbreit 1995a; Umbreit, Coates, and Vos 2001a). Only three studies reported offender opinions of their preparation for mediation; offender satisfaction with preparation ranged from 89 to 93 percent (Fercello and Umbreit 1999; Roberts 1998; Umbreit, Coates, and Vos 2001a).

20.1.3   Mediation Phase

If, after the initial separate contact, both parties express a willingness to proceed, the mediator schedules a face-to-face meeting between the victim and offender. The meeting typically begins with the mediator explaining his or her role, identifying the agenda, and stating the ground rules. The first part of the meeting focuses upon a discussion of the impact of the crime on both parties. Victims are given the unique opportunity to express their feelings directly to the offender, as well as to receive answers to many lingering questions such as "Why me?" or "How did you get into our house?" or "Were you stalking us and planning on coming back?" Victims are often relieved to finally see the offender, who usually bears little resemblance to the frightening character they may have conjured up in their minds.

The expression of feelings by the victim is typically not highly emotional and only rarely rises to the level of verbal violence. Some of the initial anger has usually been dissipated through the preliminary meeting with the mediator. Yet, it is often important that some of this intensity of feeling be recalled and expressed directly to the offender during the joint meeting. During the meeting, offenders must face the person they violated, giving them a chance to display the human dimension of their character and even to express remorse. Through open discussion of their feelings, both victim and offender deal with each other as people rather than as stereotypes or objects.

Following this sharing of one another's stories and perspectives, the second part of the meeting focuses upon a discussion of losses and the negotiation, when appropriate, of a mutually acceptable restitution agreement. Mediators do not impose a restitution settlement but rather encourage the involved parties to work out a resolution that is satisfactory to both of them. Such an agreement serves as a tangible symbol of conflict resolution and a focal point for accountability. If the victim and offender are unable to come to an agreement about the form or amount of restitution, the case is typically referred back to the referral source with a good likelihood that the offender will be placed in a different program.

However, rather than focus primarily upon restitution, most VOM programs emphasize the importance of allowing enough time to address the emotional and practical effects the crime has had on the lives of both victims and offenders. The mediation session is designed to address the needs of both victims and offenders in a manner that personalizes the process of justice by facilitating the empowerment of both parties to resolve the conflict at a community level. It is not meant to be primarily a victim assistance or offender rehabilitation process.

Attempting to address some of the needs of both parties does not mean that they are treated as if they have both equally contributed to the conflict. To the contrary, because the issue of guilt is not at question, the mediator must exercise special sensitivity when working with the victim. Victims must be presented with choices whenever possible, such as where and when to meet, whether or not to have support people present, and whether to tell their story first or listen to the offender first. Presentation of choices to both the victim and the offender as much as feasible is the essence of empowerment and respect.

Although VOM may not be appropriate for all victims and offenders, the underlying theory is that the conflict between those victims and offenders who participate in mediation can be humanized, stereotypes of each other lessened, and fear reduced. The mediation process thereby consistently offers a more satisfactory experience of justice for both the victim and offender than the traditional criminal justice process and can have a positive impact on reducing further criminal behavior (Umbreit, Coates, and Vos 2001b, 2002).

20.1.4 Follow-Up Phase

Many VOM practitioners believe that close monitoring and follow-up of cases is needed. If direct restitution was agreed upon, this often involves periodic phone contact with the victim to monitor fulfillment of the agreement. In some instances, follow-up may also include the scheduling of additional victim offender meetings when appropriate. One or more follow-up meetings between the victim and offender can play a significant role in strengthening the personal accountability of the offender to his or her victim. These follow-up meetings, typically briefer and less structured than the initial VOM session, provide an informal opportunity to review the implementation of the restitution agreement and discuss any problems that may have arisen related to the payment schedule. The meetings can also be a time for the victim and offender to simply share small talk if they feel so moved.

The need for and willingness to have follow-up meetings is tempered by the amount of restitution to be paid. If only a small amount of restitution is owed, a follow-up meeting might not be appropriate. On the other hand, if a larger amount is due, brief follow-up sessions (mid-contract and "close-out" meetings) can be quite helpful.

20.2 A Look at the Evidence

The present review examines participation rates and reasons, participant satisfaction, participant perception of fairness, restitution and repair of harm, diversion, recidivism, and cost. A total of fifty-seven studies were reviewed for the present report, including fifty-four individual studies and three meta-analyses.

20.2.1 Participation Rates and Reasons

Participation rates for crime victims are addressed in eighteen VOM studies and typically range from 40 to 60 percent, though rates as high as 90 percent have been reported. Several studies noted that victim willingness to participate was driven by a desire to receive restitution, to hold the offender accountable, to learn more about the reasons for the crime, to share their pain with the offender, to avoid court processing, to help the offender change behavior, or to see the offender adequately punished. Interestingly, victims frequently report that although restitution was the primary initial reason they elected to participate in VOM, what they appreciated most about the program was the opportunity to talk with the offender (Coates and Gehm 1985; Umbreit 1995a; Umbreit and Coates 1993).

Offenders choosing to participate often wanted to pay back the victim, to clarify matters with the victim, to apologize, to impress the court, and to connect their actions to the actual victim (Abrams and Umbreit 2002; Coates and Gehm 1985; Umbreit, Coates, and Vos 2001a; Niemeyer and Shichor 1996; Roberts 1995; Strode 1997; Umbreit 1989; Umbreit 1995a; Umbreit et al. 1987).

Among victims who elected not to participate in VOM, reasons included feeling the crime was too trivial to be worth the time, feeling fearful of meeting the offender, and wanting the offender to have a harsher punishment (Coates and Gehm 1985; Niemeyer and Shichor 1996; Umbreit 1995a). One study examining reasons victims elected not to participate reported the following rank order of reasons given: It wasn't worth the time and trouble, the matter was already taken care of, too much time had elapsed, they just wanted their money back, the system just wanted to slap the offender on the wrist, they thought the meeting wouldn't be safe, they didn't want to help the offender, and family or friends advised against it (Coates, Burns, and Umbreit 2002).

Two studies explored factors correlated with victim participation. Gehm (1990) studied 555 eligible VOM cases and found 47 percent of the victims willing to participate. Victims were more likely to participate if the offender was white (as were the victims), if the offense was a misdemeanor, and if the victim was representing an institution. Wyrick and Costanzo (1999) similarly found that property cases were more likely to reach mediation than personal offenses. They further noted an interaction between type of crime and the passage of time: The longer the time lapse between the offense and the mediation opportunity, the less likely victims of property crimes were to come to mediation, but the more likely personal crimes were to meet.

Offender reasons for not participating are less frequently explored. Some offenders have reported being advised by lawyers not to participate (Schneider 1986), and some simply didn't want to be bothered (Coates and Gehm 1985). In one study of a juvenile VOM program, fully a third of the offenders who refused participation reported that their parents did not want them to participate (Niemeyer and Shichor 1996).

20.2.2   Participant Satisfaction

A total of thirty-three of the studies reviewed reported in some way on satisfaction of victims and offenders with victim offender mediation and its outcomes. Expression of satisfaction with VOM is consistently high for both victims and offenders across sites, cultures, and seriousness of offenses. Typically, eight or nine out of ten participants report being satisfied with the process and with the resulting agreement (Carr 1998; Coates and Gehm 1985; Davis, Tichane, and Grayson 1980; Evje and Cushman 2000; Marshall 1990; Perry, Lajeunesse, and Woods 1987; Roberts 1995, 1998; Umbreit 1991; Umbreit and Coates 1992a; Umbreit, Coates, and Vos 2002; Warner 1992). Two studies of programs that utilized shuttle mediation yielded slightly lower satisfaction rates for those participants than for participants who met face-to-face (Dignan 1990; Umbreit and Roberts 1996).

Secondary analysis of satisfaction data from a U.S. study and a Canadian study yielded similarly high rates of satisfaction (Bradshaw and Umbreit 1998; Umbreit and Bradshaw 1999). Using step-wise multiple regression procedures to determine those variables most associated with victim satisfaction, the authors found that three variables emerged to explain over 40 percent of the variance. The key variables associated with victim satisfaction were (1) the victim felt good about the mediator, (2) the victim perceived the resulting restitution agreement as fair, and (3) the victim, for whatever reason, had a strong initial desire to meet the offender.

When asked, typically nine out of ten participants would recommend a VOM program to others (Coates and Gehm 1985; Evje and Cushman 2000; Umbreit 1991; Umbreit, Coates, and Vos 2001a).

These high levels of satisfaction with victim offender mediation also translated into relatively high levels of satisfaction with the criminal justice system. Where comparison groups were studied, those victims and offenders going through mediation indicated being more satisfied with the criminal justice system than those going through traditional court prosecution (Davis, Tichane, and Grayson 1980; Umbreit 1995a, 1995b; Umbreit and Coates 1992a).

In a meta-analysis covering both VOM and conferencing programs, Latimer, Dowden, and Muise (2001) found that in twelve of the thirteen VOM and conferencing programs that reported satisfaction rates, victims were more satisfied than those in traditional approaches. Satisfaction rates were somewhat higher in VOM than in conferencing; the authors felt one reason might be that conferences typically have more participants, making it more difficult to find as much satisfaction with an agreement. The meta-analysis found a "moderate to weak positive impact" on offender satisfaction as compared to offenders in nonrestorative programs.

20.2.3   Fairness

Fourteen VOM studies asked participants about the fairness of the mediation process and/or of the resulting agreement (Coates and Gehm 1985; Collins 1984; Davis, Tichane, and Grayson 1980; Evje and Cushman 2000; Roberts 1998; Strode 1997; Umbreit 1988, 1989, 1991, 1995a, 1995b; Umbreit and Coates 1992b; Umbreit, Coates, and Vos 2001a; Umbreit and Roberts 1996). Not surprisingly, given the high levels of satisfaction, the vast majority of VOM participants (typically over 80 percent) across settings, cultures, and types of offenses reported believing that the process was fair to both sides and that the resulting agreement was fair. Again, these experiences led to feelings that the overall criminal justice system was fair. In the studies that employed comparison groups, those individuals exposed to mediation came away more likely feeling that they had been treated fairly than those going through the traditional court proceedings. For example, in a study of burglary victims in Minneapolis, Umbreit found that 80 percent who went through VOM indicated that they experienced the criminal justice system as fair compared with only 37 percent of burglary victims who did not participate in VOM (Umbreit 1989).

20.2.4   Restitution and Repayment of Harm

The form of restitution, or what is called reparation in some jurisdictions, is quite varied and can include direct compensation to the victim, community service, work for the victim, and sometimes unusual paybacks devised between victim and offender. Apologies are also often included in program reports as a component of repairing the harm. In some settings, restitution amounts are established before cases are referred for mediation; in others, deciding whether the victim should receive restitution and how much is seen as an important domain for the mediation session.

Just under half the studies reviewed addressed the issue of restitution or repair of harm. Of those cases that reached a meeting, typically 90 percent or more generated agreements. Restitution of some sort was part of the vast majority of these agreements. Overall, approximately 80 to 90 percent of the contracts are reported as completed (Coates and Gehm 1985; Collins 1984; Dissel 2000; Evje and Cushman 2000; Galaway 1989; Katz 2000; Perry, Laje-unesse, and Woods 1987; Roy 1993; Umbreit 1988, 1991; Umbreit and Coates 1992a; Umbreit, Coates, and Vos 2001a; Warner 1992).

Results from comparative studies have been somewhat mixed. Most studies reported greater amounts of restitution and/or higher completion rates for VOM participants than comparison groups (Bradbury 2002; Evje and Cushman 2000; Umbreit and Coates 1992a), whereas another reported no difference (Roy 1993). One study found that restitution completion for offenders participating in face-to-face mediation was higher than for offenders who negotiated agreements through a neutral third party (Dignan 1990). The meta-analysis covering both mediation and group conferencing found that offenders participating in these programs had substantially higher completion rates than offenders processed in other ways (Latimer, Dowden, and Muise 2001).

20.2.5 Diversion

Among other reasons, many restorative programs are nominally established to divert offenders from the traditional justice system processes. Although such diversion is a laudable goal, it carries a concomitant risk of widening the net: that is, of sanctioning offenders who otherwise would not have received sanctions through traditional procedures. Only a handful of the studies reviewed here address this question.

Two mediation studies, both in the United Kingdom, have reported a net-widening impact for the intervention. One concluded that at least 60 percent of the offenders participating in mediation were true diversion from court prosecution, and that overall there was a 13 percent net-widening effect, much lower than expected (Dignan 1990). In the other, fully 43 percent of the comparison group cases were not prosecuted and received no sanction, a fairly broad net-widening result (Warner 1992).

In contrast, two U.S.-based studies found that the mediation programs successfully diverted offenders from court. One North Carolina program apparently reduced court trials by as much as two-thirds (Clarke, Valente, and Mace 1992). An Indiana-Ohio study compared consequences for seventy-three youth and adults going through VOM programs with those for a matched sample of individuals who were processed in the traditional manner (Coates and Gehm 1985). VOM offenders spent less time incarcerated than did their counterparts, and when incarcerated, they did county jail time rather than state time.

A recent study of the similar restorative process of group conferencing reported a finding that has relevance for the diversion/net-widening debate. In a recidivism study of 200 juveniles who had participated in group conferencing, Hayes and Daly (2004) performed survival analysis grouped by age at first offense. They found that if conferencing was the first intervention in the ten- to twelve-year-old age group, the offenders were less likely to reoffend than if the response was court referral or cautioning.

20.2.6   Recidivism

Restorative processes have as their goal attempting to meet the needs of all parties affected by crime: victims, offenders, and communities. Preventing recidivism is often used as a long-term measure of the "effectiveness" of such programs; clearly, such prevention benefits offenders directly and, more broadly, benefits communities. However, in the rush to demonstrate that VOM has a positive impact on offender rehabilitation, it is crucial not to lose sight of the overall balance that is the goal of restorative justice.

A large number of the studies reviewed here have addressed recidivism; we will confine our discussion to those studies that provided some type of comparison group. Studies simply reporting overall reoffending rates with no comparison will not addressed.

Although results of studies examining recidivism rates for VOM participants have been somewhat mixed, overall evidence is emerging that VOM has an impact on reducing recidivism. Several studies found lower rates for mediation participants than for offenders processed through traditional means (Katz 2000; Nugent and Paddock 1995; Schneider 1986; Stone 2000; Umbreit and Coates 1992a). In addition, five of the six programs examined by Evje and Cushman (2000) also found reduced recidivism. Two studies also found that youths who did reoffend tended to incur less serious charges than their counterparts (Nugent and Paddock 1995; Umbreit and Coates 1992a). Others reported little or no difference (Roy 1993; Stone, Helms, and Edgeworth 1998), as did one of the six programs studied by Evje and Cushman (2000). A study of a countywide restorative program that included VOM as one component found virtually equal recidivism rates between the sample and the control group (Bradbury 2002).

One U.K. study compared recidivism data on the VOM offenders who went through face-to-face mediation with those who were exposed only to shuttle mediation. The former group did somewhat better than the latter: 15.4 and 21.6 percent (Dignan 1990). As with satisfaction measures reported earlier, face-to-face mediation seems to generate better results both in the short run and in the longer run than the less personal indirect mediation. Another U.K. study examining seven varying restorative justice schemes found that "the only scheme that routinely involved victims was for the most part both lower cost and more effective than the other schemes" (Miers et al. 2001). The program reduced both the frequency and the seriousness of subsequent offenses.

A few studies have examined participants' offense rates before and after mediation. All of these studies found an overall reduction in offense rates for participating offenders (Nelson 2000; Umbreit, Coates, and Vos 2001a; Wynne and Brown 1998).

Three meta-analyses have addressed recidivism issues. Nugent et al. (1999) conducted a rigorous reanalysis of recidivism data reported in four previous studies involving a total sample of 1,298 juvenile offenders, 619 who participated in VOM and 679 who did not. Using ordinal logistical regression procedures, the authors determined that VOM youth recidivated at a statistically significant 32 percent lower rate than non-VOM youth, and when they did reoffend, they committed less serious offenses than the non-VOM youth.

In a subsequent report, Nugent, Williams, and Umbreit (2003) expanded their database to include fourteen studies. This analysis relied on a combined sample of 9,037 juveniles and similarly found that the VOM adolescents committed fewer and less serious offenses than their counterparts.

The third meta-analysis included both VOM and group conferencing, and found that the two types of programs together yielded reductions in recidivism compared to other, nonrestorative approaches, and that offenders in the two program types were significantly more successful during the follow-up periods (Latimer, Dowden, and Muise 2001).

20.2.7   Costs

The relative cost of correctional programs is difficult to assess. Several studies reviewed here addressed the issue of costs. Cost per unit case is obviously influenced by the number of cases handled and the amount of time devoted to each case. The results of a detailed cost analysis in a Scottish study were mixed (Warner 1992). In some instances, mediation was less costly than other options, and in others, more. The author noted that given the "marginal scope" of these programs, it remained difficult to project what their cost would be if implemented on a scale large enough to impact overall program administration.

Evaluation of a large-scale VOM program in California led the authors to conclude that the cost per case was reduced dramatically as the program went from being a fledgling to being a viable option (Niemeyer and Shichor 1996). Cost per case was $250. A Missouri program reported total cost per case that ranged from \$232 to \$338, but did not provide comparison data (Katz 2000).

As noted earlier, some programs have impacted total incarceration time (Coates and Gehm 1985), place/cost of incarceration (Coates and Gehm 1985), or reduction of trials (Clarke, Valente, and Mace 1992). Additionally, time spent to process a case has implications for overall cost. Stone, Helms, and Edgeworth (1998) found that the total time required to process mediated cases was only a third of that needed for nonmediated cases.

In an evaluation of a large-scale restorative program (of which VOM was one component) for youths who would have been referred to state custody, Bradbury found that the yearly cost per case was less than for the state custody program (\$48,396 versus \$65,866). Because recidivism was virtually the same between the two groups, the restorative program was less costly on the surface. However, the author concluded that because the restorative youths spent more days in the community, they posed more risk to community residents, so neither program could be designated as "clearly superior" (Bradbury 2002).

20.3   Crimes of Severe Violence

The practice of offering facilitated dialogue in crimes of severe violence is markedly different from the more typical VOM practice that has been described thus far. Rather than beginning with an offender referral, dialogue in serious and violent crimes is entirely victim-initiated. The service itself developed as a response to victims of serious and violent crimes such as assault and homicide who pressured their state victim service offices until they were permitted to meet with the offenders who harmed them or their loved ones.

Nearly all aspects of the practice of VOM in these cases extend over a longer time period than is typical in cases of less severe crimes. In most instances, there is a much longer interval between the crime and the initiation of a request for dialogue. The process of preparing the parties to meet tends to involve several sessions and stretch over a period of weeks or months, and actual meetings can last a half-day or longer. Naturally, the training of mediators to facilitate these more extensive and in-depth experiences is also longer.

Texas and Ohio were the first two states to develop and offer statewide programs for victim-offender dialogue in serious and violent crimes for victims who desire such a meeting. In a recent study focused on these two pioneering programs and their early participants, researchers interviewed forty victims and thirty-nine offenders who participated in mediation/dialogue sessions regarding serious and violent crimes (Umbreit et al. 2003). Exactly half of the crimes were murder or manslaughter, and the remaining crimes included sexual assault, felony assault/attempted murder, and theft/burglary. The interviews covered the participants' experience of the crime, their reasons for seeking and/or agreeing to meet, their preparation for the meeting, their evaluation of their preparation, their dialogue with their mediator/facilitator, their experience of the dialogue meeting, and their assessment of its impact on their life.

The three most frequently listed reasons that victims sought to meet were to seek information, to show offenders the impact of their actions, and to have some form of human contact with the person responsible for the crime. Offenders focused primarily on benefits to victims, such as the opportunity for the victim to receive an apology for the offender to help the victims heal. Offenders also often hoped that participation in VOM would contribute to their own rehabilitation or that it might change how their victims viewed them. Many also reported spiritual reasons for wanting to meet with their victim.

Both victims and offenders gave overwhelmingly positive evaluations of their preparation, their dialogue meetings, and their mediators/facilitators. The vast majority of the research participants reported that their participation in the mediation/dialogue program had a profound effect on their lives. Victims/family members and offenders alike reported feeling more at peace and better able to cope with their lives.

20.4 Conclusions

Victim offender mediation is a restorative justice process with considerable promise for repairing the harm caused by crime while holding offenders accountable and allowing those affected by the crime to have a voice in its solution. When it is practiced in accordance with its guidelines and values, the research demonstrates that VOM improves victims' involvement and healing, increases the extent to which offenders take responsibility for their behaviors and learn from their experience, offers community members a role in shaping a just response to law violation, and contributes to a more positive public attitude towards juvenile and criminal courts.

References

Abrams, L., and M. S. Umbreit. 2002. *Youthful Offenders Response to Victim Offender Conferencing in Washington County, MN*. St. Paul, MN: Center for Restorative Justice & Peacemaking.

Bazemore, G., and M. S. Umbreit. 1995. Rethinking the sanctioning function in juvenile court: Retributive or restorative responses to youth crime. *Crime and Delinquency* 41, 296.

Bradbury, B. 2002. *Deschutes County Delinquent Youth Demonstration Project: Secretary of State Audit Report # 2002-29*. Salem, OR: Office of the Secretary of State.

Bradshaw, W., and M. S. Umbreit. 1998. Crime victims meet juvenile offenders: Contributing factors to victim satisfaction with mediated dialogue. *Juvenile and Family Court Journal* 49, 3, 17.

Carr, C. 1998. *VORS Program Evaluation Report*. Inglewood, CA: Centenela Valley Juvenile Diversion Project.

Clarke, S., E. Valente, and R. Mace. 1992. *Mediation of Interpersonal Disputes: An Evaluation of North Carolina's Programs*. Chapel Hill: Institute of Government, University of North Carolina.

Coates, R.B., H. Burns, and M. S. Umbreit. 2002. *Victim Participation in Victim Offender Conferencing: Washington County, Minnesota Community Justice Program*. St. Paul, MN: Center for Restorative Justice and Peacemaking.

Coates, R. B., and J. Gehm. 1985. *Victim Meets Offender: An Evaluation of Victim-Offender Reconciliation Programs*. Valparaiso, IN: PACT Institute of Justice.

Collins, J. P. 1984. *Final Evaluation Report on the Grande Prairie Community Reconciliation Project for Young Offenders*. Ottawa: Ministry of the Solicitor General of Canada, Consultation Centre (Prairies).

Davis, R., M. Tichane, and D. Grayson. 1980. *Mediation and Arbitration as Alternatives to Prosecution in Felony Arrest Cases: An Evaluation of the Brooklyn Dispute Resolution Center*. New York: VERA Institute of Justice.

Dignan, J. 1990. *Repairing the Damage: An Evaluation of an Experimental Adult Reparation Scheme in Kettering, Northamptonshire*. Sheffield, U.K.: Centre for Criminological Legal Research, Faculty of Law, University of Sheffield.

Dissel, A. 2000. *Restoring the Harmony: A Report on a Victim Offender Conferencing Pilot Project*. Johannesburg, South Africa: Centre for the Study of Violence and Reconciliation.

Evje, A., and R. Cushman. 2000. *A Summary of the Evaluations of Six California Victim Offender Reconciliation Programs*. San Francisco: Judicial Council of California, Administrative Office of the Courts.

Fercello, C., and M. S. Umbreit. 1999. *Client Satisfaction with Victim Offender Conferences in Dakota County, Minnesota*. St. Paul, MN: Center for Restorative Justice and Peacemaking.

Galaway, B. 1989. Informal justice: Mediation between offenders and victims. In *Crime Prevention and Intervention: Legal and Ethical Problems*, ed. P. Albrecht and O. Backes, 103. New York: Walter de Gruyter.

Gehm, J. 1990. Mediated victim-offender restitution agreements: An exploratory analysis of factors related to victim participation. In *Criminal Justice, Restitution, and Reconciliation*, ed. B. Galaway and J. Hudson, 177. Monsey, NY: Criminal Justice Press.

Hayes, H., and K. Daly. 2004. Conferencing and re-offending in Queensland. *Australian and New Zealand Journal of Criminology* 37, 167.

Katz, J. 2000. *Victim Offender Mediation in Missouri's Juvenile Courts: Accountability, Restitution, and Transformation.* Jefferson City: Missouri Department of Public Safety.

Latimer, J., C. Dowden, and D. Muise. 2001. *The Effectiveness of Restorative Practices: A Meta- Analysis.* Ottawa, Canada: Department of Justice, Research and Statistics Division Methodological Series.

Marshall, T. 1990. Results of research from British experiments in restorative justice. In *Criminal Justice, Restitution, and Reconciliation*, ed. B. Galaway and J. Hudson, 83. Monsey, NY: Criminal Justice Press.

Miers, D., et al. 2001. *An Exploratory Evaluation of Restorative Justice Schemes: Executive Summary.* Crime Reduction Research Series Paper 9. London: Home Office.

Nelson, S. 2000. *Evaluation of the Restorative Justice Program.* Eugene, OR: Lane County Department of Youth Services.

Niemeyer, M., and D. Shichor. 1996. A preliminary study of a large victim/offender reconciliation program. *Federal Probation* 60, 3, 30.

Nugent, W. M., and J. Paddock. 1995. The effect of victim-offender mediation on severity of reoffense. *Mediation Quarterly* 12, 353.

Nugent, W. M., M. S. Umbreit, L. Wiinamaki, and J. Paddock. 1999. Participation in victim-offender mediation and severity of subsequent delinquent behavior: Successful replications? *Journal of Research in Social Work Practice* 11, 5.

Nugent, W. M., R. M. Williams, and M. S. Umbreit. 2003. Participation in victim-offender mediation and the prevalence and severity of subsequent delinquent behavior: A meta-analysis. *Utah Law Review* 1, 137.

Perry, L., T. Lajeunesse, and A. Woods. 1987. *Mediation Services: An Evaluation.* Manitoba, Canada: Research, Planning and Evaluation Office of the Attorney General.

Roberts, L. 1998. Victim offender mediation: An evaluation of the Pima County Juvenile Court Center's Victim Offender Mediation Program (VOMP), Masters Thesis, University of Arizona Department of Communications, Tucson.

Roberts, T. 1995. *Evaluation of the Victim Offender Mediation Project, Langley, BC: Final Report.* Victoria, BC, Canada: Focus Consultants.

Roy, S. 1993. Two Types of Juvenile Restitution Programs in Two Midwestern Counties: A Comparative Study. *Federal Probation* 57, 4, 48.

Schneider, A. 1986. Restitution and recidivism rates of juvenile offenders: Results from four experimental studies. *Criminology* 24, 533.

Stone, K. 2000. An evaluation of recidivism rates for Resolutions Northwest's Victim Offender Mediation Program, Masters Thesis, Portland State University, Portland, OR.

Stone, S., S. Helms, and P. Edgeworth. 1998. *Cobb County Juvenile Court Mediation Program Evaluation.* Carrolton: State University of West Georgia.

Strode, E. 1997. Victims of property crime meet their juvenile offenders: Victim participants' evaluation of the Dakota County (MN) Community Corrections Victim Offender Meeting Program, Masters Thesis, Smith College of Social Work, Northampton, MA.

Umbreit, M. S. 1988. Mediation of victim offender conflict. *Journal of Dispute Resolution* 35, 85.

Umbreit, M. S. 1989. Crime victims seeking fairness, not revenge: Toward restorative justice. *Federal Probation* 53, 3, 52.

Umbreit, M. S. 1991. Minnesota mediation center produces positive results. *Corrections Today* August, 194.

Umbreit, M. S. 1994. *Victim Meets Offender.* Monsey, NY: Criminal Justice Press.

Umbreit, M. S. 1995a. *Mediation of Criminal Conflict: An Assessment of Programs in Four Canadian Provinces.* St. Paul, MN: Center for Restorative Justice and Peacemaking.

Umbreit, M. S. 1995b. Restorative justice through mediation: The impact of offenders facing their victims in Oakland. *Journal of Law and Social Work* 5, 1.

Umbreit, M. S. 1997. Humanistic mediation: A transformative journey of peacemaking. *Mediation Quarterly* 14, 201.

Umbreit, M. S. 2001. *The Handbook of Victim Offender Mediation: An Essential Guide to Practice and Research.* San Francisco: Jossey-Bass.

Umbreit, M. S., and W. Bradshaw. 1999. Factors that contribute to victim satisfaction with mediated offender dialogue in Winnipeg: An emerging area of social work practice. *Journal of Law and Social Work* 9, 2, 35.

Umbreit, M. S., and R. B. Coates. 1992a. The impact of mediating victim offender conflict: An analysis of programs in three states. *Juvenile and Family Court Journal* 4, 1.

Umbreit, M. S., and R. B. Coates. 1992b. *Victim Offender Mediation: An Analysis of Programs in Four States of the U.S.* Minneapolis: Minnesota Citizens Council on Crime and Justice.

Umbreit, M. S. and R. B. Coates. 1993. Cross-site analysis of victim-offender mediation in four states. *Crime and Delinquency* 39, 565.

Umbreit, M. S., R. B. Coates, and B. Vos. 2001a. *Juvenile Victim Offender Mediation in Six Oregon Counties.* Salem, OR: Oregon Dispute Resolution Commission.

Umbreit, M. S., R. B. Coates, and B. Vos. 2001b. The impact of victim offender mediation: Two decades of research. *Federal Probation*, 65, 1, 29.

Umbreit, M. S., R. B. Coates, and B. Vos. 1999. The impact of restorative justice conferencing: A multi-national perspective. *British Journal of Community Justice* 1, 2, 21.

Umbreit, M. S., and J. Greenwood. 1999. National survey of victim offender mediation programs in the U.S. *Mediation Quarterly* 16, 235.

Umbreit, M. S., and A. W. Roberts. 1996. *Mediation of Criminal Conflict in England: An Assessment of Services in Coventry and Leeds.* St. Paul, MN: Center for Restorative Justice and Peacemaking.

Umbreit, M. S., et al. 2003. *Facing Violence: The Path of Restorative Justice and Dialogue.* Monsey, NY: Criminal Justice Press.

van Ness, D., and K. Heetderks. 2002. *Restoring Justice,* 2nd ed. Cincinnati: Anderson.

Warner, S. 1992. *Making Amends, Justice for Victims and Offenders.* Aldershot, U.K.: Avebury.

Wynne, J., and I. Brown. 1998. Can mediation cut reoffending? *Probation Journal* 45, 1, 21.

Wyrick, P., and M. Costanzo. 1999. Predictors of client participation in victim-offender mediation. *Mediation Quarterly* 16, 253.

Zehr, H. 2002. *The Little Book of Restorative Justice.* Intercourse, PA: Good Books.

Lenient Justice? Punishing White-Collar and Corporate Crime

21

HENRY N. PONTELL,
STEPHEN M. ROSOFF, AND
ANDREW PETERSON

Contents

21.1 Introduction

The term *white-collar crime* continues to be contentious in criminology. Debates regarding its definition and overall scientific merit have persisted since Sutherland introduced the concept in his 1939 presidential address to the American Society of Sociology. Some scholars use Sutherland's status-based formulation (Braithwaite 1985; Coleman 2002; Geis 1981), whereas others attempt to alter its focus and definition (Clinard and Quinney 1973; Shapiro 1990), or argue that it is a social construct that is ill framed, imprecise, and "selectively defined to fit the ideological biases of individual scholars" (Johnson and Leo 1993). Revisionists are likely to maintain that Sutherland's work represented a partisan polemic against corporations and high social status persons, despite decades of evidence that the crimes of the wealthy and of corporate organizations dwarf the harmful effects of common crime. Both the savings and loan (S&L) scandals (Pontell and Calavita 1993) and the more recent corporate and accounting meltdowns on Wall Street (Eichenwald 2005; Toffler 2003) *alone* have produced unprecedented losses due to fraud that question the common crime focus of mainstream criminological enterprise.

At the same time, the generally lenient treatment of high-status white-collar offenders has been a topic that has aroused much controversy and research among criminologists and sociologists. For example, it has been argued that one important reason for white-collar and corporate crime is the leniency accorded to such criminals. Jeffrey Reiman's (1995) pithy observation that "the rich get richer and the poor get prison" neatly summarizes the sociological contrast of the frequent indifferent response to white-collar crime with the harsh punitive treatment customarily accorded street criminals. This comparative leniency shown to white-collar offenders can be attributed to several factors related to their status and resources, as well as to the peculiar characteristics of their offenses. For one, the relatively high educational level and occupational prestige of many white-collar offenders can serve as a "status shield" that protects them from the harsh penalties applied with greater frequency to common criminals.

Weak or absent regulations are also seen as a cause of leniency, due in part to the power of corporations to influence regulatory legislation that pertains to them. In addition, given the size of what they are responsible for proactively policing, regulatory agencies are inadequately funded and understaffed, leaving much corporate crime undetected. Corporate crime is difficult—certainly much more so than most common crimes—to prove and sanction even when there is ample evidence as to its probable occurrence. The power of large corporations and wealthy defendants with highly skilled lawyers is often more than a formidable match for law enforcement agencies stretched thin by policing common crime and for prosecutors who must manage correspondingly heavy caseloads. This would appear to punctuate one of the world's worst-kept secrets: that life is seldom fair. Here again, white-collar defendants' high incomes and corporations' power and wealth enable them to secure expensive legal counsel, whose level of skill and access to defensive resources is generally unavailable to lower-class defendants. One might liken this situation to the fight between David and Goliath, but in the Bible, David won. In the contemporary world, Goliath is much more likely to be the victor. As just one indicator of this state of affairs, regulatory agencies and prosecutors often settle for promises by corporations that they will stop their offenses, which many times they do not even formally acknowledge engaging in (Rosoff, Pontell, and Tillman 2004).

It is also undoubtedly the case that many judges identify with defendants whose background and standing in the community are similar to their own. For example, when three former executives of C. R. Bard Corporation, one of the world's largest medical equipment manufacturers, were convicted in 1996 of conspiring to test unapproved heart surgery catheters in patients, the sympathetic judge reluctantly sentenced them to eighteen months in federal prison and seemed to be scolding the jury when he said, "I don't regard the defendants as being evil people or typical criminal types" (Ranalli 1996: 20). The U.S. Attorney who prosecuted the case could not have disagreed more. He characterized the callous executives as "evil people doing evil things... for money" (Ranalli 1996: 20).

Another component of leniency toward white-collar and corporate lawbreaking can be found in weak punishment. In numerous corporate scandals in the United States preceding the meltdown of Enron, including the cases of E. F. Hutton, National Medical Enterprises, Prudential Securities, and many others, millions of dollars in fines were levied, but not one single individual was ever imprisoned. Moreover, fining individuals and companies for their offenses has been noted to be a rather weak sanction for quite some time. In his seminal study involving the heavy electrical equipment antitrust cases in the 1960s, Gilbert Geis (1967) noted that a $400,000 fine against General Electric was the financial equivalent of a person earning $175,000 a year receiving a $3 parking ticket. The situation has not changed much since that time, as indicated by one contemporary example among many others.

Bank of America was fined $10 million in March 2004 for delaying the delivery of documentation on possible securities trading violations. The Securities and Exchange Commission (SEC), which levied the fine, noted it was the largest it had ever imposed for failing to produce evidence requested in an investigation. The $10 million was a lot of money in absolute terms, yet Bank of America took in $48 billion in revenue in 2003 and cleared a profit of $10.8 billion, and its total assets are almost $1 trillion. Thus the fine amounted to 0.02 percent of its revenue, less than 1 percent of its profit, and 0.001 percent of its assets. To translate the first and last figures to ones that are more understandable, the $10 million fine was equivalent to $8 for someone with an annual income of $40,000, and to $2 to someone with a net worth of $200,000. Thus fines for corporations have little impact and are often seen as just the cost of doing business (Barkan 2006: 393).

The complexity of the most consequential white-collar and corporate crimes is yet another factor that hampers the ability to prove that they in fact occurred. White-collar crimes frequently involve complicated financial transactions in which the victims are either aggregated classes of unrelated persons, such as stockholders, or large government agencies, such as the Internal Revenue Service (IRS), neither of which engender the kind of commiseration that individual victims of street crimes can elicit from judges and juries. Moreover, exactly how and which laws and regulations were violated, by whom, and whether or not intent was involved, also present formidable legal challenges. Such complicated cases are very difficult to represent to juries.

Anecdotal evidence also seems to support the proposition that white-collar criminals receive lighter sanctions. Michael Milken's initially tough ten-year sentence was later cut to three years, and he was released after serving only twenty-four months in a minimum security facility. Likewise, two of the most notorious savings and loan crooks in Texas—Don Dixon and "Fast Eddie" McBirney—whose corrupt savings and loans eventually cost U.S. taxpayers $3 billion, had their original sentences substantially reduced (Hightower 1994: 11).

21.2 Contradictions in Labeling: White-Collar Crime as a "Nonissue"

Such issues are important for understanding the sanctioning of white-collar crime, as they entail the process by which actors and events come to be labeled as criminal. Some critical crime theorists claim that "criminal definitions are applied to segments of society that have the power to shape the enforcement and administration of criminal law" (Quinney 1970: 185). Taking this a step further, Katz (1988) has effectively argued that the analysis of white-collar crime by conventional methods involving "background determinism" is inherently doomed to failure because of the contradictory relationship between white-collar crime and the enforcement mechanism to control it. That is, the phenomenon would no longer exist if enforcement became too serious, as pressure would build from conventional sectors of society to reduce the reach of the law.

Moreover, white-collar crime may often be hidden altogether for long periods of time and never be subject to sanctioning at all. In a study examining arson for profit, Barry Goetz (1997) effectively demonstrated that both resource constraints and class bias affect the recognition of white-collar crime, providing a "structural cloak" over such acts that are subsequently defined by officials as "nonissues." He showed that a number of fires in Boston that were intentionally set by landlords for insurance purposes were never recognized as such for many years, but rather were blamed on lower-class occupants of the buildings and neighborhoods. The dynamics of keeping arson for profit a "nonissue" thus illuminates a major deficiency in law and society scholarship that has traditionally focused on the "law in action" when it comes to white-collar offending. A more critical approach views the "law in inaction" as equally, if not more, important, especially regarding the non-recognition and lesser sanctioning of white-collar crime (Levi 1984; Tombs and Whyte 2003). Because most acts of white-collar and corporate lawbreaking—especially those that are the most serious in terms of fiscal and physical harm—do not officially exist without proactive enforcement, the law in inaction can play a substantial role in the nonrecognition of such acts. The law in inaction is also evident in the labeling and punishment process in terms of reduced sanctioning and leniency.

21.2.1   Differential Treatment of White-Collar Offenders?

Although sociologists and criminologists have argued that the lenient treatment of high-status, white-collar criminals can be found at all stages of the system, its effects are concentrated at two central points: the decision to prosecute and sentencing. A considerable amount of empirical work on the differential treatment of white-collar offenders has, on the whole, produced mixed conclusions. Less research has been done on the charging stage, where prosecutorial decisions are made as to whether to bring a case at all. In one of the few major studies on the topic, Hagan and Parker (1985) examined legal sanctioning of securities fraud in Canada and found that employers were less likely to be prosecuted under criminal laws than were offenders in lower-class positions. They concluded that class advantage was embedded in the organizational structure of corporations in a manner that protects employers from criminal prosecution. Shapiro (1990) later challenged this view in an analysis of sanctions imposed on securities law violators in the United States. She concluded that the apparent tendency to prosecute lower-status offenders more frequently was not due to class bias, but rather to the greater availability of alternative sanctions in cases involving higher status defendants.

Another view of such differential treatment relates to the capacity of government agencies to respond to incidents of suspected crime. This perspective sees official reaction as structured by such factors as caseload pressures and organizational resources (Pontell 1984). Such resource limitations are particularly relevant to larger, more complex white-collar crime cases that necessarily require substantial amounts of investigative and prosecutorial effort for adjudication. Commonplace organizational capacity issues and problems become glaringly apparent when massive waves of white-collar crime occur, such as in the savings and loan debacle and the recent corporate and accounting scandals in the United States (Pontell 2005; Pontell, Calavita, and Tillman 1994).

Among the three major theoretical explanations for white-collar leniency, the class-advantage argument has received the most empirical attention. A series of studies on the sentencing of white-collar offenders in U.S. federal courts has added to the debate, as they produced conflicting results. John

Hagan and his colleagues, for example, found modest but significant evidence of more lenient treatment of higher-status federal defendants (Hagan and Nagel 1982; Hagan, Nagel, and Albonetti 1980). On the other hand, Wheeler and his colleagues found that higher-status defendants in ten federal judicial districts tended to receive more, not less, punitive sentences (Wheeler, Weisburd, and Bode 1982). In a replication of the Wheeler study that focused on a single jurisdiction, Benson and Walker (1988) did not find evidence that higher-status defendants were punished more severely than lower-class ones. Yet, on the other side of the issue, Hagan and Parker (1985) found that for securities violations in Canada, employers were less likely to be charged under criminal codes, and thus received lighter sentences than did employees. Other studies in varying contexts comparing sanctions imposed on white-collar offenders and those given to traditional offenders found that the former enjoy a considerable leniency advantage (Tillman and Pontell 1992; Snider 1982).

Even with these disparate results, several of these researchers have offered similar theoretical explanations for their findings. Hagan and Parker, Wheeler et al., as well as Baker and Faulkner in a later study suggest that white-collar offenders' vulnerability to criminal sanctions may be determined by their relative position within the organization in which the crime was committed (Hagan and Parker 1985, 313; Wheeler et al. 1982, 657; Baker and Faulkner 1991). Individuals in higher positions in corporations, such as CEOs, for example, may be able to more easily evade prosecution because of their structural ability to distance themselves from crimes, leaving lower-level employees "holding the bag." This same "organizational advantage" hypothesis found support in Geis's (1967) analysis of the heavy electrical equipment industry antitrust case of 1961. That organizational structure can serve as a shield between white-collar offenders and social control mechanisms suggests the need to revise traditional class-advantage arguments to focus on how organizational position, and not simply social status, acts to shield criminality from discovery and/or prosecution.

In contrast to this class-advantage argument and its organizational variant, Shapiro has argued that it is important to recognize the availability of alternative sanctions such as civil remedies in response to white-collar offenses. From an analysis of securities violations in the United States, she argued, "any apparent discrimination against lower status offenders in prosecutorial discretion is more readily explained by greater access to legal options than by social standing" (1990: 361-362). She called for a reconceptualization of the white-collar leniency thesis, in that "arguments that attribute leniency accorded to white-collar offenders to class bias misunderstand the structural sources of leniency."

Similar assessments are found in the work of Chicago-school economists, most notably Richard Posner (1980). Drawing on Becker's (1968) work, he argued that efficient legal institutions will seek to control white-collar offenders through monetary sanctions obtained through less costly civil or administrative procedures rather than seeking imprisonment through the cumbersome criminal justice system. In a study of Medicaid fraud offenders, Tillman and Pontell (1992) found little support for this position. Physicians and other licensed health care providers convicted of Medicaid fraud rarely received harsh criminal sanctions, but neither did they typically face civil or administrative sanctions.

In contrast to both the organizational-advantage and the alternative sanctions arguments, the system capacity model focuses on the practical difficulties that confront law enforcement agents as a limiting factor in the use of criminal sanctions. White-collar crimes often require greater investigatory and prosecutorial resources as well as special expertise and coordination of law enforcement and regulatory agencies and are often exceedingly difficult to explain to juries. For these reasons, officials are reluctant to initiate criminal cases, or will do so only on ancillary matters related to the central criminal activity (e.g., tax fraud or mail fraud charges) unless the chances of conviction are high (Gurney 1985; Levi 1987; Benson et al. 1988). In broad theoretical context, white-collar crime challenges the capacity of the criminal justice system and society to effectively sanction it. "In a sense, the most serious crimes are those which attempt to make use of politically powerful or economically elite positions to frustrate detection and prosecution; white-collar crimes define the boundaries of the criminal justice system's capacities and the limits of the moral integrity in the economy and polity" (Katz 1980: 175).

The leniency hypothesis also receives support from a study of persons suspected by federal regulators in Texas and California to be involved in serious savings and loan crimes that revealed that only between 14 percent and 25 percent were ever indicted. The study also examined the sentences imposed in S&L cases involving mean losses of a half-million dollars and found that the average sentence was three years: significantly less than the average prison terms handed to convicted burglars and first-time drug offenders in federal court (Calavita, Pontell, and Tillman 1997). It would appear from these findings that burglars and first-time drug offenders are considered by the courts to be more serious threats to public security than are thrift looters, who can destabilize the entire economy.

The aforementioned study of California Medicaid providers convicted of defrauding that state's health care system produced similar findings. It reported that, when compared to a control group of first-time "blue-collar" offenders charged with grand theft (similar if not identical to the charge leveled at the Medicaid fraud offenders), the fraud defendants—many of whom were physicians—were less than half as likely to be incarcerated. This disparity is made even more conspicuous by the fact that the median financial losses from the Medicaid offenses were more than *ten times* the amount of the control group's crimes (Tillman and Pontell 1992).

On the other hand, although the findings from these kinds of focused studies may seem clear, the results yielded by broader analyses of class-based sentencing differentials are less consistent. Although many studies have supported the leniency hypothesis (e.g., Hagan and Nagel 1982; Hagan, Nagel, and Albonetti 1980), others have reported no evidence that higher-status defendants are punished any less severely than lower-status ones (Benson and Walker 1988). Some have even produced the contrary finding that higher-status defendants receive longer, not shorter, sentences (e.g., Wheeler, Weisburd, and Bode 1982; Weisburd, Waring, and Wheeler 1990). So, the issue of social status and punitive leniency remains unresolved.[1]

21.3 Punishing "Too Much"?

Given the numerous opportunities that many persons have to engage in white-collar crime, it may be surprising that more people do not. Perhaps the most obvious reason for their avoidance of such acts is the fear of punishment. For example, in the United States, despite the fact that relatively few individuals who cheat on their taxes are ever actually prosecuted, the knowledge that some are may be enough to keep most people reasonably law-abiding when they turn in their yearly tax forms. That is, many citizens refrain from cheating not simply because they have strong moral compunctions, but because the law deters them, if not the actual amount of sanctioning itself. Classical criminological notions of deterrence rest on the fundamental utilitarian premise that people will seek pleasure and avoid pain. When the potential risks associated with a behavior—such as crime—outweigh the potential gains, an individual will decide rationally to avoid the behavior. Much of criminal law is based on this assumption about human nature. However, a central concern about white-collar crime is that the risk-reward ratio is out of balance in that the potential rewards greatly outweigh the actual risks. With a low probability of apprehension and the likelihood of light punishment, white-collar crime appears to be a "rational" course of action in many cases.

In response to this situation, in 2001 the U.S. Congress adopted federal sentencing guidelines for financial crimes and updated them in 2003 in response to public outrage over the corporate and accounting scandals. The guidelines call for the adjusting of sentences based on the severity of the

[1] Using criminal defendants who are physicians as a model, Rosoff has argued that the customary "status shield" can be transformed into a target, under certain circumstances—particularly when the offense is a "common" crime rather than a white-collar crime.

fraud, most notably the estimated loss. If the amount is greater than $5,000, there are fifteen escalating categories up to "more than $400 million," with corresponding increases in sentences.

On March 25, 2004, Jamie Olis, a former accountant for Dynegy, a Houston-based energy company, was sentenced in federal court to twenty-four years and four months for fraud and conspiracy (Hays 2004). Olis had been convicted a year earlier of participating in a 2001 scheme, code-named Project Alpha, to disguise a $300 million loan as cash flow in order to help the company meet Wall Street expectations ("Olis begins prison sentence" 2004). The scheme also had helped Dynegy claim an improper $79 million tax benefit ("Olis begins prison sentence" 2004). After Project Alpha was uncovered, Jamie Olis' illegal actions eventually cost Dynegy investors more than $500 million, and the company soon unraveled (Hays 2004).

Against the advice of counsel, he had refused to settle; he believed that everything he had done was legal. Olis' own e-mails had warned colleagues to "never, never, never" share details of Project Alpha. Another of his e-mails even joked about his fear of a good prosecutor making him "cry" on the witness stand (Hays 2004). The jury found him guilty in less than two hours (Hays 2004). The judge told Olis: "I take no pleasure in sentencing you to 292 months" (quoted in Cook 2004). But the judge also declared that the punishment "reflects Congress' intent that white-collar corporate fraud defendants receive harsh sentences" (quoted in Hays 2004).

Critics of the federal sentencing guidelines argue that they have a chilling effect on productivity. Financial writer James K. Glassman (2004) labeled the reaction of politicians to the corporate scandals as "hysterical." He argued, "The penalty for failure today is not merely lower earnings; it is lawsuits, prosecution, huge fines, and long prison terms." Glassman may be correct about failure causing lawsuits and even fines; but he's mistaken about prosecution. Prison terms are not caused by mere failure; they are caused by serious criminal behavior.

Another financial author, Henry Blodget (2004), echoed Glassman's sentiments. Blodget wrote that the tough sentencing guidelines have made it "shockingly risky" to work at a major corporation. This is an unpersuasive argument built upon a persuasive premise. Certainly, the risk-reward ratio is central to capitalism. Economist John Maynard Keynes was a proponent of risk-taking, which he called "animal spirits" ("In praise of animal spirits" 1999). Historian Walter A. McDougall (2004) maintained that the U.S. economy was built by "scramblers, gamblers, scofflaws, and speculators." But there are many ways to define acceptable risk-taking, and Blodget's definition seems overly broad. He is a former dot.com analyst, who was once a major star on Wall Street—until he was barred from the securities industry for phony and self-serving research ratings (Gasparino 2005). It might just as easily be argued that Blodget and his ilk have made it "shockingly risky" to buy dot-com stocks.

Nevertheless, Blodget and Glassman's side appears to have prevailed. On November 1, 2005, the 5th U.S. Circuit Court of Appeals overturned Jamie Olis' twenty-four-year sentence (Fowler 2005: A1, A8), though it let his conviction stand. The court explicitly challenged the careful calculations set forth in the federal sentencing guidelines. In January 2005, the Supreme Court ruled 5-4 that federal judges no longer have to abide by mandatory sentencing guidelines, saying that the consideration of factors not presented to jurors violates a defendant's right to a fair trial. Thus the decision made the guidelines advisory and not mandatory (*U.S. v. Booker* 2005). If the judge chooses to impose a longer sentence, an appeals court could overturn the sentence if it determines the application was unreasonable.

The Jamie Olis sentence, along with the effective "life sentences" being served by Bernie Ebbers (WorldCom) and John Rigas (Adelphia), seem to belie traditional notions of white-collar criminals getting "slapped on the wrist." But even if some high-status defendants still do receive preferential treatment, is that necessarily a bad thing? Certain economists have challenged the presumption that differential sentencing has a deleterious effect on the justice system and on society. In a provocative article entitled, "Do we punish high income criminals too heavily?" John Lott answered his own question with an emphatic "Yes." He argued that, because wealthy defendants experience a proportionately greater decline in income following a criminal conviction than do poorer defendants, their punishment will be unduly harsh if they receive the same sentences as their low-income counterparts who are convicted of the same crimes (Lott 1992; see also Baum and Kamas 1995). The solution he recommended is to allow upper world criminals to "buy justice": that is, to use their lighter sentences to offset the more serious extralegal sanctions they face (Lott 1987). Thus, for example, if a bank president and a bank teller are each convicted of embezzlement and sentenced to two years in prison, and the bank president's income declines 90 percent (from $1 million a year to $100,000) and the teller's declines "only" 50 percent (from $20,000 a year to $10,000), according to Lott's extraordinarily curious notion of justice, the bank president should be "compensated" for his or her greater loss of income by a shorter sentence.

Critics of Lott's "wealth maximization" approach contend that using money as his unit of measure "violates the principle of the equality of individuals before the law" (Baum and Kamas 1995: 74). Furthermore, wealth maximization arguments seem to assume that wealthy offenders suffer from "collateral penalties"; that is, society punishes white-collar criminals in ways that go far beyond the courtroom, such as a dramatic alteration of their standing in the community and their ability to earn a living. One of the flaws in such reasoning is that its underlying premise may be false, at least in many cases. After interviewing several dozen convicted white-collar criminals who had completed their sentences about their postrelease lifestyles, *Forbes* magazine concluded: "U.S. society is forgiving and often forgetting about white-collar convictions" (Machan and Button 1990). One of those interviewed was David Begelman, who was convicted of embezzlement in 1978 when he ran Columbia Pictures (McClintick 1982). Within months of his conviction, he was back in the movie business, running MGM Studios, and later went on to become a successful independent film producer (McClintick 1982).

Further evidence of the forgiving attitude of business toward professionals who cheat and defraud clients is found in a Securities and Exchange Commission study of "rogue brokers," persons who had been the subject of official investigations for violating securities laws. The SEC found that many of the brokers had little difficulty securing jobs after their brushes with the law; in fact, two-thirds were still employed in the securities industry (U.S. Securities and Exchange Commission 1995). Likewise, the Medicaid fraud study cited earlier reported that only 12 percent of the convicted doctors had their licenses to practice medicine revoked (Tillman and Pontell 1992).

Moreover, in some states, the laws actually protect the wealth of convicted white-collar criminals. For example, just before Martin Siegel was indicted in New York for insider trading, he moved his family to Florida, where he purchased a $3.25 million beachfront home. It might just be that Siegel preferred mild Florida winters to those in New York. But it seems more likely that he was trying to safeguard his assets from the onslaught of impending litigation by taking advantage of a Florida law that prohibits the seizure of a person's legal residence. This archaic statute, originally enacted as a populist measure to prevent banks from displacing homesteaders, has resulted in Florida becoming a haven for white-collar criminals seeking to shelter their assets from the government by "investing" in expensive mansions ("Rich debtors finding shelter" 1993: A1).

21.4   White-Collar Crime and State Theory: Crime Control versus Damage Control

A series of studies on the savings and loan debacle in the United States examined how the state's relationship to capital was in turn related to the punishment of white-collar offenders (Calavita, Pontell, and Tillman 1997; Calavita and Pontell 1994; Calavita, Tillman, and Pontell 1997). Noting the transformation of the economic system from one based on industrial capitalism to one based on financial capitalism, criminologists have argued that this also involves the proliferation of new forms of white-collar crime that entail violations of economic regulations for personal profit at the expense of organizations, which may threaten the stability of the economy itself. Unlike older forms of white-collar offending, which typically involved crimes *by organizations* in the manufacturing sector, crimes such as "collective embezzlement" by controlling insiders of financial institutions constituted crimes *by the organization against the organization itself.* When such lawbreaking proliferated throughout the savings and loan industry, it not only decimated individual institutions but threatened the demise of the entire industry and, with it, the financial stability of the U.S. economy.

Scholars who study regulatory issues generally borrow from a structuralist approach to the state, which sees lax enforcement of social regulations as due to the necessity of the state to protect the capital accumulation process, while not concurrently interfering with profitable business enterprises (Barnett 1981; Calavita 1983; Snider 1991; Yeager 1991). Social regulations are generally aimed at the control of production processes, whereas economic regulation refers to laws that regulate the market and stabilize the economy. Active enforcement of social regulation generally occurs in response to public pressure and concerns of political stability, and it recedes when attention moves elsewhere and legitimacy is restored (Barnett 1981; Calavita 1983; Snider 1991; Yeager 1991). On the other hand, where economic regulation is concerned, the stakes are much higher, and the state is likely to take a more rigorous approach to offenses. Despite protests from those at whom such sanctions are directed, the state will more likely enforce regulations that stabilize the economy and enhance economic viability and investment. Economic regulations are central to the functioning of the economy and are thus more consistently and vigorously enforced (Barnett 1981; Snider 1991; Yeager 1991). Studies have found evidence that such enforcement discrepancies do in fact exist, including research conducted on the SEC (Yeager 1991; Shapiro 1984), and analysis of enforcement actions against the 582 largest corporations in the United States in the 1970s (Clinard and Yeager 1980).

These empirical findings are consistent with structural theories of the state and demonstrate the lenient treatment of white-collar lawbreaking claimed by Sutherland (1948) and reaffirmed in many subsequent studies. This documentation, however, may be related to the fact that the primary focus of the white-collar crime sanctioning literature has been on "social regulations" that affect profits, and not the "economic regulations" that affect the entire economy. If this is correct, then one would expect an altogether different response to massive economic crimes such as collective embezzlement in the savings and loan crisis than to traditional corporate crimes in the manufacturing sector. "Instead, extensive evidence indicates that the state not only failed to avert the crisis but was complicit in shielding thrift offenders from detection" (Calavita, Tillman, and Pontell 1997: 32). The evolution of the savings and loan crisis showed that although the state is capable of rigorous enforcement of economic regulations, it also involves political actors whose own career interests are intertwined with a variety of external influences, most notably powerful industry lobbyists. Thus, initial government action was conflicted and actually contributed to the subsequent debacle. As a consequence, the state response to the unprecedented wave of lawbreaking in the thrift industry was characterized more by "damage control" than "crime control" (Calavita and Pontell 1995). According to Calavita and her colleagues, this indicated the need for a more synthetic model of state action to explain such response when "instrumental influences on state actors can—and periodically do—neutralize that structural interest and derail the regulatory agenda" (Calavita, Tillman, and Pontell 1997: 35).

21.4.1 Punishment, Compliance, Regulation, and Change

It has been proposed that new laws that impose tougher penalties on white-collar criminals might well deter some potential offenders. More punitive federal sentencing guidelines have resulted in more white-collar crime convictions: 8,050 in 1994, up 6 percent in twenty-four months (Calavita, Tillman, and Pontell 1997). But whether this new toughness serves as a general deterrent is not at all clear, especially in light of the largest wave of business and accounting frauds in 2002—the most costly in history—that took investor confidence in the United States to its lowest levels since the Great Depression and caused trillions of dollars of market losses worldwide. Current laws likely fail to deter because white-collar offenders are aware of the frequent lack of vigorous enforcement and the relatively low probability that their crimes will be detected or punished severely. A federal prosecutor has declared: "You deal with white-collar crime the same way as street crime. You try to raise the likelihood they will be caught and punished" (quoted in Langberg 1989: 1E). Stricter application of existing guidelines would also serve to redress the sentencing imbalance between white-collar and traditional "common" criminals (*United States Code Congressional and Administrative News* 1984).

The system of regulatory codes and administrative agencies that monitor corporate conduct and respond to criminal violations is another important part of the legal apparatus. Some scholars believe that we do not need more regulation; rather, we need "smarter" regulation (Grabosky 2001). Simply applying harsher laws to corporations and individuals, they argue, will only produce a subculture of resistance within the corporate community "wherein methods of legal resistance and counterattack are incorporated into industry socialization" (Ayres and Braithwaite 1992: 20). Regulation works best when it is a "benign big gun"; that is, when regulators can speak softly but carry big sticks in the form of substantial legal penalties (Ayres and Braithwaite 1992: 20).

A hierarchical structure of sanctions also has been proposed, in which the first response to misconduct consists of advice, warnings, and persuasion, then escalates to harsher responses culminating at the top of the pyramid, in what is termed "corporate capital punishment" or the dissolution of the offending company (Fisse and Braithwaite 1993). The goal of this model is compliance: "Compliance is thus understood within a dynamic enforcement game where enforcers try to get commitment from corporations to comply with the law and can back up their negotiations with credible threats about the dangers faced by defendants if they choose to go down the path of non-compliance" (Fisse and Braithwaite 1993: 143). The strength of such a system is that it works at multiple levels and holds all the actors involved—"executive directors, accountants, brokers, legal advisers, and sloppy regulators" (Fisse and Braithwaite 1993: 230)—accountable for criminal misconduct.

In response to the corporate and accounting scandals of 2002 in the United States, Congress passed the Sarbanes-Oxley Act, the toughest piece of corporate governance legislation ever enacted. The law imposes new duties on public corporations and their executives, directors, auditors, and attorneys, as well as securities analysts. The act provides significantly expanded rulemaking by the Securities and Exchange Commission and the creation of the Public Company Accounting Oversight Board. Among the act's eleven major provisions is the requirement that corporate CEOs assume personal responsibility for the honesty of their company's financial statements. Misrepresentations could mean prison time for company executives. In the year following the enactment of Sarbanes-Oxley, more than 300 publicly traded corporations restated their earnings ("Study: More companies restating earnings" 2003).

It is far too soon to evaluate the effectiveness of this new law, but it is worth noting that, as of this writing, there have been no major accounting scandals of Enron/WorldCom magnitude since Sarbanes-Oxley was enacted. Nevertheless, smaller cases do still surface. One example involves Coca-Cola. In mid-2003, an internal auditing committee reported that the company's fountain division had improperly overvalued $9 million in equipment ("Coca-Cola says it cheated" 2003). The auditing committee also acknowledged that the fountain division had rigged a marketing test of Frozen Coke at Burger King, one of Coca-Cola's largest customers ("Coca-Cola says it cheated" 2003). The company hired people to spend up to $10,000 to buy "value meals" in the test market site of Richmond, Virginia, thus fraudulently boosting the demand for Frozen Coke. The skewed sales resulted in a $65 million Frozen Coke investment by Burger King (Weber 2003). That Coca-Cola would find it necessary to resort to such tactics, especially in the wake of the corporate and accounting scandals of 2002, is indeed a sad commentary on the business ethics of the New Millennium.

Any legal and policy changes regarding regulation and punishment as noted above also need to account for "criminogenic industries," industries whose structure and traditional practices seem to encourage, or even embrace, criminal behavior. Any successful preventive strategy must therefore seek to "deinstitutionalize" white-collar crime, that is, to remove its institutional sources. This is by no means an easy task. About 20 percent of the 1,000 largest American corporations already have "ethics officers," who help formulate codes of proper conduct (Yenkin 1993). A *Wall Street Journal* reporter, however, has written that these codes "are little more than high-sounding words on paper" (Rakstis 1990: 30).

Sociologist Amitai Etzioni has suggested that a better way to encourage ethical business conduct is to "foster associations and enforce moral codes somewhat like those of lawyers and physicians" in the business community (1993: 103). Such associations would lack legal authority, but they could discipline violators through public censure and other informal control mechanisms.

Another way to change the environment in which corporate organizations do business is to create internationally agreed-upon standards of conduct. This would be particularly important in the case of American companies that operate in (and often export white-collar crimes to) foreign countries. The most significant step in this direction has been the United Nation's attempt to draw up a code of conduct for multinational corporations that sets standards of acceptable behavior for global firms. Among other things, the code calls upon multinationals to abstain from corrupt practices, such as political bribery, and to carry out their operations in an environmentally sound manner (U.S. Congress 1990). With these same goals in mind, the Clinton administration proposed a code of ethics for American firms operating overseas. Known as the Model Business Principles, the purpose of the code was to encourage companies to adopt more scrupulous behavior abroad by "providing a safe and healthy workplace... pursuing safe environmental practices... and complying with U.S. laws prohibiting bribery" ("White House unveils" 1995).

Neither of these proposed codes established any authority to sanction violators; they were merely guidelines. Enforcement is left up to individual nations, and this could be a significant weakness. Some Third World countries, for example, have shown a willingness to tolerate egregious abuses by American corporations, either because of official corruption or out of desperation for economic growth. Nevertheless, these efforts represent a first step toward battling white-collar crime in a global economy.

Americans tend to have very strong feelings about crime and criminals but are often ambivalent in their responses to those convicted of white-collar offenses. Many corporate and white-collar lawbreakers have received the support of their colleagues and other prominent members of their community. Even after their convictions, they were quickly accepted back into society, suffering few of the stigmas and resentments that other types of convicted felons routinely experience. Indeed, it almost seems that we extend a begrudging respect to those who are clever and bold enough to fleece victims out of millions. But if there is to be effective control of white-collar crime, these attitudes must change.

Criminologist John Braithwaite argued in this regard that the broader corporate milieu needs to be transformed. He called for the creation of a "communitarian corporate culture" in which organizations draw "everyone's attention to the failings of those who fall short of corporate social responsibility standards [shaming], while continuing to offer them advice and encouragement to improve [reintegration]" (1989). A simple, yet very effective, form of "shaming" that can be employed when corporations violate the law is adverse publicity: spreading information about misconduct to consumers, who could then express their disapproval by refusing to patronize the offending company (Coffee 1981). Braithwaite's ideal corporation, "well integrated into the community and therefore amenable to the pressures of social control" (1989: 144), stands in dramatic contrast to Milton Friedman's model of an amoral corporation, divorced from obligations to the community and inevitably producing a criminogenic environment.

Another way to change the culture of tolerance for white-collar crime is to alter the socialization of future captains of industry. One logical place to look is to the elite M.B.A. programs where many American business leaders are trained. A few years ago, a class at the Columbia Business School was divided into groups for a simulated negotiation game. Each team was given time to plan its bargaining strategy in private. One group actually planted a "bug" in the room where another group was holding its strategy meeting (Marks 1990: 26). A survey of students at the University of Virginia's Darden Graduate School of Business Administration reported that "71 percent believed that being ethical can be personally damaging" (Marks 1990: 26).

A number of reformers have called for the integration of rigorous ethical analyses into the curricula of business schools (e.g., Etzioni 1993). The sad reality, however, is that by that point it may already be too late. Some M.B.A. programs have begun to offer business ethics courses, either as electives or in some cases as requirements (Fraedrich 1996: 122-123); but whether such reform will have any measurable future impact on corporate morality seems remote at best. At one leading business school, an elective called "Managing in the socially responsible corporation" is reportedly ridiculed by students as a useless "touchy-feely" course (Marks 1990). A former chairman of IBM has declared: "If an MBA candidate doesn't know the difference between honesty and crime, between lying and telling the truth, then business school, in all probability, will not produce a convert" (quoted in Mulligan 1989: F1).

Accordingly, pedagogic indoctrination would need to be expanded beyond M.B.A. programs. It has been proposed that critical analyses of commercial and governmental practices should be incorporated into classrooms at all levels of the educational system.[2] Attitudes of apathy and cynicism, captured in statements like, "What's the difference? The system's rigged anyway," or "What can you do? All politicians are corrupt," are indicative of a social resignation that is self-fulfilling and ultimately self-defeating; it allows upper world criminality to continue without resistance and with the tacit acceptance of its victims. Students and the public at large have to understand that, although business and political corruption is pervasive, it is not unstoppable. Ordinary citizens do possess the means to counter these practices, even if it is only through collective acts like voting against crooked politicians or shunning products from manufacturers that poison the environment.

21.5 Conclusions

Regarding the perceived social inequity in white-collar and common crime sentencing in the United States, the executive editor of one of the world's leading business magazines noted, "The double standard in criminal justice in this country is starker and more embedded than many realize. Bob Dylan was right. Steal a little, and they put you in jail. Steal a lot and you're likely to walk away with a lecture and a court-ordered promise not to do it again" (Leaf 2002: 63). The same writer made it abundantly clear that the social inequity in sanctioning—which is bad enough to rectify on its own—is necessarily coupled with the fact that there is a massive financial cost associated with white-collar crime that will not be substantially reduced until offenders face a consequence that might actually affect their behavior: the threat of incarceration.

Yet as discussed here, structural sources of leniency exist on many levels for white-collar and corporate crime that necessitate other control and prevention strategies. Despite the fact that vast discrepancies exist between the punishment of white-collar and corporate lawbreakers and common criminals, numerous legal, social, and resource obstacles stand in the way of easily or immediately rectifying the situation. Although retribution may be a justification for the sentencing of common criminals (and a cornerstone of conventional notions of "justice"), it is extremely problematic when applied

---

[2] For example: Denise A. Monroe (1994) has designed a creative social science lesson for elementary school teachers, from which young students can learn about defective consumer products and false advertising.

to the white-collar or corporate offender. Retributive justifications for punishment, whether applied to individuals or organizations, are hard to imagine for offenders who poison the environment and cause birth defects and death to numerous victims or who cause the loss of billions of dollars. As Braithwaite has effectively argued, this results in a two-tier system of punishment that provides retribution for the poor and gentle persuasion for the rich.

> Just deserts... only gives us the option of imposing desert successfully against the poor and unsuccessfully against the rich. The irony is that under just deserts—the philosophy of punishment which sets out with justice as its primary goal—justice is sociologically impossible (Braithwaite 1986: 55-65).

In the wake of the U.S. corporate and accounting scandals, however, there appears to be much less leniency in sentencing white-collar criminals—at least for high-profile offenders, for the time being. John Rigas, the founder of Adelphia Communications, received a fifteen-year sentence without the possibility of parole, which means that he will most likely die in prison. His son Timothy received a twenty-year prison term. Sam Waksal, head of Imclone, pled guilty to insider trading and fraud charges to avoid a jury trial, "accepting" a seven-year prison sentence and a $3 million fine. His close friend, television icon Martha Stewart, served time for lying to investigators. Bernie Ebbers, former CEO of WorldCom, was convicted on fraud charges and will most likely die in prison. Dennis Koslowski, former CEO of Tyco, was sentenced to eight to twenty-five years in prison for misappropriating the company's funds, among other charges. The trial of Kenneth Lay and Jeffrey Skilling, former top executives of Enron, resulted in both being convicted on fraud charges. Whether the outcomes of these cases represent a new dawn of long-standing intolerance and greater understanding of the damage caused by white-collar and corporate offending remains to be seen. The current attention they command, however, should not overshadow the idea that overreliance on criminal sanctioning as a response to white-collar crime, while simultaneously neglecting other causes, will not, according to the literature on the subject, be effective in preventing such offenses and the massive social damage they incur.

Whether or not these recent highly publicized sentences produce a significant deterrent effect also remains to be seen, but they may send other messages as well. One is that these terms do not represent fair outcomes, an attitude that one would be likely to encounter in many business circles. Another is that the structural aspects of corporate governance and regulation that led these individuals and many others to engage in massive frauds need much greater attention than the relatively severe sentences received by certain offenders. Knowing that essentially good people can do terrible things, perhaps even when they themselves do not see it that way, takes us only so far. Understanding the structures and contexts that allowed them to do what they did might be a more productive focus in terms of preventing future offenses. It is this aspect that typically receives the least sustained attention, as it is lost in the media frenzy to report on the personal stories and tribulations of the offenders themselves, along with how punishment has affected their lives. Their acts may be more easily forgiven precisely because they do not seem like the "typical criminal" but, in fact, resemble in most other respects the conventional citizen.

References

Ayres, I., and J. Braithwaite. 1992. *Responsive Regulation*. Oxford: Oxford University Press.

Baker, W., and R. Faulkner. 1991. The social organization of conspiracy in the heavy electrical equipment industry. *American Sociological Review* 58, 837.

Barkan, S. E. 2006. *Criminology: A Sociological Understanding*, 3rd ed. Upper Saddle River, NJ: Prentice-Hall.

Barnett, H. C. 1981. Corporate capitalism, corporate crime. *Crime & Delinquency* 27, 4, January.

Baum, S., and L. Kamas. 1995. Time, money, and optimal criminal penalties. *Contemporary Economic Policy* 13, 72, October.

Becker, G. 1968. Crime and punishment: An economic approach. *Journal of Political Economy* 76, 169.

Benson, M., and E. Walker. 1988. Sentencing the white-collar offender. *American Sociological Review* 53, 294.

Benson, M., et al. 1988. District attorneys and corporate crime: Surveying the prosecutorial gatekeepers. *Criminology* 26, 505.

Blodget, H. 2004. Zero to life. slate.msn.com, May 6.

Braithwaite, J. 1985. White-collar crime. *Annual Review of Sociology* 11, 1.

Braithwaite, J. 1986. Retributivism, punishment and privilege. In *Punishment and Privilege*, ed. W. B. Groves and G. Newman, 55-65. Albany, NY: Harrow and Heston.

Braithwaite, J. 1989. *Crime, Shame and Reintegration*. Cambridge: Cambridge University Press.

Calavita, K. 1983. The demise of the occupational safety and health administration: A case study in symbolic action. *Social Problems* 30, 437.

Calavita, K., and H. N. Pontell. 1994. The state and white-collar crime: Saving the savings and loans. *Law and Society Review* 28, 297.

Calavita, K., and H. N. Pontell. 1995. Saving the savings and loans: U.S. government response to financial crime. In *Corporate Crime: Contemporary Debates*, ed. F. Pearce and L. Snider, 199-213. Toronto: University of Toronto Press.

Calavita, K., R. H. Tillman, and H. N. Pontell. 1997a. *Big Money Crime: Fraud and Politics in the Savings and Loan Crisis*. Berkeley: University of California Press.

Calavita, K., H. N. Pontell, and R. H. Tillman. 1997b. Financial crime and the state. *Annual Review of Sociology* 23, 19.

Clinard, M. B., and R. Quinney. 1973. *Criminal Behavior Systems*, 2nd ed. New York: Holt, Rinehart, and Winston.

Clinard, M. B., and P. C. Yeager. 1980. *Corporate Crime*. New York: Free Press.

Coca-Cola says it cheated in Burger King tests. 2003. www.chron.com, June 17.

Coffee, J. 1981. No soul to damn, no body to kick: An unscandalized inquiry into the problem of corporate punishment. *Michigan Law Review* 79, 424.

Coleman, J. W. 2002. *The Criminal Elite: Understanding White-Collar Crime*, 5th ed. New York: Worth.

Cook, D. 2004. Former Dynegy executive gets 24 years. cfo.com, March 26.

Eichenwald, K. 2005. *Conspiracy of Fools*. New York: Broadway Books.

Etzioni, A. 1993. *Public Policy in a New Key*. New Brunswick, NJ: Transaction Publishers.

Fisse, B., and J. Braithwaite. 1993. *Corporations, Crime, and Accountability*. Cambridge: Cambridge University Press.

Fowler, T. 2005. Court tosses lengthy white-collar sentence. *Houston Chronicle*, November 2, A1, A8.

Fraedrich, J. P. 1996. Do the right thing: Ethics and marketing in a world gone wrong. *Journal of Marketing* 60, 122, January.

Gasparino, C. 2005. *Blood on the Street*. New York: Free Press.

Geis, G. 1967. The Heavy Electrical Equipment Antitrust Case of 1961. In *Criminal Behavior Systems*, ed. M. Clinard and R. Quinney, 140-1515. New York: Holt, Rinehart, and Winston.

Geis, G. 1981. Upperworld crime. In *Current Perspectives on Criminal Behavior*, ed. A. Blumberg, 179-198. New York: Knopf.

Glassman, J. K. 2004. Jamie Olis's tragedy, and ours. capmag.com, April 12.

Goetz, B. 1997. Organization as class bias in local law enforcement: Arson-for-profit as a "Non-Issue." *Law and Society Review* 31, 557.

Grabosky, P. 2001. The system of corporate crime control. In *Contemporary Issues in Crime and Criminal Justice: Essays in Honor of Gilbert Geis*, ed. H. N. Pontell and D. Shichor, 137-154. Upper Saddle River, NJ: Prentice-Hall.

Gurney, J. N. 1985. Factors influencing the decision to prosecute economic crime. *Criminology* 23, 609.

Hagan, J., and I. Nagel. 1982. White-collar crime, white-collar time. *American Criminal Law Review* 20, 259.

Hagan, J., I. Nagel, and C. Albonetti. 1980. Differential sentencing of white-collar offenders. *American Sociological Review* 45, 802.

Hagan, J., and P. Parker. 1985. White-collar crime and punishment: Class structure and legal sanctioning of securities violations. *American Sociological Review* 5, 302.

Hays, K. 2004. Dynegy executive gets 24 years in prison for accounting fraud. sfgate.com, March 26.

Hightower, S. 1994. S&L swindlers get early withdrawal from prison. *San Diego Union-Tribune*, July 31.

In praise of animal spirits. 1999. forbes.com, February 8.

Johnson, D. T., and R. Leo. 1993. The Yale White-Collar Crime Project: A review and critique. *Law and Social Inquiry* 18, 63.

Katz, J. 1980. The social movement against white-collar crime. In *Criminology Review Yearbook*, vol. 2, ed. E. Bittner and S. Messinger, 175. Beverly Hills, CA: Sage Publishing.

Katz, J. 1988. *Seductions of Crime: Moral and Sensual Attractions in Doing Evil.* New York: Basic Books, New York.

Langberg, M.1989. White collar crime erodes faith in business. *San Jose Mercury News,* February 12, 1E.

Leaf, C. 2002. White-collar criminals: Enough is enough. *Fortune,* 145, 63, March 25.

Levi, M. 1984. Giving creditors the business: The criminal law in inaction. *International Journal of the Sociology of Law* 12, 320.

Levi, M. 1987. *Regulating Fraud: White-Collar Crime and the Criminal Process.* London: Tavistock Publications.

Lott, J. 1987. Should the wealthy be able to "buy justice"? *Journal of Political Economy* 95, 1307.

Lott, J. 1992. Do we punish high income criminals too heavily? *Economic Inquiry* 30, 583.

Machan, D., and G. Button. 1990. Beyond the slammer. *Forbes* 284, November 26.

McClintick, D. 1982. *Indecent Exposure: A True Story of Hollywood and Wall Street.* New York: Morrow.

McDougall, W. A. 2004. *Freedom Just Around the Corner: A New American History: 1585-1828.* New York: Harper Collins.

Marks, P. 1990. Ethics and the bottom line. *Chicago Tribune Magazine* May 6, 26.

Monroe, D. A. 1994. Let the manufacturer beware. *Journal of School Health* 64, 83, February.

Mulligan, H. A. 1989. Ethics in America. *Richmond Times-Dispatch*, April 6, F1.

Olis begins prison sentence. 2004. *bizjournals.com*, May 20.

Pontell, H. N. 1984. *A Capacity to Punish: The Ecology of Crime and Punishment.* Bloomington: Indiana University Press.

Pontell, H. N. 2005. The role of fraud in major financial debacles: White-collar crime or just risky business? *Crime, Law, and Social Change* 42, 309, January.

Pontell, H. N., and K. Calavita. 1993. Organizational crime in the savings and loan industry. In *Beyond the Law: Crime in Complex Organizations: Crime and Justice,* vol. 18, ed. M. Tonry and A. J. Reiss, Jr., 203-246. Chicago: University of Chicago Press.

Pontell, H. N., K. Calavita, and R. Tillman. 1994. Corporate crime and criminal justice system capacity: Government response to financial institution fraud. *Justice Quarterly* 11, 383, September.

Posner, R. 1980. Optimal sentences for white-collar criminals. *American Criminal Law Review* 17, 409.

Quinney, R. 1970. *The Social Reality of Crime.* Boston: Little Brown.

Rakstis, T. J. 1990. The business challenge: Confronting the ethics issue. *Kiwanis Magazine* 30, September.

Ranalli, R. 1996. Execs get 18 months in med-testing flap. *Boston Herald,* August 9.

Reiman, J. 1995. *The Rich Get Richer and the Poor Get Prison: Ideology, Crime and Criminal Justice,* 4th ed. Boston: Allyn and Bacon.

Rich debtors finding shelter under a populist Florida law. 1993. *New York Times,* July 25, A1.

Rosoff, S. M., H. N. Pontell, and R. H. Tillman. 2004. *Profit Without Honor: White-Collar Crime and the Looting of America,* 3rd ed. Upper Saddle River, NJ: Prentice-Hall.

Shapiro, S. 1984. *Wayward Capitalists: Target of the Securities and Exchange Commission.* New Haven, CT: Yale University Press.

Shapiro, S. 1990. Collaring the crime, not the criminal: Liberating the concept of white-collar crime. *American Sociological Review* 55, 346.

Snider, L. 1982. Traditional and corporate theft: A comparison of sanctions. In *White-Collar and Economic Crime: Multidisciplinary and Cross-National Perspectives,* ed. P. Wickman and T. Dailey, 235-258. Lexington, MA: Lexington Books.

Snider, L. 1991. The regulatory dance: Understanding reform processes in corporate crime. *International Journal of the Sociology of Law* 19, 209.

Study: More companies restating earnings. 2003. *Boston Business Journal, bizjournals.com,* July 29.

Tillman, R., and H. N. Pontell. 1992. Is justice "collar-blind"? Punishing Medicaid provider fraud. *Criminology* 30, 401, November.

Toffler, B. L. 2003. *Final Accounting: Ambition, Greed, and the Fall of Arthur Andersen.* New York: Broadway Books.

Tombs, S., and D. Whyte. 2003. *Unmasking the Crimes of the Powerful: Scrutinizing States and Corporations.* New York: Peter Lang.

United States Code Congressional and Administrative News, vol. 4. 1984. 98th Congress, Second Session, West, St. Paul, MN.

U.S. Congress. 1990. Senate Committee on Foreign Relations, Subcommittee on International Economic Policy, Trade, Oceans and Environment, U.N. code of conduct on transnational corporations, 101st Congress, Second Session, October 11.

U.S. Securities and Exchange Commission. 1995. The large firm project. Division of Market Regulation.

U.S. v. Booker. 2005.

Weber, H. 2003. Coca-Cola admits manipulating promotion that misled Burger King. www.cbc.ca, June 20.

Weisburd, D., E. Waring, and S. Wheeler. 1990. Class, status, and the punishment of white-collar criminals. *Law and Social Inquiry* 15, 222.

Wheeler, S., D. Weisburd, and N. Bode. 1982. Sentencing the white-collar offender: Rhetoric and reality. *American Sociological Review* 50, 641.

White House unveils its overseas code of corporate conduct. 1995. *Los Angeles Times*, March 28, D1.

Yeager, P. C. 1991. *The Limits of Law: The Public Regulation of Private Pollution.* Cambridge: Cambridge University Press.

Yenkin, J. 1993. Ethics officers manage companies' morals. *Orange County Register*, August 29, Business Section, 1.

The Third Wave: American Sex Offender Policies since the 1990s

JONATHAN SIMON AND
CHRYSANTHI LEON

22

Contents

Within the booming business of penal legislation in the United States, laws (both criminal and civil) addressing criminal acts defined as sexual in nature have been especially irresistible to politicians. Laws against drug dealers, criminals who use guns, and domestic abusers have been popular as well. So have laws lengthening prison sentences and making them less revisable. In all these areas, a lively network of policy entrepreneurs have circulated versions of "tough on crime" legislation and typically enjoyed solid majority support in both political parties. Yet within this populist festival of punitiveness, no subject has been as popular a target of law as those convicted of sexual crimes (those we must struggle to avoid calling "sexual offenders").

Most of the interest has been in two policy approaches. One involves registration and notification laws that require certain subclasses of persons convicted of sexual offenses to register their current residence with local police or a state agency, to open access to all citizens to this registry of persons convicted of some subclasses of offenses, and for police or state agents to actively notify institutions and ordinary citizens in proximity to those convicted of sexual offenses who are deemed most dangerous. The second is a civil commitment procedure that allows some persons convicted of sexual offenses to be detained in a secure facility after the completion of their original sentence, if the state can demonstrate that they have an uncontrolled propensity to commit further sexual offenses. The first type of measure has been extraordinarily successful, winning adoption in every state in the United States over a period of less than five years. The second type of measure had been adopted in at least sixteen states by 2001 (Kirwin 2003: 1143), probably owing to the far greater fiscal commitment required of the adopting states. In the case of registration and notification laws, the pattern of adoption from state to state (with the encouragement, in the case of notification laws, of the federal government) has been extraordinarily swift. New Jersey enacted the first notification law in 1994, approximately three months after the highly publicized disappearance of Megan Kanka (Sullivan 1994). The federal government quickly followed, amending the Jacob Wetterling Crimes Against Children and Sexually Violent Offender Act to make participation in some level of notification a requirement for receiving federal funds from the Omnibus Crime Bill (42 U.S.C. § 14071 1996). As a result, every state and the District of Columbia had passed a version of Megan's Law by the end of 1996.

The current wave of civil commitment laws aimed at sexual crimes began in the late 1980s in response to growing popular concerns about persons convicted of sexual crimes. State officials began using existing laws to extend the incapacitation of such persons, including laws adopted by many states in the 1930s and 1940s but which had gone out of use in the 1960s. The new wave of laws, beginning with the state of Washington in 1990, were largely drafted to avoid constitutional problems that plagued the earlier generation of civil commitment laws.

It is tempting to assume that the intense response to sexual offenses is a simple consequence of the substantial weight generally given to the sexual in modern society (Foucault 1980; Simon 1996), but the degree of interest in such legislation has in fact fluctuated, as have the social meanings assigned to sexual offenses themselves. The boom in sexual offense legislation since the 1990s is actually the third wave of such legislation since the nineteenth century (Lynch 2002: 533). At the end of the nineteenth century, laws were passed in both Europe and the United States permitting the commitment of sexual offenders to specialized institutions. In this period, sexual offenses were taken as evidence of a kind of biological degeneracy or defectiveness. Commitment represented a eugenic strategy for containing that threat. In the 1930s and 1940s, when another wave of legislation spread in both Europe and the United States, sexual offenses were seen in terms of psychiatric concepts, and commitment was a mode of treatment. Since the 1990s, a third wave has spread, mainly in the United States, that is neither simply biological nor psychiatric. Informed by popular political and religious discourses, the new sexual offense laws have largely thrown off the modernist presumption evident in the first two waves, that scientific experts must mediate the extraordinary extension of repressive law in the name of prevention. The methods of risk assessment used in both registration/notification laws and civil commitment laws vary from state to state but often place judgment in the hands of prosecutors, juries, or police. The new laws operate openly with a notion of the monstrous, named as "predator." In place of society as the general beneficiary, these policies have been aimed primarily at vulnerable classes of potential victims. In this regard, they partake of the civil rights tradition in post-World War II American law.

22.1 New Sex Offender Policies and the Resurgence of Old Ones

In addition to new postincarceration "civil" controls, like registration and civil commitment laws, American jurisdictions appear to have enforced criminal laws involving sexual conduct more aggressively than in the recent past. In the United States, available data shows that the proportions of arrests and incarcerations for sexual offenses increased during the last two decades of the twentieth century, with arrest rates largely peaking in the early 1990s. Although we lack complete data for the range of offenses that may be included under the umbrella of sexual offenses, we do have somewhat stable statistics on rape and sexual assault, though how offenses have been defined and included in these categories has varied among reporting jurisdictions and over time. The Uniform Crime Reports (UCRs) show that reported rapes per 100,000 females nearly doubled from 1976 to 1992, when rates began to decline; however, the estimated number of arrests for rape during this period remains stable (Greenfeld 1997). In addition, the UCR reports that its catchall category of "other sex offenses" also showed increases in estimated arrests from 1980 to about 1992, when arrests began a slight decline (Greenfeld 1997).[1]

This arrest pattern is making a measurable if modest difference in the portion of persons convicted of sexual offenses in the stock of prison inmates. The Bureau of Justice Statistics reports a 15 percent annual increase in prisoners sentenced for violent sexual assault since 1980, as opposed to a general average growth of 7.2 percent (Greenfeld 1997). However, examination of correctional data for nonrape/other sex offenses shows a proportional increase at about the same rate as the overall increase in incarceration (Greenfeld 1997: 23). Preliminary examination of the data collected by the periodic Survey of State Inmates over roughly the same period (1974-1997) similarly shows a small proportional increase in sex offenses counted more broadly, as well as for rape alone.[2]

Though there are many conclusions we cannot confidently reach about the scope of sexual offending during this period or of the changes in law enforcement (e.g., Fisher and Cullen 2000; Lynch 1996), the longitudinal data does demonstrate that sexual offending received an increasing share of law enforcement attention through at least the mid-1990s.

22.1.1 Legal Developments in the 1990s

In the 1990s, persons convicted of sexual offenses became subject to a new breed of policies, as well as to the reintroduction of older policies that had lain dormant. The new policies have broadened the categories of crimes that require registration and community notification, and have reintroduced the possibility of preventive detention after the completion of punitive sanctions. With the approval of the Supreme Court, the new policies have broken the earlier link between treatment and control, imposing the possibility of indefinite civil commitment for a "disease" that has no "cure," and made use of actuarial models for risk assessment that rest on unproven assumptions

---

[1] This synthesis explains that "other sex offenses" include "statutory rape and offenses against chastity, common decency and morals." This definition itself lacks precision and does not address the possible variations among reporting jurisdictions and over time in interpreting how to include offenses in this category.

[2] These estimates are based on analysis of the Survey of Inmates data available from the Inter-university Consortium for Political and Social Research, study nos. 2598, 6068, 7856, and 8711.

(discussing the failure to treat: Pfaffenroth 2003; LaFond 1992; discussing assumptions: Zimring 2004).

22.1.1.1   Increasing Number of Registerable Offenses

Some classes of sex offenders have been required to register with local law enforcement for decades—in California, since as early as 1947. Part of the new wave of policies in this era included a drastic expansion of qualifying offenses. By the end of the century, people with convictions for noncontact offenses such as indecent exposure and possession of child pornography were required to register for life as sexual offenders (e.g., Cal. Pen. §§ 311, 314; Dolan 2004; Logan 2003).

22.1.1.2   Community Notification

After the widely publicized murder of seven-year-old Megan Kanka in 1994 by a convicted sexual offender, Congress passed legislation that required states to release information concerning registered sex offenders (Pub. L. 104-236, 110 Stat. 3093). The novel part of this policy is the release of information about convicted sex offenders to the public; previously, registries were for law enforcement use only.

The classification and notification systems vary from state to state, and even from county to county (Terry et al. 2003). Jurisdictional variations include the length of the registration period, whether DNA is collected, whether juvenile offenders are included, and whether offenders may petition for exemption. The forms and limits of notification also vary. In one of its most intrusive forms, notification involves proactive effort by the state to notify the public about particular offenders (e.g., Pa. Cons. State. Ann. tit. 42, §§ 9797, 9798). Special notification may also be made to officials at potentially vulnerable institutions, such as schools or daycare centers in the case of a pedophile, or a women's clinic in the case of a rapist (e.g., Okla. Stat. Ann. § 57-584.E). Law enforcement may also post flyers with information about released offenders in the neighborhoods. More commonly, police or sheriff's departments maintain a database of local offenders that the public can view by appointment and after signing a promise not to share the information. Many jurisdictions also post names and other information on a public Website. Some state courts have demanded due process protections including adversarial hearings before an independent decision maker for the strong form of notification, but little or no process in the passive forms (see *Connecticut Dep't. of Public Safety v. Doe* 2003).

Methods of risk assessment for assigning notification levels vary from state to state. In New Jersey, the home state of Megan Kanka and the first state to adopt a new law following her murder, the attorney general designated a process to be used by prosecutors throughout the state. The methodology, created by a special committee of prosecutors and psychologists, is based at least partly on the empirical research literature. The assessment is limited to factors readily ascertainable from the offenders' legal and correctional records and not from clinical assessments, but the overall formula has never been statistically validated (Witt and Barone 2004: 173).

These laws have been vigorously challenged by defense lawyers on grounds that they violated the constitutional rights against retroactive authorization of punishment and to procedural due process (Hopbell 2004; Logan 1999). Courts have universally rejected the first claim, holding that registration and notification laws do not constitute punishment, but are instead a civil disability (*Smith v. Doe* 2003). In some states, courts have been more supportive of procedural due process claims. In New Jersey, for example, the Supreme Court has required that classifying a person in the two highest risk groups for notification may be tested in an adversarial hearing before a judge, though rules of evidence do not apply and the standard for overturning the risk designation is very high *(Doe v. Poritz* 1995: 422-3; Terry and Furlong 2003: 1-13). In Massachusetts, courts have resolved that all sex offenders, regardless of risk level, must receive a hearing (e.g., *Doe v. Attorney General* 1987; *Doe v. Sex Offender Registry Board* 1997; Terry and Furlong 2003: 1-14). There is some indication that the Massachusetts paradigm may become dominant (Terry 2003).

22.1.1.3 *Civil Commitment of Sexually Violent Predators*

The new civil commitment laws for persons convicted of sexual offenses differ in a number of respects from the earlier wave of civil commitment laws enacted by states in the 1930s and 1940s. The latter laws, often called "sexual psychopath" laws, were targeted at sexual offenders whose behavior could be classified within specific psycho-pathological categories such as "repetitive compulsive"; in addition, the laws often required that candidates be amenable to treatment. Those committed under the law were placed in specialized treatment facilities as an alternative to serving time in a regular prison. The laws were designed with the aspiration of successfully treating offenders with psychopathic tendencies and incapacitating those who failed at treatment. During the height of their usage from the 1940s through the 1960s, these laws were often used on persons convicted of relatively minor offenses, or first-time offenders (Kirwin 2003: 1140).

The new laws operate as an extension to already lengthened prison sentences, rather than as an alternative to imprisonment. They no longer require that an individual targeted for incapacitation belong to a specific diagnostic (for the example of New Jersey, see Witt and Barone 2004: 172), though in most cases individuals are diagnosed with the DSM catchall categories of "paraphilia" or antisocial personality disorder NOS (not otherwise specified). The typical targets are persons convicted of repeated serious offenses.

Whereas the earlier wave of commitment laws spoke a language of then-current scientific psychology, current laws rely more upon terminology like "predator" that seems to take its cues from popular sentiment and even popular culture rather than current science.

Civil commitment laws allow the state to keep offenders who have served their full prison sentences in protective custody for as long as they are deemed dangerous. The first generation of civil commitment laws aimed at controlling dangerous sex offenders were created in response to the fear of "sexual psychopaths" in the post-war period (Freedman 1987). Most of these first-generation laws fell into disuse by the 1970s. Currently, sixteen states have civil commitment laws that apply to certain categories of recidivist sex offenders; other states are considering adding them. The U.S. Supreme Court has ruled against challenges to these laws as applied to sex offenders. The Kansas statute, upheld in *Kansas v. Hendricks* (1997), is considered the prototype, though there is variation in terms of risk assessment and judicial review.

Generally, the civil commitment of a sex offender begins with the application of an actuarial instrument for risk prediction (for example, the Rapid Risk Assessment for Sex Offense Recidivism (RRASOR), though many states are developing and testing their own instruments), a thorough case review, and a recommendation for release or for civil commitment. The prosecutor or the attorney general then has a determined period of time to decide whether to file a petition seeking civil commitment. Next, a judge determines whether probable cause exists to support a finding that the person is a "sexually violent predator" (or other term specific to that jurisdiction) and thus eligible for civil commitment. Then the individual is transferred to a secure facility for professional evaluation. After that evaluation, a hearing is held to determine beyond a reasonable doubt whether the individual meets the statutory definition of "a sexually violent predator" (in Kansas, a jury makes this decision based on this definition: "any person who has been convicted of or charged with a sexually violent offense and who suffers from a mental abnormality or personality disorder which makes the person likely to engage in the predatory acts of sexual violence" [Kan. Stat. Ann. § 59-29a02(a)-(b), 1995]).[3] Finally, if the court decides that the individual is a sexually violent predator, he or she is transferred to the custody of the state's mental health agency (in Kansas, the Secretary of Social and Rehabilitation Services). The Kansas law allows for release in one of three ways: as a result of the mandatory annual review by the court, by decision of the Secretary of Social and Rehabilitation Services, or in response to a release petition filed by the confined person.

---

[3] A "mental abnormality" is defined, in turn, as a "congenital or acquired condition affecting the emotional or volitional capacity which predisposes the person to commit sexually violent offenses in a degree constituting such person a menace to the health and safety of others" § 59-29a02(b).

In New Jersey, prisoners convicted of certain sexual crimes and coming up within ninety days of their release date are automatically put through a risk assessment by a psychologist, using a combination of actuarial, semistructured (but nonvalidated), and clinical assessment procedures, who decides whether the prisoner is committable under the state's "Sexually Violent Predator" law. If so, a second round of the same assessments is undertaken by a psychiatrist, at which point those who have been assessed as committable by both are reviewed by a committee within the prison institution, and those selected by this body are referred to the attorney general. Those prisoners that the attorney general decides to seek commitment against finally are subject to a judicial hearing (Witte and Barone 2004: 172). Thus, although risk assessment includes actuarial elements in many states, the overall process is dominated by correctional, prosecutorial, and judicial actors (including juries in some states).

Sex offender civil commitment legislation creates a wide net for the state to keep and control potential "predators." Although there is limited variation in the legal proceedings for establishing and maintaining an offender in civil commitment, most of the actual variation occurs at the risk assessment stage, beyond the bounds of legislative or judicial frameworks. Though statutes prescribe certain elements that must be considered such as actuarial predictions, in practice, the clinicians who make the recommendations often have complete leeway to include any and all information they deem relevant. Though actuarial predictions suggest a certain amount of objectivity, most risk assessments seem to be "adjusted actuarial," what the leading scholar on risk prediction calls the procedure of amending an actuarial score with clinical judgment (Hanson 1999). For example, in Minnesota, the initial screening process is based upon the MnSOST, an instrument that rates an offender based on his or her history of sexual and nonsexual offenses, number of victims, presence of "paraphilias," chemical dependency, and victim characteristics (Huot 1999: 4-6). But this limited set of factors is then expanded to include the clinician's assessment of the offender's mental state, the offender's own stated beliefs about his or her risk (both admission and resistance/denial seem to get referral), treatment history, empathy for victims, and release plans (Huot 1999). While actuarial instruments tend to be based on factors that have proven to have some empirical correlation with sexual recidivism, many of the additional factors that clinicians consider have been proven to be empirically irrelevant (e.g., Hanson and Buissiere 1998; for criticism of MnSOST, see Gunderson 2004). In New Jersey as well, psychologists and psychiatrists employed by the state blend actuarial tests with their own "clinical" assessment (Witte and Barone 2004, 172). Anecdotal evidence in California also suggests that almost all adjustments made to actuarial scores are upward, thus screening in many additional offenders.

As with notification laws, civil commitment legislation has been challenged as retroactive punishment. At least some judicial actors have been more sympathetic to this claim because of doubts that commitment is based on any finding of disease that would form the basis for civilly committing the mentally ill, as well as skepticism that the state has any real intention of providing committed persons with the treatment necessary to eventually obtain release (*Hendricks v. Kansas* 1996; *Kansas v. Hendricks* 1997, Breyer dissenting). But the U.S. Supreme Court, in a follow-up to its *Kansas v. Hendricks* decision, held that no connection with psychiatric disorder is necessary and that a very minimal prospect of treatment for release is sufficient (*Kansas v. Crane* 2002).

Although both legislatures and courts have been highly receptive to this new wave of civil commitment laws, states are only now experiencing a different set of challenges posed by the release into the community of prisoners committed under them. In California, a handful of sexual offenders have met sustained populist protests, led by radio talk show hosts and victim advocates, upon their release from California's postpunishment civil commitment program. Ironically, this handful of pariahs are the sex offenders who successfully completed the treatment program during their detention. Notably, more than one hundred other civilly committed sex offenders in California who have refused treatment have been able to convince the courts that their detention should end and have left the facility without attention or burdensome supervision (Ashley 2004). However, public outcries have hounded the "success stories" of the treatment program as they attempt to return to the community. City and county officials everywhere in the state have voiced their disapproval of the location of these releasees in their jurisdiction and especially of the lack of notice and hearing for the communities involved. In 2004, the Governor signed legislation that requires such process (Cal. Welf. & Inst. § 6608.5). These developments raise the question of whether this new generation of policies is creating more security or insecurity around sexual offenses. Having marked a large portion of those convicted of sexual crimes as "violent sexual predators," California has created a subject whose advertised dangerousness is not satisfied by the forms of expertise available to modern penology.

22.1.2 Expansion in the 2000s

Both community notification and civil commitment have proved productive fields for legislative activity. In response to popular concerns that may arise as a result of publicized crimes involving sexual conduct, legislatures can readily expand the range of sexually related crimes that render a convicted person subject to civil commitment. They can also revisit the nature of the information that registration and notification laws require such persons convicted of sexual crimes to produce or which kinds of parties are to be notified with such information. Although these two control strategies remain the largest area of legislative innovation, new legislation is constantly being introduced and enacted to enhance the state's ability to punish and surveil sexual offenders. State legislators continue to propose sexual offender legislation: In the California legislature, the pace of the introduction of bills regarding "sexual predators" has increased drastically, from six introduced in 1993-1994 to sixty-four in the 2003-2004 term. These California efforts reacted to local concerns that include responding to a particular crime by naming a new law in the victim's honor and attempts to correct perceived "loopholes" in correctional policy (Cal. Welf. & Inst. Section 6608.5). In addition to the populist efforts of local politicians, most federal crime legislation enacted in the last decade has also included at least one provision affecting sex offenders.

The PROTECT Act exemplifies the way sex offenders remain crucial to federal legislation on crime (PROTECT Act 2003). Though touted primarily for amending the U.S. Sentencing Guidelines and for institutionalizing the Amber Alert system to publicize information about abducted children, the PROTECT Act relies on public fear of sexual offenders for providing its moral force. In introducing the bill, Senator Orrin Hatch focused on the need to stop sexual offenders by cracking down on child pornography, citing the need to punish those who "satisfy their depraved desires by dealing in such filth" (Hatch 2003: S237). The findings section of the Act's title on obscenity and pornography (Title V, Sec 501) is a lengthy explication of this point, which serves as the justification for the bill's attempts to correct the Supreme Court's decision in *Ashcroft v. Free Speech Coalition* (2002), which ostensibly has weakened the state's ability to prosecute child pornographers by encouraging defendants to argue that pictured children were not real. In addition, the act makes multiple additions to existing laws such as enhanced penalties and specific inclusion of sexual crimes in other federal criminal statutes. In addition, Section 202 declares, "No statute of limitations for child abduction and sex crimes."

Recent judicial activity regarding sex offenders that has not centered on notification or commitment laws has focused on limiting extrajudicial penalties and questioning intensive conditions for postconviction supervision. For example, in response to a convicted sex offender's admission that he occasionally drove to the park and fantasized about children, the city of Lafayette, Indiana, banned him for life from city parks and schools. Using First Amendment arguments about protected thought and traditional prohibitions against the criminalization of status, the Seventh Circuit overturned the ban, stating that communities cannot punish individuals found likely to recidivate (*Doe v. Lafayette* 2003).

Convicted sex offenders released on probation or parole or from civil commitment are often subject to a lengthy list of conditions, including surveillance through electronic monitoring, ongoing psychotherapy, polygraph administration, antiandrogen therapy, curfews, total bans on Internet use, and mandatory supervision for visits with family members, even for offenders who have never victimized a relative (e.g., Kuebelbeck 1994; Podger 2001). Appellate courts have ruled on some of these conditions, though no standard has yet emerged. In the Ninth Circuit, a recent ruling determined that mandatory therapy that included polygraph testing violated a probationer's right against self-incrimination, but that a ban on Internet use was not overbroad (*U.S. v. Antelope* 2005).

22.1.3 Trends Outside the United States

A parallel shift in strategy has taken place in Germany, which long recognized nonretributive, incapacitative sanctions for dangerous offenders in lieu of regular imprisonment. Since a series of high-publicity sex crimes in the mid-1990s, Germany has targeted sex offenders with harsher retributive sentences, including compulsory treatment as a condition of parole, and eliminated the prior ten-year limit to incapacitative sanctions (Albrecht 2004).

Canada appears to utilize a wider range of responses to sexual offending, with a more therapeutic emphasis for all of its prisoners. On one end of the spectrum, a Dangerous Offenders Provision provides for civil commitment for any offender who has committed a serious injury offense if evidence shows a risk to others as well as "a pattern of repetitive and persistent behavior that is likely to lead to injury or death; the likelihood of injury through a failure to control sexual impulses; or a crime so brutal that it is unlikely the person can inhibit their behavior in the future" (R.S., c. C-34, s. 688 1977, Chapter 17, 1997). At the other end, experimentation with adapting aboriginal practices has provided a model for a Restorative Justice approach to sexual abuse, such as the Community Holistic Circle Healing approach. Offenders plead guilty and receive probation subject to their participation in the program, which involves a series of meetings between victims, offenders, family members, and others in the community (Cormier 2002). Similar restorative justice approaches are also being piloted in a few U.S. jurisdictions, but seem to have more support in places like Canada and New Zealand, which have different cultural orientations to community justice (Albany Catholic Worker Community 2004; Yantzi 1989).

22.2 Responses to Sexual Offending: Techniques and Technologies

22.2.1 Diagnosis and Treatment

The current generation of tools and techniques used to evaluate and treat accused and convicted sex offenders displays continuities with past practices (dating back to Lombrosian techniques of measurement and categorization) combined with the integration of new technologies (Horn 2003). Almost all reflect a focus on the body (rather than the mind) as a source of truth.[4]

Much of the efforts to assess and monitor sex offenders extends surveillance beyond traditional boundaries and actually enters the body—a transgression indicative of the "new surveillance" as described by Gary Marx (2003). These methods are designed to gauge or affect an individual's potential for committing a prohibited sexual act based on physical indicators that attempt to measure desire. These include testing or altering the hormones that are believed to be the physical genesis of sexually deviant behavior: blood testing, pheromone testing (in development), "chemical castration" (also known as antiandrogen therapy), and physical castration. They also include measuring response to stimuli: lie detector tests, brain scanning, voice stress analyzers, and penile plethysmography (PPG). Finally, this category can also include the practice of group therapy and other "confessional" mechanisms in which sex offenders "self-monitor" their impulses (LAO 1999; Launay 1994; Laws 1997; Laws 2004; Marshall 1999; Prentky 2000; Winslade et al. 1998).

All three types of methods, biological interventions to control impulses, stimuli response measurement, and confessional self-monitoring, are based upon an uncertain premise. The common belief about sex offenders is that they have perverse desires that they cannot help acting upon (Cleary 2004). Mental health treatment methods have shown some efficacy in helping offenders refrain from acting on their desires (e.g., Subcommittee on Crime 1996; CSOM 2001). But the belief persists that impulse control cannot be fixed, which leads to a focus on removing the impulses altogether.

The first group of management methods aims to reduce the impulse to commit sexual offenses. When this is undertaken through physical intervention, it is most often by testing the levels of the hormone androgen, which is thought to be responsible for aggressive sexual impulses. Some jurisdictions have allowed incarcerated sex offenders to elect surgical castration, known medically as "orchiectomy," in order to increase their eligibility for release. In California, at least fifteen convicted sex offenders have requested surgical castration since the passage of the 1996 Sexually Violent Predator civil commitment law, and at least three have received permission (Marosi 2001). Though California law requires some offenders to submit to chemical castration, often by taking the drug Lupron, the state mental health agency bans the surgery. So, for an offender to be surgically castrated, a judge must find

---

[4] Foucault (1977) asserted that the rise of the cellular prison in the nineteenth century reflected a shift from a strategy of producing truth through the torture of the body to a strategy of targeting the mind or soul of the offender.

him competent and the offender must pay for his own surgery (Athright 2001) But, both chemical and surgical castration are known to be reversible with the help of hormonal therapy, so even if we accept the premise that the offending is hormone-driven, castration is not a guarantee against reoffending. Instead, the push for castration seems to be another instance of appealing to populist sentiments of appropriate punishment for "monstrous" offenders.

The second group of methods that surveil into the body attempts to pinpoint the stimulus behind the person's inappropriate desires and/or to measure whether therapeutic methods have been effective. The general procedure for each of these is the same and can be described through the example of penile plethysmography (e.g., Laws 2001). The procedure begins with attaching the individual to the machine: In the case of penile plethysmography (also known as phallometry), a cuff is wrapped around a man's penis to measure his erection (no comparable instrument for women is available). Next, the administrator of the test establishes a baseline by presenting neutral stimuli, either in the form of words, pictures, sounds, or a combination of all three. After determining the "normal," nonaroused readings, the administrator will next introduce specific stimuli. For example, suppose that a subject was convicted of assaulting a young Asian boy. If the purpose of the test is to find out what else might arouse him, the administrator might first present pictures of young Asian boys and measure that reaction. This reaction could then be compared with pictures of boys and girls of other races, and with adults. Or, if the objective is to test whether or not he can control his arousal or if it has been eradicated, the administrator might present pictures of known stimuli and measure the reactions. If there is too much of an erection, he flunks the test.

Mental health professionals have raised a wide range of questions about the utility of these stimuli assessments. First is the question of the technology itself: even in best-case scenarios, skeptics question whether it really tells us what we think it does. Lie detector tests are not given much weight in contemporary courtrooms, in part because there is so much room for error. With all likelihood, these other tests that conflate physical reactions with mental processes will also be subject to skepticism as more about them is discussed and debated by defense attorneys. Second, there are numerous questions about the use of these technologies. In practice, there is great inconsistency in terms of the administration of these tests. Individual administrators have little training and have extraordinary leeway in deciding which stimuli to present, in what order, and in which combinations. To some extent, this is understandable, because each person may respond differently to stimuli—we could not expect a single image to arouse everyone in the same way. However, without standardization, the technology cannot be realistically evaluated. Third, research suggests that some subjects can learn to alter the results. This is a constant problem for administrators of these tests. Consider the college admission tests: today, most high school students take it at least four times with the hope that they will get better through practice. Similarly, with repeated tests of physical stimuli, results become less reliable. With penile plethysmography, for example, some administrators have tried "distracting" the subjects by asking them to perform simple math while they are being presented stimuli, thus decreasing the subject's ability to suppress their erections (Launay 1994). Ultimately, however, these tests must be evaluated with the understanding that their repeated use will allow some individuals to control their responses.

Finally, the last major mechanism of sex offender surveillance is psychotherapy, which often includes "cognitive restructuring," or attempts to change the mental patterns that lead to the commission of wrongful acts (Marshall et al. 2000). Variations of this kind of therapeutic approach include relapse prevention (originally developed for chemical dependency), wound therapy, and aversion therapy. Often, a component of such therapy will include group sessions in which offenders will speak to each other about their thoughts and impulses, in some ways a throwback to the common practice in the rehabilitative era, which has since fallen out of favor in every other penological context. This therapy is usually either mandated by the court during or after incarceration or understood to be an important sign of the offender's "cooperativeness," which in turn will increase chances of release from prison or postrelease conditions. The Supreme Court has ruled that the Constitution permits sanctions for sex offenders who refuse to admit past crimes as part of therapy (*McKune v. Lile* 2002). Ultimately, as critics have noted about prison therapy generally, mandatory therapy for sex offenders sets them up to say what they think they should say (Lin 2000). The case of an innocent California man highlights the fallacies of the confessional requirement: After spending nearly twenty years denying his guilt in a sexual molestation case, James Rodriguez eventually decided to comply with treatment and "acknowledge his crimes." He attended group therapy meetings and spoke with admitted pedophiles in order to learn what he needed to say about his attractions and impulses in order to satisfy officials. When it turned out that his alleged victims had fabricated their story and he was vindicated, his therapist lost faith in the system (Curtis 2004). Cognitive behavioral therapy also brings surveillance to a new level: It attempts to regulate the imagination.

22.2.2 Management

In addition to the particular methods described above, there are also comprehensive models of management such as the containment model, as well as the trial-and-error approaches of states such as California, which have recently confronted the publicized release of civilly committed sexually violent predators.

The containment approach is a synthesis of "best practices" selected from a survey of parole and probation officers who manage sex offenders. It is not an empirically based model and no state has fully implemented it, though most have adopted some of its principles. The model contains five mutually reinforcing components:

1. A philosophy that values public safety, victim protection, and reparation for victims as the paramount objectives of sex offender management
2. Implementation strategies that rely on agency coordination, multidisciplinary partnerships, and job specialization
3. A containment approach that seeks to hold sex offenders accountable through the combined use of both the offenders' internal controls and external criminal justice measures, and the use of the polygraph to monitor internal controls and compliance with external controls
4. Development and implementation of informed public policies to create and support consistent practices
5. Quality control mechanisms, including program monitoring and evaluation, that ensure prescribed policies and procedures are delivered as planned (English et al. 1996)

The rhetoric of the model is aimed at reassuring an anxious public, with vague assurances about safety and collaboration. The only clearly defined component is the third, which builds on the kinds of surveillance methods described above.

Though vague in specifying its mechanics, the containment model succeeds in institutionalizing jurisdiction-sharing between correctional officers and treatment practitioners and in elevating the status of a contested "profession." In an era in which treatment for criminal offenders is generally denigrated, sex offender treatment maintains a limited stronghold through its collaboration with corrections. The containment model also signals the quasiprofessional status of sex offender treatment. Assumptions about therapy and about the behavior and character of sex offenders make it very difficult for treatment practitioners to achieve acknowledgment as "professionals." Sex offender therapy lacks a licensing program, professional examinations, university-based professional education, or an ethics code—all traditional markers of professions. Though clinical assessments for accused sex offenders and for those facing civil commitment are generally administered by psychologists, treatment programs often use lower-status personnel such as social workers, marriage and family therapists, and polygraph administrators. But despite these complications, sex offender treatment is a growing field, in part because states that authorize the containment model and its variants also contract for treatment services, so that, although professional status may be elusive, government funding is increasingly available.

22.3   Explanations for the Trends in the Treatment of Sexual Offenses

Overall, since the beginning of the 1990s, U.S. jurisdictions have punished sexual offenses more harshly. Those convicted of sexual offenses are going to prison for longer sentences than before 1990 and, on release, face formidable restrictions, the precise nature of which is largely determined by the way prosecutors assess the general level of risk they pose to the community. Those perceived as the most dangerous are subject to civil commitment under sexual predator laws in the sixteen states that have enacted such laws. The first decade of experience in many of these states suggests the difficulty of releasing such persons once they have been identified to the public as representing an extraordinary risk of committing sexual crimes. This identification of "predators" means that states bear a heavy long-term burden of maintaining specialized detention facilities that meet judicial standards for nonpunitive detention. In states without civil commitment, those released after punishment for sexual crimes will face the likelihood of a lifetime registration requirement (violations of which are criminal offenses). In many states, their status is made readily public through open access Internet databases maintained by the state. Those considered higher risk may have their name, photograph, and neighborhood identified to neighboring residents and schools.

22.3.1   As Moral Panic

The most developed discussions of the genesis and success of sex offender policies in the twentieth century suggest that they are the result of moral panic, defined as a period or cycle of exaggerated concern over a perceived threat that results in the classifying and targeting of deviants (Goode and Ben-Yehuda 1994). The most influential work in this area has come from outside of sociology, from journalists (e.g., Miller 2002; Nathan and Snedeker 1995) and professors in other disciplines (Jenkins 1998). However, there is inadequate precision about the explanatory power of "moral panic" as a concept—especially in terms of causation and how we define such panics in terms of reach and longevity. Moreover, it is not clear whether the sustained interest in these laws can be usefully described as a moral panic. The murder of Megan Kanka and other high-profile crimes in the 1990s clearly helped galvanize media attention and probably accelerated the rise of a variety of sex offense laws on the legislative agenda. Yet the measures reflect new strategies of penal control and the emergence of new forms of expertise that have been in process since at least the 1970s.

22.3.2 As New Penology

Feeley and Simon have argued that across the criminal process, a broad shift has taken place toward a "new penology" aimed at managing the risk of dangerous classes in society (Feeley and Simon 1992; Simon 1998) This model of corrections emphasizes a managerial approach to dangerous classes over other models, such as medical or social models. New laws addressing sexual conduct in criminal acts can be seen as part of this new penology. In this account, community notification and civil commitment laws exemplify a trend toward approaching crime as a problem of managing high-risk categories and subpopulations, rather than punishing or normalizing individuals. Registration and notification laws further reflect the tendency of the new penology to emphasize technocratic performance measures over the delivery of community safety. Indeed, these measures shift political responsibility for dealing with sexual crimes from the state and the criminal justice system to families and community institutions.

22.3.3 As Populist Punitiveness and Fear of Contagion

In conjunction with Feeley and Simon's explanation of sex offenders as subjects of risk management, Mona Lynch argued that sex offender policymaking is also based upon an emotional drive (Lynch 2002). Lynch found expressions of disgust, fear of contagion, and pollution avoidance in legislative rhetoric about sex offenders. In this account, which also complemented Jenkins' use of moral panic, sex offenders play a role in constructing and preserving boundaries between the pure and the dangerous, and reflect on sociocultural anxieties and discomforts surrounding sexuality, family, and gender roles. Lynch warned that disgust-based approaches are particularly likely to result in reactionary policies and that these policies are likely to be applied to the next class of offenders who elicit our disgust.

22.4 As a Culture of Control or Governing through Crime

Sex offender policies such as community notification laws may also be explained as part of the way in which the state is increasingly engaged in governing bodies through crime discourses and the way we as citizens engage in self-government in means determined by fear of crime (Garland 2001; Simon 2000). Notification laws may be seen as "governing through crime" as they valorize and prioritize victims as ideal subjects, focus on the notion of "intolerable risks" by reifying the image of sex offenders as monstrous and unreformable, and rely upon "democratic penalty" by providing information about sex offenders to the public and then expecting parents and others to accept responsibility for protecting against victimization (Simon 2000).

22.5   Conclusion

With declining violent crime rates having lasted more then a decade in the US, and the "war on terror" eating up a larger portion of governmental budgets and public attention, the broader war on crime in America is arguably winding down after four decades. However, sexual offenders offer a small but precise target on which much of the political energy and public anxiety of the war on crime, may continue to be focused. This new target is so charged with popular fear that it is likely to be immune from the vicissitudes of actual victimization rates, or from competition with terror, global warming, and other threats. We can expect government to continue to respond to this fear with escalating strategies of surveillance and containment. The approaches cataloged here seem likely to be the building blocks of this expanding effort at social control through both civil and criminal mechanisms.

References

42 U.S.C. § 14071. 1996. The Pam Lychner Sexual Offender Tracking and Identification Act of 1996, P.L. 104-236, § 9, 110 Stat. 3098, October 3.

Albany Catholic Worker Community. 2004. Wiping away the tears: A faith community responds to clergy sexual abuse in Roman Catholic Church, *VOMA Connections*, 12.

Albrecht, H-J. 2004. Security Gaps: Responding to Dangerous Sex Offenders in the Federal Republic of Germany. *Federal Sentencing Reporter*, 16, 3, 200-207.

Ashcroft v. Free Speech Coalition. 2002. 535 U.S. 234, 122 S.Ct. 1389.

Ashley, G. 2004. Some predators freed sooner. *Contra Costa Times*, October 10.

California Penal Code §§ 311, 314.

California Welfare & Institutions Code § 6608.5.

Cleary, S. 2004. *Sex Offenders and Self-Control: Explaining Sexual Violence.* New York: LFB Scholarly Pub. LLC.

Connecticut Department of Public Safety v. Doe. 2003. 538 U.S. 1.

CSOM. 2000. Myths and facts about sex offenders. Center for Sex Offender Management, available online at http://www.csom.org/pubs/mythsfacts.pdf

Curtis, A. 2004. Sex predator is released after trying to lie his way to freedom. San Francisco: AP.

Doe v. Attorney General. 1987. 426 Mass. 136.

Doe v. Lafayette. 2003. 334 F 3d. 606, 7th Cir.

Doe v. Poritz. 1995. 662 A.2d 367, N.J.

Doe v. Sex Offender Registry Board. 1997. 1997 WL 819765, Mass. Super., December 22.

Dolan, M. 2004. Ruling widens sex offender list: Possessing child porn may require registering for life, court says in reversing 1983 decision. *Los Angeles Times,* online edition.

English, K., et al. 1996. *Managing Adult Sex Offenders on Probation and Parole: A Containment Approach.* Lexington, KY: American Parole and Probation Association.

Fisher, B. S., and F. T. Cullen. 2000. Measuring the sexual victimization of women: Evolution, current controversies, and future research. *Criminal Justice* 4, 317.

Foucault, M. 1977. *Discipline and Punish: The Birth of the Prison.* New York: Vintage Books.

Foucault, M. 1980. *The History of Sexuality,* Vol. I: *An Introduction,* trans. R. Hurley. New York: Pantheon.

Freedman, E. B. 1987. "Uncontrolled desires": The response to the sexual psychopath, 1920-1960. *The Journal of American History* 74.1, 83.

Garland, D. 2001. *The Culture of Control: Crime and Social Order in Contemporary Society.* Chicago: University of Chicago Press.

Gathright, A. 2001. Sex offender pays for his own castration. *San Francisco Chronicle,* A-15.

Goode, E., and N. Ben-Yehuda. 1994. Moral panics: Culture, politics and social construction. *Annual Review of Sociology* 20, 149.

Greenfeld, L. A. 1997. *Sex Offenses and Offenders.* Washington, DC: Bureau of Justice Statistics, Office of Justice Programs, U.S. Department of Justice.

Hanson, R. K. 1999. What do we know about risk assessment? In *The Sexual Predator: Law, Policy, Evaluation and Treatment,* ed. A. M. Schlank and F. Cohen. Kingston, NJ: Civic Research Institute, 1, 8.1-8.24.

Hanson, R. K., and M. T. Buissiere. 1998. Predicting relapse: A meta-analysis of sexual offender recidivism studies. *Journal of Consulting and Clinical Psychology* 66.2, 348.

Hanson, R. K., and D. Thornton. 2000. Improving risk assessment for sex offenders: A comparison of three actuarial studies. *Law & Human Behavior* 24, 119.

Hatch, Sen. O. 2003. Statement on the introduction of the PROTECT ACT. *Congressional Record,* S236-7, January 13.

Hendricks v. Kansas. 1996. 259 Kan. 246, S.C. Kan.

Hopbell, M. S. 2004. Balancing the protection of children against the protection of constitutional rights: The past, present and future of Megan's Law. *Duquesne Law Review* 42, 331.

Horn, D. G. 2003. *The Criminal Body: Lombroso and the Anatomy of Deviance.* New York: Routledge.

Huot, S. 1999. The referral process. In *The Sexual Predator: Law, Policy, Evaluation and Treatment*, ed. A. M. Schlank and F. Cohen. Kingston, NJ: Civic Research Institute, 1, 6.1-6.10.

Jenkins, P. 1998. *Moral Panic: Changing Concepts of the Child Molester in Modern America*. New Haven, CT: Yale University Press.

Kansas v. Hendricks. 1997. 117 S.Ct. 2072.

Kansas v. Crane. 2002. 534 U.S. 407.

Kirwin, J. 2003. One arrow in the quiver: Using civil commitment as one component of a state's response to sexual violence. *William Mitchell Law Review* 29, 1135.

Kuebelbeck, A. 1994. Ruling lets sex predators leave prison; Decision worries Minnesota officials. AP, August 17.

La Fond, J. Q. 1992. Washington's sexually violent predator law. *U. Puget Sound L. Rev.*, 15, 655.

LAO. 1999. Crosscutting issues: A "containment" strategy for adult sex offenders on parole. Legislative Analyst Office (LAO): Analysis of the Budget Bill, Sacramento, D:11-D:38.

Launay, G. 1994. The phallometric assessment of sex offenders: Some professional and research issues. *Criminal Behavior and Mental Health* 4, 48.

Laws, D. R. 2000. Direct monitoring by penile plethysmography. In *Remaking Relapse Prevention with Sex Offenders: A Sourcebook*, ed. D. R. Laws, S. M. Hudson, and T. Ward. Thousand Oaks, CA: Sage Publications.

Laws, D. R., and W. T. O'Donohue. 1997. *Sexual Deviance: Theory, Assessment, and Treatment*. New York: Guilford Press.

Lin, A. C. 2000. *Reform in the Making: The Implementation of Social Policy in Prison*. Princeton, NJ: Princeton University Press.

Logan, W. A. 1999. Liberty interests in the preventive state: Procedural due process and sex offender community notification laws. *J. Crim. L. & Criminology*, 89, 1167.

Logan, W. A. 2003. Jacob's legacy: Sex offender registration and community notification laws, practice and procedure in Minnesota. *William Mitchell Law Review* 29, 1287.

Lynch, J. P. 1996. Clarifying divergent estimates of rape from two national surveys. *Public Opinion Quarterly* 60, 410.

Lynch, M. 2002. Pedophiles and cyber-predators as contaminating forces: The language of disgust, pollution, and boundary invasions in federal debates on sex offender legislation. *Law and Social Inquiry* 27.3, 529.

McKune v. Lile. 2002. 536 U.S. 24, 122 S.Ct. 2017.

Marosi, R. 2001. Some sex offenders seeking castration in bid for freedom. *Los Angeles Times* (March 2) A1.

Marshall, W. L., et al. 1999. *Cognitive Behavioural Treatment of Sexual Offenders*. New York, Chichester, U.K.: John Wiley.

Marx, G. T. 2003. A tack in the shoe: Neutralizing and resisting the new surveillance. *Journal of Social Issues* 59.2, 369.

Miller, N. 2002. *Sex-Crime Panic: A Journey to the Paranoid Heart of the 1950s.* Los Angeles: Alyson Books.

Nathan, D., and M. R. Snedeker. 1995. *Satan's Silence: Ritual Abuse and the Making of a Modern American Witch Hunt.* New York: Basic Books.

Okla. Stat. Ann. § 57-584.E.

Pa. Cons. State. Ann. tit. 42, §§ 9797, 9798.

Pfaffenroth, P. C. 2003. The need for coherence: States' civil commitment of sex offenders in the wake of *Kansas v. Crane. Stanford Law Review* 55, 2229.

Podger, P. 2001. Serial rapist to stay confined till justices rule: State Supreme Court to hear arguments on violent sexual predator law in February. *San Francisco Chronicle*, December 13.

Prentky, R. A., and A. W. Burgess. 2000. *Forensic Management of Sexual Offenders.* New York: Klewer Academic.

PROTECT Act. 2003. Prosecutorial remedies and other tools to end the exploitation of children today, Act of 2003. *Stat.* 117, 650.

Simon, J., 1996. *Postmodern Sexualities.* New York: Routledge.

Simon, J. 1998. Managing the monstrous: Sex offenders and the new penology. *Psychology, Public Policy and Law* 4.1, 452.

Simon, J. 2000. Megan's Law: Crime and democracy in late modern America. *Law and Social Inquiry* 25.4, 1111.

Smith v. Doe. 2003. 538 U.S. 84.

Sullivan, J. F. 1994. Whitman approves stringent restrictions on sex criminals. *New York Times*, (November 1) B1.

Terry, K. J., et al. 2003. *Sex Offender Registration and Community Notification: A "Megan's Law" Sourcebook.* Kingston, NJ: Civic Research Institute.

United States v. Antelope. 2005. WL 170738 (9th Cir. (Mont.)), 5 Cal. Daily Op. Serv. 745.

United States General Accounting Office and United States Congress. 1996. Washington, DC: House Committee on the Judiciary, Subcommittee on Crime, Sex offender treatment: Research results inconclusive about what works to reduce recidivism, Report to the Chairman, Subcommittee on Crime, Committee on the Judiciary, House of Representatives.

Winslade, W. T., et al. 1998. Castrating pedophiles convicted of sex offenses against children: New treatment or old punishment? *SMULR* 51, 349, January-February.

Witt, P. H., and N. Barone. 2004. Assess sex offender risk: New Jersey's methods. *Federal Sentencing Reporter* 16.3, 170.

Yantzi, M. 1989. *Sexual Offending and Restoration.* Waterloo, Ontario and Scottsdale, PA: Herald Press.

Zgoba, K. M., W. R. Sager, and P. H. Witt. 2003. Evaluation of New Jersey's sex offender treatment program at the Adult Diagnostic and Treatment Center: Preliminary results. *Journal of Psychiatry and Law* 31, 133.

Zimring, F. E. 2004. *An American Travesty: Legal Responses to Adolescent Sexual Offending.* Chicago: University of Chicago Press.

Index

A

Abolitionist Countries, list of, 191

Abu Ghraib
- prison officers and, 42
- torture and, 522

"The Accord", barhopping and, 309

Adoptive and Safe Families Act, overview of, 134

Africa, rates of imprisonment and, 30

African Commission on Human and People's Rights, death penalty and, 175

Alarms, crime prevention and, 239

Alexander, James F., parenting interventions and, 328

Alfred the Great, birth of modern policing and, 446

Alvarez-Machain, Humberto, kidnapping of, 519

American Association of Suicidology, web sites, 89

American Bar Association, ethical standards and, 540

American police innovation
- evaluating the evidence and, 484
- focusing on repeat offenders and, 490
- hot spots policing and, 489-490
- increasing size of police agencies and, 485-486
- intensive enforcement and arrests, 486-487
- overview of, 480-481
- police crackdowns and, 489
- police effectivenecc research and, 491-495
- rapid response calls and, 486
- typology of police practices and, 481-484
- what works in policing and, 485-491

American policing, most innovative periods in, 480

American Probation and Parole Association (APPA), ISPs and, 220

Amnesty International
- decline of executions and, 169
- judicial executions recorded and, 170
- supermax facilities and, 61

Ancel, Marc, abolitionist countries and, 165

anger, political attractions and, 592

"antifencing" operations, repeat offenders and, 490

Arar, Marher, extraordinary renditions and, 521

Aristotle, virtue is "justice" and, 418

art theft, situational crime prevention, 303

Aryan Brotherhood, street gangs and, 47

Ashcroft v. Free Speech Coalition, child pornography and, 742

Assize of Clarendon, gaols and, 20

Atkins v. Virginia, execution of the mentally retarded, 182-183

Attica Prison, riot at, 47

Augustus, John, first probation officer and, 200

Australia, reintegrative shaming and, 138

Austria, suicide rates and, 80

aut dedere aut judicare, extradition and, 509

B

Badinter, Robert, capital punishment and, 178

Index

Index

771

V

van den Haag, Ernest, deterrence theorists and, 394
Van Diemen's Land, prison colony and, 204
Vehicle-Based Sanctions, overview of, 127-128
Vermont, Reparative Probation Program and, 632
Victim Impact Statement (VIS), overview of, 606
Victim Offender Mediation
    costs and, 702-703
    crimes of severe violence and, 703-704
    diversion and, 700-701
    fairness and, 699
    follow-up phase and, 696-697
    mediation phase and, 695-696
    overview of, 692
    participant satisfaction and, 698-699
    participation rates and reasons, 697
    preparation phase and, 693-695
    recidivism and, 701-702
    referral/intake phase and, 693
    restitution and repayment of harm, 699-700
Victim Offender Reconciliation Program (VORP), overview of, 618
Victim-offender mediation, restorative justice and, 629
Victimization
    concentration of, 595-606
    locus of control, victim blame, and realism, 593-595
    political attractions of passive and fearful, 590-593
    prevention of repeats and near-repeats, 602
    significance of repeat victimization and, 597
    victim and criminal justice, 606-607
    victim status as strait-jacket, 588-590
Victims
    respect for victims' interests and, 672-673
    willingness to participate in mediation and, 634
Vigilante-type activities, overview of, 404-405
Violent crime, situational prevention and, 305-310

Violent offenders
    civil commitment of sexually violent predators and, 738-741
    crimes of severe violence and, 703-704
    predatory violence and, 306
    prison population and, 38-39
    self-mutilation and, 84
Virginia, 71-point risk assessment scale, 577
Vollmer, Augustus, reform leaders and, 451
von Hirsch, Andrew
    Doing Justice and, 390
    parole supervision and, 211
Voting, felony convictions and, 66
Voting rights, disenfranchisement laws and, 133

W

Wales
    changes in the composition of the prison population, 49
    dispersal prisons and, 55
    drug offenders and, 40
    growth of imprisonment and, 39
    supermax facilities and, 61
    supermax facilities and, 59-60
Walker, Nigel, retribution and, 389
Wall Street Journal, corporate crime and, 723
Walmsley, Roy, people in penal institutions and, 199
Washington Post, extraordinary renditions and, 521
Water polo, situational crime prevention and, 308
Web sites
    American Association of Suicidology, 89
    Befrienders, 89
    Reinventing Probation Council, 223
Weber, Max, theoretical basis for bureaucracies, 453
Western Trial Systems
    common law and civil trial systems, 533-535
    defense attorneys and factual investigations, 536-538
    ethical issues for defense lawyers and prosecutors, 540-541
    international crime tribunals and, 545-548
    legal preparations for trial and, 538-540